SUSAN SONTAG

Susan Sontag

ESSAYS OF THE 1960s & 70s

Against Interpretation
Styles of Radical Will
On Photography
Illness as Metaphor
Uncollected Essays

David Rieff, *editor*

THE LIBRARY OF AMERICA

The paper used in this publication meets the
minimum requirements of the American National Standard for
Information Sciences–Permanence of Paper for Printed
Library Materials, ANSI z39.48—1984.

Distributed to the trade in the United States
by Penguin Group (USA) Inc.
and in Canada by Penguin Books Canada Ltd.

Library of Congress Control Number: 2013930952
ISBN 978-1-59853-255-5

First Printing
The Library of America—246

Contents

AGAINST INTERPRETATION
AND OTHER ESSAYS

For Paul Thek

A Note and Some Acknowledgments

The articles and reviews collected here make up a good part of the criticism I wrote between 1962 and 1965, a sharply defined period in my life. In early 1962 I finished my first novel, *The Benefactor*. In late 1965 I began a second novel. The energy, and the anxiety, that spilled over into criticism had a beginning and an end. That period of search, reflection, and discovery already seemed somewhat remote at the time of the American publication of *Against Interpretation* and seems even more so now, a year later, as the collection is about to be reissued in a paperback edition.

Although in these essays I do talk a great deal about particular works of art and, implicitly, about the tasks of the critic, I am aware that little of what is assembled in the book counts as criticism proper. Leaving aside a few pieces of journalism, most of it could perhaps be called meta-criticism—if that is not too grand a name. I was writing, with passionate partiality, about *problems* raised for me by works of art, mainly contemporary, in different genres: I wanted to expose and clarify the theoretical assumptions underlying specific judgments and tastes. Although I did not set out to devise a "position" about either the arts or modernity, some kind of general position seemed to take shape and to voice itself with increasing urgency no matter what particular work I wrote about.

I disagree now with a portion of what I wrote, but it is not the sort of disagreement that makes feasible partial changes or revisions. Although I think that I overestimated or underestimated the merit of several works I discussed, little of my present disagreement owes to a shift in particular judgments. Anyway, what value these essays may possess, the extent to which they are more than just case studies of *my* evolving sensibility, rests not on the specific appraisals made but on the interestingness of the problems raised. I don't, ultimately, care for handing out grades to works of art (which is why I mostly avoided the

3

opportunity of writing about things I didn't admire). I wrote as an enthusiast and a partisan—and with, it now seems to me, a certain naïveté. I didn't understand the gross impact which writing about new or little-known activities in the arts can have in the era of instant "communication." I didn't know—I had yet to learn, painfully—the speed at which a bulky essay in *Partisan Review* becomes a hot tip in *Time*. Despite all my exhortatory tone, I was not trying to lead anyone into the Promised Land except myself.

For me, the essays have done their work. I see the world differently, with fresher eyes; my conception of my tasks as a novelist is radically changed. I could describe the process this way. Before I wrote the essays I did not believe many of the ideas espoused in them; when I wrote them, I believed what I wrote; subsequently, I have come to disbelieve some of these same ideas again—but from a new perspective, one that incorporates and is nourished by what is true in the argument of the essays. Writing criticism has proved to be an act of intellectual disburdenment as much as of intellectual self-expression. I have the impression not so much of having, for myself, resolved a certain number of alluring and troubling problems as of having used them up. But no doubt this is illusory. The problems remain, more remains to be said about them by other curious and reflective people, and perhaps this collection of some recent thinking about the arts will have a certain relevance to that.

"Sartre's *Saint Genet*," "The Death of Tragedy," "Nathalie Sarraute and the Novel," "Going to Theater, etc.," "Notes on 'Camp,'" "Marat/Sade/Artaud," and "On Style" originally appeared in *Partisan Review*; "Simone Weil," "Camus' *Notebooks*," "Michel Leiris' *Manhood*," "The Anthropologist as Hero," and "Ionesco" appeared in *The New York Review of Books*; "The Literary Criticism of Georg Lukács" and "Reflections on *The Deputy*" in *Book Week*; "Against Interpretation" in *Evergreen Review*; "Piety Without Content," "The Artist as Exemplary Sufferer," and "Happenings: An Art of Radical Juxtaposition" in *The Second Coming*; "Godard's *Vivre Sa Vie*" in *Moviegoer*; "One Culture and the New Sensibility" (in abridged form) in *Mademoiselle*; "Jack Smith's *Flaming Creatures*" in *The Nation*; "Spiritual Style in the Films of Robert Bresson" in *The Seventh*

Art; "A Note on Novels and Films" and "Psychoanalysis and Norman O. Brown's *Life Against Death*" in *The Supplement* (*Columbia Spectator*); "The Imagination of Disaster" in *Commentary*. (Some articles appeared under different titles.) I am grateful to the editors of these magazines for permission to reprint.

It is a pleasure to have the opportunity to thank William Phillips for generous encouragement though he often disagreed with what I was saying; Annette Michelson, who has shared her erudition and taste with me in many conversations over the last seven years; and Richard Howard, who very helpfully read over most of the essays and pointed out several errors of fact and rhetoric.

Last, I wish to record my gratitude to the Rockefeller Foundation for a fellowship last year which freed me, for the first time in my life, to write full-time—during which period I wrote, among other things, some of the essays collected in this book.

S.S.

Contents

I

Against Interpretation

Content is a glimpse of something, an encounter like a flash.
It's very tiny—very tiny, content.
WILLEM DE KOONING, *in an interview*

It is only shallow people who do not judge by appearances.
The mystery of the world is the visible, not the invisible.
OSCAR WILDE, *in a letter*

THE earliest *experience* of art must have been that it was incantatory, magical; art was an instrument of ritual. (Cf. the
paintings in the caves at Lascaux, Altamira, Niaux, La Pasiega,
etc.) The earliest *theory* of art, that of the Greek philosophers,
proposed that art was mimesis, imitation of reality.

It is at this point that the peculiar question of the *value* of
art arose. For the mimetic theory, by its very terms, challenges
art to justify itself.

Plato, who proposed the theory, seems to have done so in
order to rule that the value of art is dubious. Since he considered ordinary material things as themselves mimetic objects,
imitations of transcendent forms or structures, even the best
painting of a bed would be only an "imitation of an imitation."
For Plato, art is neither particularly useful (the painting of a
bed is no good to sleep on), nor, in the strict sense, true. And
Aristotle's arguments in defense of art do not really challenge
Plato's view that all art is an elaborate *trompe l'oeil*, and therefore a lie. But he does dispute Plato's idea that art is useless.
Lie or no, art has a certain value according to Aristotle because
it is a form of therapy. Art is useful, after all, Aristotle coun-
ters, medicinally useful in that it arouses and purges dangerous
emotions.

In Plato and Aristotle, the mimetic theory of art goes hand
in hand with the assumption that art is always figurative. But
advocates of the mimetic theory need not close their eyes to
decorative and abstract art. The fallacy that art is necessarily a
"realism" can be modified or scrapped without ever moving
outside the problems delimited by the mimetic theory.

The fact is, all Western consciousness of and reflection upon
art have remained within the confines staked out by the Greek
theory of art as mimesis or representation. It is through this

theory that art as such—above and beyond given works of art—becomes problematic, in need of defense. And it is the defense of art which gives birth to the odd vision by which something we have learned to call "form" is separated off from something we have learned to call "content," and to the well-intentioned move which makes content essential and form accessory.

Even in modern times, when most artists and critics have discarded the theory of art as representation of an outer reality in favor of the theory of art as subjective expression, the main feature of the mimetic theory persists. Whether we conceive of the work of art on the model of a picture (art as a picture of reality) or on the model of a statement (art as the statement of the artist), content still comes first. The content may have changed. It may now be less figurative, less lucidly realistic. But it is still assumed that a work of art *is* its content. Or, as it's usually put today, that a work of art by definition says something. ("What X is saying is . . . ," "What X is trying to say is . . . ," "What X said is . . ." etc., etc.)

2

None of us can ever retrieve that innocence before all theory when art knew no need to justify itself, when one did not ask of a work of art what it *said* because no one knew (or thought one knew) what it *did*. From now to the end of consciousness, we are stuck with the task of defending art. We can only quarrel with one or another means of defense. Indeed, we have an obligation to overthrow any means of defending and justifying art which becomes particularly obtuse or onerous or insensitive to contemporary needs and practice.

This is the case, today, with the very idea of content itself. Whatever it may have been in the past, the idea of content is today mainly a hindrance, a nuisance, a subtle or not so subtle philistinism.

Though the actual developments in many arts may seem to be leading us away from the idea that a work of art is primarily its content, the idea still exerts an extraordinary hegemony. I want to suggest that this is because the idea is not perpetuated in the guise of a certain way of encountering works of art thoroughly ingrained among most people who take any of the arts seriously. What the overemphasis on the idea of content entails is the perennial, never consummated project of *interpretation*. And, conversely, it is the habit of approaching works of art in order to *interpret* them that sustains the fancy that there really is such a thing as the content of a work of art.

3

Of course, I don't mean interpretation in the broadest sense, the sense in which Nietzsche (rightly) says, "There are no facts, only interpretations." By interpretation, I mean here a conscious act of the mind which illustrates a certain code, certain "rules" of interpretation.

Directed to art, interpretation means plucking a set of elements (the X, the Y, the Z, and so forth) from the whole work. The task of interpretation is virtually one of translation. The interpreter says, Look, don't you see that X is really—or, really means—A? That Y is really B? That Z is really C?

What situation could prompt this curious project for transforming a text? History gives us the materials for an answer. Interpretation first appears in the culture of late classical antiquity, when the power and credibility of myth had been broken by the "realistic" view of the world introduced by scientific enlightenment. Once the question that haunts post-mythic consciousness—that of the *seemliness* of religious symbols—had been asked, the ancient texts were, in their pristine form, no longer acceptable. Then interpretation was summoned, to reconcile the ancient texts to "modern" demands. Thus, the Stoics, to accord with their view that the gods had to be moral, allegorized away the rude features of Zeus and his boisterous clan in Homer's epics. What Homer really designated by the adultery of Zeus with Leto, they explained, was the union between power and wisdom. In the same vein, Philo of Alexandria interpreted the literal historical narratives of the Hebrew Bible as spiritual paradigms. The story of the exodus from Egypt, the wandering in the desert for forty years, and the entry into the promised land, said Philo, was really an allegory of the individual soul's emancipation, tribulations, and final deliverance. Interpretation thus presupposes a discrepancy between the clear meaning of the text and the demands of (later) readers. It seeks to resolve that discrepancy. The situation is that for some reason a text has become unacceptable; yet it cannot be discarded. Interpretation is a radical strategy for conserving an old text, which is thought too precious to repudiate, by revamping it. The interpreter, without actually erasing or rewriting the text, *is* altering it. But he can't admit to doing this. He claims to be only making it intelligible, by disclosing its true meaning. However far the interpreters alter the text (another notorious example is the Rabbinic and Christian "spiritual" interpretations of the clearly erotic Song of Songs), they must claim to be reading off a sense that is already there.

Interpretation in our own time, however, is even more complex. For the contemporary zeal for the project of interpretation is often prompted not by piety toward the troublesome text (which may conceal an aggression), but by an open aggressiveness, an overt contempt for appearances. The old style of interpretation was insistent, but respectful; it erected another meaning on top of the literal one. The modern style of interpretation excavates, and as it excavates, destroys; it digs "behind" the text, to find a sub-text which is the true one. The most celebrated and influential modern doctrines, those of Marx and Freud, actually amount to elaborate systems of hermeneutics, aggressive and impious theories of interpretation. All observable phenomena are bracketed, in Freud's phrase, as *manifest content*. This manifest content must be probed and pushed aside to find the true meaning—the *latent content*—beneath. For Marx, social events like revolutions and wars; for Freud, the events of individual lives (like neurotic symptoms and slips of the tongue) as well as texts (like a dream or a work of art)—all are treated as occasions for interpretation. According to Marx and Freud, these events only *seem* to be intelligible. Actually, they have no meaning without interpretation. To understand *is* to interpret. And to interpret is to restate the phenomenon, in effect to find an equivalent for it.

Thus, interpretation is not (as most people assume) an absolute value, a gesture of mind situated in some timeless realm of capabilities. Interpretation must itself be evaluated, within a historical view of human consciousness. In some cultural contexts, interpretation is a liberating act. It is a means of revising, of transvaluing, of escaping the dead past. In other cultural contexts, it is reactionary, impertinent, cowardly, stifling.

4

Today is such a time, when the project of interpretation is largely reactionary, stifling. Like the fumes of the automobile and of heavy industry which befoul the urban atmosphere, the effusion of interpretations of art today poisons our sensibilities. In a culture whose already classical dilemma is the hypertrophy of the intellect at the expense of energy and sensual capability, interpretation is the revenge of the intellect upon art.

Even more. It is the revenge of the intellect upon the world. To interpret is to impoverish, to deplete the world—in order to set up a shadow world of "meanings." It is to turn *the* world into *this* world. ("This world"! As if there were any other.)

The world, our world, is depleted, impoverished enough. Away with all duplicates of it, until we again experience more immediately what we have.

5

In most modern instances, interpretation amounts to the philistine refusal to leave the work of art alone. Real art has the capacity to make us nervous. By reducing the work of art to its content and then interpreting *that*, one tames the work of art. Interpretation makes art manageable, conformable.

This philistinism of interpretation is more rife in literature than in any other art. For decades now, literary critics have understood it to be their task to translate the elements of the poem or play or novel or story into something else. Sometimes a writer will be so uneasy before the naked power of his art that he will install within the work itself—albeit with a little shyness, a touch of the good taste of irony—the clear and explicit interpretation of it. Thomas Mann is an example of such an overcooperative author. In the case of more stubborn authors, the critic is only too happy to perform the job.

The work of Kafka, for example, has been subjected to a mass ravishment by no less than three armies of interpreters. Those who read Kafka as a social allegory see case studies of the frustrations and insanity of modern bureaucracy and its ultimate issuance in the totalitarian state. Those who read Kafka as a psychoanalytic allegory see desperate revelations of Kafka's fear of his father, his castration anxieties, his sense of his own impotence, his thralldom to his dreams. Those who read Kafka as a religious allegory explain that K. in *The Castle* is trying to gain access to heaven, that Joseph K. in *The Trial* is being judged by the inexorable and mysterious justice of God. . . . Another *oeuvre* that has attracted interpreters like leeches is that of Samuel Beckett. Beckett's delicate dramas of the withdrawn consciousness—pared down to essentials, cut off, often represented as physically immobilized—are read as a statement about modern man's alienation from meaning or from God, or as an allegory of psychopathology.

Proust, Joyce, Faulkner, Rilke, Lawrence, Gide . . . one could go on citing author after author; the list is endless of those around whom thick encrustations of interpretation have taken hold. But it should be noted that interpretation is not simply the compliment that mediocrity pays to genius. It is, indeed, *the* modern way of understanding something, and is applied to works of every quality. Thus, in the notes that Elia Kazan published on his production of *A Streetcar Named Desire*, it becomes clear that, in order to direct the play, Kazan had to discover that Stanley Kowalski represented the sensual and vengeful barbarism that was engulfing our culture, while Blanche Du Bois was Western civilization, poetry, delicate apparel, dim lighting, refined feelings and all, though a little the worse for wear to be sure. Tennessee Williams' forceful psychological melodrama now became intelligible: it was *about* something, about the decline of Western civilization. Apparently, were it to go on being a play about a handsome brute named Stanley Kowalski and a faded mangy belle named Blanche Du Bois, it would not be manageable.

6

It doesn't matter whether artists intend, or don't intend, for their works to be interpreted. Perhaps Tennessee Williams thinks *Streetcar* is about what Kazan thinks it to be about. It may be that Cocteau in *The Blood of a Poet* and in *Orpheus* wanted the elaborate readings which have been given these films, in terms of Freudian symbolism and social critique. But the merit of these works certainly lies elsewhere than in their "meanings." Indeed, it is precisely to the extent that Williams' plays and Cocteau's films do suggest these portentous meanings that they are defective, false, contrived, lacking in conviction.

From interviews, it appears that Resnais and Robbe-Grillet consciously designed *Last Year at Marienbad* to accommodate a multiplicity of equally plausible interpretations. But the temptation to interpret *Marienbad* should be resisted. What matters in *Marienbad* is the pure, untranslatable, sensuous immediacy of some of its images, and its rigorous if narrow solutions to certain problems of cinematic form.

Again, Ingmar Bergman may have meant the tank rumbling down the empty night street in *The Silence* as a phallic symbol. But if he did, it was a foolish thought. ("Never trust the teller, trust the tale," said Lawrence.) Taken as a brute object, as an immediate sensory equivalent for the mysterious abrupt armored happenings going on inside the hotel, that sequence with the tank is the most striking moment in the film. Those who reach for a Freudian interpretation of the tank are only expressing their lack of response to what is there on the screen.

It is always the case that interpretation of this type indicates a dissatisfaction (conscious or unconscious) with the work, a wish to replace it by something else.

Interpretation, based on the highly dubious theory that a work of art is composed of items of content, violates art. It makes art into an article for use, for arrangement into a mental scheme of categories.

7

Interpretation does not, of course, always prevail. In fact, a great deal of today's art may be understood as motivated by a flight from interpretation. To avoid interpretation, art may become parody. Or it may become abstract. Or it may become ("merely") decorative. Or it may become non-art.

The flight from interpretation seems particularly a feature of modern painting. Abstract painting is the attempt to have, in the ordinary sense, no content; since there is no content, there can be no interpretation. Pop Art works by the opposite means to the same result; using a content so blatant, so "what it is," it, too, ends by being uninterpretable.

A great deal of modern poetry as well, starting from the great experiments of French poetry (including the movement that is misleadingly called Symbolism) to put silence into poems and to reinstate the *magic* of the word, has escaped from the rough grip of interpretation. The most recent revolution in contemporary taste in poetry—the revolution that has deposed Eliot and elevated Pound—represents a turning away from content in poetry in the old sense, an impatience with what made modern poetry prey to the zeal of interpreters.

I am speaking mainly of the situation in America, of course. Interpretation runs rampant here in those arts with a feeble and negligible avant-garde: fiction and the drama. Most American novelists and playwrights are really either journalists or gentlemen sociologists and psychologists. They are writing the literary equivalent of program music. And so rudimentary, uninspired, and stagnant has been the sense of what might be done with *form* in fiction and drama that even when the content isn't simply information, news, it is still peculiarly visible, handier, more exposed. To the extent that novels and plays (in America), unlike poetry and painting and music, don't reflect any interesting concern with changes in their form, these arts remain prone to assault by interpretation.

But programmatic avant-gardism—which has meant, mostly, experiments with form at the expense of content—is not the only defense against the infestation of art by interpretations. At least, I hope not. For this would be to commit art to being perpetually on the run. (It also perpetuates the very distinction between form and content which is, ultimately, an illusion.) Ideally, it is possible to elude the interpreters in another way, by making works of art whose surface is so unified and clean, whose momentum is so rapid, whose address is so direct that the work can be . . . just what it is. Is this possible now? It does happen in films, I believe. This is why cinema is the most alive, the most exciting, the most important of all art forms right now. Perhaps the way one tells how alive a particular art form is, is by the latitude it gives for making mistakes in it, and still being good. For example, a few of the films of Bergman—though crammed with lame messages about the modern spirit, thereby inviting interpretations—still triumph over the pretentious intentions of their director. In *Winter Light* and *The Silence*, the beauty and visual sophistication of the images subvert before our eyes the callow pseudo-intellectuality of the story and some of the dialogue. (The most remarkable instance of this sort of discrepancy is the work of D. W. Griffith.) In good films, there is always a directness that entirely frees us from the itch to interpret. Many old Hollywood films, like those of Cukor, Walsh, Hawks, and countless other directors, have this liberating anti-symbolic quality, no less than the best work of the new European directors, like Truffaut's *Shoot the Piano Player* and *Jules and Jim*, Godard's *Breathless* and *Vivre Sa Vie*, Antonioni's *L'Avventura*, and Olmi's *The Fiancés*.

The fact that films have not been overrun by interpreters is in part due simply to the newness of cinema as an art. It also owes to the happy accident that films for such a long time were just movies; in other words, that they were understood to be part of mass, as opposed to high, culture, and were left alone by most people with minds. Then, too, there is always something other than content in the cinema to grab hold of, for those who want to analyze. For the cinema, unlike the novel, possesses a vocabulary of forms—the explicit, complex, and discussable technology of camera movements, cutting, and composition of the frame that goes into the making of a film.

8

What kind of criticism, of commentary on the arts, is desirable today? For I am not saying that works of art are ineffable, that they cannot be described or paraphrased. They can be. The question is how. What would criticism look like that would serve the work of art, not usurp its place?

What is needed, first, is more attention to form in art. If excessive stress on *content* provokes the arrogance of interpretation, more extended and more thorough descriptions of *form* would silence. What is needed is a vocabulary—a descriptive, rather than prescriptive, vocabulary—for forms.* The best criticism, and it is uncommon, is of this sort that dissolves considerations of content into those of form. On film, drama, and

*One of the difficulties is that our idea of form is spatial (the Greek metaphors for form are all derived from notions of space). This is why we have a more ready vocabulary of forms for the spatial than for the temporal arts. The exception among the temporal arts, of course, is the drama; perhaps this is because the drama is a narrative (i.e., temporal) form that extends itself visually and

painting respectively, I can think of Erwin Panofsky's essay, "Style and Medium in the Motion Pictures," Northrop Frye's essay "A Conspectus of Dramatic Genres," Pierre Francastel's essay "The Destruction of a Plastic Space." Roland Barthes' book *On Racine* and his two essays on Robbe-Grillet are examples of formal analysis applied to the work of a single author. (The best essays in Erich Auerbach's *Mimesis*, like "The Scar of Odysseus," are also of this type.) An example of formal analysis applied simultaneously to genre and author is Walter Benjamin's essay, "The Story Teller: Reflections on the Works of Nicolai Leskov."

Equally valuable would be acts of criticism which would supply a really accurate, sharp, loving description of the appearance of a work of art. This seems even harder to do than formal analysis. Some of Manny Farber's film criticism, Dorothy Van Ghent's essay "The Dickens World: A View from Todgers'," Randall Jarrell's essay on Walt Whitman are among the rare examples of what I mean. These are essays which reveal the sensuous surface of art without mucking about in it.

9

Transparence is the highest, most liberating value in art—and in criticism—today. Transparence means experiencing the luminousness of the thing in itself, of things being what they are. This is the greatness of, for example, the films of Bresson and Ozu and Renoir's *The Rules of the Game*.

Once upon a time (say, for Dante), it must have been a revolutionary and creative move to design works of art so that they might be experienced on several levels. Now it is not. It reinforces the principle of redundancy that is the principal affliction of modern life.

Once upon a time (a time when high art was scarce), it must have been a revolutionary and creative move to interpret works of art. Now it is not. What we decidedly do not need now is

pictorially, upon a stage. . . . What we don't have yet is a poetics of the novel, any clear notion of the forms of narration. Perhaps film criticism will be the occasion of a breakthrough here, since films are primarily a visual form, yet they are also a subdivision of literature.

further to assimilate Art into Thought, or (worse yet) Art into Culture.

Interpretation takes the sensory experience of the work of art for granted, and proceeds from there. This cannot be taken for granted, now. Think of the sheer multiplication of works of art available to every one of us, superadded to the conflicting tastes and odors and sights of the urban environment that bombard our senses. Ours is a culture based on excess, on overproduction; the result is a steady loss of sharpness in our sensory experience. All the conditions of modern life—its material plenitude, its sheer crowdedness—conjoin to dull our sensory faculties. And it is in the light of the condition of our senses, our capacities (rather than those of another age), that the task of the critic must be assessed.

What is important now is to recover our senses. We must learn to *see* more, to *hear* more, to *feel* more.

Our task is not to find the maximum amount of content in a work of art, much less to squeeze more content out of the work than is already there. Our task is to cut back content so that we can see the thing at all.

The aim of all commentary on art now should be to make works of art—and, by analogy, our own experience—more, rather than less, real to us. The function of criticism should be to show *how it is what it is*, even *that it is what it is*, rather than to show *what it means*.

10

In place of a hermeneutics we need an erotics of art.

(1964)

On Style

IT would be hard to find any reputable literary critic today who would care to be caught defending *as an idea* the old antithesis of style versus content. On this issue a pious consensus prevails. Everyone is quick to avow that style and content are indissoluble, that the strongly individual style of each important writer is an organic aspect of his work and never something merely "decorative."

In the *practice* of criticism, though, the old antithesis lives on, virtually unassailed. Most of the same critics who disclaim, in passing, the notion that style is an accessory to content maintain the duality whenever they apply themselves to particular works of literature. It is not so easy, after all, to get unstuck from a distinction that practically holds together the fabric of critical discourse, and serves to perpetuate certain intellectual aims and vested interests which themselves remain unchallenged and would be difficult to surrender without a fully articulated working replacement at hand.

In fact, to talk about the style of a particular novel or poem at all as a "style," without implying, whether one wishes to or not, that style is merely decorative, accessory, is extremely hard. Merely by employing the notion, one is almost bound to invoke, albeit implicitly, an antithesis between style and something else. Many critics appear not to realize this. They think themselves sufficiently protected by a theoretical disclaimer on the vulgar filtering-off of style from content, all the while their judgments continue to reinforce precisely what they are, in theory, eager to deny.

One way in which the old duality lives on in the practice of criticism, in concrete judgments, is the frequency with which quite admirable works of art are defended as good although what is miscalled their style is acknowledged to be crude or careless. Another is the frequency with which a very complex style is regarded with a barely concealed ambivalence. Contemporary writers and other artists with a style that is intricate, hermetic, demanding—not to speak of "beautiful"—get their ration of unstinting praise. Still, it is clear that such a style is often felt to be a form of insincerity: evidence of the artist's intrusion upon

his materials, which should be allowed to deliver themselves in
a pure state.

Whitman, in the preface to the 1855 edition of *Leaves of Grass*,
expresses the disavowal of "style" which is, in most arts since
the last century, a standard ploy for ushering in a new stylistic
vocabulary. "The greatest poet has less a marked style and is
more the free channel of himself," that great and very mannered
poet contends. "He says to his art, I will not be meddlesome, I
will not have in my writing any elegance or effect or originality
to hang in the way between me and the rest like curtains. I will
have nothing hang in the way, not the richest curtains. What I
tell I tell for precisely what it is."

Of course, as everyone knows or claims to know, there is no
neutral, absolutely transparent style. Sartre has shown, in his
excellent review of *The Stranger*, how the celebrated "white
style" of Camus' novel—impersonal, expository, lucid, flat—is
itself the vehicle of Meursault's image of the world (as made up
of absurd, fortuitous moments). What Roland Barthes calls "the
zero degree of writing" is, precisely by being anti-metaphorical
and dehumanized, as selective and artificial as any traditional
style of writing. Nevertheless, the notion of a style-less, transparent art is one of the most tenacious fantasies of modern
culture. Artists and critics pretend to believe that it is no more
possible to get the artifice out of art than it is for a person to
lose his personality. Yet the aspiration lingers—a permanent dissent from modern art, with its dizzying velocity of style *changes*.

To speak of style is one way of speaking about the totality of a
work of art. Like all discourse about totalities, talk of style must
rely on metaphors. And metaphors mislead.

Take, for instance, Whitman's very material metaphor. By
likening style to a curtain, he has of course confused style with
decoration and for this would be speedily faulted by most critics.
To conceive of style as a decorative encumbrance on the matter of the work suggests that the curtain could be parted and
the matter revealed; or, to vary the metaphor slightly, that the
curtain could be rendered transparent. But this is not the only
erroneous implication of the metaphor. What the metaphor also
suggests is that style is a matter of more or less (quantity), thick
or thin (density). And, though less obviously so, this is just as

wrong as the fancy that an artist possesses the genuine option to have or not to have a style. Style is not quantitative, any more than it is superadded. A more complex stylistic convention—say, one taking prose further away from the diction and cadences of ordinary speech—does not mean that the work has "more" style.

Indeed, practically all metaphors for style amount to placing matter on the inside, style on the outside. It would be more to the point to reverse the metaphor. The matter, the subject, is on the outside; the style is on the inside. As Cocteau writes: "Decorative style has never existed. Style is the soul, and unfortunately with us the soul assumes the form of the body." Even if one were to define style as the manner of our appearing, this by no means necessarily entails an opposition between a style that one assumes and one's "true" being. In fact, such a disjunction is extremely rare. In almost every case, our manner of appearing *is* our manner of being. The mask is the face.

I should make clear, however, that what I have been saying about dangerous metaphors doesn't rule out the use of limited and concrete metaphors to describe the impact of a particular style. It seems harmless to speak of a style, drawing from the crude terminology used to render physical sensations, as being "loud" or "heavy" or "dull" or "tasteless" or, employing the image of an argument, as "inconsistent."

The antipathy to "style" is always an antipathy to a given style. There are no style-less works of art, only works of art belonging to different, more or less complex stylistic traditions and conventions.

This means that the notion of style, generically considered, has a specific, historical meaning. It is not only that styles belong to a time and a place; and that our perception of the style of a given work of art is always charged with an awareness of the work's historicity, its place in a chronology. Further: the visibility of styles is itself a product of historical consciousness. Were it not for departures from, or experimentation with, previous artistic norms which are known to us, we could never recognize the profile of a new style. Still further: the very notion of "style" needs to be approached historically. Awareness of style as a problematic and isolable element in a work of art has emerged in the audience for art only at certain historical moments—as a front behind which other issues, ultimately ethical and political, are being debated. The notion of "having a style" is one of the solutions that has arisen, intermittently since the Renaissance, to the crises that have threatened old ideas of truth, of moral rectitude, and also of naturalness.

But suppose all this is admitted. That all representation is incarnated in a given style (easy to say). That there is, therefore, strictly speaking, no such thing as realism, except as, itself, a special stylistic convention (a little harder). Still, there are styles and styles. Everyone is acquainted with movements in art—two examples: Mannerist painting of the late 16th and early 17th centuries, Art Nouveau in painting, architecture, furniture, and domestic objects—which do more than simply have "a style." Artists such as Parmigianino, Pontormo, Rosso, Bronzino, such as Gaudí, Guimard, Beardsley, and Tiffany, in some obvious way cultivate style. They seem to be preoccupied with stylistic questions and indeed to place the accent less on what they are saying than on the manner of saying it.

To deal with art of this type, which seems to demand the distinction I have been urging be abandoned, a term such as "stylization" or its equivalent is needed. "Stylization" is what is present in a work of art precisely when an artist does make the by no means inevitable distinction between matter and manner, theme and form. When that happens, when style and subject are so distinguished, that is, played off against each other, one can legitimately speak of subjects being treated (or mistreated) in a certain style. Creative mistreatment is more the rule. For when the material of art is conceived of as "subject-matter," it is also experienced as capable of being exhausted. And as subjects are understood to be fairly far along in this process of exhaustion, they become available to further and further stylization.

Compare, for example, certain silent movies of Sternberg (*Salvation Hunters*, *Underworld*, *The Docks of New York*) with the six American movies he made in the 1930s with Marlene Dietrich. The best of the early Sternberg films have pronounced stylistic features, a very sophisticated aesthetic surface. But we do not feel about the narrative of the sailor and the prostitute in *The Docks of New York* as we do about the adventures of the

Dietrich character in *Blonde Venus* or *The Scarlet Empress*, that it is an exercise in style. What informs these later films of Sternberg's is an ironic attitude toward the subject-matter (romantic love, the *femme fatale*), a judgment on the subject-matter as interesting only so far as it is transformed by exaggeration, in a word, stylized. . . . Cubist painting, or the sculpture of Giacometti, would not be an example of "stylization" as distinguished from "style" in art; however extensive the distortions of the human face and figure, these are not present to make the face and figure *interesting*. But the paintings of Crivelli and Georges de La Tour are examples of what I mean.

"Stylization" in a work of art, as distinct from style, reflects an ambivalence (affection contradicted by contempt, obsession contradicted by irony) toward the subject-matter. This ambivalence is handled by maintaining, through the rhetorical overlay that is stylization, a special distance from the subject. But the common result is that either the work of art is excessively narrow and repetitive, or else the different parts seem unhinged, dissociated. (A good example of the latter is the relation between the visually brilliant denouement of Orson Welles' *The Lady from Shanghai* and the rest of the film.) No doubt, in a culture pledged to the utility (particularly the moral utility) of art, burdened with a useless need to fence off solemn art from arts which provide amusement, the eccentricities of stylized art supply a valid and valuable satisfaction. I have described these satisfactions in another essay, under the name of "camp" taste. Yet, it is evident that stylized art, palpably an art of excess, lacking harmoniousness, can never be of the very greatest kind.

What haunts all contemporary use of the notion of style is the putative opposition between form and content. How is one to exorcise the feeling that "style," which functions like the notion of form, subverts content? One thing seems certain. No affirmation of the organic relation between style and content will really carry conviction—or guide critics who make this affirmation to the recasting of their specific discourse—until the notion of content is put in its place.

Most critics would agree that a work of art does not "contain" a certain amount of content (or function—as in the case of architecture) embellished by "style." But few address themselves to the positive consequences of what they seem to have agreed to. What is "content"? Or, more precisely, what is left of the notion of content when we have transcended the antithesis of style (or form) and content? Part of the answer lies in the fact that for a work of art to have "content" is, in itself, a rather special stylistic convention. The great task which remains to critical theory is to examine in detail the *formal* function of subject-matter.

Until this function is acknowledged and properly explored, it is inevitable that critics will go on treating works of art as "statements." (Less so, of course, in those arts which are abstract or have largely gone abstract, like music and painting and the dance. In these arts, the critics have not solved the problem; it has been taken from them.) Of course, a work of art *can* be considered as a statement, that is, as the answer to a question. On the most elementary level, Goya's portrait of the Duke of Wellington may be examined as the answer to the question: what did Wellington look like? *Anna Karenina* may be treated as an investigation of the problems of love, marriage, and adultery. Though the issue of the adequacy of artistic representation to life has pretty much been abandoned in, for example, painting, such adequacy continues to constitute a powerful standard of judgment in most appraisals of serious novels, plays, and films. In critical theory, the notion is quite old. At least since Diderot, the main tradition of criticism in all the arts, appealing to such apparently dissimilar criteria as verisimilitude and moral correctness, in effect treats the work of art as *a statement being made in the form of a work of art.*

To treat works of art in this fashion is not wholly irrelevant. But it is, obviously, putting art to use—for such purposes as inquiring into the history of ideas, diagnosing contemporary culture, or creating social solidarity. Such a treatment has little to do with what actually happens when a person possessing some training and aesthetic sensibility looks at a work of art appropriately. A work of art encountered as a work of art is an experience, not a statement or an answer to a question. Art is not only about something; it is something. A work of art is a thing *in* the world, not just a text or commentary *on* the world.

I am not saying that a work of art creates a world which is

entirely self-referring. Of course, works of art (with the important exception of music) refer to the real world—to our knowledge, to our experience, to our values. They present information and evaluations. But their distinctive feature is that they give rise not to conceptual knowledge (which *is* the distinctive feature of discursive or scientific knowledge—e.g., philosophy, sociology, psychology, history) but to something like an excitation, a phenomenon of commitment, judgment in a state of thralldom or captivation. Which is to say that the knowledge we gain through art is an experience of the form or style of knowing something, rather than a knowledge of something (like a fact or a moral judgment) in itself.

This explains the preeminence of the value of *expressiveness* in works of art; and how the value of expressiveness—that is, of style—rightly takes precedence over content (when content is, falsely, isolated from style). The satisfactions of *Paradise Lost* for us do not lie in its views on God and man, but in the superior kinds of energy, vitality, expressiveness which are incarnated in the poem.

Hence, too, the peculiar dependence of a work of art, however expressive, upon the cooperation of the person having the experience, for one may see what is "said" but remain unmoved, either through dullness or distraction. Art is seduction, not rape. A work of art proposes a type of experience designed to manifest the quality of imperiousness. But art cannot seduce without the complicity of the experiencing subject.

Inevitably, critics who regard works of art as statements will be wary of "style," even as they pay lip service to "imagination." All that imagination really means for them, anyway, is the supersensitive rendering of "reality." It is this "reality" snared by the work of art that they continue to focus on, rather than on the extent to which a work of art engages the mind in certain transformations.

But when the metaphor of the work of art as a statement loses its authority, the ambivalence toward "style" should dissolve; for this ambivalence mirrors the presumed tension between the statement and the manner in which it is stated.

In the end, however, attitudes toward style cannot be reformed merely by appealing to the "appropriate" (as opposed to utilitarian) way of looking at works of art. The ambivalence toward style is not rooted in simple error—it would then be quite easy to uproot—but in a passion, the passion of an entire culture. This passion is to protect and defend values traditionally conceived of as lying "outside" art, namely truth and morality, but which remain in perpetual danger of being compromised by art. Behind the ambivalence toward style is, ultimately, the historic Western confusion about the relation between art and morality, the aesthetic and the ethical.

For the problem of art versus morality is a pseudo-problem. The distinction itself is a trap; its continued plausibility rests on not putting the ethical into question, but only the aesthetic. To argue on these grounds at all, seeking to defend the autonomy of the aesthetic (and I have, rather uneasily, done so myself), is already to grant something that should not be granted—namely, that there exist two independent sorts of response, the aesthetic and the ethical, which vie for our loyalty when we experience a work of art. As if during the experience one really had to choose between responsible and humane conduct, on the one hand, and the pleasurable stimulation of consciousness, on the other!

Of course, we never have a purely aesthetic response to works of art—neither to a play or a novel, with its depicting of human beings choosing and acting, nor, though it is less obvious, to a painting by Jackson Pollock or a Greek vase. (Ruskin has written acutely about the moral aspects of the formal properties of painting.) But neither would it be appropriate for us to make a moral response to something in a work of art in the same sense that we do to an act in real life. I would undoubtedly be indignant if someone I knew murdered his wife and got away with it (psychologically, legally), but I can hardly become indignant, as many critics seem to be, when the hero of Norman Mailer's *An American Dream* murders his wife and goes unpunished. Divine, Darling, and the others in Genet's *Our Lady of the Flowers* are not real people whom we are being asked to decide whether to invite into our living rooms; they are figures in an imaginary landscape. The point may seem obvious, but the prevalence of genteel-moralistic judgments in contemporary literary (and film) criticism makes it worth repeating a number of times.

For most people, as Ortega y Gasset has pointed out in *The Dehumanization of Art*, aesthetic pleasure is a state of mind essentially indistinguishable from their ordinary responses. By art, they understand a means through which they are brought in contact with interesting human affairs. When they grieve and rejoice at human destinies in a play or film or novel, it is not really different from grieving and rejoicing over such events in real life—except that the experience of human destinies in art contains less ambivalence, it is relatively disinterested, and it is free from painful consequences. The experience is also, in a certain measure, more intense; for when suffering and pleasure are experienced vicariously, people can afford to be avid. But, as Ortega argues, "a preoccupation with the human content of the work [of art] is in principle incompatible with aesthetic judgment." *

Ortega is entirely correct, in my opinion. But I would not care to leave the matter where he does, which tacitly isolates aesthetic from moral response. Art is connected with morality, I should argue. One way that it is so connected is that art may yield moral *pleasure*; but the moral pleasure peculiar to art is not the pleasure of approving of acts or disapproving of them. The moral pleasure in art, as well as the moral service that art performs, consists in the intelligent gratification of consciousness.

What "morality" means is a habitual or chronic type of behavior (including feelings and acts). Morality is a code of acts, and of judgments and sentiments by which we reinforce our habits of acting in a certain way, which prescribe a standard for behaving or trying to behave toward other human beings *generally* (that

---

*Ortega continues: "A work of art vanishes from sight for a beholder who seeks in it nothing but the moving fate of John and Mary or Tristan and Isolde and adjusts his vision to this. Tristan's sorrows are sorrows and can evoke compassion only insofar as they are taken as real. But an object of art is artistic only insofar as it is not real. . . . But not many people are capable of adjusting their perceptive apparatus to the pane and the transparency that is the work of art. Instead, they look right through it and revel in the human reality with which the work deals. . . . During the 19th century artists proceeded in all too impure a fashion. They reduced the strictly aesthetic elements to a minimum and let the work consist almost entirely in a fiction of human realities. . . . Works of this kind [both Romanticism and Naturalism] are only partially works of art, or artistic objects. . . . No wonder that 19th century art has been so popular . . . it is not art but an extract from life."

is, to all who are acknowledged to be human) as if we were inspired by love. Needless to say, love is something we feel in truth for just a few individual human beings, among those who are known to us in reality and in our imagination. . . . Morality is a *form* of acting and not a particular repertoire of choices.

If morality is so understood—as one of the achievements of human will, dictating to itself a mode of acting and being in the world—it becomes clear that no generic antagonism exists between the form of consciousness, aimed at action, which is morality, and the nourishment of consciousness, which is aesthetic experience. Only when works of art are reduced to statements which propose a specific content, and when morality is identified with a particular morality (and any particular morality has its dross, those elements which are no more than a defense of limited social interest and class values)—only then can a work of art be thought to undermine morality. Indeed, only then can the full distinction between the aesthetic and the ethical be made.

But if we understand morality in the singular, as a generic decision on the part of consciousness, then it appears that our response to art is "moral" insofar as it is, precisely, the enlivening of our sensibility and consciousness. For it is sensibility that nourishes our capacity for moral choice, and prompts our readiness to act, assuming that we do choose, which is a prerequisite for calling an act moral, and are not just blindly and unreflectively obeying. Art performs this "moral" task because the qualities which are intrinsic to the aesthetic experience (disinterestedness, contemplativeness, attentiveness, the awakening of the feelings) and to the aesthetic object (grace, intelligence, expressiveness, energy, sensuousness) are also fundamental constituents of a moral response to life.

In art, "content" is, as it were, the pretext, the goal, the lure which engages consciousness in essentially *formal* processes of transformation.

This is how we can, in good conscience, cherish works of art which, considered in terms of "content," are morally objectionable to us. (The difficulty is of the same order as that involved in appreciating works of art, such as *The Divine Comedy*, whose premises are intellectually alien.) To call Leni Riefenstahl's *The*

Triumph of the Will and *The Olympiad* masterpieces is not to gloss over Nazi propaganda with aesthetic lenience. The Nazi propaganda is there. But something else is there, too, which we reject at our loss. Because they project the complex movements of intelligence and grace and sensuousness, these two films of Riefenstahl (unique among works of Nazi artists) transcend the categories of propaganda or even reportage. And we find ourselves—to be sure, rather uncomfortably—seeing "Hitler" and not Hitler, the "1936 Olympics" and not the 1936 Olympics. Through Riefenstahl's genius as a film-maker, the "content" has—let us even assume, against her intentions—come to play a purely formal role.

A work of art, so far as it is a work of art, cannot—whatever the artist's personal intentions—advocate anything at all. The greatest artists attain a sublime neutrality. Think of Homer and Shakespeare, from whom generations of scholars and critics have vainly labored to extract particular "views" about human nature, morality, and society.

Again, take the case of Genet—though here, there is additional evidence for the point I am trying to make, because the artist's intentions are known. Genet, in his writings, may seem to be asking us to approve of cruelty, treacherousness, licentiousness, and murder. But so far as he is making a work of art, Genet is not advocating anything at all. He is recording, devouring, transfiguring his experience. In Genet's books, as it happens, this very process itself is his explicit subject; his books are not only works of art but works about art. However, even when (as is usually the case) this process is not in the foreground of the artist's demonstration, it is still this, the processing of experience, to which we owe our attention. It is immaterial that Genet's characters might repel us in real life. So would most of the characters in *King Lear*. The interest of Genet lies in the manner whereby his "subject" is annihilated by the serenity and intelligence of his imagination.

Approving or disapproving morally of what a work of art "says" is just as extraneous as becoming sexually excited by a work of art. (Both are, of course, very common.) And the reasons urged against the propriety and relevance of one apply as well to the other. Indeed, in this notion of the annihilation of the subject we have perhaps the only serious criterion for distinguishing between erotic literature or films or paintings which are art and those which (for want of a better word) one has to call pornography. Pornography has a "content" and is designed to make us connect (with disgust, desire) with that content. It is a substitute for life. But art does not excite; or, if it does, the excitation is appeased, within the terms of the aesthetic experience. All great art induces contemplation, a dynamic contemplation. However much the reader or listener or spectator is aroused by a provisional identification of what is in the work of art with real life, his ultimate reaction—so far as he is reacting to the work as a work of art—must be detached, restful, contemplative, emotionally free, beyond indignation and approval. It is interesting that Genet has recently said that he now thinks that if his books arouse readers sexually, "they're badly written, because the poetic emotion should be so strong that no reader is moved sexually. Insofar as my books are pornographic, I don't reject them. I simply say that I lacked grace."

A work of art may contain all sorts of information and offer instruction in new (and sometimes commendable) attitudes. We may learn about medieval theology and Florentine history from Dante; we may have our first experience of passionate melancholy from Chopin; we may become convinced of the barbarity of war by Goya and of the inhumanity of capital punishment by *An American Tragedy*. But so far as we deal with these works as works of art, the gratification they impart is of another order. It is an experience of the qualities or forms of human consciousness.

The objection that this approach reduces art to mere "formalism" must not be allowed to stand. (That word should be reserved for those works of art which mechanically perpetuate outmoded or depleted aesthetic formulas.) An approach which considers works of art as living, autonomous models of consciousness will seem objectionable only so long as we refuse to surrender the shallow distinction of form and content. For the sense in which a work of art has no content is no different from the sense in which the world has no content. Both are. Both need no justification; nor could they possibly have any.

The hyperdevelopment of style in, for example, Mannerist painting and Art Nouveau, is an emphatic form of experiencing the world as an aesthetic phenomenon. But only a particularly

emphatic form, which arises in reaction to an oppressively dogmatic style of realism. All style—that is, all art—proclaims this.
And the world *is*, ultimately, an aesthetic phenomenon.

That is to say, the world (all there is) cannot, ultimately, be
justified. Justification is an operation of the mind which can
be performed only when we consider one part of the world in
relation to another—not when we consider all there is.

The work of art, so far as we give ourselves to it, exercises a
total or absolute claim on us. The purpose of art is not as an
auxiliary to truth, either particular and historical or eternal. "If
art is anything," as Robbe-Grillet has written, "it is everything;
in which case it must be self-sufficient, and there can be nothing beyond it."

But this position is easily caricatured, for we live in the world,
and it is in the world that objects of art are made and enjoyed.
The claim that I have been making for the autonomy of the
work of art—its freedom to "mean" nothing—does not rule out
consideration of the effect or impact or function of art, once it
be granted that in this functioning of the art object as art object
the divorce between the aesthetic and the ethical is meaningless.

I have several times applied to the work of art the metaphor
of a mode of nourishment. To become involved with a work of
art entails, to be sure, the experience of detaching oneself from
the world. But the work of art itself is also a vibrant, magical,
and exemplary object which returns us to the world in some
way more open and enriched.

Raymond Bayer has written: "What each and every aesthetic
object imposes upon us, in appropriate rhythms, is a unique
and singular formula for the flow of our energy. . . . Every
work of art embodies a principle of proceeding, of stopping,
of scanning; an image of energy or relaxation, the imprint of a
caressing or destroying hand which is [the artist's] alone." We
can call this the physiognomy of the work, or its rhythm, or,
as I would rather do, its style. Of course, when we employ the
notion of style historically, to group works of art into schools
and periods, we tend to efface the individuality of styles. But
this is not our experience when we encounter a work of art
from an aesthetic (as opposed to a conceptual) point of view.
Then, so far as the work is successful and still has the power to

communicate with us, we experience only the individuality and contingency of the style.

It is the same with our own lives. If we see them from the outside, as the influence and popular dissemination of the social sciences and psychiatry has persuaded more and more people to do, we view ourselves as instances of generalities, and in so doing become profoundly and painfully alienated from our own experience and our humanity.

As William Earle has recently noted, if *Hamlet* is "about" anything, it is about Hamlet, his particular situation, not about the human condition. A work of art is a kind of showing or recording or witnessing which gives palpable form to consciousness; its object is to make something singular explicit. So far as it is true that we cannot judge (morally, conceptually) unless we generalize, then it is also true that the experience of works of art, and what is represented in works of art, transcends judgment—though the work itself may be judged as art. Isn't this just what we recognize as a feature of the greatest art, like the *Iliad* and the novels of Tolstoy and the plays of Shakespeare? That such art overrides our petty judgments, our facile labelling of persons and acts as good or bad? And that this can happen is all to the good. (There is even a gain for the cause of morality in it.)

For morality, unlike art, *is* ultimately justified by its utility: that it makes, or is supposed to make, life more humane and livable for us all. But consciousness—what used to be called, rather tendentiously, the faculty of contemplation—can be, and is, wider and more various than action. It has its nourishment, art and speculative thought, activities which can be described either as self-justifying or in no need of justification. What a work of art does is to make us see or comprehend something singular, not judge or generalize. This act of comprehension accompanied by voluptuousness is the only valid end, and sole sufficient justification, of a work of art.

Perhaps the best way of clarifying the nature of our experience of works of art, and the relation between art and the rest of human feeling and doing, is to invoke the notion of will. It is a useful notion because will is not just a particular posture of consciousness, energized consciousness. It is also an attitude toward the world, of a subject toward the world.

The complex kind of willing that is embodied, and communicated, in a work of art both abolishes the world and encounters it in an extraordinary intense and specialized way. This double aspect of the will in art is succinctly expressed by Bayer when he says: "Each work of art gives us the schematized and disengaged memory of a volition." Insofar as it is schematized, disengaged, a memory, the willing involved in art sets itself at a distance from the world.

All of which harkens back to Nietzsche's famous statement in *The Birth of Tragedy*: "Art is not an imitation of nature but its metaphysical supplement, raised up beside it in order to overcome it."

All works of art are founded on a certain distance from the lived reality which is represented. This "distance" is, by definition, inhuman or impersonal to a certain degree; for in order to appear to us as art, the work must restrict sentimental intervention and emotional participation, which are functions of "closeness." It is the degree and manipulating of this distance, the conventions of distance, which constitute the style of the work. In the final analysis, "style" *is* art. And art is nothing more or less than various modes of stylized, dehumanized representation.

But this view—expounded by Ortega y Gasset, among others—can easily be misinterpreted, since it seems to suggest that art, so far as it approaches its own norm, is a kind of irrelevant, impotent toy. Ortega himself greatly contributes to such a misinterpretation by omitting the various dialectics between self and world involved in the experiencing of works of art. Ortega focuses too exclusively on the notion of the work of art as a certain kind of object, with its own, spiritually aristocratic, standards for being savored. A work of art *is* first of all an object, not an imitation; and it is true that all great art is founded on distance, on artificiality, on style, on what Ortega calls dehumanization. But the notion of distance (and of dehumanization, as well) is misleading, unless one adds that the movement is not just away from but toward the world. The overcoming or transcending of the world in art is also a way of encountering the world, and of training or educating the will to be in the world. It would seem that Ortega and even Robbe-Grillet, a more recent exponent of the same position, are still not wholly

free of the spell of the notion of "content." For, in order to
limit the human content of art, and to fend off tired ideologies
like humanism or socialist realism which would put art in the
service of some moral or social idea, they feel required to ignore
or scant the function of art. But art does not become function-
less when it is seen to be, in the last analysis, content-less. For
all the persuasiveness of Ortega's and Robbe-Grillet's defense
of the formal nature of art, the specter of banished "content"
continues to lurk around the edges of their argument, giving to
"form" a defiantly anemic, salutarily eviscerated look.

The argument will never be complete until "form" or "style"
can be thought of without that banished specter, without a
feeling of loss. Valéry's daring inversion—"Literature. What is
'form' for anyone else is 'content' for me"—scarcely does the
trick. It is hard to think oneself out of a distinction so habitual
and apparently self-evident. One can do so only by adopting a
different, more organic, theoretical vantage point—such as the
notion of will. What is wanted of such a vantage point is that it
do justice to the twin aspects of art: as object and as function, as
artifice and as living form of consciousness, as the overcoming
or supplementing of reality and as the making explicit of forms
of encountering reality, as autonomous individual creation and
as dependent historical phenomenon.

Art is the objectifying of the will in a thing or performance,
and the provoking or arousing of the will. From the point of
view of the artist, it is the objectifying of a volition; from the
point of view of the spectator, it is the creation of an imaginary
décor for the will.

Indeed, the entire history of the various arts could be rewritten as the history of different attitudes toward the will.
Nietzsche and Spengler wrote pioneer studies on this theme.
A valuable recent attempt is to be found in a book by Jean
Starobinski, *The Invention of Liberty*, mainly devoted to 18th
century painting and architecture. Starobinski examines the art
of this period in terms of the new ideas of self-mastery and of
mastery of the world, as embodying new relations between the
self and the world. Art is seen as the naming of emotions. Emotions, longings, aspirations, by thus being named, are virtually
invented and certainly promulgated by art: for example, the

"sentimental solitude" provoked by the gardens that were laid out in the 18th century and by much-admired ruins.

Thus, it should be clear that the account of the autonomy of art I have been outlining, in which I have characterized art as an imaginary landscape or décor of the will, not only does not preclude but rather invites the examination of works of art as historically specifiable phenomena.

The intricate stylistic convolutions of modern art, for example, are clearly a function of the unprecedented *technical* extension of the human will by technology, and the devastating commitment of human will to a novel form of social and psychological order, one based on incessant change. But it also remains to be said that the very possibility of the explosion of technology, of the contemporary disruptions of self and society, depends on the attitudes toward the will which are partly invented and disseminated by works of art at a certain historical moment, and then come to appear as a "realistic" reading of a perennial human nature.

Style is the principle of decision in a work of art, the signature of the artist's will. And as the human will is capable of an indefinite number of stances, there are an indefinite number of possible styles for works of art.

Seen from the outside, that is, historically, stylistic decisions can always be correlated with some historical development—like the invention of writing or of movable type, the invention or transformation of musical instruments, the availability of new materials to the sculptor or architect. But this approach, however sound and valuable, of necessity sees matters grossly; it treats of "periods" and "traditions" and "schools."

Seen from the inside, that is, when one examines an individual work of art and tries to account for its value and effect, every stylistic decision contains an element of arbitrariness, however much it may seem justifiable *propter hoc*. If art is the supreme game which the will plays with itself, "style" consists of the set of rules by which this game is played. And the rules are always, finally, an artificial and arbitrary limit, whether they are rules of form (like *terza rima* or the twelve-tone row or frontality) or the presence of a certain "content." The role of the arbitrary and unjustifiable in art has never been sufficiently acknowledged. Ever since the enterprise of criticism began with Aristotle's *Poetics*, critics have been beguiled into emphasizing the necessary in art. (When Aristotle said that poetry was more philosophical than history, he was justified insofar as he wanted to rescue poetry, that is, the arts, from being conceived as a type of factual, particular, descriptive statement. But what he said was misleading insofar as it suggests that art supplies something like what philosophy gives us: an argument. The metaphor of the work of art as an "argument," with premises and entailments, has informed most criticism since.) Usually critics who want to praise a work of art feel compelled to demonstrate that each part is justified, that it could not be other than it is. And every artist, when it comes to his own work, remembering the role of chance, fatigue, external distractions, knows what the critic says to be a lie, knows that it could well have been otherwise. The sense of inevitability that a great work of art projects is not made up of the inevitability or necessity of its parts, but of the whole.

In other words, what is inevitable in a work of art is the style. To the extent that a work seems right, just, unimaginable otherwise (without loss or damage), what we are responding to is a quality of its style. The most attractive works of art are those which give us the illusion that the artist had no alternatives, so wholly centered is he *in* his style. Compare that which is forced, labored, synthetic in the construction of *Madame Bovary* and of *Ulysses* with the ease and harmony of such equally ambitious works as *Les Liaisons Dangereuses* and Kafka's *Metamorphosis*. The first two books I have mentioned are great indeed. But the greatest art seems secreted, not constructed.

For an artist's style to have this quality of authority, assurance, seamlessness, inevitability does not, of course, alone put his work at the very highest level of achievement. Radiguet's two novels have it as well as Bach.

The difference that I have drawn between "style" and "stylization" might be analogous to the difference between will and willfulness.

———

An artist's style is, from a technical point of view, nothing other than the particular idiom in which he deploys the *forms* of his art. It is for this reason that the problems raised by the concept of "style" overlap with those raised by the concept of "form," and their solutions will have much in common.

For instance, one function of style is identical with, because it is simply a more individual specification of, that important function of form pointed out by Coleridge and Valéry: to preserve the works of the mind against oblivion. This function is easily demonstrated in the rhythmical, sometimes rhyming, character of all primitive, oral literatures. Rhythm and rhyme, and the more complex formal resources of poetry such as meter, symmetry of figures, antitheses, are the means that words afford for creating a memory of themselves before material signs (writing) are invented; hence everything that an archaic culture wishes to commit to memory is put in poetic form. "The form of a work," as Valéry puts it, "is the sum of its perceptible characteristics, whose physical action compels recognition and tends to resist all those varying causes of dissolution which threaten the expressions of thought, whether it be inattention, forgetfulness, or even the objections that may arise against it in the mind."

Thus, form—in its specific idiom, style—is a plan of sensory imprinting, the vehicle for the transaction between immediate sensuous impression and memory (be it individual or cultural). This mnemonic function explains why every style depends on, and can be analyzed in terms of, some principle of repetition or redundancy.

It also explains the difficulties of the contemporary period of the arts. Today styles do not develop slowly and succeed each other gradually, over long periods of time which allow the audience for art to assimilate fully the principles of repetition on which the work of art is built; but instead succeed one another so rapidly as to seem to give their audiences no breathing space to prepare. For, if one does not perceive how a work repeats itself, the work is, almost literally, not perceptible and therefore, at the same time, not intelligible. It is the perception of repetitions that makes a work of art intelligible. Until one has grasped, not the "content," but the principles of (and balance between) variety and redundancy in Merce Cunningham's "Winterbranch" or a chamber concerto by Charles Wuorinen or Burroughs' *Naked Lunch* or the "black" paintings of Ad Reinhardt, these works are bound to appear boring or ugly or confusing, or all three.

Style has other functions besides that of being, in the extended sense that I have just indicated, a mnemonic device.

For instance, every style embodies an epistemological decision, an interpretation of how and what we perceive. This is easiest to see in the contemporary, self-conscious period of the arts, though it is no less true of all art. Thus, the style of Robbe-Grillet's novels expresses a perfectly valid, if narrow, insight into relationships between persons and things: namely, that persons are also things and that things are not persons. Robbe-Grillet's behavioristic treatment of persons and refusal to "anthropomorphize" things amount to a stylistic decision—to give an exact account of the visual and topographic properties of things; to exclude, virtually, sense modalities other than sight, perhaps because the language that exists to describe them is less exact and less neutral. The circular repetitive style of Gertrude Stein's *Melanctha* expresses her interest in the dilution of immediate awareness by memory and anticipation, what she calls "association," which is obscured in language by the system of the tenses. Stein's insistence on the presentness of experience is identical with her decision to keep to the present tense, to choose commonplace short words and repeat groups of them incessantly, to use an extremely loose syntax and abjure most punctuation. Every style is a means of insisting on something.

It will be seen that stylistic decisions, by focusing our attention on some things, are also a narrowing of our attention, a refusal to allow us to see others. But the greater interestingness of one work of art over another does not rest on the greater number of things the stylistic decisions in that work allow us to attend to, but rather on the intensity and authority and wisdom of that attention, however narrow its focus.

In the strictest sense, all the contents of consciousness are ineffable. Even the simplest sensation is, in its totality, indescribable. Every work of art, therefore, needs to be understood not only as something rendered, but also as a certain handling of the ineffable. In the greatest art, one is always aware of things

that cannot be said (rules of "decorum"), of the contradiction between expression and the presence of the inexpressible.
Stylistic devices are also techniques of avoidance. The most
potent elements in a work of art are, often, its silences.

What I have said about style has been directed mainly to clearing up certain misconceptions about works of art and how to
talk about them. But it remains to be said that style is a notion
that applies to any experience (whenever we talk about its form
or qualities). And just as many works of art which have a potent
claim on our interest are impure or mixed with respect to the
standard I have been proposing, so many items in our experience which could not be classed as works of art possess some
of the qualities of art objects. Whenever speech or movement
or behavior or objects exhibit a certain deviation from the most
direct, useful, insensible mode of expression or being in the
world, we may look at them as having a "style," and being both
autonomous and exemplary.

(1965)

II

The Artist as Exemplary Sufferer

The richest style is the synthetic voice of the leading character.

PAVESE

CESARE PAVESE began writing around 1930, and the novels which have been translated and published here—*The House on the Hill, The Moon and the Bonfires, Among Women Only*, and *The Devil in the Hills*—were all written in the years 1947–49, so that a reader confined to English translations can't generalize about his work as a whole. From these four novels alone, however, it appears that his main virtues as a novelist are delicacy, economy, and control. The style is flat, dry, unemotional. One remarks the coolness of Pavese's fiction, though the subject-matter is often violent. This is because the real subject is never the violent happening (e.g. the suicide in *Among Women Only*, the war in *The Devil in the Hills*) but, rather, the cautious subjectivity of the narrator. The typical effort of a Pavese hero is lucidity; the typical problem is that of lapsed communication. The novels are about crises of conscience, and the refusal to allow crises of conscience. A certain atrophy of the emotions, an enervation of sentiment and bodily vitality, is presupposed. The anguish of prematurely disillusioned, highly civilized people alternating between irony and melancholic experiments with their own emotions is indeed familiar. But unlike other explorations of this vein of modern sensibility—for example, much of French fiction and poetry of the last eighty years—Pavese's novels are unsensational and chaste. The main action always takes place off-stage, or in the past; and erotic scenes are curiously avoided.

As if to compensate for the detached relations which his characters have with each other, Pavese typically attributes to them a deep involvement with a place—usually either the cityscape of Turin, where Pavese went to the university and lived most of his adult life, or the surrounding Piedmont countryside, where he was born and spent his childhood. This sense of place, and the desire to find and recover the meaning of a place, does not, however, give Pavese's work any of the characteristics of regional fiction, and this may in part account for the failure of his novels to arouse much enthusiasm among an English-speaking audience, nothing like that aroused by the work of Silone or Moravia, though he is a much more gifted and original writer than either of these. Pavese's sense of place and of people is not what one expects of an Italian writer. But then Pavese was a Northern Italian; Northern Italy is not the Italy of the foreign dream, and Turin is a large industrial city lacking in the historical resonance and incarnate sensuality which attracts foreigners to Italy. One finds no monuments, no local color, no ethnic charm in Pavese's Turin and Piedmont. The place is there, but as the unattainable, the anonymous, the inhuman.

Pavese's sense of the relation of people to place (the way in which people are transfixed by the impersonal force of a place) will be familiar to anyone who has seen the films of Alain Resnais and especially of Michelangelo Antonioni—*Le Amiche* (which was adapted from Pavese's best novel, *Among Women Only*), *L'Avventura*, and *La Notte*. But the virtues of Pavese's fiction are not popular virtues, any more than are the virtues of, say, Antonioni's films. (Those who don't take to Antonioni's films call them "literary" and "too subjective.") Like Antonioni's films, Pavese's novels are refined, elliptical (though never obscure), quiet, anti-dramatic, self-contained. Pavese is not a major writer, as Antonioni is a major film-maker. But he does deserve a good deal more attention in England and America than he has gotten thus far.*

*The same is true of another Italian, Tommaso Landolfi, with a large body of stories and novels, born the same year as Pavese (1908) but still living and writing. Landolfi, who is thus far represented in English by only one volume, a selection of nine of his short stories, entitled *Gogol's Wife and Other Stories*, is a very different and, at his best, more forceful writer than Pavese. His morbid wit, austere intellectuality, and rather surrealistic notions of disaster put him closer to writers like Borges and Isak Dinesen. But he and Pavese have something in common which makes the work of both unlike the fiction mainly being written today in England and America, and apparently uninteresting to the audience for that fiction. What they share is the project of a basically neutral, reserved kind of writing. In such writing, the act of relating a story is seen primarily as an act of intelligence. To narrate is palpably to employ one's intelligence; the unity of the narration characteristic of European and Latin American fiction is the unity of the narrator's intelligence. But the writing of fiction common in America today has little use for this patient, dogged, unshowy use of intelligence. American writers mostly want the facts to declare, to interpret themselves. If there is a narrative voice, it is likely to be immaculately mindless—or else strainingly clever and bouncy. Thus, most American writing is grossly rhetorical (that is, there is an overproduction of means in relation to ends), in contrast to the classical mode of European writing, which achieves its effects with an anti-rhetorical style—a style that holds back, that aims ultimately at neutral transparency. Both Pavese and Landolfi belong squarely in this anti-rhetorical tradition.

Recently Pavese's diaries from the years 1935 to 1950, when he committed suicide at the age of forty-two, have been issued in English.* They can be read without any acquaintance with Pavese's novels, as an example of a peculiarly modern literary genre—the writer's "diary" or "notebooks" or "journal."

Why do we read a writer's journal? Because it illuminates his books? Often it does not. More likely, simply because of the rawness of the journal form, even when it is written with an eye to future publication. Here we read the writer in the first person; we encounter the ego behind the masks of ego in an author's works. No degree of intimacy in a novel can supply this, even when the author writes in the first person or uses a third person which transparently points to himself. Most of Pavese's novels, including the four translated into English, are narrated in the first person. Yet we know that the "I" in Pavese's novels is not identical with Pavese himself, no more than is the "Marcel" who tells *Remembrance of Things Past* identical with Proust, nor the "K." of *The Trial* and *The Castle* identical with Kafka. We are not satisfied. It is the author naked which the modern audience demands, as ages of religious faith demanded a human sacrifice.

The journal gives us the workshop of the writer's soul. And why are we interested in the soul of the writer? Not because we are so interested in writers as such. But because of the insatiable modern preoccupation with psychology, the latest and most powerful legacy of the Christian tradition of introspection, opened up by Paul and Augustine, which equates the discovery of the self with the discovery of the suffering self. For the modern consciousness, the artist (replacing the saint) is the exemplary sufferer. And among artists, the writer, the man of words, is the person to whom we look to be able best to express his suffering.

The writer is the exemplary sufferer because he has found both the deepest level of suffering and also a professional means to sublimate (in the literal, not the Freudian, sense of sublimate) his suffering. As a man, he suffers; as a writer, he transforms his

---

* *The Burning Brand: Diaries 1935–1950* by Cesare Pavese. Translated by A. E. Murch (with Jeanne Molli). New York, Walker & Co.

suffering into art. The writer is the man who discovers the use of suffering in the economy of art—as the saints discovered the utility and necessity of suffering in the economy of salvation.

The unity of Pavese's diaries is to be found in his reflections on how to use, how to act on, his suffering. Literature is one use. Isolation is another, both as a technique for the inciting and perfecting of his art, and as a value in itself. And suicide is the third, ultimate use of suffering—conceived of not as an end to suffering, but as the ultimate way of acting on suffering.

Thus we have the following remarkable sequence of thought, in a diary entry of 1938. Pavese writes: "Literature is a defense against the attacks of life. It says to life: 'You can't deceive me. I know your habits, foresee and enjoy watching your reactions, and steal your secrets by involving you in cunning obstructions that halt your normal flow.' . . . The other defense against things in general is silence as we muster strength for a fresh leap forward. But we must impose that silence on ourselves, not have it imposed on us, not even by death. To choose a hardship for ourselves is our only defense against that hardship. . . . Those who by their very nature can suffer completely, utterly, have an advantage. This is how we can disarm the power of suffering, make it our own creation, our own choice; submit to it. A justification for suicide."

The modern form of the writer's journal shows a curious evolution if we examine some of its principal exemplars: Stendhal, Baudelaire, Gide, Kafka, and now Pavese. The uninhibited display of egotism devolves into the heroic quest for the cancellation of the self. Pavese has none of Gide's Protestant sense of his life as a work of art, his respect for his own ambition, his confidence in his own feelings, his love for himself. Nor does he have Kafka's exquisite commitment without mockery to his own anguish. Pavese, who used the "I" so freely in his novels, usually speaks of himself as "you" in his diaries. He does not describe himself, but addresses himself. He is the ironic, exhortatory, reproachful spectator of himself. The ultimate consequence of such a bracketed view of the self would seem to have been, inevitably, suicide.

The diaries are in effect a long series of self-assessments and self-interrogations. They record nothing of daily life or observed incidents; nor is there any description of family, friends, lovers, colleagues or reaction to public events (as in Gide's *Journals*). All that satisfies the more conventional expectation of the contents of a writer's journal (as in Coleridge's *Notebooks*, and again in Gide's *Journals*) are the numerous reflections on the general problems of style and literary composition, and the copious notes on the writer's reading. Pavese was very much a "good European," though he never travelled outside Italy; the diaries attest that he was at home in all of European literature and thought, and in American writing (in which he was especially interested) as well. Pavese was not simply a novelist but a *uomo di cultura*: poet, novelist, short story writer, literary critic, translator, and editor with one of Italy's leading publishers (Einaudi). Much space in the diaries is taken up by this writer-as-man-of-letters. There are sensitive and subtle comments on a lifetime of immensely varied reading that ranged from the Rig-Veda, Euripides, and Defoe to Corneille, Vico, Kierkegaard, and Hemingway. But it is not this aspect of the diaries which I am considering here, for it is not this which constitutes the specific interest that writers' journals hold for a modern audience. It should however be noted that when Pavese discusses his own writing, it is not as the writer of it but rather as a reader or critic. There is no discussion of work-in-progress, or plans and sketches for stories, novels, and poems to be written. The only work discussed is what has been finished. Another notable omission in the diaries is any reflection of Pavese's involvement in politics—neither his anti-fascist activities, for which he was imprisoned for ten months in 1935, nor his long, ambivalent, and finally disillusioned association with the Communist Party.

It might be said that there are two *personae* in the diary. Pavese the man, and Pavese the critic and reader. Or: Pavese thinking prospectively, and Pavese thinking retrospectively. There is the self-reproachful and self-exhortatory analysis of his feelings and projects; the focus of reflection is on his talents—as a writer, as a lover of women, and as a prospective suicide. Then there is all the retrospective comment: analyses of some of his completed books, and their place in his work; the notes on his reading. Insofar as the "present" of Pavese's life enters the diaries at all, it is mainly in the form of a consideration of his capabilities and prospects.

Apart from writing, there are two prospects to which Pavese continually recurs. One is the prospect of suicide, which tempted Pavese at least as early as his university years (when two of his close friends killed themselves) and is a theme to be found on almost every page of the diaries. The other is the prospect of romantic love and erotic failure. Pavese shows himself as tormented by a profound sense of sexual inadequacy, which he bulwarked by all sorts of theories about sexual technique, the hopelessness of love, and the sex war. Remarks on the predatoriness, the exploitativeness of women are interspersed with confessions of his own failure to love, or to provide sexual satisfaction. Pavese, who never married, records in the journal the reactions to a number of long affairs and casual sexual experiences, usually at the point when he is expecting trouble or after they actually have failed. The women themselves are never described; the events of the relationship are not even alluded to.

The two themes are intimately connected, as Pavese himself experienced. In the closing months of his life, in the midst of an unhappy affair with an American film star, he writes: "One does not kill oneself for love of a woman, but because love—any love—reveals us in our nakedness, our misery, our vulnerability, our nothingness . . . Deep, deep down, did I not clutch at this amazing love affair as it flew . . . to make myself revert to my old thought—my long-standing temptation, to have an excuse for thinking of it again: love and death. This is the hereditary pattern." Or again, in an ironic vein, Pavese remarks: "It is possible not to think about women, just as one does not think about death." Women and death never ceased to fascinate Pavese, and with an equal degree of anxiety and morbidity, since his main problem in both cases was whether he would be equal to the occasion.

What Pavese has to say about love is the familiar other side of romantic idealization. Pavese rediscovers, with Stendhal, that love is an essential fiction; it is not that love sometimes makes mistakes, but that it is, essentially, a mistake. What one takes to be an attachment to another person is unmasked as one more dance of the solitary ego. It is easy to see how this view of love is peculiarly congruent to the modern vocation of the writer. In the Aristotelian tradition of art as imitation, the writer was the medium or vehicle for describing the truth about something outside himself. In the modern tradition (roughly, Rousseau forward) of art as expression, the artist tells the truth about himself. Therefore it was inevitable that a theory of love as an experience or revelation of oneself, deceptively presented as an experience or revelation of the value of a loved person or object, should suggest itself. Love, like art, becomes a medium of self-expression. But because making a woman is not as solitary an act as making a novel or a poem, it is doomed to failure. A prevailing theme of serious literature and cinema today is the failure of love. (When we encounter the opposite statement, as for instance in *Lady Chatterley's Lover* or in Louis Malle's film *The Lovers*, we incline to describe it as a "fairy tale.") Love dies because its birth was an error. However, the error remains a necessary one, so long as one sees the world, in Pavese's words, as a "jungle of self-interest." The isolated ego does not cease to suffer. "Life is pain and the enjoyment of love is an anaesthetic."

A further consequence of this modern belief in the fictional nature of erotic attachment is a new self-conscious aquiescence in the inevitable attractiveness of unrequited love. As love is an emotion felt by the solitary ego and mistakenly projected outward, the impregnability of the beloved's ego exercises a hypnotic attraction for the romantic imagination. The lure of unrequited love lies in the identity of what Pavese calls "perfect behavior" and a strong, absolutely isolated, indifferent ego. "Perfect behavior is born of complete indifference," Pavese writes in his diary in 1940. "Perhaps that is why we always love madly someone who treats us with indifference; she represents 'style,' the fascination of 'class,' all that is desirable."

Many of Pavese's remarks on love seem like a case history supporting the thesis of Denis de Rougemont and other historians of the Western imagination who have traced the evolution of the Western image of sexual love since Tristan and Isolde as a "romantic agony," a death-wish. But the striking rhetorical enmeshment of the terms "writing," "sex," and "suicide" in Pavese's diaries indicates that this sensibility in its modern form is more complex. Rougemont's thesis may throw light on the Western overvaluation of love, but not on the modern pessimism about it: the view that love, and sensual fulfillment, are hopeless projects. Rougemont might well have used Pavese's own words: "Love is the cheapest of religions."

My own view is that the modern cult of love is not part of the story of a Christian heresy (Gnostic, Manichean, Catharist), as Rougemont suggests, but expresses the central and peculiarly modern preoccupation of the loss of feeling. To wish to cultivate "the art of looking at ourselves as though we were characters in one of our novels . . . as the way to put ourselves in a position to think constructively and reap the benefits" reveals Pavese speaking hopefully about a situation of self-alienation which elsewhere in the diaries is a subject of continual sorrow. For "life begins in the body," as Pavese observes in another entry; and he continually gives voice to the reproach which the body makes to the mind. If civilization may be defined as that stage of human life at which, objectively, the body becomes a problem, then our moment of civilization may be described as that stage at which we are subjectively aware of, and feel trapped by, this problem. Now we aspire to the life of the body and we reject the ascetic traditions of Judaism and Christianity, but we are still confined in the generalized sensibility which that religious tradition bequeathed us. Hence we complain; we are resigned and detached; we complain. Pavese's continual prayers for the strength to lead a life of rigorous seclusion and solitude ("The only heroic rule is to be alone, alone, alone") are entirely of a piece with his repeated complaints about his inability to feel. (See, for example, his remarks on his absence of feeling when his best friend, Leone Ginzburg, eminent professor and Resistance leader, was tortured to death by the fascists in 1940.) Here is where the modern cult of love enters: it is the main way in which we test ourselves for strength of feeling, and find ourselves deficient.

Everyone knows that we have a different, much more emphatic view of love between the sexes than the ancient Greeks and the Orientals, and that the modern view of love is an extension of the spirit of Christianity, in however attenuated and secularized a form. But the cult of love is not, as Rougemont claims, a Christian *heresy.* Christianity is, from its inception (Paul), the romantic religion. The cult of love in the West is an aspect of the cult of suffering—suffering as the supreme token of seriousness (the paradigm of the Cross). We do not find among the ancient Hebrews, Greeks, and the Orientals the same value placed on love because we do not find there the same positive value placed on suffering. Suffering was not the hallmark of seriousness; rather, seriousness was measured by one's ability to evade or transcend the penalty of suffering, by one's ability to achieve tranquillity and equilibrium. In contrast, the sensibility we have inherited identifies spirituality and seriousness with turbulence, suffering, passion. For two thousand years, among Christians and Jews, it has been spiritually fashionable to be in pain. Thus it is not love which we overvalue, but suffering—more precisely, the spiritual merits and benefits of suffering.

The modern contribution to this Christian sensibility has been to discover the making of works of art and the venture of sexual love as the two most exquisite sources of suffering. It is this that we look for in a writer's diary, and which Pavese provides in disquieting abundance.

(1962)

Simone Weil

THE culture-heroes of our liberal bourgeois civilization are anti-liberal and anti-bourgeois; they are writers who are repetitive, obsessive, and impolite, who impress by force—not simply by their tone of personal authority and by their intellectual ardor, but by the sense of acute personal and intellectual extremity. The bigots, the hysterics, the destroyers of the self—these are the writers who bear witness to the fearful polite time in which we live. Mostly it is a matter of tone: it is hardly possible to give credence to ideas uttered in the impersonal tones of sanity. There are certain eras which are too complex, too deafened by contradictory historical and intellectual experiences, to hear the voice of sanity. Sanity becomes compromise, evasion, a lie. Ours is an age which consciously pursues health, and yet only believes in the reality of sickness. The truths we respect are those born of affliction. We measure truth in terms of the cost to the writer in suffering—rather than by the standard of an objective truth to which a writer's words correspond. Each of our truths must have a martyr.

What revolted the mature Goethe in the young Kleist, who submitted his works to the elder statesman of German letters "on the knees of his heart"—the morbid, the hysterical, the sense of the unhealthy, the enormous indulgence in suffering out of which Kleist's plays and tales were mined—is just what we value today. Today Kleist gives pleasure, most of Goethe is a classroom bore. In the same way, such writers as Kierkegaard, Nietzsche, Dostoevsky, Kafka, Baudelaire, Rimbaud, Genet—and Simone Weil—have their authority with us precisely because of their air of unhealthiness. Their unhealthiness is their soundness, and is what carries conviction.

Perhaps there are certain ages which do not need truth as much as they need a deepening of the sense of reality, a widening of the imagination. I, for one, do not doubt that the sane view of the world is the true one. But is that what is always wanted, truth? The need for truth is not constant; no more than is the need for repose. An idea which is a distortion may have a greater intellectual thrust than the truth; it may better serve the needs of the spirit, which vary. The truth is balance, but the opposite of truth, which is unbalance, may not be a lie.

Thus I do not mean to decry a fashion, but to underscore the motive behind the contemporary taste for the extreme in art and thought. All that is necessary is that we not be hypocritical, that we recognize why we read and admire writers like Simone Weil. I cannot believe that more than a handful of the tens of thousands of readers she has won since the posthumous publication of her books and essays really share her ideas. Nor is it necessary—necessary to share Simone Weil's anguished and unconsummated love affair with the Catholic Church, or accept her gnostic theology of divine absence, or espouse her ideals of body denial, or concur in her violently unfair hatred of Roman civilization and the Jews. Similarly, with Kierkegaard and Nietzsche; most of their modern admirers could not, and do not embrace their ideas. We read writers of such scathing originality for their personal authority, for the example of their seriousness, for their manifest willingness to sacrifice themselves for their truths, and—only piecemeal—for their "views." As the corrupt Alcibiades followed Socrates, unable and unwilling to change his own life, but moved, enriched, and full of love, so the sensitive modern reader pays his respect to a level of spiritual reality which is not, could not, be his own.

Some lives are exemplary, others not; and of exemplary lives, there are those which invite us to imitate them, and those which we regard from a distance with a mixture of revulsion, pity, and reverence. It is, roughly, the difference between the hero and the saint (if one may use the latter term in an aesthetic, rather than a religious sense). Such a life, absurd in its exaggerations and degree of self-mutilation—like Kleist's, like Kierkegaard's— was Simone Weil's. I am thinking of the fanatical asceticism of Simone Weil's life, her contempt for pleasure and for happiness, her noble and ridiculous political gestures, her elaborate self-denials, her tireless courting of affliction; and I do not exclude her homeliness, her physical clumsiness, her migraines, her tuberculosis. No one who loves life would wish to imitate her dedication to martyrdom, or would wish it for his children or for anyone else whom he loves. Yet so far as we love seriousness, as well as life, we are moved by it, nourished by it. In the respect we pay to such lives, we acknowledge the presence of mystery in the world—and mystery is just what the secure possession of the truth, an objective truth, denies. In this sense, all truth is

superficial; and some (but not all) distortions of the truth, some
(but not all) insanity, some (but not all) unhealthiness, some
(but not all) denials of life are truth-giving, sanity-producing,
health-creating, and life-enhancing.

(1963)

Camus' Notebooks

GREAT writers are either husbands or lovers. Some writers supply the solid virtues of a husband: reliability, intelligibility, generosity, decency. There are other writers in whom one prizes the gifts of a lover, gifts of temperament rather than of moral goodness. Notoriously, women tolerate qualities in a lover—moodiness, selfishness, unreliability, brutality—that they would never countenance in a husband, in return for excitement, an infusion of intense feeling. In the same way, readers put up with unintelligibility, obsessiveness, painful truths, lies, bad grammar—if, in compensation, the writer allows them to savor rare emotions and dangerous sensations. And, as in life, so in art both are necessary, husbands and lovers. It's a great pity when one is forced to choose between them.

Again, as in life, so in art: the lover usually has to take second place. In the great periods of literature, husbands have been more numerous than lovers; in all the great periods of literature, that is, except our own. Perversity is the muse of modern literature. Today the house of fiction is full of mad lovers, gleeful rapists, castrated sons—but very few husbands. The husbands have a bad conscience, they would all like to be lovers. Even so husbandly and solid a writer as Thomas Mann was tormented by an ambivalence toward virtue, and was forever carrying on about it in the guise of a conflict between the bourgeois and the artist. But most modern writers don't even acknowledge Mann's problem. Each writer, each literary movement vies with its predecessor in a great display of temperament, obsession, singularity. Modern literature is oversupplied with madmen of genius. No wonder, then, that when an immensely gifted writer, whose talents certainly fall short of genius, arises who boldly assumes the responsibilities of sanity, he should be acclaimed beyond his purely literary merits.

I mean, of course, Albert Camus, the ideal husband of contemporary letters. Being a contemporary, he had to traffic in the madmen's themes: suicide, affectlessness, guilt, absolute terror. But he does so with such an air of reasonableness, *mesure*, effortlessness, gracious impersonality, as to place him apart from the others. Starting from the premises of a popular nihilism, he moves the reader—solely by the power of his own tranquil voice and tone—to humanist and humanitarian conclusions in no way entailed by his premises. This illogical leaping of the abyss of nihilism is the gift for which readers are grateful to Camus. This is why he evoked feelings of real affection on the part of his readers. Kafka arouses pity and terror, Joyce admiration, Proust and Gide respect, but no modern writer that I can think of, except Camus, has aroused love. His death in 1960 was felt as a personal loss by the whole literate world.

Whenever Camus is spoken of there is a mingling of personal, moral, and literary judgment. No discussion of Camus fails to include, or at least suggest, a tribute to his goodness and attractiveness as a man. To write about Camus is thus to consider what occurs between the image of a writer and his work, which is tantamount to the relation between morality and literature. For it is not only that Camus himself is always thrusting the moral problem upon his readers. (All his stories, plays, and novels relate the career of a responsible sentiment, or the absence of it.) It is because his work, solely as a literary accomplishment, is not major enough to bear the weight of admiration that readers want to give it. One *wants* Camus to be a truly great writer, not just a very good one. But he is not. It might be useful here to compare Camus with George Orwell and James Baldwin, two other husbandly writers who essay to combine the role of artist with civic conscience. Both Orwell and Baldwin are better writers in their essays than they are in their fiction. This disparity is not to be found in Camus, a far more important writer. But what is true is that Camus' art is always in the service of certain intellectual conceptions which are more fully stated in the essays. Camus' fiction is illustrative, philosophical. It is not so much about its characters—Meursault, Caligula, Jan, Clamence, Dr. Rieux—as it is about the problems of innocence and guilt, responsibility and nihilistic indifference. The three novels, the stories, and the plays have a thin, somewhat skeletal quality which makes them a good deal less than absolutely first-rate, judged by the standards of art. Unlike Kafka, whose most illustrative and symbolic fictions are at the same time autonomous acts of the imagination, Camus' fiction continually betrays its source in an intellectual concern.

What of Camus' essays, political articles, addresses, literary criticism, journalism? It is extremely distinguished work. But was Camus a thinker of importance? The answer is no. Sartre, however distasteful certain of his political sympathies are to his English-speaking audience, brings a powerful and original mind to philosophical, psychological, and literary analysis. Camus, however attractive his political sympathies, does not. The celebrated philosophical essays (*The Myth of Sisyphus, The Rebel*) are the work of an extraordinarily talented and literate epigone. The same is true of Camus as a historian of ideas and as a literary critic. Camus is at his best when he disburdens himself of the baggage of existentialist culture (Nietzsche, Kierkegaard, Dostoevsky, Heidegger, Kafka) and speaks in his own person. This happens in the great essay against capital punishment, "Reflections on the Guillotine," and in the casual writings, like the essay-portraits of Algiers, Oran, and other Mediterranean places.

Neither art nor thought of the highest quality is to be found in Camus. What accounts for the extraordinary appeal of his work is beauty of another order, moral beauty, a quality unsought by most 20th century writers. Other writers have been more engaged, more moralistic. But none have appeared more beautiful, more convincing in their profession of moral interest. Unfortunately, moral beauty in art—like physical beauty in a person—is extremely perishable. It is nowhere so durable as artistic or intellectual beauty. Moral beauty has a tendency to decay very rapidly into sententiousness or untimeliness. This happens with special frequency to the writer, like Camus, who appeals directly to a generation's image of what is exemplary in a man in a given historical situation. Unless he possesses extraordinary reserves of artistic originality, his work is likely to seem suddenly denuded after his death. For a few, this decay overtook Camus within his own lifetime. Sartre, in the famous debate that ended their famous friendship, noted cruelly but truthfully that Camus carried about with him "a portable pedestal." Then came that deadly honor, the Nobel Prize. And shortly before his death, one critic was predicting for Camus the same fate as that of Aristides: that we would tire of hearing him called "the Just."

Perhaps it is always dangerous for a writer to inspire gratitude in his readers, gratitude being one of the most vehement but also the shortest-lived of the sentiments. But one cannot dismiss such unkind remarks simply as the revenge of the grateful. If Camus' moral earnestness at times ceased to enthrall and began to irritate, it is because there was a certain intellectual weakness in it. One sensed in Camus, as one senses in James Baldwin, the presence of an entirely genuine, and historically relevant, passion. But also, as with Baldwin, that passion seemed to transmute itself too readily into stately language, into an inexhaustible self-perpetuating oratory. The moral imperatives—love, moderation—offered to palliate intolerable historical or metaphysical dilemmas were too general, too abstract, too rhetorical.

Camus is the writer who for a whole literate generation was the heroic figure of a man living in a state of permanent spiritual revolution. But he is also the man who advocated that paradox: a civilized nihilism, an absolute revolt that acknowledges limits—and converted the paradox into a recipe for good citizenship. What intricate goodness, after all! In Camus' writing, goodness is forced to search simultaneously for its appropriate act and for its justifying reason. So is revolt. In 1939, in the midst of reflections on the war, which had just begun, the young Camus interrupted himself in his *Notebooks* to remark: "I am seeking reasons for my revolt which nothing has so far justified." His radical stance preceded the reasons which justified it. More than a decade later, in 1951, Camus published *The Rebel*. The refutation of revolt in that book was, equally, a gesture of temperament, an act of self-persuasion.

What is remarkable is that, given Camus' refined temperament, it was possible for him to act, to make real historical choices, as wholeheartedly as he did. It should be remembered that Camus had to make no less than three model decisions in his brief lifetime—to participate personally in the French Resistance, to disassociate himself from the Communist Party, and to refuse to take sides in the Algerian revolt—and that he acquitted himself admirably, in my opinion, in two out of the three. Camus' problem in the last years of his life was not that he became religious, or that he subsided into bourgeois humanitarian seriousness, or that he lost his socialist nerve. It was, rather, that he was hoist on the petard of his own virtue. A writer who acts as public conscience needs extraordinary nerve and fine instincts, like a boxer. After a time, these instincts inevitably falter. He also needs to be emotionally tough. Camus was not that tough, not tough in the way that Sartre is. I do not underestimate the courage involved in disavowing the pro-Communism

of many French intellectuals in the late forties. As a moral judgment, Camus' decision was right then, and since the death of
Stalin he has been vindicated many times over in a political
sense as well. But moral and political judgment do not always so
happily coincide. His agonizing inability to take a stand on the
Algerian question—the issue on which he, as both Algerian and
Frenchman, was uniquely qualified to speak—was the final and
unhappy testament of his moral virtue. Throughout the fifties,
Camus declared that his private loyalties and sympathies made
it impossible for him to render decisive political judgment. Why
is so much demanded of a writer, he asked plaintively. While
Camus clung to his silence, both Merleau-Ponty, who had followed Camus out of the *Temps Modernes* group over the issue
of Communism, and Sartre himself, gathered influential signa-
tories for two historic manifestoes protesting the continuation
of the Algerian War. It is a harsh irony that both Merleau-
Ponty, whose general political and moral outlook was so close
to that of Camus, and Sartre, whose political integrity Camus
had seemed to demolish a decade before, were in a position to
lead French intellectuals of conscience to the inevitable stand,
the only stand, the one everyone hoped Camus would take.

   In a perceptive review of one of Camus' books some years
ago, Lionel Abel spoke of him as the man who incarnates the
Noble Feeling, as distinct from the Noble Act. This is exactly
right, and does not mean that there was some sort of hypocrisy
in Camus' morality. It means that action is not Camus' first concern. The ability to act, or to refrain from acting, is secondary
to the ability or inability to feel. It is less an intellectual position
which Camus elaborated than an exhortation to feel—with all
the risks of political impotence that this entailed. Camus' work
reveals a temperament in search of a situation, noble feelings
in search of noble acts. Indeed, this disjunction is precisely the
subject of Camus' fiction and philosophical essays. There one
finds the prescription of an attitude (noble, stoical, at the same
time detached and compassionate) tacked on to the description of excruciating events. The attitude, the noble feeling, is
not genuinely linked to the event. It is a transcendence of the
event, more than a response to it or a solution of it. Camus' life
and work are not so much about morality as they are about the
pathos of moral positions. This pathos is Camus' modernity.

And his ability to suffer this pathos in a dignified and virile way is what made his readers love and admire him.

Again one comes back to the man, who was so strongly loved and yet so little known. There is something disembodied in Camus' fiction; and in the voice, cool and serene, of the famous essays. This, despite the unforgettable photographs, with their beautifully informal presence. A cigarette dangles between the lips, whether he wears a trench-coat, a sweater and open shirt, or a business suit. It is in many ways an almost ideal face: boyish, good-looking but not too good-looking, lean, rough, the expression both intense and modest. One wants to know this man.

In the *Notebooks, 1935–1942,** the first of three volumes to be published comprising the notebooks which Camus kept from 1935 until his death, his admirers will naturally hope to find a generous sense of the man and the work which has moved them. I am sorry to have to say, first of all, that the translation by Philip Thody is poor work. It is repeatedly inaccurate, sometimes to the point of seriously misconstruing Camus' sense. It is heavy-handed, and quite fails to find the equivalent in English to Camus' compressed, off-hand, and very eloquent style. The book also has an obtrusive academic apparatus which may not annoy some readers; it did annoy me. (For an idea of how Camus should sound in English, curious readers might look up the accurate and sensitive translation by Anthony Hartley of sections of the *Notebooks* which appeared in *Encounter* two years ago.) Yet no translation, whether faithful or tone-deaf, can make the *Notebooks* less interesting than they are, or more interesting either. These are not great literary journals, like those of Kafka and Gide. They do not have the white-hot intellectual brilliance of Kafka's *Diaries.* They lack the cultural sophistication, the artistic diligence, the human density of Gide's *Journals.* They are comparable, say to the *Diaries* of Cesare Pavese, except that they lack the element of personal exposure, of psychological intimacy.

Camus' *Notebooks* contain an assortment of things. They are

---

* *Notebooks, 1935–1942,* by Albert Camus. Translated from the French by Philip Thody. New York, Knopf.

literary work-books, quarries for his writings, in which phrases, scraps of overheard conversation, ideas for stories, and sometimes whole paragraphs later incorporated into the novels and essays, were first jotted down. These sections of the *Notebooks* are sketchy stuff, and for that reason I doubt if they will be terribly exciting even to aficionados of Camus' fiction, despite the zealous annotation and correlation with the published works supplied by Mr. Thody. The *Notebooks* also contain a miscellany of reading notes (Spengler, Renaissance history, etc.) of a rather limited range—the vast reading that went into writing *The Rebel* is certainly not recorded here—and a number of maxims and reflections on psychological and moral themes. Some of these reflections have a great deal of boldness and finesse. They are worth reading, and they might help dispel one current image of Camus—according to which he was a sort of Raymond Aron, a man deranged by German philosophy belatedly converting to Anglo-Saxon empiricism and common sense under the name of "Mediterranean" virtue. The *Notebooks*, at least this first volume, exude an endearing atmosphere of domesticated Nietzscheanism. The young Camus writes as a French Nietzsche, melancholy where Nietzsche is savage, stoical where Nietzsche is outraged, impersonal and objective in tone where Nietzsche is personal and subjective to the point of mania. And lastly, the *Notebooks* are full of personal comments—declarations and resolutions, one might better describe them—of a markedly impersonal nature.

Impersonality is perhaps the most telling thing about Camus' *Notebooks*; they are so anti-autobiographical. It is hard to remember, when reading the *Notebooks*, that Camus was a man who had a very interesting life, a life (unlike that of many writers) interesting not only in an interior but also in an outward sense. Scarcely anything of this life is preserved in the *Notebooks*. There is nothing about his family, to whom he was closely attached. Neither is there any mention of the events which took place in this period: his work with the Théâtre de l'Équipe, his first and second marriages, his membership in the Communist Party, his career as an editor of a left-wing Algerian newspaper.

Of course, a writer's journal must not be judged by the standards of a diary. The notebooks of a writer have a very special function: in them he builds up, piece by piece, the identity of a writer to himself. Typically, writers' notebooks are crammed with statements about the will: the will to write, the will to love, the will to renounce love, the will to go on living. The journal is where a writer is heroic to himself. In it he exists solely as a perceiving, suffering, struggling being. That is why all the personal comments in Camus' *Notebooks* are of so impersonal a nature, and completely exclude the events and the people in his life. Camus writes about himself only as a solitary—a solitary reader, voyeur, sun-and-sea worshipper, and walker in the world. In this he is being very much the writer. Solitariness is the indispensable metaphor of the modern writer's consciousness, not only to self-declared emotional misfits like Pavese, but even to as sociable and socially conscientious a man as Camus.

Thus the *Notebooks*, while absorbing reading, do not resolve the question of Camus' permanent stature or deepen our sense of him as a man. Camus was, in the words of Sartre, "the admirable conjunction of a man, of an action, and of a work." Today only the work remains. And whatever that conjunction of man, action, and work inspired in the minds and hearts of his thousands of readers and admirers cannot be wholly reconstituted by experience of the work alone. It would have been an important and happy occurrence if Camus' *Notebooks* had survived their author to give us more than they do of the man, but unfortunately they do not.

(1963)

Michel Leiris' Manhood

ARRIVING in translation in the year 1963, Michel Leiris' brilliant autobiographical narrative, *L'Age d'Homme*, is at first rather puzzling. *Manhood*, as it is called in English, appears without any covering note.* There is no way for the reader to find out that Leiris, now in his sixties and the author of some twenty books, none of which are yet in English, is an important poet and senior survivor of the Surrealist generation in Paris in the 1920s, and a fairly eminent anthropologist. Nor does the American edition explain that *Manhood* is not recent—that it was in fact written in the early 1930s, first published in 1939, and republished with an important prefatory essay, "Literature Considered as a Bullfight," in 1946, when it had a great *succès de scandale*. Although autobiographies can enthrall even though we have no prior interest—or reason for becoming interested—in the writer, the fact that Leiris is unknown here complicates matters, because his book is very much part of a life-history as well as a life-work.

In 1929, Leiris suffered a severe mental crisis, which included becoming impotent, and underwent a year or so of psychiatric treatment. In 1930, when he was thirty-four years old, he began *Manhood*. At that time, he was a poet, strongly influenced by Apollinaire and by his friend Max Jacob; he had already published several volumes of poetry, the first of which is *Simulacre* (1925); and in the same year that he began *Manhood*, he wrote a remarkable novel in the Surrealist manner, *Aurora*. But shortly after beginning *Manhood* (it was not finished until 1935), Leiris entered upon a new career—as an anthropologist. He made a field trip to Africa (Dakar and Djibouti) in 1931–33, and upon his return to Paris joined the staff of the Musée de l'Homme, where he remains, in an important curatorial post, to the present day. No trace of this startling shift—from bohemian and poet to scholar and museum bureaucrat—is recorded in the wholly intimate disclosures of *Manhood*. There is nothing in the book of the accomplishments of the poet or the anthropologist. One feels there cannot be; to have recorded them would mar the impression of failure.

---

* *Manhood* by Michel Leiris. Translated from the French by Richard Howard. New York, Grossman.

Instead of a history of his life, Leiris gives us a catalogue of its limitations. *Manhood* begins not with "I was born in . . ." but with a matter-of-fact description of the author's body. We learn in the first pages of Leiris' incipient baldness, of a chronic inflammation of the eyelids, of his meager sexual capacities, of his tendency to hunch his shoulders when sitting and to scratch his anal region when he is alone, of a traumatic tonsillectomy undergone as a child, of an equally traumatic infection in his penis; and, subsequently, of his hypochondria, of his cowardice in all situations of the slightest danger, of his inability to speak any foreign language fluently, of his pitiful incompetence in physical sports. His character, too, is described under the aspect of limitation: Leiris presents it as "corroded" with morbid and aggressive fantasies concerning the flesh in general and women in particular. *Manhood* is a manual of abjection—anecdotes and fantasies and verbal associations and dreams set down in the tones of a man, partly anesthetized, curiously fingering his own wounds.

One may think of Leiris' book as an especially powerful instance of the venerable preoccupation with sincerity peculiar to French letters. From Montaigne's *Essays* and Rousseau's *Confessions* through Stendhal's journals to the modern confessions of Gide, Jouhandeau, and Genet, the great writers of France have been concerned to a singular extent with the detached presentation of intimate feelings, particularly those connected with sexuality and ambition. In the name of sincerity, both in autobiographical form and the in form of fiction (as in Constant, Laclos, Proust), French writers have been coolly exploring erotic manias, and speculating on techniques of emotional disengagement. It is this long-standing preoccupation with sincerity—over and beyond emotional expressiveness—that gives a severity, a certain classicism even, to most French works of the romantic period. But to see Leiris' book simply in this way does it an injustice. *Manhood* is odder, harsher, than such a lineage suggests. Far more than any avowals to be found in the great French autobiographical documents of incestuous feelings, sadism, homosexuality, masochism, and crass promiscuity, what Leiris admits to is obscene and repulsive. It is not especially what Leiris has done that shocks. Action is not his forte, and his vices are those of a fearfully cold sensual temperament—wormy failures and deficiencies more often than lurid acts. It is because Leiris' attitude is unredeemed by the slightest tinge of self-respect. This lack of esteem or respect for himself is obscene. All the other great confessional works of French letters proceed out of self-love, and have the clear purpose of defending and justifying the self. Leiris loathes himself, and can neither defend nor justify. *Manhood* is an exercise in shamelessness—a sequence of self-exposures of a craven, morbid, damaged temperament. It is not incidentally, in the course of his narration, that Leiris reveals what is disgusting about himself. What is disgusting is the *topic* of his book.

One may well ask: who cares? *Manhood* undoubtedly has a certain value as a clinical document; it is full of lore for the professional student of mental aberration. But the book would not be worth attention did it not have value as literature. This, I think, it does—though, like so many modern works of literature, it makes its way as anti-literature. (Indeed, much of the modern movement in the arts presents itself as anti-art.) Paradoxically, it is just its animus to the idea of literature that makes *Manhood*—a very carefully (though not beautifully) written and subtly executed book—interesting as literature. In the same way, it is precisely through *Manhood's* unstated rejection of the rationalist project of self-understanding that Leiris makes his contribution to it.

The question that Leiris answers in *Manhood* is not an intellectual one. It is what we would call a psychological—and the French, a moral—question. Leiris is not trying to understand himself. Neither has he written *Manhood* to be forgiven, or to be loved. Leiris writes to appall, and thereby to receive from his readers the gift of a strong emotion—the emotion needed to defend himself against the indignation and disgust he expects to arouse in his readers. Literature becomes a mode of psychotechnics. As he explains in the prefatory essay "*De la Littérature Considérée comme une Tauromachie*," to be a writer, a man of letters, is not enough. It is boring, pallid. It lacks danger. Leiris must feel, as he writes, the equivalent of the bullfighter's knowledge that he risks being gored. Only then is writing worthwhile. But how can the writer achieve this invigorating sense of mortal danger? Leiris' answer is: through self-exposure, through *not* defending himself; not through fabricating works of art, objectifications of himself, but through laying himself—his own person—on the line of fire. But we, the readers, the spectators of this bloody act, know that when it is performed well (think of how the bullfight is discussed as a preeminently aesthetic, ceremonial act) it becomes, whatever the disavowals of literature—literature.

A writer who subscribes to a program similar to Leiris' for creating literature inadvertently, out of self-laceration and self-exposure, is Norman Mailer. For some years now Mailer has conceived of writing as a blood sport (more often in the image of boxing than bullfighting), and insisted that the better writer is the man who dares more, who risks more. For this reason, Mailer has used himself increasingly as the subject of his essays and quasi-fiction. But there are big differences between Mailer and Leiris, and they are revealing. In Mailer, this enthusiasm for danger appears much of the time in a base form—as megalomania, and a tiresome competitiveness with other writers. In Leiris' writings, there is no awareness of a literary scene, of other writers, fellow-toreros competing for the most ravishing danger. (On the contrary, Leiris, who has known practically everybody, painters as well as writers, is extremely deferential when he discusses the work and person of his friends.) Mailer in his writings is ultimately more concerned with success than with danger; danger is only a means to success. Leiris in his writings is not concerned with success at all. Mailer records in his recent essays and public appearances his perfecting of himself as a virile instrument of letters; he is perpetually in training, getting ready to launch himself from his own missile pad into a high, beautiful orbit; even his failures may yet be turned to successes. Leiris records the defeats of his own virility; completely incompetent in the arts of the body, he is perpetually in training to extinguish himself; even his successes look to him like failures. Perhaps the essential contrast between the optimistic, populist temperament of most American writers and the drastically alienated posture of the best European writers can be seen here. Leiris is a much more subjective, less ideological writer than Mailer. Mailer shows us how his private travails and weaknesses produce the strength of his public work—and wants to engage the reader in this process of transformation. But Leiris doesn't see any continuity between his public self, distinguished as that may be, and his private weaknesses. While Mailer's motives for self-exposure may be described as spiritual (not to mention worldly) ambitiousness—a desire to prove himself through repeated ordeals—Leiris' motives are more desperate: he wishes to prove, not that he is heroic, but that he is at all. Leiris loathes his physical cowardice and ineptness. Yet far from wishing to exonerate himself for his ugly failings, what he seems to wish is to convince himself that this unsatisfactory body—and this unseemly character—really exist. Haunted by a sense of the unreality of the world, and ultimately of himself, Leiris searches for a strong, unequivocal feeling. But, like a regular textbook romantic, the only emotion Leiris acknowledges is the one which involves a risk of death. "With a bitterness that I never suspected before, I have just realized that all I need in order to save myself is a certain fervor," he writes in *Manhood*, "but that this world lacks anything for which I would give my life." All emotions are mortal to Leiris, or they are nothing. What is real is defined as that which involves the risk of death. One knows from his books that Leiris has made several serious attempts at suicide; it might be said that, for him, life becomes real only when placed under the threat of suicide. The same is true of the vocation of literature. In a view like Leiris', literature has value only as a means of enhancing virility, or as a means of suicide.

Needless to say, it does neither. Literature usually begets literature. Whatever the therapeutic value of his self-exposure in *Manhood*, Leiris' mode of operating upon himself did not end with this book. His literary work since the war does not show a resolution of the problems set forth in *Manhood*, only further types of complication. Under the general title *La Règle du Jeu* (The Rules of the Game), Leiris has been writing essays on sense memories of his childhood, private images of death, sexual fantasies, the associative meanings of certain words—more discursive and more complex autobiographical forays than *Manhood*. Two of the projected three volumes have appeared: *Biffures* (Deletions) in 1948, and *Fourbis* (Odds and Ends) in 1961. The mocking titles tell the story. In *Fourbis*, one finds again the old complaint: "If there is nothing in love—or taste—for which I am ready to face death, I am only stirring up empty space and everything cancels itself out, myself included." The same theme is continued in his recent *Vivantes Cendres, Innommées* (Living Ashes, Unnamed), a cycle of peoms which are a "journal" of Leiris' attempted suicide in 1958, and illustrated with line drawings by his friend Giacometti. For, it seems, the greatest problem Leiris faces is the chronic thinness of his emotions. The life which he dissects in all his books is polarized between what he calls his "huge capacity for boredom, from which everything else proceeds," and a staggering burden of morbid fantasies, memories of childhood injuries, fear of punishment, and failure ever to be at home in his own body. By writing about his weaknesses Leiris courts the punishment which he dreads, hoping that he will rouse in himself an unprecedented courage. One has the impression of a man flogging himself just in order to make his lungs consent to draw air.

The tone of *Manhood*, however, is anything but vehement. Leiris speaks somewhere in the book of preferring English clothes, of affecting a sober and correct style "actually a little stiff and even funereal—which corresponds so well, I believe, to my temperament." This is not a bad description of the style of his book. The extreme coldness of his sexual disposition, he explains, entails a profound distaste for the feminine, the liquid, the emotional; a lifelong fantasy is that of his own body becoming petrified, crystalline, mineralized. Everything that is impersonal and cold fascinates Leiris. For example, he is attracted to prostitution because of its character as a ritual; and "brothels are like museums," he explains. It seems his choice of the profession of anthropology also owes to the same taste: he is attracted by the extreme *formalism* of primitive societies. This is evident in the book which Leiris wrote about his two-year field trip, *L'Afrique Fantôme* (1934), as well as in several excellent anthropological monographs. Leiris' love of formalism, reflected in the cool underplayed style of *Manhood*, explains a seeming paradox. For it is surely remarkable that the man who has dedicated himself to ruthless self-exposure has written a brilliant monograph on the use of masks in African religious rituals ("Possession and Its Theatrical Aspects among the Ethiopians of Gondar," 1958), that the man who has carried the notion of candor to its most painful limits has also concerned himself professionally with the idea of secret languages ("The Secret Language of the Dogons of Sanga," 1948).

This coolness of tone—combined with a great intelligence and subtlety about motives—makes *Manhood* an attractive book in a fairly familiar sense. To its other qualities, though, we may react with impatience, for they violate many preconceptions. Apart from the brilliant prefatory essay, *Manhood* meanders, circles, and doubles back; there is no reason for it to end where it does; such types of insight are interminable. The book has no movement or direction and provides no consummation or climax. *Manhood* is another of those very modern books which are fully intelligible only as part of the project of a life: we are to take the book as an action, giving on to other actions. This type of literature, item by item, rather than retrospectively viewed as part of a body of work, is often hermetic and opaque, sometimes boring. Now, it is not hard to make out a defense for hermeticism and opaqueness as a possible condition for literary works of an extreme density. But what about boredom? Can that ever be justified? I think it can, sometimes. (Is it the obligation of great art to be continually interesting? I think not.) We should acknowledge certain uses of boredom as one of the most creative stylistic features of modern literature—as the conventionally ugly and messy have already become essential resources of modern painting, and silence (since Webern) a positive, structural element in contemporary music.

                                                                (1964)

The Anthropologist as Hero

The paradox is irresoluble: the less one culture communicates with another, the less likely they are to be corrupted, one by the other; but on the other hand, the less likely it is, in such conditions, that the respective emissaries of these cultures will be able to seize the richness and significance of their diversity. The alternative is inescapable: either I am a traveller in ancient times, and faced with a prodigious spectacle which would be almost entirely unintelligible to me and might, indeed, provoke me to mockery or disgust; or I am a traveller of my own day, hastening in search of a vanished reality. In either case I am the loser . . . for today, as I go groaning among the shadows, I miss, inevitably, the spectacle that is now taking shape.

from *Tristes Tropiques*

MOST serious thought in our time struggles with the feeling of homelessness. The felt unreliability of human experience brought about by the inhuman acceleration of historical change has led every sensitive modern mind to the recording of some kind of nausea, of intellectual vertigo. And the only way to cure this spiritual nausea seems to be, at least initially, to exacerbate it. Modern thought is pledged to a kind of applied Hegelianism: seeking its Self in its Other. Europe seeks itself in the exotic—in Asia, in the Middle East, among pre-literate peoples, in a mythic America; a fatigued rationality seeks itself in the impersonal energies of sexual ecstasy or drugs; consciousness seeks its meaning in unconsciousness; humanistic problems seek their oblivion in scientific "value neutrality" and quantification. The "other" is experienced as a harsh purification of "self." But at the same time the "self" is busily colonizing all strange domains of experience. Modern sensibility moves between two seemingly contradictory but actually related impulses: surrender to the exotic, the strange, the other; and the domestication of the exotic, chiefly through science.

Although philosophers have contributed to the statement and understanding of this intellectual homelessness—and, in my opinion, only those modern philosophers who do so have an urgent claim on our interest—it is mainly poets, novelists, a few painters who have *lived* this tortured spiritual impulse, in willed derangement and in self-imposed exile and in compulsive travel. But there are other professions whose conditions of life have been made to bear witness to this vertiginous modern attraction

71

to the alien. Conrad in his fiction, and T. E. Lawrence, Saint-Exupéry, Montherlant among others in their lives as well as their writing, created the métier of the adventurer as a spiritual vocation. Thirty-five years ago, Malraux chose the profession of the archaeologist, and went to Asia. And, more recently, Claude Lévi-Strauss has invented the profession of the anthropologist as a total occupation, one involving a spiritual commitment like that of the creative artist or the adventurer or the psychoanalyst.

Unlike the writers mentioned above, Lévi-Strauss is not a man of letters. Most of his writings are scholarly, and he has always been associated with the academic world. At present, since 1960, he holds a very grand academic post, the newly created chair of social anthropology at the Collège de France, and heads a large and richly endowed research institute. But his academic eminence and ability to dispense patronage are scarcely adequate measures of the formidable position he occupies in French intellectual life today. In France, where there is more awareness of the adventure, the *risk* involved in intelligence, a man can be both a specialist and the subject of general and intelligent interest and controversy. Hardly a month passes in France without a major article in some serious literary journal, or an important public lecture, extolling or attacking the ideas and influence of Lévi-Strauss. Apart from the tireless Sartre and the virtually silent Malraux, he is the most interesting intellectual "figure" in France today.

So far, Lévi-Strauss is hardly known in this country. A collection of previously scattered essays on the methods and concepts of anthropology, brought out in 1958 and entitled *Anthropologie Structurale*, and his *Le Totémisme Aujourd'hui* (1962) have been translated in the last year. Still to appear are another collection of essays, more philosophical in character, entitled *La Pensée Sauvage* (1962); a book published by UNESCO in 1952 called *Race et Histoire*; and the brilliant work on the kinship systems of primitives, *Les Structures Élémentaires de la Parenté* (1949).* Some of these writings presuppose more familiarity with anthropological literature and with the concepts of linguistics, sociology, and psychology than the ordinary cultivated reader

---

*In 1965, Lévi-Strauss published *Le Cru et le Cuit*, a lengthy study of the "mythologies" of food preparation among primitive peoples.

has. But it would be a great pity if Lévi-Strauss' work, when it is all translated, were to find no more than a specialist audience in this country. For Lévi-Strauss has assembled, from the vantage point of anthropology, one of the few interesting and possible intellectual positions—in the most general sense of that phrase. And one of his books is a masterpiece. I mean the incomparable *Tristes Tropiques*, a book that became a best-seller when published in France in 1955, but when translated into English and brought out here in 1961 was shamefully ignored. *Tristes Tropiques* is one of the great books of our century. It is rigorous, subtle, and bold in thought. It is beautifully written. And, like all great books, it bears an absolutely personal stamp; it speaks with a human voice.

Ostensibly *Tristes Tropiques* is the record, or memoir rather, written over fifteen years after the event, of the author's experience in the "field." Anthropologists are fond of likening field research to the puberty ordeal which confers status upon members of certain primitive societies. Lévi-Strauss' ordeal was in Brazil, before the Second World War. Born in 1908 and of the intellectual generation and circle which included Sartre, Beauvoir, Merleau-Ponty, and Paul Nizan, he studied philosophy in the late twenties, and, like them, taught for a while in a provincial lycée. Dissatisfied with philosophy he soon gave up his teaching post, returned to Paris to study law, then began the study of anthropology, and in 1935 went to São Paulo as Professor of Anthropology. From 1935 to 1939, during the long university vacations from November to March and for one period of more than a year, Lévi-Strauss lived among Indian tribes in the interior of Brazil. *Tristes Tropiques* offers a record of his encounters with these tribes—the nomadic, missionary-murdering Nambikwara, the Tupi-Kawahib whom no white man had ever seen before, the materially splendid Bororo, the ceremonious Caduveo who produce huge amounts of abstract painting and sculpture. But the greatness of *Tristes Tropiques* lies not simply in this sensitive reportage, but in the way Lévi-Strauss *uses* his experience—to reflect on the nature of landscape, on the meaning of physical hardship, on the city in the Old World and the New, on the idea of travel, on sunsets, on modernity, on the connection between literacy and power. The key to the book is Chapter Six, "How I Became an Anthropologist," where

Lévi-Strauss finds in the history of his own choice a case study of the unique spiritual hazards to which the anthropologist subjects himself. *Tristes Tropiques* is an intensely personal book. Like Montaigne's *Essays* and Freud's *Interpretation of Dreams*, it is an intellectual autobiography, an exemplary personal history in which a whole view of the human situation, an entire sensibility, is elaborated.

The profoundly intelligent sympathy which informs *Tristes Tropiques* makes other memoirs about life among pre-literate peoples seem ill-at-ease, defensive, provincial. Yet sympathy is modulated throughout by a hard-won impassivity. In her autobiography Simone de Beauvoir recalls Lévi-Strauss as a young philosophy student-teacher expounding "in his detached voice, and with a deadpan expression . . . the folly of the passions." Not for nothing is *Tristes Tropiques* prefaced by a motto from Lucretius' *De Rerum Natura*. Lévi-Strauss' aim is very much like that of Lucretius, the Graecophile Roman who urged the study of the natural sciences as a mode of ethical psychotherapy. The aim of Lucretius was not independent scientific knowledge, but the reduction of emotional anxiety. Lucretius saw man as torn between the pleasure of sex and the pain of emotional loss, tormented by superstitions inspired by religion, haunted by the fear of bodily decay and death. He recommended scientific knowledge, which teaches intelligent detachment, equanimity. Scientific knowledge is, for Lucretius, a mode of psychological gracefulness. It is a way of learning to let go.

Lévi-Strauss sees man with a Lucretian pessimism, and a Lucretian feeling for knowledge as both consolation and necessary disenchantment. But for him the demon is history—not the body or the appetites. The past, with its mysteriously harmonious structures, is broken and crumbling before our eyes. Hence, the tropics are *tristes*. There were nearly twenty thousand of the naked, indigent, nomadic, handsome Nambikwaras in 1915, when they were first visited by white missionaries; when Lévi-Strauss arrived in 1938 there were no more than two thousand of them; today they are miserable, ugly, syphilitic, and almost extinct. Hopefully, anthropology brings a reduction of historical anxiety. It is interesting that Lévi-Strauss describes himself as an ardent student of Marx since the age of seventeen ("Rarely do I tackle a problem in sociology or ethnology without having first set my mind in motion by reperusal of a page or two from the *18th Brumaire of Louis Bonaparte* or the *Critique of Political Economy*") and that many of Lévi-Strauss' students are reported to be former Marxists, come as it were to lay their piety at the altar of the past since it cannot be offered to the future. Anthropology is necrology. "Let's go and study the primitives," say Lévi-Strauss and his pupils, "before they disappear."

It is strange to think of these ex-Marxists—philosophical optimists if ever such have existed—submitting to the melancholy spectacle of the crumbling prehistoric past. They have moved not only from optimism to pessimism, but from certainty to systematic doubt. For, according to Lévi-Strauss, research in the field, "where every ethnological career begins, is the mother and nursemaid of doubt, the philosophical attitude par excellence." In Lévi-Strauss' program for the practicing anthropologist in *Structural Anthropology*, the Cartesian method of doubt is installed as a permanent agnosticism. "This 'anthropological doubt' consists not merely in knowing that one knows nothing but in resolutely exposing what one knows, even one's own ignorance, to the insults and denials inflicted on one's dearest ideas and habits by those ideas and habits which may contradict them to the highest degree."

To be an anthropologist is thus to adopt a very ingenious stance vis-à-vis one's own doubts, one's own intellectual uncertainties. Lévi-Strauss makes it clear that for him this is an eminently *philosophical* stance. At the same time, anthropology reconciles a number of divergent personal claims. It is one of the rare intellectual vocations which do not demand a sacrifice of one's manhood. Courage, love of adventure, and physical hardiness—as well as brains—are called upon. It also offers a solution to that distressing by-product of intelligence, alienation. Anthropology conquers the estranging function of the intellect by institutionalizing it. For the anthropologist, the world is professionally divided into "home" and "out there," the domestic and the exotic, the urban academic world and the tropics. The anthropologist is not simply a neutral observer. He is a man in control of, and even consciously exploiting, his own intellectual alienation. A *technique de dépaysement*, Lévi-Strauss calls his profession in *Structual Anthropology*. He takes for granted the philistine formulas of modern scientific "value neutrality."

What he does is to offer an exquisite, aristocratic version of this neutrality. The anthropologist in the field becomes the very model of the 20th century consciousness: a "critic at home" but a "conformist elsewhere." Lévi-Strauss acknowledges that this paradoxical spiritual state makes it impossible for the anthropologist to be a citizen. The anthropologist, so far as his own country is concerned, is sterilized politically. He cannot seek power, he can only be a critical dissenting voice. Lévi-Strauss himself, although in the most generic and very French way a man of the Left (he signed the famous Manifesto of the 121, which recommended civil disobedience in France in protest against the Algerian War), is by French standards an apolitical man. Anthropology, in Lévi-Strauss' conception, is a technique of political disengagement; and the anthropologist's vocation requires the assumption of a profound detachment. "Never can he feel himself 'at home' anywhere; he will always be, psychologically speaking, an amputee."

Certainly the earliest visitors to pre-literate peoples were far from being detached. The original field workers in what was then called ethnology were missionaries, bent on redeeming the savage from his follies and making him over into a civilized Christian. To cover the bosoms of the women, put pants on the men, and send them all to Sunday school to mumble the gospel was the aim of an army of stony-eyed spinsters from Yorkshire and rawboned farmers' sons from the American Midwest. Then there were the secular humanists—impartial, respectful, hands-off observers who did not come to sell Christ to the savages but to preach "reason," "tolerance," and "cultural pluralism" to the bourgeois literary public back home. And back home there were the great consumers of anthropological data, building rationalist world views, like Frazer and Spencer and Robertson Smith and Freud. But always anthropology has struggled with an intense, fascinated *repulsion* towards its subject. The horror of the primitive (naïvely expressed by Frazer and Lévy-Bruhl) is never far from the anthropologist's consciousness. Lévi-Strauss marks the furthest reach of the conquering of the aversion. The anthropologist in the manner of Lévi-Strauss is a new breed altogether. He is not, like recent generations of American anthropologists, simply a modest data-collecting "observer." Nor does he have any axe—Christian, rationalist, Freudian, or otherwise—

to grind. Essentially he is engaged in saving his own soul, by a curious and ambitious act of intellectual catharsis.

The anthropologist—and herein lies his essential difference, according to Lévi-Strauss, from the sociologist—is an *eye-witness*. "It is sheer illusion that anthropology can be taught purely theoretically." (One wonders why a Max Weber writing about ancient Judaism or Confucian China is permissible, if a Frazer describing scapegoat rituals among the Tagbanua tribe in the Philippines is not.) Why? Because anthropology, for Lévi-Strauss, is an intensely personal kind of intellectual discipline, like psychoanalysis. A spell in the field is the exact equivalent of the training analysis undergone by candidate psychoanalysts. The purpose of field work, Lévi-Strauss writes, is to "create that psychological revolution which marks the decisive turning point in the training of the anthropologist." And no written tests, but only the judgment of "experienced members of the profession" who have undergone the same psychological ordeal, can determine "if and when" a candidate anthropologist "has, as a result of field work, accomplished that inner revolution that will really make him into a new man."

However, it must be emphasized that this literary-sounding conception of the anthropologist's calling—the twice-born spiritual adventure, pledged to a systematic *déracinement*—is complemented in most of Lévi-Strauss' writings by an insistence on the most unliterary techniques of analysis and research. His important essay on myth in *Structural Anthropology* outlines a technique for analyzing and recording the elements of myths so that these can be processed by a computer. European contributions to what in America are called the "social sciences" are in exceedingly low repute in this country, for their insufficient empirical documentation, for their "humanist" weakness for covert culture criticism, for their refusal to embrace the techniques of quantification as an essential tool of research. Lévi-Strauss' essays in *Structural Anthropology* certainly escape these strictures. Indeed, far from disdaining the American fondness for precise quantitative measurement of traditional problems, Lévi-Strauss finds it not sophisticated or methodologically rigorous enough. Somewhat at the expense of the French school (Durkheim, Mauss, and their followers) to whom he is closely allied, Lévi-Strauss pays lavish tribute throughout the essays in *Structural Anthropology* to the work of American anthropologists—particularly Lowie, Boas, and Kroeber.* But his nearest affinity is to the more avant-garde methodologies of economics, neurology, linguistics, and game theory. For Lévi-Strauss, there is no doubt that anthropology must be a science, rather than a humanistic study. The question is only how. "For centuries," he writes, "the humanities and the social sciences have resigned themselves to contemplate the world of the natural and exact sciences as a kind of paradise which they will never enter." But recently, a doorway to paradise has been opened by the linguists, like Roman Jakobson and his school. Linguists now know how to reformulate their problems so that they can "have a machine built by an engineer and make a kind of experiment, completely similar to a natural-science experiment," which will tell them "if the hypothesis is worthwhile or not." Linguists—as well as economists and game theorists—have shown the anthropologist "a way to get out of the confusion resulting from too much acquaintance and familiarity with concrete data."

Thus the man who submits himself to the exotic to confirm his own inner alienation as an urban intellectual ends by aiming to vanquish his subject by translating it into a purely formal

---

*Lévi-Strauss relates in *Tristes Tropiques* that although he had long been familiar with the writings of the French anthropologists and sociologists, it was a reading of Lowie's *Primitive Society* in 1934 or 1935 which effected his conversion from philosophy to anthropology. "Thus began my long intimacy with Anglo-American anthropology . . . I started as an avowed anti-Durkheimian and the enemy of any attempt to put sociology to metaphysical uses."

Nevertheless, Lévi-Strauss has made it clear that he considers himself the true legate of the Durkheim-Mauss tradition, and recently has not hesitated to situate his work in relation to the philosophical problems posed by Marx, Freud, and Sartre. And, on the level of technical analysis, he is fully aware of his debt to the French writers, particularly by way of the *Essai sur Quelques Formes Primitives de Classification* (1901–2) by Durkheim and Mauss, and Mauss' *Essai sur le Don* (1924). From the first essay, Lévi-Strauss derives the starting point of the studies of taxonomy and the "concrete science" of primitives in *La Pensée Sauvage*. From the second essay, in which Mauss puts forth the proposition that kinship relations, relations of economic and ceremonial exchange, and linguistic relations are fundamentally of the same order, Lévi-Strauss derives the approach most fully exemplified in *Les Structures Élémentaires de la Parenté*. To Durkheim and Mauss, he repeatedly says, he owes the decisive insight that *"la pensée dite primitive était une pensée quantifiée."*

code. The ambivalence toward the exotic, the primitive, is not overcome after all, but only given a complex restatement. The anthropologist, as a man, is engaged in saving his own soul. But he is also committed to recording and understanding his subject by a very high-powered mode of formal analysis—what Lévi-Strauss calls "structural" anthropology—which obliterates all traces of his personal experience and truly effaces the human features of his subject, a given primitive society.

In *La Pensée Sauvage*, Lévi-Strauss calls his thought "*anecdotique et géometrique.*" The essays in *Structural Anthropology* show mostly the geometrical side of his thought; they are applications of a rigorous formalism to traditional themes—kinship systems, totemism, puberty rites, the relation between myth and ritual, and so forth. A great cleansing operation is in process, and the broom that sweeps everything clean is the notion of "structure." Lévi-Strauss strongly dissociates himself from what he calls the "naturalistic" trend of British anthropology, represented by such leading figures as Malinowski and Radcliffe-Brown. British anthropologists have been the most consistent proponents of "functional analysis," which interprets the variety of custom as different strategies for producing universal social ends. Thus, Malinowski thought that empirical observation of a single primitive society would make it possible to understand the "universal motivations" present in all societies. According to Lévi-Strauss, this is nonsense. Anthropology cannot aim to understand anything more than its own proper subject. Nothing can be inferred from anthropological material for psychology or sociology, for anthropology cannot possibly get complete knowledge of the societies it studies. Anthropology (the comparative study of "structures" rather than "functions") can neither be a descriptive nor an inductive science; it occupies itself with only the formal features which differentiate one society from another. It has properly no interest in the biological basis, psychological content, or social function of institutions and customs. Thus, while Malinowski and Radcliffe-Brown argue, for example, that biological ties are the origin of the model for every kinship tie, "structuralists" like Lévi-Strauss, following Kroeber and Lowie, emphasize the artificiality of kinship rules. They would discuss kinship in terms of notions which admit of mathematical treatment. Lévi-Strauss and the structuralists, in short, would view society like a game, which there is no one right way to play; different societies assign different moves to the players. The anthropologist can regard a ritual or a taboo simply as a set of rules, paying little attention to "the nature of the partners (either individuals or groups) whose play is being patterned after these rules." Lévi-Strauss' favorite metaphor or model for analyzing primitive institutions and beliefs is a language. And the analogy between anthropology and linguistics is the leading theme of the essays in *Structural Anthropology*. All behavior, according to Lévi-Strauss, is a language, a vocabulary and grammar of order; anthropology proves nothing about human nature except the need for order itself. There is no universal truth about the relations between, say, religion and social structure. There are only models showing the variability of one in relation to the other.

To the general reader, perhaps the most striking example of Lévi-Strauss' theoretical agnosticism is his view of myth. He treats myth as a purely formal mental operation, without any psychological content or any necessary connection with rite. Specific narratives are exposed as logical designs for the description and possibly the softening of the rules of the social game when they give rise to a tension or contradiction. For Lévi-Strauss, the logic of mythic thought is fully as rigorous as that of modern science. The only difference is that this logic is applied to different problems. Contrary to Mircea Eliade, his most distinguished opponent in the theory of primitive religion, Lévi-Strauss argues that the activity of the mind in imposing form on content is fundamentally the same for all minds, archaic and modern. Lévi-Strauss sees no difference in quality between the scientific thinking of modern "historical" societies and the mythic thinking of prehistoric communities.

The demonic character which history and the notion of historical consciousness has for Lévi-Strauss is best exposed in his brilliant and savage attack on Sartre, the last chapter of *La Pensée Sauvage*. I am not persuaded by Lévi-Strauss' arguments against Sartre. But I should say that he is, since the death of Merleau-Ponty, the most interesting and challenging critic of Sartrean existentialism and phenomenology.

Sartre, not only in his ideas but in his entire sensibility, is the antithesis of Lévi-Strauss. With his philosophical and political dogmatisms, his inexhaustible ingenuity and complexity, Sartre always has the manners (which are often bad manners) of the enthusiast. It is entirely apt that the writer who has aroused Sartre's greatest enthusiasm is Jean Genet, a baroque and didactic and insolent writer whose ego effaces all objective narrative; whose characters are stages in a masturbatory revel; who is the master of games and artifices, of a rich, overrich style stuffed with metaphors and conceits. But there is another tradition in French thought and sensibility—the cult of aloofness, *l'esprit géometrique*. This tradition is represented, among the new novelists, by Nathalie Sarraute, Alain Robbe-Grillet, and Michel Butor, so different from Genet in their search for an infinite precision, their narrow dehydrated subject-matter and cool microscopic styles, and, among film-makers, by Alain Resnais. The formula for this tradition—in which I would locate Lévi-Strauss, as I would put Sartre with Genet—is the mixture of pathos and coldness.

Like the formalists of the "new novel" and film, Lévi-Strauss' emphasis on "structure," his extreme formalism and intellectual agnosticism, are played off against an immense but thoroughly subdued pathos. Sometimes the result is a masterpiece like *Tristes Tropiques*. The very title is an understatement. The tropics are not merely sad. They are in agony. The horror of the rape, the final and irrevocable destruction of pre-literate peoples taking place throughout the world today—which is the true subject of Lévi-Strauss' book—is told at a certain distance, the distance of a personal experience of fifteen years ago, and with a sureness of feeling and fact that allows the readers' emotions more rather than less freedom. But in the rest of his books, the lucid and anguished observer has been taken in hand, purged, by the severity of theory.

Exactly in the same spirit as Robbe-Grillet disavows the traditional empirical content of the novel (psychology, social observation), Lévi-Strauss applied the methods of "structural analysis" to traditional materials of empirical anthropology. Customs, rites, myths, and taboo are a language. As in language, where the sounds which make up words are, taken in themselves, meaningless, so the parts of a custom or a rite or a myth (according to Lévi-Strauss) are meaningless in themselves. When analyzing the Oedipus myth, he insists that the parts of the myth (the lost child, the old man at the crossroad, the marriage with the mother, the blinding, etc.) mean nothing. Only when put together in the total context do the parts have a meaning—the meaning that a logical model has. This degree of intellectual agnosticism is surely extraordinary. And one does not have to espouse a Freudian or a sociological interpretation of the elements of myth to contest it.

Any serious critique of Lévi-Strauss, however, must deal with the fact that, ultimately, his extreme formalism is a moral choice, and (more surprisingly) a vision of social perfection. Radically anti-historicist, he refuses to differentiate between "primitive" and "historical" societies. Primitives have a history; but it is unknown to us. And historical consciousness (which they do not have), he argues in the attack on Sartre, is not a privileged mode of consciousness. There are only what he revealingly calls "hot" and "cold" societies. The hot societies are the modern ones, driven by the demons of historical progress. The cold societies are the primitive ones, static, crystalline, harmonious. Utopia, for Lévi-Strauss, would be a great lowering of the historical temperature. In his inaugural lecture at the Collège de France, Lévi-Strauss outlined a post-Marxist vision of freedom in which man would finally be freed from the obligation to progress, and from "the age-old curse which forced it to enslave men in order to make progress possible." Then:

> history would henceforth be quite alone, and society, placed outside and above history, would once again be able to assume that regular and quasi-crystalline structure which, the best-preserved primitive societies teach us, is not contradictory to humanity. It is in this admittedly Utopian view that social anthropology would find its highest justification, since the forms of life and thought which it studies would no longer be of mere historic and comparative interest. They would correspond to a permanent possibility of man, over which social anthropology would have a mission to stand watch, especially in man's darkest hours.

The anthropologist is thus not only the mourner of the cold world of the primitives, but its custodian as well. Lamenting among the shadows, struggling to distinguish the archaic from the pseudo-archaic, he acts out a heroic, diligent, and complex modern pessimism.

(1963)

The Literary Criticism of Georg Lukács

THE Hungarian philosopher and literary critic Georg Lukács is the senior figure living today within the borders of the Communist world who speaks a Marxism that it is possible for intelligent non-Marxists to take seriously.

I do not believe (as many do) that Lukács is the figure who speaks the *most* interesting or plausible form of Marxism today, much less that he is (as he has been called) "the greatest Marxist since Marx." But there can be no doubt that he has a special eminence and claim to our attention. Not only is he the mentor of new intellectual stirrings in Eastern Europe and Russia; outside of Marxist circles as well, Lukács has counted for a long time. His early writings, for instance, are the source of many of the ideas of Karl Mannheim (on the sociology of art, culture, and knowledge), and through Mannheim upon all of modern sociology; he has also had a great influence on Sartre, and through him on French existentialism.

He was born Georg von Lukács, of a wealthy, recently ennobled Jewish banking family, in Hungary in 1885. From the start, his intellectual career was an extraordinary one. While still in his teens he wrote, gave public lectures, founded a theater, and launched a liberal journal. When he came to Germany to study at the Universities of Berlin and Heidelberg, he astonished his great teachers, Max Weber and Georg Simmel, by his brilliance. His main interest was literature, but he was interested in everything else as well. His doctoral dissertation, in 1907, was *The Metaphysics of Tragedy.* His first major work, in 1908, was a two-volume *History of the Evolution of the Modern Drama.* In 1911, he published a collection of literary essays, *The Soul and Its Forms*; in 1916, *The Theory of the Novel.* Some time during the First World War he moved from neo-Kantianism, his earliest philosophical view, to the philosophy of Hegel, and thence to Marxism. He joined the Communist Party in 1918 (dropping the *von* before his name).

From here on, Lukács' career is a stunning testament to the difficulties of a free intellectual committed to a view which has taken on more and more the character of a closed system, and, in addition, living in a society which listens to what intellectuals say and write with the utmost gravity. For, from the beginning,

Lukács' interpretation of Marxist theory was free-wheeling, speculative.

Shortly after joining the Party, Lukács, for the first of two times in his life, took part in a revolution. Returning to Hungary, he became Minister of Education in the brief Communist dictatorship of Béla Kun in 1919. After the Kun regime was overthrown, he escaped to Vienna, where he lived for the next ten years. His most important book of this period was a philosophical discussion of Marxist theory, the now almost legendary *History and Class Consciousness* (1923)—of all his works, perhaps the one most esteemed by non-Marxists, and for which he immediately came under strong and unremitting attack from within the Communist movement.

The controversy over this book marked the defeat of Lukács in his battle with Kun for leadership of the Hungarian Communist Party, a battle which was fought in those years of exile in Vienna. After being attacked throughout the Communist world by everyone from Lenin, Bukharin, and Zinoviev on down, he was expelled from the central committee of the Hungarian party, and deprived of the editorship of his magazine *Kommunismus*. But throughout this decade Lukács defended his books, standing firm and retracting nothing.

Then, in 1930, after a year in Berlin, he went to Moscow for a year to do research on the staff of the famous Marx-Engels Institute (whose brilliant director, D. Ryazanoff, was to disappear in the purges of the late thirties). What was happening, subjectively, to Lukács at this time is not known. The facts are that, after returning to Berlin in 1931, he went back to Moscow in 1933, when Hitler came to power; and the same year publicly repudiated in the most abject terms the *History and Class Consciousness* and all his previous writings as infected by "bourgeois idealism."

Lukács lived on as a refugee in Moscow for twelve years; even after his recantation, and numerous attempts to bring his work more into line with Communist orthodoxy, he remained in disfavor. Nevertheless, unlike Ryazanoff, he survived the terrible purges. One of his finest books, *The Young Hegel*, dates from this period (it was written in 1938, but not published until a decade later), as well as a vile simplistic tract against modern philosophy, *The Destruction of Reason* (1945). The contrast between these two books is typical of the vast fluctuations of quality in Lukács' later work.

In 1945, when the war was over and a Communist government assumed power in Hungary, Lukács returned permanently to his native country to teach at the University of Budapest. Among the books he wrote in the succeeding decade are *Goethe and His Time* (1947) and *Thomas Mann* (1949). Then, at the age of seventy-one, came a second and incredibly moving venture into revolutionary politics, when Lukács emerged as one of the leaders of the revolution of 1956, and was named a minister in Imre Nagy's government. Deported to Rumania and put under house arrest after the suppression of the revolution, he was permitted to return to Budapest four months later to resume teaching and to continue publishing both at home and in Western Europe. Only Lukács' age and his immense international prestige, one supposes, saved him from the fate of Imre Nagy. At any rate, among all the leaders of the revolution, he alone was never put on trial nor has he publicly recanted.

Immediately after the revolution he published *Realism in Our Time* (1956), and last year brought out the first part, consisting of two huge volumes, of his long-awaited *Aesthetics*. He continues to be attacked by cultural bureaucrats and older Communist critics, though much more in, say, East Germany than at home, under the increasingly liberal regime of Kadar. His early writings (which he still strenuously repudiates) are increasingly studied in England and Western Europe and Latin America—he is widely translated in French and Spanish—in the light of the new interest in the early writings of Marx; while for many of the new generation of intellectuals in Eastern Europe, it is the later work which is the touchstone for the cautious but inexorable overthrow of the ideas and practices of Stalinism.

Obviously, Lukács has a great talent for personal and political survival—that is, for being many things to many different men. He has, in effect, accomplished the difficult feat of being both marginal and central in a society which makes the position of the marginal intellectual almost intolerable. To do this, however, he has had to spend a great deal of his life in one or another form of exile. Of the external exile, I have already spoken. But there is also a kind of internal exile, evident in his choice of subjects to write about. The writers Lukács is most devoted to are Goethe, Balzac, Scott, Tolstoy. By virtue of his age, and the possession of a sensibility formed before the advent of the canon of Communist culture, Lukács has been able to protect himself by (intellectually) emigrating out of the present. The only modern writers who receive his unqualified approval are those who, essentially, continue the 19th century tradition of the novel—Mann, Galsworthy, Gorky, and Roger Martin du Gard.

But this commitment to 19th century literature and philosophy is not just an aesthetic choice (as, indeed, there can be no purely aesthetic choices in a Marxist—or a Christian, or a Platonic—view of art). The standard by which Lukács judges the present is a moral one, and it is notable that this standard is drawn from the past. The wholeness of the vision of the past is what Lukács means when he speaks of "realism."

Another way Lukács has partly emigrated from the present is in his choice of the language in which to write. Only his first two books are in Hungarian. The rest—some thirty books and fifty essays—are in German; and to continue writing in German in the Hungary of today is decidedly a polemical act. By concentrating on 19th century literature and stubbornly retaining German as the language in which he writes, Lukács has continued to propose, as a Communist, European and humanist—as opposed to nationalist and doctrinaire—values; living as he does in a Communist and provincial country, he has remained a genuinely European intellectual figure. Needless to say, knowledge of him here is long overdue.

It is perhaps unfortunate, though, that the two works which hereby introduce Lukács to an American public are both works of literary criticism, and both of the "late" rather than "early" Lukács.* *Studies in European Realism*, a collection of eight essays dealing mainly with Balzac, Stendhal, Tolstoy, Zola, and Gorky, was written in Russia during the late thirties, at the time of the purges, and bears the scars of that awful period in the form of several passages of a crude political nature; Lukács published it

---

* *Studies in European Realism*, translated by Edith Bone. New York, Grosset & Dunlap. *Realism in Our Time*, translated by John and Necke Mander. New York, Harper. (*Essays on Thomas Mann* was translated and published in England in 1964. *The Historical Novel*, written in 1936, has also recently been translated.)

in 1948. *Realism in Our Time* is a shorter work, written in the fifties, less academic in style and more sprightly and rapid in argument; in the three essays, Lukács reviews the alternatives for literature today and rejects both "modernism" and "socialist realism" in favor of what he calls "critical realism"—essentially the tradition of the 19th century novel.

I say this choice of books may be unfortunate because, while here is a quite accessible Lukács, not hard to read, as he is in his philosophical writings, we are forced to react to him as a literary critic alone. What is Lukács' intrinsic value and quality as a literary critic? Sir Herbert Read has praised him lavishly; Thomas Mann called him "the most important literary critic of today"; George Steiner regards him as "the only major German literary critic of our epoch" and claims that "among critics, only Sainte-Beuve and Edmund Wilson have matched the breadth of Lukács' response" to literature; and Alfred Kazin clearly regards him as a very able, sound, and important guide to the great tradition of the 19th century novel. But do the present books support these claims? I think not. Indeed, I rather suspect that the current vogue for Lukács—promoted by such effusions as the essays of George Steiner and Alfred Kazin offered as prefaces to the present translations—is motivated more by cultural good will than by strictly literary criteria.

It is easy to sympathize with Lukács' boosters. I, too, am inclined to give Lukács all the benefit of the doubt, if only in protest against the sterilities of the Cold War which have made it impossible to discuss Marxism seriously for the last decade or more. But we may be generous toward the "late" Lukács only at the price of not taking him altogether seriously, of subtly patronizing him by treating his moral fervor aesthetically, as style rather than idea. My own inclination is to take him at his word. Then, what about the fact that Lukács rejects Dostoevsky, Proust, Kafka, Beckett, almost all modern literature? It is scarcely adequate to remark, as Steiner does in his introduction, that "Lukács is a radical moralist . . . like [the] Victorian critics. . . . In this great Marxist, there is an old-style Puritan."

This type of shallow, knowing comment, by which notorious radicalisms are domesticated, amounts to a surrender of judgment. It is cute or appealing to discover that Lukács—like Marx, like Freud—is morally conventional, even positively prudish, only if one has started with a cliché about an intellectual bogey-man. The point is: Lukács does treat literature as a branch of moral argument. Is the way he does it plausible, powerful? Does it allow for sensitive and discriminating and true literary judgments? I, for one, find Lukács' writings of the 1930s, 1940s, and 1950s to be seriously marred, not by his Marxism but by the coarseness of his argument.

Any critic is entitled to wrong judgments, of course. But certain lapses of judgment indicate the radical failure of an entire sensibility. And a writer who—as Lukács does—dismisses Nietzsche as merely a forerunner of Nazism, who criticizes Conrad for not "portraying the totality of life" (Conrad "is really a short-story writer rather than a novelist"), is not just making isolated mistakes of judgment, but proposing standards that ought not to be assented to.

Nor can I agree, as Kazin in his introduction seems to suggest, that, regardless of where Lukács went wrong, where he is right he is sound. Admirable as the 19th century realist tradition in the novel may be, the standards of admiration which Lukács proposes are unnecessarily coarse. For everything depends on Lukács' view that "the business of the critic is the relation between ideology (in the sense of *Weltanschauung*) and artistic creation." Lukács is committed to a version of the mimetic theory of art which is simply far too crude. A book is a "portrayal"; it "depicts," it "paints a picture"; the artist is a "spokesman." The great realist tradition of the novel does not need to be defended in these terms.

Both of the present books, "late" writings, lack intellectual subtlety. Of the two, *Realism in Our Time* is by far the better. The first essay in particular, "The Ideology of Modernism," is a powerful, in many ways brilliant, attack. Lukács' thesis is that modernist literature (he sweeps Kafka, Joyce, Moravia, Benn, Beckett, and a dozen others into this net) is really allegorical in character; he goes on to develop the connection between allegory and the refusal of historical consciousness. The next essay, "Franz Kafka or Thomas Mann?" is a cruder, and less interesting, restatement of the same thesis. The final essay, "Critical Realism and Socialist Realism," refutes from a Marxist point of view the base doctrines of art which were part of the Stalin era.

But even this book disappoints in many ways. The notion about allegory in the first essay is based on ideas of the late

Walter Benjamin, and the quotations from Benjamin's essay on allegory leap off the page as examples of a type of writing and reasoning much finer than that of Lukács. Ironically, Benjamin, who died in 1940, is one of the critics influenced by the "early" Lukács. But, irony aside, the truth is that Benjamin is a great critic (it is he who deserves the title "the only major German literary critic of our epoch"), and the "late" Lukács is not. Benjamin shows us what Lukács as a literary critic might have been.

Writers like Sartre, in France, and the German school of neo-Marxist critics whose most illustrious members, besides Benjamin, are Theodor Adorno and Herbert Marcuse, have developed the Marxist (more accurately, the radical Hegelian) position as a mode of philosophical and cultural analysis capable, among other things, of doing justice to at least certain aspects of modern literature. It is against these writers that Lukács must be compared, and found wanting. I am sympathetic to the reasons and experiences which underlie Lukács' reactionary aesthetic sensibility, and respectful even of his chronic moralizing and the burden of ideology which he valiantly carries, in part, to assist in the taming of its philistinism. But as I cannot accept either the intellectual premises of Lukács' taste or its consequences, his sweeping strictures against the greatest works of contemporary literature, neither can I pretend that, for me, these do not vitiate his entire later critical work.

For his new American audience, the best service to Lukács would be to translate the earlier books, *The Forms of the Soul* (which includes his thesis on tragedy), *The Theory of the Novel*, and, of course, *History and Class Consciousness*. Besides this, the best service to the vitality and scope inherent in the Marxist position on art would be to translate the German and French critics I have mentioned—above all, Benjamin. Only when all the important writings of this group are taken together can we properly evaluate Marxism as an important position vis-à-vis art and culture.

(1964)

POSTSCRIPT:

Karl Mannheim, in his review (published in 1920) of Lukács' *Theory of the Novel*, described it as "an attempt at interpreting aesthetic phenomena, particularly the novel, from a higher point of view, that of the philosophy of history." For Mannheim, "Lukács' book moves in the right direction." Putting aside the judgments of right and wrong, such a direction is clearly a limiting one, I should say. More precisely, both the strength and the limitation of the Marxist approach to art arise from its commitment to a "higher point of view." There is no question in the writings of the critics I have cited (the early Lukács, Benjamin, Adorno, etc.) of a narrow forcing of art *per se* into the service of a particular moral or historical tendency. But none of these critics, even at their best, are free of certain notions which in the end serve to perpetuate an ideology that, for all its attractiveness when considered as a catalogue of ethical duties, has failed to comprehend in other than a dogmatic and disapproving way the texture and qualities, the peculiar vantage point, of contemporary society. I mean "humanism." Despite their commitment to the notion of historical progress, the neo-Marxist critics have shown themselves to be singularly insensitive to most of the interesting and creative features of contemporary culture in non-socialist countries. In their general lack of interest in avant-garde art, in their blanket indictment of contemporary styles of art and life of very different quality and import (as "alienated," "dehumanized," "mechanized"), they reveal themselves as little different in spirit from the great conservative critics of modernity who wrote in the 19th century such as Arnold, Ruskin, and Burckhardt. It is odd, and disquieting, that such strongly apolitical critics as Marshall McLuhan have got so much better grasp on the texture of contemporary reality.

The variety of particular judgments made by the neo-Marxist critics may seem to indicate less unanimity of sensibility than I have argued. But when one notes the recurrence of the same terms of praise throughout, the differences seem slight. True, Schoenberg is defended by Adorno in his *Philosophy of New Music*—but in the name of "progress." (Adorno complements his defense of Schoenberg with an attack on Stravinsky, whom he unfairly identifies with just one period, the neo-classical. For raiding the past, for making musical pastiches—an analogous case could be made against Picasso—Stravinsky is labeled as a "reactionary," in the end, a "fascist.") However, Kafka is attacked by Lukács for the qualities which, *mutatis mutandis*, in the history of music, would have made him in Adorno's terms a "progressive." Kafka is a reactionary because of the allegorical, that is, the dehistoricized, texture of his writings, while Mann is a progressive because of his realism, that is, his sense of history. But I imagine that Mann's writings—old-fashioned in their form, riddled with parody and irony—could, if the discussion were set up differently, be labeled as reactionary. In the one case, "reaction" is identified with an inauthentic relation to the past; in the other, with abstractness. Using either standard—despite the exceptions allowed by individual taste—these critics must be generally inhospitable to or obtuse about modern art. Mostly, they don't get any nearer to it than they have to. The only contemporary novelist the French neo-Marxist critic Lucien Goldmann has written on at any length is André Malraux. Even the extraordinary Benjamin, who wrote with equal brilliance on Goethe, Leskov, and Baudelaire, did not deal with any 20th century writers. And the cinema, the only wholly new major art form of our century, to which he did devote the better part of an important essay, was singularly misunderstood and unappreciated by Benjamin. (He thought the movies embodied the abolition of tradition and historical consciousness, and therefore—once again!—fascism.)

What all the culture critics who descend from Hegel and Marx have been unwilling to admit is the notion of art as autonomous (not merely historically interpretable) form. And since the peculiar spirit which animates the modern movements in the arts is based on, precisely, the rediscovery of the power (including the emotional power) of the formal properties of art, these critics are poorly situated to come to sympathetic terms with modern works of art, except through their "content." Even form is viewed by the historicist critics as a kind of content. This is very clear in *The Theory of the Novel*, where Lukács' analysis of the various literary genres—epic, lyric, novel—proceeds by an explication of the attitude toward social change incarnated in the form. A similar prejudice is less explicit, but equally pervasive, in the writings of many American literary critics—who get their Hegelianism partly from Marx but mainly from sociology.

There is certainly much that is valuable in the historicist approach. But if form may be understood as a certain kind of content, it is equally true (and perhaps more important to say now) that all content may be considered as a device of form.

Only when the historicist critics and all their progeny are able to accommodate into their views a large measure of devotion to works of art as, above all, works of art (rather than as sociological, cultural, moral, or political documents) will they be open to more than a few of the many great works of art which are of the 20th century, and will they develop—this is mandatory for any responsible critic today—an intelligent involvement with the problems and objectives of "modernism" in the arts.

(1965)

Sartre's Saint Genet

S *aint Genet* is a cancer of a book, grotesquely verbose, its cargo of brilliant ideas borne aloft by a tone of viscous solemnity and by ghastly repetitiveness. One knows that the book began as an introductory essay to the collected edition of Genet's works published by Gallimard—some fifty pages, perhaps—and grew to its present length, whereupon it was issued in 1952 as a separate volume, the first, of the Collected Genet.* To read it, familiarity with Genet's writings in prose, most as yet untranslated, is surely essential. Even more important, the reader must come equipped with sympathy for Sartre's way of explicating a text. Sartre breaks every rule of decorum established for the critic; this is criticism by immersion, without guidelines. The book simply plunges into Genet; there is little discernible organization to Sartre's argument; nothing is made easy or clear. One should perhaps be grateful that Sartre stops after six hundred and twenty-five pages. The indefatigable act of literary and philosophical disembowelment which he practices on Genet could just as well have gone on for a thousand pages. Yet, Sartre's exasperating book is worth all one's effort of attention. *Saint Genet* is not one of the truly great, mad books; it is too long and too academic in vocabulary for that. But it is crammed with stunning and profound ideas.

What made the book grow and grow is that Sartre, the philosopher, could not help (however reverentially) upstaging Genet, the poet. What began as an act of critical homage and recipe for the bourgeois literary public's "good use of Genet" turned into something more ambitious. Sartre's enterprise is really to exhibit his own philosophical style—compounded of the phenomenological tradition from Descartes through Husserl and Heidegger, plus a liberal admixture of Freud and revisionist Marxism—while writing about a specific figure. In this instance, the person whose acts are made to yield the value of Sartre's philosophical vocabulary is Genet. In a previous effort at "existential psychoanalysis," published in 1947 and kept to a more digestible length, it was Baudelaire. In this earlier essay,

---

* Saint Genet, by Jean-Paul Sartre. Translated by Bernard Frechtman. New York, George Braziller.

Sartre was much more concerned with specifically psychological issues, such as Baudelaire's relation to his mother and his
mistresses. The present study of Genet is more philosophical
because, to put it bluntly, Sartre admires Genet in a way that
he does not admire Baudelaire. It would seem that, for Sartre,
Genet deserves something more than perceptive psychologizing. He merits philosophical diagnosis.

And a philosophical dilemma accounts for the length—and
the breathlessness—of the book. All thought, as Sartre knows,
universalizes. Sartre wants to be concrete. He wants to reveal
Genet, not simply to exercise his own tireless intellectual facility.
But he cannot. His enterprise is fundamentally impossible. He
cannot catch the real Genet; he is always slipping back into the
categories of Foundling, Thief, Homosexual, Free Lucid Individual, Writer. Somewhere Sartre knows this, and it torments
him. The length, and the inexorable tone, of *Saint Genet* are
really the product of intellectual agony.

The agony comes from the philosopher's commitment to
impose meaning upon action. Freedom, the key notion of existentialism, reveals itself in *Saint Genet*, even more clearly than
in *Being and Nothingness*, as a compulsion to assign meaning,
a refusal to let the world alone. According to Sartre's phenomenology of action, to act is to change the world. Man, haunted
by the world, acts. He acts in order to modify the world in view
of an end, an ideal. An act is therefore intentional, not accidental, and an accident is not to be counted as an act. Neither the
gestures of personality nor the works of the artist are simply
to be experienced. They must be understood, they must be
interpreted as modifications of the world. Thus, throughout
Saint Genet, Sartre continually moralizes. He moralizes upon
the acts of Genet. And since Sartre's book was written at a time
when Genet was chiefly a writer of prose narratives (among the
plays, only the first two, *The Maids* and *Deathwatch*, had been
written), and since these narratives are all autobiographical and
written in the first person, Sartre need not separate the personal from the literary act. Although Sartre occasionally refers
to things which he knows through his own friendship with
Genet, it is almost entirely the man revealed by his books of
whom Sartre speaks. It is a monstrous figure, real and surreal at
the same time, all of whose acts are seen by Sartre as meaningful, intentional. This is what gives *Saint Genet* a quality that is

clotted and ghostly. The name "Genet" repeated thousands of times throughout the book never seems to be the name of a real person. It is the name given to an infinitely complex process of philosophical transfiguration.

Given all these ulterior intellectual motives, it is surprising how well Sartre's enterprise serves Genet. This is because Genet himself, in his writings, is notably and explicitly involved in the enterprise of self-transfiguration. Crime, sexual and social degradation, above all murder, are understood by Genet as occasions for glory. It did not require much ingenuity on Sartre's part to propose that Genet's writings are an extended treatise on abjection—conceived as a spiritual method. The "sanctity" of Genet, created by an onanistic meditation upon his own degradation and the imaginative annihilation of the world, is the explicit subject of his prose works. What remained for Sartre was to draw out the implications of what is explicit in Genet. Genet may never have read Descartes, Hegel, or Husserl. But Sartre is right, entirely right, in finding a relation in Genet to the ideas of Descartes, Hegel, and Husserl. As Sartre brilliantly observes: "Abjection is a methodical conversion, like Cartesian doubt and Husserlian *epoché*: it establishes the world as a closed system which consciousness regards from without, in the manner of the divine understanding. The superiority of this method to the other two lies in its being lived in pain and pride. It therefore does not lead to the transcendental and universal consciousness of Husserl, the formal and abstract thinking of the Stoics, or the substantial *cogito* of Descartes, but to an individual existence at its highest degree of tension and lucidity."

As I have said, the only work of Sartre's comparable to *Saint Genet* is the dazzling essay on Baudelaire. Baudelaire is analyzed as a man in revolt whose life is continually lived in bad faith. His freedom is not creative, rebellious though it may have been, because it never finds its own set of values. Throughout his life the profligate Baudelaire needed bourgeois morality to condemn him. Genet is a true revolutionist. In Genet, freedom is won for freedom's sake. Genet's triumph, his "sanctity," is that he broke through the social framework against unbelievable odds to found his own morality. Sartre shows us Genet making a lucid, coherent system out of *le mal*. Unlike Baudelaire, Genet is free of self-deception.

Saint Genet is a book about the dialectic of freedom, and is, formally at least, set in the Hegelian mold. What Sartre wants to show is how Genet, by means of action and reflection, has spent his whole life attaining the lucid free act. Cast from his birth in the role of the Other, the outcast, Genet chose himself. This original choice is asserted through three different metamorphoses—the criminal, the aesthete, the writer. Each one is necessary to fulfill freedom's demand for a push beyond the self. Each new level of freedom carries with it a new knowledge of the self. Thus the whole discussion of Genet may be read as a dark travesty on Hegel's analysis of the relations between self and other. Sartre speaks of the works of Genet as being, each one of them, small editions of *The Phenomenology of Mind*. Absurd as it sounds, Sartre is correct. But it is also true that all of Sartre's writings as well are versions, editions, commentaries, satires on Hegel's great book. This is the bizarre point of connection between Sartre and Genet; two more different human beings it would be hard to imagine.

In Genet, Sartre has found his ideal subject. To be sure, he has drowned in him. Nevertheless, *Saint Genet* is a marvelous book, full of truths about moral language and moral choice. (Take, as only one instance, the insight that "evil is the systematic substitution of the abstract for the concrete.") And the analyses of Genet's narratives and plays are consistently perceptive. On Genet's most daring book, *Funeral Rites*, Sartre is particularly striking. And he is certainly capable of appraisal, as well as explication, as in the entirely just comment that "The style of *Our Lady of the Flowers*, which is a dream poem, a poem of futility, is very slightly marred by a kind of onanistic complacency. It does not have the spirited tone of the works that follow." Sartre does say many foolish, superfluous things in *Saint Genet*. But everything true and interesting that can be said about Genet is in this book as well.

It is also a crucial book for the understanding of Sartre at his best. After *Being and Nothingness*, Sartre stood at the crossroads. He could move from philosophy and psychology to an ethics. Or he could move from philosophy and psychology to a politics, a theory of group action and history. As everyone knows, and many deplore, Sartre chose the second path; and the result is the *Critique of Dialectical Reason*, published in 1960. *Saint Genet* is his complex gesture in the direction he did not go.

Of all the philosophers in the Hegelian tradition (and I include Heidegger), Sartre is the man who has understood the dialectic between self and other in Hegel's *Phenomenology* in the most interesting and usable fashion. But Sartre is not simply Hegel with knowledge of the flesh, any more than he deserves to be written off as a French disciple of Heidegger. Sartre's great book, *Being and Nothingness*, is heavily indebted to the language and problems of Hegel, Husserl, and Heidegger, to be sure. But it has a fundamentally different intention from theirs. Sartre's work is not contemplative, but is moved by a great psychological urgency. His pre-war novel, *Nausea*, really supplies the key to all his work. Here is stated the fundamental problem of the assimilability of the world in its repulsive, slimy, vacuous, or obtrusively substantial thereness—the problem which moves all of Sartre's writings. *Being and Nothingness* is an attempt to develop a language to cope with, to record the gestures of, a consciousness tormented by disgust. This disgust, this experience of the superfluity of things and of moral values, is simultaneously a psychological crisis and a metaphysical problem.

Sartre's solution is nothing if not impertinent. Corresponding to the primitive rite of anthropophagy, the eating of human beings, is the philosophical rite of cosmophagy, the eating of the world. The hallmark of the philosophical tradition to which Sartre is heir starts with consciousness as the sole given. Sartre's solution to the anguish of consciousness confronted by the brute reality of things is cosmophagy, the devouring of the world by consciousness. More exactly, consciousness is understood as both world-constituting and world-devouring. All relations—especially, in the most brilliant passages in *Being and Nothingness*, the erotic—are analyzed as gestures of consciousness, appropriations of the other in the interminable self-definition of the self.

In *Being and Nothingness*, Sartre reveals himself as a psychologist of the first rank—worthy to rank with Dostoevsky, Nietzsche, and Freud. And the focus of the Baudelaire essay is the analysis of Baudelaire's work and biography, treated as texts equivalent from a symptomatic point of view, disclosing fundamental psychological gestures. What makes *Saint Genet* even more interesting than the Baudelaire essay (though, at the same time, more unmanageable as well) is that, through thinking about Genet, Sartre has gone beyond the notion of action as a mode of psychological self-conservation. Through Genet, Sartre has glimpsed something of the autonomy of the aesthetic. More exactly, he has redemonstrated the connection between the aesthetic dimension and freedom, rather differently argued by Kant. The artist who is the subject of *Saint Genet* is not psychologized away. Genet's works are interpreted in terms of a saving ritual, a ceremony of consciousness. That this ceremony is essentially onanistic, is curiously apt. According to European philosophy since Descartes, world-creating has been the principal activity of consciousness. Now, a disciple of Descartes has interpreted world-creating as a form of world-procreating, as masturbation.

Sartre correctly describes Genet's spiritually most ambitious book, *Funeral Rites,* as "a tremendous effort of transubstantiation." Genet relates how he transformed the whole world into the corpse of his dead lover, Jean Decarnin, and this young corpse into his own penis. "The Marquis de Sade dreamt of extinguishing the fires of Etna with his sperm," Sartre observes. "Genet's arrogant madness goes further: he jerks off the Universe." Jerking off the universe is perhaps what all philosophy, all abstract thought is about: an intense, and not very sociable pleasure, which has to be repeated again and again. It is a rather good description, anyway, of Sartre's own phenomenology of consciousness. And, certainly, it is a perfectly fair description of what Genet is about.

(1963)

Nathalie Sarraute and the Novel

A NEW mode of didacticism has conquered the arts, is indeed the "modern" element in art. Its central dogma is the idea that art must evolve. Its result is the work whose main intention is to advance the history of the genre, to break ground in matters of technique. The paramilitary imagery of *avant-garde* and *arrière-garde* perfectly expresses the new didacticism. Art is the army by which human sensibility advances implacably into the future, with the aid of ever newer and more formidable techniques. This mainly negative relation of individual talent to tradition, which gives rise to the rapid and built-in obsolescence of each new item of technique, and each new use of materials, has vanquished the conception of art as giving familiar pleasure, and produced a body of work which is principally didactic and admonitory. As everyone knows by now, the point of Duchamp's "Nude Descending a Staircase" is not so much to represent anything, much less a nude, descending a staircase, as to teach a lesson on how natural forms may be broken into a series of kinetic planes. The point of the prose works of Stein and Beckett is to show how diction, punctuation, syntax, and narrative order can be recast to express continuous impersonal states of consciousness. The point of the music of Webern and Boulez is to show how, for example, the rhythmical function of silence and the structural role of tone colors can be developed.

The victory of the modern didacticism has been most complete in music and painting, where the most respected works are those which give little pleasure on first hearing and seeing (except to a small and highly trained audience) but make important advances in the technical revolutions which have taken place in these arts. Compared with music and painting, the novel, like the cinema, lags well to the rear of the battlefield. A body of "difficult" novels comparable to Abstract Expressionist painting and *musique concrète* has not overrun the territory of critically respectable fiction. On the contrary, most of the novel's few brave ventures to the front line of modernism get marooned there. After a few years they seem merely idiosyncratic, for no troops follow the brave CO and back him up. Novels which, in the order of difficulty and of merit, are comparable to the music of Gian-Carlo Menotti and the painting of Bernard Buffet, are garnished with the highest critical acclaim. The ease of access and lack of rigor that causes embarrassment in music and painting are no embarrassment in the novel, which remains intransigently *arrière-garde*.

Yet, middle-class art form or no, there is no genre in greater need of sustained reexamination and renovation. The novel is (along with opera) the archetypal art form of the 19th century, perfectly expressing that period's wholly mundane conception of reality, its lack of really ambitious spirituality, its discovery of the "interesting" (that is, of the commonplace, the inessential, the accidental, the minute, the transient), its affirmation of what E. M. Cioran calls "destiny in lower case." The novel, as all the critics who praise it never tire of reminding us and upbraiding contemporary writers who deviate, is about man-in-society; it brings alive a chunk of the world and sets its "characters" within that world. Of course, one can treat the novel as the successor to the epic and the picaresque tale. But everyone knows that this inheritance is superficial. What animates the novel is something wholly missing from these older narrative forms: the discovery of psychology, the transposition of motives into "experiences." This passion for the documentation of "experience," for facts, made the novel the most open of all art forms. Every art form works with some implicit standard of what is elevated and what is vulgar—except the novel. It could accommodate any level of language, any plot, any ideas, any information. And this, of course, was its eventual undoing as a serious art form. Sooner or later discriminating readers could no longer be expected to become interested in one more leisurely "story," in half a dozen more private lives laid open for their inspection. (They found the movies doing this, with more freedom and with more vigor.) While music and the plastic arts and poetry painfully dug themselves out of the inadequate dogmas of the 19th century "realism," by a passionate commitment to the idea of progress in art and a hectic quest for new idioms and new materials, the novel has proved unable to assimilate whatever of genuine quality and spiritual ambition has been performed in its name in the 20th century. It has sunk to the level of an art form deeply, if not irrevocably, compromised by philistinism.

When one thinks of giants like Proust, Joyce, the Gide of

Lafcadio, Kafka, the Hesse of *Steppenwolf*, Genet, or lesser but nonetheless masterly writers such as Machado de Assis, Svevo, Woolf, Stein, the early Nathanael West, Céline, Nabokov, the early Pasternak, the Djuna Barnes of *Nightwood*, Beckett (to mention only some), one thinks of writers who close off rather than inaugurate, who cannot be learned from, so much as imitated, and whom one imitates at the peril of merely repeating what they have done. One hesitates to blame or praise critics for anything that happens in an art form, whether for good or bad. Yet it is hard not to conclude that what the novel has lacked, and what it must have if it is to continue as a generally (as opposed to sporadically) serious art form, is any sustained distance from its 19th century premises. (The great flowering of literary criticism in England and America in the last thirty years, which began with the criticism of poetry and then passed on to the novel, precisely does *not* contain such a reevaluation. It is a philosophically naïve criticism, unquestioning and uncritical of the prestige of "realism.")

This coming-of-age of the novel will entail a commitment to all sorts of questionable notions, like the idea of "progress" in the arts and the defiantly aggressive ideology expressed in the metaphor of the avant-garde. It will restrict the novel's audience because it will demand accepting new pleasures—such as the pleasure of solving a problem—to be gotten from prose fiction and learning how to get them. (It may mean, for example, that we shall have to read aloud as well as with the eye, and it will certainly mean that we must expect to read a novel a number of times to understand it fully or to feel ourselves competent to judge it. We have already accepted this idea of repeated looking or hearing or reading with serious contemporary poetry, painting, sculpture, and music.) And it will make self-conscious aestheticians, didactic explorers, of all who wish seriously to practice the form. (All "modern" artists are aestheticians.) This surrender of the novel's commitment to facileness, to easy availability and the perpetuation of an outmoded aesthetic, will undoubtedly give rise to a great many boring and pretentious books; and one may well come to wish the old unself-consciousness back again. But the price must be paid. Readers must be made to see, by a new generation of critics

who may well have to force this ungainly period of the novel
down their throats by all sorts of seductive and partly fraudulent
rhetoric, the necessity of this move. And the sooner the better.

For until we have a *continuous* serious "modern" tradition
of the novel, venturesome novelists will work in a vacuum.
(Whether critics will decide not to call these prose fiction novels any more doesn't matter. Nomenclature has not proved
an obstacle in painting or music or poetry, although it has in
sculpture, so that we now tend to drop that word in favor of
words like "construction" and "assemblage.") We shall continue
to have monstrous hulks, like abandoned tanks, lying about
the landscape. An example, perhaps the greatest example, is
Finnegans Wake—still largely unread and unreadable, left to
the care of academic exegetes who may decipher the book for
us, but cannot tell us why it should be read or what we can
learn from it. That Joyce expected his readers to devote their
whole lives to his book may seem an outrageous demand; but
it is a logical one, considering the singularity of his work. And
the fate of Joyce's last book presages the obtuse reception of a
number of its less mammoth but equally plotless successors in
English—the books of Stein, Beckett, and Burroughs come to
mind. No wonder these stand out, as stark isolated forays, on
an eerily pacified battleground.

Lately, however, the situation appears to be changing. A
whole school—should I say a battalion?—of important and challenging novels is being produced in France. There are actually
two waves here. The earlier was led by Maurice Blanchot,
Georges Bataille, and Pierre Klossowski; most of these books
were written in the 1940s and are as yet untranslated into English. Better known, and mostly translated, are a "second wave"
of books written in the 1950s, by (among others) Michel Butor,
Alain Robbe-Grillet, Claude Simon, and Nathalie Sarraute. All
these writers—and they differ greatly from each other, in intention and achievement—have this in common: they reject the
idea of the "novel" whose task is to tell a story and delineate
characters according to the conventions of 19th century realism,
and all they abjure is summed up in the notion of "psychology."
Whether they try to transcend psychology by Heidegger's phenomenology (a powerful influence) or undercut it by behavioristic, external description, the results are at least negatively

similar, and constitute the first body of work on the form of the novel which gives promise of telling us something useful about the new forms which fiction may take.

But perhaps the more valuable achievement to come out of France for the novel has been a whole body of criticism inspired by the new novelists (and, in some cases, written by them) which amounts to a most impressive attempt to think systematically about the genre. This criticism—I am thinking of essays by Maurice Blanchot, Roland Barthes, E. M. Cioran, Alain Robbe-Grillet, Nathalie Sarraute, Michel Butor, Michel Foucault, and others—is, by far, the most interesting literary criticism today. And nothing prevents novelists in the English-speaking world from drawing sustenance from the brilliant re-examination of the premises of the novel expounded by these critics, but doing work in the novel very different from that of the French novelists. The reason these essays may prove more valuable than the novels is that they propose standards that are ampler and more ambitious than anything yet achieved by any writer. (Robbe-Grillet, for example, admits that his novels are inadequate illustrations of the diagnoses and recommendations put forth in his essays.)

This is, to me, the importance of the appearance in English of *The Age of Suspicion*, a collection of Nathalie Sarraute's essays in which, ostensibly, the theory behind her novels is fully set forth.* Whether or not one enjoys or admires Sarraute's novels (I really like only *Portrait of a Man Unknown* and *The Planetarium*), whether or not she really practices what she preaches (in a crucial respect, I think she does not), the essays broach a number of criticisms of the traditional novel which seem to me a good beginning for the theoretical reconsideration long overdue on this side of the Atlantic.

Perhaps the best approach to Sarraute's polemic for an English-speaking reader would be to compare it with two other manifestoes on what the novel should be, Virginia Woolf's "Mr. Bennett and Mrs. Brown" and Mary McCarthy's "The Fact in Fiction." Sarraute scorns as "naïve" Virginia Woolf's dismissal of

---

* *The Age of Suspicion* by Nathalie Sarraute. Translated by Maria Jolas. New York, Braziller.

naturalism and objective realism, her call to the modern novel-ist to examine "the dark places of psychology." But Sarraute is equally hard on the position represented by Mary McCarthy's essay, which may be read as a rebuttal of Virginia Woolf, call-ing as it does for a return to the old novelistic virtues of setting forth a real world, giving a sense of verisimilitude, and con-structing memorable characters.

Sarraute's case against realism is a convincing one. Reality is not that unequivocal; life is not that lifelike. The immedi-ate cozy recognition that the lifelike in most novels induces is, and should be, suspect. (Truly, as Sarraute says, the genius of the age is suspicion. Or, if not its genius, at least its besetting vice.) I wholeheartedly sympathize with what she objects to in the old-fashioned novel: *Vanity Fair* and *Buddenbrooks*, when I reread them recently, however marvellous they still seemed, also made me wince. I could not stand the omnipotent author showing me that's how life is, making me compassionate and tearful; with his obstreperous irony, his confidential air of per-fectly knowing his characters and leading me, the reader, to feel I knew them too. I no longer trust novels which fully satisfy my passion to understand. Sarraute is right, too, that the novel's traditional machinery for furnishing a scene, and describing and moving about characters, does not justify itself. Who really cares about the furniture of so-and-so's room, or whether he lit a cigarette or wore a dark gray suit or uncovered the typewriter after sitting down and before inserting a sheet of paper in the typewriter? Great movies have shown that the cinema can invest pure physical action—whether fleeting and small-scale like the wig-changing in *L'Avventura*, or important like the advance through the forest in *The Big Parade*—with more immediate magic than words ever can, and more economically, too.

More complex and problematic, however, is Sarraute's insis-tence that psychological analysis in the novel is equally obsolete and misguided. "The word 'psychology,'" Sarraute says, "is one that no present-day writer can hear spoken with regard to him-self without averting his gaze and blushing." By psychology in the novel, she means Woolf, Joyce, Proust: novels which explore a substratum of hidden thoughts and feelings beneath action, the depiction of which replaces the concern with character and plot. All Joyce brought up from these depths, she remarks, was an uninterrupted flow of words. And Proust, too, failed. In the end Proust's elaborate psychological dissections recompose themselves into realistic characters, in which the practiced reader "immediately recognizes a rich man of the world in love with a kept woman, a prominent, awkward, gullible doctor, a parvenu bourgeoise or a snobbish 'great lady,' all of which will soon take their places in the vast collection of fictitious characters that people his imaginary museum."

Actually Sarraute's novels are not so unlike Joyce's (and Woolf's) as she thinks, and her rejection of psychology is far from total. What she wants herself is precisely the psychological, but (and this is the basis of her complaint against Proust) without the possibility of any conversion back into "character" and "plot." She is against psychological *dissection*, for that assumes there is a body to dissect. She is against a provisional psychology, against psychology as a new means to the old end. The use of the psychological microscope must not be intermittent, a device merely in the furthering of the plot. This means a radical recasting of the novel. Not only must the novelist not tell a story; he must not distract the reader with gross events like a murder or a great love. The more minute, the less sensational the event the better. (Thus *Martereau* consists of the ruminations of a nameless young man, an interior decorator, about the artistic aunt and rich businessman uncle with whom he lives, and about an older, not-so-well-off man named Martereau, concerning why and in what circumstances he feels comfortable with them, and why and when he feels he is succumbing to the force of their personalities and the objects with which they surround themselves. The aunt and uncle's project of buying a house in the country provides the only "action" of the book, and if for a time it is suspected that Martereau has defrauded the uncle in the matter of the house, you can bet that in the end all suspicions are allayed. In *The Planetarium* something does happen. A social-climbing young man, shamelessly trying to gain admittance to the circle of a rich, vain, and very famous woman writer, actually does manage to dispossess his doting, gullible aunt from her five-room apartment.) But Sarraute's characters do not really ever act. They scheme, they throb, they shudder—under the impact of the minutiae of daily life. These preliminaries and gropings toward action are the real subjects of her novels. Since analysis is out—that is, the speak-ing, interpreting author is out—Sarraute's novels are logically written only in the first person, even when the interior musings use "she" and "he."

What Sarraute proposes is a novel written in continuous monologue, in which dialogue between characters is a func-tional extension of monologue, "real" speech a continuation of silent speech. This kind of dialogue she calls "sub-conversation." It is comparable to theatrical dialogue in that the author does not intervene or interpret, but unlike theatrical dialogue it is not broken up or assigned to clearly separable characters. (She has some particularly sharp and mocking words to say about the creaky *he said*'s, *she replied*'s, *so-and-so declared*'s with which most novels are strewn.) Dialogue must "become vibrant and swollen with those tiny inner movements that propel and extend it." The novel must disavow the means of classical psychology—introspection—and proceed instead by immer-sion. It must plunge the reader "into the stream of those subter-ranean dramas of which Proust only had time to obtain a rapid aerial view, and concerning which he observed and reproduced nothing but the broad motionless outlines." The novel must record without comment the direct and purely sensory contact with things and persons which the "I" of the novelist experi-ences. Abstaining from all creating of likenesses (Sarraute hands that over to the cinema), the novel must preserve and promote "that element of indetermination, of opacity and mystery that one's own actions always have for the one who lives them."

There is something exhilarating in Sarraute's program for the novel, which insists on an unlimited respect for the complexity of human feelings and sensations. But there is, for me, a certain softness in her argument, based as it is on a diagnosis of psy-chology that is both excessively doctrinaire in its remedy and equivocal. A view which regards "the efforts of Henry James or Proust to take apart the delicate wheelworks of our inner mechanisms" as wielding a pick and shovel has dazzling stan-dards of psychological refinement indeed. Who would contra-dict Sarraute when she characterizes the feelings as an immense mobile mass in which almost anything can be found; or when she says that no theory, least of all a cipher like psychoanalysis, can give an account of all its movements? But Sarraute is only attacking psychology in the novel on behalf of a better, closer technique of psychological description.

Her views of the complexity of feeling and sensation are one thing, her program for the novel another. True, all accounts of motivation simplify. But, admitting that, there still remain many choices available to the novelist besides seeking a more refined and microscopic way of representing motives. Certain kinds of overviews, for example—which scant the minutiae of feeling altogether—are, I am sure, at least as valid a solution to the problem Sarraute raises as the technique of dialogue and narration which she takes as the logical consequence of her critique. Character may be (as Sarraute insists) an ocean, a confluence of tides and streams and eddies, but I do not see the privileged value of immersion. Skin-diving has its place, but so has oceanic cartography, what Sarraute contemptuously dismisses as "the aerial view." Man is a creature who is designed to live on the surface; he lives in the depths—whether terrestrial, oceanic, or psychological—at his peril. I do not share her contempt for the novelist's effort to transmute the watery shapeless depths of experience into solid stuff, to impose outlines, to give fixed shape and sensuous body to the world. That it's boring to do it in the old ways goes without saying. But I cannot agree that it should not be done at all.

Sarraute invites the writer to resist the desire to amuse his contemporaries, to reform them, to instruct them, or to fight for their emancipation; and simply, without trimming or smoothing or overcoming contradictions, to present "reality" (the word is Sarraute's) as he sees it, with as great a sincerity and sharpness of vision as he is capable. I will not here dispute the question of whether the novel should amuse, reform, or instruct (why should it not, so long as it justifies itself as a work of art?) but only point out what a tendentious definition of reality she proposes. Reality, for Sarraute, means a reality that is rid of the "preconceived ideas and ready-made images that encase it." It is opposed to "the surface reality that everyone can easily see and which, for want of anything better, everyone uses." According to Sarraute, for a writer to be in contact with reality he must "attain something that is thus far unknown, which, it seems to him, he is the first to have seen."

But what is the point of this multiplication of realities? For truly, it is the plural rather than the singular that Sarraute should have used. If each writer must "bring to light this fragment of reality that is his own"—and all the whales and sharks have been catalogued; it is new species of plankton she is after—then the writer not only is a maker of fragments, but is condemned to being an exponent only of what is original in his own subjectivity. When he comes to the literary arena bearing his jar of tiny, and as yet uncatalogued, marine specimens, are we to welcome him in the name of science? (The writer as marine biologist.) Of sport? (The writer as deep-sea diver.) Why does he deserve an audience? How many fragments of reality do readers of novels need?

By invoking the notion of reality at all, Sarraute has, in fact, narrowed and compromised her argument when she need not have done so. The metaphor of the work of art as a representation of reality should be retired for a while; it has done good service throughout the history of the analysis of works of art, but now it can scarcely fail to skirt the important issues. In Sarraute's exposition, it has the unfortunate result of giving further life to the tedious alternatives of subjectivity versus objectivity, the original versus what is preconceived and ready-made. There is no reason why the novelist cannot make new arrangements and transformations of what everybody has seen, and restrict himself precisely to preconceived ideas and ready-made images.

Sarraute's allegiance to this rather vacuous notion of reality (a reality lying in the depths rather than the surface) is also responsible for the unnecessarily grim tone of some of her admonitions. Her chilly dismissal of the possibility of the writer's providing "aesthetic enjoyment" to his readers is mere rhetoric, and does serious injustice to the position she, in part, ably represents. The writer, she says, must renounce "all desire to write 'beautifully' for the pleasure of doing so, to give aesthetic enjoyment to himself or to his readers." Style is "capable of beauty only in the sense that any athlete's gesture is beautiful; the better it is adapted to its purpose, the greater the beauty." The purpose, remember, is the recording of the writer's unique apprehension of an unknown reality. But there is absolutely no reason to equate "aesthetic enjoyment," which every work of art is by definition designed to supply, with the notion of a frivolous, decorative, merely "beautiful" style. . . . It really is science, or better yet sport, that Sarraute has in mind as model for the novel. The final justification for the novelist's quest as Sarraute characterizes it—what for her frees the novel from all moral and social purposes—is that the novelist is after truth (or a fragment of it), like the scientist, and after functional exercise, like the athlete. And there is nothing, in principle, so objectionable about these models, except their meaning for her. For all the basic soundness of Sarraute's critique of the old-fashioned novel, she still has the novelist chasing after "truth" and "reality."

Sarraute's manifesto must thus be finally judged to do less justice to the position she is defending than that position deserves. A more rigorous and searching account of this position may be found in Robbe-Grillet's essays "On Several Dated Notions" and "Nature, Humanism, and Tragedy." These appeared in 1957 and 1958, respectively, while Sarraute's were published between 1950 and 1955, and collected in book form in 1956; and Robbe-Grillet has cited Sarraute in a way that might lead one to think that he is a later exponent of the same position. But Robbe-Grillet's complex criticism of the notions of tragedy and of humanism, the unremitting clarity with which he demolishes the old shibboleth of form versus content (his willingness, for example, to declare that the novel, so far as it belongs in the domain of art, has no content), the compatibility of his aesthetic with technical innovations in the novel quite different from those he has chosen, put his arguments on a far higher level than those of Sarraute. Robbe-Grillet's essays are truly radical and, if one grants but a single of his assumptions, carry one all the way to conviction. Sarraute's essays, useful as they may be to introduce the literate English-speaking public to the important critique of the traditional novel which has been launched in France, in the end hedge and compromise.

Undoubtedly, many people will feel that the prospects for the novel laid out by the French critics are rather bleak; and wish that the armies of art would go on fighting on other battlefronts and leave the novel alone. (In the same mood, some of us wish we were endowed with a good deal less of the excruciating psychological self-consciousness that is the burden of educated people in our time.) But the novel as a form of art has nothing to lose, and everything to gain, by joining the revolution that has already swept over most of the other arts. It is time that the

novel became what it is not, in England and America, with rare
and unrelated exceptions: a form of art which people with serious and sophisticated taste in the other arts can take seriously.

(1963; revised 1965)

III

Ionesco

IT IS fitting that a playwright whose best works apotheosize the platitude has compiled a book on the theater crammed with platitudes.* I quote, at random:

> Didacticism is above all an attitude of mind and an expression of the will to dominate.
>
> A work of art really is above all an adventure of the mind.
>
> Some have said that Boris Vian's *The Empire Builders* was inspired by my own *Amédée*. Actually, no one is inspired by anyone except by his own self and his own anguish.
>
> I detect a crisis of thought, which is manifested by a crisis of language; words no longer meaning anything.
>
> No society has even been able to abolish human sadness; no political system can deliver us from the pain of living, from our fear of death, our thirst for the absolute.

What is one to make of a view at once so lofty and so banal? As if this were not enough, Ionesco's essays are laden with superfluous self-explication and unctuous vanity. Again, at random:

> I can affirm that neither the public nor the critics have influenced me.
>
> Perhaps I am socially minded in spite of myself.
>
> With me every play springs from a kind of self-analysis.
>
> I am not an ideologue, for I am straightforward and objective.
>
> The world ought not to interest me so much. In reality, I am obsessed with it.

Etcetera, etcetera. Ionesco's essays on the theater offer a good deal of such, presumably unconscious, humor.

There are, to be sure, some ideas in *Notes and Counter Notes* worth taking seriously, none of them original with Ionesco. One is the idea of the theater as an instrument which, by dislocating the real, freshens the sense of reality. Such a function for the theater plainly calls not only for a new dramaturgy, but for a new body of plays. "No more masterpieces," Artaud demanded in *The Theatre and Its Double*, the most daring and profound manifesto of the modern theater. Like Artaud, Ionesco scorns the "literary" theater of the past: he likes to read Shakespeare

---

* *Notes and Counter Notes: Writings on the Theatre* by Eugène Ionesco. Translated by Donald Watson. New York, Grove.

and Kleist but not to see them performed, while Corneille, Molière, Ibsen, Strindberg, Pirandello, Giraudoux and company bore him either way. If the old-fashioned theater pieces must be done at all, Ionesco suggests (as did Artaud) a certain trick. One should play "against" the text: by grafting a serious, formal production onto a text that is absurd, wild, comic, or by treating a solemn text in the spirit of buffoonery. Along with the rejection of the literary theater—the theater of plot and individual character—Ionesco calls for the scrupulous avoidance of all psychology, for psychology means "realism," and realism is dull and confines the imagination. His rejection of psychology permits the revival of a device common to all non-realistic theatrical traditions (it is equivalent to frontality in naïve painting), in which the characters turn to face the audience (rather than each other), stating their names, identities, habits, tastes, acts. . . . All this, of course, is very familiar: the canonical modern style in the theater. Most of the interesting ideas in *Notes and Counter Notes* are watered-down Artaud; or rather Artaud spruced up and made charming, ingratiating; Artaud without his hatreds, Artaud without his madness. Ionesco comes closest to being original in certain remarks about humor, which he understands as poor mad Artaud did not at all. Artaud's notion of a Theater of Cruelty emphasized the darker registers of fantasy: frenzied spectacle, melodramatic deeds, bloody apparitions, screams, transports. Ionesco, noting that any tragedy becomes comic simply if it is speeded up, has devoted himself to the violently comic. Instead of the cave or the palace or the temple or the heath, he sets most of his plays in the living room. His comic terrain is the banality and oppressiveness of the "home"—be it the bachelor's furnished room, the scholar's study, the married couple's parlor. Underneath the forms of conventional life, Ionesco would demonstrate, lies madness, the obliteration of personality.

But Ionesco's plays, it seems to me, need little explanation. If an account of his work is desired, Richard N. Coe's excellent short book on Ionesco, published in 1961 in the English *Writers and Critics* series, offers a far more coherent and compact defense of the plays than anything in *Notes and Counter Notes.* The interest of Ionesco on Ionesco is not for its author's theory of theater, but for what the book suggests about the puzzling thinness—puzzling considering their richness of theme—of Ionesco's plays. The tone of the book tells a great deal. For behind the relentless egotism of Ionesco's writings on the theater—the allusions to unending battles with obtuse critics and a bovine public—is an insistent, plaintive uneasiness. Ionesco protests, incessantly, that he has been misunderstood. Therefore, everything he says at one point in *Notes and Counter Notes*, he takes back on another page. (Though these writings span the years 1951–61, there is no development in the argument.) His plays are avant-garde theater; there is no such thing as avant-garde theater. He is writing social criticism; he is not writing social criticism. He is a humanist; he is morally and emotionally estranged from humanity. Throughout, he writes as a man sure—whatever you say of him, whatever he says of himself—that his true gifts are misunderstood.

What is Ionesco's accomplishment? Judging by the most exacting standards, he has written one really remarkable and beautiful play, *Jack, or the Submission* (1950); one brilliant lesser work, *The Bald Soprano*, his first play (written 1948–49); and several effective short plays which are pungent reprises of the same material, *The Lesson* (1950), *The Chairs* (1951), and *The New Tenant* (1953). All these plays—Ionesco is a prolific writer—are "early" Ionesco. The later works are marred by a diffuseness in the dramatic purpose and an increasing, unwieldy self-consciousness. The diffuseness can be clearly seen in *Victims of Duty* (1952), a work with some powerful sections but unhappily overexplicit. Or one can compare his best play, *Jack*, with a short sequel using the same characters, *The Future Is in Eggs* (1951). *Jack* abounds with splendid harsh fantasy, ingenious and logical; it alone, of all Ionesco's plays, gives us something up to the standard of Artaud: the Theater of Cruelty as Comedy. But in *The Future Is in Eggs*, Ionesco has embarked upon the disastrous course of his later writings, railing against "views" and tediously attributing to his characters a concern with the state of the theater, the nature of language, and so forth. Ionesco is an artist of considerable gifts who has been victimized by "ideas." His work has become water-logged with them; his talents have coarsened. In *Notes and Counter Notes* we have a chunk of that endless labor of self-explication and self-vindication as a playwright and thinker which occupies the whole of his play, *Improvisation*, which dictates the intrusive remarks on playwriting in *Victims of Duty* and *Amédée*, which inspires the oversimplified critique of modern society in *The Killer* and *Rhinoceros*.

Ionesco's original artistic impulse was his discovery of the poetry of banality. His first play, *The Bald Soprano*, was written almost by accident, he says, after he discovered the Smiths and the Martins *en famille* in the Assimil phrase book he bought when he decided to study English. And all the subsequent plays of Ionesco continued at least to open with a volleying back and forth of clichés. By extension, the discovery of the poetry of cliché led to the discovery of the poetry of meaninglessness— the convertibility of all words into one another. (Thus, the litany of "*chat*" at the end of *Jack*.) It has been said that Ionesco's early plays are "about" meaninglessness, or "about" non-communication. But this misses the important fact that in much of modern art one can no longer really speak of subject-matter in the old sense. Rather, the subject-matter is the technique. What Ionesco did—no mean feat—was to appropriate for the theater one of the great technical discoveries of modern poetry: that all language can be considered from the outside, as by a stranger. Ionesco disclosed the *dramatic* resources of this attitude, long known but hitherto confined to modern poetry. His early plays are not "about" meaninglessness. They are attempts to use meaninglessness theatrically.

Ionesco's discovery of the cliché meant that he declined to see language as an instrument of communication or self-expression, but rather as an exotic substance secreted—in a sort of trance—by interchangeable persons. His next discovery, also long familiar in modern poetry, was that he could treat language as a palpable thing. (Thus, the teacher kills the student in *The Lesson* with the word "knife.") The key device for making language into a thing is repetition. This verbal repetition is dramatized further by another persistent motif of Ionesco's plays: the cancerous, irrational multiplication of material things. (Thus: the egg in *The Future Is in Eggs*; the chairs in *The Chairs*; the furniture in *The New Tenant*; the boxes in *The Killer*; the cups in *Victims of Duty*; the noses and fingers of Roberta II in *Jack*; the corpse in *Amédée, or How to Get Rid of It*.) These repeating words, these demonically proliferating things, can only be exorcised as in a dream, by being obliterated. Logically, poetically—and *not* because of any "ideas" Ionesco has about the nature of individual and society—his plays must end either in a *da capo* repetition, or in incredible violence. Some typical endings are: massacre of the audience (the proposed end of *The Bald Soprano*), suicide (*The Chairs*), entombment and silence (*The New Tenant*), unintelligibility and animal moans (*Jack*), monstrous physical coercion (*Victims of Duty*), the collapse of the stage (*The Future Is in Eggs*). In Ionesco's plays, the recurrent nightmare is of a wholly clogged, overrun world. (The nightmare is explicit with respect to the furniture in *The New Tenant*, the rhinoceroses in *Rhinoceros*.) The plays therefore must end in either chaos or non-being, destruction or silence.

These discoveries of the poetry of cliché and of language-as-thing gave Ionesco some remarkable theatrical material. But then ideas were born, a theory about the meaning of this theater of meaninglessness took up residence in Ionesco's work. The most fashionable modern experiences were invoked. Ionesco and his defenders claimed that he had begun with his experience of the meaninglessness of contemporary existence, and developed his theater of cliché to express this. It seems more likely that he began with the discovery of the poetry of banality, and then, alas, called on a theory to bulwark it. This theory amounts to the hardiest clichés of the criticism of "mass society," all scrambled together—alienation, standardization, dehumanization. To sum up this dreadfully familiar discontent, Ionesco's favorite word of abuse is "bourgeois," or sometimes "petty bourgeois." Ionesco's bourgeois has little in common with that favorite target of Leftist rhetoric, although perhaps he has adopted it from that source. For Ionesco, "bourgeois" means everything he doesn't like: it means "realism" in the theater (something like the way Brecht used "Aristotelian"); it means ideology; it means conformism. Of course, none of this would have mattered were it merely a question of Ionesco's pronouncements on his work. What mattered is that increasingly it began to infect his work. More and more, Ionesco tended to "indicate" shamelessly what he was doing. (One cringes when, at the end of *The Lesson*, the professor dons a swastika armband as he prepares to dispose of the corpse of his student.) Ionesco began with a fantasy, the vision of a world inhabited by language puppets. He was not criticizing anything, much less discovering what in an early essay he called "The Tragedy of Language." He was just discovering one way in which language could be used. Only afterward was a set of crude, simplistic attitudes extracted from this artistic discovery—attitudes about the contemporary standardization and dehumanization of man, all laid at the feet of a stuffed ogre called the "bourgeois," "Society," etc. The time then came for the affirmation of individual man against this ogre. Thus Ionesco's work passed through an unfortunate and familiar double phase: first, works of anti-theater, parody; then, the socially constructive plays. These later plays are thin stuff. And the weakest in all his *oeuvre* are the Bérenger plays— *The Killer* (1957), *Rhinoceros* (1960), and *The Pedestrian of the Air* (1962)—where Ionesco (as he said) created in Bérenger an alter ego, an Everyman, a beleaguered hero, a character "to rejoin humanity." The difficulty is that affirmation of man cannot simply be willed, either in morals or in art. If it is merely willed, the result is always unconvincing, and usually pretentious.

In this, Ionesco's development is just the reverse of Brecht's. Brecht's early works—*Baal, In the Jungle of Cities*—give way to the "positive" plays which are his masterpieces: *The Good Woman of Setzuan*, *The Caucasian Chalk Circle*, *Mother Courage*. But then—quite apart from the theories they espouse— Brecht is simply a much greater writer than Ionesco. To Ionesco, of course, he represents the arch-villain, the arch-bourgeois. He is political. But Ionesco's attacks on Brecht and the Brechtians—and on the idea of a politically committed art—are trivial. Brecht's political attitudes are, at best, the occasion for his humanism. They allow him to focus and expand his drama. The choice Ionesco insists on, between political affirmation and affirmation of man, is spurious, and dangerous besides.

Compared with Brecht, Genet, and Beckett, Ionesco is a minor writer even at his best. His work does not have the same weight, the same full-bloodedness, the same grandeur and relevance. Ionesco's plays, especially the shorter ones (the form for which his gifts are most suited), have their considerable virtues: charm, wit, a nice feeling for the macabre; above all, theatricality. But the recurrent themes—identities slipping out of gear, the monstrous proliferation of things, the gruesomeness of togetherness—are rarely so moving, so appalling, as they might be. Perhaps it is because—with the exception of *Jack*, where Ionesco lets his fantasy have its head—the terrible is always, somehow, circumscribed by the cute. Ionesco's morbid farces are the boulevard comedies of the avant-garde sensibility; as one English critic has pointed out, little really separates Ionesco's whimsy of conformity from Feydeau's whimsy of adultery. Both are skillful, cold, self-referring.

To be sure, Ionesco's plays—and writings about the theater—pay strenuous lip service to the emotions. Of *The Bald Soprano*, for instance, Ionesco says that it is about "talking and saying nothing because [of] the absence of any inner life." The Smiths and the Martins represent man totally absorbed in his social context, they "have forgotten the meaning of emotion." But what of the numerous descriptions which Ionesco gives in *Notes and Counter Notes* of his own inability to feel—an inability which he regards as rescuing him from being, rather than turning him into, a mass man? It is not protest against passionlessness which moves Ionesco, but a kind of misanthropy, which he has covered over with fashionable clichés of cultural diagnosis. The sensibility behind this theater is tight, defensive, and riddled with sexual disgust. Disgust is the powerful motor in Ionesco's plays: out of disgust, he makes comedies of the distasteful.

Disgust with the human condition is perfectly valid material for art. But disgust for ideas, expressed by a man with little talent for ideas, is another matter. This is what mars many of Ionesco's plays and makes his collection of writings on the theater irritating rather than amusing. Disgusted with ideas as one more foul human excrescence, Ionesco flails about in this repetitious book, at once assuming and disavowing all positions. The unifying theme of *Notes and Counter Notes* is his desire to maintain a position that is not a position, a view that is no view—in a word, to be intellectually invulnerable. But this is impossible, since initially he experiences an idea only as a cliché: "systems of thought on all sides are nothing more than alibis, something to hide reality (another cliché word) from us." By a sickening glide in the argument, ideas somehow become identified with politics, and all politics identified with a fascistic nightmare world. When Ionesco says, "I believe that what separates us all from one another is simply society itself, or, if you like, politics," he is expressing his anti-intellectualism rather than a position about politics. This can be seen with special clarity in the most interesting section in the book (pp. 87–108), the so-called London Controversy, an exchange of essays and letters with Kenneth Tynan, representing ostensibly a Brechtian point of view, which first appeared in the English weekly *The Observer* in 1958. The high moment of this controversy is a noble and eloquent letter from Orson Welles, who points out that the separation between art and politics cannot emerge, much less prosper, except in a certain kind of society. As Welles wrote, "Whatever is valuable is likely to have a rather shopsoiled name," and all freedoms—including Ionesco's privilege to shrug his shoulders at politics—"were, at one time or another, political achievements." It is not "politics which is the arch-enemy of art; it is neutrality . . . [which is] a political position like any other. . . . If we are doomed indeed, let M. Ionesco go down fighting with the rest of us. He should have the courage of our platitudes."

What is disconcerting about Ionesco's work is, then, the intellectual complacency it sponsors. I have no quarrel with works of art that contain no ideas at all; on the contrary, much of the greatest art is of this kind. Think of the films of Ozu, Jarry's *Ubu Roi*, Nabokov's *Lolita*, Genet's *Our Lady of the Flowers*—to take four modern examples. But the intellectual blankness is one (often very salutary) thing, intellectual surrender is another. In Ionesco's case, the intellect that has surrendered is not interesting, relying as it does on a view of the world that sets up an opposition between the wholly monstrous and the wholly banal. At first we may take pleasure in the monstrousness of the monstrous, but finally we are left with the banality of banality.

(1964)

Reflections on The Deputy

THE supreme tragic event of modern times is the murder of the six million European Jews. In a time which has not lacked in tragedies, this event most merits that unenviable honor—by reason of its magnitude, unity of theme, historical meaningfulness, and sheer opaqueness. For no one understands this event. The murder of the six million Jews cannot be wholly accounted for either in terms of passions, private or public, or of error, or of madness, or of moral failure, or of overwhelming and irresistible social forces. Some twenty years after, there is more controversy about it than ever. What happened? How did it happen? How could it have been allowed to happen? Who are responsible? This great event is a wound that will not heal; even the balm of intelligibility is denied to us.

Yet, if we did know more, that would not suffice. In saying this event was "tragic," we allow other demands than those for factual historical understanding. By tragic, I mean an event—piteous and terrifying in the extreme—whose causation is supercharged and overdetermined, and which is of an exemplary or edifying nature that imposes a solemn duty upon the survivors to confront and assimilate it. In calling the murder of the six million a tragedy, we acknowledge a motive beyond the intellectual (knowing what happened and how) or the moral (catching the criminals and bringing them to justice) for comprehending it. We acknowledge that the event is, in some sense, incomprehensible. Ultimately, the only response is to continue to hold the event in mind, to remember it. This capacity to assume the burden of memory is not always practical. Sometimes remembering alleviates grief or guilt; sometimes it makes it worse. Often, it may not do any good to remember. But we may feel that it is *right*, or fitting, or proper. This moral function of remembering is something that cuts across the different worlds of knowledge, action and art.

We live in a time in which tragedy is not an art form but a form of history. Dramatists no longer write tragedies. But we do possess works of art (not always recognized as such) which reflect or attempt to resolve the great historical tragedies of our time. Among the unacknowledged art forms which have been devised or perfected in the modern era for this purpose are the psychoanalytic session, the parliamentary debate, the political rally, and the political trial. And as the supreme tragic event of modern times is the murder of the six million European Jews, one of the most interesting and moving works of art of the past ten years is the trial of Adolf Eichmann in Jerusalem in 1961.

As Hannah Arendt and others have pointed out, the juridical basis of the Eichmann trial, the relevance of all the evidence presented and the legitimacy of certain procedures, are open to question on strictly legal grounds. But the truth is that the Eichmann trial not only did not, but could not have conformed to legal standards only. It was not Eichmann alone who was on trial. He stood trial in a double role: as both the particular and the generic; both the man, laden with hideous specific guilt, and the cipher, standing for the whole history of anti-Semitism, which climaxed in this unimaginable martyrdom.

The trial was thus an occasion for attempting to make comprehensible the incomprehensible. To this end, while the impassive bespectacled Eichmann sat in his bullet-proof glass cage—tight-lipped, but for all that like one of the great shrieking but unheard creatures from the paintings of Francis Bacon—a great collective dirge was enacted in the courtroom. Masses of facts about the extermination of the Jews were piled into the record; a great outcry of historical agony was set down. There was, needless to say, no strictly legal way of justifying this. The function of the trial was like that of the tragic drama: above and beyond judgment and punishment, catharsis.

The very modern feeling for due process which the trial appealed to was no doubt genuine, but the ancient connections between the theater and the courtroom went deeper. The trial is preeminently a theatrical form (in fact, the very first account in history of a trial comes from the drama—it is in the third play, *The Eumenides*, of Aeschylus' trilogy, the *Oresteia*). And as the trial is preeminently a theatrical form, the theater is a courtroom. The classical form of the drama is always a contest between protagonist and antagonist; the resolution of the play is the "verdict" on the action. All the great stage tragedies take this form of a trial of the protagonist—the peculiarity of the tragic form of judgment being that it is possible to lose the case (i.e., be condemned, suffer, die) and somehow triumph nonetheless.

The Eichmann trial was such a drama. It was not a tragedy itself, but the attempt, dramatically, to deal with and resolve a tragedy. It was, in the profoundest sense, theater. And, as such, it must be judged by other criteria in addition to those of legality and of morality. Because its purposes were not simply those of a historical inquest into the facts, an attempt to determine guilt and affix punishment, the trial of Eichmann did not always "work." But the problem of the Eichmann trial was not its deficient legality, but the contradiction between its juridical form and its dramatic function. As Harold Rosenberg has pointed out: "The trial undertook the function of tragic poetry, that of making the pathetic and terrifying past live again in the mind. But it had to carry out this function on a world stage ruled by the utilitarian code." There was a fundamental paradox in the Eichmann trial: it was primarily a great act of commitment through memory and the renewal of grief, yet it clothed itself in the forms of legality and scientific objectivity. The trial is a dramatic form which imparts to events a certain provisional neutrality; the outcome remains to be decided; the very word "defendant" implies that a defense is possible. In this sense, though Eichmann, as everyone expected, was condemned to death, the form of the trial favored Eichmann. Perhaps this is why many feel, in retrospect, that the trial was a frustrating experience, an anticlimax.

It remains to be seen whether art of a more easily recognizable type—art which need not pretend to be neutral—can do better. By far the most celebrated of all the works of art which take up the same functions of historical memory served by the Eichmann trial is *The Deputy (Der Stellvertreter)*, the lengthy play by the young German playwright Rolf Hochhuth.* Here we have a work of art as we ordinarily understand it—a work for the familiar theater of 8:30 curtains and intermissions, rather than for the austere public stage of the courtroom. Here there are actors, rather than real murderers and real survivors from hell. Yet it is not false to compare it with the Eichmann trial, because *The Deputy* is first of all a compilation, a record. Eichmann himself and many other real persons of the period are

---

* *The Deputy* by Rolf Hochhuth. Translated by Richard and Clara Winston. New York, Grove.

represented in the play; the speeches of the characters are drawn from historical records.

In modern times, this use of the theater as a forum for public, moral judgment has been shunted aside. The theater has largely become a place in which private quarrels and agonies are staged; the verdict which events render upon characters in most modern plays has no relevance beyond the play itself. *The Deputy* breaks with the completely private boundaries of most modern theater. And as it would be obtuse to refuse to evaluate the Eichmann trial as a public work of art, it would be frivolous to judge *The Deputy* simply as a work of art.

Some art—but not all—elects as its central purpose *to tell the truth*; and it must be judged by its fidelity to the truth, and by the relevance of the truth which it tells. By these standards, *The Deputy* is an important play. The case against the Nazi party, the SS, the German business elite, and most of the German people—none of which is slighted by Hochhuth—is too well known to need anyone's assent. But *The Deputy* also stresses, and this is the controversial part of the play, a strong case for the complicity of the German Catholic Church and of Pope Pius XII. This case I am convinced is true, and well taken. (See the ample documentation which Hochhuth has provided at the end of the play, and the excellent book by Guenter Lewy, *The Catholic Church and Nazi Germany*.) And the importance, historical and moral, of this difficult truth at the present time cannot be overestimated.

In a preface (unfortunately not translated) to the German edition of the play, the director Erwin Piscator, who gave *The Deputy* its first production in Berlin, wrote that he saw Hochhuth's play as a successor to the historical dramas of Shakespeare and Schiller and the epic theater of Brecht. All questions of quality aside, these comparisons—with classical historical drama and with epic theater when it deals with historical subjects—are misleading. It is the whole point of Hochhuth's play that he has barely transformed his material. Unlike the plays of Shakespeare or Schiller or Brecht, Hochhuth's play stands or falls by its fidelity to the complete historical truth.

This documentary intention of the play also indicates its limitations. The fact is that as not all works of art aim at educating and directing conscience, not all works of art which successfully perform a moral function greatly satisfy as art. I can think of only one dramatic work of the type of *The Deputy*, the short film *Night and Fog* by Alain Resnais, which satisfies equally as a moral act and as a work of art. *Night and Fog*, also a memorial to the tragedy of the six million, is highly selective, emotionally relentless, historically scrupulous, and—if the word seems not outrageous—beautiful. *The Deputy* is not a beautiful play. Nor does one necessarily ask that it be. Nevertheless, since one can assume the immense interest and moral importance of the play, the aesthetic questions need to be faced. Whatever *The Deputy* is as a moral event, it is not playwriting of the highest order.

There is the matter of length, for example. I don't find *The Deputy*'s length objectionable. Probably it is, indeed, one of those works of art—like Dreiser's *An American Tragedy*, the operas of Wagner, the best plays of O'Neill—which positively benefit from their outlandish length. The language, though, is a genuine liability. In this English version, it is flat, neither formal nor truly idiomatic. ("The Legation is extraterritorial—be off with you/ Or I'll send for the police.") Hochhuth may have arranged his lines in free-verse form on the page to emphasize the seriousness of his subject, or to reveal the banality of Nazi rhetoric. But I can't imagine any plausible way of *speaking* these lines that conveys the effect (either one) that the author intended. A greater artistic fault is the thick chunks of documentation with which Hochhuth has loaded the play. *The Deputy* is clogged with undigested exposition. There are, to be sure, a number of extremely powerful scenes, particularly those involving the demonic SS doctor. Yet the fact remains that one of the principal and recurrent—and almost, by nature, undramatic—reasons for characters confronting each other in a scene is *to inform each other of something*. Hundreds of names, facts, statistics, reports of conversations, items of current news have been pumped into the dialogue. If the reading of *The Deputy*—I have not yet seen it performed—is tremendously moving, it is because of the weight of its subject, not because of its style or dramaturgy, both of which are extremely conventional.

I imagine that *The Deputy* could be highly satisfying on the stage. But its theatrical effectiveness depends on the director possessing an unusual kind of moral and aesthetic tact. A good production of *The Deputy*, I would think, must be ingeniously stylized. Yet in summoning the resources of the advanced modern theater, with its bent toward the ritualistic rather than the realistic, the director must beware of undermining the power of the play, which lies in its factual authority, its evocation of a concrete historicity. This seems to me just what Hochhuth has inadvertently done in the one suggestion he makes for *The Deputy*'s staging. Listing the characters, Hochhuth has made certain groupings of the shorter roles; all the roles in a single grouping are to be played by the same actor. Thus, the same actor is to play both Pius XII and Baron Rutta of the Reich's Armament Cartel. Another grouping allows a Father in the Papal Legation, an SS sergeant, and a Jewish Kapo all to be played by a single actor. "For recent history," Hochhuth explains, "has taught us that in the age of universal military conscription it is not necessarily to anyone's credit or blame, or even a question of character, which uniform one wears or whether one stands on the side of the victims or the executioners." I can't believe that Hochhuth really subscribes to this facile, fashionable view of the interchangeability of persons and roles (his whole play precisely contradicts this view) and I should resent seeing it embodied in the staging as Hochhuth suggests. The same objection would not apply, however, to the superficially similar theatrical idea devised by Peter Brook for his production of the play in Paris: that the actors all wear identical blue cotton suits, over which, when identification is needed, are slipped the cardinal's scarlet coat, the priest's soutane, the Nazi officer's swastika armband, and so on.

That Hochhuth's play has been the occasion of riots in Berlin, Paris, London, almost everywhere it has been performed, because it depicts (not just reports) the late Pius XII refusing to use the influence of the Catholic Church and oppose, either openly or through private diplomatic channels, the Nazi policy toward the Jews, is irrefutable indication of the valuable site which *The Deputy* occupies—between art and life. (In Rome, the play was closed by the police on the day it was to open.)

There is good reason to believe that protests by the Church might have saved many lives. Within Germany, when the Catholic hierarchy strongly opposed Hitler's euthanasia program for elderly and incurably ill Aryans—the trial run for the Final Solution of the Jewish Problem—it was stopped. And the precedent of political neutrality cannot be allowed to stand as the Vatican's excuse, since the Vatican had made forceful pronouncements on such matters of international politics as the Russian invasion of Finland. Most damaging to the case of those who regard the play as a calumny on Pius XII are extant documents which indicate that the Pope, like many conservative European rulers of the time, did approve of Hitler's war against Russia and for that reason hesitated to oppose the German government actively. For the scene that depicts this fact, Hochhuth's play has been slandered by many Catholics as an anti-Catholic tract. But either what Hochhuth reports is true or it is not. And, assuming that Hochhuth has his facts (and his notion of Christian courage) right, a good Catholic is no more bound to defend all the actions of Pius XII than he is to admire the libertine Popes of the Renaissance. Dante, whom no one would accuse of being anti-Catholic, consigned Celestine V to hell. Why may not a modern Christian—Hochhuth is a Lutheran—hold up as a standard to the then incumbent Deputy or Vicar of Christ the behavior of the Berlin provost, Bernard Lichtenberg (who publicly prayed for the Jews from his pulpit and volunteered to accompany the Jews to Dachau), or the Franciscan monk, Father Maximilian Kolbe (who died hideously in Auschwitz)?

In any case, the attack on the Pope is scarcely the only subject of *The Deputy*. The Pope appears in only one scene of the play. The action centers on the two heroes—the Jesuit priest Riccardo Fontana (mainly based on Provost Lichtenberg, with something of Father Kolbe) and the remarkable Kurt Gerstein, who joined the SS in order to gather facts to lay before the Papal Nuncio in Berlin. Hochhuth has not placed Gerstein and Fontana (Lichtenberg) in any "grouping," to be played along with other roles by the same actor. There is nothing interchangeable about these men. Thus, the main point that *The Deputy* makes is not a recriminatory one. It is not only an attack on the hierarchy of the German Catholic Church and on the Pope and his advisors, but a statement that genuine honor and decency—though these may entail martyrdom—are possible, and mandatory for a Christian. Precisely because there were Germans who did choose, Hochhuth is saying, we have a right to accuse the others who refused to choose, to speak out, of an unforgivable cowardice.

(1964)

The Death of Tragedy

MODERN discussions of the possibility of tragedy are not exercises in literary analysis; they are exercises in cultural diagnostics, more or less disguised. The subject of literature has pre-empted much of the energy that formerly went into philosophy, until that subject was purged by the empiricists and logicians. The modern dilemmas of feeling, action, and belief are argued out on the field of literary masterpieces. Art is seen as a mirror of human capacities in a given historical period, as the pre-eminent form by which a culture defines itself, names itself, dramatizes itself. In particular, questions about the death of literary forms—is the long narrative poem still possible, or is it dead? the novel? verse drama? tragedy?—are of the greatest moment. The burial of a literary form is a moral act, a high achievement of the modern morality of honesty. For, as an act of self-definition, it is also a self-entombment.

Such burials are customarily accompanied by all the displays of mourning; for we mourn ourselves, when we name the lost potential of sensibility and attitude which the defunct form incarnated. In his *Birth of Tragedy*, which is really about the death of tragedy, Nietzsche blamed the radically new prestige of knowledge and conscious intelligence—which arose in ancient Greece with the figure of Socrates—for the waning of instinct and of the sense of reality which made tragedy impossible. All subsequent discussions of the topic have been similarly elegiac, or at least defensive: either mourning the death of tragedy, or hopefully trying to make "modern" tragedy out of the naturalistic-sentimental theater of Ibsen and Chekhov, of O'Neill, Miller, and Williams. It is one of the singular merits of Lionel Abel's book* that the customary accent of lament is missing. Nobody writes tragedies any more? Very well. Abel invites his readers to leave the funeral parlor and come to a party, a party celebrating the dramatic form which is ours, has been ours in fact for three hundred years: the metaplay.

Indeed there is hardly reason to mourn, since the corpse was only a distant relative. Tragedy, says Abel, is not and never has

---

* *Metatheatre: A New View of Dramatic Form*, by Lionel Abel. New York, Hill & Wang.

been the characteristic form of Western theater; most Western dramatists, bent on writing tragedy, have been unable to do so. Why? In a word: self-consciousness. First, the self-consciousness of the dramatist himself, and then that of his protagonists. "The Western playwright is unable to believe in the reality of a character who is lacking in self-consciousness. Lack of self-consciousness is as characteristic of Antigone, Oedipus, and Orestes, as self-consciousness is characteristic of Hamlet, that towering figure of Western metatheatre." Thus, it is the metaplay—plots that depict the self-dramatization of conscious characters, a theater whose leading metaphors state that life is a dream and the world is a stage—which has occupied the dramatic imagination of the West to the same degree that the Greek dramatic imagination was occupied with tragedy. Two important historical observations follow from this thesis. One is that tragedy is simply much rarer than has been supposed— the Greek plays, one play of Shakespeare (*Macbeth*), and a few plays of Racine. Tragedy is not the characteristic form of the Elizabethan or Spanish theater. Most Elizabethan serious drama consists of failed tragedies (*Lear, Doctor Faustus*) or successful metaplays (*Hamlet, The Tempest*). The other point relates to contemporary drama. In Abel's account, Shakespeare and Calderón are the two great sources of a tradition which is gloriously revived in the "modern" theater of Shaw, Pirandello, Beckett, Ionesco, Genet, and Brecht.

As a piece of cultural diagnostics, Abel's book is in the grand continental tradition of meditation on the tribulations of subjectivity and self-consciousness, inaugurated by the romantic poets and Hegel and continued by Nietzsche, Spengler, the early Lukács, and Sartre. Their problems, their terminology loom behind Abel's spare, untechnical essays. Where the Europeans are heavy, he travels light, without footnotes; where they write tomes, he has written a set of blunt essays; and where they are gloomy, he is crisply sanguine. In short, Abel has expounded a continental argument in the American manner: he has written the first American-style existentialist tract. His argument is clean-cut, pugnacious, prone to slogans, oversimplified—and, in the main, absolutely right. His book does not plumb the windy depths (but they are depths) of Lucien Goldmann's great work on Pascal, Racine, and the idea of tragedy, *Le Dieu Caché*, which I would guess Abel has learned from. But its virtues, not the least of which are directness and brevity, are formidable. To an English-speaking audience unfamiliar with the writing of Lukács, Goldmann, Brecht, Duerrenmatt, *et al.*, the very problems that Abel raises should come as a revelation. Abel's book is far more stimulating than George Steiner's *Death of Tragedy* and Martin Esslin's *The Theater of the Absurd*. Indeed, no recent English or American writer on the theater has done anything as interesting or sophisticated.

As I have suggested, the diagnosis presupposed in *Metatheatre* —that modern man lives with an increasing burden of subjectivity, at the expense of his sense of the reality of the world—is not new. Nor do works for the theater constitute the main texts which disclose this attitude and its correlative idea, reason as self-manipulation and role-playing. The two greatest documents of this attitude are Montaigne's *Essays* and Machiavelli's *The Prince*—both manuals of strategy which assume a gulf between the "public self" (the role) and the "private self" (the true self). The value of Abel's book lies in the forthright application of this diagnosis to the drama. He is quite right, for example, in arguing that most of the plays of Shakespeare which their author, and everyone else since, have called tragedies are not, strictly speaking, tragedies at all. In fact, Abel could have gone even further. Not only are most of the putative tragedies really "metaplays"; so are most of the histories and comedies. The principal plays of Shakespeare are plays about self-consciousness, about characters not *acting* so much as *dramatizing themselves* in roles. Prince Hal is the man of perfected self-consciousness and self-control, triumphing over the man of rash, unself-conscious integrity, Hotspur, and over the sentimental, cowardly, self-conscious man of pleasure, Falstaff. Achilles and Oedipus do not see themselves as, but *are*, hero and king. But Hamlet and Henry V see themselves as acting parts—the part of the avenger, the part of the heroic and confident king leading his troops to battle. Shakespeare's fondness for the play-within-a-play and for putting his characters into disguise for long stretches of the story clearly partakes of the style of metatheater. From Prospero to the Police Chief in Genet's *The Balcony*, the personages of metatheater are characters in search of an action.

I have said that Abel's main thesis is right. But it is also, with respect to three issues, mistaken or incomplete.

First, his thesis would be more complete, and I think some-what altered, if Abel had considered what comedy is. Without wanting to suggest that comedy and tragedy divide the dra-matic universe between them, I would argue that they are best defined in relation to each other. The omission of comedy is particularly striking when one recalls that counterfeit, deceit, role-playing, manipulation, self-dramatization—basic elements of what Abel calls metatheater—are staples of comedy since Aristophanes. Comic plots are stories either of conscious self-manipulation and role-playing (*Lysistrata*, *The Golden Ass*, *Tar-tuffe*) or else of improbably unself-conscious—underconscious, one might say—characters (Candide, Buster Keaton, Gulliver, Don Quixote) playing strange roles which they assent to with a cheerful dumbness that secures their invulnerability. It might well be argued that the form which Abel calls the metaplay, particularly in its modern versions, represents a fusion of the posthumous spirit of tragedy with the most ancient principles of comedy. Some modern metaplays, such as Ionesco's, are obvi-ously comedies. It is hard, too, to deny that Beckett is writing, in *Waiting for Godot*, *Krapp's Last Tape*, and *Happy Days*, a kind of *comédie noire*.

Second, Abel considerably oversimplifies, and I think indeed misrepresents, the vision of the world which is necessary for the writing of tragedies. He says: "One cannot create tragedy with-out accepting some implacable values as true. Now the Western imagination has, on the whole, been liberal and skeptical; it has tended to regard *all* implacable values as false." This statement seems to me wrong and, where it is not wrong, superficial. (Abel is here perhaps too much under the influence of Hegel's analy-sis of tragedy, and that of Hegel's popularizers.) What are the implacable values of Homer? Honor, status, personal courage—the values of an aristocratic military class? But this is not what the *Iliad* is about. It would be more correct to say, as Simone Weil does, that the *Iliad*—as pure an example of the tragic vi-sion as one can find—is about the emptiness and arbitrariness of the world, the ultimate meaninglessness of all moral values, and the terrifying rule of death and inhuman force. If the fate of Oedipus was represented and experienced as tragic, it is not because he, or his audience, believed in "implacable values," but precisely because a crisis had overtaken those values. It is not the implacability of "values" which is demonstrated by tragedy, but the implacability of the world. The story of Oedipus is tragic insofar as it exhibits the brute opaqueness of the world, the collision of subjective intention with objective fate. After all, in the deepest sense, Oedipus is innocent; he is wronged by the gods, as he himself says in *Oedipus at Colonus.* Tragedy is a vision of nihilism, a heroic or ennobling vision of nihilism.

It is also untrue that Western culture has been on the whole liberal and skeptical. Post-Christian Western culture, yes. Montaigne, Machiavelli, the Enlightenment, the psychiatric culture of personal autonomy and health of the 20th century, yes. But what of the dominant religious traditions of Western culture? Were Paul, Augustine, Dante, Pascal, and Kierkegaard liberal skeptics? Hardly. Therefore one must ask, why was there no Christian tragedy?—a question Abel does not raise in his book, though Christian tragedy would seem to be inevitable if one stops at the assertion that belief in implacable values is the necessary ingredient for making tragedies.

As everyone knows, there was no Christian tragedy, strictly speaking, because the content of Christian values—for it is a question of *what* values, however implacably held; not any will do—is inimical to the pessimistic vision of tragedy. Hence, Dante's theological poem is a "comedy," as is Milton's. That is, as Christians, Dante and Milton make sense out of the world. In the world envisaged by Judaism and Christianity, there are no free-standing arbitrary events. All events are part of the plan of a just, good, providential deity; every crucifixion must be topped by a resurrection. Every disaster or calamity must be seen either as leading to a greater good or else as just and adequate punishment fully merited by the sufferer. This moral adequacy of the world asserted by Christianity is precisely what tragedy denies. Tragedy says there are disasters which are not fully merited, that there is ultimate injustice in the world. So one might say that the final optimism of the prevailing religious traditions of the West, their will to see meaning in the world, prevented a rebirth of tragedy under Christian auspices—as, in Nietzsche's argument, reason, the fundamentally optimistic spirit of Socrates, killed tragedy in ancient Greece. The liberal, skeptical era of metatheater only inherits this will to make sense from Judaism and Christianity. Despite the exhaustion of religious sentiments, the will to make sense and find meaning prevails, although contracted to the idea of an action as the projection of one's idea of oneself.

The third caveat I would make is to Abel's treatment of the modern metaplays, those plays which have all too often been thrown together under the patronizing label "theater of the absurd." Abel is right to point out that these plays are, formally, in an old tradition. Yet the considerations of form which Abel addresses in his essays must not obscure differences in range and tone, which he slights. Shakespeare and Calderón construct metatheatrical *jeux d'esprit* in the bosom of a world rich in established feelings and a sense of openness. The metatheater of Genet and Beckett reflects the feelings of an era whose greatest artistic pleasure is self-laceration, an era suffocated by the sense of eternal return, an era which experiences innovation as an act of terror. That life is a dream, all the metaplays presuppose. But there are restful dreams, troubled dreams, and nightmares. The modern dream—which the modern metaplays project—is a nightmare, a nightmare of repetition, stalled action, exhausted feeling. There are discontinuities between the modern nightmare and the Renaissance dream which Abel (like, more recently, Jan Kott) neglects, at the price of misreading the texts.

For Brecht, particularly, whom Abel includes among the modern metadramatists, the category is misleading. At times Abel seems to use "naturalistic play" rather than "tragedy" as a foil for metatheater. Brecht's plays are anti-naturalistic, didactic. But unless Abel is willing to call *The Play of Daniel* a metaplay— because it has on-stage musicians, and a narrator who explains everything to the audience, and invites them to see the play as a play, a performance—I cannot see that Brecht fits very well into the category. And much of Abel's discussion of Brecht is unhappily disfigured by callow Cold War platitudes. Abel argues that Brecht's plays must be metaplays because to write tragedies one must believe that "individuals are real" and one must "believe in the importance of moral suffering." (Does Abel mean the moral importance of suffering?) Since Brecht was a Communist, and since Communists do "not believe in the individual or in moral experience" (what does it mean, to "believe" in moral

experience? does Abel mean moral principles?), Brecht lacked
the essential equipment to write tragedies; therefore, dogmatic
as he was, Brecht could only write metatheater—that is, make
"all human actions, reactions, and expressions of feeling theatrical." This is nonsense. There is no more moralizing doctrine
abroad today than Communism, no more sturdy exponent of
"implacable values." What else is meant when Western liberals
vulgarly call Communism a "secular religion"? And as for the
familiar accusation that Communism does not believe in the
individual, this is equally nonsense. It is not so much Marxist
theory as the sensibility and historic traditions of the countries
in which Communism has taken power that do not and never
have held the so-called Western idea of the individual, which
separates off the "private" from the "public" self, seeing the
private self as the true self which only lends itself grudgingly to
the activities of public life. Neither did the Greeks, the creators
of tragedy, possess a notion of the individual in the modern
Western sense. There is a deep confusion in Abel's argument—
his historical generalizations are mostly superficial—when he
tries to make the absence of the individual the criterion of metatheater.

Admittedly Brecht was a sly, ambivalent guardian of Communist "morality." But the secret of his plays is to be sought
in his idea of the theater as a moralizing instrument. Hence
his use of stage techniques borrowed from the non-naturalistic
theater of China and Japan, and his famous theory of stage production and acting—the Alienation Effect—which aims to enforce a detached, intellectual attitude upon the audience. (The
Alienation Effect seems to be mainly a method of writing plays
and of staging them, non-naturalistically; its effect as a method
of acting, from what I have seen of the Berliner Ensemble, is
mainly to moderate, to tone down, the naturalistic style of acting—not fundamentally to contradict it.) By assimilating Brecht
to the metadramatists, with whom he surely shares something,
Abel obscures the difference between Brecht's didacticism and
the studied neutrality—the mutual cancellation of all values—
which is represented by the true metadramatists. It is something like the difference between Augustine and Montaigne.
Both the *Confessions* and the *Essays* are didactic autobiographies;
but while the author of the *Confessions* sees his life as a drama

illustrating the linear movement of consciousness from egocentricity to theocentricity, the author of the *Essays* sees his life as a dispassionate, varied exploration of the innumerable styles of being a self. Brecht has as little in common with Beckett, Genet, and Pirandello as Augustine's exercise in self-analysis has with Montaigne's.

(1963)

Going to Theater, etc.

THE theater has a long history as a public art. But, outside the provinces of socialist realism, there are few plays today dealing with social-and-topical problems. The best modern plays are those devoted to raking up private, rather than public, hells. The public voice in the theater today is crude and raucous, and, all too often, weak-minded.

The most notable example of weak-mindedness around at the moment is Arthur Miller's new play, *After the Fall*, which opened the first season of the Lincoln Center Repertory Theater. Miller's play stands or falls on the authenticity of its moral seriousness, and on its being about "big" issues. But, unfortunately, Miller chose as the method of his play the garrulous monologue of the psychoanalytic confessional, and falteringly designated the audience as the Great Listener. "The action of the play takes place in the mind and memory of Quentin, a contemporary man." The Everymanish hero (remember Willy Loman) and the timeless, placeless interior setting give the show away: whatever stirring public issues *After the Fall* may confront, they are treated as the furniture of a mind. That places an awful burden on Miller's "Quentin, a contemporary man," who must literally hold the world in his head. To pull that one off, it has to be a very good head, a very interesting and intelligent one. And the head of Miller's hero isn't any of these things. Contemporary man (as Miller represents him) seems stuck in an ungainly project of self-exoneration. Self-exoneration, of course, implies self-exposure; and there is a lot of that in *After the Fall*. Many people are willing to give Miller a good deal of credit for the daring of his self-exposure—as husband, lover, political man, and artist. But self-exposure is commendable in art only when it is of a quality and complexity that allows other people to learn about themselves from it. In this play, Miller's self-exposure is mere self-indulgence.

After the Fall does not present an action, but ideas about action. Its psychological ideas owe more to Franzblau than to Freud. (Quentin's mother wanted him to have beautiful penmanship, to take revenge through her son upon her successful but virtually illiterate businessman husband.) As for its political ideas, where politics has not yet been softened up by psychiatric charity, Miller still writes on the level of a left-wing newspaper cartoon. To pass muster at all, Quentin's young German girl friend—this in the mid-1950s—has to turn out to have been a courier for the 20th of July officers' plot; "they were all hanged." Quentin's political bravery is demonstrated by his triumphantly interrupting the harangue of the chairman of the House Committee on Un-American Activities to ask, "How many Negroes do you allow to vote in your patriotic district?" This intellectual weak-mindedness of *After the Fall* leads, as it always does, to moral dishonesty. *After the Fall* claims to be nothing less than modern man taking inventory of his humanity—asking where he is guilty, where innocent, where responsible. What I find objectionable is not the peculiar conjunction of issues, apparently the exemplary issues of the mid-20th century (Communism, Marilyn Monroe, the Nazi extermination camps), which Quentin, this writer *manqué* pretending throughout the play to be a lawyer, has recapitulated in his own person. I object to the fact that in *After the Fall* all these issues are on the same level—not unexpectedly, since they are all in the mind of Quentin. The shapely corpse of Maggie–Marilyn Monroe sprawls on the stage throughout long stretches of the play in which she has no part. In the same spirit a raggedy oblong made of plaster and barbed wire—it represents the concentration camps, I hasten to explain—remains suspended high at the back of the stage, occasionally lit by a spot when Quentin's monologue swings back to Nazis, etc. *After the Fall*'s quasi-psychiatric approach to guilt and responsibility elevates personal tragedies, and demeans public ones—to the same dead level. Somehow—staggering impertinence!—it all seems pretty much the same: whether Quentin is responsible for the deterioration and suicide of Maggie, and whether he (modern man) is responsible for the unimaginable atrocities of the concentration camps.

Putting the story inside Quentin's head has, in effect, allowed Miller to short-circuit any serious exploration of his material, though he obviously thought this device would "deepen" his story. Real events become the ornaments and intermittent fevers of consciousness. The play is peculiarly loose-jointed, repetitive, indirect. The "scenes" go on and off—jumping back and forth, to and from Quentin's first marriage, his second marriage (to Maggie), his indecisive courtship of his German wife-to-be, his childhood, the quarrels of his hysterical, oppressive parents, his agonizing decision to defend an ex-Communist law-school teacher and friend against a friend who has "named names." All "scenes" are fragments, pushed out of Quentin's mind when they become too painful. Only deaths, inevitably offstage, seem to move Quentin's life along: the Jews (the word "Jews" is never mentioned) died long ago; his mother dies; Maggie kills herself with an overdose of barbiturates; the law professor throws himself under a subway train. Throughout the play, Quentin seems much more a sufferer than an active agent in his own life—yet this is precisely what Miller never acknowledges, never lets Quentin see as his problem. Instead, he continually exonerates Quentin (and, by implication, the audience) in the most conventional way. For all troubling decisions, and all excruciating memories, Miller issues Quentin the same moral solvent, the same consolation. I (we) am (are) *both* guilty and innocent, both responsible and not responsible. Maggie was right when she denounced Quentin as cold and unforgiving; but Quentin was justified in giving up on the insatiable, deranged, self-destructive Maggie. The professor who refused to "name names" before the House Un-American Activities Committee was right; but the colleague who did testify cooperatively had a certain nobility, too. And (choicest of all), as Quentin realizes while touring Dachau with his Good German girl friend, any one of us could have been a victim there; but we could as well have been one of the murderers, too.

The circumstances and production of the play are marked by certain perverse strokes of realism that underscore the bad faith, the have-it-both-ways temper of the play. That vast sloping stage painted slate gray and empty of props, the mind of contemporary man, is so pointedly bare that one can't help jumping when Quentin, sitting much of the time stage-front on a box-like form and chain smoking, suddenly deposits the ashes in some mysterious pocket ashtray in the abutment. One is jarred again at the sight of Barbara Loden made up like Marilyn Monroe, displaying the mannerisms of Monroe and bearing a certain physical resemblance to Monroe (though lacking the fullness of figure needed to complete the illusion). But perhaps the most appalling combination of reality and play lies in the fact that *After the Fall* is directed by Elia Kazan, well known to be the model for the colleague who named names before the Committee. As I recalled the story of the turbulent relations between Miller and Kazan, I felt the same queasiness as when I first saw *Sunset Boulevard*, with its dizzying parody of and daring references to the real career and former relationships of Gloria Swanson, the old movie queen making a comeback, and Erich Von Stroheim, the forgotten great director. Whatever bravery *After the Fall* possesses is neither intellectual nor moral; it is the bravery of a species of personal perversity. But it is far inferior to *Sunset Boulevard*: it does not acknowledge its morbidity, its qualities of personal exorcism. *After the Fall* insists, as it were, to the bitter end, on being serious, on dealing with big social and moral themes; and as such, it must be judged sadly wanting, in both intelligence and moral honesty.

Since it insists on being serious, I suspect that *After the Fall* will seem just as belabored, trite, and dated in a few years as O'Neill's *Marco Millions*, the second play in the Lincoln Center Repertory, does now. Both plays are disfigured by a distressing (though, one imagines, unconscious) complicity with what they profess to attack. The attack which *Marco Millions* launched upon the philistine values of American business civilization itself reeks of philistinism; *After the Fall* is a long sermon in favor of being tough with oneself, but the argument is soft as mush. It is indeed difficult to choose between the two plays, or their productions. I don't know which is more heavy-handed: Marco Polo's Babbittish exuberance over the wonders of Cathay ("Sure is a nice little palace you got here, Khan"— Americans are crude and materialistic, see?) or the weird declamations, at times archly poetic and stilted, at times WEVD soap opera, of Miller's hero Quentin (Americans are tormented and complex, see?). I don't know which I found more monotonous, less ingratiating as an acting performance—Jason Robards Jr.'s depleted, gauche Quentin or Hal Holbrook's hysterically boyish Marco Polo. I could hardly tell Zohra Lampert when she was the Bronxy chick who keeps running into Quentin's head to slobber all over him for giving her the courage to have a nose job from Zohra Lampert when she was supposed to be that elegant lovelorn flower of the Orient, Princess Kukachin, in *Marco Millions*. True, Elia Kazan's staging of *After the Fall* was stark and *moderne* and repetitive, while José Quintero's staging of *Marco Millions* was tricky and pretty and had the advantage of Beni Montresor's lovely costumes, though the stage was so badly lit you couldn't be sure of what you saw. But the difference in the productions seemed trivial, when you consider that Kazan had toiled over a bad play, and Quintero over a play so juvenile that no production, however good, could redeem it. The Lincoln Center Repertory group (our National Theater?) is a stunning disappointment. It's hard to believe that all its vaunted freedom from Broadway commercialism has begotten are passably acted productions of this wretched play by Miller, a play by O'Neill so bad it isn't even of historical interest, and a fatuous comedy by S. N. Behrman that makes *After the Fall* and *Marco Millions* look like works of genius.

If *After the Fall* fails as a serious play because of its intellectual softness, Rolf Hochhuth's *The Deputy* fails because of its intellectual simplicity and artistic naïveté. But this is failure of another order. *The Deputy* has been put into awkward English and, clearly, Hochhuth couldn't care less about the truth of Aristotle's observation that poetry is more philosophical than historical; Hochhuth's characters are little more than mouthpieces for the exposition of historical facts, exhibits of the collision of moral principles. But after the way in which Miller turns all events into their subjective reverberations, the artistic weakness of *The Deputy* seems almost condonable. *The Deputy* has all the directness toward its subject that Arthur Miller's play lacks. Its virtue is precisely that it refuses to be subtle about the murder of the six million Jews.

But the production by Herman Shumlin is as far from Hochhuth's play (as written) as that play (as written) is from being a great play. Hochhuth's crude but powerful six to eight hour documentary in play form has been put through Shumlin's Broadway Blendor and emerges as a two hour and fifteen minute comic strip, and a dull one to boot—the story of a handsome, well-born hero, a couple of villains, and a few fence-sitters, titled The Story of Father Fontana, or Will the Pope Speak?

I'm not of course insisting that the whole six to eight hours must be played. The play as written is repetitive. But a theater public that is willing to sit through four or five hours of O'Neill could surely be persuaded to sit through—say—four hours of

Hochhuth's play. And it is not hard to imagine a four-hour version that would do justice to the narrative. From the present Broadway version, one would never guess that the noble SS Lieutenant Kurt Gerstein (a true person) is as important a character and as much the hero of *The Deputy* as the Jesuit Father Fontana (a composite figure based on two heroic priests of the period). Neither Eichmann, nor the notorious Professor Hirt, nor the Krupp industrialist—all important characters in Hochhuth's play as he wrote it—appears at all in the Broadway version. (Among the dropped scenes, one particularly misses Act I, Scene 2, the party given by Eichmann.) By concentrating exclusively on the story of Fontana's vain appeals to the Pope, Shumlin has gone far toward burying the historical memories which Hochhuth's play aims to keep alive. But this drastic simplification of Hochhuth's historical argument is not even the worst offense of Shumlin's version. The worst offense is the refusal to dramatize anything really painful to watch. Certain scenes in *The Deputy* are excruciating to read. None of this—the terror and torture, the gruesome boasts and banter, even the recitals of unimaginable statistics—has been retained. The entire horror of the murder of the six million has been reduced to one scene of police interrogation of some Jewish converts to Catholicism, plus a single image repeated three times in the course of the play: a line of bent, ragged figures shuffles across the dark rear of the stage; midstage stands an SS man, his back to the audience, yelling something that sounds like "Move along now!" A conventional image; an entirely palatable image; an image which neither stirs, nor disgusts, nor terrifies. Even Fontana's long monologue, the speechifying scene on the freightcar headed for Auschwitz—the seventh of the eight scenes in Shumlin's emasculated version—was cut just before opening night. Now the play moves directly from the confrontation between the Pope and Father Fontana at the Vatican to the final scene in Auschwitz, of which all that's left is the amateurish philosophical debate between the demonic SS doctor and Fontana, who has donned the yellow star and elected martyrdom in the gas chambers. The reunion of Gerstein and Fontana, their appalling discovery that Jacobson has been captured, the torture of Carlotta, the death of Fontana—all are omitted.

Although the decisive damage is already done by the version

which Shumlin has carved from the play, it should be noted that the production is in most ways inadequate as well. Rouben Ter-Arutunian's slim allusive sets belong to another director; they are lost on a production utterly lacking in the slightest subtlety or stylization. The actors are no more but no less inept and unskillful than the average Broadway cast. As usual, there is the same over-statement of emotions, the same monotony of move-ment, the same mélange of accents, the same flatness of style that makes for the low level of American acting. The leads, who are English, seem more gifted—though their performances are thin. Emlyn Williams plays Pope Pius XII with a hesitant stiff-ness of movement and speech, presumably designed to indicate Papal solemnity, which aroused my suspicion that he was indeed the late Pope, exhumed for the occasion, and in an understand-ably fragile condition. At the least, he looked suspiciously like the life-size statue of Pius XII behind glass near the entrance of Saint Patrick's Cathedral. Jeremy Brett, who plays Father Fon-tana, has an agreeable presence and lovely diction, though he floundered badly when he had to convey real despair or terror.

These recent plays—and some others, like *Dylan*, which it would be a mercy to pass over in silence—illustrate once again that the American theater is ruled by an extraordinary, irrepress-ible zest for intellectual simplification. Every idea is reducible to a cliché, and the function of a cliché is to castrate an idea. Now, intellectual simplification has its uses, its value. It is, for example, absolutely indispensable to comedy. But it is inimi-cal to the serious. At present, the seriousness of the American theater is worse than frivolity.

The hope for intelligence in the theater is not through con-ventional "seriousness," whether in the form of analysis (bad example: *After the Fall*), or the documentary (weak example: *The Deputy*). It is rather, I think, through comedy. The figure in the modern theater who best understood this was Brecht. But comedy, too, has its enormous perils. The danger here is not so much intellectual simplification as failure of tone and taste. It may be that not all subjects can be given a comic treatment.

This question of the adequacy of tone and taste to serious subject-matter is, of course, not confined to the theater alone. There is an excellent illustration of the advantages of comedy, and of its peculiar dilemmas—if I may pass to the movies for a moment—in two films recently showing in New York, Charlie Chaplin's *The Great Dictator* and Stanley Kubrick's *Doctor Strangelove: Or How I Learned to Stop Worrying and Love the Bomb*. The virtues and failures of both films seem to me oddly comparable, and instructive.

In the case of *The Great Dictator*, the problem is easily discernible. The entire conception of the comedy is totally, painfully, insultingly inadequate to the reality it purports to represent. The Jews are Jews, and they live in what Chaplin calls the Ghetto. But their oppressors don't display the swastika but the emblem of the double cross; and the dictator is not Adolf Hitler but a balletic buffoon with a mustache named Adenoid Hynkel. Oppression in *The Great Dictator* is uniformed bullies throwing so many tomatoes at Paulette Goddard that she has to wash her laundry all over again. It is impossible to see *The Great Dictator* in 1964 without thinking of the hideous reality behind the movie, and one is depressed by the shallowness of Chaplin's political vision. One cringes at that embarrassing final speech, when the Little Jewish Barber steps up to the podium in place of Der Phooey to call for "progress," "liberty," "brotherhood," "one world," even "science." And to watch Paulette Goddard looking up at the dawn and smiling through her tears—in 1940!

The problem of *Doctor Strangelove* is more complex, though it may well be that in twenty years it will seem as simple as *The Great Dictator*. If the positive assertions at the close of *The Great Dictator* seem facile and insulting to its subject, so may the display of negative thinking of *Doctor Strangelove* soon (if it does not already) seem equally facile. But this does not explain its appeal now. Liberal intellectuals who saw *Doctor Strangelove* during its many preview showings last October and November marvelled at its political daring, and feared that the film would run into terrible difficulties (mobs of American Legion types storming the theaters, etc.). As it turned out, everybody, from *The New Yorker* to the *Daily News*, has had kind words for *Doctor Strangelove*; there are no pickets; and the film is breaking records at the box-office. Intellectuals and adolescents both love it. But the sixteen-year-olds who are lining up to see it understand the film, and its real virtues, better than the intellectuals, who vastly overpraise it. For *Doctor Strangelove* is not, in fact, a political film at all. It uses the OK targets of left-liberals (the defense establishment, Texas, chewing gum, mechanization, American vulgarity) and treats them from an entirely post-political, *Mad Magazine* point of view. *Doctor Strangelove* is really a very cheerful film. Certainly, its fullbloodedness contrasts favorably with what is (in retrospect) the effeteness of Chaplin's film. The end of *Doctor Strangelove*, with its matter-of-fact image of apocalypse and flip soundtrack ("We'll Meet Again"), reassures in a curious way, for nihilism is our contemporary form of moral uplift. As *The Great Dictator* was Popular Front optimism for the masses, so *Doctor Strangelove* is nihilism for the masses, a philistine nihilism.

What is good in *The Great Dictator* are the solitary autistic acts of grace, like Hynkel playing with the balloon-globe; and the "little man" humor, as in the sequence where the Jews draw lots for a suicidal mission out of slices of a pie, and Chaplin ends up with all the tokens in his slice. These are the perennial elements of comedy, as developed by Chaplin, over which has been pasted this unsatisfactory political cartoon. Similarly, what is good in *Doctor Strangelove* has to do with another perennial source of comedy, mental aberration. The best things in the film are the fantasies of contamination expounded by the psychotic Gen. Jack D. Ripper (played with excruciating brilliance by Sterling Hayden), the super-American clichés and body movements of Gen. Buck Turgidson, a Ring Lardneresque businessman-military type (put together by George C. Scott), and the euphoric satanism of Doctor Strangelove himself, the Nazi scientist with the right arm that hates him (Peter Sellers). The specialty of silent-film comedy (and *The Great Dictator* is still, essentially, a silent film) is the purely visual crossing of grace, folly, and pathos. *Doctor Strangelove* works another classic vein of comedy, as much verbal as visual—the idea of humors. (Hence the joke names of characters in *Doctor Strangelove*, exactly as in Ben Jonson.) But notice that both films rely on the same device for distancing the audience's feelings: employing the same actor to play several key roles. Chaplin plays both the Little Jewish Barber and the dictator Hynkel. Sellers plays the relatively sane British officer, the weak American president, and the Nazi scientist; he was originally supposed to take a fourth role as well—that of the Texan, played in the film by Slim

Pickens, who commands the plane which drops the H-Bomb that sets off the Russian Doomsday Machine. Without this device of the same actor playing morally opposed roles, and so subliminally undermining the reality of the entire plot, the precarious ascendancy of comic detachment over the morally ugly or the terrifying in both films would be lost.

Doctor Strangelove fails most obviously in scale. Much (though not all) of its comedy seems to me repetitive, juvenile, ham-handed. And when comedy fails, seriousness begins to leak back in. One begins to ask serious questions about the misanthropy which is the only perspective from which the topic of mass annihilation is comic. . . . For me, the only successful spectacle shown this winter dealing with public issues was a work which was both a pure documentary *and* a comedy—Daniel Talbot and Emile de Antonio's editing into a ninety-minute film of the TV kinescopes of the 1954 Army-McCarthy hearings. Viewed in 1964, the hearings make a quite different impression. All the good guys come off badly—Army Secretary Stevens, Senator Symington, lawyer Welch, and the rest, looked like dopes, stuffed shirts, ninnies, prigs, or opportunists—while the film irresistibly encourages us to relish the villains aesthetically. Roy Cohen, with his swarthy face, slicked-down hair, and double-breasted, pin-stripe suit, looked like a period punk from a Warner Brothers' crime movie of the early thirties; McCarthy, unshaven, fidgety, giggling, looked and acted like W. C. Fields in his most alcoholic, vicious, and inaudible roles. In that it aestheticized a weighty public event, *Point of Order* was the real *comédie noire* of the season, as well as the best political drama.

(*Spring 1964*)

2

The currency of exchange for most social and moral attitudes is that ancient device of the drama: personifications, masks. Both for play and for edification, the mind sets up these figures, simple and definite, whose identity is easily stated, who arouse quick loves and hates. Masks are a peculiarly effective, shorthand way of defining virtue and vice.

Once a grotesque, a figure of folly—childlike, lawless, lascivious—"the Negro" is fast becoming the American theater's leading mask of virtue. For definiteness of outline, being black, he even surpasses "the Jew," who has an ambiguous physical identity. (It was part of the lore of the advanced position on Jewishness that Jews didn't have to look like "Jews." But Negroes always look like "Negroes," unless, of course, they are unauthentic.) And for sheer pain and victimage, the Negro is far ahead of any other contender in America. In just a few short years, the old liberalism, whose archetypal figure was the Jew, has been challenged by the new militancy, whose hero is the Negro. But while the temper which gives rise to the new militancy—and to "the Negro" as hero—may indeed scorn the ideas of liberalism, one feature of the liberal sensibility hangs on. We still tend to choose our images of virtue from among our victims.

In the theater, as among educated Americans generally, liberalism has suffered an ambiguous rout. That large streak of moralism, of preachiness in such plays as *Waiting for Lefty*, *Watch on the Rhine*, *Tomorrow the World*, *Deep Are the Roots*, *The Crucible*—the classics of Broadway liberalism—would be unacceptable now. But what was wrong with these plays, from the most contemporary point of view, is not that they aimed to convert their audiences, rather than simply entertaining them. It was, rather, that they were too optimistic. They thought problems could be solved. James Baldwin's *Blues for Mister Charlie* is a sermon, too. To make it official, Baldwin has said that the play is loosely inspired by the Emmett Till case, and one may read, on the theater program under the director's name, that the play is "dedicated to the memory of Medgar Evers, and his widow and his children, and to the memory of the dead children of Birmingham." But it is a sermon of a new type. In *Blues for Mister Charlie*, Broadway liberalism has been vanquished by Broadway racism. Liberalism preached politics, that is, solutions. Racism regards politics as superficial (and seeks some deeper level); it emphasizes what is unalterable. Across a virtually impassable gulf, the new mask of "the Negro," manly, toughened, but ever vulnerable, faces his antipode, another new mask, "the white" (sub-genus: "the white liberal")—who is pasty-faced, graceless, lying, sexually dull, murderous.

No one in his right mind would wish the old masks back. But this does not make the new masks wholly convincing. And whoever accepts them should notice that the new mask of "the Negro" has become visible only at the price of emphasizing the fatality of racial antagonisms. If D. W. Griffith could call his famous white supremacist film about the origins of the Ku Klux Klan *The Birth of a Nation*, then James Baldwin could, with more justice to the overt political message of his *Blues for Mister Charlie* ("Mister Charlie" is Negro slang for "white man"), have as well called his play "The Death of a Nation." Baldwin's play, which takes place in a small Southern town, opens with the death of its brash, tormented Negro jazz musician hero, Richard, and ends with the acquittal of his white murderer, a resentful inarticulate young buck named Lyle, and the moral collapse of the local liberal, Parnell. There is the same insistence on the painful ending, even more starkly presented, in LeRoi Jones' one-act play *Dutchman*, now running off-Broadway. In *Dutchman*, a young Negro sitting on the subway reading and minding his own business is first accosted, then elaborately teased and taunted to the point of rage, then suddenly knifed by a twitchy young hustler; while his body is being disposed of by the other passengers, whites, the girl turns her attention to a new young Negro who has just boarded the train. In the new post-liberal morality plays, it is essential that virtue be defeated. Both *Blues for Mister Charlie* and *Dutchman* turn on a shocking murder—even though, in the case of *Dutchman*, the murder is simply not credible in terms of the more or less realistic action that has gone before, and seems crude (dramatically), tacked on, willed. Only murder releases one from the mandate to be moderate. It is essential, dramatically, that the white man win. Murder justifies the author's rage, and disarms the white audience, who have to learn what's coming to *them*.

For it is indeed an extraordinary sermon that is being preached. Baldwin is not interested in dramatizing the incontestable fact that white Americans have brutally mistreated Negro Americans. What is being demonstrated is not the social guilt of the whites, but their inferiority as human beings. This means, above all, their sexual inferiority. While Richard jeers about his unsatisfying experiences with white women up North, it turns out that the only passions—in one instance carnal, in the other romantic—ever felt by the two white men who figure importantly in the play, Lyle and Parnell, have been with Negro women. Thus, the oppression by whites of Negroes becomes a classic case of resentment as described by Nietzsche. It is eerie to sit in the ANTA Theatre on 52nd Street and hear that audience—sizably Negro, but still preponderantly white—cheer and laugh and break into applause at every line cursing white America. After all, it's not some exotic Other from across the seas who is being abused—like the rapacious Jew or the treacherous Italian of the Elizabethan drama. It is the majority of the members of the audience themselves. Social guilt would not be enough to explain this remarkable acquiescence of the majority in their own condemnation. Baldwin's plays, like his essays and novels, have undoubtedly touched a nerve other than political. Only by tapping the sexual insecurity that grips most educated white Americans could Baldwin's virulent rhetoric have seemed so reasonable.

But after the applause and cheers, what? The masks which the Elizabethan theater proposed were exotic, fantastic, playful. Shakespeare's audience did not come streaming out of the Globe Theatre to butcher a Jew or string up a Florentine. The morality of *The Merchant of Venice* is not incendiary, but merely simplifying. But the masks which *Blues for Mister Charlie* holds up for our scorn are our reality. And Baldwin's rhetoric *is* incendiary, though let loose in a carefully fireproofed situation. The result is not any idea of action—but a vicarious pleasure in the rage vented on the stage, with no doubt an undertow of anxiety.

Considered as art, *Blues for Mister Charlie* runs aground for some of the same reasons it stalls as propaganda. Baldwin might have done something much better with the agitprop scheme of his play (noble, handsome Negro student youth pitted against stupid, vicious town whites), for to that in itself I have no objection. Some of the greatest art arises out of moral simplification. But this play gets bogged down in repetitions, incoherence, and in all sorts of loose ends of plot and motive. For example: it is hard to believe that in a town beset by civil rights agitation and with a race murder on its hands, the white liberal, Parnell, could move so freely, with so little recrimination, from one community to another. Again: it is not credible that Lyle, who is Parnell's close friend, and his wife aren't bewildered and irate when Parnell secures Lyle's arraignment on the charge of murder. Perhaps this remarkable equanimity owes to the place of love in Baldwin's rhetoric. Love is always on the horizon, a universal solvent almost in the manner of Paddy Chayefsky. Again: from what we are shown of the romance struck up between Richard and Juanita—which begins only a few days before Richard is killed—it is unconvincing that Juanita should proclaim that what she has learned from Richard is how to love. (The truth seems rather that Richard was just beginning to learn to love, for the first time, from her.) More important: the whole confrontation between Richard and Lyle, with its explicit tones of masculine sexual rivalry, seems inadequately motivated. Richard simply has not enough reason, except that the author wants to say these things, to introduce the theme of sexual envy on all the occasions that he does. And quite apart from any consideration of the sentiments expressed, it is grotesque, humanly and dramatically, for Richard's dying words, as he crawls at Lyle's feet with three bullets in his gut, to be: "White man! I don't want nothing from you. You ain't got nothing to give me! You can't talk because nobody won't talk to you. You can't dance because you've got nobody to dance with . . . Okay. Okay. Okay. Keep your old lady home, you hear? Don't let her near no nigger. She might get to like it. You might get to like it, too."

Perhaps the origin of what seems forced, hysterical, unconvincing in *Blues for Mister Charlie*—and in *Dutchman*—is a rather complex displacement of the play's true subject. Race conflict is what the plays are supposed to be about. Yet also, in both plays, the racial problem is drawn mainly in terms of sexual attitudes. Baldwin has been very plain about the reason for this. White America, he charges, has robbed the Negro of his masculinity. What whites withhold from Negroes, and what Negroes aspire to, is sexual recognition. The withholding of this recognition—and its converse, treating the Negro as a mere object of lust—is the heart of the Negro's pain. As stated in Baldwin's essays, the argument strikes home. (And it doesn't hinder one's considering other consequences, political and economic, of the Negro's oppression.) But what one reads in Baldwin's last novel, or sees on the stage in *Blues for Mister Charlie*, is considerably less persuasive. In Baldwin's novel and play, it seems to me, the racial situation has become a kind of code, or metaphor for sexual conflict. But a sexual problem cannot be wholly masked as a racial problem. Different tonalities, different specifics of emotion are involved.

The truth is that *Blues for Mister Charlie* isn't really about what it claims to be about. It is supposed to be about racial strife. But it is really about the anguish of tabooed sexual longings, about the crisis of identity which comes from confronting these longings, and about the rage and destructiveness (often, self-destructiveness) by which one tries to surmount this crisis. It has, in short, a psychological subject. The surface may be Odets, but the interior is pure Tennessee Williams. What Baldwin has done is to take the leading theme of the serious theater of the fifties—sexual anguish—and work it up as a political play. Buried in *Blues for Mister Charlie* is the plot of several successes of the last decade: the gruesome murder of a handsome virile young man by those who envy him his virility.

The plot of *Dutchman* is similar, except that here there is an added fillip of anxiety. In place of the veiled homoerotic hang-ups of *Blues for Mister Charlie*, there is class anxiety. As his contribution to the mystique of Negro sexuality, Jones brings up the question—which is never raised in *Blues for Mister Charlie*—of being authentically Negro. (Baldwin's play takes place in the South; perhaps one can only have such a problem up North.) Clay, the hero of *Dutchman*, is a middle-class Negro from New Jersey, who has gone to college and wanted to write poetry like Baudelaire, and has Negro friends who speak with English accents. In the early part of the play, he is in limbo. But in the end, poked and prodded by Lula, Clay strips down to his true self; he stops being nice, well-spoken, reasonable, and assumes his full Negro identity: that is, he announces the homicidal rage toward whites that Negroes bear in their hearts, whether they act on it or not. He will not kill, he says. Whereupon, he is killed.

Dutchman is, of course, a smaller work than *Blues for Mister Charlie*. In only one act and with only two speaking characters, it is a descendant of the sexual duels to the death dramatized by Strindberg. At its best, in some of the early exchanges between Lula and Clay, it is neat and powerful. But as a whole—and one does look back on the play in the light of the astonishing fantasy revealed at the end—it is altogether too frantic, too overstated. Robert Hooks played Clay with some subtlety, but I found the spasmic sexual contortions and raucousness in Jennifer West's performance as Lula almost unbearable. There is a smell of a new, rather verbose style of emotional savagery in *Dutchman* that, for want of a better name, I should have to call Albee-esque. Undoubtedly, we shall see more of it. . . . In contrast, *Blues for Mister Charlie* is a long, overlong, rambling work which is virtually an anthology, a summa of the trends of serious big American plays of the last thirty years. It has lots of moral uplift. It carries on the good fight to talk dirty on the legitimate stage to new, splendid victories. And it adopts a complex, pretentious form of narration—the story is told in clumsy flashbacks, with the ornament of a non-functioning chorus, some kind of world-historical disc jockey ensconced stage-right, wearing earphones and fiddling with his apparatus all evening. The production itself, directed by Burgess Meredith, wobbles through several different styles. The realistic parts come off best. In roughly the last third of the play, which takes place in the courtroom, the play founders completely; all pretense at verisimilitude is dropped, there being no fidelity to courtroom rituals observed even in darkest Mississippi, and the play crumbles into bits of internal monologue, whose subjects have little bearing on the present action, which is Lyle's trial. In the last part of *Blues for Mister Charlie*, Baldwin seems bent on dissipating the play's dramatic power; the director needed only to follow. Despite the flabbiness of the direction, though, there are a number of affecting performances. Rip Torn, a sexy aggressive Lyle, rather upstaged the other actors; he was fun to watch. Al Freeman, Jr., was appealing as Richard, though he was saddled with some remarkably maudlin lines, especially in the Moment of Truth With Father scene, which has been obligatory in the serious Broadway theater for the last decade. Diana Sands, one of the loveliest actresses around, did well with the underrealized role of Juanita, except in what has been the most praised part of her performance, her downstage-center-and-face-the-audience aria of lament for Richard, which I thought terribly forced. As Parnell, Pat Hingle, an actor spectacularly embalmed in his own mannerisms, is still the very same indecisive lumbering old dear that he was last year as Nina Leeds' husband in the Actors Studio production of *Strange Interlude*.

The best occasions in the theater in the last months were free-wheeling efforts, which made wholly comic use of the mask, the cliché of character.

At a small theater on East Fourth Street on two Monday evenings in late March, two short plays, *The General Returns From One Place to Another* by Frank O'Hara and *The Baptism* by LeRoi Jones, were performed. The O'Hara is a set of skits involving a kind of General MacArthur type and his entourage in perpetual orbit around the Pacific; the Jones play (like his *Dutchman*) starts more or less realistically, and ends in fantasy; it is about sex and religion and takes place in an evangelical church. Neither the O'Hara nor the Jones seemed very interesting as plays, but then, there is more to theater than plays, that is, than literature. Their main interest for me was as vehicles for the incredible Taylor Mead, poet and "Underground" movie actor. (He has been in Ron Rice's *Flower Thief.*) Mead is a skinny, balding, pot-bellied, round-shouldered, droopy, very pale young man—a sort of consumptive, faggot Harry Langdon. How it is possible for such a physically self-effacing, underprivileged-looking fellow to be so immensely attractive on the stage is hard to explain. But one simply cannot take one's eyes off him. In *The Baptism*, Mead is delightfully inventive and funny as a homosexual in long red underwear camping-in in the church, prancing, wisecracking, kibbitzing, flirting, while all the spiritual doings are taking place. In *The General Returns From One Place to Another*, he was more varied, and even more captivating. Rather than a role, this part is more like a set of charades: the General saluting while his pants are falling down, the General courting an inane widow who keeps popping up along his route, the General making a political speech, the General mowing down a field of flowers with his swagger stick, the General trying to crawl into a sleeping bag, the General dressing down his two adjutants, and so on. It was not, of course, what Mead did, but the somnambulistic concentration with which he did it. The source of his art is the deepest and purest of all: he just gives himself, wholly and without reserve, to some bizarre autistic fantasy. Nothing is more attractive in a person, but it is extremely rare after the age of four. This is the quality Harpo Marx has; Langdon and Keaton among the great silent comics have it; so do those four wonderful floppy Raggedy Andy dolls, the Beatles. Tammy Grimes projects something of it in her very stylized and exciting performance in an otherwise unremarkable Broadway musical now running, *High Spirits*, which is based on Noel Coward's *Blithe Spirit*. (The marvelous Bea Lillie is in it, too; but either she doesn't have enough scope for her gifts in this play or she just isn't up to form.)

What all these performers, from Buster Keaton to Taylor Mead, have in common is their total lack of self-consciousness, in the pursuit of some absolutely invented idea of action. With even a touch of self-consciousness, the effect is spoiled. It becomes insincere, distasteful, even grotesque. I am speaking of course of something rarer than acting ability. And since the ordinary conditions of work in the theater promote a great deal of self-consciousness, one is at least as likely to find this kind of thing in informal circumstances, such as those in which *The General* and *The Baptism* were put on. I am not sure whether Taylor Mead's performances would have prospered in another setting.

My favorite theatrical event of recent months, though, did survive the jump from semi-amateur production to off-Broadway; at least it was still surviving the last time I saw it. *Home Movies* opened in March in the choir loft of the Judson Memorial Church off Washington Square and eventually moved to the Provincetown Playhouse. The scene is A Home. The characters are: a Margaret Dumont mother; a super-athletic mustachioed father; a shrivelled whiny virgin daughter; a girlish youth; a red-cheeked stuttering poet sporting a muffler; a pair of bouncy clericals named Father Shenanigan and Sister Thalia; and an affable Negro delivery man with a thick foot-long pencil. Certain gestures are made in the direction of a plot. The father is believed dead, mother and daughter are lamenting his absence, friends of the family and clergy are paying condolence calls, and in the middle of it all father is delivered, alive and kicking, in a wardrobe. But it doesn't matter. In *Home Movies*, only the present exists—charming people coming and going, reclining in various tableaux, and singing at each other. There is a fast and witty script by Rosalyn Drexler, in which the oldest cliché and the fanciest fancy are meant to be uttered with the same solemnity. "It's the truth," says one character. "Yes," answers another, "a terrible truth like a rash." The gentleness and warmth of *Home Movies* delighted me even more than its wit; and this seemed the work of the adorable music composed by Al Carmines (who is assistant minister at the Judson Memorial Church) and played by him on the piano. The best numbers are a tango sung and danced by Sister Thalia (Sheindi Tokayer) and Father Shenanigan (Al Carmines), the winsome strip tease done by Peter (Freddy Herko) and the duets between him and Mrs. Verdun (Gretel Cummings); and the song "Peanut Brittle" belted out by the maid Violet (Barbara Ann Teer). *Home Movies* is great fun. The people on the stage look happy to be doing what they are doing, too. One could hardly ask for more in the theater—except for great plays, great actors, and great spectacles. Lacking these, one hopes for vitality and joy; and these seem more likely to turn up on out-of-the-way stages, like the Judson Memorial Church or the Sierra Leone pavilion at the World's Fair, than in midtown or even off-Broadway theaters. It helps that neither *Home Movies*, nor *The General* or *The Baptism*, is, strictly, a play. They are theatrical events of a use-and-throw-away kind—spoofs, joyous and insouciant, full of irreverence for "the theater" and "the play." Something similar is taking place with the movies: there is more vitality and art in the Maysles brothers' film on the Beatles in America, *What's Happening*, than in all American story films made this year.

Last, and I suppose least, a few words about two Shakespeare productions.

From John Gielgud's excellent essay, "The Hamlet Tradition—Some Notes on Costume, Scenery and Stage," published in 1937, one could educe most of the particular mistakes in Gielgud's present production of *Hamlet* in New York. For instance, Gielgud cautions against playing Act I, Scene 2—the scene in which Hamlet, Claudius, and Gertrude all appear for the first time—as a family quarrel, rather than a formal privy council meeting, the first (according to tradition) held after the accession of Claudius to the throne. Yet this is just what Gielgud has allowed in the New York production, with Claudius and Gertrude looking like a weary suburban couple having it out with a spoiled only son. Another instance: in staging the

Ghost, Gielgud in his essay argues convincingly against increasing ghostliness by using a miked voice coming from offstage,
rather than the voice of the actor who is on stage and being
seen by the audience. Everything must work toward making the
Ghost as real as possible. But in the present production, Gielgud has forfeited the entire physical presence of the Ghost. This
time the Ghost is really ghostly: a taped voice, Gielgud's own,
resonating hollowly through the theater, and a giant silhouette
thrown on the rear wall of the stage. . . . But it is a waste of
time to look for reasons for this or that feature of the current
production. The overall impression is of complete indifference,
as if the play hadn't really been directed at all—except that one
gathers that some of the dullness, at least the visual dullness,
is actually deliberate. There is the matter of the clothes: most
of the actors, whether courtiers or soldiers, wear old slacks and
sweaters and windbreakers, though Hamlet's pants and shirt
match (they're black), and Claudius and Polonius wear natty
business suits, and Gertrude and Ophelia have long skirts (Gertrude has a mink, too), and the Player King and Queen have
gorgeous costumes and gold masks. This silly conceit appears to
be the one idea in the present production, and is called "playing
Hamlet in rehearsal clothes."

The production affords exactly two pleasures. Hearing John
Gielgud's voice on tape, even thus Cineramarized, reminded
one of how beautiful Shakespeare's verse sounds when it is spoken with grace and intelligence. And the excellent George Rose,
in the brief role of the gravedigger, rendered all the delights of
Shakespeare's prose. The rest of the performances gave only various degrees of pain. Everyone spoke too fast; that fault apart,
some performances rose to the height of mediocrity, while
others, for example the performances of Laertes and Ophelia,
deserve to be singled out as particularly immature, unfelt. It
might be mentioned, though, that Eileen Herlie, who does a
perfunctory Gertrude, gave a striking performance in the same
role in Olivier's movie some fifteen years ago. And that Richard
Burton, who does as little as possible with the part of Hamlet,
is indeed a very handsome man. Correction: he does play the
whole of Hamlet's death scene standing, when he could have
sat down.

But no sooner had one recovered from Gielgud's effrontery

in presenting a Shakespeare play absolutely nude, without any interpretation at all, than a Shakespeare production arrived which, putting the best face on it, was marred by overinterpretation and too much thought. This was Peter Brook's celebrated *King Lear* which was staged at Stratford-on-Avon two years ago, was received with great acclaim in Paris, throughout Eastern Europe, and in Russia, and played—more or less inaudibly—in the New York State Theater (which, it is now discovered, was designed for music and ballet) at Lincoln Center. If Gielgud's *Hamlet* was without thought or style, Brook's *King Lear* came laden with ideas. One read that, inspired by a recent essay by Jan Kott, the Polish Shakespearean scholar, comparing Shakespeare and Beckett, Brook had decided to play *King Lear* as *End-Game*, so to speak. Gielgud has mentioned, in an interview this April in England, that Brook told him it was his controversial "Japanese" *King Lear* (sets and costumes by Noguchi) in 1955 which gave him the basic idea for the current production. And by consulting the "Lear Log" of Charles Marowitz, Brook's assistant at Stratford in 1962, one can find other influences, too. But in the end none of the ideas that fed into the production matter. What matters is what one saw and, hopefully, heard. What I saw was rather dull—if you liked it, it was austere—and arbitrary, too. I can't see what is gained by going against the emotional climaxes of the play—leveling off Lear's tirades, bringing the Gloucester plot almost to equal scale with the Lear plot, cutting out "humanist" passages such as where Regan's servants move to aid the newly blinded Gloucester and where Edmund attempts to revoke the execution of Cordelia and Lear ("Some good I mean to do, Despite of mine own nature"). There were a number of graceful and intelligent performances—Edmund, Gloucester, the Fool. But all the actors seemed to work under an almost palpable constraint, the desire simultaneously to make explicit and to underplay, which must have been what led Brook, in one of the most curious choices of the production, to keep the stage fully lit and bare during the storm scenes. Paul Scofield's Lear is an admirably studied performance. On Lear's great age—with its egotism, its awkward movements and appetites—he is especially good. But I cannot see the point of his throwing so much of the role away, Lear's madness for instance, by arbitrary vocal mannerisms that deadened the full emotional power of his lines. The only performance which seemed to me to survive this strange, crippling interpretation which Brook has imposed on his actors—even, to thrive on it—was Irene Worth's complex and partly sympathetic Goneril. Miss Worth appeared to have searched every corner of her role and, unlike Scofield, to have found more, rather than less, than others had before.

(Summer 1964)

Marat/Sade/Artaud

The Primary and most beautiful of Nature's qualities is motion,
which agitates her at all times. But this motion is simply the
perpetual consequence of crimes; and it is conserved by means
of crimes alone.

SADE

Everything that acts is a cruelty. It is upon this idea of extreme
action, pushed beyond all limits, that theatre must be rebuilt.

ARTAUD

THEATRICALITY and insanity—the two most potent subjects of the contemporary theater—are brilliantly fused in
Peter Weiss' play, *The Persecution and Assassination of Marat
as Performed by the Inmates of the Asylum at Charenton under
the Direction of the Marquis de Sade.* The subject is a dramatic
performance staged before the audience's eyes; the scene is a
madhouse. The historical facts behind the play are that in the
insane asylum just outside Paris where Sade was confined by
order of Napoleon for the last eleven years of his life (1803–14),
it was the enlightened policy of the director, M. Coulmier, to
allow Charenton's inmates to stage theatrical productions of
their own devising which were open to the Parisian public. In
these circumstances Sade is known to have written and put on
several plays (all lost), and Weiss' play ostensibly re-creates such
a performance. The year is 1808 and the stage is the stark tiled
bath-house of the asylum.

Theatricality permeates Weiss' cunning play in a peculiarly
modern sense: most of *Marat/Sade* consists of a play-within-
a-play. In Peter Brook's production, which opened in London
last August, the aged, disheveled, flabby Sade (acted by Patrick
Magee) sits quietly on the left side of the stage—prompting
(with the aid of a fellow-patient who acts as stage manager
and narrator), supervising, commenting. M. Coulmier, dressed
formally and wearing some sort of honorific red sash, attended
by his elegantly dressed wife and daughter, sits throughout the
performance on the right side of the stage. There is also an
abundance of theatricality in a more traditional sense: the emphatic appeal to the senses with spectacle and sound. A quartet
of inmates with string hair and painted faces, wearing colored
sacks and floppy hats, sing sardonic loony songs while the action

described by the songs is mimed; their motley getup contrasts with the shapeless white tunics and strait-jackets, the whey-colored faces of most of the rest of the inmates who act in Sade's passion play on the French Revolution. The verbal action, conducted by Sade, is repeatedly interrupted by brilliant bits of acting-out performed by the lunatics, the most forceful of which is a mass guillotining sequence, in which some inmates make metallic rasping noises, bang together parts of the in-genious set, and pour buckets of paint (blood) down drains, while other madmen gleefully jump into a pit in the center of the stage, leaving their heads piled above stage level, next to the guillotine.

In Brook's production, insanity proves the most authoritative and sensuous kind of theatricality. Insanity establishes the inflec-tion, the intensity of *Marat/Sade*, from the opening image of the ghostly inmates who are to act in Sade's play, crouching in foetal postures or in a catatonic stupor or trembling or perform-ing some obsessive ritual, then stumbling forward to greet the affable M. Coulmier and his family as they enter the stage and mount the platform where they will sit. Insanity is the register of the intensity of the individual performances as well: of Sade, who recites his long speeches with a painful clenched singsong deliberateness; of Marat (acted by Clive Revill), swathed in wet cloths (a treatment for his skin disease) and encased throughout the action in a portable metal bathtub, even in the midst of the most passionate declamation staring straight ahead as though he were already dead; of Charlotte Corday, Marat's assassin, who is played by a beautiful somnambule who periodically goes blank, forgets her lines, even lies down on the stage and has to be awakened by Sade; of Duperret, the Girondist deputy and lover of Corday, played by a lanky stiff-haired patient, an erotomaniac, who is constantly breaking down in his role of gentleman and lover and lunging lustfully toward the patient playing Corday (in the course of the play, he has to be put in a strait-jacket); of Simone Everard, Marat's mistress and nurse, played by an almost wholly disabled patient who can barely speak and is limited to jerky idiot movements as she changes Marat's dressings. Insanity becomes the privileged, most au-thentic metaphor for passion; or, what's the same thing in this case, the logical terminus of any strong emotion. Both dream (as in the "Marat's Nightmare" sequence) and dream-like states must end in violence. Being "calm" amounts to a failure to understand one's real situation. Thus, the slow-motion staging of Corday's murder of Marat (history, i.e. theater) is followed by the inmates shouting and singing of the fifteen bloody years since then, and ends with the "cast" assaulting the Coulmiers as they attempt to leave the stage.

It is through its depiction of theatricality and insanity that Weiss' play is also a play of ideas. The heart of the play is a running debate between Sade, in his chair, and Marat, in his bath, on the meaning of the French Revolution, that is, on the psychological and political premises of modern history, but seen through a very modern sensibility, one equipped with the hindsight afforded by the Nazi concentration camps. But *Marat/Sade* does not lend itself to being formulated as a particular theory about modern experience. Weiss' play seems to be more about the range of sensibility that concerns itself with, or is at stake in, the modern experience, than it is about an argument or an interpretation of that experience. Weiss does not present ideas as much as he immerses his audience in them. Intellectual debate is the material of the play, but it is not its subject or its end. The Charenton setting insures that this debate takes place in a constant atmosphere of barely suppressed violence: all ideas are volatile at this temperature. Again, insanity proves to be the most austere (even abstract) and drastic mode of expressing in theatrical terms the reenacting of ideas, as members of the cast reliving the Revolution run amuck and have to be restrained and the cries of the Parisian mob for liberty are suddenly metamorphosed into the cries of the patients howling to be let out of the asylum.

Such theater, whose fundamental action is the irrevocable careening toward extreme states of feeling, can end in only two ways. It can turn in on itself and become formal, and end in strict *da capo* fashion, with its own opening lines. Or it can turn outward, breaking the "frame," and assault the audience. Ionesco has admitted that he originally envisaged his first play, *The Bald Soprano*, ending with a massacre of the audience; in another version of the same play (which now ends *da capo*), the author was to leap on the stage, and shout imprecations at the audience till they fled the theater. Brook, or Weiss, or both, have devised for the end of *Marat/Sade* an equivalent of the same hostile gesture toward the audience. The inmates, that is, the "cast" of Sade's play, have gone berserk and assaulted the Coulmiers; but this riot—that is, the play—is broken off by the entry of the stage manager of the Aldwych Theater, in modern skirt, sweater, and gym shoes. She blows a whistle; the actors abruptly stop, turn, and face the audience; but when the audience applauds, the company responds with a slow ominous handclap, drowning out the "free" applause and leaving everyone pretty uncomfortable.

My own admiration for, and pleasure in, *Marat/Sade* is virtually unqualified. The play that opened in London last August, and will, it's rumored, soon be seen in New York, is one of the great experiences of anyone's theater-going lifetime. Yet almost everyone, from the daily reviewers to the most serious critics, has voiced serious reservations about, if not outright dislike for, Brook's production of Weiss' play. Why?

Three ready-made ideas seem to me to underlie most caviling at Weiss' play in Brook's production of it.

The connection between theater and literature. One ready-made idea: a work of theater is a branch of literature. The truth is, some works of theater may be judged primarily as works of literature, others not.

It is because this is not admitted, or generally understood, that one reads all too frequently the statement that while *Marat/Sade* is, theatrically, one of the most stunning things anyone has seen on the stage, it's a "director's play," meaning a first-rate production of a second-rate play. A well-known English poet told me he detested the play for this reason: because although he thought it marvelous when he saw it, he *knew* that if it hadn't had the benefit of Peter Brook's production, he wouldn't have liked it. It's also reported that the play in Konrad Swinarski's production last year in West Berlin made nowhere near the striking impression it does in the current production in London.

Granted, *Marat/Sade* is not the supreme masterpiece of contemporary dramatic literature, but it is scarcely a second-rate play. Considered as a text alone, *Marat/Sade* is both sound and exciting. It is not the play which is at fault, but a narrow vision of theater which insists on one image of the director—as servant to the writer, bringing out meanings already resident in the text.

After all, to the extent that it is true that Weiss' text, in Adrian Mitchell's graceful translation, is enhanced greatly by being joined with Peter Brook's staging, what of it? Apart from a theater of dialogue (of language) in which the text is primary, there is also a theater of the senses. The first might be called "play," the second "theater work." In the case of a pure theater work, the writer who sets down words which are to be spoken by actors and staged by a director loses his primacy. In this case, the "author" or "creator" is, to quote Artaud, none other than "the person who controls the direct handling of the stage." The director's art is a material art—an art in which he deals with the bodies of actors, the props, the lights, the music. And what Brook has put together is particularly brilliant and inventive— the rhythm of the staging, the costumes, the ensemble mime scenes. In every detail of the production—one of the most re- markable elements of which is the clangorous tuneful music (by Richard Peaslee) featuring bells, cymbals, and the organ—there is an inexhaustible material inventiveness, a relentless address to the senses. Yet, something about Brook's sheer virtuosity in stage effects offends. It seems, to most people, to overwhelm the text. But perhaps that's just the point.

I'm not suggesting that *Marat/Sade* is simply theater of the senses. Weiss has supplied a complex and highly literate text which demands to be responded to. But *Marat/Sade* also de- mands to be taken on the sensory level as well, and only the sheerest prejudice about what theater must be (the prejudice, namely, that a work of theater is to be judged, in the last analy- sis, as a branch of literature) lies behind the demand that the written, and subsequently spoken, text of a theater work carry the whole play.

The connection between theater and psychology. Another ready- made idea: drama consists of the revelation of character, built on the conflict of realistically credible motives. But the most interesting modern theater is a theater which goes beyond psy- chology.

Again, to cite Artaud: "We need true action, but without prac- tical consequences. It is not on the social level that the action of theater unfolds. Still less on the ethical and psychological

levels. . . . This obstinacy in making characters talk about feelings, passions, desires, and impulses of a strictly psychological
order, in which a single word is to compensate for innumerable
gestures, is the reason . . . the theater has lost its true *raison
d'être*."

It's from this point of view, tendentiously formulated by Artaud,
that one may properly approach the fact that Weiss has situated his argument in an insane asylum. The fact is that with
the exception of the audience-figures on stage—M. Coulmier,
who frequently interrupts the performance to remonstrate with
Sade, and his wife and daughter, who have no lines—all the
characters in the play are mad. But the setting of *Marat/Sade*
does not amount to a statement that the world is insane. Nor
is it an instance of a fashionable interest in the psychology of
psychopathic behavior. On the contrary, the concern with insanity in art today usually reflects the desire to go beyond psychology. By representing characters with deranged behavior or
deranged styles of speech, such dramatists as Pirandello, Genet,
Beckett, and Ionesco make it unnecessary for their characters
to embody in their acts or voice in their speech sequential and
credible accounts of their motives. Freed from the limitations
of what Artaud calls "psychological and dialogue painting of
the individual," the dramatic representation is open to levels of
experience which are more heroic, more rich in fantasy, more
philosophical. The point applies, of course, not only to the
drama. The choice of "insane" behavior as the subject-matter
of art is, by now, the virtually classic strategy of modern artists
who wish to transcend traditional "realism," that is, psychology.

Take the scene to which many people particularly objected,
in which Sade persuades Charlotte Corday to whip him (Peter
Brook has her do it with her hair)—while he, meanwhile, continues to recite, in agonized tones, some point about the Revolution, and the nature of human nature. The purpose of this
scene is surely not to inform the audience that, as one critic
put it, Sade is "sick, sick, sick"; nor is it fair to reproach Weiss'
Sade, as the same critic does, with "using the theater less to
advance an argument than to excite himself." (Anyway, why not
both?) By combining rational or near-rational argument with
irrational behavior, Weiss is not inviting the audience to make
a judgment on Sade's character, mental competence, or state

of mind. Rather, he is shifting to a kind of theater focused not on characters, but on intense transpersonal emotions borne by characters. He is providing a kind of vicarious emotional experience (in this case, frankly erotic) from which the theater has shied away too long.

Language is used in *Marat/Sade* primarily as a form of incantation, instead of being limited to the revelation of character and the exchange of ideas. This use of language as incantation is the point of another scene which many who saw the play have found objectionable, upsetting, and gratuitous—the bravura soliloquy of Sade, in which he illustrates the cruelty in the heart of man by relating in excruciating detail the public execution by slow dismemberment of Damiens, the would-be assassin of Louis XV.

The connection between theater and ideas. Another readymade idea: a work of art is to be understood as being "about" or representing or arguing for an "idea." That being so, an implicit standard for a work of art is the value of the ideas it contains, and whether these are clearly and consistently expressed.

It is only to be expected that *Marat/Sade* would be subjected to these standards. Weiss' play, theatrical to its core, is also full of intelligence. It contains discussions of the deepest issues of contemporary morality and history and feeling that put to shame the banalities peddled by such would-be diagnosticians of these issues as Arthur Miller (see his current *After the Fall* and *Incident at Vichy*), Friedrich Duerrenmatt (*The Visit*, *The Physicists*), and Max Frisch (*The Firebugs*, *Andorra*). Yet, there is no doubt that *Marat/Sade* is intellectually puzzling. Argument is offered, only (seemingly) to be undermined by the context of the play—the insane asylum, and the avowed theatricality of the proceedings. People do seem to represent positions in Weiss' play. Roughly, Sade represents the claim of the permanence of human nature, in all its vileness, against Marat's revolutionary fervor and his belief that man can be changed by history. Sade thinks that "the world is made of bodies," Marat that it is made of forces. Secondary characters, too, have their moments of passionate advocacy: Duperret hails the eventual dawn of freedom, the priest Jacques Roux denounces Napoleon. But Sade and "Marat" are both madmen, each in a different style; "Charlotte Corday" is a sleepwalker, "Duperret" has satyriasis;

"Roux" is hysterically violent. Doesn't this undercut their arguments? And, apart from the question of the context of insanity in which the ideas are presented, there is the device of the play-within-a-play. At one level, the running debate between Sade and Marat, in which the moral and social idealism attributed to Marat is countered by Sade's trans-moral advocacy of the claims of individual passion, seems a debate between equals. But, on another level, since the fiction of Weiss' play is that it is Sade's script which Marat is reciting, presumably Sade carries the argument. One critic goes so far as to say that because Marat has to double as a puppet in Sade's psychodrama, and as Sade's opponent in an evenly matched ideological contest, the debate between them is stillborn. And, lastly, some critics have attacked the play on the grounds of its lack of historical fidelity to the actual views of Marat, Sade, Duperret, and Roux.

These are some of the difficulties which have led people to charge *Marat/Sade* with being obscure or intellectually shallow. But most of these difficulties, and the objections made to them, are misunderstandings—misunderstandings of the connection between the drama and didacticism. Weiss' play cannot be treated like an argument of Arthur Miller, or even of Brecht. We have to do here with a kind of theater as different from these as Antonioni and Godard are from Eisenstein. Weiss' play contains an argument, or rather it employs the material of intellectual debate and historical reevaluation (the nature of human nature, the betrayal of the Revolution, etc.). But Weiss' play is only secondarily an argument. There is another use of ideas to be reckoned with in art: ideas as sensory stimulants. Antonioni has said of his films that he wants them to dispense with "the superannuated casuistry of positives and negatives." The same impulse discloses itself in a complex way in *Marat/Sade*. Such a position does not mean that these artists wish to dispense with ideas. What it does mean is that ideas, including moral ideas, are proffered in a new style. Ideas may function as décor, props, sensuous material.

One might perhaps compare the Weiss play with the long prose narratives of Genet. Genet is not really arguing that "cruelty is good" or "cruelty is holy" (a moral statement, albeit the opposite of traditional morality), but rather shifting the argument to another plane, from the moral to the aesthetic. But this is not quite the case with *Marat/Sade*. While the "cruelty" in *Marat/Sade* is not, ultimately, a moral issue, it is not an aesthetic one either. It is an ontological issue. While those who propose the aesthetic version of "cruelty" interest themselves in the richness of the surface of life, the proponents of the ontological version of "cruelty" want their art to act out the widest possible context for human action, at least a wider context than that provided by realistic art. That wider context is what Sade calls "nature" and what Artaud means when he says that "everything that acts is a cruelty." There is a moral vision in art like *Marat/Sade*, though clearly it cannot (and this has made its audience uncomfortable) be summed up with the slogans of "humanism." But "humanism" is not identical with morality. Precisely, art like *Marat/Sade* entails a rejection of "humanism," of the task of moralizing the world and thereby refusing to acknowledge the "crimes" of which Sade speaks.

I have repeatedly cited the writings of Artaud on the theater in discussing *Marat/Sade*. But Artaud—unlike Brecht, the other great theoretician of 20th century theater—did not create a body of work to illustrate his theory and sensibility.

Often, the sensibility (the theory, at a certain level of discourse) which governs certain works of art is formulated before there exist substantial works to embody that sensibility. Or, the theory may apply to works other than those for which they are developed. Thus, right now in France writers and critics such as Alain Robbe-Grillet (*Pour un Nouveau Roman*), Roland Barthes (*Essais Critiques*), and Michel Foucault (essays in *Tel Quel* and elsewhere) have worked out an elegant and persuasive anti-rhetorical aesthetic for the novel. But the novels produced by the *nouveau roman* writers and analyzed by them are in fact not as important or satisfying an illustration of this sensibility as certain films, and, moreover, films by directors, Italian as well as French, who have no connection with this school of new French writers, such as Bresson, Melville, Antonioni, Godard, and Bertolucci (*Before the Revolution*).

Similarly, it seems doubtful that the only stage production which Artaud personally supervised, of Shelley's *The Cenci*, or the 1948 radio broadcast *Pour en Finir avec le Jugement de Dieu*, came close to following the brilliant recipes for the theater in his writings, any more than did his public readings of Seneca's tragedies. We have up to now lacked a full-fledged example of Artaud's category, "the theater of cruelty." The closest thing to it are the theatrical events done in New York and elsewhere in the last five years, largely by painters (such as Allan Kaprow, Claes Oldenburg, Jim Dine, Bob Whitman, Red Grooms, Robert Watts) and without text or at least intelligible speech, called Happenings. Another example of work in a quasi-Artaudian spirit: the brilliant staging by Lawrence Kornfield and Al Carmines of Gertrude Stein's prose poem "What Happened," at the Judson Memorial Church last year. Another example: the final production of The Living Theater in New York, Kenneth H. Brown's *The Brig*, directed by Judith Malina.

All the works I have mentioned so far suffer, though, apart from all questions of individual execution, from smallness of scope and conception—as well as a narrowness of sensory means. Hence, the great interest of *Marat/Sade*, for it, more than any modern theater work I know of, comes near the scope, as well as the intent, of Artaud's theater. (I must reluctantly except, because I have never seen it, what sounds like the most interesting and ambitious theater group in the world today—the Theater Laboratory of Jerzy Grotowski in Opole, Poland. For an account of this work, which is an ambitious extension of Artaudian principles, see the *Tulane Drama Review*, Spring 1965.)

Yet Artaud's is not the only major influence reflected in the Weiss-Brook production. Weiss is reported to have said that in this play he wished—staggering ambition!—to combine Brecht and Artaud. And, to be sure, one can see what he means. Certain features of *Marat/Sade* are reminiscent of Brecht's theater—constructing the action around a debate on principles and reasons; the songs; the appeals to the audience through an M.C. And these blend well with the Artaudian texture of the situation and the staging. Yet the matter is not that simple. Indeed, the final question that Weiss' play raises is precisely the one of the ultimate compatibility of these two sensibilities and ideals. How *could* one reconcile Brecht's conception of a didactic theater, a theater of intelligence, with Artaud's theater of magic, of gesture, of "cruelty," of feeling?

The answer seems to be that, if one could effect such a

reconciliation or synthesis, Weiss' play has taken a big step toward doing so. Hence the obtuseness of the critic who complained: "Useless ironies, insoluble conundrums, double meanings which could be multiplied indefinitely: Brecht's machinery without Brecht's incisiveness or firm commitment," forgetting about Artaud altogether. If one does put the two together, one sees that new perceptions must be allowed, new standards devised. For isn't an Artaudian theater of commitment, much less "firm commitment," a contradiction in terms? Or is it? The problem is not solved by ignoring the fact that Weiss in *Marat/Sade* means to employ ideas in a fugue form (rather than as literal assertions), and thereby necessarily refers beyond the arena of social material and didactic statement. A misunderstanding of the artistic aims implicit in *Marat/Sade* due to a narrow vision of the theater accounts for most of the critics' dissatisfaction with Weiss' play—an ungrateful dissatisfaction, considering the extraordinary richness of the text and of the Brook production. That the ideas taken up in *Marat/Sade* are not resolved, in an intellectual sense, is far less important than the extent to which they do work together in the sensory arena.

(1965)

IV

Spiritual Style in the
Films of Robert Bresson

SOME art aims directly at arousing the feelings; some art
appeals to the feelings through the route of the intelligence. There is art that involves, that creates empathy. There is
art that detaches, that provokes reflection.

Great reflective art is not frigid. It can exalt the spectator,
it can present images that appall, it can make him weep. But
its emotional power is mediated. The pull toward emotional
involvement is counterbalanced by elements in the work that
promote distance, disinterestedness, impartiality. Emotional
involvement is always, to a greater or lesser degree, postponed.

The contrast can be accounted for in terms of techniques or
means—even of ideas. No doubt, though, the sensibility of the
artist is, in the end, decisive. It is a reflective art, a detached art
that Brecht is advocating when he talks about the "Alienation
Effect." The didactic aims which Brecht claimed for his theater
are really a vehicle for the cool temperament that conceived
those plays.

2

In the film, the master of the reflective mode is Robert Bresson.

Though Bresson was born in 1911, his extant work in the cinema has all been done in the last twenty years, and consists of six
feature films. (He made a short film in 1934 called *Les Affaires
Publiques*, reportedly a comedy in the manner of René Clair, all
copies of which have been lost; did some work on the scripts of
two obscure commercial films in the mid-thirties; and in 1940
was assistant director to Clair on a film that was never finished.)
Bresson's first full-length film was begun when he returned to
Paris in 1941 after spending eighteen months in a German
prison camp. He met a Dominican priest and writer, Father
Bruckberger, who suggested that they collaborate on a film
about Bethany, the French Dominican order devoted to the
care and rehabilitation of women ex-convicts. A scenario was
written, Jean Giraudoux was enlisted to write the dialogue, and
the film—at first called *Béthanie*, and finally, at the producers'

insistence, *Les Anges du Péché* (The Angels of Sin)—was released in 1943. It was enthusiastically acclaimed by the critics and had a success with the public as well.

The plot of his second film, begun in 1944 and released in 1945, was a modern version of one of the interpolated stories in Diderot's great anti-novel *Jacques le Fataliste*; Bresson wrote the scenario and Jean Cocteau the dialogue. Bresson's first success was not repeated, however. *Les Dames du Bois de Boulogne* (sometimes called, here, *The Ladies of the Park*) was panned by the critics and failed at the box-office, too.

Bresson's third film, *Le Journal d'un Curé de Campagne* (*The Diary of a Country Priest*), did not appear until 1951; his fourth film, *Un Condamné à Mort s'est Échappé* (called, here, *A Man Escaped*), in 1956; his fifth film, *Pickpocket*, in 1959; and his sixth film, *Procès de Jeanne d'Arc* (The Trial of Joan of Arc), in 1962. All have had a certain success with critics but scarcely any with the public—with the exception of the last film, which most critics disliked, too. Once hailed as the new hope of the French cinema, Bresson is now firmly labeled as an esoteric director. He has never had the attention of the art-house audience that flocks to Buñuel, Bergman, Fellini—though he is a far greater director than these; even Antonioni has almost a mass audience compared with Bresson's. And, except among a small coterie, he has had only the scantest critical attention.

The reason that Bresson is not generally ranked according to his merits is that the tradition to which his art belongs, the reflective or contemplative, is not well understood. Particularly in England and America, Bresson's films are often described as cold, remote, overintellectualized, geometrical. But to call a work of art "cold" means nothing more or less than to compare it (often unconsciously) to a work that is "hot." And not all art is—or could be—hot, any more than all persons have the same temperament. The generally accepted notions of the range of temperament in art are provincial. Certainly, Bresson is cold next to Pabst or Fellini. (So is Vivaldi cold next to Brahms, and Keaton cold next to Chaplin.) One has to understand the aesthetics—that is, find the beauty—of such coldness. And Bresson offers a particularly good case for sketching such an aesthetic, because of his range. Exploring the possibilities of a reflective, as opposed to an emotionally immediate, art, Bresson moves

from the diagrammatic perfection of *Les Dames du Bois de Boulogne* to the almost lyrical, almost "humanistic" warmth of *Un
Condamné à Mort s'est Échappé*. He also shows—and this is
instructive, too—how such art can become too rarefied, in his
last film, *Procès de Jeanne d'Arc*.

3

In reflective art, the *form* of the work of art is present in an
emphatic way.

The effect of the spectator's being aware of the form is to
elongate or to retard the emotions. For, to the extent that we
are conscious of form in a work of art, we become somewhat
detached; our emotions do not respond in the same way as they
do in real life. Awareness of form does two things simultaneously: it gives a sensuous pleasure independent of the "content," and it invites the use of intelligence. It may be a very
low order of reflection which is invited, as, for instance, by the
narrative form (the interweaving of the four separate stories) of
Griffith's *Intolerance*. But it is reflection, nonetheless.

The typical way in which "form" shapes "content" in art is by
doubling, duplicating. Symmetry and the repetition of motifs
in painting, the double plot in Elizabethan drama, and rhyme
schemes in poetry are a few obvious examples.

The evolution of forms in art is partly independent of the
evolution of subject-matters. (The history of forms is dialectical. As types of sensibility become banal, boring, and are
overthrown by their opposites, so forms in art are, periodically, exhausted. They become banal, unstimulating, and are
replaced by new forms which are at the same time anti-forms.)
Sometimes the most beautiful effects are gained when the material and the form are at cross purposes. Brecht does this often:
placing a hot subject in a cold frame. Other times, what satisfies
is that the form is perfectly appropriate to the theme. This is
the case with Bresson.

Why Bresson is not only a much greater, but also a more
interesting director than, say, Buñuel is that he has worked out
a form that perfectly expresses and accompanies what he wants
to say. In fact, it *is* what he wants to say.

Here, one must carefully distinguish between form and manner. Welles, the early René Clair, Sternberg, Ophuls are examples

of directors with unmistakable stylistic inventions. But they never created a rigorous narrative form. Bresson, like Ozu, has. And the form of Bresson's films is designed (like Ozu's) to discipline the emotions at the same time that it arouses them: to induce a certain tranquillity in the spectator, a state of spiritual balance that is itself the subject of the film.

Reflective art is art which, in effect, imposes a certain discipline on the audience—postponing easy gratification. Even boredom can be a permissible means of such discipline. Giving prominence to what is artifice in the work of art is another means. One thinks here of Brecht's idea of theater. Brecht advocated strategies of staging—like having a narrator, putting musicians on stage, interposing filmed scenes—and a technique of acting so that the audience could distance itself, and not become uncritically "involved" in the plot and the fate of the characters. Bresson wishes distance, too. But his aim, I would imagine, is not to keep hot emotions cool so that intelligence can prevail. The emotional distance typical of Bresson's films seems to exist for a different reason altogether: because all identification with characters, deeply conceived, is an impertinence—an affront to the mystery that is human action and the human heart.

But—all claims for intellectual coolness or respect for the mystery of action laid aside—surely Brecht knew, as must Bresson, that such distancing is a source of great emotional power. It is precisely the defect of the naturalistic theater and cinema that, giving itself too readily, it easily consumes and exhausts its effects. Ultimately, the greatest source of emotional power in art lies not in any particular subject-matter, however passionate, however universal. It lies in form. The detachment and retarding of the emotions, through the consciousness of form, makes them far stronger and more intense in the end.

4

Despite the venerable critical slogan that film is primarily a visual medium, and despite the fact that Bresson was a painter before he turned to making films, form for Bresson is not mainly visual. It is, above all, a distinctive form of narration. For Bresson film is not a plastic but a narrative experience.

Bresson's form fulfills beautifully the prescription of Alexandre

Astruc, in his famous essay "Le Camera-Stylo," written in the late forties. According to Astruc, the cinema will, ideally, become a language.

> By a language I mean the form in which and through which an artist can express his thoughts, however abstract they may be, or translate his obsessions, just as in an essay or a novel . . . The film will gradually free itself from the tyranny of the visual, of the image for its own sake, of the immediate and concrete anecdote, to become a means of writing as supple and subtle as the written word . . . What interests us in the cinema today is the creation of this language.

Cinema-as-language means a break with the traditional dramatic and visual way of telling a story in film. In Bresson's work, this creation of a language for films entails a heavy emphasis on the word. In the first two films, where the action is still relatively dramatic, and the plot employs a group of characters,* language (in the literal sense) appears in the form of dialogue. This dialogue definitely calls attention to itself. It is very theatrical dialogue, concise, aphoristic, deliberate, literary. It is the opposite of the improvised-sounding dialogue favored by the new French directors—including Godard in *Vivre Sa Vie* and *Une Femme Mariée*, the most Bressonian of the New Wave films.

But in the last four films, in which the action has contracted from that which befalls a group to the fortunes of the lonely self, dialogue is often displaced by first-person narration. Sometimes the narration can be justified as providing links between scenes. But, more interestingly, it often doesn't tell us anything we don't know or are about to learn. It "doubles" the action. In this case, we usually get the word first, then the scene. For example, in *Pickpocket*: we see the hero writing (and hear his voice reading) his memoirs. Then we see the event which he has already curtly described.

---

*Even here, though, there is a development. In *Les Anges du Péché*, there are five main characters—the young novice Anne-Marie, another novice Madeleine, the Prioress, the Prioress' assistant Mother Saint-Jean, and the murderess Thérèse—as well as a great deal of background: the daily life of the convent, and so forth. In *Les Dames du Bois de Boulogne*, there is already a simplification, less background. Four characters are clearly outlined—Hélène, her former lover Jean, Agnès, and Agnès' mother. Everyone else is virtually invisible. We never see the servants' faces, for instance.

But sometimes we get the scene first, then the explanation, the description of what has just happened. For example, in *Le Journal d'un Curé de Campagne*, there is a scene in which the priest calls anxiously on the Vicar of Torcy. We see the priest wheeling his bicycle up to the Vicar's door, then the housekeeper answering (the Vicar is obviously not at home, but we don't hear the housekeeper's voice), then the door shutting, and the priest leaning against it. Then, we hear: "I was so disappointed, I had to lean against the door." Another example: in *Un Condamné à Mort s'est Échappé*, we see Fontaine tearing up the cloth of his pillow, then twisting the cloth around wire which he has stripped off the bed frame. Then, the voice: "I twisted it strongly."

The effect of this "superfluous" narration is to punctuate the scene with intervals. It puts a brake on the spectator's direct imaginative participation in the action. Whether the order is from comment to scene or from scene to comment, the effect is the same: such doublings of the action both arrest and intensify the ordinary emotional sequence.

Notice, too, that in the first type of doubling—where we hear what's going to happen before we see it—there is a deliberate flouting of one of the traditional modes of narrative involvement: suspense. Again, one thinks of Brecht. To eliminate suspense, at the beginning of a scene Brecht announces, by means of placards or a narrator, what is to happen. (Godard adopts this technique in *Vivre Sa Vie*.) Bresson does the same thing, by jumping the gun with narration. In many ways, the perfect story for Bresson is that of his last film, *Procès de Jeanne d'Arc*—in that the plot is wholly known, foreordained; the words of the actors are not invented but those of the actual trial record. Ideally, there is no suspense in a Bresson film. Thus, in the one film where suspense should normally play a large role, *Un Condamné à Mort s'est Échappé*, the title deliberately—even awkwardly—gives the outcome away: we know Fontaine is going to make it.* In this respect, of course, Bresson's escape film differs from Jacques Becker's last work, *Le Trou* (called, here, *Nightwatch*), though in other ways Becker's excellent film

---

*The film has a co-title, which expresses the theme of inexorability: *Le Vent Souffle où il Veut*.

owes a great deal to *Un Condamné à Mort s'est Échappé*. (It is to Becker's credit that he was the only prominent person in the French film world who defended *Les Dames du Bois de Boulogne* when it came out.)

Thus, form in Bresson's films is anti-dramatic, though strongly linear. Scenes are cut short, and set end to end without obvious emphasis. In *Le Journal d'un Curé de Campagne*, there must be thirty such short scenes. This method of constructing the story is most rigorously observed in *Procès de Jeanne d'Arc*. The film is composed of static, medium shots of people talking; the scenes are the inexorable sequence of Jeanne's interrogations. The principle of eliding anecdotal material—in *Un Condamné à Mort s'est Échappé*, for instance, one knows little about why Fontaine is in prison in the first place—is here carried to its extreme. There are no interludes of any sort. An interrogation ends; the door slams behind Jeanne; the scene fades out. The key clatters in the lock; another interrogation; again the door clangs shut; fadeout. It is a very dead-pan construction, which puts a sharp brake on emotional involvement.

Bresson also came to reject the species of involvement created in films by the expressiveness of the acting. Again, one is reminded of Brecht by Bresson's particular way of handling actors, in the exercise of which he has found it preferable to use non-professionals in major roles. Brecht wanted the actor to "report" a role rather than "be" it. He sought to divorce the actor from indentifying with the role, as he wanted to divorce the spectator from identifying with the events that he saw being "reported" on the stage. "The actor," Brecht insists, "must remain a demonstrator; he must present the person demonstrated as a stranger, he must not suppress the '*he* did that, *he* said that' element in his performance." Bresson, working with non-professional actors in his last four films (he used professionals in *Les Anges du Péché* and *Les Dames du Bois de Boulogne*), also seems to be striving for the same effect of strangeness. His idea is for the actors not to act out their lines, but simply to say them with as little expression as possible. (To get this effect, Bresson rehearses his actors for several months before shooting begins.) Emotional climaxes are rendered very elliptically.

But the reason is really quite different in the two cases. The reason that Brecht rejected acting reflects his idea of the relation of dramatic art to critical intelligence. He thought that the emotional force of the acting would get in the way of the ideas represented in plays. (From what I saw of the work of the Berliner Ensemble six years ago, though, it didn't seem to me that the somewhat low-keyed acting really diminished emotional involvement; it was the highly stylized staging which did that.) The reason that Bresson rejects acting reflects his notion of the purity of the art itself. "Acting is for the theater, which is a bastard art," he has said. "The film can be a true art because in it the author takes fragments of reality and arranges them in such a way that their juxtaposition transforms them." Cinema, for Bresson, is a total art, in which acting corrodes. In a film,

> each shot is like a word, which means nothing by itself, or rather means so many things that in effect it is meaningless. But a word in a poem is transformed, its meaning made precise and unique, by its placing in relation to the words around it: in the same way a shot in a film is given its meaning by its context, and each shot modifies the meaning of the previous one until with the last shot a total, unparaphrasable meaning has been arrived at. Acting has nothing to do with that, it can only get in the way. Films can only be made by bypassing the will of those who appear in them; using not what they do, but what they are.

In sum: there are spiritual resources beyond effort, which appear only when effort is stilled. One imagines that Bresson never treats his actors to an "interpretation" of their roles: Claude Laydu, who plays the priest in *Le Journal d'un Curé de Campagne*, has said that while he was making the film he was never told to try to represent sanctity, though that is what it appears, when viewing the film, that he does. In the end, everything depends on the actor, who either has this luminous presence or doesn't. Laydu has it. So does François Leterrier, who is Fontaine in *Un Condamné à Mort s'est Échappé*. But Martin Lassalle as Michel in *Pickpocket* conveys something wooden, at times evasive. With Florence Carrez in *Procès de Jeanne d'Arc*, Bresson has experimented with the limit of the unexpressive. There is no acting at all; she simply reads the lines. It could have worked. But it doesn't—because she is the least luminous of all the presences Bresson has "used" in his later films. The thinness of Bresson's last film is, partly, a failure of communicated intensity on the part of the actress who plays Jeanne, upon whom the film depends.

5

All of Bresson's films have a common theme: the meaning of confinement and liberty. The imagery of the religious vocation and of crime are used jointly. Both lead to "the cell."

The plots all have to do with incarceration and its sequel. *Les Anges du Péché* takes place mostly inside a convent. Thérèse, an ex-convict who (unknown to the police) has just murdered the lover who betrayed her, is delivered into the hands of the Bethany nuns. One young novice, who tries to create a special relationship with Thérèse and, learning her secret, to get her to surrender herself voluntarily to the police, is expelled from the convent for insubordination. One morning, she is found dying in the convent garden. Thérèse is finally moved, and the last shot is of her extending her hands to the policeman's manacles. . . . In *Les Dames du Bois de Boulogne*, the metaphor of confinement is repeated several times. Hélène and Jean have been confined in their love; he urges her to return to the world now that she is "free." But she doesn't, and instead devotes herself to setting a trap for him—a trap which requires that she find two pawns (Agnès and her mother), whom she virtually confines in an apartment while they await her orders. Like *Les Anges du Péché*, this is the story of the redemption of a lost girl. In *Les Anges du Péché*, Thérèse is liberated by accepting imprisonment; in *Les Dames du Bois de Boulogne*, Agnès is imprisoned, and then, arbitrarily, as by a miracle, is forgiven, set free. . . . In *Le Journal d'un Curé de Campagne*, the emphasis has shifted. The bad girl, Chantal, is kept in the background. The drama of confinement is in the priest's confinement in himself, his despair, his weakness, his mortal body. ("I was a prisoner of the Holy Agony.") He is liberated by accepting his senseless and agonizing death from stomach cancer. . . . In *Un Condamné à Mort s'est Échappé*, which is set in a German-run prison in occupied France, confinement is most literally represented. So is liberation: the hero triumphs over himself (his despair, the temptation of inertia) and escapes. The obstacles are embodied both in material things and in the incalculability of the human beings in the vicinity of the solitary hero. But Fontaine risks trusting the two strangers in the courtyard at the beginning of his imprisonment, and his trust is not betrayed. And because he risks trusting the youthful collaborationist who is thrown into his cell with him on the eve of his escape (the alternative is to kill the boy), he is able to get out. . . . In *Pickpocket*, the hero is a young recluse who lives in a closet of a room, a petty criminal who, in Dostoevskian fashion, appears to crave punishment. Only at the end, when he has been caught and is in jail, talking through the bars with the girl who has loved him, is he depicted as being, possibly, able to love. . . . In *Procès de Jeanne d'Arc*, again the entire film is set in prison. As in *Le Journal d'un Curé de Campagne*, Jeanne's liberation comes through a hideous death; but Jeanne's martyrdom is much less affecting than the priest's, because she is so depersonalized (unlike Falconetti's Jeanne in Dreyer's great film) that she does not seem to mind dying.

The nature of drama being conflict, the real drama of Bresson's stories is interior conflict: the fight against oneself. And all the static and formal qualities of his films work to that end. Bresson has said, of his choice of the highly stylized and artificial plot of *Les Dames du Bois de Boulogne*, that it allowed him to "eliminate anything which might distract from the interior drama." Still, in that film and the one before it, interior drama is represented in an exterior form, however fastidious and stripped down. *Les Anges du Péché* and *Les Dames du Bois de Boulogne* depict conflicts of wills among the various characters as much or more than they concern a conflict within the self.

It is only in the films following *Les Dames du Bois de Boulogne* that Bresson's drama has been really interiorized. The theme of *Le Journal d'un Curé de Campagne* is the young priest's conflict with himself: only secondarily is this acted out in his relation with the Vicar of Torcy, with Chantal, and with the Countess, Chantal's mother. This is even clearer in *Un Condamné à Mort s'est Échappé*—where the principal character is literally isolated in a cell, struggling against despair. Solitude and interior conflict pair off in another way in *Pickpocket*, where the solitary hero refuses despair only at the price of refusing love, and gives himself over to masturbatory acts of theft. But in the last film, where we know the drama should be taking place, there is scarcely any evidence of it. Conflict has been virtually suppressed; it must be inferred. Bresson's Jeanne is an automaton of grace. But, however interior the drama, there must be drama. This is what *Procès de Jeanne d'Arc* withholds.

Notice, though, that the "interior drama" which Bresson

seeks to depict does not mean *psychology*. In realistic terms, the
motives of Bresson's characters are often hidden, sometimes
downright incredible. In *Pickpocket*, for instance, when Michel
sums up his two years in London with "I lost all my money on
gambling and women," one simply does not believe it. Nor is
it any more convincing that during this time the good Jacques,
Michel's friend, has made Jeanne pregnant and then deserted
her and their child.

Psychological implausibility is scarcely a virtue; and the narrative passages I have just cited are flaws in *Pickpocket*. But
what is central to Bresson and, I think, not to be caviled at,
is his evident belief that psychological analysis is superficial.
(Reason: it assigns to action a paraphrasable meaning that true
art transcends.) He does not intend his characters to be implausible, I'm sure; but he does, I think, intend them to be opaque.
Bresson is interested in the forms of spiritual action—in the
physics, as it were, rather than in the psychology of souls. Why
persons behave as they do is, ultimately, not to be understood.
(Psychology, precisely, does claim to understand.) Above all,
persuasion is inexplicable, unpredictable. That the priest *does*
reach the proud and unyielding Countess (in *Le Journal d'un
Curé de Campagne*), that Jeanne *doesn't* persuade Michel (in
Pickpocket) are just facts—or mysteries, if you like.

Such a physics of the soul was the subject of Simone Weil's
most remarkable book, *Gravity and Grace*. And the following
sentences of Simone Weil's—

> All the natural movements of the soul are controlled by laws
> analogous to those of physical gravity. Grace is the only exception.
>   Grace fills empty spaces, but it can only enter where there is
> a void to receive it, and it is grace itself which makes this void.
>   The imagination is continually at work filling up all the fissures
> through which grace might pass.

supply the three basic theorems of Bresson's "anthropology."
Some souls are heavy, others light; some are liberated or capable
of being liberated, others not. All one can do is be patient, and
as empty as possible. In such a regimen there is no place for
the imagination, much less for ideas and opinions. The ideal is
neutrality, transparence. This is what is meant when the Vicar
of Torcy tells the young priest in *Le Journal d'un Curé de Campagne*, "A priest has no opinions."

Except in an ultimate unrepresentable sense, a priest has no attachments either. In the quest for spiritual lightness ("grace"), attachments are a spiritual encumbrance. Thus, the priest, in the climactic scene of *Le Journal d'un Curé de Campagne*, forces the Countess to relinquish her passionate mourning for her dead son. True contact between persons is possible, of course; but it comes not through will but unasked for, through grace. Hence in Bresson's films human solidarity is represented only at a distance—as it is between the priest and the Vicar of Torcy in *Le Journal d'un Curé de Campagne*, or between Fontaine and the other prisoners in *Un Condamné à Mort s'est Échappé*. The actual coming together of two people in a relation of love can be stated, ushered in, as it were, before our eyes: Jean crying out "Stay! I love you!" to the nearly dead Agnès in *Les Dames du Bois de Boulogne*; Fontaine putting his arm around Jost in *Un Condamné à Mort s'est Échappé*; Michel in *Pickpocket* saying to Jeanne through prison bars, "How long it has taken me to come to you." But we do not see love lived. The moment in which it is declared terminates the film.

In *Un Condamné à Mort s'est Échappé*, the elderly man in the adjoining cell asks the hero, querulously, "Why do you fight?" Fontaine answers, "To fight. To fight against myself." The true fight against oneself is against one's heaviness, one's gravity. And the instrument of this fight is the idea of work, a project, a task. In *Les Anges du Péché*, it is Anne-Marie's project of "saving" Thérèse. In *Les Dames du Bois de Boulogne*, it is the revenge plot of Hélène. These tasks are cast in traditional form—constantly referring back to the intention of the character who performs them, rather than decomposed into separately engrossing acts of behavior. In *Le Journal d'un Curé de Campagne* (which is transitional in this respect) the most affecting images are not those of the priest in his role, struggling for the souls of his parishioners, but of the priest in his homely moments: riding his bicycle, removing his vestments, eating bread, walking. In Bresson's next two films, work has dissolved into the idea of the-infinite-taking-of-pains. The project has become totally concrete, incarnate, and at the same time more impersonal. In *Un Condamné à Mort s'est Échappé*, the most powerful scenes are those which show the hero absorbed in his labors: Fontaine scraping at his door with the spoon, Fontaine sweeping the wood shavings which have fallen on the floor into a tiny pile with a single straw pulled from his broom. ("One month of patient work—my door opened.") In *Pickpocket*, the emotional center of the film is where Michel is wordlessly, disinterestedly, taken in hand by a professional pickpocket and initiated into the real art of what he has only practiced desultorily: difficult gestures are demonstrated, the necessity of repetition and routine is made clear. Large sections of *Un Condamné à Mort s'est Échappé* and *Pickpocket* are wordless; they are about the beauties of personality effaced by a project. The face is very quiet, while other parts of the body, represented as humble servants of projects, become expressive, transfigured. One remembers Thérèse kissing the white feet of the dead Anne-Marie at the end of *Les Anges du Péché*, the bare feet of the monks filing down the stone corridor in the opening sequence of *Procès de Jeanne d'Arc*. One remembers Fontaine's large graceful hands at their endless labors in *Un Condamné à Mort s'est Échappé*, the ballet of agile thieving hands in *Pickpocket*.

Through the "project"—exactly contrary to "imagination"— one overcomes the gravity that weighs down the spirit. Even *Les Dames du Bois de Boulogne*, whose story seems most un-Bressonian, rests on this contrast between a project and gravity (or, immobility). Hélène has a project—revenging herself on Jean. But she is immobile, too—from suffering and vengefulness. Only in *Procès de Jeanne d'Arc*, the most Bressonian of stories, is this contrast (to the detriment of the film) not exploited. Jeanne has no project. Or if she may be said to have a project, her martyrdom, we only know about it; we are not privy to its development and consummation. She *appears* to be passive. If only because Jeanne is not portrayed for us in her solitude, alone in her cell, Bresson's last film seems, next to the others, so undialectical.

6

Jean Cocteau has said (*Cocteau on the Film*, A Conversation Recorded by André Fraigneau, 1951) that minds and souls today "live without a syntax, that is to say, without a moral system. This moral system has nothing to do with morality proper, and should be built up by each one of us as an inner style, without which no outer style is possible." Cocteau's films may be understood as portraying this inwardness which is the true morality; so may Bresson's. Both are concerned, in their films, with depicting spiritual style. This similarity is less than obvious because Cocteau conceives of spiritual style aesthetically, while in at least three of his films (*Les Anges du Péché*, *Le Journal d'un Curé de Campagne*, and *Procès de Jeanne d'Arc*) Bresson seems committed to an explicit religious point of view. But the difference is not as great as it appears. Bresson's Catholicism is a language for rendering a certain vision of human action, rather than a "position" that is stated. (For contrast, compare the direct piety of Rossellini's *The Flowers of Saint Francis* and the complex debate on faith expounded in Melville's *Leon Morin, Prêtre*.) The proof of this is that Bresson is able to say the same thing without Catholicism—in his three other films. In fact, the most entirely successful of all Bresson's films—*Un Condamné à Mort s'est Échappé*—is one which, while it has a sensitive and intelligent priest in the background (one of the prisoners), bypasses the religious way of posing the problem. The religious vocation supplies one setting for ideas about gravity, lucidity, and martyrdom. But the drastically secular subjects of crime, the revenge of betrayed love, and solitary imprisonment also yield the same themes.

Bresson is really more like Cocteau than appears—an ascetic Cocteau, Cocteau divesting himself of sensuousness, Cocteau without poetry. The aim is the same: to build up an image of spiritual style. But the sensibility, needless to say, is altogether different. Cocteau's is a clear example of the homosexual sensibility that is one of the principal traditions of modern art: both romantic and witty, langorously drawn to physical beauty and yet always decorating itself with stylishness and artifice. Bresson's sensibility is anti-romantic and solemn, pledged to ward off the easy pleasures of physical beauty and artifice for a pleasure which is more permanent, more edifying, more sincere.

In the evolution of this sensibility, Bresson's cinematic means become more and more chaste. His first two films, which were photographed by Philippe Agostini, stress visual effects in a way that the other four do not. Bresson's very first film, *Les Anges du Péché*, is more conventionally beautiful than any which have followed. And in *Les Dames du Bois de Boulogne*, whose beauty is more muted, there are lyrical camera movements, like the shot which follows Hélène running down the stairs to arrive at the same time as Jean, who is descending in an elevator, and stunning cuts, like the one which moves from Hélène alone in her bedroom, stretched out on the bed, saying, "I will be revenged," to the first shot of Agnès, in a crowded nightclub, wearing tights and net stockings and top hat, in the throes of a sexy dance. Extremes of black and white succeed one another with great deliberateness. In *Les Anges du Péché*, the darkness of the prison scene is set off by the whiteness of the convent wall and of the nuns' robes. In *Les Dames du Bois de Boulogne*, the contrasts are set by clothes even more than by interiors. Hélène always wears long black velvet dresses, whatever the occasion. Agnès has three costumes: the scant black dancing outfit in which she appears the first time, the light-colored trench-coat she wears during most of the film, and the white wedding dress at the end. . . . The last four films, which were photographed by L. H. Burel, are much less striking visually, less chic. The photography is almost self-effacing. Sharp contrasts, as between black and white, are avoided. (It is almost impossible to imagine a Bresson film in color.) In *Le Journal d'un Curé de Campagne*, for instance, one is not particularly aware of the blackness of the priest's habit. One barely notices the bloodstained shirt and dirty pants which Fontaine has on throughout *Un Condamné à Mort s'est Échappé*, or the drab suits which Michel wears in *Pickpocket*. Clothes and interiors are as neutral, inconspicuous, functional as possible.

Besides refusing the visual, Bresson's later films also renounce "the beautiful." None of his non-professional actors are handsome in an outward sense. One's first feeling, when seeing Claude Laydu (the priest in *Le Journal d'un Curé de Campagne*), François Leterrier (Fontaine in *Un Condamné à Mort s'est Échappé*), Martin Lassalle (Michel in *Pickpocket*), and Florence Carrez (Jeanne in *Procès de Jeanne d'Arc*), is how plain they are. Then, at some point or other, one begins to see the face as strikingly beautiful. The transformation is most profound, and satisfying, with François Leterrier as Fontaine. Here lies an important difference between the films of Cocteau and Bresson, a difference which indicates the special place of *Les Dames du Bois de Boulogne* in Bresson's work; for this film (for which Cocteau wrote the dialogue) is in this respect very Cocteauish.

Maria Casarès' black-garbed demonic Hélène is, visually and emotionally, of a piece with her brilliant performance in Cocteau's *Orphée* (1950). Such a hard-edge character, a character with a "motive" that remains constant throughout the story, is very different from the treatment of character, typical of Bresson, in *Le Journal d'un Curé de Campagne, Un Condamné à Mort s'est Échappé*, and *Pickpocket*. In the course of each of these three films, there is a subliminal revelation: a face which at first seems plain reveals itself to be beautiful; a character which at first seems opaque becomes oddly and inexplicably transparent. But in Cocteau's films—and in *Les Dames du Bois de Boulogne*—neither character nor beauty is revealed. They are there to be assumed, to be transposed into drama.

While the spiritual style of Cocteau's heroes (who are played, usually, by Jean Marais) tends toward narcissism, the spiritual style of Bresson's heroes is one variety or other of unself-consciousness. (Hence the role of the project in Bresson's films: it absorbs the energies that would otherwise be spent on the self. It effaces personality, in the sense of personality as what is idiosyncratic in each human being, the limit inside which we are locked.) Consciousness of self is the "gravity" that burdens the spirit; the surpassing of the consciousness of self is "grace," or spiritual lightness. The climax of Cocteau's films is a voluptuous movement: a falling down, either in love (*Orphée*) or death (*L'Aigle à Deux Têtes, L'Éternel Retour*); or a soaring up (*La Belle et la Bête*). With the exception of *Les Dames du Bois de Boulogne* (with its final glamorous image, shot from above, of Jean bending over Agnès, who lies on the floor like a great white bird), the end of Bresson's films is counter-voluptuous, reserved.

While Cocteau's art is irresistibly drawn to the logic of dreams, and to the truth of invention over the truth of "real life," Bresson's art moves increasingly away from the story and toward documentary. *Le Journal d'un Curé de Campagne* is a fiction, drawn from the superb novel of the same name by Georges Bernanos. But the journal device allows Bresson to relate the fiction in a quasi-documentary fashion. The film opens with a shot of a notebook and a hand writing in it, followed by a voice on the sound track reading what has been written. Many scenes start with the priest writing in his journal. The film ends with a letter from a friend to the Vicar of Torcy relating the priest's death—we hear the words while the whole screen is occupied with the silhouette of a cross. Before *Un Condamné à Mort s'est Échappé* begins we read the words on the screen: "This story actually happened. I have set it down without embellishment," and then: "Lyons, 1943." (Bresson had the original of Fontaine constantly present while the film was being made, to check on its accuracy.) *Pickpocket*, again a fiction, is told—partly—through journal form. Bresson returned to documentary in *Procès de Jeanne d'Arc*, this time with the greatest severity. Even music, which aided in setting tone in the earlier films, has been discarded. The use of the Mozart Mass in C minor in *Un Condamné à Mort s'est Échappé*, of Lully in *Pickpocket*, is particularly brilliant; but all that survives of music in *Procès de Jeanne d'Arc* is the drum beat at the opening of the film.

Bresson's attempt is to insist on the irrefutability of what he is presenting. Nothing happens by chance; there are no alternatives, no fantasy; everything is inexorable. Whatever is not necessary, whatever is merely anecdotal or decorative, must be left out. Unlike Cocteau, Bresson wishes to pare down—rather than to enlarge—the dramatic and visual resources of the cinema. (In this, Bresson again reminds one of Ozu, who in the course of his thirty years of film-making renounced the moving camera, the dissolve, the fade.) True, in the last, most ascetic of all his films, Bresson seems to have left out too much, to have over-refined his conception. But a conception as ambitious as this cannot help but have its extremism, and Bresson's "failures" are worth more than most directors' successes. For Bresson, art is the discovery of what is necessary—of that, and nothing more. The power of Bresson's six films lies in the fact that his purity and fastidiousness are not just an assertion about the resources of the cinema, as much of modern painting is mainly a comment in paint about painting. They are at the same time an idea about life, about what Cocteau called "inner style," about the most serious way of being human.

(1964)

Godard's Vivre Sa Vie

PREFACE: Vivre Sa Vie *invites a rather theoretical treatment, because it is—intellectually, aesthetically—extremely complex. Godard's films are about ideas, in the best, purest, most sophisticated sense in which a work of art can be "about" ideas. I have discovered, while writing these notes, that in an interview in the Paris weekly,* L'Express, *July 27, 1961, he said: "My three films all have, at bottom, the same subject. I take an individual who has an idea, and who tries to go to the end of his idea." Godard said this after he had made, besides a number of short films,* À Bout de Souffle *(1959) with Jean Seberg and Jean-Paul Belmondo,* Le Petit Soldat *(1960) with Michel Subor and Anna Karina, and* Une Femme est Une Femme *(1961) with Karina, Belmondo, and Jean-Claude Brialy. How this is true of* Vivre Sa Vie, *his fourth film, which he made in 1962, is what I have attempted to show.*

NOTE: *Godard, who was born in Paris in 1930, has now completed ten feature films. After the four mentioned above, he made* Les Carabiniers *(1962–63) with Marino Mase and Albert Juross,* Le Mépris *(1963) with Brigitte Bardot, Jack Palance, and Fritz Lang,* Bande à Part *(1964) with Karina, Sami Frey, and Claude Brasseur,* Une Femme Mariée *(1964) with Macha Méril and Bernard Noël,* Alphaville *(1965) with Karina, Eddie Constantine, and Akim Tamiroff, and* Pierrot le Fou *(1965) with Karina and Belmondo. Six of the films have been shown in America. The first called* Breathless *here, is by now established as an art-house classic; the eighth,* The Married Woman, *has had a mixed reception; but the others, under the titles* A Woman Is a Woman, My Life to Live, Contempt, *and* Band of Outsiders, *have been both critical and box-office flops. The brilliance of* À Bout de Souffle *is now obvious to everybody and I shall explain my esteem for* Vivre Sa Vie. *While I am not claiming that all his other work is on the same level of excellence, there is no film of Godard's which does not have many remarkable passages of the highest quality. The obtuseness of serious critics here to the merits of* Le Mépris, *a deeply flawed but nonetheless extraordinarily ambitious and original film, seems to me particularly lamentable.*

I

"The cinema is still a form of graphic art," Cocteau wrote in his *Journals*. "Through its mediation, I write in pictures, and secure for my own ideology a power in actual fact. I show what others tell. In *Orphée*, for example, I do not narrate the passing through mirrors; I show it, and in some manner, I prove it. The means I use are not important, if my characters perform publicly what I want them to perform. The greatest power of a film is to be indisputable with respect to the actions it determines and which are carried out before our eyes. It is normal for the witness of an action to transform it for his own use, to distort it, and to testify to it inaccurately. But the action was carried out, and is carried out as often as the machine resurrects it. It combats inexact testimonies and false police reports."

2

All art may be treated as a mode of proof, an assertion of accuracy in the spirit of maximum vehemence. Any work of art may be seen as an attempt to be indisputable with respect to the actions it represents.

3

Proof differs from analysis. Proof establishes that something happened. Analysis shows why it happened. Proof is a mode of argument that is, by definition, complete; but the price of its completeness is that proof is always formal. Only what is already contained in the beginning is proven at the end. In analysis, however, there are always further angles of understanding, new realms of causality. Analysis is substantive. Analysis is a mode of argument that is, by definition, always incomplete; it is, properly speaking, interminable.

The extent to which a given work of art is designed as a mode of proof is, of course, a matter of proportion. Surely, some works of art are more directed toward proof, more based on considerations of form, than others. But still, I should argue, all art tends toward the formal, toward a completeness that must be formal rather than substantive—endings that exhibit grace and design, and only secondarily convince in terms of psychological motives or social forces. (Think of the barely credible but immensely satisfying endings of most of Shakespeare's plays, particularly the comedies.) In great art, it is form—or, as I call it here, the desire to prove rather than the desire to analyze—that is ultimately sovereign. It is form that allows one to terminate.

4

An art concerned with proof is formal in two senses. Its subject is the form (above and beyond the matter) of events, and the forms (above and beyond the matter) of consciousness. Its means are formal; that is, they include a conspicuous element of design (symmetry, repetition, inversion, doubling, etc.). This can be true even when the work is so laden with "content" that it virtually proclaims itself as didactic—like Dante's *Divine Comedy*.

5

Godard's films are particularly directed toward proof, rather than analysis. *Vivre Sa Vie* is an exhibit, a demonstration. It shows that something happened, not *why* it happened. It exposes the inexorability of an event.

For this reason, despite appearances, Godard's films are drastically untopical. An art concerned with social, topical issues can never simply show that something is. It must indicate *how*. It must show *why*. But the whole point of *Vivre Sa Vie* is that it does not explain anything. It rejects causality. (Thus, the ordinary causal sequence of narrative is broken in Godard's film by the extremely arbitrary decomposition of the story into twelve episodes—episodes which are serially, rather than causally, related.) *Vivre Sa Vie* is certainly not "about" prostitution, any more than *Le Petit Soldat* is "about" the Algerian War. Neither does Godard in *Vivre Sa Vie* give us any explanation, of an ordinary recognizable sort, as to what led the principal character, Nana, ever to become a prostitute. Is it because she couldn't borrow 2,000 francs toward her back rent from her former husband or from one of her fellow clerks at the record store in which she works and was locked out of her apartment? Hardly that. At least, not that alone. But we scarcely know any more than this. All Godard shows us is that she did become a prostitute. Again, Godard does not show us why, at the end of the film, Nana's pimp Raoul "sells" her, or what has happened between them, or what lies behind the final gun battle in the street in which Nana is killed. He only shows us that she is sold, that she does die. He does not analyze. He proves.

6

Godard uses two means of proof in *Vivre Sa Vie*. He gives us a collection of images illustrating what he wants to prove, and a series of "texts" explaining it. In keeping the two elements separate, Godard's film employs a genuinely novel means of exposition.

7

Godard's intention is Cocteau's. But Godard discerns difficulties, where Cocteau saw none. What Cocteau wanted to show, to be indisputable with reference to, was magic—things like the reality of fascination, the eternal possibility of metamorphosis. (Passing through mirrors, etc.) What Godard wishes to show is the opposite: the anti-magical, the structure of lucidity. This is why Cocteau used techniques that, by means of the alikeness of images, bind together events—to form a total sensuous whole. Godard makes no effort to exploit the beautiful in this sense. He uses techniques that would fragment, dissociate, alienate, break up. Example: the famous staccato editing (jump cuts *et al.*) in *À Bout de Souffle*. Another example: the division of *Vivre Sa Vie* into twelve episodes, with long titles like chapter headings at the beginning of each episode, telling us more or less what is going to happen.

The rhythm of *Vivre Sa Vie* is stopping-and-starting. (In another style, this is also the rhythm of *Le Mépris*.) Hence, *Vivre Sa Vie* is divided into separate episodes. Hence, too, the repeated halting and resuming of the music in the credit sequence; and the abrupt presentation of Nana's face—first in left profile, then (without transition) full face, then (again without transition) in right profile. But, above all, there is the dissociation of word and image which runs through the entire film, permitting quite separate accumulations of intensity for both idea and feeling.

8

Throughout the history of film, image and word have worked in tandem. In the silent film, the word—set down in the form of titles—alternated with, literally linked together, the sequences of images. With the advent of sound films, image and word became simultaneous rather than successive. While in silent films the word could be either comment on the action or dialogue by the participants in the action, in sound films the word became (except for documentaries) almost exclusively, certainly preponderantly dialogue.

Godard restores the dissociation of word and image characteristic of silent film, but on a new level. *Vivre Sa Vie* is clearly composed of two discrete types of material, the seen and the heard. But in the distinguishing of these materials, Godard is very ingenious, even playful. One variant is the television documentary or *cinéma vérité* style of Episode VIII—while one is taken, first, on a car ride through Paris, then sees, in rapid montage, shots of a dozen clients, one hears a dry flat voice rapidly detailing the routine, hazards, and appalling arduousness of the prostitute's vocation. Another variant is in Episode XII, where the happy banalities exchanged by Nana and her young lover are projected on the screen in the form of subtitles. The speech of love is not *heard* at all.

9

Thus, *Vivre Sa Vie* must be seen as an extension of a particular cinematic genre: the narrated film. There are two standard forms of this genre, which gives us images plus a text. In one, an impersonal voice, the author, as it were, narrates the film. In the other, we hear the interior monologue of the main character, narrating the events as we see them happening to him.

Two examples of the first type, featuring an anonymous commenting voice which oversees the action, are Resnais' *L'Année Dernière à Marienbad* and Melville's *Les Enfants Terribles.* An example of the second type, featuring an interior monologue of the main character, is Franju's *Thérèse Desqueyroux.* Probably the greatest examples of the second type, in which the entire action is recited by the hero, are Bresson's *Le Journal d'un Curé de Campagne* and *Un Condamné à Mort s'est Échappé.*

Godard used the technique brought to perfection by Bresson in his second film, *Le Petit Soldat*, made in 1960 in Geneva though not released (because for three years it was banned by the French censors) until January 1963. The film is the sequence of the reflections of the hero, Bruno Forestier, a man embroiled in a right-wing terrorist organization who is assigned the job of killing a Swiss agent for the FLN. As the film opens, one hears Forestier's voice saying: "The time for action is passed. I have grown older. The time for reflection has come." Bruno is a photographer. He says, "To photograph a face is to photograph the soul behind it. Photography is truth. And the cinema is the truth twenty-four times a second." This central passage in *Le Petit Soldat*, in which Bruno meditates on the relation between the image and truth, anticipates the complex meditation on the relation between language and truth in *Vivre Sa Vie*.

Since the story itself in *Le Petit Soldat*, the factual connections between the characters, are mostly conveyed through Forestier's monologue, Godard's camera is freed to become an instrument of contemplation—of certain aspects of events, and of characters. Quiet "events"—Karina's face, the façade of buildings, passing through the city by car—are *studied* by the camera, in a way that somewhat isolates the violent action. The images seem arbitrary sometimes, expressing a kind of emotional neutrality; at other times, they indicate an intense involvement. It is as though Godard hears, then looks at what he hears.

In *Vivre Sa Vie*, Godard takes this technique of hearing first, then seeing, to new levels of complexity. There is no longer a single unified point of view, either the protagonist's voice (as in *Le Petit Soldat*) or a godlike narrator, but a series of documents (texts, narrations, quotations, excerpts, set pieces) of various description. These are primarily words; but they may also be wordless sounds, or even wordless images.

10

All the essentials of Godard's technique are present in the opening credit sequence and in the first episode. The credits occur over a left profile view of Nana, so dark that it is almost a silhouette. (The title of the film is *Vivre Sa Vie. A Film in Twelve*

Episodes.) As the credits continue, she is shown full face, and then from the right side, still in deep shadow. Occasionally she blinks or shifts her head slightly (as if it were uncomfortable to hold still so long), or wets her lips. Nana is posing. She is being seen.

Next we are given the first titles. "Episode I: Nana and Paul. Nana Feels Like Giving Up." Then the images begin, but the emphasis is on what is heard. The film proper opens in the midst of a conversation between Nana and a man; they are seated at the counter of a café; their backs are to the camera; besides their conversation, we hear the noises of the barman, and snatches of the voices of other customers. As they talk, always facing away from the camera, we learn that the man (Paul) is Nana's husband, that they have a child, and that she has recently left both husband and child to try to become an actress. In this brief public reunion (it is never clear on whose initiative it came about) Paul is stiff and hostile, but wants her to come back; Nana is oppressed, desperate, and revolted by him. After weary, bitter words, Nana says to Paul, "The more you talk, the less it means." Throughout this opening sequence, Godard systematically deprives the viewer. There is no crosscutting. The viewer is not allowed to see, to become involved. He is only allowed to hear.

Only after Nana and Paul break off their fruitless conversation to leave the counter and play a game at the pinball machine, do we see them. Even here, the emphasis remains on hearing. As they go on talking, we continue to see Nana and Paul mainly from behind. Paul has stopped pleading and being rancorous. He tells Nana of the droll theme his father, a schoolteacher, received from one of his pupils on an assigned topic, The Chicken. "The chicken has an inside and an outside," wrote the little girl. "Remove the outside and you find the inside. Remove the inside, and you find the soul." On these words, the image dissolves and the episode ends.

I I

The story of the chicken is the first of many "texts" in the film which establish what Godard wants to say. For the story of the chicken, of course, is the story of Nana. (There is a pun in

French—the French *poule* being something like, but a good
deal rougher than, the American "chick.") In *Vivre Sa Vie*, we
witness the stripping down of Nana. The film opens with Nana
having divested herself of her outside: her old identity. Her new
identity, within a few episodes, is to be that of a prostitute. But
Godard's interest is in neither the psychology nor the sociology
of prostitution. He takes up prostitution as the most radical
metaphor for the separating out of the elements of a life—as a
testing ground, a crucible for the study of what is essential and
what is superfluous in a life.

12

The whole of *Vivre Sa Vie* may be seen as a text. It is a text in,
a study of, lucidity; it is about seriousness.

And it "uses" texts (in the more literal sense), in all but two
of its twelve episodes. The little girl's essay on the chicken told
by Paul in Episode I. The passage from the pulp magazine
story recited by the salesgirl in Episode II. ("You exaggerate
the importance of logic.") The excerpt from Dreyer's *Jeanne
d'Arc* which Nana watches in Episode III. The story of the
theft of 1,000 francs which Nana relates to the police inspector
in Episode IV. (We learn that her full name is Nana Klein and
that she was born in 1940.) Yvette's story—how she was abandoned by Raymond two years ago—and Nana's speech in reply
("I am responsible") in Episode VI. The letter of application
Nana composes to the madam of a brothel in Episode VII. The
documentary narration of the life and routine of the prostitute
in Episode VIII. The record of dance music in Episode IX. The
conversation with the philosopher in Episode XI. The excerpt
from the story by Edgar Allan Poe ("The Oval Portrait") read
aloud by Luigi in Episode XII.

13

The most elaborate, intellectually, of all the texts in the film is
the conversation in Episode XI between Nana and a philosopher
(played by the philosopher, Brice Parain) in a café. They discuss
the nature of language. Nana asks why one can't live without
words; Parain explains that it is because talking equals thinking,

and thinking talking, and there is no life without thought. It is not a question of speaking or not speaking, but of speaking well. Speaking well demands an ascetic discipline (*une ascèse*), detachment. One has to understand, for one thing, that there is no going straight at the truth. One needs error.

Early in their conversation, Parain relates the story of Dumas' Porthos, the man of action, whose first thought killed him. (Running away from a dynamite charge he had planted, Porthos suddenly wondered how one could walk, how anyone ever placed one foot in front of the other. He stopped. The dynamite exploded. He was killed.) There is a sense in which this story, too, like the story of the chicken, is about Nana. And through both the story and the Poe tale told in the next (and last) episode, we are being prepared—formally, not substantively—for Nana's death.

14

Godard takes his motto for this film-essay on freedom and responsibility from Montaigne: "Lend yourself to others; give yourself to yourself." The life of the prostitute is, of course, the most radical metaphor for the act of lending oneself to others. But if we ask, how has Godard shown us Nana keeping herself for herself, the answer is: he has *not* shown it. He has, rather, expounded on it. We don't know Nana's motives except at a distance, by inference. The film eschews all psychology; there is no probing of states of feeling, of inner anguish.

Nana knows herself to be free, Godard tells us. But that freedom has no psychological interior. Freedom is not an inner, psychological something—but more like physical grace. It is being *what*, *who* one is. In Episode I, Nana says to Paul, "I want to die." In Episode II, we see her desperately trying to borrow money, trying unsuccessfully to force her way past the concierge and get into her own apartment. In Episode III, we see her weeping in the cinema over Jeanne d'Arc. In Episode IV, at the police station, she weeps again as she relates the humiliating incident of the theft of 1,000 francs. "I wish I were someone else," she says. But in Episode V ("On the Street. The First Client") Nana has become what she is. She has entered the road that leads to her affirmation and to her death. Only as prostitute

do we see a Nana who can affirm herself. This is the meaning of
Nana's speech to her fellow prostitute Yvette in Episode VI, in
which she declares serenely, "I am responsible. I turn my head,
I am responsible. I lift my hand, I am responsible."

Being free means being responsible. One is free, and therefore responsible, when one realizes that things are as they are.
Thus, the speech to Yvette ends with the words: "A plate is a
plate. A man is a man. Life is . . . life."

15

That freedom has no psychological interior—that the soul is
something to be found not upon but after stripping away the
"inside" of a person—is the radical spiritual doctrine which
Vivre Sa Vie illustrates.

One would guess that Godard is quite aware of the difference
between his sense of the "soul" and the traditional Christian
one. The difference is precisely underscored by the quotation
from Dreyer's *Jeanne d'Arc*; for the scene which we see is the
one in which the young priest (played by Antonin Artaud)
comes to tell Jeanne (Mlle Falconetti) that she is to be burned
at the stake. Her martyrdom, Jeanne assures the distraught
priest, is really her deliverance. While the choice of a quotation
from a film does distance our emotional involvement with these
ideas and feelings, the reference to martyrdom is not ironic in
this context. Prostitution, as *Vivre Sa Vie* allows us to see it, has
entirely the character of an ordeal. "Pleasure isn't all fun," as the
title to Episode X announces laconically. And Nana does die.

The twelve episodes of *Vivre Sa Vie* are Nana's twelve stations
of the cross. But in Godard's film the values of sanctity and martyrdom are transposed to a totally secular plane. Godard offers
us Montaigne instead of Pascal, something akin to the mood
and intensity of Bressonian spirituality but without Catholicism.

16

The one false step in *Vivre Sa Vie* comes at the end, when
Godard breaks the unity of his film by referring to it from the
outside, as maker. Episode XII begins with Nana and Luigi
in a room together; he is a young man with whom she has

apparently fallen in love (we have seen him once before, in Episode IX, when Nana meets him in a billiard parlor and flirts with him). At first the scene is silent, and the dialogue—"Shall we go out?" "Why don't you move in with me?" etc.—rendered in subtitles. Then Luigi, lying on the bed, begins to read aloud from Poe's "The Oval Portrait," a story about an artist engaged in painting a portrait of his wife; he strives for the perfect likeness, but at the moment he finally achieves it his wife dies. The scene fades out on these words, and opens to show Raoul, Nana's pimp, roughly forcing her through the courtyard of her apartment house, pushing her into a car. After a car ride (one or two brief images), Raoul hands Nana over to another pimp; but it is discovered that the money exchanged is not enough, guns are drawn, Nana is shot, and the last image shows the cars speeding away and Nana lying dead in the street.

What is objectionable here is not the abruptness of the ending. It is the fact that Godard is clearly making a reference outside the film, to the fact that the young actress who plays Nana, Anna Karina, is his wife. He is mocking his own tale, which is unforgivable. It amounts to a peculiar failure of nerve, as if Godard did not dare to let us have Nana's death—in all its horrifying arbitrariness—but had to provide, at the last moment, a kind of subliminal causality. (The woman is my wife.—The artist who portrays his wife kills her.—Nana must die.)

17

This one lapse aside, *Vivre Sa Vie* seems to me a perfect film. That is, it sets out to do something that is both noble and intricate, and wholly succeeds in doing it. Godard is perhaps the only director today who is interested in "philosophical films" and possesses an intelligence and discretion equal to the task. Other directors have had their "views" on contemporary society and the nature of our humanity; and sometimes their films survive the ideas they propose. Godard is the first director fully to grasp the fact that, in order to deal seriously with ideas, one must create a new film language for expressing them—if the ideas are to have any suppleness and complexity. This he has been trying to do in different ways: in *Le Petit Soldat*, *Vivre Sa Vie*, *Les Carabiniers*, *Le Mépris*, *Une Femme Mariée*, and

Alphaville—Vivre Sa Vie being, I think, his most successful film. For this conception, and the formidable body of work in which he has pursued it, Godard is in my opinion the most important director to have emerged in the last ten years.

APPENDIX: The advertisement drawn up by Godard when the film was first released in Paris:

VIVRE SA VIE

Un	Une
Film	Série
Sur	D'Aventures
La	Qui
Prostitution	Lui
Qui	Font
Raconte	Connaître
Comment	Tous
Une	Les
Jeune	Sentiments
Et	Humains
Jolie	Profonds
Vendeuse	Possibles
Parisienne	Et
Donne	Qui
Son	Ont
Corps	Eté
Mais	Filmés
Garde	Par
Son	Jean-Luc
Ame	Godard
Alors	Et
Qu'elle	Joués
Traverse	Par
Comme	Anna Karina
Des	Vivre
Apparences	Sa Vie

(1964)

The Imagination of Disaster

THE typical science fiction film has a form as predictable as a Western, and is made up of elements which, to a practiced eye, are as classic as the saloon brawl, the blonde schoolteacher from the East, and the gun duel on the deserted main street.

One model scenario proceeds through five phases.

(1) The arrival of the thing. (Emergence of the monsters, landing of the alien spaceship, etc.) This is usually witnessed or suspected by just one person, a young scientist on a field trip. Nobody, neither his neighbors nor his colleagues, will believe him for some time. The hero is not married, but has a sympathetic though also incredulous girl friend.

(2) Confirmation of the hero's report by a host of witnesses to a great act of destruction. (If the invaders are beings from another planet, a fruitless attempt to parley with them and get them to leave peacefully.) The local police are summoned to deal with the situation and massacred.

(3) In the capital of the country, conferences between scientists and the military take place, with the hero lecturing before a chart, map, or blackboard. A national emergency is declared. Reports of further destruction. Authorities from other countries arrive in black limousines. All international tensions are suspended in view of the planetary emergency. This stage often includes a rapid montage of news broadcasts in various languages, a meeting at the UN, and more conferences between the military and the scientists. Plans are made for destroying the enemy.

(4) Further atrocities. At some point the hero's girl friend is in grave danger. Massive counter-attacks by international forces, with brilliant displays of rocketry, rays, and other advanced weapons, are all unsuccessful. Enormous military casualties, usually by incineration. Cities are destroyed and/or evacuated. There is an obligatory scene here of panicked crowds stampeding along a highway or a big bridge, being waved on by numerous policemen who, if the film is Japanese, are immaculately white-gloved, preternaturally calm, and call out in dubbed English, "Keep moving. There is no need to be alarmed."

(5) More conferences, whose motif is: "They must be vulnerable to something." Throughout the hero has been working in

his lab to this end. The final strategy, upon which all hopes depend, is drawn up; the ultimate weapon—often a super-powerful, as yet untested, nuclear device—is mounted. Countdown. Final repulse of the monster or invaders. Mutual congratulations, while the hero and girl friend embrace cheek to cheek and scan the skies sturdily. "But have we seen the last of them?"

The film I have just described should be in color and on a wide screen. Another typical scenario, which follows, is simpler and suited to black-and-white films with a lower budget. It has four phases.

(1) The hero (usually, but not always, a scientist) and his girl friend, or his wife and two children, are disporting themselves in some innocent ultra-normal middle-class surroundings—their house in a small town, or on vacation (camping, boating). Suddenly, someone starts behaving strangely; or some innocent form of vegetation becomes monstrously enlarged and ambulatory. If a character is pictured driving an automobile, something gruesome looms up in the middle of the road. If it is night, strange lights hurtle across the sky.

(2) After following the thing's tracks, or determining that It is radioactive, or poking around a huge crater—in short, conducting some sort of crude investigation—the hero tries to warn the local authorities, without effect; nobody believes anything is amiss. The hero knows better. If the thing is tangible, the house is elaborately barricaded. If the invading alien is an invisible parasite, a doctor or friend is called in, who is himself rather quickly killed or "taken possession of" by the thing.

(3) The advice of whoever further is consulted proves useless. Meanwhile, It continues to claim other victims in the town, which remains implausibly isolated from the rest of the world. General helplessness.

(4) One of two possibilities. Either the hero prepares to do battle alone, accidentally discovers the thing's one vulnerable point, and destroys it. Or, he somehow manages to get out of town and succeeds in laying his case before competent authorities. They, along the lines of the first script but abridged, deploy a complex technology which (after initial setbacks) finally prevails against the invaders.

———

Another version of the second script opens with the scientist-hero in his laboratory, which is located in the basement or on the grounds of his tasteful, prosperous house. Through his experiments, he unwittingly causes a frightful metamorphosis in some class of plants or animals which turn carnivorous and go on a rampage. Or else, his experiments have caused him to be injured (sometimes irrevocably) or "invaded" himself. Perhaps he has been experimenting with radiation, or has built a machine to communicate with beings from other planets or transport him to other places or times.

Another version of the first script involves the discovery of some fundamental alteration in the conditions of existence of our planet, brought about by nuclear testing, which will lead to the extinction in a few months of all human life. For example: the temperature of the earth is becoming too high or too low to support life, or the earth is cracking in two, or it is gradually being blanketed by lethal fallout.

A third script, somewhat but not altogether different from the first two, concerns a journey through space—to the moon, or some other planet. What the space-voyagers discover commonly is that the alien terrain is in a state of dire emergency, itself threatened by extra-planetary invaders or nearing extinction through the practice of nuclear warfare. The terminal dramas of the first and second scripts are played out there, to which is added the problem of getting away from the doomed and/or hostile planet and back to Earth.

I am aware, of course, that there are thousands of science fiction novels (their heyday was the late 1940s), not to mention the transcriptions of science fiction themes which, more and more, provide the principal subject-matter of comic books. But I propose to discuss science fiction films (the present period began in 1950 and continues, considerably abated, to this day) as an independent sub-genre, without reference to other media—and, most particularly, without reference to the novels from which, in many cases, they were adapted. For, while novel and film may share the same plot, the fundamental difference between the resources of the novel and the film makes them quite dissimilar.

Certainly, compared with the science fiction novels, their film counterparts have unique strengths, one of which is the

immediate representation of the extraordinary: physical deformity and mutation, missile and rocket combat, toppling skyscrapers. The movies are, naturally, weak just where the science
fiction novels (some of them) are strong—on science. But in
place of an intellectual work-out, they can supply something the
novels can never provide—sensuous elaboration. In the films it
is by means of images and sounds, not words that have to be
translated by the imagination, that one can participate in the
fantasy of living through one's own death and more, the death
of cities, the destruction of humanity itself.

Science fiction films are not about science. They are about
disaster, which is one of the oldest subjects of art. In science
fiction films disaster is rarely viewed intensively; it is always extensive. It is a matter of quantity and ingenuity. If you will, it is
a question of scale. But the scale, particularly in the wide-screen
color films (of which the ones by the Japanese director Inoshiro
Honda and the American director George Pal are technically
the most convincing and visually the most exciting), does raise
the matter to another level.

Thus, the science fiction film (like that of a very different
contemporary genre, the Happening) is concerned with the
aesthetics of destruction, with the peculiar beauties to be found
in wreaking havoc, making a mess. And it is in the imagery of
destruction that the core of a good science fiction film lies.
Hence, the disadvantage of the cheap film—in which the monster appears or the rocket lands in a small dull-looking town.
(Hollywood budget needs usually dictate that the town be in
the Arizona or California desert. In *The Thing From Another
World* [1951] the rather sleazy and confined set is supposed to
be an encampment near the North Pole.) Still, good black-
and-white science fiction films have been made. But a bigger
budget, which usually means color, allows a much greater play
back and forth among several model environments. There is
the populous city. There is the lavish but ascetic interior of a
spaceship—either the invaders' or ours—replete with stream-
lined chromium fixtures and dials and machines whose complexity is indicated by the number of colored lights they flash
and strange noises they emit. There is the laboratory crowded
with formidable boxes and scientific apparatus. There is a comparatively old-fashioned-looking conference room, where the
scientists unfurl charts to explain the desperate state of things to

the military. And each of these standard locales or backgrounds is subject to two modalities—intact and destroyed. We may, if we are lucky, be treated to a panorama of melting tanks, flying bodies, crashing walls, awesome craters and fissures in the earth, plummeting spacecraft, colorful deadly rays; and to a symphony of screams, weird electronic signals, the noisiest military hardware going, and the leaden tones of the laconic denizens of alien planets and their subjugated earthlings.

Certain of the primitive gratifications of science fiction films—for instance, the depiction of urban disaster on a colossally magnified scale—are shared with other types of films. Visually there is little difference between mass havoc as represented in the old horror and monster films and what we find in science fiction films, except (again) scale. In the old monster films, the monster always headed for the great city, where he had to do a fair bit of rampaging, hurling busses off bridges, crumpling trains in his bare hands, toppling buildings, and so forth. The archetype is King Kong, in Schoedsack and Cooper's great film of 1933, running amok, first in the native village (trampling babies, a bit of footage excised from most prints), then in New York. This is really no different in spirit from the scene in Inoshiro Honda's *Rodan* (1957) in which two giant reptiles—with a wingspan of 500 feet and supersonic speeds—by flapping their wings whip up a cyclone that blows most of Tokyo to smithereens. Or the destruction of half of Japan by the gigantic robot with the great incinerating ray that shoots forth from his eyes, at the beginning of Honda's *The Mysterians* (1959). Or, the devastation by the rays from a fleet of flying saucers of New York, Paris, and Tokyo, in *Battle in Outer Space* (1960). Or, the inundation of New York in *When Worlds Collide* (1951). Or, the end of London in 1966 depicted in George Pal's *The Time Machine* (1960). Neither do these sequences differ in aesthetic intention from the destruction scenes in the big sword, sandal, and orgy color spectaculars set in Biblical and Roman times—the end of Sodom in Aldrich's *Sodom and Gomorrah*, of Gaza in De Mille's *Samson and Delilah*, of Rhodes in *The Colossus of Rhodes*, and of Rome in a dozen Nero movies. Griffith began it with the Babylon sequence in *Intolerance*, and to this day there is nothing like the thrill of watching all those expensive sets come tumbling down.

In other respects as well, the science fiction films of the 1950s take up familiar themes. The famous 1930s movie serials and comics of the adventures of Flash Gordon and Buck Rogers, as well as the more recent spate of comic book super-heroes with extraterrestrial origins (the most famous is Superman, a found-ling from the planet Krypton, currently described as having been exploded by a nuclear blast), share motifs with more recent science fiction movies. But there is an important difference. The old science fiction films, and most of the comics, still have an essentially innocent relation to disaster. Mainly they offer new versions of the oldest romance of all—of the strong invulner-able hero with a mysterious lineage come to do battle on behalf of good and against evil. Recent science fiction films have a decided grimness, bolstered by their much greater degree of visual credibility, which contrasts strongly with the older films. Modern historical reality has greatly enlarged the imagination of disaster, and the protagonists—perhaps by the very nature of what is visited upon them—no longer seem wholly innocent.

The lure of such generalized disaster as a fantasy is that it releases one from normal obligations. The trump card of the end-of-the-world movies—like *The Day the Earth Caught Fire* (1962)—is that great scene with New York or London or Tokyo discovered empty, its entire population annihilated. Or, as in *The World, The Flesh, and The Devil* (1957), the whole movie can be devoted to the fantasy of occupying the deserted metropolis and starting all over again, a world Robinson Crusoe.

Another kind of satisfaction these films supply is extreme moral simplification—that is to say, a morally acceptable fantasy where one can give outlet to cruel or at least amoral feelings. In this respect, science fiction films partly overlap with horror films. This is the undeniable pleasure we derive from looking at freaks, beings excluded from the category of the human. The sense of superiority over the freak conjoined in varying propor-tions with the titillation of fear and aversion makes it possible for moral scruples to be lifted, for cruelty to be enjoyed. The same thing happens in science fiction films. In the figure of the monster from outer space, the freakish, the ugly, and the preda-tory all converge—and provide a fantasy target for righteous bellicosity to discharge itself, and for the aesthetic enjoyment of suffering and disaster. Science fiction films are one of the purest forms of spectacle; that is, we are rarely inside anyone's feelings.

(An exception is Jack Arnold's *The Incredible Shrinking Man* [1957].) We are merely spectators; we watch.

But in science fiction films, unlike horror films, there is not much horror. Suspense, shocks, surprises are mostly abjured in favor of a steady, inexorable plot. Science fiction films invite a dispassionate, aesthetic view of destruction and violence—a *technological* view. Things, objects, machinery play a major role in these films. A greater range of ethical values is embodied in the décor of these films than in the people. Things, rather than the helpless humans, are the locus of values because we experience them, rather than people, as the sources of power. According to science fiction films, man is naked without his artifacts. *They* stand for different values, they are potent, they are what get destroyed, and they are the indispensable tools for the repulse of the alien invaders or the repair of the damaged environment.

The science fiction films are strongly moralistic. The standard message is the one about the proper, or humane, use of science, versus the mad, obsessional use of science. This message the science fiction films share in common with the classic horror films of the 1930s, like *Frankenstein, The Mummy, Island of Lost Souls, Dr. Jekyll and Mr. Hyde*. (Georges Franju's brilliant *Les Yeux Sans Visage* [1959], called here *The Horror Chamber of Doctor Faustus*, is a more recent example.) In the horror films, we have the mad or obsessed or misguided scientist who pursues his experiments against good advice to the contrary, creates a monster or monsters, and is himself destroyed—often recognizing his folly himself, and dying in the successful effort to destroy his own creation. One science fiction equivalent of this is the scientist, usually a member of a team, who defects to the planetary invaders because "their" science is more advanced than "ours."

This is the case in *The Mysterians*, and, true to form, the ren-egade sees his error in the end, and from within the Mysterian space ship destroys it and himself. In *This Island Earth* (1955), the inhabitants of the beleaguered planet Metaluna propose to conquer earth, but their project is foiled by a Metalunan scientist named Exeter who, having lived on earth a while and learned to love Mozart, cannot abide such viciousness. Exeter

plunges his spaceship into the ocean after returning a glamorous pair (male and female) of American physicists to earth. Metaluna dies. In *The Fly* (1958), the hero, engrossed in his base-
ment-laboratory experiments on a matter-transmitting machine,
uses himself as a subject, exchanges head and one arm with a
housefly which had accidentally gotten into the machine, becomes a monster, and with his last shred of human will destroys
his laboratory and orders his wife to kill him. His discovery, for
the good of mankind, is lost.

Being a clearly labeled species of intellectual, scientists in science fiction films are always liable to crack up or go off the deep
end. In *Conquest of Space* (1955), the scientist-commander of
an international expedition to Mars suddenly acquires scruples
about the blasphemy involved in the undertaking, and begins
reading the Bible mid-journey instead of attending to his duties.
The commander's son, who is his junior officer and always addresses his father as "General," is forced to kill the old man
when he tries to prevent the ship from landing on Mars. In
this film, both sides of the ambivalence toward scientists are
given voice. Generally, for a scientific enterprise to be treated
entirely sympathetically in these films, it needs the certificate of
utility. Science, viewed without ambivalence, means an efficacious response to danger. Disinterested intellectual curiosity
rarely appears in any form other than caricature, as a maniacal
dementia that cuts one off from normal human relations. But
this suspicion is usually directed at the scientist rather than his
work. The creative scientist may become a martyr to his own
discovery, through an accident or by pushing things too far. But
the implication remains that other men, less imaginative—in
short, technicians—could have administered the same discovery better and more safely. The most ingrained contemporary
mistrust of the intellect is visited, in these movies, upon the
scientist-as-intellectual.

The message that the scientist is one who releases forces
which, if not controlled for good, could destroy man himself
seems innocuous enough. One of the oldest images of the
scientist is Shakespeare's Prospero, the overdetached scholar
forcibly retired from society to a desert island, only partly in
control of the magic forces in which he dabbles. Equally classic is the figure of the scientist as satanist (*Doctor Faustus*, and
stories of Poe and Hawthorne). Science is magic, and man has

always known that there is black magic as well as white. But it is not enough to remark that contemporary attitudes—as reflected in science fiction films—remain ambivalent, that the scientist is treated as both satanist and savior. The proportions have changed, because of the new context in which the old admiration and fear of the scientist are located. For his sphere of influence is no longer local, himself or his immediate community. It is planetary, cosmic.

One gets the feeling, particularly in the Japanese films but not only there, that a mass trauma exists over the use of nuclear weapons and the possibility of future nuclear wars. Most of the science fiction films bear witness to this trauma, and, in a way, attempt to exorcise it.

The accidental awakening of the super-destructive monster who has slept in the earth since prehistory is, often, an obvious metaphor for the Bomb. But there are many explicit references as well. In *The Mysterians*, a probe ship from the planet Mysteroid has landed on earth, near Tokyo. Nuclear warfare having been practiced on Mysteroid for centuries (their civilization is "more advanced than ours"), ninety percent of those now born on the planet have to be destroyed at birth, because of defects caused by the huge amounts of Strontium 90 in their diet. The Mysterians have come to earth to marry earth women, and possibly to take over our relatively uncontaminated planet. . . . In *The Incredible Shrinking Man*, the John Doe hero is the victim of a gust of radiation which blows over the water, while he is out boating with his wife; the radiation causes him to grow smaller and smaller, until at the end of the movie he steps through the fine mesh of a window screen to become "the infinitely small." . . . In *Rodan*, a horde of monstrous carnivorous prehistoric insects, and finally a pair of giant flying reptiles (the prehistoric Archeopteryx), are hatched from dormant eggs in the depths of a mine shaft by the impact of nuclear test explosions, and go on to destroy a good part of the world before they are felled by the molten lava of a volcanic eruption. . . . In the English film, *The Day the Earth Caught Fire*, two simultaneous hydrogen bomb tests by the United States and Russia change by 11 degrees the tilt of the earth on its axis and alter the earth's orbit so that it begins to approach the sun.

Radiation casualties—ultimately, the conception of the whole

world as a casualty of nuclear testing and nuclear warfare—is
the most ominous of all the notions with which science fiction films deal. Universes become expendable. Worlds become
contaminated, burnt out, exhausted, obsolete. In *Rocketship
X-M* (1950) explorers from the earth land on Mars, where they
learn that atomic warfare has destroyed Martian civilization.
In George Pal's *The War of the Worlds* (1953), reddish spindly
alligator-skinned creatures from Mars invade the earth because
their planet is becoming too cold to be inhabitable. In *This
Island Earth*, also American, the planet Metaluna, whose population has long ago been driven underground by warfare, is
dying under the missile attacks of an enemy planet. Stocks of
uranium, which power the force field shielding Metaluna, have
been used up; and an unsuccessful expedition is sent to earth to
enlist earth scientists to devise new sources for nuclear power.
In Joseph Losey's *The Damned* (1961), nine icy-cold radioactive
children are being reared by a fanatical scientist in a dark cave
on the English coast to be the only survivors of the inevitable
nuclear Armageddon.

There is a vast amount of wishful thinking in science fiction
films, some of it touching, some of it depressing. Again and
again, one detects the hunger for a "good war," which poses
no moral problems, admits of no moral qualifications. The
imagery of science fiction films will satisfy the most bellicose
addict of war films, for a lot of the satisfactions of war films
pass, untransformed, into science fiction films. Examples: the
dogfights between earth "fighter rockets" and alien spacecraft
in the *Battle in Outer Space* (1960); the escalating firepower
in the successive assaults upon the invaders in *The Mysterians*,
which Dan Talbot correctly described as a non-stop holocaust;
the spectacular bombardment of the underground fortress of
Metaluna in *This Island Earth*.

Yet at the same time the bellicosity of science fiction films
is neatly channeled into the yearning for peace, or for at least
peaceful coexistence. Some scientist generally takes sententious
note of the fact that it took the planetary invasion to make the
warring nations of the earth come to their senses and suspend
their own conflicts. One of the main themes of many science fiction films—the color ones usually, because they have the budget

and resources to develop the military spectacle—is this UN fantasy, a fantasy of united warfare. (The same wishful UN theme cropped up in a recent spectacular which is not science fiction, *Fifty-Five Days in Peking* [1963]. There, topically enough, the Chinese, the Boxers, play the role of Martian invaders who unite the earthmen, in this case the United States, England, Russia, France, Germany, Italy, and Japan.) A great enough disaster cancels all enmities and calls upon the utmost concentration of earth resources.

Science—technology—is conceived of as the great unifier. Thus the science fiction films also project a Utopian fantasy. In the classic models of Utopian thinking—Plato's Republic, Campanella's City of the Sun, More's Utopia, Swift's land of the Houyhnhnms, Voltaire's Eldorado—society had worked out a perfect consensus. In these societies reasonableness had achieved an unbreakable supremacy over the emotions. Since no disagreement or social conflict was intellectually plausible, none was possible. As in Melville's *Typee*, "they all think the same." The universal rule of reason meant universal agreement. It is interesting, too, that societies in which reason was pictured as totally ascendant were also traditionally pictured as having an ascetic or materially frugal and economically simple mode of life. But in the Utopian world community projected by science fiction films, totally pacified and ruled by scientific consensus, the demand for simplicity of material existence would be absurd.

Yet alongside the hopeful fantasy of moral simplification and international unity embodied in the science fiction films lurk the deepest anxieties about contemporary existence. I don't mean only the very real trauma of the Bomb—that it has been used, that there are enough now to kill everyone on earth many times over, that those new bombs may very well be used. Besides these new anxieties about physical disaster, the prospect of universal mutilation and even annihilation, the science fiction films reflect powerful anxieties about the condition of the individual psyche.

For science fiction films may also be described as a popular mythology for the contemporary *negative* imagination about the impersonal. The other-world creatures that seek to take "us" over are an "it," not a "they." The planetary invaders are usually zombie-like. Their movements are either cool, mechanical, or lumbering, blobby. But it amounts to the same thing. If they are non-human in form, they proceed with an absolutely regular, unalterable movement (unalterable save by destruction). If they are human in form—dressed in space suits, etc.— then they obey the most rigid military discipline, and display no personal characteristics whatsoever. And it is this regime of emotionlessness, of impersonality, of regimentation, which they will impose on the earth if they are successful. "No more love, no more beauty, no more pain," boasts a converted earthling in *The Invasion of the Body Snatchers* (1956). The half-earthling, half-alien children in *The Children of the Damned* (1960) are absolutely emotionless, move as a group and understand each other's thoughts, and are all prodigious intellects. They are the wave of the future, man in his next stage of development.

These alien invaders practice a crime which is worse than murder. They do not simply kill the person. They obliterate him. In *The War of the Worlds*, the ray which issues from the rocket ship disintegrates all persons and objects in its path, leaving no trace of them but a light ash. In Honda's *The H-Man* (1959), the creeping blob melts all flesh with which it comes in contact. If the blob, which looks like a huge hunk of red Jello and can crawl across floors and up and down walls, so much as touches your bare foot, all that is left of you is a heap of clothes on the floor. (A more articulated, size-multiplying blob is the villain in the English film *The Creeping Unknown* [1956].) In another version of this fantasy, the body is preserved but the person is entirely reconstituted as the automatized servant or agent of the alien powers. This is, of course, the vampire fantasy in new dress. The person is really dead, but he doesn't know it. He is "undead," he has become an "unperson." It happens to a whole California town in *The Invasion of the Body Snatchers*, to several earth scientists in *This Island Earth*, and to assorted innocents in *It Came From Outer Space*, *Attack of the Puppet People* (1958), and *The Brain Eaters* (1958). As the victim always backs away from the vampire's horrifying embrace, so in science fiction films the person always fights being "taken over"; he wants to retain his humanity. But once the deed has been done, the victim is eminently satisfied with his condition. He has not been converted from human amiability to monstrous "animal" bloodlust (a metaphoric exaggeration of sexual desire), as in the old vampire fantasy. No, he has simply become far more efficient—the very model of technocratic man, purged of emotions, volitionless, tranquil, obedient to all orders. (The dark secret behind human nature used to be the upsurge of the animal—as in *King Kong*. The threat to man, his availability to dehumanization, lay in his own animality. Now the danger is understood as residing in man's ability to be turned into a machine.)

The rule, of course, is that this horrible and irremediable form of murder can strike anyone in the film except the hero. The hero and his family, while greatly threatened, always escape this fate and by the end of the film the invaders have been repulsed or destroyed. I know of only one exception, *The Day Mars Invaded Earth* (1963), in which after all the standard struggles the scientist-hero, his wife, and their two children are "taken over" by the alien invaders—and that's that. (The last minutes of the film show them being incinerated by the Martians' rays and their ash silhouettes flushed down their empty swimming pool, while their simulacra drive off in the family car.) Another variant but upbeat switch on the rule occurs in *The Creation of the Humanoids* (1964), where the hero discovers at the end of the film that he, too, has been turned into a metal robot, complete with highly efficient and virtually indestructible mechanical insides, although he didn't know it and detected no difference in himself. He learns, however, that he will shortly be upgraded into a "humanoid" having all the properties of a real man.

Of all the standard motifs of science fiction films, this theme of dehumanization is perhaps the most fascinating. For, as I have indicated, it is scarcely a black-and-white situation, as in the old vampire films. The attitude of the science fiction films toward depersonalization is mixed. On the one hand, they deplore it as the ultimate horror. On the other hand, certain characteristics of the dehumanized invaders, modulated and disguised—such as the ascendancy of reason over feelings, the idealization of teamwork and the consensus-creating activities of science, a marked degree of moral simplification—are precisely traits of the savior-scientist. It is interesting that when the scientist in these films is treated negatively, it is usually done through the portrayal of an individual scientist who holes up in his laboratory and neglects his fiancée or his loving wife and children, obsessed by his daring and dangerous experiments. The scientist as a loyal member of a team, and therefore considerably less individualized, is treated quite respectfully.

There is absolutely no social criticism, of even the most implicit kind, in science fiction films. No criticism, for example, of the conditions of our society which create the impersonality and dehumanization which science fiction fantasies displace onto the influence of an alien It. Also, the notion of science as a social activity, interlocking with social and political interests, is unacknowledged. Science is simply either adventure (for good or evil) or a technical response to danger. And, typically, when the fear of science is paramount—when science is conceived of as black magic rather than white—the evil has no attribution beyond that of the perverse will of an individual scientist. In science fiction films the antithesis of black magic and white is drawn as a split between technology, which is beneficent, and the errant individual will of a lone intellectual.

Thus, science fiction films can be looked at as thematically central allegory, replete with standard modern attitudes. The theme of depersonalization (being "taken over") which I have been talking about is a new allegory reflecting the age-old awareness of man that, sane, he is always perilously close to insanity and unreason. But there is something more here than just a recent, popular image which expresses man's perennial, but largely unconscious, anxiety about his sanity. The image derives most of its power from a supplementary and historical anxiety, also not experienced *consciously* by most people, about the depersonalizing conditions of modern urban life. Similarly, it is not enough to note that science fiction allegories are one of the new myths about—that is, one of the ways of accommodating to and negating—the perennial human anxiety about death. (Myths of heaven and hell, and of ghosts, had the same function.) For, again, there is a historically specifiable twist which intensifies the anxiety. I mean, the trauma suffered by everyone in the middle of the 20th century when it became clear that, from now on to the end of human history, every person would spend his individual life under the threat not only of individual death, which is certain, but of something almost insupportable psychologically—collective incineration and extinction which could come at any time, virtually without warning.

From a psychological point of view, the imagination of disaster does not greatly differ from one period in history to another. But from a political and moral point of view, it does. The expectation of the apocalypse may be the occasion for a radical disaffiliation from society, as when thousands of Eastern European Jews in the 17th century, hearing that Sabbatai Zevi had been proclaimed the Messiah and that the end of the world was imminent, gave up their homes and businesses and began the trek to Palestine. But people take the news of their doom in diverse ways. It is reported that in 1945 the populace of Berlin received without great agitation the news that Hitler had decided to kill them all, before the Allies arrived, because they had not been worthy enough to win the war. We are, alas, more in the position of the Berliners of 1945 than of the Jews of 17th century Eastern Europe; and our response is closer to theirs, too. What I am suggesting is that the imagery of disaster in science fiction is above all the emblem of an *inadequate response*. I don't mean to bear down on the films for this. They themselves are only a sampling, stripped of sophistication, of the inadequacy of most people's response to the unassimilable terrors that infect their consciousness. The interest of the films, aside from their considerable amount of cinematic charm, consists in this intersection between a naïve and largely debased commercial art product and the most profound dilemmas of the contemporary situation.

Ours is indeed an age of extremity. For we live under continual threat of two equally fearful, but seemingly opposed, destinies: unremitting banality and inconceivable terror. It is fantasy, served out in large rations by the popular arts, which allows most people to cope with these twin specters. For one job that fantasy can do is to lift us out of the unbearably humdrum and to distract us from terrors—real or anticipated—by an escape into exotic, dangerous situations which have last-minute happy endings. But another of the things that fantasy can do is to normalize what is psychologically unbearable, thereby inuring us to it. In one case, fantasy beautifies the world. In the other, it neutralizes it.

The fantasy in science fiction films does both jobs. The films reflect world-wide anxieties, and they serve to allay them. They inculcate a strange apathy concerning the processes of radiation, contamination, and destruction which I for one find haunting and depressing. The naïve level of the films neatly tempers the sense of otherness, of alien-ness, with the grossly familiar. In particular, the dialogue of most science fiction films, which is of a monumental but often touching banality, makes them wonderfully, unintentionally funny. Lines like "Come quickly, there's a monster in my bathtub," "We must do something about this," "Wait, Professor. There's someone on the telephone," "But that's incredible," and the old American stand-by, "I hope it works!" are hilarious in the context of picturesque and deafening holocaust. Yet the films also contain something that is painful and in deadly earnest.

There is a sense in which all these movies are in complicity with the abhorrent. They neutralize it, as I have said. It is no more, perhaps, than the way all art draws its audience into a circle of complicity with the thing represented. But in these films we have to do with things which are (quite literally) unthinkable. Here, "thinking about the unthinkable"—not in the way of Herman Kahn, as a subject for calculation, but as a subject for fantasy—becomes, however inadvertently, itself a somewhat questionable act from a moral point of view. The films perpetuate clichés about identity, volition, power, knowledge, happiness, social consensus, guilt, responsibility which are, to say the least, not serviceable in our present extremity. But collective nightmares cannot be banished by demonstrating that they are, intellectually and morally, fallacious. This nightmare—the one reflected, in various registers, in the science fiction films—is too close to our reality.

(1965)

Jack Smith's Flaming Creatures

T HE only thing to be regretted about the close-ups of limp penises and bouncing breasts, the shots of masturbation and oral sexuality, in Jack Smith's *Flaming Creatures* is that they make it hard simply to talk about this remarkable film; one has to *defend* it. But in defending as well as talking about the film, I don't want to make it seem less outrageous, less shocking than it is. For the record: in *Flaming Creatures*, a couple of women and a much larger number of men, most of them clad in flamboyant thrift-shop women's clothes, frolic about, pose and posture, dance with one another, enact various scenes of voluptuousness, sexual frenzy, romance, and vampirism—to the accompaniment of a sound track which includes some Latin pop favorites (*Siboney, Amapola*), rock-'n'-roll, scratchy violin playing, bullfight music, a Chinese song, the text of a wacky ad for a new brand of "heart-shaped lipstick" being demonstrated on the screen by a host of men, some in drag and some not, and the chorale of flutey shrieks and screams which accompany the group rape of a bosomy young woman, rape happily converting itself into an orgy. Of course, *Flaming Creatures* is outrageous, and intends to be. The very title tells us that.

As it happens, *Flaming Creatures* is not pornographic, if pornography be defined as the manifest intention and capacity to excite sexually. The depiction of nakedness and various sexual embraces (with the notable omission of straight screwing) is both too full of pathos and too ingenuous to be prurient. Rather than being sentimental or lustful, Smith's images of sex are alternately childlike and witty.

The police hostility to *Flaming Creatures* is not hard to understand. It is, alas, inevitable that Smith's film will have to fight for its life in the courts. What is disappointing is the indifference, the squeamishness, the downright hostility to the film evinced by almost everyone in the mature intellectual and artistic community. Almost its only supporters are a loyal coterie of film-makers, poets, and young "Villagers." *Flaming Creatures* has not yet graduated from being a cult object, the prize exhibit of the New American Cinema group whose house organ is the magazine *Film Culture*. Everyone should be grateful to Jonas Mekas, who almost single-handedly, with tenacity and even

heroism, has made it possible to see Smith's film and many other
new works. Yet it must be admitted that the pronouncements of
Mekas and his entourage are shrill and often positively alienating. It is absurd of Mekas to argue that this new group of films,
which includes *Flaming Creatures*, is a totally unprecedented
departure in the history of cinema. Such truculence does Smith
a disservice, making it unnecessarily hard to grasp what is of
merit in *Flaming Creatures*. For *Flaming Creatures* is a small
but valuable work in a particular tradition, the poetic cinema
of shock. In this tradition are to be found Buñuel's *Un Chien
Andalou* and *L'Âge d'Or*, parts of Eisenstein's first film, *Strike*,
Tod Browning's *Freaks*, Jean Rouch's *Les Maîtres-Fous*, Franju's
Le Sang des Bêtes, Lenica's *Labyrinth*, the films of Kenneth
Anger (*Fireworks*, *Scorpio Rising*), and Noël Burch's *Noviciat*.

The older avant-garde film-makers in America (Maya Deren,
James Broughton, Kenneth Anger) turned out short films
which were technically quite studied. Given their very low bud-
gets, the color, camera work, acting, and synchronization of
image and sound were as professional as possible. The hallmark
of one of the two new avant-garde styles in American cinema
(Jack Smith, Ron Rice, *et al.*, but not Gregory Markopoulos
or Stan Brakhage) is its willful technical crudity. The newer
films—both the good ones and the poor, uninspired work—
show a maddening indifference to every element of technique,
a studied primitiveness. This is a very contemporary style, and
very American. Nowhere in the world has the old cliché of European romanticism—the assassin mind versus the spontaneous
heart—had such a long career as in America. Here, more than
anywhere else, the belief lives on that neatness and carefulness
of technique interfere with spontaneity, with truth, with immediacy. Most of the prevailing techniques (for even to be against
technique demands a technique) of avant-garde art express this
conviction. In music, there is aleatory performance now as well
as composition, and new sources of sound and new ways of
mutilating the old instruments; in painting and sculpture, there
is the favoring of impermanent or found materials, and the
transformation of objects into perishable (use-once-and-throw-
away) environments or "happenings." In its own way *Flaming
Creatures* illustrates this snobbery about the coherence and
technical finish of the work of art. There is, of course, no story

in *Flaming Creatures*, no development, no necessary order of the seven (as I count them) clearly separable sequences of the film. One can easily doubt that a certain piece of footage was indeed intended to be overexposed. Of no sequence is one convinced that it had to last this long, and not longer or shorter. Shots aren't framed in the traditional way; heads are cut off; extraneous figures sometimes appear on the margin of the scene. The camera is hand-held most of the time, and the image often quivers (where this is wholly effective, and no doubt deliberate, is in the orgy sequence).

But in *Flaming Creatures*, amateurishness of technique is not frustrating, as it is in so many other recent "underground" films. For Smith is visually very generous; at practically every moment there is simply a tremendous amount to see on the screen. And then, there is an extraordinary charge and beauty to his images, even when the effect of the strong ones is weakened by the ineffective ones, the ones that might have been better through planning. Today indifference to technique is often accompanied by bareness; the modern revolt against calculation in art often takes the form of aesthetic asceticism. (Much of Abstract Expressionist painting has this ascetic quality.) *Flaming Creatures*, though, issues from a different aesthetic: it is crowded with visual material. There are no ideas, no symbols, no commentary on or critique of anything in *Flaming Creatures*. Smith's film is strictly a treat for the senses. In this it is the very opposite of a "literary" film (which is what so many French avant-garde films were). It is not in the knowing about, or being able to interpret, what one sees, that the pleasure of *Flaming Creatures* lies; but in the directness, the power, and the lavish quantity of the images themselves. Unlike most serious modern art, this work is not about the frustrations of consciousness, the dead ends of the self. Thus Smith's crude technique serves, beautifully, the sensibility embodied in *Flaming Creatures*—a sensibility which disclaims ideas, which situates itself beyond negation.

Flaming Creatures is that rare modern work of art: it is about joy and innocence. To be sure, this joyousness, this innocence is composed out of themes which are—by ordinary standards—perverse, decadent, at the least highly theatrical and artificial. But this, I think, is precisely how the film comes by its beauty and modernity. *Flaming Creatures* is a lovely specimen of what currently, in one genre, goes by the flippant name of "pop art." Smith's film has the sloppiness, the arbitrariness, the looseness of pop art. It also has pop art's gaiety, its ingenuousness, its exhilarating freedom from moralism. One great virtue of the pop-art movement is the way it blasts through the old imperative about taking a *position* toward one's subject matter. (Needless to say, I'm not denying that there are certain events about which it is necessary to take a position. An extreme instance of a work of art dealing with such events is *The Deputy*. All I'm saying is that there are some elements of life—above all, sexual pleasure—about which it isn't necessary to have a position.) The best works among those that are called pop art intend, precisely, that we abandon the old task of always either approving or disapproving of what is depicted in art—or, by extension, experienced in life. (This is why those who dismiss pop art as a symptom of a new conformism, a cult of acceptance of the artifacts of mass civilization, are being obtuse.) Pop art lets in wonderful and new mixtures of attitude, which would before have seemed contradictions. Thus *Flaming Creatures* is a brilliant spoof on sex and at the same time full of the lyricism of erotic impulse. Simply in a visual sense, too, it is full of contradictions. Very studied visual effects (lacy textures, falling flowers, tableaux) are introduced into disorganized, clearly improvised scenes in which bodies, some shapely and convincingly feminine and others scrawny and hairy, tumble, dance, make love.

One can regard Smith's film as having, for its subject, the poetry of transvestitism. *Film Culture*, in awarding *Flaming Creatures* its Fifth Independent Film Award, said of Smith: "He has struck us with not the mere pity or curiosity of the perverse, but the glory, the pageantry of Transylvestia and the magic of Fairyland. He has lit up a part of life, although it is a part which most men scorn." The truth is that *Flaming Creatures* is much more about intersexuality than about homosexuality. Smith's vision is akin to the vision in Bosch's paintings of a paradise and a hell of writhing, shameless, ingenious bodies. Unlike those serious and stirring films about the beauties and terrors of homoerotic love, Kenneth Anger's *Fireworks* and Genet's *Chant d'Amour*, the important fact about the figures in Smith's film is that one cannot easily tell which are men and which are women. These are "creatures," flaming out in intersexual, polymorphous joy. The film is built out of a complex web of ambiguities and ambivalences, whose primary image is the confusion of male and female flesh. The shaken breast and the shaken penis become interchangeable with each other.

Bosch constructed a strange, aborted, ideal nature against which he situated his nude figures, his androgynous visions of pain and pleasure. Smith has no literal background (it's hard to tell in the film whether one is indoors or outdoors), but instead the thoroughly artificial and invented landscape of costume, gesture, and music. The myth of intersexuality is played out against a background of banal songs, ads, clothes, dances, and above all, the repertory of fantasy drawn from corny movies. The texture of *Flaming Creatures* is made up of a rich collage of "camp" lore: a woman in white (a transvestite) with drooping head holding a stalk of lilies; a gaunt woman seen emerging from a coffin, who turns out to be a vampire and, eventually, male; a marvelous Spanish dancer (also transvestite) with huge dark eyes, black lace mantilla and fan; a tableau from the *Sheik of Araby*, with reclining men in burnooses and an Arab temptress stolidly exposing one breast; a scene between two women, reclining on flowers and rags, which recalls the dense, crowded texture of the movies in which Sternberg directed Dietrich in the early thirties. The vocabulary of images and textures on which Smith draws includes pre-Raphaelite languidness; Art Nouveau; the great exotica styles of the twenties, the Spanish and the Arab; and the modern "camp" way of relishing mass culture.

Flaming Creatures is a triumphant example of an aesthetic vision of the world—and such a vision is perhaps always, at its core, epicene. But this type of art has yet to be understood in this country. The space in which *Flaming Creatures* moves is not the space of moral ideas, which is where American critics have traditionally located art. What I am urging is that there is not only moral space, by whose laws *Flaming Creatures* would indeed come off badly; there is also aesthetic space, the space of pleasure. Here Smith's film moves and has its being.

(1964)

Resnais' Muriel

M*uriel* is the most difficult, by far, of Resnais' three feature
films, but it is clearly drawn from the same repertoire of
themes as the first two. Despite the special mannerisms of the
very independent scriptwriters he has employed—Marguerite
Duras in *Hiroshima, Mon Amour*, Alain Robbe-Grillet in
L'Année Dernière à Marienbad, and Jean Cayrol in *Muriel*—all
three films share a common subject: the search for the inexpressible past. Resnais' new film even has a co-title to this effect,
like an old-fashioned novel. It is called *Muriel, ou Le Temps d'un
Retour*.

In *Hiroshima, Mon Amour*, the subject is the collation of two
disjunct and clashing pasts. The story of the film is the unsuccessful attempt of the two principals, a Japanese architect and
a French actress, to extract from their pasts the substance of
feeling (and concordance of memory) that could sustain a love
in the present. At the beginning of the film, they are in bed.
They spend the rest of the film literally reciting themselves to
each other. But they fail to transcend their "statements," their
guilt and separateness.

L'Année Dernière à Marienbad is another version of the same
theme. But here the theme is put in a deliberately theatrical,
static setting, at a tangent to both the brash modern ugliness
of the new Hiroshima and the solid provincial authenticity of
Nevers. This story entombs itself in an outlandish, beautiful,
barren place and plays out the theme of *le temps retrouvé* with
abstract personages, who are denied a solid consciousness or
memory or past. *Marienbad* is a formal inversion of the idea
of *Hiroshima*, with more than one note of melancholic parody
of its own theme. As the idea of *Hiroshima* is the weight of
the inescapably remembered past, so the idea of *Marienbad*
is the openness, the abstractness of memory. The claim of the
past upon the present is reduced to a cipher, a ballet, or—in
the controlling image of the film—a game, whose results are
entirely determined by the first move (if he who makes the first
move knows what he is doing). The past is a fantasy of the present, according to both *Hiroshima* and *Marienbad*. *Marienbad*
develops the meditation on the form of memory implicit in *Hiroshima*, cutting away the ideological clothing of the first film.

The reason *Muriel* is difficult is that it attempts to do both what *Hiroshima* and what *Marienbad* did. It attempts to deal with substantive issues—the Algerian War, the OAS, the racism of the colons—even as *Hiroshima* dealt with the bomb, pacifism, and collaboration. But it also, like *Marienbad*, attempts to project a purely abstract drama. The burden of this double intention—to be both concrete and abstract—doubles the technical virtuosity and complexity of the film.

Again, the story concerns a group of people haunted by their memories. Hélène Aughain, a fortyish widow living in the provincial city of Boulogne, impulsively summons a former lover whom she has not seen in twenty years to visit her. Her motive is never named; in the film, it has the character of a gratuitous act. Hélène runs a touch-and-go antique furniture business from her apartment, gambles compulsively, and is badly in debt. Living with her in a painful loving stalemate is her uncommunicative stepson, Bernard Aughain, another memory addict, who has recently returned from serving in the army in Algeria. Bernard is unable to forget his share in a crime: the torturing of an Algerian political prisoner, a girl named Muriel. He is not merely too distraught to work; he is in an agony of restlessness. On the pretext of visiting a nonexistent fiancée in the town (whom he has named Muriel), he often flees his stepmother's modern apartment, where every item of furniture is beautiful and for sale, to a room he maintains in the ruins of the old family apartment, which was bombed during World War II. . . . The film opens with the arrival from Paris of Hélène's old lover, Alphonse. He is accompanied by his mistress, Françoise, whom he passes off as his niece. It ends, several months later, the unsuccessful reunion of Hélène and Alphonse having run its course. Alphonse and Françoise, their relationship permanently embittered, leave for Paris. Bernard—after shooting the boyhood friend who, as a soldier, led the torture of Muriel and who is now a civilian member of the OAS underground in France—says good-bye to his stepmother. In a coda, we are shown the arrival in Hélène's empty apartment of the wife of Alphonse, Simone, who has come to reclaim her husband.

Unlike *Hiroshima* and *Marienbad*, *Muriel* directly suggests an elaborate plot and complex interrelationships. (In the sketch above I have omitted important minor characters, including

friends of Hélène, who figure in the film.) Yet, for all this complexity, Resnais conscientiously avoids direct narration. He gives
us a chain of short scenes, horizontal in emotional tone, which
focus on selected undramatic moments in the lives of the four
main characters: Hélène and her stepson and Alphonse and
Françoise eating together; Hélène going up, or coming down,
the steps of the gambling casino; Bernard riding his bicycle in
the town; Bernard going horseback riding on the cliffs outside
the town; Bernard and Françoise walking and talking; and so
forth. The film is not really hard to follow. I have seen it twice,
and expected after I saw it once that I would see more in it
the second time. I didn't. *Muriel*, like *Marienbad*, should not
puzzle, because there is nothing "behind" the lean, staccato
statements that one sees. They can't be deciphered, because
they don't say more than they say. It is rather as if Resnais had
taken a story, which could be told quite straightforwardly, and
cut it against the grain. This "against the grain" feeling—the
sense of being shown the action at an angle—is the peculiar
mark of *Muriel*. It is Resnais' way of making a realistic story
over into an examination of the *form* of emotions.

Thus, although the story is not difficult to follow, Resnais'
techniques for telling it deliberately estrange the viewer from
the story. Most conspicuous of these techniques is his elliptical, off-center conception of a scene. The film opens with
the strained good-byes of Hélène and a demanding client
at the threshold of Hélène's apartment; then there is a brief
exchange between the harried Hélène and the disgruntled Bernard. Throughout both sequences, Resnais denies the viewer
a chance to orient himself visually in traditional story terms.
We are shown a hand on the doorknob, the vacant insincere
smile of the client, a coffee pot boiling. The way the scenes are
photographed and edited decomposes, rather than explains, the
story. Then Hélène hurries off to the station to meet Alphonse,
whom she finds accompanied by Françoise, and leads them
from the station back to her apartment on foot. On this walk
from the station—it is night—Hélène is nervously chattering
about Boulogne, which was mostly destroyed during the war
and has been rebuilt in a bright functional modern style; and
shots of the city in the daytime are interspersed with shots of the
three walking through the city at night. Hélène's voice bridges

this high-speed visual alternation. In Resnais' films, all speech, including dialogue, tends to become narration—to hover over the visible action, rather than to issue directly from it.

The extremely rapid cutting of *Muriel* is unlike the jumpy, jazzy cutting of Godard in *Breathless* and *Vivre Sa Vie*. Godard's abrupt cutting pulls the viewer into the story, makes him restless and heightens his appetite for action, creating a kind of visual suspense. When Resnais cuts abruptly, he pulls the viewer away from the story. His cutting acts as a brake on the narrative, a kind of aesthetic undertow, a sort of filmic alienation effect.

Resnais' use of speech has a similar "alienating" effect on the viewer's feelings. Because his main characters have something not only benumbed but positively hopeless about them, their words are never emotionally moving. Speaking in a Resnais film is typically an occasion of frustration—whether it is the trance-like recitation of the uncommunicable distress of an event in the past; or the truncated, distracted words his characters address to each other in the present. (Because of the frustrations of speech, eyes have great authority in Resnais' films. A standard dramatic moment, insofar as he allows such a thing, is a few banal words followed by silence and a look.) Happily, there is nothing in *Muriel* of the insufferable incantatory style of the dialogue of *Hiroshima* and the narration of *Marienbad*. Apart from a few stark, unanswered questions, the characters in *Muriel* mostly speak in dull, evasive phrases, especially when they are very unhappy. But the firm prosiness of the dialogue in *Muriel* is not intended to *mean* anything different from the awful poetizing of the earlier two long films. Resnais proposes the same subject in all his films. All his films are about the *inexpressible*. (The main topics which are inexpressible are two: guilt and erotic longing.) And the twin notion to inexpressibility is banality. In high art, banality is the modesty of the inexpressible. "Ours is really *une histoire banale*," the anguished Hélène says ruefully at one moment to the suave, furtive Alphonse. "The story of Muriel can't be told," says Bernard to a stranger in whom he has confided his excruciating memory. The two declarations really amount to the same thing.

Resnais' techniques, despite the visual brilliance of his films, seem to me to owe more to literature than to the tradition of the cinema as such. (Bernard, in *Muriel*, is a film-maker—he is collecting "evidence," as he calls it, about the case of Muriel—for the same reason that the central consciousness in so many modern novels is that of a character who is a writer.) Most literary of all is Resnais' formalism. Formalism itself is not literary. But to appropriate a complex and specific narrative in order deliberately to obscure it—to write an abstract text on top of it, as it were—is a very literary procedure. There *is* a story in *Muriel*, the story of a troubled middle-aged woman attempting to reinstate the love of twenty years ago and a young ex-soldier wracked by guilt over his complicity in a barbarous war. But *Muriel* is designed so that, at any given moment of it, it's not about anything at all. At any given moment it is a formal composition; and it is to this end that individual scenes are shaped so obliquely, the time sequence scrambled, and dialogue kept to a minimum of informativeness.

This is exactly the point of many new novels coming out of France today—to suppress the story, in its traditional psychological or social meaning, in favor of a formal exploration of the structure of an emotion or event. Thus, the real concern of Michel Butor in his novel *La Modification* is not to show whether the hero will or will not leave his wife to live with his mistress, and even less to base some theory of love on his decision. What interests Butor is the "modification" itself, the formal structure of the man's behavior. It's exactly in this spirit that Resnais handles the story of *Muriel*.

The typical formula of the new formalists of the novel and film is a mixture of coldness and pathos: coldness enclosing and subduing an immense pathos. Resnais' great discovery is the application of this formula to "documentary" material, to true events locked in the historical past. Here—in Resnais' short films, particularly *Guernica*, *Van Gogh*, and above all, *Night and Fog*—the formula works brilliantly, educating and liberating the viewer's feelings. *Night and Fog* shows us Dachau, ten years later. The camera moves about (the film is in color), nosing out the grass growing up between the cracks in the masonry of the crematoria. The ghastly serenity of Dachau—now a hollow, silent, evacuated shell—is posed against the unimaginable reality of what went on there in the past; this past is represented by a quiet voice describing life in the camps and reciting the statistics of extermination (text by Jean Cayrol), and some interpolated black-and-white newsreel footage of the camp when it was liberated. (This is the parent of the scene in *Muriel* when Bernard recites the story of the torture and murder of Muriel, while running off a home-movie type film of his smiling uniformed comrades in Algeria. Muriel herself is never shown.) The triumph of *Night and Fog* is its absolute control, its supreme refinement in dealing with a subject that incarnates the purest, most agonizing pathos. For the danger of such a subject is that it can numb, instead of stir, our feelings. Resnais has overcome this danger by adopting a distance from his subject which is not sentimental, and which yet does not cheat the horror of its horrifyingness. *Night and Fog* is overwhelming in its directness, yet full of tact about the unimaginable.

But in Resnais' three feature films, the same strategy is not so apt or satisfying. It would be too simple to say that it is because the lucid and brilliantly compassionate documentarist has been superseded by the aesthete, the formalist. (After all, films *are* an art.) But there is an undeniable loss of power, since Resnais wants very much to have it both ways—as "*homme de gauche*" and as formalist. The aim of formalism is to break up content, to *question* content. The questionable reality of the past is the subject of all Resnais' films. More exactly, for Resnais, the past is that reality which is both unassimilable and dubious. (The new formalism of the French novels and films is thus a dedicated agnosticism about reality itself.) But at the same time, Resnais does believe in, and want us to share in a certain attitude toward, the past insofar as it has the signature of history. This does not create a problem in *Night and Fog*, where the memory of the past is situated objectively, outside the film, so to speak, in an impersonal narrator. But when Resnais decided to take as his subject, not "a memory," but "remembering," and to situate memories in characters within the film, a muted collision between the aims of formalism and the ethic of engagement occurred. The result of using admirable sentiments—like guilt for the bomb (in *Hiroshima*) and for the French atrocities in Algeria (*Muriel*)—as subjects for aesthetic demonstration is a palpable strain and diffuseness in the structure, as if Resnais did not know where the center of his film really was. Thus, the disturbing anomaly of *Hiroshima* is the implicit equating of the grandiose horror of the Japanese hero's memory, the bombing and its mutilated victims, with the comparatively insignificant horror from the past that plagues the French heroine, an affair with a German soldier during the war for which, after the liberation, she was humiliated by having her head shaved.

I have said that not a memory but remembering is Resnais' subject: nostalgia itself becomes an object of nostalgia, the memory of an unrecapturable feeling becomes the subject of feeling. The only one of Resnais' feature films which does not reveal this confusion about its center is *Marienbad*. Here, a strong emotion—the pathos of erotic frustration and longing— is raised to the level of a meta-emotion by being set in a place that has the character of an abstraction, a vast palace peopled with *haute couture* mannequins. This method is plausible because it is a totally ahistorical, apolitical memory which Resnais has located in what is a kind of generalized Past. But abstraction through generality, at least in this film, seems to produce a certain deflection of energy. The mood is stylized reticence, but one does not feel, sufficiently, the pressure of what the characters are being reticent about. *Marienbad* has its center, but the center seems frozen. It has an insistent, sometimes sluggish stateliness in which visual beauty and exquisiteness of composition are continually undermined by a lack of emotional tension.

There is greater energy in *Muriel*, which is a far more ambitious film. For Resnais has come back to the problem which, given his sensibility *and* the themes he wishes to pursue, he cannot evade: the reconciliation of formalism and the ethic of engagement. He cannot be said to have solved the problem, and in an ultimate sense *Muriel* must be judged a noble failure, but he has shown a good deal more about the problem and the complexities of any solution to it. He does not make the mistake of implicitly coordinating historical atrocity with a private grief (as in *Hiroshima*). Both simply exist, in an extended network of relationships whose psychological "insides" we never know. For Resnais has sought to represent his materials, the burden of an anguishing memory of participation in a real historical event (Bernard in Algeria) and the inexplicit anguish of a purely private past (Hélène and her affair with Alphonse) in a manner which is both abstract and concrete. It is neither the understated documentary realism of his rendering of the city of Hiroshima, nor the sensuous realism of the photography of Nevers; nor is it the abstract museum stillness, embodied in the exotic locale of *Marienbad*. Abstraction in *Muriel* is subtler and more complex because it is discovered in the real everyday world rather than by departing from it in time (the flashbacks in *Hiroshima*) or in space (the château of *Marienbad*). It is conveyed in the rigor of its compositional sense, first of all, but this is to be found in all Resnais' films. And it is in the rapid cutting-away-from-scenes which I have already mentioned, a rhythm new in Resnais' films; and in the use of color. About the last, much could be said. Sacha Vierny's color photography in *Muriel* stuns and delights, giving one that sense of having never before appreciated the resources of color in the cinema that such films as *Gate of Hell* and Visconti's *Senso* once also did. But the impact of the colors in Resnais' film is not just that they are beautiful. It is the aggressive inhuman intensity they possess, which gives to quotidian objects, up-to-date kitchenware, modern apartment buildings and stores, a peculiar abstractness and distance.

Another resource for intensification through abstractness is the music of Hans Werner Henze for voice and orchestra, one of those rare film scores that stands as a musical composition by itself. Sometimes the music is used for conventional dramatic purposes: to confirm or comment on what is happening. Thus, in the scene when Bernard shows the crude film he made of his ex-comrades in Algeria, cavorting and smiling, the music becomes harsh and jolting—contradicting the innocence of the image. (We know these are the soldiers who share with Bernard the guilt of Muriel's death.) But the more interesting use which Resnais makes of the music is as a structural element in the narration. The atonal vocal line sung by Rita Streich is sometimes used, like the dialogue, to soar over the action. It is through the music that we know when Hélène is most tormented by her barely named emotions. And, in its most powerful use, the music constitutes a kind of purified dialogue, displacing speech altogether. In the brief wordless final scene, when Simone comes looking for her husband in Hélène's apartment and finds no one, the music becomes her speech; voice and orchestra rise to a crescendo of lament.

But, for all the beauty and effectiveness of the resources I have mentioned (and those I have not mentioned, which include acting performances of great clarity, restraint, and intelligence*), the problem of *Muriel*—and of Resnais' work—remains. A cleavage of intention, which Resnais has thus far failed to transcend, has given rise to a multiplicity of devices, each one justifiable and largely successful, but the whole giving an unpleasant feeling of clutteredness. Perhaps this is why *Muriel*, however admirable, is not a very likable film. The trouble, let me repeat, is not formalism. Bresson's *Les Dames du Bois de Boulogne* and Godard's *Vivre Sa Vie*—to mention only two great films in the formalist tradition—are emotionally exalting, even when they are being most dead-pan and cerebral. But *Muriel* is somehow depressing, weighty. Its virtues, such as its intelligence and its extraordinary rewards on a purely visual level, still retain something (though a good deal less) of that preciousness, that studied air, that artiness that infests *Hiroshima* and *Marienbad*. Resnais knows all about beauty. But his films lack tonicity and vigor, directness of address. They are cautious, somehow, overburdened and synthetic. They do not go to the end, either of the idea or of the emotion which inspires them, which all great art must do.

(1963)

---

*Most of the principals of *Muriel* are remarkable as actors and in the clarity of their physical presences. But it must be noted that, unlike the other two feature films of Resnais, *Muriel* is dominated by a single performance, that of Delphine Seyrig as Hélène. In this film (but not in *Marienbad*) Seyrig has the nourishing irrelevant panoply of mannerisms of a star, in the peculiarly cinematic sense of that word. That is to say, she doesn't simply play (or even perfectly fill) a role. She becomes an independent aesthetic object in herself. Each detail of her appearance—her graying hair, her tilted loping walk, her wide-brimmed hats and smartly dowdy suits, her gauche manner in enthusiasm and regret—is unnecessary and indelible.

A Note on Novels and Films

THE fifty years of the cinema present us with a scrambled recapitulation of the more than two hundred year history of the novel. In D. W. Griffith, the cinema had its Samuel Richardson; the director of *Birth of a Nation* (1915), *Intolerance* (1916), *Broken Blossoms* (1919), *Way Down East* (1920), *One Exciting Night* (1922), and hundreds of other films voiced many of the same moral conceptions and occupied an approximately similar position with respect to the development of the film art as the author of *Pamela* and *Clarissa* did with respect to the development of the novel. Both Griffith and Richardson were innovators of genius; both had intellects of supreme vulgarity and even inanity; and the work of both men reeks of a fervid moralizing about sexuality and violence whose energy comes from suppressed voluptuousness. The central figure in Richardson's two novels, the pure young virgin assailed by the brute-seducer, finds its exact counterpart—stylistically and conceptually—in the Pure Young Girl, the Perfect Victim, of Griffith's many films, played often either by Lillian Gish (who is famous for these roles) or by the now-forgotten but much better actress, Mae Marsh. Like Richardson, Griffith's moral drivel (expressed in his inimitable and lengthy titles written in a brand of English all his own, replete with capital letters for the names of all the virtues and sins) concealed an essential lasciviousness; and, like Richardson, what is best in Griffith is his extraordinary capacity for representing the most tremulous feminine sentiments in all their *longueurs*, which the banality of his "ideas" does not obscure. Like Richardson, too, the world of Griffith seems cloying and slightly mad to modern taste. Yet it was these two who discovered "psychology" for the respective genres in which they are the pioneers.

Of course, not every great film director can be matched with a great novelist. The comparisons cannot be pressed too literally. Nevertheless, the cinema has had not only its Richardson, but its Dickens, its Tolstoy, its Balzac, its Proust, its Nathanael West. And then there are the curious marriages of style and conception in the cinema. The masterpieces that Erich Von Stroheim directed in Hollywood in the 1920s (*Blind Husbands*, *Foolish Wives*, *Greed*, *The Merry Widow*, *Wedding March*, *Queen*

Kelly) might be described as an improbable and brilliant synthesis of Anthony Hope and Balzac.

This is not to assimilate the cinema to the novel, or even to claim that the cinema can be analyzed in the same terms as a novel. The cinema has its own methods and logic of representation, which one does not exhaust by saying that they are primarily visual. The cinema presents us with a new language, a way of talking about emotion through the direct experience of the language of faces and gestures. Nevertheless, there are useful analogies which may be drawn between the cinema and the novel—far more, it seems to me, than between the cinema and the theater. Like the novel, the cinema presents us with a view of an action which is absolutely under the control of the director (writer) at every moment. Our eye cannot wander about the screen, as it does about the stage. The camera is an absolute dictator. It shows us a face when we are to see a face, and nothing else; a pair of clenched hands, a landscape, a speeding train, the façade of a building in the middle of a tête-à-tête, when and only when it wants us to see these things. When the camera moves we move, when it remains still we are still. In a similar way the novel presents a selection of the thoughts and descriptions which are relevant to the writer's conception, and we must follow these serially, as the author leads us; they are not spread out, as a background, for us to contemplate in the order we choose, as in painting or the theater.

A further caveat. Traditions exist within the cinema—less frequently exploited than that tradition which plausibly can be compared with the novel—which are analogous to literary forms other than the novel. Eisenstein's *Strike, Potemkin, Ten Days That Shook the World, The Old and the New*; Pudovkin's *The Mother, The End of St. Petersburg, Storm Over Asia*; Kurosawa's *The Seven Samurai, The Throne of Blood, The Hidden Fortress*; Inagaki's *Chushingura*; Okamoto's *Samurai Assassin*; most films of John Ford (*The Searchers*, etc.) belong rather to a conception of the cinema as epic. There is also a tradition of the cinema as poetry; many of the "avant-garde" short films which were made in France in the 1920s (Buñuel's *Un Chien Andalou* and *L'Age d'Or*; Cocteau's *Le Sang d'un Poète*; Jean Renoir's *La Petite Marchande d'Allumettes*; Antonin Artaud's *La Coquille et le Clergyman*) are best compared with the work of Baudelaire, Rimbaud, Mallarmé, and Lautréamont. Nevertheless, the dominant tradition in the film has centered upon the more or less novelistic unfolding of plot and idea, employing highly individuated characters located in a precise social setting.

Of course, the cinema does not obey the same schedule of contemporaneity as the novel; thus, it would appear anachronistic to us if someone wrote a novel like Jane Austen, but it would be very "advanced" if someone makes a film which is the cinematic equivalent of Jane Austen. This is no doubt because the history of films is so much shorter than the history of narrative fiction; and has emerged under the peculiarly accelerated tempo at which the arts move in our century. Thus its various possibilities overlap and double back on each other. Another reason is the fact that cinema, as a late-comer to the serious arts, is in a position to raid the other arts and can deploy even relatively stale elements in innumerable fresh combinations. Cinema is a kind of pan-art. It can use, incorporate, engulf virtually any other art: the novel, poetry, theater, painting, sculpture, dance, music, architecture. Unlike opera, which is a (virtually) frozen art form, the cinema is and has been a fruitfully conservative medium of ideas and styles of emotion. All the trappings of melodrama and high emotion may be found in the most recent and sophisticated cinema (for example, Visconti's *Senso* and *Rocco and His Brothers*), while these have been banished from most recent sophisticated novels.

One link between novels and films that is frequently made, however, does not seem very useful. That is the old saw about dividing directors into those who are primarily "literary" and those who are primarily "visual." Actually, there are few directors whose work can be so simply characterized. A distinction at least as useful is that between films which are "analytic" and those which are "descriptive" and "expository." Examples of the first would be the films of Carné, Bergman (especially *Through a Glass Darkly*, *Winter Light*, and *The Silence*), Fellini, and Visconti; examples of the second would be the films of Antonioni, Godard, and Bresson. The first kind could be described as psychological films, those concerned with the revelation of the characters' motives. The second kind is anti-psychological, and deals with the transaction between feeling and things; the persons are opaque, "in situation." The same contrast could be carried through in the novel. Dickens and Dostoevsky are examples of the first; Stendhal of the second.

(1961)

V

Piety Without Content

As we may learn from such disparate sources as the *Oresteia* and *Psycho*, matricide is of all possible individual crimes the most insupportable psychologically. And, of all possible crimes which an entire culture can commit, the one most difficult to bear, psychologically, is deicide. We live in a society whose entire way of life testifies to the thoroughness with which the deity has been dispatched, but philosophers, writers, men of conscience everywhere squirm under the burden. For it is a far simpler matter to plot and commit a crime than it is to live with it afterwards.

While the act of killing the Judeo-Christian God was still under way, antagonists on both sides took up their positions with a great deal of sureness and self-righteousness. But once it was clear that the deed had been done, the battle lines began to blur. In the 19th century, melancholy attempts at promoting a revived pagan religion to replace the vanquished Biblical tradition (Goethe, Hölderlin) and tremulous hopes that something humane could be saved (George Eliot, Matthew Arnold) are heard amidst the loud and somewhat shrill voices of the victors proclaiming the triumph of reason and maturity over faith and childishness, and the inevitable advance of humanity under the banner of science. In the 20th century, the sturdy Voltairean optimism of the rationalist attack on religion is even less convincing and less attractive, though we still find it in conscientiously emancipated Jews like Freud and, among American philosophers, in Morris Cohen and Sidney Hook. It seems that such optimism is possible only to those whom the "bad tidings," the *dysangel* of which Nietzsche speaks, that God is dead, have not reached.

More common in our own generation, particularly in America in the backwash of broken radical political enthusiasms, is a stance that can only be called religious fellow-travelling. This is a piety without content, a religiosity without either faith or observance. It includes in differing measures both nostalgia and relief: nostalgia over the loss of the sense of sacredness and relief that an intolerable burden has been lifted. (The conviction that what befell the old faiths could not be avoided was held with a nagging sense of impoverishment.) Unlike political fellow-travelling, religious fellow-travelling does not proceed from the attraction which a massive and increasingly successful idealism exercises, an attraction which is powerfully felt at the same time that one cannot completely identify with the movement. Rather, religious fellow-travelling proceeds from a sense of the weakness of religion: knowing the good old cause is down, it seems superfluous to kick it. Modern religious fellow-travelling is nourished on the awareness that the contemporary religious communities are on the defensive; thus to be anti-religious (like being a feminist) is old hat. Now one can afford to look on sympathetically and derive nourishment from whatever one can find to admire. Religions are converted into "religion," as painting and sculpture of different periods and motives are converted into "art." For the modern post-religious man the religious museum, like the world of the modern spectator of art, is without walls; he can pick and choose as he likes, and be committed to nothing except his own reverent spectatorship.

Religious fellow-travelling leads to several highly undesirable consequences. One is that the sense of what religions are and have been historically becomes coarse and intellectually dishonest. It is understandable, if not sound, when Catholic intellectuals attempt to reclaim Baudelaire, Rimbaud, and James Joyce—passionate atheists all—as true, if highly tormented, sons of the Church. But the same strategy is entirely indefensible on the part of the religious fellow-travellers operating within the Nietzschean "God is dead," who apparently see no harm in making everybody religious. They stand for no tradition to which they seek to reclaim errant members. They merely collect exemplars of seriousness, or moral earnestness, or intellectual passion, which is what they identify the religious possibility with today.

The present book under review* is just such an example of religious fellow-travelling, worth examining because it clearly reflects the lack of intellectual definition in this attitude which is so widespread. It consists of an assemblage of writings by

* *Religion from Tolstoy to Camus.* Selected and introduced by Walter Kaufmann. New York, Harper.

twenty-three authors "from Tolstoy to Camus," selected and edited by Walter Kaufmann, an associate professor of philosophy at Princeton.

Of the order of the book one need not speak since it has no order, except a vague chronological one. There are a few selections with which one could hardly quarrel, such as the two chapters "Rebellion" and "The Grand Inquisitor" from *The Brothers Karamazov* (certainly Kaufmann is correct in saying that one cannot understand the Grand Inquisitor story without the preceding disquisition by Ivan on the sufferings of children), the excerpts from Nietzsche's *The Antichrist* and Freud's *The Future of an Illusion*, and William James' essay "The Will to Believe." There are also a few imaginative choices of writings which deserve to be better known: e.g. the Syllabus of Errors of Pope Pius IX, the exchange of letters between Karl Barth and Emil Brunner on the Church's stand against Communism, and the essay of W. K. Clifford which prompted the famous reply of William James. But the majority of the selections seem ill-chosen. Oscar Wilde cannot be regarded seriously as a religious writer. Neither is there any justification for Morton Scott Enslin's chapter on the New Testament, a conventionally sound account of the gospels and their historical setting, which is entirely out of place in an anthology of religious *thought*. The choices of Wilde and Enslin illustrate the two poles of irrelevance into which Kaufmann's book falls: frivolity and academicism.*

---

*Kaufmann claims that he has presented "a heterogenous group, selected not to work toward some predetermined conclusion but to give a fair idea of the complexity of our story," but it's just this that he hasn't done. It is unfair to represent Catholicism by papal encyclicals plus two and one half pages by Maritain of neo-Scholastic argument on "the contingent and the necessary," which will be largely unintelligible to the audience to whom this anthology is directed. Selections from Gabriel Marcel, or Simone Weil, or some of the letters exchanged between Paul Claudel and André Gide on the latter's possible conversion, or Newman on "the grammar of assent," or Lord Acton, or Bernanos' *Diary of a Country Priest*—any of these would be more interesting and richer than what Kaufmann has given. Protestantism is more generously, but still inadequately, represented—by two sermons of Pastor Niemöller, a weak excerpt from Paul Tillich (one of the essays in *The Protestant Era* would have been far more appropriate here), the least interesting chapter from Albert Schweitzer's epochal book on eschatology in the New Testament, the Barth-Brunner correspondence, and the tame selection from Enslin mentioned above. Again, one may ask, why these? Why not something substantive from Barth

Kaufmann says in his introduction: "Almost all the men included were 'for' religion, though not the popular religion which scarcely any great religious figure has ever admired." But what does it mean to be "for" religion? Does the notion "religion" have any serious *religious* meaning at all? Put another way: can one teach or invite people to be sympathetic to religion-in-general? What does it mean to be "religious"? Obviously it is not the same thing as being "devout" or "orthodox." My own view is that one cannot be religious in general any more than one can speak language in general; at any given moment one speaks French or English or Swahili or Japanese, but not "language." Similarly one is not "a religionist," but a believing Catholic, Jew, Presbyterian, Shintoist, or Tallensi. Religious beliefs may be options, as William James described them, but they are not generalized options. It is easy, of course, to misunderstand this point. I don't mean to say that one must be orthodox as a Jew, a Thomist as a Catholic, or a fundamentalist as a Protestant. The history of every important religious community is a complex one, and (as Kaufmann suggests) those figures who are afterwards acknowledged as great religious teachers have generally been in critical opposition to popular religious practices and to much within the past traditions of their own faiths. Nevertheless, for a believer the concept of "religion" (and of deciding to become religious) makes no sense as a category. (For the rationalist critic, from Lucretius to Voltaire to Freud, the term does have a certain polemical sense when, typically, he opposes "religion" on the one hand to "science" or "reason" on the other.) Neither does it make sense as a concept

---

or Bultmann? For Judaism, Kaufmann makes only the obvious choice, Martin Buber, represented by a chapter on the Hassidim. Why not more nourishing Buber, say, a chapter from *I and Thou* or *Between Man and Man*, or, better yet, a text by Franz Rosenzweig or Gershom Scholem? Of the fiction, why is there only Tolstoy and Dostoevsky? Why not Hesse (say, *The Journey to the East*) or some of Kafka's parables or D. H. Lawrence's *Apocalypse*? The emphasis on Camus, whose name appears in the title and whose great essay against capital punishment closes the book, seems particularly mysterious. Camus was not, nor ever claimed to be, religious. In fact, one of the points he makes in his essay is that capital punishment derives its only plausible rationale as a religious punishment and is therefore entirely inappropriate and ethically obscene in our present post-religious, secularized society.

of objective sociological and historical inquiry. To be religious is always to be in some sense an adherent (even as a heretic) to a specific symbolism and a specific historic community, whatever the interpretation of these symbols and this historic community the believer may adopt. It is to be involved in specific beliefs and practices, not just to give assent to the philosophical assertions that a being whom we may call God exists, that life has meaning, etc. Religion is not equivalent to the theistic proposition.

The significance of Kaufmann's book is that it is one more example of a prevailing modern attitude which seems to me, at best, soft-headed and, more often, intellectually presumptuous. The attempts of modern secular intellectuals to help the faltering authority of "religion" ought to be rejected by every sensitive believer, and by every honest atheist. God-in-his-heaven, moral certitude, and cultural unity cannot be restored by nostalgia; the suspenseful piety of religious fellow-travelling demands a resolution, by acts of either commitment or disavowal. The presence of a religious faith may indeed be of unquestionable psychological benefit to the individual and of unquestionable social benefit to a society. But we shall never have the fruit of the tree without nourishing its roots as well; we shall never restore the prestige of the old faiths by demonstrating their psychological and sociological benefits.

Neither is it worth dallying with the lost religious consciousness because we unreflectively equate religion with *seriousness*, seriousness about the important human and moral issues. Most secular Western intellectuals have not really thought through or lived out the atheist option; they are only on the verge of it. Seeking to palliate a harsh choice, they often argue that all highmindedness and profundity has religious roots or can be viewed as a "religious" (or crypto-religious) position. The concern with the problems of despair and self-deception which Kaufmann singles out in *Anna Karenina* and *The Death of Ivan Ilyich* do not make Tolstoy in these writings a spokesman "for" religion, any more than they do Kafka, as Günther Anders has shown. If, finally, what we admire in religion is its "prophetic" or "critical" stance, as Kaufmann suggests, and we wish to salvage that (cf. also Erich Fromm's Terry lectures, *Psychoanalysis and Religion*, with its distinction between "humanistic" or good and "authoritarian" or bad religion), then we are deluding ourselves. The critical stance of the Old Testament prophets demands the priesthood, the cult, the specific history of Israel; it is rooted in that matrix. One cannot detach criticism from its roots and, ultimately, from that party to which it sets itself in antagonism. Thus Kierkegaard observed in his *Journals* that Protestantism makes no sense alone, without the dialectical opposition to Catholicism. (When there are no priests it makes no sense to protest that every layman is a priest; when there is no institutionalized other-worldliness, it makes no religious sense to denounce monasticism and asceticism and recall people to this world and to their mundane vocations.) The voice of the genuine critic always deserves the most *specific* hearing. It is simply misleading and vulgar to say of Marx, as Edmund Wilson in *To the Finland Station* and many others have done, that he was really a latter-day prophet; no more than it is true of Freud, though here people are following the cue of Freud's own rather ambivalent self-identification with Moses. The decisive element in Marx and Freud is the critical and entirely secular attitude which they took to all human problems. For their energies as persons and for their immense moral seriousness as thinkers, surely a better epithet of commendation can be found than these tired evocations of the prestige of the religious teacher. If Camus is a serious writer and worthy of respect, it is because he seeks to reason according to the post-religious premises. He does not belong in the "story" of modern religion.

If this is granted, we will become much clearer about the attempts which have been made to work out the serious consequences of atheism for reflective thought and personal morality. The heritage of Nietzsche constitutes one such tradition: the essays of E. M. Cioran, for example. The French *moraliste* and *anti-moraliste* tradition—Laclos, Sade, Breton, Sartre, Camus, Georges Bataille, Lévi-Strauss—constitutes another. The Hegelian-Marxist tradition is a third. And the Freudian tradition, which includes not only the work of Freud, but also that of dissidents such as Wilhelm Reich, Herbert Marcuse (*Eros and Civilization*) and Norman Brown (*Life Against Death*), is another. The creative phase of an idea coincides with the period during which it insists, cantankerously, on its boundaries, on what makes it different; but an idea becomes false and impotent when it seeks reconciliation, at cut-rate prices, with other ideas. Modern seriousness, in numerous traditions, exists. Only a bad intellectual end is served when we blur all boundaries and call it religious, too.

(1961)

Psychoanalysis and Norman O. Brown's
Life Against Death

THE publication of Norman O. Brown's *Life Against Death* (1959) in a paperback edition is a noteworthy event. Together with Herbert Marcuse's *Eros and Civilization* (1955), it represents a new seriousness about Freudian ideas which reveals most previous writing on Freud published in America, be it the right-wing scholasticism of the psychoanalytic journals or the left-wing cultural studies of the Freudian "revisionists" (Fromm, Horney, etc.), as theoretically irrelevant or, at best, superficial. But, more important than its value as a reinterpretation of the most influential mind of our culture is its boldness as a discussion of the fundamental problems—about the hypocrisy of our culture, about art, money, religion, work, about sex and the motives of the body. Serious thinking about these problems—rightly, in my opinion, centered on the meaning of sexuality and of human freedom—has been continuous in France since Sade, Fourier, Cabanis, and Enfantin; it is to be found today in such disparate works as the sections on the body and on concrete relations with others of Sartre's *Being and Nothingness*, in the essays of Maurice Blanchot, in *L'Histoire d'O*, in the plays and prose of Jean Genet.

But in America, the twin subjects of eroticism and liberty are just beginning to be treated in a serious way. Most of us still feel required to fight the stale battle against inhibitions and prudery, taking sexuality for granted as something which merely needs a freer expression. A country in which the vindication of so sexually reactionary a book as *Lady Chatterley's Lover* is a serious matter is plainly at a very elementary stage of sexual maturity. Lawrence's ideas on sex are seriously marred by his class-romanticism, by his mystique of male separateness, by his puritanical insistence on genital sexuality; and many of his recent literary defenders have admitted this. Yet Lawrence must still be defended, especially when many who reject him have retreated to an even more reactionary position than his: treating sex as a matter-of-fact adjunct to love. The truth is that love is more sexual, more bodily than even Lawrence imagined. And the revolutionary implications of sexuality in contemporary society are far from being fully understood.

Norman Brown's book is a step in this direction. *Life Against Death* cannot fail to shock, if it is taken personally; for it is a book which does not aim at eventual reconciliation with the views of common sense. Another distinction which it possesses: it shows, convincingly, that psychoanalysis is not to be written off—as many contemporary intellectuals have done—as one more vulgar and conformist "ism" (along with Marxism, original sin-ism, existentialism, Zen Buddhism, etc., etc.). The disenchantment with psychoanalysis which animates the most sophisticated voices of our culture is understandable; it is difficult not to reject a view which has become both so official and so bland. The vocabulary of psychoanalysis has become the routine weapon of personal aggression, and the routine way of formulating (and therefore defending oneself against) anxiety, in the American middle classes. Being psychoanalyzed has become as much a bourgeois institution as going to college; and psychoanalytic ideas, incarnated in Broadway plays, in television, in the movies, confront us everywhere. The trouble with psychoanalytic ideas, as it now appears to many, is that they constitute a form of retreat from, and, therefore, conformity to, the real world. Psychoanalytic treatment does not challenge society; it returns us to the world, only a little better able to bear it, and without hope. Psychoanalysis is understood as anti-Utopian and anti-political—a desperate, but fundamentally pessimistic, attempt to safeguard the individual against the oppressive but inevitable claims of society.

But the disenchantment of American intellectuals with psychoanalytic ideas, as with the earlier disenchantment with Marxist ideas (a parallel case), is premature. Marxism is not Stalinism or the suppression of the Hungarian revolution; psychoanalysis is not the Park Avenue analyst or the psychoanalytic journals or the suburban matron discussing her child's Oedipus complex. Disenchantment is the characteristic posture of contemporary American intellectuals, but disenchantment is often the product of laziness. We are not tenacious enough about ideas, as we have not been serious or honest enough about sexuality.

This is the importance of Brown's *Life Against Death*, as well as of Marcuse's *Eros and Civilization*. Brown, like Marcuse, pursues Freud's ideas as a general theory of human nature—not as a therapy which returns people to the society which enforces their conflicts. Psychoanalysis is conceived by Brown not as a mode of treatment to smooth away the neurotic edges of discontent, but as a project for the transformation of human culture, and as a new and higher level in human consciousness as a whole. Freud's psychological categories are thus correctly seen, in the terminology of Marcuse, as political categories.

The step which Brown takes, which moves beyond Freud's own conception of what he was doing, is to show that psychological categories are also bodily categories. For Brown, psychoanalysis (and he does not mean the institutions of current-day psychoanalysis) promises nothing less than the healing of the split between the mind and the body: the transformation of the human ego into a body ego, and the resurrection of the body that is promised in Christian mysticism (Boehme) and in Blake, Novalis, and Rilke. We are nothing but body; all values are bodily values, says Brown. He invites us to accept the androgynous mode of being and the narcissistic mode of self-expression that lie hidden in the body. According to Brown, mankind is unalterably, in the unconscious, in revolt against sexual differentiation and genital organization. The core of human neurosis is man's incapacity to live in the body—to live (that is, to be sexual) and to die.

In a time in which there is nothing more common or more acceptable than criticism of our society and revulsion against civilization, it is well to distinguish the arguments of Brown (and Marcuse) from the general run of criticism, which is either childishly nihilistic or ultimately conformist and irrelevant (or often both). And since both books are sharply critical of Freud at many points, it is also important to distinguish them from other attempts to modify Freudian theory and to extend it as a theory of human nature and a moral critique of society. Both Brown and Marcuse offer the sharpest opposition to the bland "revisionist" interpretation of Freud which rules American cultural and intellectual life—on Broadway, in the nursery, at the cocktail parties, and in the suburban marriage bed. This "revisionist" Freudianism (Fromm to Paddy Chayevsky) passes for a criticism of mechanized, anxious, television-brainwashed America. It seeks to reinstate the value of the individual against the mass society; it offers the worthy ideal of fulfillment through love. But the revisionist critique is superficial. To assert the claims of love, when love is understood as comfort, protection against loneliness, ego-security—while leaving all the claims of sublimation unchallenged—hardly does justice to Freud. It is no accident that Freud chose to use the word sex when, as he himself declared, he might as well have used "love." Freud insisted on sex; he insisted on the body. Few of his followers understood his meaning, or saw its applications in a theory of culture; two exceptions were Ferenczi and the ill-fated Wilhelm Reich. The fact that both Reich and Ferenczi, in Brown's account, misunderstood the implications of Freud's thought—mainly, in their acceptance of the primacy of the orgasm—is less important than the fact that they grasped the critical implications of the Freudian ideas. They are far truer to Freud than the orthodox psychoanalysts who, as a result of their inability to transform psychoanalysis into social criticism, send human desire back into repression again.

Of course, to some extent, the master does deserve the disciples he gets. The contemporary appearance of psychoanalysis as a form of expensive spiritual counselling on techniques of adjustment and reconciliation to culture proceeds from the limits in Freud's own thought, which Brown points out in careful detail. Revolutionary mind that he was, Freud nevertheless supported the perennial aspirations of repressive culture. He accepted the inevitability of culture as it is, with its two characteristics—"a strengthening of the intellect, which is beginning to govern instinctual life, and an internalization of the aggressive impulses, with all its consequent advantages and disadvantages." Those who think of Freud as the champion of libidinal expressiveness may be surprised at what he calls "the psychological ideal," for it is none other than "the primacy of the intellect."

More generally, Freud is heir to the Platonic tradition of Western thought in its two paramount, and related, assumptions: the dualism of mind and body, and the self-evident value (both theoretical and practical) of self-consciousness. The first assumption is reflected in Freud's own acceptance of the view that sexuality is "lower" and the sublimations in art, science, and culture "higher." Added to this is the pessimistic view of sexuality which regards the sexual as precisely the area of vulnerability in human personality. The libidinal impulses are in uncontrollable conflict in themselves, a prey to frustration, aggression, and internalization in guilt; and the repressive agency of culture is necessary to harness the self-repressive mechanisms installed in human nature itself. The second assumption is reflected in the way in which the Freudian therapy assumes the curative value of self-consciousness, of knowing in detail how and in what way we are ill. Bringing to light the hidden motives must, Freud thought, automatically dispel them. Neurotic illness, in his conception, is a form of amnesia, a forgetting (bungled repression) of the painful past. Not to know the past is to be in bondage to it, while to remember, to know, is to be set free.

Brown criticizes both of these assumptions of Freud. We are not body versus mind, he says; this is to deny death, and therefore to deny life. And self-consciousness, divorced from the experiences of the body, is also equated with the life-denying denial of death. Brown's argument, too involved to summarize here, does not entail a repudiation of the value of consciousness or reflectiveness. Rather, a necessary distinction is made. What is wanted, in his terminology, is not Apollonian (or sublimation) consciousness, but Dionysian (or body) consciousness.

The terms "Apollonian" and "Dionysian" will inevitably remind one of Nietzsche, and the association is appropriate. The key to this reinterpretation of Freud is Nietzsche. It is interesting, however, that Brown does not link his discussion to Nietzsche, but rather to the eschatological tradition within Christianity.

> The specialty of Christian eschatology lies precisely in its rejection of the Platonic hostility to the human body and to 'matter,' its refusal to identify the Platonic path of sublimation with ultimate salvation, and its affirmation that eternal life can only be life in a body. Christian asceticism can carry punishment of the fallen body to heights inconceivable to Plato, but Christian hope is for the redemption of that fallen body. Hence the affirmation of Tertullian—'The body will rise again, all of the body, the identical body, the entire body.' The medieval Catholic synthesis between Christianity and Greek philosophy, with its notion of an immortal soul, compromised and confused the issue; only Protestantism carries the full burden of the peculiar Christian faith. Luther's break with the doctrine of sublimation (good works) is decisive, but the theologian of the resurrected body is the cobbler of Görlitz, Jacob Boehme.

The polemical drive, if not the exquisite detail, of Brown's book can be seen from this passage. It is at the same time an analysis of the whole range of Freudian theory, a theory of instinct and culture, and a set of historical case studies. Brown's commitment to Protestantism as the herald of a culture which has transcended sublimation is, however, historically dubious. To make only the most obvious criticism, Protestantism is also Calvinism, and the Calvinist ethic (as Max Weber has shown) provided the most powerful impetus for the ideals of sublimation and self-repression which are incarnated in modern urban culture.

Nevertheless, by putting his ideas in the framework of Christian eschatology (rather than in the terms of the passionate atheists like Sade, Nietzsche, and Sartre), Brown raises some additional issues of great importance. The genius of Christianity has been its development, from Judaism, of a historical view of the world and the human condition. And Brown's analysis, by allying itself with some of the submerged promises of Christian eschatology, opens up the possibility of a psychoanalytic theory of history which does not simply reduce cultural history to the psychology of individuals. The originality of *Life Against Death* consists in its working out a point of view which is simultaneously historical and psychological. Brown demonstrates that the psychological point of view does not necessarily imply a rejection of history, in terms of its eschatological aspirations, and a resignation to the "limits of human nature" and the necessity of repression through the agency of culture.

If this is so, however, we must reconsider the meaning of eschatology, or Utopianism, itself. Traditionally, eschatology has taken the form of an expectation of the future transcendence of the human condition for all mankind in inexorably advancing history. And it is against this expectation, whether in the form of Biblical eschatology, enlightenment, progressivism, or the theories of Marx and Hegel, that modern "psychological" critics have taken their largely conservative stand. But not all eschatological theories are theories of history. There is another kind of eschatology, which might be called the eschatology of immanence (as opposed to the more familiar eschatology of transcendence). It is this hope that Nietzsche, the greatest critic of the Platonic devaluation of the world (and of its heir, that "popular Platonism" known as Christianity), expressed in his theory of the "eternal return" and the "will to power."

However, for Nietzsche, the promise of fulfilled immanence was available only to the few, the masters, and rested on a perpetuation or freezing of the historical impasse of a master-slave society; there could be no collective fulfillment. Brown rejects the logic of public domination which Nietzsche accepted as the inevitable price for the fulfillment of the few. The highest praise one can give to Brown's book is that, apart from its all-important attempt to penetrate and further the insights of Freud, it is the first major attempt to formulate an eschatology of immanence in the seventy years since Nietzsche.

(1961)

Happenings: An Art
of Radical Juxtaposition

T HERE has appeared in New York recently a new, and still
esoteric, genre of spectacle. At first sight apparently a cross
between art exhibit and theatrical performance, these events
have been given the modest and somewhat teasing name of
"Happenings." They have taken place in lofts, small art galleries, backyards, and small theaters before audiences averag-
ing between thirty and one hundred persons. To describe a
Happening for those who have not seen one means dwelling
on what Happenings are not. They don't take place on a stage
conventionally understood, but *in* a dense object-clogged setting which may be made, assembled, or found, or all three.
In this setting a number of participants, *not* actors, perform
movements and handle objects antiphonally and in concert to
the accompaniment (sometimes) of words, wordless sounds,
music, flashing lights, and odors. The Happening has no plot,
though it is an action, or rather a series of actions and events. It
also shuns continuous rational discourse, though it may contain
words like "Help!", "*Voglio un bicchiere di acqua*," "Love me,"
"Car," "One, two, three . . ." Speech is purified and condensed
by disparateness (there is only the speech of need) and then
expanded by ineffectuality, by the lack of relation between the
persons enacting the Happening.

Those who do Happenings in New York—but they are not
just a New York phenomenon; similar activities have been reported in Osaka, Stockholm, Cologne, Milan, and Paris by
groups unrelated to each other—are young, in their late twenties or early thirties. They are mostly painters (Allan Kaprow,
Jim Dine, Red Grooms, Robert Whitman, Claes Oldenburg,
Al Hansen, George Brecht, Yoko Ono, Carolee Schneemann)
and a few musicians (Dick Higgins, Philip Corner, LaMonte
Young). Allan Kaprow, the man who more than anyone else is
responsible for stating and working out the genre, is the only
academic among them; he formerly taught art and art history
at Rutgers and now teaches at the State University of New York
on Long Island. For Kaprow, a painter and (for a year) a student of John Cage, doing Happenings since 1957 has replaced

painting; Happenings are, as he puts it, what his painting has become. But for most of the others, this is not the case; they have continued to paint or compose music in addition to occasionally producing a Happening or performing in the Happening devised by a friend.

The first Happening in public was Allan Kaprow's *Eighteen Happenings in Six Parts*, presented in October, 1959, at the opening of the Reuben Gallery, which Kaprow, among others, helped to form. For a couple of years, the Reuben Gallery, the Judson Gallery, and later the Green Gallery, were the principal showcases of Happenings in New York by Kaprow, Red Grooms, Jim Dine, Robert Whitman, and others; in the recent years, the only series of Happenings were those of Claes Oldenburg, presented every weekend in the three tiny back rooms of his "store" on East Second Street. In the five years since the Happenings have been presented in public, the group has enlarged from an original circle of close friends, and the members have diverged in their conceptions; no statement about what Happenings are as a genre will be acceptable to all the people now doing them. Some Happenings are more sparse, others more crowded with incident; some are violent, others are witty; some are like haiku, others are epic; some are vignettes, others more theatrical. Nevertheless, it is possible to discern an essential unity in the form, and to draw certain conclusions about the relevance of Happenings to the arts of painting and theater. Kaprow, by the way, has written the best article yet to appear on Happenings, their meaning in general in the context of the contemporary art scene, and their evolution for him in particular, in the May, 1961, *Art News*, to which the reader is referred for a fuller description of what literally "happens" than I shall attempt in this article.

Perhaps the most striking feature of the Happening is its treatment (this is the only word for it) of the audience. The event seems designed to tease and abuse the audience. The performers may sprinkle water on the audience, or fling pennies or sneeze-producing detergent powder at it. Someone may be making near-deafening noises on an oil drum, or waving an acetylene torch in the direction of the spectators. Several radios may be playing simultaneously. The audience may be made to stand uncomfortably in a crowded room, or fight for space to stand on boards laid in a few inches of water. There is no attempt to cater to the audience's desire to see everything. In fact this is often deliberately frustrated, by performing some of the events in semi-darkness or by having events go on in different rooms simultaneously. In Allan Kaprow's *A Spring Happening*, presented in March, 1961, at the Reuben Gallery, the spectators were confined inside a long box-like structure resembling a cattle car; peep-holes had been bored in the wooden walls of this enclosure through which the spectators could strain to see the events taking place outside; when the Happening was over, the walls collapsed, and the spectators were driven out by someone operating a power lawnmower.

(This abusive involvement of the audience seems to provide, in default of anything else, the dramatic spine of the Happening. When the Happening is more purely spectacle, and the audience simply spectators, as in Allan Kaprow's *The Courtyard*, presented in November, 1962, at the Renaissance House, the event is considerably less dense and compelling.)

Another striking feature of Happenings is their treatment of time. The duration of a Happening is unpredictable; it may be anywhere from ten to forty-five minutes; the average one is about a half-hour in length. I have noticed, in attending a fair number of them over the last two years, that the audience of Happenings, a loyal, appreciative, and for the most part experienced audience, frequently does not know when they are over, and has to be signalled to leave. The fact that in the audiences one sees mostly the same faces again and again indicates this is not due to a lack of familiarity with the form. The unpredictable duration, and content, of each individual Happening is essential to its effect. This is because the Happening has no plot, no story, and therefore no element of suspense (which would then entail the satisfaction of suspense).

The Happening operates by creating an asymmetrical network of surprises, without climax or consummation; this is the alogic of dreams rather than the logic of most art. Dreams have no sense of time. Neither do the Happenings. Lacking a plot and continuous rational discourse, they have no past. As the name itself suggests, Happenings are always in the present tense. The same words, if there are any, are said over and over; speech is reduced to a stutter. The same actions, too, are frequently repeated throughout a single Happening—a kind of gestural stutter, or done in slow motion, to convey a sense of the arrest of time. Occasionally the entire Happening takes a circular form, opening and concluding with the same act or gesture.

One way in which the Happenings state their freedom from time is in their deliberate impermanence. A painter or sculptor who makes Happenings does not make anything that can be purchased. One cannot buy a Happening; one can only support it. It is consumed on the premises. This would seem to make Happenings a form of theater, for one can only attend a theatrical performance, but can't take it home. But in the theater, there is a text, a complete "score" for the performance which is printed, can be bought, read, and has an existence independent of any performance of it. Happenings are not theater either, if by theater we mean plays. However, it is not true (as some Happening-goers suppose) that Happenings are improvised on the spot. They are carefully rehearsed for any time from a week to several months—though the script or score is minimal, usually no more than a page of general directions for movements and descriptions of materials. Much of what goes on in the performance has been worked out or choreographed in rehearsal by the performers themselves; and if the Happening is done for several evenings consecutively it is likely to vary a good deal from performance to performance, far more than in the theater. But while the same Happening might be given several nights in a row, it is not meant to enter into a repertory which can be repeated. Once dismantled after a given performance or series of performances, it is never revived, never performed again. In part, this has to do with the deliberately occasional materials which go into Happenings—paper, wooden crates, tin cans, burlap sacks, foods, walls painted for the occasion—materials which are often literally consumed, or destroyed, in the course of the performance.

What is primary in a Happening is materials—and their modulations as hard and soft, dirty and clean. This preoccupation with materials, which might seem to make the Happenings more like painting than theater, is also expressed in the use or treatment of persons as material objects rather than "characters." The people in the Happenings are often made to look like objects, by enclosing them in burlap sacks, elaborate paper wrappings, shrouds, and masks. (Or, the person may be used as a still-life, as in Allan Kaprow's *Untitled Happening*, given in the basement boiler room of the Maidman Theater in March, 1962, in which a naked woman lay on a ladder strung above the space in which the Happenings took place.) Much of the action, violent and otherwise, of Happenings involves this use of the person as a material object. There is a great deal of violent using of the physical persons of the performers by the person himself (jumping, falling) and by each other (lifting, chasing, throwing, pushing, hitting, wrestling); and sometimes a slower, more sensuous use of the person (caressing, menacing, gazing) by others or by the person himself. Another way in which people are employed is in the discovery or the impassioned, repetitive use of materials for their sensuous properties rather than their conventional uses: dropping pieces of bread into a bucket of water, setting a table for a meal, rolling a huge paper-screen hoop along the floor, hanging up laundry. Jim Dine's *Car Crash*, done at the Reuben Gallery in November, 1960, ended with a man smashing and grinding pieces of colored chalk into a blackboard. Simple acts like coughing and carrying, a man shaving himself, or a group of people eating, will be prolonged, repetitively, to a point of demoniacal frenzy.

Of the materials used, it might be noted that one cannot distinguish among set, props, and costumes in a Happening, as one can in the theater. The underwear or thrift-shop oddments which a performer may wear are as much a part of the whole composition as the paint-spattered papier-mâché shapes which protrude from the wall or the trash which is strewn on the floor. Unlike the theater and like some modern painting, in the Happening objects are not *placed*, but rather scattered about and heaped together. The Happening takes place in what can best be called an "environment," and this environment typically is messy and disorderly and crowded in the extreme, constructed of some materials which are rather fragile, such as paper and cloth, and others which are chosen for their abused, dirty, and dangerous condition. The Happenings thereby register (in a real, not simply an ideological way) a protest against the museum conception of art—the idea that the job of the artist is to make things to be preserved and cherished. One cannot hold on to a Happening, and one can only cherish it as one cherishes a firecracker going off dangerously close to one's face.

Happenings have been called by some "painters' theater," which means—aside from the fact that most of the people who do them are painters—that they can be described as animated paintings, more accurately as "animated collages" or "*trompe l'oeil* brought to life." Further, the appearance of Happenings can be described as one logical development of the New York school of painting of the fifties. The gigantic size of many of the canvases painted in New York in the last decade, designed to overwhelm and envelop the spectator, plus the increasing use of materials other than paint to adhere to, and later extend from, the canvas, indicate the latent intention of this type of painting to project itself into a three-dimensional form. This is exactly what some people started to do. The crucial next step was taken with the work done in the middle and late fifties by Robert Rauschenberg, Allan Kaprow, and others in a new form called "assemblages," a hybrid of painting, collage, and sculpture, using a sardonic variety of materials, mainly in the state of debris, including license plates, newspaper clippings, pieces of glass, machine parts, and the artist's socks. From the assemblage to the whole room or "environment" is only one further step. The final step, the Happening, simply puts people into the environment and sets it in motion. There is no doubt that much of the style of the Happening—its general look of messiness, its fondness for incorporating ready-made materials of no artistic prestige, particularly the junk of urban civilization—owes to the experience and pressures of New York painting. (It should be mentioned, however, that Kaprow for one thinks the use of urban junk is not a necessary element of the Happening form, and contends that Happenings can as well be composed and put on in pastoral surroundings, using the "clean" materials of nature.)

Thus recent painting supplies one way of explaining the look and something of the style of Happenings. Yet it does not explain their form. For this we must look beyond painting and particularly to Surrealism. By Surrealism, I do not mean a specific movement in painting inaugurated by André Breton's manifesto in 1924 and to which we associate the names of Max Ernst, Dalí, de Chirico, Magritte, and others. I mean a mode of sensibility which cuts across all the arts in the 20th century. There is a Surrealist tradition in the theater, in painting, in poetry, in the cinema, in music, and in the novel; even in architecture there is, if not a tradition, at least one candidate, the Spanish architect Gaudí. The Surrealist tradition in all these arts is united by the idea of destroying conventional meanings, and creating new meanings or counter-meanings through radical juxtaposition (the "collage principle"). Beauty, in the words of Lautréamont, is "the fortuitous encounter of a sewing machine and an umbrella on a dissecting table." Art so understood is obviously animated by aggression, aggression toward the presumed conventionality of its audience and, above all, aggression toward the medium itself. The Surrealist sensibility aims to shock, through its techniques of radical juxtaposition. Even one of the classical methods of psychoanalysis, free association, can be interpreted as another working-out of the Surrealist principle of radical juxtaposition. By its accepting as relevant every unpremeditated statement made by the patient, the Freudian technique of interpretation shows itself to be based on the same logic of coherence behind contradiction to which we are accustomed in modern art. Using the same logic, the Dadaist Kurt Schwitters made his brilliant *Merz* constructions of the early twenties out of deliberately unartistic materials; one of his collages, for example, is assembled from the gutter-pickings of a single city block. This recalls Freud's description of his method as divining meaning from "the rubbish-heap . . . of our observations," from the collation of the most insignificant details; as a time limit the analyst's daily hour with the patient is no less arbitrary than the space limit of one block from whose gutter the rubbish was selected; everything depends on the creative accidents of arrangement and insight. One may also see a kind of involuntary collage-principle in many of the artifacts of the modern city: the brutal disharmony of buildings in size and style, the wild juxtaposition of store signs, the clamorous layout of the modern newspaper, etc.

The art of radical juxtaposition can serve different uses, however. A great deal of the content of Surrealism has served the purposes of wit—either the delicious joke in itself of what is inane, childish, extravagant, obsessional; or social satire. This is particularly the purpose of Dada, and of the Surrealism that is represented in the International Surrealist Exhibition in Paris in January, 1938, and the exhibits in New York in 1942 and 1960. Simone de Beauvoir in the second volume of her memoirs describes the 1938 spook-house as follows:

In the entrance hall stood one of Dalí's special creations: a taxi cab, rain streaming out of it, with a blonde, swooning female dummy posed inside, surrounded by a sort of lettuce-and-chicory salad all smothered with snails. The "Rue Surréaliste" contained other similar figures, clothed or nude, by Man Ray, Max Ernst, Dominguez, and Maurice Henry. Masson's [was] a face imprisoned in a cage and gagged with a pansy. The main salon had been arranged by Marcel Duchamp to look like a grotto; it contained, among other things, a pond and four beds grouped around a brazier, while the ceiling was covered with coal bags. The whole place smelled of Brazilian coffee, and various objects loomed up out of the carefully contrived semi-darkness: a fur-lined dish, an occasional table with the legs of a woman. On all sides ordinary things like walls and doors and flower vases were breaking free from human restraint. I don't think surrealism had any direct influence on us, but it had impregnated the very air we breathed. It was the surrealists, for instance, who made it fashionable to frequent the Flea Market where Sartre and Olga and I often spent our Sunday afternoons.

The last line of this quote is particularly interesting, for it recalls how the Surrealist principle has given rise to a certain kind of witty appreciation of the derelict, inane, *démodé* objects of modern civilization—the taste for a certain kind of passionate non-art that is known as "camp." The fur-lined teacup, the portrait executed out of Pepsi-Cola bottle caps, the perambulating toilet bowl, are attempts to create objects which have built into them a kind of wit which the sophisticated beholder with his eyes opened by camp can bring to the enjoyment of Cecil B. DeMille movies, comic books, and *art nouveau* lampshades. The main requirement for such wit is that the objects not be high art or good taste in any normally valued sense; the more despised the material or the more banal the sentiments expressed, the better.

But the Surrealist principle can be made to serve other purposes than wit, whether the disinterested wit of sophistication or the polemical wit of satire. It can be conceived more seriously, therapeutically—for the purpose of reeducating the senses (in art) or the character (in psychoanalysis). And finally, it can be made to serve the purposes of terror. If the meaning of modern art is its discovery beneath the logic of everyday life of the alogic of dreams, then we may expect the art which has the freedom of dreaming also to have its emotional range. There are witty dreams, solemn dreams, and there are nightmares.

The examples of terror in the use of the Surrealist principle are more easily illustrated in arts with a dominant figurative tradition, like literature and the film, than in music (Varèse, Scheffer, Stockhausen, Cage) or painting (de Kooning, Bacon). In literature, one thinks of Lautréamont's *Maldoror* and Kafka's tales and novels and the morgue poems of Gottfried Benn. From the film, examples are two by Buñuel and Dalí, *Un Chien Andalou* and *L'Âge d'Or*, Franju's *Le Sang des Bêtes*, and, more recently, two short films, the Polish *Life Is Beautiful* and the American Bruce Connor's *A Movie*, and certain moments in the films of Alfred Hitchcock, H. G. Clouzot, and Kon Ichikawa. But the best understanding of the Surrealist principle employed for the purposes of terrorization is to be found in the writings of Antonin Artaud, a Frenchman who had four important and model careers: as a poet, a lunatic, a film actor, and a theoretician of the theater. In his collection of essays, *The Theater and Its Double*, Artaud envisages nothing less than a complete repudiation of the modern Western theater, with its cult of masterpieces, its primary emphasis on the written text (the word), its tame emotional range. Artaud writes: "The theater must make itself the equal of life—not an individual life, that individual aspect of life in which *characters* triumph, but the sort of liberated life which sweeps away human individuality." This transcendence of the burden and limitations of personal individuality—also a hopeful theme in D. H. Lawrence and Jung—is executed through recourse to the preeminently collective contents of dreaming. Only in our dreams do we nightly strike below the shallow level of what Artaud calls, contemptuously, "psychological and social man." But dreaming does not mean for Artaud simply poetry, fantasy; it means violence, insanity, nightmare. The connection with the dream will necessarily give rise to what Artaud calls a "*theater of cruelty*," the title of two of his manifestoes. The theater must furnish "the spectator with the truthful precipitates of dreams, in which his taste for crime, his erotic obsessions, his savagery, his chimeras, his Utopian sense of life and matter, even his cannibalism, pour out, on a level not counterfeit and illusory, but interior. . . . The theater, like dreams, must be bloody and inhuman."

The prescriptions which Artaud offers in *The Theater and Its Double* describe better than anything else what Happenings are. Artaud shows the connection between three typical features of the Happening: first, its supra-personal or impersonal treatment of persons; second, its emphasis on spectacle and sound, and disregard for the word; and third, its professed aim to assault the audience.

The appetite for violence in art is hardly a new phenomenon. As Ruskin noted in 1880 in the course of an attack on "the modern novel" (his examples are *Guy Mannering* and *Bleak House!*), the taste for the fantastic, the *outré*, the rejected, and the willingness to be shocked are perhaps the most remarkable characteristics of modern audiences. Inevitably, this drives the artist to ever greater and more intense attempts to arouse a reaction from his audience. The question is only whether a reaction need always be provoked by terrorization. It seems to be the implicit consensus of those who do Happenings that other kinds of arousal (for example, sexual arousal) are in fact less effective, and that the last bastion of the emotional life is fear.

Yet it is also interesting to note that this art form which is designed to stir the modern audience from its cozy emotional anesthesia operates with images of anesthetized persons, acting in a kind of slow-motion disjunction with each other, and gives us an image of action characterized above all by ceremoniousness and ineffectuality. At this point the Surrealist arts of terror link up with the deepest meaning of comedy: the assertion of invulnerability. In the heart of comedy, there is emotional anesthesia. What permits us to laugh at painful and grotesque events is that we observe that the people to whom these events happen are really underreacting. No matter how much they scream or prance about or inveigh to heaven or lament their misfortune, the audience knows they are really not feeling very much. The protagonists of great comedy all have something of the automaton or robot in them. This is the secret of such different examples of comedy as Aristophanes' *The Clouds*, *Gulliver's Travels*, Tex Avery cartoons, *Candide*, *Kind Hearts and Coronets*, the films of Buster Keaton, *Ubu Roi*, the Goon Show. The secret of comedy is the dead-pan—or the exaggerated reaction or the misplaced reaction that is a parody of a true response. Comedy, as much as tragedy, works by a certain stylization of emotional response. In the case of tragedy, it is by a heightening of the norm of feeling; in the case of comedy, it is by underreacting and misreacting according to the norms of feeling.

Surrealism is perhaps the farthest extension of the idea of

comedy, running the full range from wit to terror. It is "comic" rather than "tragic" because Surrealism (in all its examples, which include Happenings) stresses the extremes of disrelation—which is preeminently the subject of comedy, as "relatedness" is the subject and source of tragedy. I, and other people in the audience, often laugh during Happenings. I don't think this is simply because we are embarrassed or made nervous by violent and absurd actions. I think we laugh because what goes on in the Happenings is, in the deepest sense, funny. This does not make it any less terrifying. There is something that moves one to laughter, if only our social pieties and highly conventional sense of the serious would allow it, in the most terrible of modern catastrophes and atrocities. There is something comic in modern experience as such, a demonic, not a divine comedy, precisely to the extent that modern experience is characterized by meaningless mechanized situations of disrelation.

Comedy is not any less comic because it is punitive. As in tragedy, every comedy needs a scapegoat, someone who will be punished and expelled from the social order represented mimetically in the spectacle. What goes on in the Happenings merely follows Artaud's prescription for a spectacle which will eliminate the stage, that is, the distance between spectators and performers, and "will physically envelop the spectator." In the Happenings this scapegoat is the audience.

(1962)

Notes on "Camp"

MANY things in the world have not been named; and many things, even if they have been named, have never been described. One of these is the sensibility—unmistakably modern, a variant of sophistication but hardly identical with it—that goes by the cult name of "Camp."

A sensibility (as distinct from an idea) is one of the hardest things to talk about; but there are special reasons why Camp, in particular, has never been discussed. It is not a natural mode of sensibility, if there be any such. Indeed the essence of Camp is its love of the unnatural: of artifice and exaggeration. And Camp is esoteric—something of a private code, a badge of identity even, among small urban cliques. Apart from a lazy two-page sketch in Christopher Isherwood's novel *The World in the Evening* (1954), it has hardly broken into print. To talk about Camp is therefore to betray it. If the betrayal can be defended, it will be for the edification it provides, or the dignity of the conflict it resolves. For myself, I plead the goal of self-edification, and the goad of a sharp conflict in my own sensibility. I am strongly drawn to Camp, and almost as strongly offended by it. That is why I want to talk about it, and why I can. For no one who wholeheartedly shares in a given sensibility can analyze it; he can only, whatever his intention, exhibit it. To name a sensibility, to draw its contours and to recount its history, requires a deep sympathy modified by revulsion.

Though I am speaking about sensibility only—and about a sensibility that, among other things, converts the serious into the frivolous—these are grave matters. Most people think of sensibility or taste as the realm of purely subjective preferences, those mysterious attractions, mainly sensual, that have not been brought under the sovereignty of reason. They *allow* that considerations of taste play a part in their reactions to people and to works of art. But this attitude is naïve. And even worse. To patronize the faculty of taste is to patronize oneself. For taste governs every free—as opposed to rote—human response. Nothing is more decisive. There is taste in people, visual taste, taste in emotion—and there is taste in acts, taste in morality. Intelligence, as well, is really a kind of taste: taste in ideas. (One of the facts to be reckoned with is that taste tends to develop

259

very unevenly. It's rare that the same person has good visual taste *and* good taste in people *and* taste in ideas.)

Taste has no system and no proofs. But there is something like a logic of taste: the consistent sensibility which underlies and gives rise to a certain taste. A sensibility is almost, but not quite, ineffable. Any sensibility which can be crammed into the mold of a system, or handled with the rough tools of proof, is no longer a sensibility at all. It has hardened into an idea. . . .

To snare a sensibility in words, especially one that is alive and powerful,* one must be tentative and nimble. The form of jottings, rather than an essay (with its claim to a linear, consecutive argument), seemed more appropriate for getting down something of this particular fugitive sensibility. It's embarrassing to be solemn and treatise-like about Camp. One runs the risk of having, oneself, produced a very inferior piece of Camp.

These notes are for Oscar Wilde.

"One should either be a work of art, or wear a work of art."
    —*Phrases & Philosophies for the Use of the Young*

1. To start very generally: Camp is a certain mode of aestheticism. It is *one* way of seeing the world as an aesthetic phenomenon. That way, the way of Camp, is not in terms of beauty, but in terms of the degree of artifice, of stylization.

2. To emphasize style is to slight content, or to introduce an attitude which is neutral with respect to content. It goes without saying that the Camp sensibility is disengaged, depoliticized— or at least apolitical.

3. Not only is there a Camp vision, a Camp way of looking at things. Camp is as well a quality discoverable in objects and the behavior of persons. There are "campy" movies, clothes, furniture, popular songs, novels, people, buildings. . . . This distinction is important. True, the Camp eye has the power to transform experience. But not everything can be seen as Camp. It's not *all* in the eye of the beholder.

---

*The sensibility of an era is not only its most decisive, but also its most perishable, aspect. One may capture the ideas (intellectual history) and the behavior (social history) of an epoch without ever touching upon the sensibility or taste which informed those ideas, that behavior. Rare are those historical studies— like Huizinga on the late Middle Ages, Febvre on 16th century France—which do tell us something about the sensibility of the period.

4. Random examples of items which are part of the canon of Camp:

Zuleika Dobson
Tiffany lamps
Scopitone films
The Brown Derby restaurant on Sunset Boulevard in LA
The Enquirer, headlines and stories
Aubrey Beardsley drawings
Swan Lake
Bellini's operas
Visconti's direction of *Salomé* and *'Tis Pity She's a Whore*
certain turn-of-the-century picture postcards
Schoedsack's *King Kong*
the Cuban pop singer La Lupe
Lynd Ward's novel in woodcuts, *Gods' Man*
the old Flash Gordon comics
women's clothes of the twenties (feather boas, fringed and
    beaded dresses, etc.)
the novels of Ronald Firbank and Ivy Compton-Burnett
stag movies seen without lust

5. Camp taste has an affinity for certain arts rather than others. Clothes, furniture, all the elements of visual décor, for instance, make up a large part of Camp. For Camp art is often decorative art, emphasizing texture, sensuous surface, and style at the expense of content. Concert music, though, because it is contentless, is rarely Camp. It offers no opportunity, say, for a contrast between silly or extravagant content and rich form. . . . Sometimes whole art forms become saturated with Camp. Classical ballet, opera, movies have seemed so for a long time. In the last two years, popular music (post rock-'n'-roll, what the French call *yé yé*) has been annexed. And movie criticism (like lists of "The 10 Best Bad Movies I Have Seen") is probably the greatest popularizer of Camp taste today, because most people still go to the movies in a high-spirited and unpretentious way.

6. There is a sense in which it is correct to say: "It's too good to be Camp." Or "too important," not marginal enough. (More on this later.) Thus, the personality and many of the works of Jean Cocteau are Camp, but not those of André Gide; the

operas of Richard Strauss, but not those of Wagner; concoctions of Tin Pan Alley and Liverpool, but not jazz. Many examples of Camp are things which, from a "serious" point of view, are either bad art or kitsch. Not all, though. Not only is Camp not necessarily bad art, but some art which can be approached as Camp (example: the major films of Louis Feuillade) merits the most serious admiration and study.

"The more we study Art, the less we care for Nature."
—*The Decay of Lying*

7. All Camp objects, and persons, contain a large element of artifice. Nothing in nature can be campy. . . . Rural Camp is still man-made, and most campy objects are urban. (Yet, they often have a serenity—or a naïveté—which is the equivalent of pastoral. A great deal of Camp suggests Empson's phrase, "urban pastoral.")

8. Camp is a vision of the world in terms of style—but a particular kind of style. It is the love of the exaggerated, the "off," of things-being-what-they-are-not. The best example is in Art Nouveau, the most typical and fully developed Camp style. Art Nouveau objects, typically, convert one thing into something else: the lighting fixtures in the form of flowering plants, the living room which is really a grotto. A remarkable example: the Paris Métro entrances designed by Hector Guimard in the late 1890s in the shape of cast-iron orchid stalks.

9. As a taste in persons, Camp responds particularly to the markedly attenuated and to the strongly exaggerated. The androgyne is certainly one of the great images of Camp sensibility. Examples: the swooning, slim, sinuous figures of pre-Raphaelite painting and poetry; the thin, flowing, sexless bodies in Art Nouveau prints and posters, presented in relief on lamps and ashtrays; the haunting androgynous vacancy behind the perfect beauty of Greta Garbo. Here, Camp taste draws on a mostly unacknowledged truth of taste: the most refined form of sexual attractiveness (as well as the most refined form of sexual pleasure) consists in going against the grain of one's sex. What is most beautiful in virile men is something feminine; what is most beautiful in feminine women is something masculine. . . . Allied to the Camp taste for the androgynous is something that seems quite different but isn't: a relish for the exaggeration of sexual characteristics and personality mannerisms. For obvious reasons,

the best examples that can be cited are movie stars. The corny flamboyant femaleness of Jayne Mansfield, Gina Lollobrigida, Jane Russell, Virginia Mayo; the exaggerated he-man-ness of Steve Reeves, Victor Mature. The great stylists of temperament and mannerism, like Bette Davis, Barbara Stanwyck, Tallulah Bankhead, Edwige Feuillère.

10. Camp sees everything in quotation marks. It's not a lamp, but a "lamp"; not a woman, but a "woman." To perceive Camp in objects and persons is to understand Being-as-Playing-a-Role. It is the farthest extension, in sensibility, of the metaphor of life as theater.

11. Camp is the triumph of the epicene style. (The convertibility of "man" and "woman," "person" and "thing.") But all style, that is, artifice, is, ultimately, epicene. Life is not stylish. Neither is nature.

12. The question isn't, "Why travesty, impersonation, theatricality?" The question is, rather, "When does travesty, impersonation, theatricality acquire the special flavor of Camp?" Why is the atmosphere of Shakespeare's comedies (*As You Like It*, etc.) not epicene, while that of *Der Rosenkavalier* is?

13. The dividing line seems to fall in the 18th century; there the origins of Camp taste are to be found (Gothic novels, Chinoiserie, caricature, artificial ruins, and so forth). But the relation to nature was quite different then. In the 18th century, people of taste either patronized nature (Strawberry Hill) or attempted to remake it into something artificial (Versailles). They also indefatigably patronized the past. Today's Camp taste effaces nature, or else contradicts it outright. And the relation of Camp taste to the past is extremely sentimental.

14. A pocket history of Camp might, of course, begin farther back—with the mannerist artists like Pontormo, Rosso, and Caravaggio, or the extraordinarily theatrical painting of Georges de La Tour, or Euphuism (Lyly, etc.) in literature. Still, the soundest starting point seems to be the late 17th and early 18th century, because of that period's extraordinary feeling for artifice, for surface, for symmetry; its taste for the picturesque and the thrilling, its elegant conventions for representing instant feeling and the total presence of character—the epigram and the rhymed couplet (in words), the flourish (in gesture and in music). The late 17th and early 18th century is the great period of Camp: Pope, Congreve, Walpole, etc., but

not Swift; *les précieux* in France; the rococo churches of Munich; Pergolesi. Somewhat later: much of Mozart. But in the 19th century, what had been distributed throughout all of high culture now becomes a special taste; it takes on overtones of the acute, the esoteric, the perverse. Confining the story to England alone, we see Camp continuing wanly through 19th century aestheticism (Burne-Jones, Pater, Ruskin, Tennyson), emerging full-blown with the Art Nouveau movement in the visual and decorative arts, and finding its conscious ideologists in such "wits" as Wilde and Firbank.

15. Of course, to say all these things are Camp is not to argue they are simply that. A full analysis of Art Nouveau, for instance, would scarcely equate it with Camp. But such an analysis cannot ignore what in Art Nouveau allows it to be experienced as Camp. Art Nouveau is full of "content," even of a political-moral sort; it was a revolutionary movement in the arts, spurred on by a utopian vision (somewhere between William Morris and the Bauhaus group) of an organic politics and taste. Yet there is also a feature of the Art Nouveau objects which suggests a disengaged, unserious, "aesthete's" vision. This tells us something important about Art Nouveau—and about what the lens of Camp, which blocks out content, is.

16. Thus, the Camp sensibility is one that is alive to a double sense in which some things can be taken. But this is not the familiar split-level construction of a literal meaning, on the one hand, and a symbolic meaning, on the other. It is the difference, rather, between the thing as meaning something, anything, and the thing as pure artifice.

17. This comes out clearly in the vulgar use of the word Camp as a verb, "to camp," something that people do. To camp is a mode of seduction—one which employs flamboyant mannerisms susceptible of a double interpretation; gestures full of duplicity, with a witty meaning for cognoscenti and another, more impersonal, for outsiders. Equally and by extension, when the word becomes a noun, when a person or a thing is "a camp," a duplicity is involved. Behind the "straight" public sense in which something can be taken, one has found a private zany experience of the thing.

"To be natural is such a very difficult pose to keep up."
                                        —*An Ideal Husband*

18. One must distinguish between naïve and deliberate Camp. Pure Camp is always naïve. Camp which knows itself to be Camp ("camping") is usually less satisfying.

19. The pure examples of Camp are unintentional; they are dead serious. The Art Nouveau craftsman who makes a lamp with a snake coiled around it is not kidding, nor is he trying to be charming. He is saying, in all earnestness: Voilà! the Orient! Genuine Camp—for instance, the numbers devised for the Warner Brothers musicals of the early thirties (*42nd Street*; *The Golddiggers of 1933*; . . . *of 1935*; . . . *of 1937*; etc.) by Busby Berkeley—does not *mean* to be funny. Camping—say, the plays of Noel Coward—does. It seems unlikely that much of the traditional opera repertoire could be such satisfying Camp if the melodramatic absurdities of most opera plots had not been taken seriously by their composers. One doesn't need to know the artist's private intentions. The work tells all. (Compare a typical 19th century opera with Samuel Barber's *Vanessa*, a piece of manufactured, calculated Camp, and the difference is clear.)

20. Probably, intending to be campy is always harmful. The perfection of *Trouble in Paradise* and *The Maltese Falcon*, among the greatest Camp movies ever made, comes from the effortless smooth way in which tone is maintained. This is not so with such famous would-be Camp films of the fifties as *All About Eve* and *Beat the Devil*. These more recent movies have their fine moments, but the first is so slick and the second so hysterical; they want so badly to be campy that they're continually losing the beat. . . . Perhaps, though, it is not so much a question of the unintended effect versus the conscious intention, as of the delicate relation between parody and self-parody in Camp. The films of Hitchcock are a showcase for this problem. When self-parody lacks ebullience but instead reveals (even sporadically) a contempt for one's themes and one's materials—as in *To Catch a Thief*, *Rear Window*, *North by Northwest*—the results are forced and heavy-handed, rarely Camp. Successful Camp—a movie like Carné's *Drôle de Drame*; the film performances of Mae West and Edward Everett Horton; portions of the Goon Show—even when it reveals self-parody, reeks of self-love.

21. So, again, Camp rests on innocence. That means Camp discloses innocence, but also, when it can, corrupts it. Objects, being objects, don't change when they are singled out by the Camp vision. Persons, however, respond to their audiences.

Persons begin "camping": Mae West, Bea Lillie, La Lupe, Tallulah Bankhead in *Lifeboat*, Bette Davis in *All About Eve*. (Persons can even be induced to camp without their knowing it. Consider the way Fellini got Anita Ekberg to parody herself in *La Dolce Vita*.)

22. Considered a little less strictly, Camp is either completely naïve or else wholly conscious (when one plays at being campy). An example of the latter: Wilde's epigrams themselves.

"It's absurd to divide people into good and bad. People are either charming or tedious."

—Lady Windemere's Fan

23. In naïve, or pure, Camp, the essential element is seriousness, a seriousness that fails. Of course, not all seriousness that fails can be redeemed as Camp. Only that which has the proper mixture of the exaggerated, the fantastic, the passionate, and the naïve.

24. When something is just bad (rather than Camp), it's often because it is too mediocre in its ambition. The artist hasn't attempted to do anything really outlandish. ("It's too much," "It's too fantastic," "It's not to be believed," are standard phrases of Camp enthusiasm.)

25. The hallmark of Camp is the spirit of extravagance. Camp is a woman walking around in a dress made of three million feathers. Camp is the paintings of Carlo Crivelli, with their real jewels and *trompe-l'oeil* insects and cracks in the masonry. Camp is the outrageous aestheticism of Sternberg's six American movies with Dietrich, all six, but especially the last, *The Devil Is a Woman*. . . . In Camp there is often something *démesuré* in the quality of the ambition, not only in the style of the work itself. Gaudí's lurid and beautiful buildings in Barcelona are Camp not only because of their style but because they reveal— most notably in the Cathedral of the Sagrada Familia—the ambition on the part of one man to do what it takes a generation, a whole culture to accomplish.

26. Camp is art that proposes itself seriously, but cannot be taken altogether seriously because it is "too much." *Titus Andronicus* and *Strange Interlude* are almost Camp, or could be played as Camp. The public manner and rhetoric of de Gaulle, often, are pure Camp.

27. A work can come close to Camp, but not make it, because it succeeds. Eisenstein's films are seldom Camp because,
despite all exaggeration, they do succeed (dramatically) without
surplus. If they were a little more "off," they could be great
Camp—particularly *Ivan the Terrible I & II*. The same for
Blake's drawings and paintings, weird and mannered as they
are. They aren't Camp; though Art Nouveau, influenced by
Blake, is.

What is extravagant in an inconsistent or an unpassionate
way is not Camp. Neither can anything be Camp that does not
seem to spring from an irrepressible, a virtually uncontrolled
sensibility. Without passion, one gets pseudo-Camp—what is
merely decorative, safe, in a word, chic. On the barren edge of
Camp lie a number of attractive things: the sleek fantasies of
Dalí, the haute couture preciosity of Albicocco's *The Girl with
the Golden Eyes*. But the two things—Camp and preciosity—
must not be confused.

28. Again, Camp is the attempt to do something extraordinary. But extraordinary in the sense, often, of being special,
glamorous. (The curved line, the extravagant gesture.) Not
extraordinary merely in the sense of effort. Ripley's Believe-
It-Or-Not items are rarely campy. These items, either natural
oddities (the two-headed rooster, the eggplant in the shape of
a cross) or else the products of immense labor (the man who
walked from here to China on his hands, the woman who en-
graved the New Testament on the head of a pin), lack the visual
reward—the glamour, the theatricality—that marks off certain
extravagances as Camp.

29. The reason a movie like *On the Beach*, books like *Winesburg, Ohio* and *For Whom the Bell Tolls* are bad to the point of
being laughable, but not bad to the point of being enjoyable,
is that they are too dogged and pretentious. They lack fantasy.
There is Camp in such bad movies as *The Prodigal* and *Samson
and Delilah*, the series of Italian color spectacles featuring the
super-hero Maciste, numerous Japanese science fiction films
(*Rodan*, *The Mysterians*, *The H-Man*) because, in their relative
unpretentiousness and vulgarity, they are more extreme and irresponsible in their fantasy—and therefore touching and quite
enjoyable.

30. Of course, the canon of Camp can change. Time has a

great deal to do with it. Time may enhance what seems simply dogged or lacking in fantasy now because we are too close to it, because it resembles too closely our own everyday fantasies, the fantastic nature of which we don't perceive. We are better able to enjoy a fantasy as fantasy when it is not our own.

31. This is why so many of the objects prized by Camp taste are old-fashioned, out-of-date, *démodé*. It's not a love of the old as such. It's simply that the process of aging or deterioration provides the necessary detachment—or arouses a necessary sympathy. When the theme is important, and contemporary, the failure of a work of art may make us indignant. Time can change that. Time liberates the work of art from moral relevance, delivering it over to the Camp sensibility. . . . Another effect: time contracts the sphere of banality. (Banality is, strictly speaking, always a category of the contemporary.) What was banal can, with the passage of time, become fantastic. Many people who listen with delight to the style of Rudy Vallee revived by the English pop group, The Temperance Seven, would have been driven up the wall by Rudy Vallée in his heyday.

Thus, things are campy, not when they become old—but when we become less involved in them, and can enjoy, instead of be frustrated by, the failure of the attempt. But the effect of time is unpredictable. Maybe "Method" Acting (James Dean, Rod Steiger, Warren Beatty) will seem as Camp some day as Ruby Keeler's does now—or as Sarah Bernhardt's does, in the films she made at the end of her career. And maybe not.

32. Camp is the glorification of "character." The statement is of no importance—except, of course, to the person (Loïe Fuller, Gaudí, Cecil B. De Mille, Crivelli, de Gaulle, etc.) who makes it. What the Camp eye appreciates is the unity, the force of the person. In every move the aging Martha Graham makes she's being Martha Graham, etc., etc. . . . This is clear in the case of the great serious idol of Camp taste, Greta Garbo. Garbo's incompetence (at the least, lack of depth) as an *actress* enhances her beauty. She's always herself.

33. What Camp taste responds to is "instant character" (this is, of course, very 18th century); and, conversely, what it is not stirred by is the sense of the development of character. Character is understood as a state of continual incandescence— a person being one, very intense thing. This attitude toward

character is a key element of the theatricalization of experience embodied in the Camp sensibility. And it helps account for the fact that opera and ballet are experienced as such rich treasures of Camp, for neither of these forms can easily do justice to the complexity of human nature. Wherever there is development of character, Camp is reduced. Among operas, for example, *La Traviata* (which has some small development of character) is less campy than *Il Trovatore* (which has none).

"Life is too important a thing ever to talk seriously about it."
—*Vera, or The Nihilists*

34. Camp taste turns its back on the good-bad axis of ordinary aesthetic judgment. Camp doesn't reverse things. It doesn't argue that the good is bad, or the bad is good. What it does is to offer for art (and life) a different—a supplementary—set of standards.

35. Ordinarily we value a work of art because of the seriousness and dignity of what it achieves. We value it because it succeeds—in being what it is and, presumably, in fulfilling the intention that lies behind it. We assume a proper, that is to say, straightforward relation between intention and performance. By such standards, we appraise *The Iliad*, Aristophanes' plays, The Art of the Fugue, *Middlemarch*, the paintings of Rembrandt, Chartres, the poetry of Donne, *The Divine Comedy*, Beethoven's quartets, and—among people—Socrates, Jesus, St. Francis, Napoleon, Savonarola. In short, the pantheon of high culture: truth, beauty, and seriousness.

36. But there are other creative sensibilities besides the seriousness (both tragic and comic) of high culture and of the high style of evaluating people. And one cheats oneself, as a human being, if one has *respect* only for the style of high culture, whatever else one may do or feel on the sly.

For instance, there is the kind of seriousness whose trademark is anguish, cruelty, derangement. Here we do accept a disparity between intention and result. I am speaking, obviously, of a style of personal existence as well as of a style in art; but the examples had best come from art. Think of Bosch, Sade, Rimbaud, Jarry, Kafka, Artaud, think of most of the important works of art of the 20th century, that is, art whose goal is not that of creating harmonies but of overstraining the medium and introducing more and more violent, and unresolvable, subject-matter. This sensibility also insists on the principle that an *oeuvre* in the old sense (again, in art, but also in life) is not possible. Only "fragments" are possible. . . . Clearly, different standards apply here than to traditional high culture. Something is good not because it is achieved, but because another kind of truth about the human situation, another experience of what it is to be human—in short, another valid sensibility—is being revealed.

And third among the great creative sensibilities is Camp: the sensibility of failed seriousness, of the theatricalization of experience. Camp refuses both the harmonies of traditional seriousness, and the risks of fully identifying with extreme states of feeling.

37. The first sensibility, that of high culture, is basically moralistic. The second sensibility, that of extreme states of feeling, represented in much contemporary "avant-garde" art, gains power by a tension between moral and aesthetic passion. The third, Camp, is wholly aesthetic.

38. Camp is the consistently aesthetic experience of the world. It incarnates a victory of "style" over "content," "aesthetics" over "morality," of irony over tragedy.

39. Camp and tragedy are antitheses. There is seriousness in Camp (seriousness in the degree of the artist's involvement) and, often, pathos. The excruciating is also one of the tonalities of Camp; it is the quality of excruciation in much of Henry James (for instance, *The Europeans*, *The Awkward Age*, *The Wings of the Dove*) that is responsible for the large element of Camp in his writings. But there is never, never tragedy.

40. Style is everything. Genet's ideas, for instance, are very Camp. Genet's statement that "the only criterion of an act is its elegance"* is virtually interchangeable, as a statement, with Wilde's "in matters of great importance, the vital element is not sincerity, but style." But what counts, finally, is the style in which ideas are held. The ideas about morality and politics in, say, *Lady Windermere's Fan* and in *Major Barbara* are Camp, but not just because of the nature of the ideas themselves. It is

---

*Sartre's gloss on this in *Saint Genet* is: "Elegance is the quality of conduct which transforms the greatest amount of being into appearing."

those ideas, held in a special playful way. The Camp ideas in *Our Lady of the Flowers* are maintained too grimly, and the writing itself is too successfully elevated and serious, for Genet's books to be Camp.

41. The whole point of Camp is to dethrone the serious. Camp is playful, anti-serious. More precisely, Camp involves a new, more complex relation to "the serious." One can be serious about the frivolous, frivolous about the serious.

42. One is drawn to Camp when one realizes that "sincerity" is not enough. Sincerity can be simple philistinism, intellectual narrowness.

43. The traditional means for going beyond straight seriousness—irony, satire—seem feeble today, inadequate to the culturally oversaturated medium in which contemporary sensibility is schooled. Camp introduces a new standard: artifice as an ideal, theatricality.

44. Camp proposes a comic vision of the world. But not a bitter or polemical comedy. If tragedy is an experience of hyperinvolvement, comedy is an experience of underinvolvement, of detachment.

"I adore simple pleasures, they are the last refuge of the complex."
                                        —*A Woman of No Importance*

45. Detachment is the prerogative of an elite; and as the dandy is the 19th century's surrogate for the aristocrat in matters of culture, so Camp is the modern dandyism. Camp is the answer to the problem: how to be a dandy in the age of mass culture.

46. The dandy was overbred. His posture was disdain, or else *ennui*. He sought rare sensations, undefiled by mass appreciation. (Models: Des Esseintes in Huysmans' *À Rebours*, *Marius the Epicurean*, Valéry's *Monsieur Teste*.) He was dedicated to "good taste."

The connoisseur of Camp has found more ingenious pleasures. Not in Latin poetry and rare wines and velvet jackets, but in the coarsest, commonest pleasures, in the arts of the masses. Mere use does not defile the objects of his pleasure, since he learns to possess them in a rare way. Camp—Dandyism in the age of mass culture—makes no distinction between the unique object and the mass-produced object. Camp taste transcends the nausea of the replica.

47. Wilde himself is a transitional figure. The man who, when he first came to London, sported a velvet beret, lace shirts, velveteen knee-breeches and black silk stockings, could never depart too far in his life from the pleasures of the old-style dandy; this conservatism is reflected in *The Picture of Dorian Gray*. But many of his attitudes suggest something more modern. It was Wilde who formulated an important element of the Camp sensibility—the equivalence of all objects—when he announced his intention of "living up" to his blue-and-white china, or declared that a doorknob could be as admirable as a painting. When he proclaimed the importance of the necktie, the boutonniere, the chair, Wilde was anticipating the democratic *esprit* of Camp.

48. The old-style dandy hated vulgarity. The new-style dandy, the lover of Camp, appreciates vulgarity. Where the dandy would be continually offended or bored, the connoisseur of Camp is continually amused, delighted. The dandy held a perfumed handkerchief to his nostrils and was liable to swoon; the connoisseur of Camp sniffs the stink and prides himself on his strong nerves.

49. It is a feat, of course. A feat goaded on, in the last analysis, by the threat of boredom. The relation between boredom and Camp taste cannot be overestimated. Camp taste is by its nature possible only in affluent societies, in societies or circles capable of experiencing the psychopathology of affluence.

"What is abnormal in Life stands in normal relations to Art. It is the only thing in Life that stands in normal relations to Art."
       —*A Few Maxims for the Instruction of the Over-Educated*

50. Aristocracy is a position vis-à-vis culture (as well as vis-à-vis power), and the history of Camp taste is part of the history of snob taste. But since no authentic aristocrats in the old sense exist today to sponsor special tastes, who is the bearer of this taste? Answer: an improvised self-elected class, mainly homosexuals, who constitute themselves as aristocrats of taste.

51. The peculiar relation between Camp taste and homosexuality has to be explained. While it's not true that Camp taste *is* homosexual taste, there is no doubt a peculiar affinity and overlap. Not all liberals are Jews, but Jews have shown a peculiar

affinity for liberal and reformist causes. So, not all homosexuals have Camp taste. But homosexuals, by and large, constitute the vanguard—and the most articulate audience—of Camp. (The analogy is not frivolously chosen. Jews and homosexuals are the outstanding creative minorities in contemporary urban culture. Creative, that is, in the truest sense: they are creators of sensibilities. The two pioneering forces of modern sensibility are Jewish moral seriousness and homosexual aestheticism and irony.)

52. The reason for the flourishing of the aristocratic posture among homosexuals also seems to parallel the Jewish case. For every sensibility is self-serving to the group that promotes it. Jewish liberalism is a gesture of self-legitimization. So is Camp taste, which definitely has something propagandistic about it. Needless to say, the propaganda operates in exactly the opposite direction. The Jews pinned their hopes for integrating into modern society on promoting the moral sense. Homosexuals have pinned their integration into society on promoting the aesthetic sense. Camp is a solvent of morality. It neutralizes moral indignation, sponsors playfulness.

53. Nevertheless, even though homosexuals have been its vanguard, Camp taste is much more than homosexual taste. Obviously, its metaphor of life as theater is peculiarly suited as a justification and projection of a certain aspect of the situation of homosexuals. (The Camp insistence on not being "serious," on playing, also connects with the homosexual's desire to remain youthful.) Yet one feels that if homosexuals hadn't more or less invented Camp, someone else would. For the aristocratic posture with relation to culture cannot die, though it may persist only in increasingly arbitrary and ingenious ways. Camp is (to repeat) the relation to style in a time in which the adoption of style—as such—has become altogether questionable. (In the modern era, each new style, unless frankly anachronistic, has come on the scene as an anti-style.)

"One must have a heart of stone to read the death of Little Nell without laughing."

—In conversation

54. The experiences of Camp are based on the great discovery that the sensibility of high culture has no monopoly upon refinement. Camp asserts that good taste is not simply good

taste; that there exists, indeed, a good taste of bad taste. (Genet talks about this in *Our Lady of the Flowers*.) The discovery of the good taste of bad taste can be very liberating. The man who insists on high and serious pleasures is depriving himself of pleasure; he continually restricts what he can enjoy; in the constant exercise of his good taste he will eventually price himself out of the market, so to speak. Here Camp taste supervenes upon good taste as a daring and witty hedonism. It makes the man of good taste cheerful, where before he ran the risk of being chronically frustrated. It is good for the digestion.

55. Camp taste is, above all, a mode of enjoyment, of appreciation—not judgment. Camp is generous. It wants to enjoy. It only seems like malice, cynicism. (Or, if it is cynicism, it's not a ruthless but a sweet cynicism.) Camp taste doesn't propose that it is in bad taste to be serious; it doesn't sneer at someone who succeeds in being seriously dramatic. What it does is to find the success in certain passionate failures.

56. Camp taste is a kind of love, love for human nature. It relishes, rather than judges, the little triumphs and awkward intensities of "character." . . . Camp taste identifies with what it is enjoying. People who share this sensibility are not laughing at the thing they label as "a camp," they're enjoying it. Camp is a *tender* feeling.

(Here, one may compare Camp with much of Pop Art, which—when it is not just Camp—embodies an attitude that is related, but still very different. Pop Art is more flat and more dry, more serious, more detached, ultimately nihilistic.)

57. Camp taste nourishes itself on the love that has gone into certain objects and personal styles. The absence of this love is the reason why such kitsch items as *Peyton Place* (the book) and the Tishman Building aren't Camp.

58. The ultimate Camp statement: it's good *because* it's awful. . . . Of course, one can't always say that. Only under certain conditions, those which I've tried to sketch in these notes.

(1964)

One Culture and the New Sensibility

I N THE last few years there has been a good deal of discussion of a purported chasm which opened up some two centuries ago, with the advent of the Industrial Revolution, between "two cultures," the literary-artistic and the scientific. According to this diagnosis, any intelligent and articulate modern person is likely to inhabit one culture to the exclusion of the other. He will be concerned with different documents, different techniques, different problems; he will speak a different language. Most important, the type of effort required for the mastery of these two cultures will differ vastly. For the literary-artistic culture is understood as a general culture. It is addressed to man insofar as he is man; it is culture or, rather, it promotes culture, in the sense of culture defined by Ortega y Gasset: that which a man has in his possession when he has forgotten everything that he has read. The scientific culture, in contrast, is a culture for specialists; it is founded on remembering and is set down in ways that require complete dedication of the effort to comprehend. While the literary-artistic culture aims at internalization, ingestion—in other words, cultivation—the scientific culture aims at accumulation and externalization in complex instruments for problem-solving and specific techniques for mastery.

Though T. S. Eliot derived the chasm between the two cultures from a period more remote in modern history, speaking in a famous essay of a "dissociation of sensibility" which opened up in the 17th century, the connection of the problem with the Industrial Revolution seems well taken. There is a historic antipathy on the part of many literary intellectuals and artists to those changes which characterize modern society—above all, industrialization and those of its effects which everyone has experienced, such as the proliferation of huge impersonal cities and the predominance of the anonymous style of urban life. It has mattered little whether industrialization, the creature of modern "science," is seen on the 19th and early 20th century model, as noisy smoky artificial processes which defile nature and standardize culture, or on the newer model, the clean automated technology that is coming into being in the second half of the 20th century. The judgment has been mostly the same. Literary men, feeling that the status of humanity itself was being

challenged by the new science and the new technology, ab-
horred and deplored the change. But the literary men, whether
one thinks of Emerson and Thoreau and Ruskin in the 19th
century, or of 20th century intellectuals who talk of modern society as being in some new way incomprehensible, "alienated,"
are inevitably on the defensive. They know that the scientific
culture, the coming of the machine, cannot be stopped.

The standard response to the problem of "the two cultures"—
and the issue long antedates by many decades the crude and
philistine statement of the problem by C. P. Snow in a famous
lecture some years ago—has been a facile defense of the function of the arts (in terms of an ever vaguer ideology of "humanism") or a premature surrender of the function of the arts to
science. By the second response, I am not referring to the philistinism of scientists (and those of their party among artists and
philosophers) who dismiss the arts as imprecise, untrue, at best
mere toys. I am speaking of serious doubts which have arisen
among those who are passionately engaged in the arts. The role
of the individual artist, in the business of making unique objects
for the purpose of giving pleasure and educating conscience
and sensibility, has repeatedly been called into question. Some
literary intellectuals and artists have gone so far as to prophesy
the ultimate demise of the art-making activity of man. Art, in
an automated scientific society, would be unfunctional, useless.

But this conclusion, I should argue, is plainly unwarranted.
Indeed, the whole issue seems to me crudely put. For the question of "the two cultures" assumes that science and technology
are changing, in motion, while the arts are static, fulfilling some
perennial generic human function (consolation? edification?
diversion?). Only on the basis of this false assumption would
anyone reason that the arts might be in danger of becoming
obsolete.

Art does not progress, in the sense that science and technology do. But the arts do develop and change. For instance, in
our own time, art is becoming increasingly the terrain of specialists. The most interesting and creative art of our time is
not open to the generally educated; it demands special effort;
it speaks a specialized language. The music of Milton Babbitt
and Morton Feldman, the painting of Mark Rothko and Frank
Stella, the dance of Merce Cunningham and James Waring

demand an education of sensibility whose difficulties and length of apprenticeship are at least comparable to the difficulties of mastering physics or engineering. (Only the novel, among the arts, at least in America, fails to provide similar examples.) The parallel between the abstruseness of contemporary art and that of modern science is too obvious to be missed. Another likeness to the scientific culture is the history-mindedness of contemporary art. The most interesting works of contemporary art are full of references to the history of the medium; so far as they comment on past art, they demand a knowledge of at least the recent past. As Harold Rosenberg has pointed out, contemporary paintings are themselves acts of criticism as much as of creation. The point could be made as well of much recent work in the films, music, the dance, poetry, and (in Europe) literature. Again, a similarity with the style of science—this time, with the accumulative aspect of science—can be discerned.

The conflict between "the two cultures" is in fact an illusion, a temporary phenomenon born of a period of profound and bewildering historical change. What we are witnessing is not so much a conflict of cultures as the creation of a new (potentially unitary) kind of sensibility. This new sensibility is rooted, as it must be, in *our* experience, experiences which are new in the history of humanity—in extreme social and physical mobility; in the crowdedness of the human scene (both people and material commodities multiplying at a dizzying rate); in the availability of new sensations such as speed (physical speed, as in airplane travel; speed of images, as in the cinema); and in the pan-cultural perspective on the arts that is possible through the mass reproduction of art objects.

What we are getting is not the demise of art, but a transformation of the function of art. Art, which arose in human society as a magical-religious operation, and passed over into a technique for depicting and commenting on secular reality, has in our own time arrogated to itself a new function—neither religious, nor serving a secularized religious function, nor merely secular or profane (a notion which breaks down when its opposite, the "religious" or "sacred," becomes obsolescent). Art today is a new kind of instrument, an instrument for modifying consciousness and organizing new modes of sensibility. And the means for practicing art have been radically extended.

Indeed, in response to this new function (more felt than clearly articulated), artists have had to become self-conscious aestheticians: continually challenging their means, their materials and methods. Often, the conquest and exploitation of new materials and methods drawn from the world of "non-art"—for example, from industrial technology, from commercial processes and imagery, from purely private and subjective fantasies and dreams— seems to be the principal effort of many artists. Painters no longer feel themselves confined to canvas and paint, but employ hair, photographs, wax, sand, bicycle tires, their own toothbrushes and socks. Musicians have reached beyond the sounds of the traditional instruments to use tampered instruments and (usually on tape) synthetic sounds and industrial noises.

All kinds of conventionally accepted boundaries have thereby been challenged: not just the one between the "scientific" and the "literary-artistic" cultures, or the one between "art" and "non-art"; but also many established distinctions within the world of culture itself—that between form and content, the frivolous and the serious, and (a favorite of literary intellectuals) "high" and "low" culture.

The distinction between "high" and "low" (or "mass" or "popular") culture is based partly on an evaluation of the difference between unique and mass-produced objects. In an era of mass technological reproduction, the work of the serious artist had a special value simply because it was unique, because it bore his personal, individual signature. The works of popular culture (and even films were for a long time included in this category) were seen as having little value because they were manufactured objects, bearing no individual stamp—group concoctions made for an undifferentiated audience. But in the light of contemporary practice in the arts, this distinction appears extremely shallow. Many of the serious works of art of recent decades have a decidedly impersonal character. The work of art is reasserting its existence as "object" (even as manufactured or mass-produced object, drawing on the popular arts) rather than as "individual personal expression."

The exploration of the impersonal (and trans-personal) in contemporary art is the new classicism; at least, a reaction against what is understood as the romantic spirit dominates most of the interesting art of today. Today's art, with its insistence on coolness, its refusal of what it considers to be sentimentality, its spirit of exactness, its sense of "research" and "problems," is closer to the spirit of science than of art in the old-fashioned sense. Often, the artist's work is only his idea, his concept. This is a familiar practice in architecture, of course. And one remembers that painters in the Renaissance often left parts of their canvases to be worked out by students, and that in the flourishing period of the concerto the cadenza at the end of the first movement was left to the inventiveness and discretion of the performing soloist. But similar practices have a different, more polemical meaning today, in the present post-romantic era of the arts. When painters such as Josef Albers, Ellsworth Kelly, and Andy Warhol assign portions of the work, say, the painting in of the colors themselves, to a friend or the local gardener; when musicians such as Stockhausen, John Cage, and Luigi Nono invite collaboration from performers by leaving opportunities for random effects, switching around the order of the score, and improvisations—they are changing the ground rules which most of us employ to recognize a work of art. They are saying what art need not be. At least, not necessarily.

The primary feature of the new sensibility is that its model product is not the literary work, above all, the novel. A new non-literary culture exists today, of whose very existence, not to mention significance, most literary intellectuals are entirely unaware. This new establishment includes certain painters, sculptors, architects, social planners, film-makers, TV technicians, neurologists, musicians, electronics engineers, dancers, philosophers, and sociologists. (A few poets and prose writers can be included.) Some of the basic texts for this new cultural alignment are to be found in the writings of Nietzsche, Wittgenstein, Antonin Artaud, C. S. Sherrington, Buckminster Fuller, Marshall McLuhan, John Cage, André Breton, Roland Barthes, Claude Lévi-Strauss, Sigfried Giedion, Norman O. Brown, and Gyorgy Kepes.

Those who worry about the gap between "the two cultures," and this means virtually all literary intellectuals in England and America, take for granted a notion of culture which decidedly needs reexamining. It is the notion perhaps best expressed by Matthew Arnold (in which the central cultural act is the making of literature, which is itself understood as the criticism of culture). Simply ignorant of the vital and enthralling (so called "avant-garde") developments in the other arts, and blinded by their personal investment in the perpetuation of the older notion of culture, they continue to cling to literature as the model for creative statement.

What gives literature its preeminence is its heavy burden of "content," both reportage and moral judgment. (This makes it possible for most English and American literary critics to use literary works mainly as texts, or even pretexts, for social and cultural diagnosis—rather than concentrating on the properties of, say, a given novel or a play, as an art work.) But the model arts of our time are actually those with much less content, and a much cooler mode of moral judgment—like music, films, dance, architecture, painting, sculpture. The practice of these arts—all of which draw profusely, naturally, and without embarrassment, upon science and technology—are the locus of the new sensibility.

The problem of "the two cultures," in short, rests upon an uneducated, uncontemporary grasp of our present cultural situation. It arises from the ignorance of literary intellectuals (and of scientists with a shallow knowledge of the arts, like the scientist-novelist C. P. Snow himself) of a new culture, and its emerging sensibility. In fact, there can be no divorce between science and technology, on the one hand, and art, on the other, any more than there can be a divorce between art and the forms of social life. Works of art, psychological forms, and social forms all reflect each other, and change with each other. But, of course, most people are slow to come to terms with such changes—especially today, when the changes are occurring with an unprecedented rapidity. Marshall McLuhan has described human history as a succession of acts of technological extension of human capacity, each of which works a radical change upon our environment and our ways of thinking, feeling, and valuing. The tendency, he remarks, is to upgrade the old environment into art form (thus Nature became a vessel of aesthetic and spiritual values in the new industrial environment) "while the new conditions are regarded as corrupt and degrading." Typically, it is only certain artists in any given era who "have the resources and temerity to live in immediate contact with the environment of their age . . . That is why they may seem to be 'ahead of their time' . . . More timid people prefer to accept the . . . previous environment's values as the continuing reality of their time. Our natural bias is to accept the new gimmick (automation, say) as a thing that can be accommodated in the old ethical order." Only in the terms of what McLuhan calls the old ethical order does the problem of "the two cultures" appear to be a genuine problem. It is not a problem for most of the creative artists of our time (among whom one could include very few novelists) because most of these artists have broken, whether they know it or not, with the Matthew Arnold notion of culture, finding it historically and humanly obsolescent.

The Matthew Arnold notion of culture defines art as the criticism of life—this being understood as the propounding of moral, social, and political ideas. The new sensibility understands art as the extension of life—this being understood as the representation of (new) modes of vivacity. There is no necessary denial of the role of moral evaluation here. Only the scale has changed; it has become less gross, and what it sacrifices in discursive explicitness it gains in accuracy and subliminal power. For we are what we are able to see (hear, taste, smell, feel) even more powerfully and profoundly than we are what furniture of ideas we have stocked in our heads. Of course, the proponents of "the two cultures" crisis continue to observe a desperate contrast between unintelligible, morally neutral science and technology, on the one hand, and morally committed, human-scale art on the other. But matters are not that simple, and never were. A great work of art is never simply (or even mainly) a vehicle of ideas or of moral sentiments. It is, first of all, an object modifying our consciousness and sensibility, changing the composition, however slightly, of the humus that nourishes all specific ideas and sentiments. Outraged humanists, please note. There is no need for alarm. A work of art does not cease being a moment in the conscience of mankind, when moral conscience is understood as only one of the functions of consciousness.

Sensations, feelings, the abstract forms and styles of sensibility count. It is to these that contemporary art addresses itself. The basic unit for contemporary art is not the idea, but the analysis of and extension of sensations. (Or if it is an "idea," it is about the form of sensibility.) Rilke described the artist as someone who works "toward an extension of the regions of the individual senses"; McLuhan calls artists "experts in sensory awareness." And the most interesting works of contemporary art (one can begin at least as far back as French symbolist poetry) are adventures in sensation, new "sensory mixes." Such art is, in principle, experimental—not out of an elitist disdain for what is accessible to the majority, but precisely in the sense that science is experimental. Such an art is also notably apolitical and undidactic, or, rather, infra-didactic.

When Ortega y Gasset wrote his famous essay *The Dehumanization of Art* in the early 1920s, he ascribed the qualities of modern art (such as impersonality, the ban on pathos, hostility to the past, playfulness, willful stylization, absence of ethical and political commitment) to the spirit of youth which he thought dominated our age.* In retrospect, it seems this "dehumanization" did not signify the recovery of childlike innocence, but was rather a very adult, knowing response. What other response than anguish, followed by anesthesia and then by wit and the elevating of intelligence over sentiment, is possible as a response to the social disorder and mass atrocities of our time, and—equally important for our sensibilities, but less often remarked on—to the unprecedented change in what rules our environment from the intelligible and visible to that which is only with difficulty intelligible, and is invisible? Art, which I have characterized as an instrument for modifying and educating sensibility and consciousness, now operates in an environment which cannot be grasped by the senses.

Buckminster Fuller has written:

In World War I industry suddenly went from the visible to the invisible base, from the track to the trackless, from the wire to the wireless, from visible structuring to invisible structuring in alloys. The big thing about World War I is that *man went off the sensorial spectrum forever* as the prime criterion of accrediting innovations . . . All major advances since World War I have been in the infra and the ultrasensorial frequencies of the electromagnetic spectrum. All the important technical affairs of men today are invisible . . . The old masters, who were sensorialists, have

---

*Ortega remarks, in this essay: "Were art to redeem man, it could do so only by saving him from the seriousness of life and restoring him to an unexpected boyishness."

unleashed a Pandora's box of non-sensorially controllable phenomena, which they had avoided accrediting up to that time . . .
Suddenly they lost their true mastery, because from then on they
didn't personally understand what was going on. If you don't
understand you cannot master . . . Since World War I, the old
masters have been extinct . . .

But, of course, art remains permanently tied to the senses. Just
as one cannot float colors in space (a painter needs some sort of
surface, like a canvas, however neutral and textureless), one cannot have a work of art that does not impinge upon the human
sensorium. But it is important to realize that human sensory
awareness has not merely a biology but a specific history, each culture placing a premium on certain senses and inhibiting others.
(The same is true for the range of primary human emotions.)
Here is where art (among other things) enters, and why the interesting art of our time has such a feeling of anguish and crisis
about it, however playful and abstract and ostensibly neutral
morally it may appear. Western man may be said to have been
undergoing a massive sensory anesthesia (a concomitant of the
process that Max Weber calls "bureaucratic rationalization")
at least since the Industrial Revolution, with modern art functioning as a kind of shock therapy for both confounding and
unclosing our senses.

One important consequence of the new sensibility (with its
abandonment of the Matthew Arnold idea of culture) has already been alluded to—namely, that the distinction between
"high" and "low" culture seems less and less meaningful. For
such a distinction—inseparable from the Matthew Arnold
apparatus—simply does not make sense for a creative community of artists and scientists engaged in programming sensations,
uninterested in art as a species of moral journalism. Art has
always been more than that, anyway.

Another way of characterizing the present cultural situation,
in its most creative aspects, would be to speak of a new attitude
toward pleasure. In one sense, the new art and the new sensibility take a rather dim view of pleasure. (The great contemporary
French composer, Pierre Boulez, entitled an important essay
of his twelve years ago, "Against Hedonism in Music.") The
seriousness of modern art precludes pleasure in the familiar

sense—the pleasure of a melody that one can hum after leaving the concert hall, of characters in a novel or play whom one can recognize, identify with, and dissect in terms of realistic psychological motives, of a beautiful landscape or a dramatic moment represented on a canvas. If hedonism means sustaining the old ways in which we have found pleasure in art (the old sensory and psychic modalities), then the new art is anti-hedonistic. Having one's sensorium challenged or stretched hurts. The new serious music hurts one's ears, the new painting does not graciously reward one's sight, the new films and the few interesting new prose works do not go down easily. The commonest complaint about the films of Antonioni or the narratives of Beckett or Burroughs is that they are hard to look at or to read, that they are "boring." But the charge of boredom is really hypocritical. There is, in a sense, no such thing as boredom. Boredom is only another name for a certain species of frustration. And the new languages which the interesting art of our time speaks are frustrating to the sensibilities of most educated people.

But the purpose of art is always, ultimately, to give pleasure—though our sensibilities may take time to catch up with the forms of pleasure that art in a given time may offer. And, one can also say that, balancing the ostensible anti-hedonism of serious contemporary art, the modern sensibility is more involved with pleasure in the familiar sense than ever. Because the new sensibility demands less "content" in art, and is more open to the pleasures of "form" and style, it is also less snobbish, less moralistic—in that it does not demand that pleasure in art necessarily be associated with edification. If art is understood as a form of discipline of the feelings and a programming of sensations, then the feeling (or sensation) given off by a Rauschenberg painting might be like that of a song by the Supremes. The brio and elegance of Budd Boetticher's *The Rise and Fall of Legs Diamond* or the singing style of Dionne Warwick can be appreciated as a complex and pleasurable event. They are experienced without condescension.

This last point seems to me worth underscoring. For it is important to understand that the affection which many younger artists and intellectuals feel for the popular arts is not a new philistinism (as has so often been charged) or a species of anti-intellectualism or some kind of abdication from culture. The fact that many of the most serious American painters, for example, are also fans of "the new sound" in popular music is *not* the result of the search for mere diversion or relaxation; it is not, say, like Schoenberg also playing tennis. It reflects a new, more open way of looking at the world and at things in the world, our world. It does not mean the renunciation of all standards: there is plenty of stupid popular music, as well as inferior and pretentious "avant-garde" paintings, films, and music. The point is that there *are* new standards, new standards of beauty and style and taste. The new sensibility is defiantly pluralistic; it is dedicated both to an excruciating seriousness and to fun and wit and nostalgia. It is also extremely history-conscious; and the voracity of its enthusiasms (and of the supercession of these enthusiasms) is very high-speed and hectic. From the vantage point of this new sensibility, the beauty of a machine or of the solution to a mathematical problem, of a painting by Jasper Johns, of a film by Jean-Luc Godard, and of the personalities and music of the Beatles is equally accessible.

(1965)

STYLES OF RADICAL WILL

For Joseph Chaikin

Contents

I

I

The Aesthetics of Silence

I

EVERY era has to reinvent the project of "spirituality" for itself. (Spirituality = plans, terminologies, ideas of deportment aimed at resolving the painful structural contradictions inherent in the human situation, at the completion of human consciousness, at transcendence.)

In the modern era, one of the most active metaphors for the spiritual project is "art." The activities of the painter, the musician, the poet, the dancer, once they were grouped together under that generic name (a relatively recent move), have proved a particularly adaptable site on which to stage the formal dramas besetting consciousness, each individual work of art being a more or less astute paradigm for regulating or reconciling these contradictions. Of course, the site needs continual refurbishing. Whatever goal is set for art eventually proves restrictive, matched against the widest goals of consciousness. Art, itself a form of mystification, endures a succession of crises of demystification; older artistic goals are assailed and, ostensibly, replaced; outworn maps of consciousness are redrawn. But what supplies all these crises with their energy—an energy held in common, so to speak—is the very unification of numerous, quite disparate activities into a single genus. At the moment when "art" comes into being, the modern period of art begins. From then on, any of the activities therein subsumed becomes a profoundly *problematic* activity, all of whose procedures and, ultimately, whose very right to exist can be called into question.

From the promotion of the arts into "art" comes the leading myth about art, that of the absoluteness of the artist's activity. In its first, more unreflective version, the myth treated art as an *expression* of human consciousness, consciousness seeking to know itself. (The evaluative standards generated by this version of the myth were fairly easily arrived at: some expressions were more complete, more ennobling, more informative, richer than others.) The later version of the myth posits a more complex, tragic relation of art to consciousness. Denying that art is mere expression, the later myth rather relates art to the mind's need or capacity for self-estrangement. Art is no longer understood as consciousness expressing and therefore, implicitly, affirming itself. Art is not consciousness per se, but rather its antidote— evolved from within consciousness itself. (The evaluative standards generated by this version of the myth proved much harder to get at.)

The newer myth, derived from a post-psychological conception of consciousness, installs within the activity of art many of the paradoxes involved in attaining an absolute state of being described by the great religious mystics. As the activity of the mystic must end in a *via negativa*, a theology of God's absence, a craving for the cloud of unknowing beyond knowledge and for the silence beyond speech, so art must tend toward anti-art, the elimination of the "subject" (the "object," the "image"), the substitution of chance for intention, and the pursuit of silence.

In the early, linear version of art's relation to consciousness, a struggle was discerned between the "spiritual" integrity of the creative impulses and the distracting "materiality" of ordinary life, which throws up so many obstacles in the path of authentic sublimation. But the newer version, in which art is part of a dialectical transaction with consciousness, poses a deeper, more frustrating conflict. The "spirit" seeking embodiment in art clashes with the "material" character of art itself. Art is unmasked as gratuitous, and the very concreteness of the artist's tools (and, particularly in the case of language, their historicity) appears as a trap. Practiced in a world furnished with second-hand perceptions, and specifically confounded by the treachery of words, the artist's activity is cursed with mediacy. Art becomes the enemy of the artist, for it denies him the realization— the transcendence—he desires.

Therefore, art comes to be considered something to be overthrown. A new element enters the individual artwork and becomes constitutive of it: the appeal (tacit or overt) for its own abolition—and, ultimately, for the abolition of art itself.

2

The scene changes to an empty room.

Rimbaud has gone to Abyssinia to make his fortune in the slave trade. Wittgenstein, after a period as a village schoolteacher, has chosen menial work as a hospital orderly. Duchamp has turned to chess. Accompanying these exemplary renunciations of a vocation, each man has declared that he regards his previous achievements in poetry, philosophy, or art as trifling, of no importance.

But the choice of permanent silence doesn't negate their work. On the contrary, it imparts retroactively an added power and authority to what was broken off—disavowal of the work becoming a new source of its validity, a certificate of unchallengeable seriousness. That seriousness consists in not regarding art (or philosophy practiced as an art form: Wittgenstein) as something whose seriousness lasts forever, an "end," a permanent vehicle for spiritual ambition. The truly serious attitude is one that regards art as a "means" to something that can perhaps be achieved only by abandoning art; judged more impatiently, art is a false way or (the word of the Dada artist Jacques Vaché) a stupidity.

Though no longer a confession, art is more than ever a deliverance, an exercise in asceticism. Through it, the artist becomes purified—of himself and, eventually, of his art. The artist (if not art itself) is still engaged in a progress toward "the good." But whereas formerly the artist's good was mastery of and fulfillment in his art, now the highest good for the artist is to reach the point where those goals of excellence become insignificant to him, emotionally and ethically, and he is more satisfied by being silent than by finding a voice in art. Silence in this sense, as termination, proposes a mood of ultimacy antithetical to the mood informing the self-conscious artist's traditional serious use of silence (beautifully described by Valéry and Rilke): as a zone of meditation, preparation for spiritual ripening, an ordeal that ends in gaining the right to speak.

So far as he is serious, the artist is continually tempted to sever the dialogue he has with an audience. Silence is the furthest extension of that reluctance to communicate, that ambivalence about making contact with the audience which is a leading motif of modern art, with its tireless commitment to the "new" and/or "esoteric." Silence is the artist's ultimate other-worldly gesture: by silence, he frees himself from servile bondage to the world, which appears as patron, client, consumer, antagonist, arbiter, and distorter of his work.

Still, one cannot fail to perceive in this renunciation of "society" a highly social gesture. The cues for the artist's eventual liberation from the need to practice his vocation come from observing his fellow artists and measuring himself against them. An exemplary decision of this sort can be made only after the artist has demonstrated that he possesses genius and exercised that genius authoritatively. Once he has surpassed his peers by the standards which he acknowledges, his pride has only one place left to go. For, to be a victim of the craving for silence is to be, in still a further sense, superior to everyone else. It suggests that the artist has had the wit to ask more questions than other people, and that he possesses stronger nerves and higher standards of excellence. (That the artist *can* persevere in the interrogation of his art until he or it is exhausted scarcely needs proving. As René Char has written, "No bird has the heart to sing in a thicket of questions.")

3

The exemplary modern artist's choice of silence is rarely carried to this point of final simplification, so that he becomes literally silent. More typically, he continues speaking, but in a manner that his audience can't hear. Most valuable art in our time has been experienced by audiences as a move into silence (or unintelligibility or invisibility or inaudibility); a dismantling of the artist's competence, his responsible sense of vocation—and therefore as an aggression against them.

Modern art's chronic habit of displeasing, provoking, or frustrating its audience can be regarded as a limited, vicarious participation in the ideal of silence which has been elevated as a major standard of "seriousness" in contemporary aesthetics.

But it is also a contradictory form of participation in the ideal of silence. It is contradictory not only because the artist continues making works of art, but also because the isolation of the work from its audience never lasts. With the passage of time and the intervention of newer, more difficult works, the artist's transgression becomes ingratiating, eventually legitimate. Goethe accused Kleist of having written his plays for an "invisible theatre." But eventually the invisible theatre becomes "visible." The ugly and discordant and senseless become "beautiful." The history of art is a sequence of successful transgressions.

The characteristic aim of modern art, to be *unacceptable* to its audience, inversely states the unacceptability to the artist of the very presence of an audience—audience in the modern sense, an assembly of voyeuristic spectators. At least since Nietzsche observed in *The Birth of Tragedy* that an audience of spectators as we know it, those present whom the actors ignore, was unknown to the Greeks, a good deal of contemporary art seems moved by the desire to eliminate the audience from art, an enterprise that often presents itself as an attempt to eliminate "art" altogether. (In favor of "life"?)

Committed to the idea that the power of art is located in its power to *negate*, the ultimate weapon in the artist's inconsistent war with his audience is to verge closer and closer to silence. The sensory or conceptual gap between the artist and his audience, the space of the missing or ruptured dialogue, can also constitute the grounds for an ascetic affirmation. Beckett speaks of "my dream of an art unresentful of its insuperable indigence and too proud for the farce of giving and receiving." But there is no abolishing a minimal transaction, a minimal exchange of gifts—just as there is no talented and rigorous asceticism that, whatever its intention, doesn't produce a gain (rather than a loss) in the capacity for pleasure.

And none of the aggressions committed intentionally or inadvertently by modern artists has succeeded in either abolishing the audience or transforming it into something else, a community engaged in a common activity. They cannot. As long as art is understood and valued as an "absolute" activity, it will be a separate, elitist one. Elites presuppose masses. So far as the best art defines itself by essentially "priestly" aims, it presupposes and confirms the existence of a relatively passive, never fully initiated, voyeuristic laity that is regularly convoked to watch, listen, read, or hear—and then sent away.

The most the artist can do is to modify the different terms in this situation vis-à-vis the audience and himself. To discuss the idea of silence in art is to discuss the various alternatives within this essentially unalterable situation.

4

How literally does silence figure in art?

Silence exists as a *decision*—in the exemplary suicide of the artist (Kleist, Lautréamont), who thereby testifies that he has gone "too far"; and in the already cited model renunciations by the artist of his vocation.

Silence also exists as a *punishment*—self-punishment, in the exemplary madness of artists (Hölderlin, Artaud) who demonstrate that sanity itself may be the price of trespassing the accepted frontiers of consciousness; and, of course, in penalties (ranging from censorship and physical destruction of artworks to fines, exile, prison for the artist) meted out by "society" for the artist's spiritual nonconformity or subversion of the group sensibility.

Silence doesn't exist in a literal sense, however, as the *experience* of an audience. It would mean that the spectator was aware of no stimulus or that he was unable to make a response. But this can't happen; nor can it even be induced programmatically. The non-awareness of any stimulus, the inability to make a response, can result only from a defective presence on the part of the spectator, or a misunderstanding of his own reactions (misled by restrictive ideas about what would be a "relevant" response). As long as audiences, by definition, consist of sentient beings in a "situation," it is impossible for them to have no response at all.

Nor can silence, in its literal state, exist as the *property* of an artwork—even of works like Duchamp's readymades or Cage's *4'33"*, in which the artist has ostentatiously done no more to satisfy any established criteria of art than set the object in a gallery or situate the performance on a concert stage. There is no neutral surface, no neutral discourse, no neutral theme, no neutral form. Something is neutral only with respect to something else—like an intention or an expectation. As a property of the work of art itself, silence can exist only in a cooked or non-literal sense. (Put otherwise: if a work exists at all, its silence is only one element in it.) Instead of raw or achieved silence, one finds various moves in the direction of an ever receding horizon of silence—moves which, by definition, can never be fully consummated. One result is a type of art that many people characterize pejoratively as dumb, depressed, acquiescent, cold. But these private qualities exist in a context of the artist's objective intention, which is always discernible. Cultivating the metaphoric silence suggested by conventionally lifeless subjects (as in much of Pop Art) and constructing "minimal" forms that seem to lack emotional resonance are in themselves vigorous, often tonic choices.

And, finally, even without imputing objective intentions to the artwork, there remains the inescapable truth about perception: the positivity of all experience at every moment of it. As Cage has insisted, "There is no such thing as silence. Something is always happening that makes a sound." (Cage has described how, even in a soundless chamber, he still heard two things: his heartbeat and the coursing of the blood in his head.) Similarly, there is no such thing as empty space. As long as a human eye is looking, there is always something to see. To look at something which is "empty" is still to be looking, still to be seeing something—if only the ghosts of one's own expectations. In order to perceive fullness, one must retain an acute sense of the emptiness which marks it off; conversely, in order to perceive emptiness, one must apprehend other zones of the world as full. (In *Through the Looking Glass*, Alice comes upon a shop "that seemed to be full of all manner of curious things—but the oddest part of it all was that whenever she looked hard at any shelf, to make out exactly what it had on it, that particular shelf was always quite empty, though the others round it were crowded full as they could hold.")

"Silence" never ceases to imply its opposite and to depend on its presence: just as there can't be "up" without "down" or "left" without "right," so one must acknowledge a surrounding environment of sound or language in order to recognize silence. Not only does silence exist in a world full of speech and other sounds, but any given silence has its identity as a stretch of time being perforated by sound. (Thus, much of the beauty of Harpo Marx's muteness derives from his being surrounded by manic talkers.)

A genuine emptiness, a pure silence is not feasible—either conceptually or in fact. If only because the artwork exists in a world furnished with many other things, the artist who creates silence or emptiness must produce something dialectical: a full void, an enriching emptiness, a resonating or eloquent silence. Silence remains, inescapably, a form of speech (in many instances, of complaint or indictment) and an element in a dialogue.

5

Programs for a radical reduction of means and effects in art— including the ultimate demand for the renunciation of art itself—can't be taken at face value, undialectically. Silence and allied ideas (like emptiness, reduction, the "zero degree") are boundary notions with a very complex set of uses, leading terms of a particular spiritual and cultural rhetoric. To describe silence as a rhetorical term is, of course, not to condemn this rhetoric as fraudulent or in bad faith. In my opinion, the myths of silence and emptiness are about as nourishing and viable as might be devised in an "unwholesome" time—which is, of necessity, a time in which "unwholesome" psychic states furnish the ener- gies for most superior work in the arts. Yet one can't deny the pathos of these myths.

This pathos appears in the fact that the idea of silence allows, essentially, only two types of valuable development. Either it is taken to the point of utter self-negation (as art) or else it is practiced in a form that is heroically, ingeniously inconsistent.

6

The art of our time is noisy with appeals for silence.

A coquettish, even cheerful nihilism. One recognizes the im- perative of silence, but goes on speaking anyway. Discovering that one has nothing to say, one seeks a way to say *that*.

Beckett has expressed the wish that art would renounce all further projects for disturbing matters on "the plane of the feasible," that art would retire, "weary of puny exploits, weary of pretending to be able, of being able, of doing a little better the same old thing, of going further along a dreary road." The alternative is an art consisting of "the expression that there is nothing to express, nothing from which to express, no power to express, no desire to express, together with the obligation to express." From where does this obligation derive? The very aesthetics of the death wish seems to make of that wish something incorrigibly lively.

Apollinaire says, "J'ai fait des gestes blancs parmi les solitudes." But he *is* making gestures.

Since the artist can't embrace silence literally and remain an artist, what the rhetoric of silence indicates is a determination to pursue his activity more deviously than before. One way is indicated by Breton's notion of the "full margin." The artist is enjoined to devote himself to filling up the periphery of the art space, leaving the central area of usage blank. Art becomes privative, anemic—as suggested by the title of Duchamp's only effort at film-making, "Anemic Cinema," a work from 1924–26. Beckett projects the idea of an "impoverished painting," painting which is "authentically fruitless, incapable of any image whatsoever." Jerzy Grotowski's manifesto for his Theatre Laboratory in Poland is called "Plea for a Poor Theatre." These programs for art's impoverishment must not be understood simply as terroristic admonitions to audiences, but rather as strategies for improving the audience's experience. The notions of silence, emptiness, and reduction sketch out new prescriptions for looking, hearing, etc.—which either promote a more immediate, sensuous experience of art or confront the artwork in a more conscious, conceptual way.

7

Consider the connection between the mandate for a reduction of means and effects in art, whose horizon is silence, and the faculty of attention. In one of its aspects, art is a technique for focusing attention, for teaching skills of attention. (While the whole of the human environment might be so described—as a pedagogic instrument—this description particularly applies to works of art.) The history of the arts is tantamount to the discovery and formulation of a repertory of objects on which to lavish attention. One could trace exactly and in order how the eye of art has panned over our environment, "naming," making its limited selection of things which people then become aware of as significant, pleasurable, complex entities. (Oscar

Wilde pointed out that people didn't see fogs before certain nineteenth-century poets and painters taught them how to; and surely, no one saw as much of the variety and subtlety of the human face before the era of the movies.)

Once the artist's task seemed to be simply that of opening up new areas and objects of attention. That task is still acknowledged, but it has become problematic. The very faculty of attention has come into question, and been subjected to more rigorous standards. As Jasper Johns says: "Already it's a great deal to see anything *clearly*, for we don't see *anything* clearly."

Perhaps the quality of the attention one brings to bear on something will be better (less contaminated, less distracted), the less one is offered. Furnished with impoverished art, purged by silence, one might then be able to begin to transcend the frustrating selectivity of attention, with its inevitable distortions of experience. Ideally, one should be able to pay attention to everything.

The tendency is toward less and less. But never has "less" so ostentatiously advanced itself as "more."

In the light of the current myth, in which art aims to become a "total experience," soliciting total attention, the strategies of impoverishment and reduction indicate the most exalted ambition art could adopt. Underneath what looks like a strenuous modesty, if not actual debility, is to be discerned an energetic secular blasphemy: the wish to attain the unfettered, unselective, total consciousness of "God."

8

Language seems a privileged metaphor for expressing the mediated character of art-making and the artwork. On the one hand, speech is both an immaterial medium (compared with, say, images) and a human activity with an apparently essential stake in the project of transcendence, of moving beyond the singular and contingent (all words being abstractions, only roughly based on or making reference to concrete particulars). On the other hand, language is the most impure, the most contaminated, the most exhausted of all the materials out of which art is made.

This dual character of language—its abstractness, and its "fallenness" in history—serves as a microcosm of the unhappy character of the arts today. Art is so far along the labyrinthine pathways of the project of transcendence that one can hardly conceive of it turning back, short of the most drastic and punitive "cultural revolution." Yet at the same time, art is foundering in the debilitating tide of what once seemed the crowning achievement of European thought: secular historical consciousness. In little more than two centuries, the consciousness of history has transformed itself from a liberation, an opening of doors, blessed enlightenment, into an almost insupportable burden of self-consciousness. It's scarcely possible for the artist to write a word (or render an image or make a gesture) that doesn't remind him of something already achieved.

As Nietzsche says: "Our pre-eminence: we live in the age of comparison, we can verify as has never been verified before." Therefore "we enjoy differently, we suffer differently: our instinctive activity is to compare an unheard number of things."

Up to a point, the community and historicity of the artist's means are implicit in the very fact of intersubjectivity: each person is a being-in-a-world. But today, particularly in the arts using language, this normal state of affairs is felt as an extraordinary, wearying problem.

Language is experienced not merely as something shared but as something corrupted, weighed down by historical accumulation. Thus, for each conscious artist, the creation of a work means dealing with two potentially antagonistic domains of meaning and their relationships. One is his own meaning (or lack of it); the other is the set of second-order meanings that both extend his own language and encumber, compromise, and adulterate it. The artist ends by choosing between two inherently limiting alternatives, forced to take a position that is either servile or insolent. Either he flatters or appeases his audience, giving them what they already know, or he commits an aggression against his audience, giving them what they don't want.

Modern art thus transmits in full the alienation produced by historical consciousness. Whatever the artist does is in (usually conscious) alignment with something else already done, producing a compulsion to be continually checking his situation, his own stance against those of his predecessors and contemporaries. To compensate for this ignominious enslavement to history, the artist exalts himself with the dream of a wholly ahistorical, and therefore unalienated, art.

9

Art that is "silent" constitutes one approach to this visionary, ahistorical condition.

Consider the difference between *looking* and *staring*. A look is voluntary; it is also mobile, rising and falling in intensity as its foci of interest are taken up and then exhausted. A stare has, essentially, the character of a compulsion; it is steady, unmodulated, "fixed."

Traditional art invites a look. Art that is silent engenders a stare. Silent art allows—at least in principle—no release from attention, because there has never, in principle, been any soliciting of it. A stare is perhaps as far from history, as close to eternity, as contemporary art can get.

10

Silence is a metaphor for a cleansed, non-interfering vision, appropriate to artworks that are unresponsive before being seen, unviolable in their essential integrity by human scrutiny. The spectator would approach art as he does a landscape. A landscape doesn't demand from the spectator his "understanding," his imputations of significance, his anxieties and sympathies; it demands, rather, his absence, it asks that he not add anything to *it*. Contemplation, strictly speaking, entails self-forgetfulness on the part of the spectator: an object worthy of contemplation is one which, in effect, annihilates the perceiving subject.

Toward such an ideal plenitude to which the audience can add nothing, analogous to the aesthetic relation to nature, a great deal of contemporary art aspires—through various strategies of blandness, of reduction, of deindividuation, of alogicality. In principle, the audience may not even add its thought. All objects, rightly perceived, are already full. This is what Cage must mean when, after explaining that there is no such thing as silence because something is always happening that makes a sound, he adds, "No one can have an idea once he starts really listening."

Plenitude—experiencing all the space as filled, so that ideas cannot enter—means impenetrability. A person who becomes silent becomes opaque for the other; somebody's silence opens up an array of possibilities for interpreting that silence, for imputing speech to it.

The way in which this opaqueness induces spiritual vertigo is the theme of Bergman's *Persona*. The actress's deliberate silence has two aspects: Considered as a decision apparently relating to herself, the refusal to speak is apparently the form she has given to the wish for ethical purity; but it is also, as behavior, a means of power, a species of sadism, a virtually inviolable position of strength from which she manipulates and confounds her nurse-companion, who is charged with the burden of talking.

But the opaqueness of silence can be conceived more positively, as free from anxiety. For Keats, the silence of the Grecian urn is a locus of spiritual nourishment: "unheard" melodies endure, whereas those that pipe to "the sensual ear" decay. Silence is equated with arresting time ("slow time"). One can stare endlessly at the Grecian urn. Eternity, in the argument of Keats' poem, is the only interesting stimulus to thought and also the sole occasion for coming to the end of mental activity, which means interminable, unanswered questions ("Thou, silent form, dost tease us out of thought/As doth eternity"), in order to arrive at a final equation of ideas ("Beauty is truth, truth beauty") which is both absolutely vacuous and completely full. Keats' poem quite logically ends in a statement that will seem, if the reader hasn't followed his argument, like empty wisdom, a banality. As time, or history, is the medium of definite, determinate thought, the silence of eternity prepares for a thought beyond thought, which must appear from the perspective of traditional thinking and the familiar uses of the mind as no thought at all—though it may rather be the emblem of new, "difficult" thinking.

I I

Behind the appeals for silence lies the wish for a perceptual and cultural clean slate. And, in its most hortatory and ambitious version, the advocacy of silence expresses a mythic project of total liberation. What's envisaged is nothing less than the liberation of the artist from himself, of art from the particular artwork, of art from history, of spirit from matter, of the mind from its perceptual and intellectual limitations.

As some people know now, there are ways of thinking that we don't yet know about. Nothing could be more important or precious than that knowledge, however unborn. The sense of urgency, the spiritual restlessness it engenders, cannot be appeased, and continues to fuel the radical art of this century. Through its advocacy of silence and reduction, art commits an act of violence upon itself, turning art into a species of auto-manipulation, of conjuring—trying to bring these new ways of thinking to birth.

Silence is a strategy for the transvaluation of art, art itself being the herald of an anticipated radical transvaluation of human values. But the success of this strategy must mean its eventual abandonment, or at least its significant modification.

Silence is a prophecy, one which the artist's actions can be understood as attempting both to fulfill and to reverse.

As language points to its own transcendence in silence, silence points to its own transcendence—to a speech beyond silence.

But can the whole enterprise become an act of bad faith if the artist knows *this*, too?

I 2

A famous quotation: "Everything that can be thought at all can be thought clearly. Everything that can be said at all can be said clearly. But not everything that can be thought can be said."

Notice that Wittgenstein, with his scrupulous avoidance of the psychological issue, doesn't ask why, when, and in what circumstances someone would *want* to put into words "everything that can be thought" (even if he could), or even to utter (whether clearly or not) "everything that could be said."

13

Of everything that's said, one can ask: *why?* (Including: why should I say *that*? And: why should I say anything at all?)

Moreover, strictly speaking, nothing that's *said* is true. (Though a person can *be* the truth, one can't ever say it.)

Still, things that are said can sometimes be helpful—which is what people ordinarily mean when they regard something *said* as being true. Speech can enlighten, relieve, confuse, exalt, infect, antagonize, gratify, grieve, stun, animate. While language is regularly used to inspire to action, some verbal statements, either written or oral, are themselves the performing of an action (as in promising, sweating, bequeathing). Another use of speech, if anything more common than that of provoking actions, is to provoke further speech. But speech can silence, too. This indeed is how it must be: without the polarity of silence, the whole system of language would fail. And beyond its generic function as the dialectical opposite of speech, silence—like speech—also has more specific, less inevitable uses.

One use for silence: certifying the absence or renunciation of thought. Silence is often employed as a magical or mimetic procedure in repressive social relationships, as in the Jesuit regulations about speaking to superiors and in the disciplining of children. (This should not be confused with the practice of certain monastic disciplines, such as the Trappist order, in which silence is both an ascetic act and bears witness to the condition of being perfectly "full.")

Another, apparently opposed, use for silence: certifying the completion of thought. In the words of Karl Jaspers, "He who has the final answers can no longer speak to the other, breaking off genuine communication for the sake of what he believes in."

Still another use for silence: providing time for the continuing or exploring of thought. Notably, speech closes off thought. (An example: the enterprise of criticism, in which there seems no way for a critic not to assert that a given artist is *this*, he's *that*, etc.) But if one decides an issue isn't closed, it's not. This is presumably the rationale behind the voluntary experiments in silence that some contemporary spiritual athletes, like Buckminster Fuller, have undertaken, and the element of wisdom in the otherwise mainly authoritarian, philistine silence of the orthodox Freudian psychoanalyst. Silence keeps things "open."

Still another use for silence: furnishing or aiding speech to attain its maximum integrity or seriousness. Everyone has experienced how, when punctuated by long silences, words weigh more; they become almost palpable. Or how, when one talks less, one begins feeling more fully one's physical presence in a given space. Silence undermines "bad speech," by which I mean dissociated speech—speech dissociated from the body (and, therefore, from feeling), speech not organically informed by the sensuous presence and concrete particularity of the speaker and by the individual occasion for using language. Unmoored from the body, speech deteriorates. It becomes false, inane, ignoble, weightless. Silence can inhibit or counteract this tendency, providing a kind of ballast, monitoring and even correcting language when it becomes inauthentic.

Given these perils to the authenticity of language (which doesn't depend on the character of any isolated statement or even group of statements, but on the relation of speaker, utterance, and situation), the imaginary project of saying clearly "everything that can be said" suggested by Wittgenstein's remarks looks fearfully complicated. (How much time would one have? Would one have to speak quickly?) The philosopher's hypothetical universe of clear speech (which assigns to silence only "that whereof one cannot speak") would seem to be a moralist's, or a psychiatrist's, nightmare—at the least a place no one should lightheartedly enter. Is there anyone who *wants* to say "everything that could be said"? The psychologically plausible answer would seem to be no. But yes is plausible, too—as a rising ideal of modern culture. Isn't that what many people *do* want today—to say everything that can be said? But this aim cannot be maintained without inner conflict. In part inspired by the spread of the ideals of psychotherapy, people are yearning to say "everything" (thereby, among other results, further undermining the crumbling distinction between public and private endeavors, between information and secrets). But in an overpopulated world being connected by global electronic communication and jet travel at a pace too rapid and violent for an organically sound person to assimilate without shock, people are also suffering from a revulsion at any further proliferation of speech and images. Such different factors as the unlimited "technological reproduction" and near universal diffusion of printed language and speech as well as images (from "news" to "art objects"), and the degeneration of public language within the realms of politics and advertising and entertainment, have produced, especially among the better-educated inhabitants of modern mass society, a devaluation of language. (I should argue, contrary to McLuhan, that a devaluation of the power and credibility of images has taken place no less profound than, and essentially similar to, that afflicting language.) And, as the prestige of language falls, that of silence rises.

I am alluding, at this point, to the sociological context of the contemporary ambivalence toward language. The matter, of course, goes much deeper than this. In addition to the specific sociological determinants, one must recognize the operation of something like a perennial discontent with language that has been formulated in each of the major civilizations of the Orient and Occident, whenever thought reaches a certain high, *excruciating* order of complexity and spiritual seriousness.

Traditionally, it has been through the religious vocabulary, with its meta-absolutes of "sacred" and "profane," "human" and "divine," that the disaffection with language itself has been charted. In particular, the antecedents of art's dilemmas and strategies are to be found in the radical wing of the mystical tradition. (Cf., among Christian texts, the *Mystica Theologia* of Dionysius the Areopagite, the anonymous *Cloud of Unknowing*, the writings of Jakob Boehme and Meister Eckhart; and parallels in Zen, Taoist, and Sufi texts.) The mystical tradition has always recognized, in Norman Brown's phrase, "the neurotic character of language." (According to Boehme, Adam spoke a language different from all known languages. It was "sensual speech," the unmediated expressive instrument of the senses, proper to being integrally part of sensuous nature—that is, still employed by all the animals except that sick animal, man. This, which Boehme calls the only "natural language," the sole language free from distortion and illusion, is what man will speak again when he recovers paradise.) But in our time, the most striking developments of such ideas have been made by artists (and certain psychotherapists) rather than by the timid legatees of the religious traditions.

Explicitly in revolt against what is deemed the desiccated, categorized life of the ordinary mind, the artist issues his own call for a revision of language. A good deal of contemporary art is moved by this quest for a consciousness purified of contaminated language and, in some versions, of the distortions produced by conceiving the world exclusively in conventional verbal (in their debased sense, "rational" or "logical") terms. Art itself becomes a kind of counterviolence, seeking to loosen the grip upon consciousness of the habits of lifeless, static verbalization, presenting models of "sensual speech."

If anything, the volume of discontent has been turned up since the arts inherited the problem of language from religious discourse. It's not just that words, ultimately, are inadequate to the highest aims of consciousness; or even that they get in the way. Art expresses a double discontent. We lack words, and we have too many of them. It raises two complaints about language. Words are too crude. And words are also too busy—inviting a hyperactivity of consciousness that is not only dysfunctional, in terms of human capacities of feeling and acting, but actively deadens the mind and blunts the senses.

Language is demoted to the status of an event. Something takes place in time, a voice speaking which points to the before and to what comes after an utterance: silence. Silence, then, is both the precondition of speech and the result or aim of properly directed speech. On this model, the artist's activity is the creating or establishing of silence; the efficacious artwork leaves silence in its wake. Silence, administered by the artist, is part of a program of perceptual and cultural therapy, often on the model of shock therapy rather than of persuasion. Even if the artist's medium is words, he can share in this task: language can be employed to check language, to express muteness. Mallarmé thought it was the job of poetry, using words, to clean up our word-clogged reality—by creating silences around things. Art must mount a full-scale attack on language itself, by means of language and its surrogates, on behalf of the standard of silence.

14

In the end, the radical critique of consciousness (first delineated by the mystical tradition, now administered by unorthodox psychotherapy and high modernist art) always lays the blame on language. Consciousness, experienced as a burden, is conceived of as the memory of all the words that have ever been said.

Krishnamurti claims that we must give up psychological, as distinct from factual, memory. Otherwise, we keep filling up the new with the old, closing off experience by hooking each experience onto the last.

We must destroy continuity (which is insured by psychological memory), by going to the *end* of each emotion or thought.

And after the end, what supervenes (for a while) is silence.

15

In his Fourth Duino Elegy, Rilke gives a metaphoric statement of the problem of language and recommends a procedure for approaching as near the horizon of silence as he considers feasible. A prerequisite of "emptying out" is to be able to perceive what one is "full of," what words and mechanical gestures one is stuffed with, like a doll; only then, in polar confrontation with the doll, does the "angel" appear, a figure representing an equally inhuman though "higher" possibility, that of an entirely unmediated, translinguistic apprehension. Neither doll nor angel, human beings remain situated within the kingdom of language. But for nature, then things, then other people, then the textures of ordinary life to be experienced from a stance other than the crippled one of mere spectatorship, language must regain its chastity. As Rilke describes it in the Ninth Elegy, the redemption of language (which is to say, the redemption of the world through its interiorization in consciousness) is a long, infinitely arduous task. Human beings are so "fallen" that they must start with the simplest linguistic act: the naming of things. Perhaps no more than this minimal function can be preserved from the general corruption of discourse. Language may very well have to remain within a permanent state of reduction. Though perhaps, when this spiritual exercise of confining language to naming is perfected, it may be possible to pass on to other, more ambitious uses of language, nothing must be attempted which will allow consciousness to become reestranged from itself.

For Rilke the overcoming of the alienation of consciousness is conceivable; and not, as in the radical myths of the mystics, through transcending language altogether. It suffices to cut back drastically the scope and use of language. A tremendous spiritual preparation (the contrary of "alienation") is required for this deceptively simple act of naming. It is nothing less than the scouring and harmonious sharpening of the senses (the very opposite of such violent projects, with roughly the same end and informed by the same hostility to verbal-rational culture, as "systematically deranging the senses").

Rilke's remedy lies halfway between exploiting the numbness of language as a gross, fully installed cultural institution and yielding to the suicidal vertigo of pure silence. But this middle ground of reducing language to naming can be claimed in quite another way than his. Contrast the benign nominalism proposed by Rilke (and proposed and practiced by Francis Ponge) with the brutal nominalism adopted by many other artists. The more familiar recourse of modern art to the aesthetics of the inventory is not made—as in Rilke—with an eye to "humanizing" things, but rather to confirming their inhumanity, their impersonality, their indifference to and separateness from human concerns. (Examples of the "inhumane" preoccupation with naming: Roussel's *Impressions of Africa*; the silkscreen paintings and early films of Andy Warhol; the early novels of Robbe-Grillet, which attempt to confine the function of language to bare physical description and location.)

Rilke and Ponge assume that there *are* priorities: rich as opposed to vacuous objects, events with a certain allure. (This is the incentive for trying to peel back language, allowing the "things" themselves to speak.) More decisively, they assume that if there are states of false (language-clogged) consciousness, there are also authentic states of consciousness—which it's the function of art to promote. The alternative view denies the traditional hierarchies of interest and meaning, in which some things have more "significance" than others. The distinction between true and false experience, true and false consciousness is also denied: in principle, one should desire to pay attention to everything. It's this view, most elegantly formulated by Cage though its practice is found everywhere, that leads to the art of the inventory, the catalogue, surfaces; also "chance." The function of art isn't to sanction any specific experience, except the state of being open to the multiplicity of experience—which ends in practice by a decided stress on things usually considered trivial or unimportant.

The attachment of contemporary art to the "minimal" narrative principle of the catalogue or inventory seems almost to parody the capitalist world-view, in which the environment is atomized into "items" (a category embracing things and persons, works of art and natural organisms), and in which every item is a commodity—that is, a discrete, portable object. A general leveling of value is encouraged in the art of inventory, which is itself only one of the possible approaches to an ideally uninflected discourse. Traditionally, the effects of an artwork have been unevenly distributed, to induce in the audience a certain sequence of experience: first arousing, then manipulating, and eventually fulfilling emotional expectations. What is proposed now is a discourse without emphases in this traditional sense. (Again, the principle of the stare as opposed to the look.)

Such art could also be described as establishing great "distance" (between spectator and art object, between the spectator and his emotions). But, psychologically, distance often is linked with the most intense state of feeling, in which the coolness or impersonality with which something is treated measures the insatiable interest that thing has for us. The distance that a great deal of "anti-humanist" art proposes is actually equivalent to obsession—an aspect of the involvement in "things" of which the "humanist" nominalism of Rilke has no intimation.

16

"There is something strange in the acts of writing and speaking," Novalis wrote in 1799. "The ridiculous and amazing mistake people make is to believe they use words in relation to things. They are unaware of the nature of language—which is to be its own and only concern, making it so fertile and splendid a mystery. When someone talks just for the sake of talking he is saying the most original and truthful thing he can say."

Novalis' statement may help explain an apparent paradox: that in the era of the widespread advocacy of art's silence, an increasing number of works of art babble. Verbosity and repetitiveness are particularly noticeable in the temporal arts of prose fiction, music, film, and dance, many of which cultivate a kind of ontological stammer—facilitated by their refusal of the incentives for a clean, anti-redundant discourse supplied by linear, beginning-middle-and-end construction. But actually, there's no contradiction. For the contemporary appeal for silence has never indicated merely a hostile dismissal of language. It also signifies a very high estimate of language—of its powers, of its past health, and of the current dangers it poses to a free consciousness. From this intense and ambivalent valuation proceeds the impulse for a discourse that appears both irrepressible (and, in principle, interminable) and strangely inarticulate, painfully reduced. Discernible in the fictions of Stein, Burroughs, and Beckett is the subliminal idea that it might be possible to out-talk language, or to talk oneself into silence.

This is not a very promising strategy, considering what results might reasonably be anticipated from it. But perhaps not so odd, when one observes how often the aesthetic of silence appears alongside a barely controlled abhorrence of the void.

Accommodating these two contrary impulses may produce the need to fill up all the spaces with objects of slight emotional weight or with large areas of barely modulated color or evenly detailed objects, or to spin a discourse with as few possible inflections, emotive variations, and risings and fallings of emphasis. These procedures seem analogous to the behavior of an obsessional neurotic warding off a danger. The acts of such a person must be repeated in the identical form, because the danger remains the same; and they must be repeated endlessly, because the danger never seems to go away. But the emotional fires feeding the art-discourse analogous to obsessionalism may be turned down so low one can forget they're there. Then all that's left to the ear is a kind of steady hum or drone. What's left to the eye is the neat filling of a space with things, or, more accurately, the patient transcription of the surface detail of things.

In this view, the "silence" of things, images, and words is a prerequisite for their proliferation. Were they endowed with a more potent, individual charge, each of the various elements of the artwork would claim more psychic space and then their total number might have to be reduced.

17

Sometimes the accusation against language is not directed against all of language but only against the written word. Thus Tristan Tzara urged the burning of all books and libraries to bring about a new era of oral legends. And McLuhan, as everyone knows, makes the sharpest distinction between written language (which exists in "visual space") and oral speech (which exists in "auditory space"), praising the psychic and cultural advantages of the latter as the basis for sensibility.

If written language is singled out as the culprit, what will be sought is not so much the reduction as the metamorphosis of language into something looser, more intuitive, less organized and inflected, non-linear (in McLuhan's terminology) and—noticeably—more verbose. But, of course, it is just these qualities that characterize many of the great prose narratives of our time. Joyce, Stein, Gadda, Laura Riding, Beckett, and Burroughs employ a language whose norms and energies come from oral speech, with its circular repetitive movements and essentially first-person voice.

"Speaking for the sake of speaking is the formula of deliverance," Novalis said. (Deliverance from what? From speaking? From art?)

In my opinion, Novalis has succinctly described the proper approach of the writer to language and offered the basic criterion for literature as an art. But to what extent oral speech is the privileged model for the speech of literature as an art is still an open question.

18

A corollary of the growth of this conception of art's language as autonomous and self-sufficient (and, in the end, self-reflective) is a decline in "meaning" as traditionally sought in works of art. "Speaking for the sake of speaking" forces us to relocate the meaning of linguistic or para-linguistic statements. We are led to abandon meaning (in the sense of references to entities outside the artwork) as the criterion for the language of art in favor of "use." (Wittgenstein's famous thesis, "the meaning is the use," can and should be rigorously applied to art.)

"Meaning" partially or totally converted into "use" is the secret behind the widespread strategy of *literalness*, a major development of the aesthetics of silence. A variant on this: hidden literality, exemplified by such different writers as Kafka and Beckett. The narratives of Kafka and Beckett seem puzzling because they appear to invite the reader to ascribe high-powered symbolic and allegorical meanings to them and, at the same time, repel such ascriptions. Yet when the narrative is examined, it discloses no more than what it literally means. The power of their language derives precisely from the fact that the meaning is so bare.

The effect of such bareness is often a kind of anxiety—like the anxiety produced when familiar things aren't in their place or playing their accustomed role. One may be made as anxious by unexpected literalness as by the Surrealists' "disturbing" objects and unexpected scale and condition of objects conjoined in an imaginary landscape. Whatever is wholly mysterious is at once both psychically relieving and anxiety-provoking. (A perfect machine for agitating this pair of contrary emotions: the Bosch drawing in a Dutch museum that shows trees furnished with two ears at the sides of their trunks, as if they were listening to the forest, while the forest floor is strewn with eyes.) Before a fully conscious work of art, one feels something like the mixture of anxiety, detachment, pruriency, and relief that a physically sound person feels when he glimpses an amputee. Beckett speaks favorably of a work of art which would be a "total object, complete with missing parts, instead of partial object. Question of degree."

But exactly what is a totality and what constitutes completeness in art (or anything else)? That problem is, in principle, unresolvable. Whatever way a work of art is, it could have been—could be—different. The necessity of *these* parts in this order is never given; it is conferred.

The refusal to admit this essential contingency (or openness) is what inspires the audience's will to confirm the closedness of a work by interpreting it, and what creates the feeling common among reflective artists and critics that the artwork is always somehow in arrears of or inadequate to its "subject." But unless one is committed to the idea that art "expresses" something, these procedures and attitudes are far from inevitable.

19

This tenacious concept of art as "expression" has given rise to the most common, and dubious, version of the notion of silence—which invokes the idea of "the ineffable." The theory supposes that the province of art is "the beautiful," which implies effects of unspeakableness, indescribability, ineffability. Indeed, the search to express the inexpressible is taken as the very criterion of art; and sometimes becomes the occasion for a strict—and to my mind untenable—distinction between prose literature and poetry. It is from this position that Valéry advanced his famous argument (repeated in a quite different context by Sartre) that the novel is not, strictly speaking, an art form at all. His reason is that since the aim of prose is to communicate, the use of language in prose is perfectly straightforward. Poetry, being an art, should have quite different aims: to express an experience which is essentially ineffable; using language to express muteness. In contrast to prose writers, poets are engaged in subverting their own instrument and seeking to pass beyond it.

This theory, so far as it assumes that art is concerned with beauty, is not very interesting. (Modern aesthetics is crippled by its dependence upon this essentially vacant concept. As if art were "about" beauty, as science is "about" truth!) But even if the theory dispenses with the notion of beauty, there is still a more serious objection. The view that expressing the ineffable is an essential function of poetry (considered as a paradigm of all the arts) is naïvely unhistorical. The ineffable, while surely a perennial category of consciousness, has certainly not always made its home in the arts. Its traditional shelter was in religious discourse and, secondarily (as Plato relates in his 7th Epistle), in philosophy. The fact that contemporary artists are concerned with silence—and, therefore, in one extension, with the ineffable— must be understood historically, as a consequence of the prevailing contemporary myth of the "absoluteness" of art. The value placed on silence doesn't arise by virtue of the *nature* of art, but derives from the contemporary ascription of certain "absolute" qualities to the art object and to the activity of the artist.

The extent to which art *is* involved with the ineffable is more specific, as well as contemporary: art, in the modern conception, is always connected with systematic transgressions of a formal sort. The systematic violation of older formal conventions practiced by modern artists gives their work a certain aura of the unspeakable—for instance, as the audience uneasily senses the negative presence of what else could be, but isn't being, said; and as any "statement" made in an aggressively new or difficult form tends to seem equivocal or merely vacant. But these features of ineffability must not be acknowledged at the expense of one's awareness of the positivity of the work of art. Contemporary art, no matter how much it has defined itself by a taste for negation, can still be analyzed as a set of assertions of a formal kind.

For instance, each work of art gives us a form or paradigm or model of *knowing* something, an epistemology. But viewed as a spiritual project, a vehicle of aspirations toward an absolute, what any work of art supplies is a specific model for meta-social or meta-ethical *tact*, a standard of decorum. Each artwork indicates the unity of certain preferences about what can and cannot be said (or represented). At the same time that it may make a tacit proposal for upsetting previously consecrated rulings on what can be said (or represented), it issues its own set of limits.

20

Contemporary artists advocate silence in two styles: loud and soft.

The loud style is a function of the unstable antithesis of "plenum" and "void." The sensuous, ecstatic, translinguistic apprehension of the plenum is notoriously fragile: in a terrible, almost instantaneous plunge it can collapse into the void of negative silence. With all its awareness of risk-taking (the hazards of spiritual nausea, even of madness), this advocacy of silence tends to be frenetic and overgeneralizing. It is also frequently apocalyptic and must endure the indignity of all apocalyptic thinking: namely, to prophesy the end, to see the day come, to outlive it, and then to set a new date for the incineration of consciousness and the definitive pollution of language and exhaustion of the possibilities of art-discourse.

The other way of talking about silence is more cautious. Basically, it presents itself as an extension of a main feature of traditional classicism: the concern with modes of propriety, with standards of seemliness. Silence is only "reticence" stepped up to the nth degree. Of course, in the translation of this concern from the matrix of traditional classical art, the tone has changed—from didactic seriousness to ironic openmindedness.

But while the clamorous style of proclaiming the rhetoric of silence may seem more passionate, its more subdued advocates (like Cage, Johns) are saying something equally drastic. They are reacting to the same idea of art's absolute aspirations (by programmatic disavowals of art); they share the same disdain for the "meanings" established by bourgeois-rationalist culture, indeed for culture itself in the familiar sense. What is voiced by the Futurists, some of the Dada artists, and Burroughs as a harsh despair and perverse vision of apocalypse is no less serious for being proclaimed in a polite voice and as a sequence of playful affirmations. Indeed, it could be argued that silence is likely to remain a viable notion for modern art and consciousness only if deployed with a considerable, near systematic irony.

21

It is in the nature of all spiritual projects to tend to consume themselves—exhausting their own sense, the very meaning of the terms in which they are couched. (This is why "spirituality" must be continually reinvented.) All genuinely ultimate projects of consciousness eventually become projects for the unraveling of thought itself.

Art conceived as a spiritual project is no exception. As an abstracted and fragmented replica of the positive nihilism expounded by the radical religious myths, the serious art of our time has moved increasingly toward the most excruciating inflections of consciousness. Conceivably, irony is the only feasible counterweight to this grave use of art as the arena for the ordeal of consciousness. The present prospect is that artists will go on abolishing art, only to resurrect it in a more retracted version. As long as art bears up under the pressure of chronic interrogation, it would seem desirable that some of the questions have a certain playful quality.

But this prospect depends, perhaps, on the viability of irony itself.

From Socrates on, there are countless witnesses to the value of irony for the private individual: as a complex, serious method of seeking and holding one's truth, and as a means of saving one's sanity. But as irony becomes the good taste of what is, after all, an essentially collective activity—the making of art—it may prove less serviceable.

One need not judge as categorically as Nietzsche, who thought the spread of irony throughout a culture signified the floodtide of decadence and the approaching end of that culture's vitality and powers. In the post-political, electronically connected cosmopolis in which all serious modern artists have taken out premature citizenship, certain organic connections between culture and "thinking" (and art is certainly now, mainly, a form of thinking) appear to have been broken, so that Nietzsche's diagnosis may need to be modified. But if irony has more positive resources than Nietzsche acknowledged, there still remains a question as to how far the resources of irony can be stretched. It seems unlikely that the possibilities of continually undermining one's assumptions can go on unfolding indefinitely into the future, without being eventually checked by despair or by a laugh that leaves one without any breath at all.

(1967)

The Pornographic Imagination

N O ONE should undertake a discussion of pornography before acknowledging the pornograph*ies*—there are at least
three—and before pledging to take them on one at a time.
There is a considerable gain in truth if pornography as an item
in social history is treated quite separately from pornography
as a psychological phenomenon (according to the usual view,
symptomatic of sexual deficiency or deformity in both the producers and the consumers), and if one further distinguishes
from both of these another pornography: a minor but interesting modality or convention within the arts.

It's the last of the three pornographies that I want to focus
upon. More narrowly, upon the literary genre for which, lacking
a better name, I'm willing to accept (in the privacy of serious
intellectual debate, not in the courts) the dubious label of pornography. By literary genre I mean a body of work belonging to
literature considered as an art, and to which inherent standards
of artistic excellence pertain. From the standpoint of social and
psychological phenomena, all pornographic texts have the same
status; they are documents. But from the standpoint of art,
some of these texts may well become something else. Not only
do Pierre Louÿ's *Trois Filles de leur Mère*, Georges Bataille's *Histoire de l'Oeil* and *Madame Edwarda*, the pseudonymous *Story
of O* and *The Image* belong to literature, but it can be made
clear why these books, all five of them, occupy a much higher
rank as literature than *Candy* or Oscar Wilde's *Teleny* or the Earl
of Rochester's *Sodom* or Apollinaire's *The Debauched Hospodar*
or Cleland's *Fanny Hill*. The avalanche of pornographic potboilers marketed for two centuries under and now, increasingly,
over the counter no more impugns the status as literature of
the first group of pornographic books than the proliferation of
books of the caliber of *The Carpetbaggers* and *Valley of the Dolls*
throws into question the credentials of *Anna Karenina* and *The
Great Gatsby* and *The Man Who Loved Children*. The ratio of
authentic literature to trash in pornography may be somewhat
lower than the ratio of novels of genuine literary merit to the
entire volume of sub-literary fiction produced for mass taste.
But it is probably no lower than, for instance, that of another
somewhat shady sub-genre with a few first-rate books to its

credit, science fiction. (As literary forms, pornography and science fiction resemble each other in several interesting ways.) Anyway, the quantitative measure supplies a trivial standard. Relatively uncommon as they may be, there are writings which it seems reasonable to call pornographic—assuming that the stale label has any use at all—which, at the same time, cannot be refused accreditation as serious literature.

The point would seem to be obvious. Yet, apparently, that's far from being the case. At least in England and America, the reasoned scrutiny and assessment of pornography is held firmly within the limits of the discourse employed by psychologists, sociologists, historians, jurists, professional moralists, and social critics. Pornography is a malady to be diagnosed and an occasion for judgment. It's something one is for or against. And taking sides about pornography is hardly like being for or against aleatoric music or Pop Art, but quite a bit like being for or against legalized abortion or federal aid to parochial schools. In fact, the same fundamental approach to the subject is shared by recent eloquent defenders of society's right and obligation to censor dirty books, like George P. Elliott and George Steiner, and those like Paul Goodman, who foresee pernicious consequences of a policy of censorship far worse than any harm done by the books themselves. Both the libertarians and the would-be censors agree in reducing pornography to pathological symptom and problematic social commodity. A near unanimous consensus exists as to what pornography is—this being identified with notions about the *sources* of the impulse to produce and consume these curious goods. When viewed as a theme for psychological analysis, pornography is rarely seen as anything more interesting than texts which illustrate a deplorable arrest in normal adult sexual development. In this view, all pornography amounts to is the representation of the fantasies of infantile sexual life, these fantasies having been edited by the more skilled, less innocent consciousness of the masturbatory adolescent, for purchase by so-called adults. As a social phenomenon—for instance, the boom in the production of pornography in the societies of Western Europe and America since the eighteenth century—the approach is no less unequivocally clinical. Pornography becomes a group pathology, the disease of a whole culture, about whose cause everyone is pretty well agreed. The mounting output of dirty books is attributed to a festering legacy of Christian sexual repression and to sheer physiological ignorance, these ancient disabilities being now compounded by more proximate historical events, the impact of drastic dislocations in traditional modes of family and political order and unsettling change in the roles of the sexes. (The problem of pornography is one of "the dilemmas of a society in transition," Goodman said in an essay several years ago.) Thus, there is a fairly complete consensus about the *diagnosis* of pornography itself. The disagreements arise only in the estimate of the psychological and social *consequences* of its dissemination, and therefore in the formulating of tactics and policy.

The more enlightened architects of moral policy are undoubtedly prepared to admit that there is something like a "pornographic imagination," although only in the sense that pornographic works are tokens of a radical failure or deformation of the imagination. And they may grant, as Goodman, Wayland Young, and others have suggested, that there also exists a "pornographic society": that, indeed, ours is a flourishing example of one, a society so hypocritically and repressively constructed that it must inevitably produce an effusion of pornography as both its logical expression and its subversive, demotic antidote. But nowhere in the Anglo-American community of letters have I seen it argued that some pornographic books are interesting and important works of art. So long as pornography is treated as only a social and psychological phenomenon and a locus for moral concern, how could such an argument ever be made?

2

There's another reason, apart from this categorizing of pornography as a topic of analysis, why the question whether or not works of pornography can be literature has never been genuinely debated. I mean the view of literature itself maintained by most English and American critics—a view which in excluding pornographic writings *by definition* from the precincts of literature excludes much else besides.

Of course, no one denies that pornography constitutes a branch of literature in the sense that it appears in the form of printed books of fiction. But beyond that trivial connection, no more is allowed. The fashion in which most critics construe the nature of prose literature, no less than their view of the nature of pornography, inevitably puts pornography in an adverse relation to literature. It is an airtight case, for if a pornographic book is defined as one not belonging to literature (and vice versa), there is no need to examine individual books.

Most mutually exclusive definitions of pornography and literature rest on four separate arguments. One is that the utterly singleminded way in which works of pornography address the reader, proposing to arouse him sexually, is antithetical to the complex function of literature. It may then be argued that pornography's aim, inducing sexual excitement, is at odds with the tranquil, detached involvement evoked by genuine art. But this turn of the argument seems particularly unconvincing, considering the respected appeal to the reader's moral feelings intended by "realistic" writing, not to mention the fact that some certified masterpieces (from Chaucer to Lawrence) contain passages that do properly excite readers sexually. It is more plausible just to emphasize that pornography still possesses only one "intention," while any genuinely valuable work of literature has many.

Another argument, made by Adorno among others, is that works of pornography lack the beginning-middle-and-end form characteristic of literature. A piece of pornographic fiction concocts no better than a crude excuse for a beginning; and once having begun, it goes on and on and ends nowhere.

Another argument: pornographic writing can't evidence any care for its means of expression as such (the concern of literature), since the aim of pornography is to inspire a set of nonverbal fantasies in which language plays a debased, merely instrumental role.

Last and most weighty is the argument that the subject of literature is the relation of human beings to each other, their complex feelings and emotions; pornography, in contrast, disdains fully formed persons (psychology and social portraiture), is oblivious to the question of motives and their credibility and reports only the motiveless tireless transactions of depersonalized organs.

Simply extrapolating from the conception of literature maintained by most English and American critics today, it would follow that the literary value of pornography has to be nil. But these paradigms don't stand up to close analysis in themselves, nor do they even fit their subject. Take, for instance, *Story of O*. Though the novel is clearly obscene by the usual standards, and more effective than many in arousing a reader sexually, sexual arousal doesn't appear to be the sole function of the situations portrayed. The narrative does have a definite beginning, middle, and end. The elegance of the writing hardly gives the impression that its author considered language a bothersome necessity. Further, the characters do possess emotions of a very intense kind, although obsessional and indeed wholly asocial ones; characters do have motives, though they are not psychiatrically or socially "normal" motives. The characters in *Story of O* are endowed with a "psychology" of a sort, one derived from the psychology of lust. And while what can be learned of the characters within the situations in which they are placed is severely restricted—to modes of sexual concentration and explicitly rendered sexual behavior—O and her partners are no more reduced or foreshortened than the characters in many nonpornographic works of contemporary fiction.

Only when English and American critics evolve a more sophisticated view of literature will an interesting debate get underway. (In the end, this debate would be not only about pornography but about the whole body of contemporary literature insistently focused on extreme situations and behavior.) The difficulty arises because so many critics continue to identify with prose literature itself the particular literary conventions of "realism" (what might be crudely associated with the major tradition of the nineteenth-century novel). For examples of alternative literary modes, one is not confined only to much of the greatest twentieth-century writing—to *Ulysses*, a book not about characters but about media of transpersonal exchange, about all that lies outside individual psychology and personal need; to French Surrealism and its most recent offspring, the New Novel; to German "expressionist" fiction; to the Russian postnovel represented by Biely's *St. Petersburg* and by Nabokov; or to the nonlinear, tenseless narratives of Stein and Burroughs. A definition of literature that faults a work for being rooted in "fantasy" rather than in the realistic rendering of how lifelike persons in familiar situations live with each other couldn't even handle such venerable conventions as the pastoral, which depicts relations between people that are certainly reductive, vapid, and unconvincing.

An uprooting of some of these tenacious clichés is long overdue: it will promote a sounder reading of the literature of the past as well as put critics and ordinary readers better in touch with contemporary literature, which includes zones of writing that structurally resemble pornography. It is facile, virtually meaningless, to demand that literature stick with the "human." For the matter at stake is not "human" versus "inhuman" (in which choosing the "human" guarantees instant moral self-congratulation for both author and reader) but an infinitely varied register of forms and tonalities for transposing *the human voice* into prose narrative. For the critic, the proper question is not the relationship between the book and "the world" or "reality" (in which each novel is judged as if it were a unique item, and in which the world is regarded as a far less complex place than it is) but the complexities of consciousness itself, as the medium through which a world exists at all and is constituted, and an approach to single books of fiction which doesn't slight the fact that they exist in dialogue with each other. From this point of view, the decision of the old novelists to depict the unfolding of the destinies of sharply individualized "characters" in familiar, socially dense situations within the conventional notation of chronological sequence is only one of many possible decisions, possessing no inherently superior claim to the allegiance of serious readers. There is nothing innately more "human" about these procedures. The presence of realistic characters is not, in itself, something wholesome, a more nourishing staple for the moral sensibility.

The only sure truth about characters in prose fiction is that they are, in Henry James' phrase, "a compositional resource." The presence of human figures in literary art can serve many purposes. Dramatic tension or three-dimensionality in the rendering of personal and social relations is often *not* a writer's aim, in which case it doesn't help to insist on that as a generic standard. Exploring ideas is as authentic an aim of prose fiction, although by the standards of novelistic realism this aim severely limits the presentation of lifelike persons. The constructing or imaging of something inanimate, or of a portion of the world of nature, is also a valid enterprise, and entails an appropriate rescaling of the human figure. (The form of the pastoral involves both these aims: the depiction of ideas and of nature. Persons are used only to the extent that they constitute a certain kind of landscape, which is partly a stylization of "real" nature and partly a neo-Platonic landscape of ideas.) And equally valid as a subject for prose narrative are the extreme states of human feeling and consciousness, those so peremptory that they exclude the mundane flux of feelings and are only contingently linked with concrete persons—which is the case with pornography.

One would never guess from the confident pronouncements on the nature of literature by most American and English critics that a vivid debate on this issue had been proceeding for several generations. "It seems to me," Jacques Rivière wrote in the *Nouvelle Revue Française* in 1924, "that we are witnessing a very serious crisis in the concept of what literature is." One of several responses to "the problem of the possibility and the limits of literature," Rivière noted, is the marked tendency for "art (if even the word can still be kept) to become a completely nonhuman activity, a supersensory function, if I may use that term, a sort of creative astronomy." I cite Rivière not because his essay, "Questioning the Concept of Literature," is particularly original or definitive or subtly argued, but simply to recall an ensemble of radical notions about literature which were almost critical commonplaces forty years ago in European literary magazines.

To this day, though, that ferment remains alien, unassimilated, and persistently misunderstood in the English and American world of letters: suspected as issuing from a collective cultural failure of nerve, frequently dismissed as outright perversity or obscurantism or creative sterility. The better English-speaking critics, however, could hardly fail to notice how much great twentieth-century literature subverts those ideas received from certain of the great nineteenth-century novelists on the nature of literature which they continue to echo in 1967. But the critics' awareness of genuinely new literature was usually tendered in a spirit much like that of the rabbis a century before the beginning of the Christian era who, humbly acknowledging the spiritual inferiority of their own age to the age of the great prophets, nevertheless firmly closed the canon of prophetic books and declared—with more relief, one suspects, than regret—the era of prophecy ended. So has the age of what in Anglo-American criticism is still called, astonishingly enough, "experimental" or "avant-garde" writing been repeatedly declared closed. The ritual celebration of each contemporary genius's undermining of the older notions of literature was often accompanied by the nervous insistence that the writing brought forth was, alas, the last of its noble, sterile line. Now, the results of this intricate, one-eyed way of looking at modern literature have been several decades of unparalleled interest and brilliance in English and American—particularly American—criticism. But it is an interest and brilliance reared on bankruptcy of taste and something approaching a fundamental dishonesty of method. The critics' retrograde awareness of the impressive new claims staked out by modern literature, linked with their chagrin over what was usually designated as "the rejection of reality" and "the failure of the self" endemic in that literature, indicates the precise point at which most talented Anglo-American literary criticism leaves off considering structures of literature and transposes itself into criticism of culture.

I don't wish to repeat here the arguments that I have advanced elsewhere on behalf of a different critical approach. Still, some allusion to that approach needs to be made. To discuss even a single work of the radical nature of *Histoire de l'Oeil* raises the question of literature itself, of prose narrative considered as an art form. And books like those of Bataille could not have been written except for that agonized reappraisal of the nature of literature which has been preoccupying literary Europe for more than half a century; but lacking that context, they must prove almost unassimilable for English and American readers—except as "mere" pornography, inexplicably fancy trash. If it is even necessary to take up the issue of whether or not pornography and literature are antithetical, if it is at all necessary to assert that works of pornography *can* belong to literature, then the assertion must imply an overall view of what art is.

To put it very generally: art (and art-making) is a form of consciousness; the materials of art are the variety of forms of consciousness. By no *aesthetic* principle can this notion of the materials of art be construed as excluding even the extreme forms of consciousness that transcend social personality or psychological individuality.

In daily life, to be sure, we may acknowledge a moral obligation to inhibit such states of consciousness in ourselves. The obligation seems pragmatically sound, not only to maintain social order in the widest sense but to allow the individual to establish and maintain a humane contact with other persons (though that contact can be renounced, for shorter or longer periods). It's well known that when people venture into the far reaches of consciousness, they do so at the peril of their sanity, that is, of their humanity. But the "human scale" or humanistic standard proper to ordinary life and conduct seems misplaced when applied to art. It oversimplifies. If within the last century art conceived as an autonomous activity has come to be invested with an unprecedented stature—the nearest thing to a sacramental human activity acknowledged by secular society—it is because one of the tasks art has assumed is making forays into and taking up positions on the frontiers of consciousness (often very dangerous to the artist as a person) and reporting back what's there. Being a freelance explorer of spiritual dangers, the artist gains a certain license to behave differently from other people; matching the singularity of his vocation, he may be decked out with a suitably eccentric life style, or he may not. His job is inventing trophies of his experiences—objects and gestures that fascinate and enthrall, not merely (as prescribed by older notions of the artist) edify or entertain. His principal means of fascinating is to advance one step further in the dialectic of outrage. He seeks to make his work repulsive, obscure, inaccessible; in short, to give what is, or seems to be, *not* wanted. But however fierce may be the outrages the artist perpetrates upon his audience, his credentials and spiritual authority ultimately depend on the audience's sense (whether something known or inferred) of the outrages he commits upon himself. The exemplary modern artist is a broker in madness.

The notion of art as the dearly purchased outcome of an immense spiritual risk, one whose cost goes up with the entry and participation of each new player in the game, invites a revised set of critical standards. Art produced under the aegis of this conception certainly is not, cannot be, "realistic." But words like "fantasy" or "surrealism," that only invert the guidelines of realism, clarify little. Fantasy too easily declines into "mere" fantasy; the clincher is the adjective "infantile." Where does fantasy, condemned by psychiatric rather than artistic standards, end and imagination begin?

Since it's hardly likely that contemporary critics seriously mean to bar prose narratives that are unrealistic from the domain of literature, one suspects that a special standard is being applied to sexual themes. This becomes clearer if one thinks of another kind of book, another kind of "fantasy." The ahistorical dreamlike landscape where action is situated, the peculiarly congealed time in which acts are performed—these occur almost as often in science fiction as they do in pornography. There is nothing conclusive in the well-known fact that most men and women fall short of the sexual prowess that people in pornography are represented as enjoying; that the size of organs, number and duration of orgasms, variety and feasibility of sexual powers, and amount of sexual energy all seem grossly exaggerated. Yes, and the spaceships and the teeming planets depicted in science-fiction novels don't exist either. The fact that the site of narrative is an ideal *topos* disqualifies neither pornography nor science fiction from being literature. Such negations of real, concrete, three-dimensional social time, space, and personality—and such "fantastic" enlargements of human energy—are rather the ingredients of another kind of literature, founded on another mode of consciousness.

The materials of the pornographic books that count as literature are, precisely, one of the extreme forms of human consciousness. Undoubtedly, many people would agree that the sexually obsessed consciousness can, in principle, enter into literature as an art form. Literature about lust? Why not? But then they usually add a rider to the agreement which effectually nullifies it. They require that the author have the proper "distance" from his obsessions for their rendering to count as literature. Such a standard is sheer hypocrisy, revealing once again that the values commonly applied to pornography are, in the end, those belonging to psychiatry and social affairs rather than to art. (Since Christianity upped the ante and concentrated on sexual behavior as the root of virtue, everything pertaining to sex has been a "special case" in our culture, evoking peculiarly inconsistent attitudes.) Van Gogh's paintings retain their status as art even if it seems his manner of painting owed less to a conscious choice of representational means than to his being deranged and actually seeing reality the way he painted it. Similarly, *Histoire de l'Oeil* does not become case history rather than art because, as Bataille reveals in the extraordinary autobiographical essay appended to the narrative, the book's obsessions are indeed his own.

What makes a work of pornography part of the history of art rather than of trash is not distance, the superimposition of a consciousness more conformable to that of ordinary reality upon the "deranged consciousness" of the erotically obsessed. Rather, it is the originality, thoroughness, authenticity, and power of that deranged consciousness itself, as incarnated in a work. From the point of view of art, the exclusivity of the consciousness embodied in pornographic books is in itself neither anomalous nor anti-literary.

Nor is the purported aim or effect, whether it is intentional or not, of such books—to excite the reader sexually—a defect. Only a degraded and mechanistic idea of sex could mislead someone into thinking that being sexually stirred by a book like *Madame Edwarda* is a simple matter. The singleness of intention often condemned by critics is, when the work merits treatment as art, compounded of many resonances. The physical sensations involuntarily produced in someone reading the book carry with them something that touches upon the reader's whole experience of his humanity—and his limits as a personality and as a body. Actually, the singleness of pornography's intention is spurious. But the aggressiveness of the intention is not. What seems like an end is as much a means, startlingly and oppressively concrete. The end, however, is less concrete. Pornography is one of the branches of literature—science fiction is another—aiming at disorientation, at psychic dislocation.

In some respects, the use of sexual obsessions as a subject for literature resembles the use of a literary subject whose validity far fewer people would contest: religious obsessions. So compared, the familiar fact of pornography's definite, aggressive impact upon its readers looks somewhat different. Its celebrated intention of sexually stimulating readers is really a species of proselytizing. Pornography that is serious literature aims to "excite" in the same way that books which render an extreme form of religious experience aim to "convert."

3

Two French books recently translated into English, *Story of O* and *The Image*, conveniently illustrate some issues involved in this topic, barely explored in Anglo-American criticism, of pornography as literature.

Story of O by "Pauline Réage" appeared in 1954 and immediately became famous, partly due to the patronage of Jean Paulhan, who wrote the preface. It was widely believed that Paulhan himself had written the book—perhaps because of the precedent set by Bataille, who had contributed an essay (signed with his own name) to his *Madame Edwarda* when it was first published in 1937 under the pseudonym "Pierre Angelique," and also because the name Pauline suggested Paulhan. But Paulhan has always denied that he wrote *Story of O*, insisting that it was indeed written by a woman, someone previously unpublished and living in another part of France, who insisted on remaining unknown. While Paulhan's story did not halt speculation, the conviction that he was the author eventually faded. Over the years, a number of more ingenious hypotheses, attributing the book's authorship to other notables on the Paris literary scene, gained credence and then were dropped. The real identity of "Pauline Réage" remains one of the few well-kept secrets in contemporary letters.

The Image was published two years later, in 1956, also under a pseudonym, "Jean de Berg." To compound the mystery, it was dedicated to and had a preface by "Pauline Réage," who has not been heard from since. (The preface by "Réage" is terse and forgettable; the one by Paulhan is long and very interesting.) But gossip in Paris literary circles about the identity of "Jean de Berg" is more conclusive than the detective work on "Pauline Réage." One rumor only, which names the wife of an influential younger novelist, has swept the field.

It is not hard to understand why those curious enough to speculate about the two pseudonyms should incline toward some name from the established community of letters in France. For either of these books to be an amateur's one-shot seems scarcely conceivable. Different as they are from each other, *Story of O* and *The Image* both evince a quality that can't be ascribed simply to an abundance of the usual writerly endowments of sensibility, energy, and intelligence. Such gifts, very much in evidence, have themselves been processed through a dialogue of artifices. The somber self-consciousness of the narratives could hardly be further from the lack of control and craft usually considered the expression of obsessive lust. Intoxicating as is their subject (if the reader doesn't cut off and find it just funny or sinister), both narratives are more concerned with the "use" of erotic material than with the "expression" of it. And this use is preeminently—there is no other word for it—literary. The imagination pursuing its outrageous pleasures in *Story of O* and *The Image* remains firmly anchored to certain notions of the *formal* consummation of intense feeling, of procedures for exhausting an experience, that connect as much with literature and recent literary history as with the ahistorical domain of eros. And why not? Experiences aren't pornographic; only images and representations—structures of the imagination— are. That is why a pornographic book often can make the reader think of, mainly, other pornographic books, rather than sex unmediated—and this not necessarily to the detriment of his erotic excitement.

For instance, what resonates throughout *Story of O* is a voluminous body of pornographic or "libertine" literature, mostly trash, in both French and English, going back to the eighteenth century. The most obvious reference is to Sade. But here one must not think only of the writings of Sade himself, but of the reinterpretation of Sade by French literary intellectuals after World War II, a critical gesture perhaps comparable in its importance and influence upon educated literary taste and upon the actual direction of serious fiction in France to the reappraisal of James launched just before World War II in the United States, except that the French reappraisal has lasted longer and seems to have struck deeper roots. (Sade, of course, had never been forgotten. He was read enthusiastically by Flaubert, Baudelaire, and most of the other radical geniuses of French literature of the late nineteenth century. He was one of the patron saints of the Surrealist movement, and figures importantly in the thought of Breton. But it was the discussion of Sade after 1945 that really consolidated his position as an inexhaustible point of departure for radical thinking about the human condition. The well-known essay of Beauvoir, the indefatigable scholarly biography undertaken by Gilbert Lely, and writings as yet un-translated of Blanchot, Paulhan, Bataille, Klossowski, and Leiris are the most eminent documents of the postwar reevaluation which secured this astonishingly hardy modification of French literary sensibility. The quality and theoretical density of the French interest in Sade remains virtually incomprehensible to English and American literary intellectuals, for whom Sade is perhaps an exemplary figure in the history of psychopathology, both individual and social, but inconceivable as someone to be taken seriously as a "thinker.")

But what stands behind *Story of O* is not only Sade, both the problems he raised and the ones raised in his name. The book is also rooted in the conventions of the "libertine" potboilers written in nineteenth-century France, typically situated in a fantasy England populated by brutal aristocrats with enormous sexual equipment and violent tastes, along the axis of sadomas-ochism, to match. The name of O's second lover-proprietor, Sir Stephen, clearly pays homage to this period fantasy, as does the figure of Sir Edmond of *Histoire de l'Oeil*. And it should be stressed that the allusion to a stock type of pornographic trash stands, as a literary reference, on exactly the same footing as the anachronistic setting of the main action, which is lifted straight from Sade's sexual theatre. The narrative opens in Paris (O joins her lover René in a car and is driven around) but most of the subsequent action is removed to more familiar if less plausible territory: that conveniently isolated château, luxuriously fur-nished and lavishly staffed with servants, where a clique of rich men congregate and to which women are brought as virtual slaves to be the objects, shared in common, of the men's brutal and inventive lust. There are whips and chains, masks worn by the men when the women are admitted to their presence, great fires burning in the hearth, unspeakable sexual indigni-ties, floggings and more ingenious kinds of physical mutilation, several lesbian scenes when the excitement of the orgies in the great drawing room seems to flag. In short, the novel comes equipped with some of the creakiest items in the repertoire of pornography.

How seriously can we take this? A bare inventory of the plot might give the impression that *Story of O* is not so much por-nography as meta-pornography, a brilliant parody. Something

similar was urged in defense of *Candy* when it was published
here several years ago, after some years of modest existence in
Paris as a more or less official dirty book. *Candy* wasn't pornography, it was argued, but a spoof, a witty burlesque of the
conventions of cheap pornographic narrative. My own view is
that *Candy* may be funny, but it's still pornography. For pornography isn't a form that can parody itself. It is the nature of
the pornographic imagination to prefer ready-made conventions of character, setting, and action. Pornography is a theatre
of types, never of individuals. A parody of pornography, so far
as it has any real competence, always remains pornography. Indeed, parody is one common form of pornographic writing.
Sade himself often used it, inverting the moralistic fictions of
Richardson in which female virtue always triumphs over male
lewdness (either by saying no or by dying afterwards). With
Story of O, it would be more accurate to speak of a "use" rather
than of a parody of Sade.

The tone alone of *Story of O* indicates that whatever in the
book might be read as parody or antiquarianism—a manda-
rin pornography?—is only one of several elements forming the
narrative. (Although sexual situations encompassing all the ex-
pectable variations of lust are graphically described, the prose
style is rather formal, the level of language dignified and almost
chaste.) Features of the Sadean staging are used to shape the
action, but the narrative's basic line differs fundamentally from
anything Sade wrote. For one thing, Sade's work has a built-
in open-endedness or principle of insatiability. His *120 Days of
Sodom*, probably the most ambitious pornographic book ever
conceived (in terms of scale), a kind of summa of the pornographic imagination; stunningly impressive and upsetting, even
in the truncated form, part narrative and part scenario, in which
it has survived. (The manuscript was accidentally rescued from
the Bastille after Sade had been forced to leave it behind when
he was transferred in 1789 to Charenton, but Sade believed
until his death that his masterpiece had been destroyed when
the prison was razed.) Sade's express train of outrages tears
along an interminable but level track. His descriptions are too
schematic to be sensuous. The fictional actions are illustrations,
rather, of his relentlessly repeated ideas. Yet these polemical
ideas themselves seem, on reflection, more like principles of
a dramaturgy than a substantive theory. Sade's ideas—of the

person as a "thing" or an "object," of the body as a machine and of the orgy as an inventory of the hopefully indefinite possibilities of several machines in collaboration with each other—seem mainly designed to make possible an endless, nonculminating kind of ultimately affectless activity. In contrast, *Story of O* has a definite movement; a logic of events, as opposed to Sade's static principle of the catalogue or encyclopedia. This plot movement is strongly abetted by the fact that, for most of the narrative, the author tolerates at least a vestige of "the couple" (O and René, O and Sir Stephen)—a unit generally repudiated in pornographic literature.

And, of course, the figure of O herself is different. Her feelings, however insistently they adhere to one theme, have some modulation and are carefully described. Although passive, O scarcely resembles those ninnies in Sade's tales who are detained in remote castles to be tormented by pitiless noblemen and satanic priests. And O is represented as active, too: literally active, as in the seduction of Jacqueline, and more important, profoundly active in her own passivity. O resembles her Sadean prototypes only superficially. There is no personal consciousness, except that of the author, in Sade's books. But O does possess a consciousness, from which vantage point her story is told. (Although written in the third person, the narrative never departs from O's point of view or understands more than she understands.) Sade aims to neutralize sexuality of all its personal associations, to represent a kind of impersonal—or pure—sexual encounter. But the narrative of "Pauline Réage" does show O reacting in quite different ways (including love) to different people, notably to René, to Sir Stephen, to Jacqueline, and to Anne-Marie.

Sade seems more representative of the major conventions of pornographic writing. So far as the pornographic imagination tends to make one person interchangeable with another and all people interchangeable with things, it's not functional to describe a person as O is described—in terms of a certain state of her will (which she's trying to discard) and of her understanding. Pornography is mainly populated by creatures like Sade's Justine, endowed with neither will nor intelligence nor even, apparently, memory. Justine lives in a perpetual state of astonishment, never learning anything from strikingly repetitious violations of her innocence. After each fresh betrayal she gets in place for another round, as uninstructed by her experience as ever, ready to trust the next masterful libertine and have her trust rewarded by a renewed loss of liberty, the same indignities, and the same blasphemous sermons in praise of vice.

For the most part, the figures who play the role of sexual objects in pornography are made of the same stuff as one principal "humour" of comedy. Justine is like Candide, who is also a cipher, a blank, an eternal naïf incapable of learning anything from his atrocious ordeals. The familiar structure of comedy which features a character who is a still center in the midst of outrage (Buster Keaton is a classic image) crops up repeatedly in pornography. The personages in pornography, like those of comedy, are seen only from the outside, behavioristically. By definition, they can't be seen in depth, so as truly to engage the audience's feelings. In much of comedy, the joke resides precisely in the *disparity* between the understated or anesthetized feeling and a large outrageous event. Pornography works in a similar fashion. The gain produced by a deadpan tone, by what seems to the reader in an ordinary state of mind to be the incredible *under*reacting of the erotic agents to the situations in which they're placed, is not the release of laughter. It's the release of a sexual reaction, originally voyeuristic but probably needing to be secured by an underlying direct identification with one of the participants in the sexual act. The emotional flatness of pornography is thus neither a failure of artistry nor an index of principled inhumanity. The arousal of a sexual response in the reader *requires* it. Only in the absence of directly stated emotions can the reader of pornography find room for his own responses. When the event narrated comes already festooned with the author's explicitly avowed sentiments, by which the reader may be stirred, it then becomes harder to be stirred by the event itself.*

---

*This is very clear in the case of Genet's books, which, despite the explicitness of the sexual experiences related, are not sexually arousing for most readers. What the reader knows (and Genet has stated it many times) is that Genet himself was sexually excited while writing *The Miracle of the Rose*, *Our Lady of the Flowers*, etc. The reader makes an intense and unsettling contact with Genet's erotic excitement, which is the energy that propels these metaphor-studded narratives; but, at the same time, the author's excitement precludes the reader's own. Genet was perfectly correct when he said that his books were not pornographic.

Silent film comedy offers many illustrations of how the formal principle of continual agitation or perpetual motion (slapstick) and that of the deadpan really converge to the same end—a deadening or neutralization or distancing of the audience's emotions, its ability to identify in a "humane" way and to make moral judgments about situations of violence. The same principle is at work in all pornography. It's not that the characters in pornography cannot conceivably possess any emotions. They can. But the principles of underreacting and frenetic agitation make the emotional climate self-canceling, so that the basic tone of pornography is affectless, emotionless.

However, degrees of this affectlessness can be distinguished. Justine is the stereotype sex-object figure (invariably female, since most pornography is written by men or from the stereotyped male point of view): a bewildered victim, whose consciousness remains unaltered by her experiences. But O is an adept; whatever the cost in pain and fear, she is grateful for the opportunity to be initiated into a mystery. That mystery is the loss of the self. O learns, she suffers, she changes. Step by step she becomes more what she is, a process identical with the emptying out of herself. In the vision of the world presented by *Story of O*, the highest good is the transcendence of personality. The plot's movement is not horizontal, but a kind of ascent through degradation. O does not simply become identical with her sexual availability, but wants to reach the perfection of becoming an object. Her condition, if it can be characterized as one of dehumanization, is not to be understood as a by-product of her enslavement to René, Sir Stephen, and the other men at Roissy, but as the point of her situation, something she seeks and eventually attains. The terminal image for her achievement comes in the last scene of the book: O is led to a party, mutilated, in chains, unrecognizable, costumed (as an owl)—so convincingly no longer human that none of the guests thinks of speaking to her directly.

O's quest is neatly summed up in the expressive letter which serves her for a name. "O" suggests a cartoon of her sex, not her individual sex but simply woman; it also stands for a nothing. But what *Story of O* unfolds is a spiritual paradox, that of the full void and of the vacuity that is also a plenum. The power of the book lies exactly in the anguish stirred up by the continuing presence of this paradox. "Pauline Réage" raises, in a far more organic and sophisticated manner than Sade does with his clumsy expositions and discourses, the question of the status of human personality itself. But whereas Sade is interested in the obliteration of personality from the viewpoint of power and liberty, the author of *Story of O* is interested in the obliteration of personality from the viewpoint of happiness. (The closest statement of this theme in English literature: certain passages in Lawrence's *The Lost Girl.*)

For the paradox to gain real significance, however, the reader must entertain a view of sex different from that held by most enlightened members of the community. The prevailing view—an amalgam of Rousseauist, Freudian, and liberal social thought—regards the phenomenon of sex as a perfectly intelligible, although uniquely precious, source of emotional and physical pleasure. What difficulties arise come from the long deformation of the sexual impulses administered by Western Christianity, whose ugly wounds virtually everyone in this culture bears. First, guilt and anxiety. Then, the reduction of sexual capacities—leading if not to virtual impotence or frigidity, at least to the depletion of erotic energy and the repression of many natural elements of sexual appetite (the "perversions"). Then the spill-over into public dishonesties in which people tend to respond to news of the sexual pleasures of others with envy, fascination, revulsion, and spiteful indignation. It's from this pollution of the sexual health of the culture that a phenomenon like pornography is derived.

I don't quarrel with the historical diagnosis contained in this account of the deformations of Western sexuality. Nevertheless, what seems to me decisive in the complex of views held by most educated members of the community is a more questionable assumption—that human sexual appetite is, if untampered with, a natural pleasant function; and that "the obscene" is a convention, the fiction imposed upon nature by a society convinced there is something vile about the sexual functions and, by extension, about sexual pleasure. It's just these assumptions that are challenged by the French tradition represented by Sade, Lautréamont, Bataille, and the authors of *Story of O* and *The Image*. Their work suggests that "the obscene" is a primal notion of human consciousness, something much more profound than the backwash of a sick society's aversion to the body. Human sexuality is, quite apart from Christian repressions, a highly questionable phenomenon, and belongs, at least potentially, among the extreme rather than the ordinary experiences of humanity. Tamed as it may be, sexuality remains one of the demonic forces in human consciousness—pushing us at intervals close to taboo and dangerous desires, which range from the impulse to commit sudden arbitrary violence upon another person to the voluptuous yearning for the extinction of one's consciousness, for death itself. Even on the level of simple physical sensation and mood, making love surely resembles having an epileptic fit at least as much, if not more, than it does eating a meal or conversing with someone. Everyone has felt (at least in fantasy) the erotic glamour of physical cruelty and an erotic lure in things that are vile and repulsive. These phenomena form part of the genuine spectrum of sexuality, and if they are not to be written off as mere neurotic aberrations, the picture looks different from the one promoted by enlightened public opinion, and less simple.

One could plausibly argue that it is for quite sound reasons that the whole capacity for sexual ecstasy is inaccessible to most people—given that sexuality is something, like nuclear energy, which may prove amenable to domestication through scruple, but then again may not. That few people regularly, or perhaps ever, experience their sexual capacities at this unsettling pitch doesn't mean that the extreme is not authentic, or that the possibility of it doesn't haunt them anyway. (Religion is probably, after sex, the second oldest resource which human beings have available to them for blowing their minds. Yet among the multitudes of the pious, the number who have ventured very far into that state of consciousness must be fairly small, too.) There is, demonstrably, something incorrectly designed and potentially disorienting in the human sexual capacity—at least in the capacities of man-in-civilization. Man, the sick animal, bears within him an appetite which can drive him mad. Such is the understanding of sexuality—as something beyond good and evil, beyond love, beyond sanity; as a resource for ordeal and for breaking through the limits of consciousness—that informs the French literary canon I've been discussing.

The *Story of O*, with its project for completely transcending personality, entirely presumes this dark and complex vision of sexuality so far removed from the hopeful view sponsored by American Freudianism and liberal culture. The woman who is given no other name than O progresses simultaneously toward her own extinction as a human being and her fulfillment as a sexual being. It's hard to imagine how anyone would ascertain whether there exists truly, empirically, anything in "nature" or human consciousness that supports such a split. But it seems understandable that the possibility has always haunted man, as accustomed as he is to decrying such a split.

O's project enacts, on another scale, that performed by the existence of pornographic literature itself. What pornographic literature does is precisely to drive a wedge between one's existence as a full human being and one's existence as a sexual being—while in ordinary life a healthy person is one who prevents such a gap from opening up. Normally we don't experience, at least don't want to experience, our sexual fulfillment as distinct from or opposed to our personal fulfillment. But perhaps in part they are distinct, whether we like it or not. Insofar as strong sexual feeling does involve an obsessive degree of attention, it encompasses experiences in which a person can feel he is losing his "self." The literature that goes from Sade through Surrealism to these recent books capitalizes on that mystery; it isolates the mystery and makes the reader aware of it, invites him to participate in it.

This literature is both an invocation of the erotic in its darkest sense and, in certain cases, an exorcism. The devout, solemn mood of *Story of O* is fairly unrelieved; a work of mixed moods on the same theme, a journey toward the estrangement of the self from the self, is Buñuel's film *L'Age d'Or*. As a literary form, pornography works with two patterns—one equivalent to tragedy (as in *Story of O*) in which the erotic subject-victim heads inexorably toward death, and the other equivalent to comedy (as in *The Image*) in which the obsessional pursuit of sexual exercise is rewarded by a terminal gratification, union with the uniquely desired sexual partner.

4

The writer who renders a darker sense of the erotic, its perils of fascination and humiliation, than anyone else is Bataille. His *Histoire de l'Oeil* (first published in 1928) and *Madame Edwarda** qualify as pornographic texts insofar as their theme is an all-engrossing sexual quest that annihilates every consideration of persons extraneous to their roles in the sexual dramaturgy, and the fulfillment of this quest is depicted graphically. But this description conveys nothing of the extraordinary quality of these books. For sheer explicitness about sexual organs and acts is not necessarily obscene; it only becomes so when delivered in a particular tone, when it has acquired a certain moral resonance. As it happens, the sparse number of sexual acts and quasi-sexual defilements related in Bataille's novellas can hardly compete with the interminable mechanistic inventiveness of the *120 Days of Sodom*. Yet because Bataille possessed a finer and more profound sense of transgression, what he describes seems somehow more potent and outrageous than the most lurid orgies staged by Sade.

One reason that *Histoire de l'Oeil* and *Madame Edwarda* make such a strong and upsetting impression is that Bataille understood more clearly than any other writer I know of that what pornography is really about, ultimately, isn't sex but death. I am not suggesting that every pornographic work speaks, either overtly or covertly, of death. Only works dealing with that specific and sharpest inflection of the themes of lust, "the obscene," do. It's toward the gratifications of death, succeeding and surpassing those of eros, that every truly obscene quest tends. (An example of a pornographic work whose subject is not the "obscene" is Louÿ's jolly saga of sexual insatiability, *Trois Filles de leur Mèère*. *The Image* presents a less clear-cut case. While the enigmatic transactions between the three characters are charged with a sense of the obscene—more like a premonition,

---

*Unfortunately, the only translation available in English of what purports to be *Madame Edwarda*, that included in *The Olympia Reader*, pp. 662–672, published by Grove Press in 1965, just gives half the work. Only the *récit* is translated. But *Madame Edwarda* isn't a *récit* padded out with a preface also by Bataille. It is a two-part invention—essay and *récit*—and one part is almost unintelligible without the other.

since the obscene is reduced to being only a constituent of voyeurism—the book has an unequivocally happy ending, with the narrator finally united with Claire. But *Story of O* takes the same line as Bataille, despite a little intellectual play at the end: the book closes ambiguously, with several lines to the effect that two versions of a final suppressed chapter exist, in one of which O received Sir Stephen's permission to die when he was about to discard her. Although this double ending satisfyingly echoes the book's opening, in which two versions "of the same beginning" are given, it can't, I think, lessen the reader's sense that O is death-bound, whatever doubts the author expresses about her fate.)

Bataille composed most of his books, the chamber music of pornographic literature, in *récit* form (sometimes accompanied by an essay). Their unifying theme is Bataille's own consciousness, a consciousness in an acute, unrelenting state of agony; but as an equally extraordinary mind in an earlier age might have written a theology of agony, Bataille has written an erotics of agony. Willing to tell something of the autobiographical sources of his narratives, he appended to *Histoire de l'Oeil* some vivid imagery from his own outrageously terrible childhood. (One memory: his blind, syphilitic, insane father trying unsuccessfully to urinate.) Time has neutralized these memories, he explains; after many years, they have largely lost their power over him and "can only come to life again, deformed, hardly recognizable, having in the course of this deformation taken on an obscene meaning." Obscenity, for Bataille, simultaneously revives his most painful experiences and scores a victory over that pain. The obscene, that is to say, the extremity of erotic experience, is the root of vital energies. Human beings, he says in the essay part of *Madame Edwarda*, live only through excess. And pleasure depends on "perspective," or giving oneself to a state of "open being," open to death as well as to joy. Most people try to outwit their own feelings; they want to be receptive to pleasure but keep "horror" at a distance. That's foolish, according to Bataille, since horror reinforces "attraction" and excites desire.

What Bataille exposes in extreme erotic experience is its subterranean connection with death. Bataille conveys this insight not by devising sexual acts whose consequences are lethal, thereby littering his narratives with corpses. (In the terrifying *Histoire de l'Oeil*, for instance, only one person dies; and the book ends with the three sexual adventurers, having debauched their way through France and Spain, acquiring a yacht in Gibraltar to pursue their infamies elsewhere.) His more effective method is to invest each action with a weight, a disturbing gravity, that feels authentically "mortal."

Yet despite the obvious differences of scale and finesse of execution, the conceptions of Sade and Bataille have some resemblances. Like Bataille, Sade was not so much a sensualist as someone with an intellectual project: to explore the scope of transgression. And he shares with Bataille the same ultimate identification of sex and death. But Sade could never have agreed with Bataille that "the truth of eroticism is tragic." People often die in Sade's books. But these deaths always seem unreal. They're no more convincing than those mutilations inflicted during the evening's orgies from which the victims recover completely the next morning following the use of a wondrous salve. From the perspective of Bataille, a reader can't help being caught up short by Sade's bad faith about death. (Of course, many pornographic books that are much less interesting and accomplished than those of Sade share this bad faith.)

Indeed, one might speculate that the fatiguing repetitiveness of Sade's books is the consequence of his imaginative failure to confront the inevitable goal or haven of a truly systematic venture of the pornographic imagination. Death is the only end to the odyssey of the pornographic imagination when it becomes systematic; that is, when it becomes focused on the pleasures of transgression rather than mere pleasure itself. Since he could not or would not arrive at his ending, Sade stalled. He multiplied and thickened his narrative; tediously reduplicated orgiastic permutations and combinations. And his fictional alter egos regularly interrupted a bout of rape or buggery to deliver to their victims his latest reworkings of lengthy sermons on what real "Enlightenment" means—the nasty truth about God, society, nature, individuality, virtue. Bataille manages to eschew anything resembling the counter-idealisms which are Sade's blasphemies (and which thereby perpetuate the banished idealism lying behind those fantasies); his blasphemies are autonomous.

Sade's books, the Wagnerian music dramas of pornographic literature, are neither subtle nor compact. Bataille achieves his effects with far more economical means: a chamber ensemble of non-interchangeable personages, instead of Sade's operatic multiplication of sexual virtuosi and career victims. Bataille renders his radical negatives through extreme compression. The gain, apparent on every page, enables his lean work and gnomic thought to go further than Sade's. Even in pornography, less can be more.

Bataille also has offered distinctly original and effective solutions to one perennial problem of pornographic narration: the ending. The most common procedure has been to end in a way that lays no claim to any internal necessity. Hence, Adorno could judge it the mark of pornography that it has neither beginning nor middle nor end. But Adorno is being unperceptive. Pornographic narratives do end—admittedly with abruptness and, by conventional novel standards, without motivation. This is not necessarily objectionable. (The discovery, midway in a science-fiction novel, of an alien planet may be no less abrupt or unmotivated.) Abruptness, an endemic facticity of encounters and chronically renewing encounters, is not some unfortunate defect of the pornographic narration which one might wish removed in order for the books to qualify as literature. These features are constitutive of the very imagination or vision of the world which goes into pornography. They supply, in many cases, exactly the ending that's needed.

But this doesn't preclude other types of endings. One notable feature of *Histoire de l'Oeil* and, to a lesser extent, *The Image*, considered as works of art, is their evident interest in more systematic or rigorous kinds of ending which still remain within the terms of the pornographic imagination—not seduced by the solutions of a more realistic or less abstract fiction. Their solution, considered very generally, is to construct a narrative that is, from the beginning, more rigorously controlled, less spontaneous and lavishly descriptive.

In *The Image* the narrative is dominated by a single metaphor, "the image" (though the reader can't understand the full meaning of the title until the end of the novel). At first, the metaphor appears to have a clear single application. "Image" seems to mean "flat" object or "two-dimensional surface" or "passive reflection"—all referring to the girl Anne whom Claire instructs the narrator to use freely for his own sexual purposes, making the girl into "a perfect slave." But the book is broken exactly in the middle ("Section V" in a short book of ten sections) by an enigmatic scene that introduces another sense of "image." Claire, alone with the narrator, shows him a set of strange photographs of Anne in obscene situations; and these are described in such a way as to insinuate a mystery in what has been a brutally straightforward, if seemingly unmotivated, situation. From this cæsura to the end of the book, the reader will have simultaneously to carry the awareness of the fictionally actual "obscene" situation being described and to keep attuned to hints of an oblique mirroring or duplication of that situation. That burden (the two perspectives) will be relieved only in the final pages of the book, when, as the title of the last section has it, "Everything Resolves Itself." The narrator discovers that Anne is not the erotic plaything of Claire donated gratuitously to him, but Claire's "image" or "projection," sent out ahead to teach the narrator how to love *her*.

The structure of *Histoire de l'Oeil* is equally rigorous, and more ambitious in scope. Both novels are in the first person; in both, the narrator is male, and one of a trio whose sexual interconnections constitute the story of the book. But the two narratives are organized on very different principles. "Jean de Berg" describes how something came to be known that was not known by the narrator; all the pieces of action are clues, bits of evidence; and the ending is a surprise. Bataille is describing an action that is really intrapsychic: three people sharing (without conflict) a single fantasy, the acting out of a collective perverse will. The emphasis in *The Image* is on behavior, which is opaque, unintelligible. The emphasis in *Histoire de l'Oeil* is on fantasy first, and then on its correlation with some spontaneously "invented" act. The development of the narrative follows the phases of acting out. Bataille is charting the stages of the gratification of an erotic obsession which haunts a number of commonplace objects. His principle of organization is thus a spatial one: a series of things, arranged in a definite sequence, are tracked down and exploited, in some convulsive erotic act. The obscene playing with or defiling of these objects, and of people in their vicinity, constitutes the action of the novella.

When the last object (the eye) is used up in a transgression more daring than any preceding, the narrative ends. There can be no revelation or surprises in the story, no new "knowledge," only further intensifications of what is already known. These seemingly unrelated elements really are related; indeed, all versions of the same thing. The egg in the first chapter is simply the earliest version of the eyeball plucked from the Spaniard in the last.

Each specific erotic fantasy is also a generic fantasy—of performing what is "forbidden"—which generates a surplus atmosphere of excruciating restless sexual intensity. At times the reader seems to be witness to a heartless debauched fulfillment; at other times, simply in attendance at the remorseless progress of the negative. Bataille's works, better than any others I know of, indicate the aesthetic possibilities of pornography as an art form: *Histoire de l'Oeil* being the most accomplished artistically of all the pornographic prose fictions I've read, and *Madame Edwarda* the most original and powerful intellectually.

To speak of the aesthetic possibilities of pornography as an art form and as a form of thinking may seem insensitive or grandiose when one considers what acutely miserable lives people with a full-time specialized sexual obsession usually lead. Still, I would argue that pornography yields more than the truths of individual nightmare. Convulsive and repetitious as this form of the imagination may be, it does generate a vision of the world that can claim the interest (speculative, aesthetic) of those who are not erotomanes. Indeed, this interest resides in precisely what are customarily dismissed as the *limits* of pornographic thinking.

5

The prominent characteristics of all products of the pornographic imagination are their energy and their absolutism.

The books generally called pornographic are those whose primary, exclusive, and overriding preoccupation is with the depiction of sexual "intentions" and "activities." One could also say sexual "feelings," except that the word seems redundant. The feelings of the personages deployed by the pornographic imagination are, at any given moment, either identical with their "behavior" or else a preparatory phase, that of "intention," on the verge of breaking into "behavior" unless physically thwarted. Pornography uses a small crude vocabulary of feeling, all relating to the prospects of action: feeling one would like to act (lust); feeling one would not like to act (shame, fear, aversion). There are no gratuitous or non-functioning feelings; no musings, whether speculative or imagistic, which are irrelevant to the business at hand. Thus, the pornographic imagination inhabits a universe that is, however repetitive the incidents occurring within it, incomparably economical. The strictest possible criterion of relevance applies: everything must bear upon the erotic situation.

The universe proposed by the pornographic imagination is a total universe. It has the power to ingest and metamorphose and translate all concerns that are fed into it, reducing everything into the one negotiable currency of the erotic imperative. All action is conceived of as a set of sexual *exchanges*. Thus, the reason why pornography refuses to make fixed distinctions between the sexes or allow any kind of sexual preference or sexual taboo to endure can be explained "structurally." The bisexuality, the disregard for the incest taboo, and other similar features common to pornographic narratives function to multiply the possibilities of exchange. Ideally, it should be possible for everyone to have a sexual connection with everyone else.

Of course the pornographic imagination is hardly the only form of consciousness that proposes a total universe. Another is the type of imagination that has generated modern symbolic logic. In the total universe proposed by the logician's imagination, all statements can be broken down or chewed up to make it possible to rerender them in the form of the logical language; those parts of ordinary language that don't fit are simply lopped off. Certain of the well-known states of the religious imagination, to take another example, operate in the same cannibalistic way, engorging all materials made available to them for retranslation into phenomena saturated with the religious polarities (sacred and profane, etc.).

The latter example, for obvious reasons, touches closely on the present subject. Religious metaphors abound in a good deal of modern erotic literature—notably in Genet—and in some works of pornographic literature, too. *Story of O* makes heavy use of religious metaphors for the ordeal that O undergoes. O "wanted to believe." Her drastic condition of total personal servitude to those who use her sexually is repeatedly described as a mode of salvation. With anguish and anxiety, she surrenders herself; and "henceforth there were no more hiatuses, no dead time, no remission." While she has, to be sure, entirely lost her freedom, O has gained the right to participate in what is described as virtually a sacramental rite.

> The word "open" and the expression "opening her legs" were, on her lover's lips, charged with such uneasiness and power that she could never hear them without experiencing a kind of internal prostration, a sacred submission, as though a god, and not he, had spoken to her.

Though she fears the whip and other cruel mistreatments before they are inflicted on her, "yet when it was over she was happy to have gone through it, happier still if it had been especially cruel and prolonged." The whipping, branding, and mutilating are described (from the point of view of *her* consciousness) as ritual ordeals which test the faith of someone being initiated into an ascetic spiritual discipline. The "perfect submissiveness" that her original lover and then Sir Stephen demand of her echoes the extinction of the self explicitly required of a Jesuit novice or Zen pupil. O is "that absent-minded person who has yielded up her will in order to be totally remade," to be made fit to serve a will far more powerful and authoritative than her own.

As might be expected, the straightforwardness of the religious metaphors in *Story of O* has evoked some correspondingly straight readings of the book. The novelist Mandiargues, whose preface precedes Paulhan's in the American translation, doesn't hesitate to describe *Story of O* as "a mystic work," and therefore "not, strictly speaking, an erotic book." What *Story of O* depicts "is a complete spiritual transformation, what others would call an *ascesis*." But the matter is not so simple. Mandiargues is correct in dismissing a psychiatric analysis of O's state of mind that would reduce the book's subject to, say, "masochism." As Paulhan says, "the heroine's ardor" is totally inexplicable in terms of the conventional psychiatric vocabulary. The fact that the novel employs some of the conventional motifs and trappings of the theatre of sadomasochism has itself to be explained. But Mandiargues has fallen into an error almost as reductive and only slightly less vulgar. Surely, the only alternative to the psychiatric reductions is not the religious vocabulary. But that only these two foreshortened alternatives exist testifies once again to the bone-deep denigration of the range and seriousness of sexual experience that still rules this culture, for all its much-advertised new permissiveness.

My own view is that "Pauline Réage" wrote an erotic book. The notion implicit in *Story of O* that eros is a sacrament is not the "truth" behind the literal (erotic) sense of the book—the lascivious rites of enslavement and degradation performed upon O—but, exactly, a metaphor for it. Why say something stronger, when the statement can't really *mean* anything stronger? But despite the virtual incomprehensibility to most educated people today of the substantive experience behind religious vocabulary, there is a continuing piety toward the grandeur of emotions that went into that vocabulary. The religious imagination survives for most people as not just the primary but virtually the only credible instance of an imagination working in a total way.

No wonder, then, that the new or radically revamped forms of the total imagination which have arisen in the past century—notably, those of the artist, the erotomane, the left revolutionary, and the madman—have chronically borrowed the prestige of the religious vocabulary. And total experiences, of which there are many kinds, tend again and again to be apprehended only as revivals or translations of the religious imagination. To try to make a fresh way of talking at the most serious, ardent, and enthusiastic level, heading off the religious encapsulation, is one of the primary intellectual tasks of future thought. As matters stand, with everything from *Story of O* to Mao reabsorbed into the incorrigible survival of the religious impulse, all thinking and feeling gets devalued. (Hegel made perhaps the grandest attempt to create a post-religious vocabulary, out of philosophy, that would command the treasures of passion and credibility and emotive appropriateness that were gathered into the religious vocabulary. But his most interesting followers steadily undermined the abstract meta-religious language in which he had bequeathed his thought, and concentrated instead on the specific social and practical applications of his revolutionary form of process-thinking, historicism. Hegel's failure lies like a gigantic disturbing hulk across the intellectual landscape. And no one has been big enough, pompous enough, or energetic enough since Hegel to attempt the task again.)

And so we remain, careening among our overvaried choices of kinds of total imagination, of species of total seriousness. Perhaps the deepest spiritual resonance of the career of pornography in its "modern" Western phase under consideration here (pornography in the Orient or the Moslem world being something very different) is this vast frustration of human passion and seriousness since the old religious imagination, with its secure monopoly on the total imagination, began in the late eighteenth century to crumble. The ludicrousness and lack of skill of most pornographic writing, films, and painting is obvious to everyone who has been exposed to them. What is less often remarked about the typical products of the pornographic imagination is their pathos. Most pornography—the books discussed here cannot be excepted—points to something more general than even sexual damage. I mean the traumatic failure of modern capitalist society to provide authentic outlets for the perennial human flair for high-temperature visionary obsessions, to satisfy the appetite for exalted self-transcending modes of concentration and seriousness. The need of human beings to transcend "the personal" is no less profound than the need to be a person, an individual. But this society serves that need poorly. It provides mainly demonic vocabularies in which to situate that need and from which to initiate action and construct rites of behavior. One is offered a choice among vocabularies of thought and action which are not merely self-transcending but self-destructive.

6

But the pornographic imagination is not just to be understood as a form of psychic absolutism—some of whose products we might be able to regard (in the role of connoisseur, rather than client) with more sympathy or intellectual curiosity or aesthetic sophistication.

Several times before in this essay I have alluded to the possibility that the pornographic imagination says something worth listening to, albeit in a degraded and often unrecognizable form. I've urged that this spectacularly cramped form of the human imagination has, nevertheless, its peculiar access to some truth. This truth—about sensibility, about sex, about individual personality, about despair, about limits—can be shared when it projects itself into art. (Everyone, at least in dreams, has inhabited the world of the pornographic imagination for some hours or days or even longer periods of his life; but only the full-time residents make the fetishes, the trophies, the art.) That discourse one might call the poetry of transgression is also knowledge. He who transgresses not only breaks a rule. He goes somewhere that the others are not; and he knows something the others don't know.

Pornography, considered as an artistic or art-producing form of the human imagination, is an expression of what William James called "morbid-mindedness." But James was surely right when he gave as part of the definition of morbid-mindedness that it ranged over "a wider scale of experience" than healthy-mindedness.

What can be said, though, to the many sensible and sensitive people who find depressing the fact that a whole library of pornographic reading material has been made, within the last few years, so easily available in paperback form to the very young? Probably one thing: that their apprehension is justified, but may not be in scale. I am not addressing the usual complainers, those who feel that since sex after all *is* dirty, so are books reveling in sex (dirty in a way that a genocide screened nightly on TV, apparently, is not). There still remains a sizeable minority of people who object to or are repelled by pornography not because they think it's dirty but because they know that pornography can be a crutch for the psychologically deformed and a brutalization of the morally innocent. I feel an aversion to pornography for those reasons, too, and am uncomfortable about the consequences of its increasing availability. But isn't the worry somewhat misplaced? What's really at stake? A concern about the uses of knowledge itself. There's a sense in which *all* knowledge is dangerous, the reason being that not everyone is in the same condition as knowers or potential knowers. Perhaps most people don't need "a wider scale of experience." It may be that, without subtle and extensive psychic preparation, any widening of experience and consciousness is destructive for most people. Then we must ask what justifies the reckless unlimited confidence we have in the present mass availability of other kinds of knowledge, in our optimistic acquiescence in the transformation of and extension of human capacities by machines. Pornography is only one item among the many dangerous commodities being circulated in this society and, unattractive as it may be, one of the less lethal, the less costly to the community in terms of human suffering. Except perhaps in a small circle of writer-intellectuals in France, pornography is an inglorious and mostly despised department of the imagination. Its mean status is the very antithesis of the considerable spiritual prestige enjoyed by many items which are far more noxious.

In the last analysis, the place we assign to pornography depends on the goals we set for our own consciousness, our own experience. But the goal A espouses for his consciousness may *not* be one he's pleased to see B adopt, because he judges that B isn't qualified or experienced or subtle enough. And B may be dismayed and even indignant at A's adopting goals that he himself professes; when A holds them, they become presumptuous or shallow. Probably this chronic mutual suspicion of our neighbor's capacities—suggesting, in effect, a hierarchy of competence with respect to human consciousness—will never be settled to everyone's satisfaction. As long as the quality of people's consciousness varies so greatly, how could it be?

In an essay on the subject some years ago, Paul Goodman wrote: "The question is not *whether* pornography, but the quality of the pornography." That's exactly right. One could extend the thought a good deal further. The question is not *whether* consciousness or *whether* knowledge, but the quality of the consciousness and of the knowledge. And that invites consideration of the quality or fineness of the human subject—the most problematic standard of all. It doesn't seem inaccurate to say most people in this society who aren't actively mad are, at best, reformed or potential lunatics. But is anyone supposed to act on this knowledge, even genuinely live with it? If so many are teetering on the verge of murder, dehumanization, sexual deformity and despair, and we were to act on that thought, then censorship much more radical than the indignant foes of pornography ever envisage seems in order. For if that's the case, not only pornography but all forms of serious art and knowledge—in other words, all forms of truth—are suspect and dangerous.

(1967)

"Thinking Against Oneself": Reflections on Cioran

What is the good of passing from one untenable position to another, of seeking justification always on the same plane?

SAMUEL BECKETT

Every now and then it is possible   to have absolutely nothing; the possibility of nothing.

JOHN CAGE

OURS is a time in which every intellectual or artistic or moral event is absorbed by a predatory embrace of consciousness: historicizing. Any statement or act can be assessed as a necessarily transient "development" or, on a lower level, belittled as mere "fashion." The human mind possesses now, almost as second nature, a perspective on its own achievements that fatally undermines their value and their claim to truth. For over a century, this historicizing perspective has occupied the very heart of our ability to *understand* anything at all. Perhaps once a marginal tic of consciousness, it's now a gigantic, uncontrollable gesture—the gesture whereby man indefatigably patronizes himself.

We understand something by locating it in a multi-determined temporal continuum. Existence is no more than the precarious attainment of relevance in an intensely mobile flux of past, present, and future. But even the most relevant events carry within them the form of their obsolescence. Thus, a single work is eventually a contribution to a body of work; the details of a life form part of a life history; an individual life history appears unintelligible apart from social, economic, and cultural history; and the life of a society is the sum of "preceding conditions." Meaning drowns in a stream of becoming: the senseless and overdocumented rhythm of advent and supersession. The becoming of man is the history of the exhaustion of his possibilities.

Yet there is no outflanking the demon of historical consciousness by turning the corrosive historicizing eye on *it*. Unfortunately, that succession of exhausted possibilities (unmasked and discredited by thought and history itself) in which man now situates himself appears to be more than simply a mental "attitude"—which could be annulled by refocusing the mind.

The best of the intellectual and creative speculation carried on in the West over the past hundred and fifty years seems incontestably the most energetic, dense, subtle, sheerly interesting, and *true* in the entire lifetime of man. And yet the equally incontestable result of all this genius is our sense of standing in the ruins of thought and on the verge of the ruins of history and of man himself. (Cogito ergo boom.) More and more, the shrewdest thinkers and artists are precocious archaeologists of these ruins-in-the-making, indignant or stoical diagnosticians of defeat, enigmatic choreographers of the complex spiritual movements useful for individual survival in an era of permanent apocalypse. The time of new collective visions may well be over: by now both the brightest and the gloomiest, the most foolish and the wisest, have been set down. But the need for individual spiritual counsel has never seemed more acute. *Sauve qui peut.*

The rise of historical consciousness is, of course, linked with the collapse, sometime in the early nineteenth century, of the venerable enterprise of philosophical system-building. Since the Greeks, philosophy (whether fused with religion or conceived as an alternative, secular wisdom) had been for the most part a collective or supra-personal vision. Claiming to give an account of "what is" in its various epistemological and ontological layers, philosophy secondarily insinuated an implicitly futuristic standard of how things "ought to be"—under the aegis of notions like order, harmony, clarity, intelligibility, and consistency. But the survival of these collective impersonal visions depends on philosophical statements being couched in such a way as to admit of multiple interpretations and applications, so that their bluff can't be called by unforeseen events. Renouncing the advantages of myth, which had developed a highly sophisticated *narrative* mode of accounting for change and for conceptual paradox, philosophy proliferated a new rhetorical mode: abstraction. Upon this abstract, atemporal discourse—with its claim to be able to describe the non-concrete "universals" or stable forms that underpin the mutable world—the authority of philosophy has always rested. More generally, the very possibility of the objective, formalized visions of Being and of human knowledge proposed by traditional philosophy depends on a

particular relation between permanent structures and change in
human experience, in which "nature" is the dominant theme and
change is recessive. But this relation was upset—permanently?—
around the time climaxed by the French Revolution, when "history" finally pulled up alongside "nature" and then took the
lead.

At the point that history usurped nature as the decisive
framework for human experience, man began to think historically about his experience, and the traditional ahistorical categories of philosophy became hollowed out. The only thinker to
meet this awesome challenge head-on was Hegel, who thought
he could salvage the philosophical enterprise from this radical
reorientation of human consciousness by presenting philosophy
as, in fact, no more and no less than the *history* of philosophy.
Still, Hegel could not help presenting his own system as true—
that is, as beyond history—because of its incorporation of the
historical perspective. So far as Hegel's system was true then,
it ended philosophy. Only the last philosophical system was
philosophy, truly conceived. So "the eternal" is reestablished
once more, after all; and history comes (or will come) to an
end. But history did not stop. Mere time proved Hegelianism
bankrupt as a system, though not as a method. (As a method,
proliferating into all the sciences of man, it confirmed and gave
the largest single intellectual impetus to the consolidation of
historical consciousness.)

After Hegel's effort, this quest for the eternal—once so glamorous and inevitable a gesture of consciousness—now stood
exposed, as the root of philosophical thinking, in all its pathos
and childishness. Philosophy dwindled into an outmoded fantasy of the mind, part of the provincialism of the spirit, the
childhood of man. However firmly philosophical statements
might cohere into an argument, there seemed no way of dis-
pelling the radical question that had arisen as to the "value" of
the terms composing the statements, no way of restoring a vast
loss of confidence in the verbal currency in which philosophical arguments had been transacted. Confounded by the new
surge of an increasingly secularized, drastically more competent
and efficient human will bent on controlling, manipulating,
and modifying "nature," its ventures into concrete ethical and

political prescription badly lagging behind the accelerating historical change of the human landscape (among which changes must be counted the sheer accumulation of concrete empirical knowledge stored in printed books and documents), the leading words of philosophy came to seem excessively overdetermined. Or, what amounts to the same thing, they seem undernourished, emptied of meaning.

Subjected to the attritions of change on this unprecedented scale, philosophy's traditionally "abstract" leisurely procedures no longer appeared to address themselves to anything; they weren't substantiated any more by the sense that intelligent people had of their experience. Neither as a description of Being (reality, the world, the cosmos) nor, in the alternative conception (in which Being, reality, the world, the cosmos are taken as what lies "outside" the mind) that marks the first great retrenchment of the philosophical enterprise, as a description of mind only, did philosophy inspire much trust in its capacity to fulfill its traditional aspiration: that of providing the formal models for *understanding* anything. At the least, some kind of further retrenchment or relocation of discourse was felt to be necessary.

One response to the collapse of philosophical system building in the nineteenth century was the rise of ideologies—aggressively anti-philosophical systems of thought, taking the form of various "positive" or descriptive sciences of man. Comte, Marx, Freud, and the pioneer figures of anthropology, sociology, and linguistics immediately come to mind.

Another response to the debacle was a new kind of philosophizing: personal (even autobiographical), aphoristic, lyrical, anti-systematic. Its foremost exemplars: Kierkegaard, Nietzsche, Wittgenstein. Cioran is the most distinguished figure in this tradition writing today.

The starting point for this modern post-philosophic tradition of philosophizing is the awareness that the traditional forms of philosophical discourse have been broken. The leading possibilities that remain are mutilated, incomplete discourse (the aphorism, the note or jotting) or discourse that has risked metamorphosis into other forms (the parable, the poem, the philosophical tale, the critical exegesis).

Cioran has apparently chosen the essay form. Between 1949 and 1964, five collections have appeared: *Précis de Décomposition* (1949), *Syllogismes de l'Amertume* (1952), *Le Tentation d'Exister* (1956), *Histoire et Utopie* (1960), and *La Chute dans le Temps* (1964). But these are curious essays by ordinary standards—meditative, disjunctive in argument, essentially aphoristic in style. One recognizes, in this Roumanian-born writer who studied philosophy at the University of Bucharest and who has lived in Paris since 1937 and writes in French, the convulsive manner characteristic of German neo-philosophical thinking, whose motto is: aphorism or eternity. (Examples: the philosophical aphorisms of Lichtenberg and Novalis; Nietzsche of course; passages in Rilke's *Duino Elegies*; and Kafka's *Reflections on Love, Sin, Hope, Death, the Way.*)

Cioran's method of broken argument is not the objective kind of aphoristic writing of La Rochefoucauld or Gracián, whose stopping and starting movement mirrors the disjunctive aspects of "the world," but rather bears witness to the impasse of the speculative mind, which moves outward only to be checked and broken off by the complexity of its own stance. For Cioran the aphoristic style is less a principle of reality than a principle of knowing: that it's the destiny of every profound idea to be quickly checkmated by another idea, which it itself has implicitly generated.

Still hoping to command something resembling its former prestige, philosophy now undertakes to give evidence incessantly of its own good faith. Though the existing range of conceptual tools for philosophy could no longer be felt to carry meaning in themselves, they might be recertified: through the passion of the thinker.

Philosophy is conceived as the personal task of the thinker. Thought becomes "thinking," and thinking—by a further turn of the screw—is redefined as worthless unless an extreme act, a risk. Thinking becomes confessional, exorcistic: an inventory of the most personal exacerbations of thinking.

Notice that the Cartesian leap is retained as the first move.

Existence is still defined as thinking. The difference is that it's not any kind of cogitation, but only a certain kind of *difficult* thinking. Thought and existence are neither brute facts nor logical givens, but paradoxical, unstable situations. Hence, the possibility of conceiving the essay that gives the title to one of Cioran's books and to the first collection of his work in English, *The Temptation to Exist*. "To exist," Cioran says in that essay, "is a habit I do not despair of acquiring."

Cioran's subject: on being a *mind*, a consciousness tuned to the highest pitch of refinement. The final justification of his writings, if one may guess at it: something close to the thesis given its classical statement in Kleist's "On the Puppet Theatre." In that essay Kleist says that, however much we may long to repair the disorders in the natural harmony of man created by consciousness, this is not to be accomplished by a surrender of consciousness. There is no return, no going back to innocence. We have no choice but to go to the end of thought, there (perhaps), in total self-consciousness, to recover grace and innocence.

In Cioran's writings, therefore, the mind is a voyeur.

But not upon "the world." Upon itself. Cioran is, to a degree reminiscent of Beckett, concerned with the absolute integrity of thought. That is, with the reduction or circumscription of thought to thinking about thinking. "The only free mind," Cioran remarks, is "the one that, pure of all intimacy with being or objects, plies its own vacuity."

Yet, throughout, this act of mental disembowelment retains its "Faustian" or "Western" passionateness. Cioran will allow no possibility that anyone born into this culture can attain—as a way out of the trap—an "Eastern" abnegation of mind. (Compare Cioran's self-consciously futile longing for the East with Lévi-Strauss' affirmative nostalgia for "neolithic consciousness.")

Philosophy becomes tortured thinking. Thinking that devours itself—and continues intact and even flourishes, in spite (or perhaps because) of these repeated acts of self-cannibalism. In the passion play of thought, the thinker plays the roles of both protagonist and antagonist. He is both suffering Prometheus and the remorseless eagle who consumes his perpetually regenerated entrails.

Impossible states of being, unthinkable thoughts are Cioran's material for speculation. (Thinking against oneself, etc.) But he comes after Nietzsche, who set down almost the whole of Cioran's position a century ago. An interesting question: why does a subtle, powerful mind consent to say what has, for the most part, already been said? In order to make those ideas genuinely his own? Because, while they were true when originally set down, they have since become *more* true?

Whatever the answer, the "fact" of Nietzsche has undeniable consequences for Cioran. He must tighten the screws, make the argument denser. More excruciating. More rhetorical.

Characteristically, Cioran begins an essay where another writer would end it. Beginning with the conclusion, he goes on from there.

His kind of writing is meant for readers who in a sense already know what he says; they have traversed these vertiginous thoughts for themselves. Cioran doesn't make any of the usual efforts to "persuade," with his oddly lyrical chains of ideas, his merciless irony, his gracefully delivered allusions to nothing less than the whole of European thought since the Greeks. An argument is to be "recognized," and without too much help. Good taste demands that the thinker furnish only pithy glimpses of intellectual and spiritual torment. Hence, Cioran's tone—one of immense dignity, dogged, sometimes playful, often haughty. But despite all that may appear as arrogance, there is nothing complacent in Cioran, unless it be his very sense of futility and his uncompromisingly elitist attitude toward the life of the mind.

As Nietzsche wanted to will his moral solitude, Cioran wants to will the difficult. Not that the essays are hard to read, but their moral point, so to speak, is the unending disclosure of difficulty. The argument of a typical Cioran essay might be described as a network of proposals for thinking—along with dissipations of the grounds for continuing to hold these ideas, not to mention the grounds for "acting" on the basis of them. By his complex intellectual formulation of intellectual impasses, Cioran constructs a closed universe—of the difficult—that is the subject of his lyricism.

Cioran is one of the most *delicate* minds of real power writing today. Nuance, irony, and refinement are the essence of his thinking. Yet he declares in the essay "On a Winded Civilization": "Men's minds need a simple truth, an answer which delivers them from their questions, a gospel, a tomb. The moments of refinement conceal a death-principle: nothing is more fragile than subtlety."

A contradiction? Not exactly. It is only the familiar double standard of philosophy since its debacle: upholding one standard (health) for the culture at large, another (spiritual ambition) for the solitary philosopher. The first standard demands what Nietzsche called the sacrifice of the intellect. The second standard demands the sacrifice of health, of mundane happiness, often of participation in family life and other community institutions, perhaps even of sanity. The philosopher's aptitude for martyrdom is almost part of his good manners, in this tradition of philosophizing since Kierkegaard and Nietzsche. And one of the commonest indications of his good taste as a philosopher is an avowed contempt for philosophy. Thus, Wittgenstein's idea that philosophy is something like a disease and the job of the philosopher is to study philosophy as the physician studies malaria, not to pass it on but to cure people of it.

But whether such behavior is diagnosed as the self-hatred of the philosopher or as merely a certain coquetry of the void, more than inconsistency must be allowed here. In Cioran's case, his disavowals of mind are not less authentic because they're delivered by someone who makes such strenuous professional use of the mind. Consider the impassioned counsels in an essay of 1952, "Some Blind Alleys: A Letter"—in which Cioran, a steadily published writer in France, puts himself in the curious position of reproaching a friend about to become that "monster," an author, and violate his admirable "detachment, scorn, and silence" by describing them in a book. Cioran is not just displaying a facile ambivalence toward his own vocation, but voicing the painful, genuinely paradoxical experience that the free intellect can have of itself when it commits itself to writing and acquires an audience. Anyway, it is one thing to choose martyrdom and compromise for oneself; quite another, to advise a friend to do likewise. And since for Cioran the use of the mind is a martyrdom, using one's mind in public—more specifically, being a writer—becomes a problematic, partly shameful act; always suspect; in the last analysis, something obscene, socially as well as individually.

Cioran is another recruit to the melancholy parade of European intellectuals in revolt against the intellect—the rebellion of idealism against "idealism"—whose greatest figures are Nietzsche and Marx. A good part of his argument on this theme differs little from what has already been stated by countless poets and philosophers in the last century and this—not to mention the sinister, traumatic amplification of these charges against the intellect in the rhetoric and practice of fascism. But the fact that an important argument is not new doesn't mean that one is exempted from taking it seriously. And what could be more relevant than the thesis, reworked by Cioran, that the free use of the mind is ultimately anti-social, detrimental to the health of the community?

In a number of essays, but most clearly in "On a Winded Civilization" and "A Little Theory of Destiny," Cioran ranges himself firmly on the side of the critics of the Enlightenment. "Since the Age of the Enlightenment," he writes, "Europe has ceaselessly sapped her idols in the name of tolerance." But these idols or "prejudices—organic fictions of a civilization—assure its duration, preserve its physiognomy. It must respect them." Elsewhere in the first of the essays mentioned above: "A minimum of unconsciousness is necessary if one wants to stay inside history." Foremost among "the diseases that undermine a civilization" is the hypertrophy of thought itself, which leads to the disappearance of the capacity for "inspired stupidity . . . fruitful exaltation, never compromised by a consciousness drawn and quartered." For any civilization "vacillates as soon as it exposes the errors which permitted its growth and its luster, as soon as it calls into question its own truths." And Cioran goes on, all too familiarly, to lament the suppression of the barbarian, of the non-thinker, in Europe. "All his instincts are throttled by his decency," is his comment on the Englishman. Protected from ordeal, "sapped by nostalgia, that generalized ennui," the average European is now monopolized and obsessed by "the concept of *living well* (that mania of declining periods)." Already

Europe has passed to "a provincial destiny." The new masters of the globe are the less civilized peoples of America and Russia and, waiting in the wings of history, the hordes of violent millions from still less civilized "suburbs of the globe" in whose hands the future resides.

Much of the old argument comes without transformation at Cioran's hands. The old heroism, the denunciation of the mind by the mind, served up once again in the name of the antitheses: heart versus head, instinct versus reason. "Too much lucidity" results in a loss of equilibrium. (One of the arguments behind Cioran's expressed mistrust, in "Blind Alleys" and "Style as Risk," of the book, the linguistic communication, literature itself—at least in the present age.)

But at least one of the familiar antitheses—thought versus action—is refined. In "On a Winded Civilization," Cioran shares the standard view of the nineteenth-century romantics, and is mainly concerned with the toll that the exercise of the mind takes on the ability to act. "To act is one thing; to know one is acting is another. When lucidity invests the action, insinuates itself into it, action is undone and, with it, prejudice, whose function consists, precisely, in subordinating, in enslaving consciousness to action." In "Thinking Against Oneself," however, the antithesis of thought and action is rendered in a more subtle and original manner. Thought is not simply that which impedes the direct, energetic performance of an act. Here, Cioran is more concerned with the inroads that action makes upon thought. Pointing out that "the sphere of consciousness shrinks in action," he supports the idea of a "liberation" from action as the only genuine mode of human freedom.

And even in the relatively simplistic argument of "On a Winded Civilization," when Cioran does invoke that exemplary European figure, "the tired intellectual," it's not simply to inveigh against the vocation of the intellectual, but to try to locate the exact difference between two states well worth distinguishing: being civilized and that mutilation of the organic person sometimes, tendentiously, called being "overcivilized." One may quarrel about the term, but the condition exists and is rampant—common among professional intellectuals, though scarcely confined to them. And, as Cioran correctly points out, a principal danger of being overcivilized is that one all too easily relapses, out of sheer exhaustion and the unsatisfied need to be "stimulated," into a vulgar and passive barbarism. Thus, "the man who unmasks his fictions" through an indiscriminate pursuit of the lucidity that is promoted by modern liberal culture "renounces his own resources and, in a sense, himself. Consequently, he will accept other fictions which will deny him, since they will not have cropped up from his own depths." Therefore, he concludes, "no man concerned with his own equilibrium may exceed a certain degree of lucidity and analysis."

Yet this counsel of moderation does not, in the end, limit Cioran's own enterprise. Saturated with a sense of the well-advertised and (in his belief) irreversible decline of European civilization, this model European thinker becomes, it would seem, emancipated from responsibility to his own health as well as his society's. For all his scorn for the enervated condition and the provincial destiny of the civilization of which he is a member, Cioran is also a gifted elegist of that civilization. Among the last, perhaps, of the elegists of the passing of "Europe"—of the European suffering, of European intellectual courage, of European vigor, of European overcomplexity. And determined, himself, to pursue that venture to its end.

His sole ambition: "to be abreast of the Incurable."

A doctrine of spiritual strenuousness. "Since every form of life betrays and corrupts Life, the man who is genuinely alive assumes a maximum of incompatibilities, works relentlessly at pleasure and pain alike. . . ." (I am quoting from "The Temptation to Exist.") And there can be no doubt in Cioran's thought that this most ambitious of all states of consciousness, while remaining truer to Life in the generic sense, to the full range of human prospects, is paid for dearly on the level of mundane existence. In terms of action, it means the acceptance of futility. Futility must be seen not as a frustration of one's hopes and aspirations, but as a prized and defended vantage point for the athletic leap of consciousness into its own complexity. It is of this desirable state that Cioran is speaking when he says: "Futility is the most difficult thing in the world." It requires that we "must sever our roots, must become metaphysically foreigners."

That Cioran conceives of this as being so formidable and difficult a task testifies perhaps to his own residual, unquenchable good health. It also may explain why his essay "A People of Solitaries" is, to my mind, one of the few things Cioran has ever written that falls well below his usual standard of brilliance and perspicacity. Writing on the Jews, who "represent the alienated condition par excellence" for Cioran no less than for Hegel and a host of intervening writers, Cioran displays a startling moral insensitivity to the contemporary aspects of his theme. Even without the example of Sartre's near-definitive treatment of the same subject in *Anti-Semite and Jew*, one could scarcely help finding Cioran's essay surprisingly cursory and highhanded.

A strange dialectic in Cioran: familiar elements fused in a complex mix. On the one hand, the traditional Romantic and vitalist contempt for "intellectuality" and for the hypertrophy of the mind at the expense of the body and the feelings and of the capacity for action. On the other hand, an exaltation of the life of the mind at the expense of body, feelings, and the capacity for action that could not be more radical and imperious.

The nearest model for this paradoxical attitude toward consciousness is the Gnostic-mystical tradition that, in Western Christianity, descends from Dionysius the Areopagite and the author of *The Cloud of Unknowing*.

And what Cioran says of the mystic applies perfectly to his own thought. "The mystic, in most cases, invents his adversaries . . . his thought asserts the existence of others by calculation, by artifice: it is a strategy of no consequence. His thought boils down, in the last instance, to a polemic with himself: he seeks to be, he becomes a crowd, even if it is only by making himself one new mask after the other, multiplying his faces: in which he resembles his Creator, whose histrionics he perpetuates."

Despite the irony in this passage, Cioran's envy of the mystics, whose enterprise so resembles his—"to find what escapes or survives the disintegration of his experiences: the residue of intemporality under the ego's vibrations"—is frank and unmistakable. Yet, like his master Nietzsche, Cioran remains nailed to the cross of an atheist spirituality. And his essays are best read as a manual of such an atheist spirituality. "Once we have ceased linking our secret life to God, we can ascend to ecstasies as effective as those of the mystics and conquer this world without recourse to the Beyond," is the opening sentence of the last paragraph of the essay "Dealing with the Mystics."

Politically, Cioran must be described as a conservative. Liberal humanism is for him simply not a viable or interesting option at all, and he regards the hope of radical revolution as something to be outgrown by the mature mind. (Thus, speaking of Russia in "A Little Theory of Destiny," he remarks: "The aspiration to 'save' the world is a morbid phenomenon of a people's youth.")

It may be relevant to recall that Cioran was born (in 1911) in Roumania, virtually all of whose distinguished expatriate intellectuals have been either apolitical or overtly reactionary; and that his only other book, besides the five collections of essays, is an edition of the writings of Joseph de Maistre (published in 1957), for which he wrote the introduction and selected the texts.* While he never develops anything like an explicit theology of counterrevolution in the manner of Maistre, those arguments seem close to Cioran's tacit position. Like Maistre, Donoso Cortés, and, more recently, Eric Voegelin, Cioran possesses what might be described—viewed from one angle—as a right-wing "Catholic" sensibility. The modern habit of fomenting revolutions against the established social order in the name of justice and equality is dismissed as a kind of childish fanaticism, much as an old cardinal might regard the activities of some uncouth millennarian sect. Within the same framework, one can locate Cioran's description of Marxism as "that sin of optimism," and his stand against the Enlightenment ideals of "tolerance" and freedom of thought. (It's perhaps worth noting, too, that Cioran is the son of a Greek Orthodox priest.)

Yet, while Cioran projects a recognizable political stance, though one present only implicitly in most of the essays, his approach is not, in the end, grounded in a religious commitment. However much his political-moral sympathies have in common with the right-wing Catholic sensibility, Cioran himself, as I have already said, is committed to the paradoxes of an atheist theology. Faith alone, he argues, solves nothing.

Perhaps what prevents Cioran from making the commitment, even in a secular form, to something like the Catholic theology of order is that he understands too well and shares too many of

*He has also published an essay on Machiavelli and one on St.-John Perse— both as yet uncollected.

the spiritual presuppositions of the Romantic movement. Critic of left-wing revolution that he may be, and a slightly snobbish analyst of the fact "that rebellion enjoys an undue privilege among us," Cioran cannot disavow the lesson that "almost all our discoveries are due to our violences, to the exacerbations of our instability." Thus, alongside the conservative implications of some of the essays, with their scornful treatment of the phenomenology of uprootedness, one must set the ironic-positive attitude toward rebellion expressed in "Thinking Against Oneself," an essay which concludes with the admonition that, "since the Absolute corresponds to a meaning we have not been able to cultivate, let us surrender to all rebellions: they will end by turning against themselves, against us. . . ."

Cioran is clearly unable to withhold admiration from what is extravagant, willful, extreme—one example of which is the extravagant, willful *ascesis* of the great Western mystics. Another is the fund of extremity stored up in the experience of the great madmen. "We derive our vitality from our store of madness," he writes in "The Temptation to Exist." Yet, in the essay on the mystics, he speaks of "our capacity to fling ourselves into a madness that is *not sacred*. In the unknown, we can go as far as the saints, without making use of their means. It will be enough for us to constrain reason to a long silence."

What makes Cioran's position not truly conservative in the modern sense is that his is, above all, an aristocratic stance. See, for only one illustration of the resources of this stance, his essay, "Beyond the Novel," in which the novel is eloquently and persuasively condemned for its spiritual vulgarity—for its devotion to what Cioran calls "destiny in lower case."

Throughout Cioran's writings, what is being posed is the problem of *spiritual good taste*. Avoiding vulgarity and the dilution of the self is the prerequisite for the arduous double task of maintaining an intact self which one is able fully to affirm and yet, at the same time, transcend. Cioran can even defend the emotion of self-pity: for the person who can no longer complain or lament has ceased, by rejecting his miseries and relegating them "outside his nature and outside his voice . . . to communicate with his life, which he turns into an object." It may seem outrageous for Cioran to advocate, as he often does, resisting the vulgar temptation to be happy and of the "impasse of happiness." But such judgments seem far from an unfeeling affectation, once one grants him his impossible project: "to be *nowhere*, when no external condition obliges you to do so . . . to extricate oneself from the world—what a labor of abolition!"

More realistically, perhaps the best to be hoped for is a series of situations, a life, a milieu, which leave part of the venturesome consciousness free for its labors. One may recall Cioran's description of Spain in "A Little Theory of Destiny": "They live in a kind of melodious asperity, a *tragic non-seriousness*, which saves them from vulgarity, from happiness, and from success."

Certainly, Cioran's writings suggest, the role of the writer isn't likely to provide this kind of spiritual leverage. In "Advantages of Exile" and the brief "Verbal Demiurgy," he describes how the vocation of literature, particularly that of the poet, creates insurmountable conditions of inauthenticity. One may suffer, but when one deposits this suffering in literature, the result is "an accumulation of confusions, an inflation of horrors, of *frissons* that *date*. One cannot keep renewing Hell, whose very character is monotony. . . ."

Whether the vocation of the philosopher is any less compromised can hardly be proved. (Reason is dying, Cioran says in "Style as Risk," in both philosophy and art.) But at least philosophy, I imagine Cioran feels, maintains somewhat higher standards of decorum. Untempted by the same kind of fame or emotional rewards that can descend on the poet, the philosopher can perhaps better comprehend and respect the modesty of the inexpressible.

When Cioran describes Nietzsche's philosophy as "a sum of attitudes"—mistakenly scrutinized by scholars for the constants that the philosopher has rejected—it's clear that he accepts the Nietzschean standard, with its critique of "truth" as system and consistency, as his own.

In "Blind Alleys," Cioran speaks of "the stupidities inherent in the cult of truth." The implication, here and elsewhere, is that what the true philosopher says isn't something "true" but rather something necessary or liberating. For "the truth" is identified with depersonalization.

Once again, the line from Nietzsche to Cioran cannot be

overemphasized. And for both writers, the critique of "truth" is intimately connected with the attitude toward "history."

Thus, one cannot understand Nietzsche's questioning of the value of truth in general and of the usefulness of historical truth in particular without grasping the link between the two notions. Nietzsche doesn't reject historical thinking because it is false. On the contrary, it must be rejected because it is true—a debilitating truth that has to be overthrown to allow a more inclusive orientation for human consciousness.

As Cioran says in "The Temptation to Exist": "History is merely an inessential mode of being, the most effective form of our infidelity to ourselves, a metaphysical refusal." And, in "Thinking Against Oneself," he refers to "history, man's aggression against himself."

Granted that the stamp of Nietzsche appears both on the form of Cioran's thinking and on his principal attitudes, where he most resembles Nietzsche is in his temperament. It's the temperament or personal style shared with Nietzsche that explains the connections, in Cioran's work, between such disparate materials as: the emphasis on the strenuousness of an ambitious spiritual life; the project of self-mastery through "thinking against oneself"; the recurrent Nietzschean thematics of strength versus weakness, health versus sickness; the savage and sometimes shrill deployment of irony (quite different from the near systematic, dialectical interplay of irony and seriousness to be found in Kierkegaard's writings); the preoccupation with the struggle against banality and boredom; the ambivalent attitude toward the poet's vocation; the seductive but always finally resisted lure of religious consciousness; and, of course, the hostility toward history and to most aspects of "modern" life.

What's missing in Cioran's work is anything comparable to Nietzsche's heroic effort to surmount nihilism (the doctrine of eternal recurrence).

And where Cioran most differs from Nietzsche is in not following Nietzsche's critique of Platonism. Contemptuous of history, yet haunted by time and mortality, Nietzsche still refused anything harking back to the rhetoric established by Plato for going beyond time and death, and indeed worked hard at exposing what he thought the essential fraud and bad faith involved in the Platonic intellectual transcendence. Cioran, apparently, hasn't been convinced by Nietzsche's arguments. All the venerable Platonic dualisms reappear in Cioran's writings, essential links of the argument, used with no more than an occasional hint of ironic reserve. One finds time versus eternity, mind versus body, spirit versus matter; and the more modern ones, too: life versus Life, and being versus existence. How seriously these dualisms are intended is hard to decide.

Could one regard the Platonist machinery in Cioran's thought as an aesthetic code? Or, alternatively, as a kind of moral therapy? But Nietzsche's critique of Platonism would still apply and still remain unanswered.

The only figure in the world of Anglo-American letters embarked on a theoretical enterprise comparable in intellectual power and scope to Cioran's is John Cage.

Also a thinker in the post- and anti-philosophical tradition of broken, aphoristic discourse, Cage shares with Cioran a revulsion against "psychology" and against "history" and a commitment to a radical transvaluation of values. But while comparable in range, interest, and energy to Cioran's, Cage's thought mainly offers the most radical contrast to it. From what must be assumed to be the grossest difference of temperament, Cage envisages a world in which most of Cioran's problems and tasks simply don't exist. Cioran's universe of discourse is occupied with the themes of sickness (individual and social), impasse, suffering, mortality. What his essays offer is diagnosis and, if not outright therapy, at least a manual of spiritual good taste through which one might be helped to keep one's life from being turned into an object, a thing. Cage's universe of discourse—no less radical and spiritually ambitious than Cioran's—refuses to admit these themes.

In contrast to Cioran's unrelenting elitism, Cage envisages a totally democratic world of the spirit, a world of "natural activity" in which "it is understood that everything is clean: there is no dirt." In contrast to Cioran's baroque standards of good and bad taste in intellectual and moral matters, Cage maintains there is no such thing as good or bad taste. In contrast to Cioran's vision of error and decline and (possible) redemption of

one's acts, Cage proposes the perennial possibility of errorless
behavior, if only we will allow it to be so. "Error is a fiction,
has no reality in fact. Errorless music is written by not giving
a thought to cause and effect. Any other kind of music always
has mistakes in it. In other words there is no split between spirit
and matter." And elsewhere in the same book from which these
quotes are taken, *Silence:* "How can we speak of error when it
is understood 'psychology never again'?" In contrast to Cioran's goal of infinite adaptability and intellectual agility (how
to find the correct vantage point, the right place to stand in a
treacherous world), Cage proposes for our experience a world
in which it's never preferable to do other than we are doing or
be elsewhere than we are. "It is only irritating," he says, "to
think one would like to be somewhere else. Here we are now."

What becomes clear, in the context of this comparison, is
how devoted Cioran is to the *will* and its capacity to transform
the world. Compare Cage's: "Do you only take the position
of doing nothing, and things will of themselves become transformed." What different views can follow the radical rejection
of history is seen by thinking first of Cioran and then of Cage,
who writes: "To be & be the present. Would it be a repetition?
Only if we thought we owned it, but since we don't, it is free
& so are we."

Reading Cage, one becomes aware how much Cioran is still
confined within the premises of the historicizing consciousness;
how inescapably he continues to repeat these gestures, much as
he longs to transcend them. Of necessity then, Cioran's thought
is halfway between anguished reprise of these gestures and a
genuine transvaluation of them. Perhaps, for a unified transvaluation, one must look to those thinkers like Cage who—whether
from spiritual strength or from spiritual insensitivity is a secondary issue—are able to jettison far more of the inherited anguish
and complexity of this civilization. Cioran's fierce, tensely argued
speculations sum up brilliantly the decaying urgencies of Western thought, but offer us no relief from them beyond the considerable satisfactions of the understanding. Relief, of course,
is scarcely Cioran's intention. His aim is diagnosis. For relief, it
may be that one must abandon the pride of knowing and feeling
so much—a local pride that has cost everyone hideously by now.

Novalis wrote that "philosophy is properly home-sickness;

the wish to be everywhere at home." If the human mind can be everywhere at home, it must in the end give up its local "European" pride and something else—that will seem strangely unfeeling and intellectually simplistic—must be allowed in. "All that is necessary," says Cage with his own devastating irony, "is an empty space of time and letting it act in its magnetic way."

(1967)

II

Theatre and Film

Does there exist an unbridgeable gap, even opposition, between the two arts? Is there something genuinely "theatrical," different in kind from what is genuinely "cinematic"?

Virtually all opinion holds that there is. A commonplace of discussion has it that film and theatre are distinct and even antithetical arts, each giving rise to its own standards of judgment and canons of form. Thus Erwin Panofsky argues in his celebrated essay "Style and Medium in the Motion Pictures" (1934, rewritten in 1956) that one of the criteria for evaluating a movie is its freedom from the impurities of theatricality, and that, to talk about film, one must first define "the basic nature of the medium." Those who think prescriptively about the nature of live drama, less confident in the future of that art than the *cinéphiles* in theirs, rarely take a comparably exclusivist line.

The history of cinema is often treated as the history of its emancipation from theatrical models. First of all from theatrical "frontality" (the unmoving camera reproducing the situation of the spectator of a play fixed in his seat), then from theatrical acting (gestures needlessly stylized, exaggerated—needlessly, because now the actor could be seen "close up"), then from theatrical furnishings (unnecessary distancing of the audience's emotions, disregarding the opportunity to immerse the audience in reality). Movies are regarded as advancing from theatrical stasis to cinematic fluidity, from theatrical artificiality to cinematic naturalness and immediateness. But this view is far too simple.

Such oversimplification testifies to the ambiguous scope of the camera eye. Because the camera *can* be used to project a relatively passive, unselective kind of vision—as well as the highly selective ("edited") vision generally associated with movies—cinema is a medium as well as an art, in the sense that it can encapsulate any of the performing arts and render it in a film transcription. (This "medium" or non-art aspect of film attained its routine incarnation with the advent of television. There, movies themselves became another performing art to be transcribed, miniaturized on film.) One *can* film a play or ballet or opera or sporting event in such a way that film becomes, relatively speaking, a transparency, and it seems correct to say that one is seeing the event filmed. But theatre is never a "medium." Thus, because one can make a movie of a play but not a play of a movie, cinema had an early but fortuitous connection with the stage. Some of the earliest films were filmed plays. Duse and Bernhardt are on film—marooned in time, absurd, touching; there is a 1913 British film of Forbes-Robertson playing Hamlet, a 1923 German film of *Othello* starring Emil Jannings. More recently, the camera has preserved Helene Weigel's performance of *Mother Courage* with the Berliner Ensemble, the Living Theatre production of *The Brig* (filmed by the Mekas brothers), and Peter Brook's staging of Weiss' *Marat/Sade*.

But from the beginning, even within the confines of the notion of film as a "medium" and the camera as a "recording" instrument, other events than those occurring in theatres were taken down. As with still photography, some of the events captured on moving photographs were staged but others were valued precisely because they were *not* staged—the camera being the witness, the invisible spectator, the invulnerable voyeuristic eye. (Perhaps public happenings, "news," constitute an intermediate case between staged and unstaged events; but film as "newsreel" generally amounts to using film as a "medium.") To create on film a *document* of a transient reality is a conception quite unrelated to the purposes of theatre. It only appears related when the "real event" being recorded happens to be a theatrical performance. In fact, the first use of the motion-picture camera was to make a documentary record of unstaged, casual reality; Lumière's films from the 1890's of crowd scenes in Paris and New York antedate any filming of plays.

The other paradigmatic non-theatrical use of film, which dates from the earliest period of movie-making with the celebrated work of Méliès, is the creation of illusion, the construction of fantasy. To be sure, Méliès (like many directors after him) conceived of the rectangle of the screen on analogy with the proscenium stage. And not only were the events staged; they were the very stuff of invention: impossible journeys, imaginary objects, physical metamorphoses. But this, even adding the fact that Méliès situated his camera in front of the action and hardly moved it, does not make his films theatrical in an invidious sense. In their treatment of persons as things (physical objects) and in their disjunctive presentation of time and space, Méliès' films are quintessentially "cinematic"—so far as there is such a thing.

If the contrast between theatre and films doesn't lie in the materials represented or depicted in a simple sense, this contrast survives in more generalized forms.

According to some influential accounts, the boundary is virtually an ontological one. Theatre deploys artifice while cinema is committed to reality, indeed to an ultimately physical reality which is "redeemed," to use Siegfried Kracauer's striking word, by the camera. The aesthetic judgment that follows from this venture in intellectual map-making is that films shot in real-life settings are better (i.e., more cinematic) than those shot in a studio. Taking Flaherty and Italian neo-realism and the *cinéma-vérité* of Rouch and Marker and Ruspoli as preferred models, one would judge rather harshly the era of wholly studio-made films inaugurated around 1920 by *The Cabinet of Dr. Caligari*, films with ostentatiously artificial décor and landscapes, and applaud the direction taken at the same period in Sweden, where many films with strenuous natural settings were being shot on location. Thus, Panofsky attacks *Dr. Caligari* for "pre-stylizing reality," and urges upon cinema "the problem of manipulating and shooting unstylized reality in such a way that the result has style."

But there is no reason to insist on a single model for film. And it is helpful to notice how the apotheosis of realism in cinema, which gives the greatest prestige to "unstylized reality," covertly advances a definite political-moral position. Films have been rather too often acclaimed as the democratic art, the preeminent art of mass society. Once one takes this description seriously, one tends (like Panofsky and Kracauer) to wish that movies continue to reflect their origins in a vulgar level of the arts, to remain loyal to their vast unsophisticated audience. Thus, a vaguely Marxist orientation collaborates with a fundamental tenet of romanticism. Cinema, at once high art and popular art, is cast as the art of the authentic. Theatre, by contrast, means dressing up, pretense, lies. It smacks of aristocratic taste and the class society. Behind the objection of critics to the stagy sets of *Dr. Caligari*, the improbable costumes and florid acting of Renoir's *Nana*, the talkiness of Dreyer's *Gertrud* as "theatrical" lay the judgment that such films were false, that they exhibited a sensibility both pretentious and reactionary which was out of step with the democratic and more mundane sensibility of modern life.

Anyway, whether aesthetic defect or no in the particular case, the synthetic "look" in films is not necessarily a misplaced theatricalism. From the beginning of film history, there were painters and sculptors who claimed that cinema's true future resided in artifice, construction. Not figurative narration or storytelling of any kind (either in a relatively realistic or in a "surrealistic" vein) but abstraction was film's true destiny. Thus, Theo van Doesburg in his essay of 1929, "Film as Pure Form," envisages film as the vehicle of "optical poetry," "dynamic light architecture," "the creation of a moving ornament." Films will realize "Bach's dream of finding an optical equivalent for the temporal structure of a musical composition." Though only a few film-makers— for example, Robert Breer—continue to pursue this conception of film, who can deny its claim to be cinematic?

Could anything be more alien to the nature of theatre than such a degree of abstraction? Let's not answer that question too quickly.

Panofsky derives the difference between theatre and film as a difference between the *formal* conditions of seeing a play and those of seeing a movie. In the theatre, "space is static, that is, the space represented on the stage, as well as the spatial relation of the beholder to the spectacle, is unalterably fixed," while in the cinema, "the spectator occupies a fixed seat, but only physically, not as the subject of an aesthetic experience." In the theatre, the spectator cannot change his angle of vision. In the cinema, the spectator is "aesthetically . . . in permanent motion as his eye identifies with the lens of the camera, which permanently shifts in distance and direction."

True enough. But the observation does not warrant a radical dissociation of theatre and film. Like many critics, Panofsky has a "literary" conception of the theatre. In contrast to theatre, conceived of as basically dramatized literature (texts, words), stands cinema, which he assumes to be primarily "a visual experience." This means defining cinema by those means perfected in the period of silent films. But many of the most interesting movies today could hardly be described adequately as images with sound added. And the most lively work in the theatre is being done by people who envisage theatre as more than, or different from, "plays" from Aeschylus to Tennessee Williams.

Given his view, Panofsky is as eager to hold the line against the infiltration of theatre by cinema as the other way around. In the theatre, unlike movies, "the setting of the stage cannot change during one act (except for such incidentals as rising moons or gathering clouds and such illegitimate reborrowings from film as turning wings or gliding backdrops)." Not only does Panofsky assume that theatre means plays, but by the aesthetic standard he tacitly proposes, the model play would approach the condition of *No Exit*, and the ideal set would be either a realistic living room or a blank stage. No less arbitrary is his complementary view of what is illegitimate in film: all elements not demonstrably subordinate to the image, more precisely, the *moving* image. Thus Panofsky asserts: "Wherever a poetic emotion, a musical outburst, or a literary conceit (even, I am grieved to say, some of the wisecracks of Groucho Marx) entirely loses contact with visible movement, they strike the sensitive spectator as, literally, out of place." What then of the films of Bresson and Godard, with their allusive, thoughtful texts and their characteristic refusal to be primarily a visual experience? How could one explain the extraordinary rightness of Ozu's relatively immobilized camera?

Part of Panofsky's dogmatism in decrying the theatrical taint in movies can be explained by recalling that the first version of his essay appeared in 1934 and undoubtedly reflects the recent experience of seeing a great many bad movies. Compared with the level that film reached in the late 1920's, it is undeniable that the average quality of films declined sharply in the early sound period. Although a number of fine, audacious films were made during the very first years of sound, the general decline had become clear by 1933 or 1934. The sheer dullness of most films of this period can't be explained simply as a regression to theatre. Still, it's a fact that film-makers in the 1930's did turn much more frequently to plays than they had in the preceding decade—filming stage successes such as *Outward Bound, Rain, Dinner at Eight, Blithe Spirit, Faisons un Rêve, Twentieth Century, Boudu Sauvé des Eaux*, the Pagnol trilogy, *She Done Him Wrong, Die Dreigroschenoper, Anna Christie, Holiday, Animal Crackers, The Petrified Forest*, and many, many more. Most of these films are negligible as art; a few are first-rate. (The same can be said of the plays, though there is scant correlation between the merits of the movies and of the stage "originals.") However, their virtues and faults cannot be sorted out into a cinematic versus a theatrical element. Usually, the success of movie versions of plays is measured by the extent to which the script rearranges and displaces the action and deals less than respectfully with the spoken text—as do certain English films of plays by Wilde and Shaw, the Olivier Shakespeare films (at least *Henry V*), and Sjöberg's *Miss Julie*. But the basic disapproval of films which betray their origins in plays remains. (A recent example: the outrage and hostility which greeted Dreyer's masterly *Gertrud*, because of its blatant fidelity to the 1904 Danish play on which it is based, with characters conversing at length and quite formally, with little camera movement and most scenes filmed in medium shot.)

My own view is that films with complex or formal dialogue, films in which the camera is static or in which the action stays indoors, are not necessarily theatrical—whether derived from plays or not. *Per contra*, it is no more part of the putative "essence" of movies that the camera must rove over a large physical area than it is that the sound element in a film must always be subordinate to the visual. Though most of the action of Kurosawa's *The Lower Depths*, a fairly faithful transcription of Gorky's play, is confined to one large room, this film is just as cinematic as the same director's *Throne of Blood*, a very free and laconic adaption of *Macbeth*. The claustrophobic intensity of Melville's *Les Enfants Terribles* is as peculiar to the movies as the kinetic élan of Ford's *The Searchers* or the opening train journey in Renoir's *La Bête Humaine*.

A film does become theatrical in an invidious sense when the narration is coyly self-conscious. Compare Autant-Lara's *Occupe-toi d'Amélie*, a brilliant cinematic use of the conventions and materials of boulevard theatre, with Ophuls' clumsy use of similar conventions and materials in *La Ronde*.

In his book *Film and Theatre* (1936), Allardyce Nicoll argues that the difference between the two arts, both forms of dramaturgy, is that they use different kinds of characters. "Practically all effectively drawn stage characters are types [while] in the cinema we demand individualization . . . and impute greater power of independent life to the figures on the screen." (Panofsky, by the way, makes exactly the same contrast but in reverse: that the nature of films, unlike that of plays, requires flat or stock characters.)

Nicoll's thesis is not as arbitrary as it may at first appear. A little-remarked fact about movies is that the moments that are plastically and emotionally most successful, and the most effective elements of characterization, often consist precisely of "irrelevant" or unfunctional details. (One random example: the ping-pong ball the schoolmaster toys with in Ivory's *Shakespeare Wallah.*) Movies thrive on the narrative equivalent of a technique familiar from painting and photography: off-centering. Hence, the pleasing disunity or fragmentariness of the characters of many of the greatest films, which is probably what Nicoll means by "individualization." In contrast, linear coherence of detail (the gun on the wall in the first act that must go off by the end of the third) is the rule in Occidental narrative theatre, and gives rise to the impression of the unity of the characters (a unity that may be equivalent to the construction of a "type").

But, even with these adjustments, Nicoll's thesis doesn't work so far as it rests on the idea that "when we go to the theatre, we expect theatre and nothing else." For what is this theater-and-nothing-else if not the old notion of artifice? (As if art were ever anything else, some arts being artificial but others not.) According to Nicoll, when we sit in a theatre "in every way the 'falsity' of a theatrical production is borne in upon us, so that we are prepared to demand nothing save a theatrical truth." Quite a different situation obtains in the cinema, Nicoll holds. Every member of the movie audience, no matter how sophisticated, is on essentially the same level; we all believe that the camera cannot lie. As the film actor and his role are identical, the image cannot be dissociated from what is imaged. We experience what cinema gives us as the truth of life.

But couldn't theatre dissolve the distinction between the

truth of artifice and the truth of life? Isn't that just what theatre as ritual seeks to do? Isn't that the aim of theatre conceived as an *exchange* with an audience?—something that films can never be.

Panofsky may be obtuse when he decries the theatrical taint in movies, but he is sound when he points out that, historically, theatre is only one of the arts feeding into cinema. As he remarks, it is apt that films came to be known popularly as moving pictures rather than as "photoplays" or "screen plays." Cinema derives less from the theatre, from a performance art, an art that already moves, than it does from forms of art which were stationary. Nineteenth-century historical paintings, sentimental postcards, the museum of wax figures à la Madame Tussaud, and comic strips are the sources Panofsky cites. Another model, which he surprisingly fails to mention, is the early narrative uses of still photography—like the family photo album. The stylistics of description and scene-building developed by certain nineteenth-century novelists, as Eisenstein pointed out in his brilliant essay on Dickens, supplied still another prototype for cinema.

Movies are images (usually photographs) that move, to be sure. But the distinctive cinematic unit is not the image but the principle of connection between the images: the relation of a "shot" to the one that preceded it and the one that comes after. There is no peculiarly "cinematic" as opposed to "theatrical" mode of linking images.

If an irreducible distinction between theatre and cinema does exist, it may be this. Theatre is confined to a logical or *continuous* use of space. Cinema (through editing, that is, through the change of shot—which is the basic unit of film construction) has access to an alogical or *discontinuous* use of space.

In the theatre, actors are either in the stage space or "off." When "on," they are always visible or visualizable in contiguity with each other. In the cinema, no such relation is necessarily visible or even visualizable. (Example: the last shot of Paradjanov's *Shadows of Our Forgotten Ancestors*.) Some of the films considered objectionably theatrical are those which seem to emphasize spatial continuities, like Hitchcock's virtuoso *Rope* or the daringly anachronistic *Gertrud*. But closer analysis of both these films would show how complex their treatment of space is. The long takes increasingly favored in sound films are, in themselves, neither more nor less cinematic than the short takes characteristic of silents.

Thus, cinematic virtue does not reside in the fluidity of the movement of the camera or in the mere frequency of the change of shot. It consists in the arrangement of screen images and (now) of sounds. Méliès, for example, though he didn't go beyond the static positioning of his camera, had a very striking conception of how to *link* screen images. He grasped that editing offered an equivalent to the magician's sleight of hand—thereby establishing that one of the distinctive aspects of film (unlike theatre) is that anything can happen, that there is nothing that cannot be represented convincingly. Through editing, Méliès presents discontinuities of physical substance and behavior. In his films, the discontinuities are, so to speak, practical, functional; they accomplish a transformation of ordinary reality. But the continuous *re*invention of space (as well as the option of temporal indeterminacy) peculiar to film narration does not pertain only to the cinema's ability to fabricate "visions," to show the viewer a radically altered world. The most "realistic" use of the motion-picture camera also involves a discontinuous account of space, insofar as all film narration has a "syntax," composed of the rhythm of associations and disjunctions. (As Cocteau has written, "My primary concern in a film is to prevent the images from flowing, to oppose them to each other, to anchor them and join them without destroying their relief." But such a conception of film syntax need hardly entail, as Cocteau thinks, rejecting movies as "mere entertainment instead of a vehicle for thought.")

In marking the boundary between theatre and film, the issue of the continuity of space seems to me more fundamental than the obvious contrast between theatre as an organization of movement in three-dimensional space (like dance) and cinema as an organization of plane space (like painting). The theatre's capacities for manipulating space and time are simply much cruder and more labored than those of film. Theatre cannot equal the cinema's facilities for the strictly controlled repetition of images, for the duplication or matching of word and image, and for the juxtaposition and overlapping of images.

(With advanced lighting techniques and an adept use of scrim, one can now "dissolve in" or "dissolve out" on the stage. But no technique could provide an equivalent on the stage of the "lap dissolve.")

Sometimes the division between theatre and film is located as the difference between the play and the film script. Theatre has been described as a mediated art, presumably because it usually consists of a preexistent play mediated by a particular performance which offers one of many possible interpretations of the play. Film, in contrast, is regarded as unmediated—because of its larger-than-life scale and more unrefusable impact on the eye, and because (in Panofsky's words) "the medium of the movies is physical reality as such" and the characters in a movie "have no aesthetic existence outside the actors." But there is an equally valid sense which shows movies to be the mediated art and theatre the unmediated one. We see what happens on the stage with our own eyes. We see on the screen what the camera sees.

In the cinema, narration proceeds by ellipsis (the "cut" or change of shot); the camera eye is a unified point of view that continually displaces itself. But the change of shot can provoke questions, the simplest of which is: from *whose* point of view is the shot seen? And the ambiguity of point of view latent in all cinematic narration has no equivalent in the theatre. Indeed, one should not underestimate the aesthetically positive role of *disorientation* in the cinema. Examples: Busby Berkeley dollying back from an ordinary-looking stage already established as some thirty feet deep to disclose a stage area three hundred feet square; Resnais panning from character X's point of view a full 360 degrees to come to rest upon X's face.

Much also may be made of the fact that, in its concrete existence, cinema is an *object* (a product, even) while theatre results in a *performance*. Is this so important? In a way, no. Art in all its forms, whether objects (like films or painting) or performances (like music or theatre), is first a mental act, a fact of consciousness. The object aspect of film and the performance aspect of theatre are only means—means to the experience which is not only "of" but "through" the film and the theatre event. Each subject of an aesthetic experience shapes it to his own measure. With respect to any *single* experience, it hardly matters that a film is identical from one projection of it to another while theatre performances are highly mutable.

The difference between object art and performance art underlies Panofsky's observation that "the screenplay, in contrast to the theatre play, has no aesthetic existence independent of its performance," so that characters in movies *are* the stars who enact them. It is because each film is an object, a totality that is set, that movie roles are identical with the actors' performances; while in the theatre (in the Occident, an artistic totality that is generally additive rather than organic) only the written play is "fixed," an object (literature) and therefore existing apart from any staging of it.

But these qualities of theatre and film are not, as Panofsky apparently thought, unalterable. Just as movies needn't necessarily be designed to be shown at all in theatre situations (they can be intended for more continuous and casual viewing: in the living room, in the bedroom, or on public surfaces like the façades of buildings), so a movie *may* be altered from one projection to the next. Harry Smith, when he runs off his films, makes each projection an unrepeatable performance. And, again, theatre is not just about preexisting plays which get produced over and over, well or badly. In Happenings, street or guerilla theatre, and certain other recent theatre events, the "plays" are identical with their productions in precisely the same sense as the screenplay is identical with the unique film made from it.

Despite these developments, however, a large difference still remains. Because films are objects, they are totally manipulable, totally calculable. Films resemble books, another portable art-object; making a film, like writing a book, means constructing an inanimate thing, every element of which is determinate. Indeed, this determinacy has or can have a quasi-mathematical form in films, as it does in music. (A shot lasts a certain number of seconds, "matching" two shots requires a change of angle of so many degrees.) Given the total determinacy of the result on celluloid (whatever the extent of the director's conscious intervention), it was inevitable that some film directors would want to devise schemas to make their intentions more exact. Thus, it was neither perverse nor primitive of Busby Berkeley to have used only one camera to shoot the whole of each of his mammoth dance numbers. Every "setup" was designed to be shot from only one, exactly calculated angle. Working on a far more self-conscious level of artistry than Busby Berkeley, Bresson has declared that, for him, the director's task consists in finding the single way of doing each shot that is correct. No image is justified in itself, according to Bresson, but rather in the exactly specifiable relation it bears to the chronologically adjacent images—which relation constitutes its "meaning."

But theatre allows only the loosest approximation to this sort of formal concern and to this degree of aesthetic responsibility on the part of the director, which is why French critics justly speak of the director of a film as its "author." Because they are performances, events that are always "live," what takes place on a theatre stage is not subject to an equivalent degree of control and cannot admit a comparably exact integration of effects.

It would be foolish to conclude that superior films are those resulting from the greatest amount of conscious planning on the part of the director or those which objectify a complex plan (though the director may not have been aware of it, and proceeded in what seemed to him an intuitive or instinctive way). Plans may be faulty or ill-conceived or sterile. More important, the cinema admits of a number of quite different kinds of sensibility. One gives rise to the kind of formalized art to which cinema (unlike theatre) is naturally adapted. Another has produced an impressive body of "improvised" cinema. (This should be distinguished from the work of some film-makers, notably Godard, who have become fascinated with the "look" of improvised, documentary cinema, used for formalistic ends.)

Nevertheless, it seems indisputable that cinema, not only potentially but by its nature, is a more rigorous art than theatre. This capacity for formal rigor, combined with the accessibility of mass audiences, has given cinema an unquestioned prestige and attractiveness as an art form. Despite the extreme emotional resources of "pure theatre" demonstrated by Julian Beck and Judith Malina's Living Theatre and Jerzy Grotowski's Theatre Laboratory, theatre as an art form gives the general impression of having a problematic future.

More than a failure of nerve must account for the fact that theatre, this seasoned art, occupied since antiquity with all sorts of local offices—enacting sacred rites, reinforcing communal loyalty, guiding morals, provoking the therapeutic discharge of violent emotions, conferring social status, giving practical instruction, affording entertainment, dignifying celebrations, subverting established authority—is now on the defensive before movies, this brash art with its huge, amorphous, passive audience. But the fact is undeniable. Meanwhile, movies continue to maintain their astonishing pace of formal articulation. (Take the commercial cinema of Europe, Japan, and the United States since 1960, and consider what the audiences of these films in less than a decade have become habituated to in the way of increasingly elliptical storytelling and visualization.)

But note: this youngest of the arts is also the most heavily burdened with memory. Cinema is a time machine. Movies preserve the past, while theatres—no matter how devoted to the classics, to old plays—can only "modernize." Movies resurrect the beautiful dead; present, intact, vanished or ruined environments; embody without irony styles and fashions that seem funny today; solemnly ponder irrelevant or naïve problems. The historical particularity of the reality registered on celluloid is so vivid that practically all films older than four or five years are saturated with pathos. (The pathos I am describing is not simply that of old photographs, for it overtakes animated cartoons and drawn, abstract films as well as ordinary movies.) Films age (being objects) as no theatre event does (being always new). There is no pathos of mortality in theatre's "reality" as such, nothing in our response to a good performance of a Mayakovsky play comparable to the aesthetic role of the emotion of nostalgia when we see in 1966 a film by Pudovkin.

Also worth noting: compared with the theatre, innovations in cinema seem to be assimilated more efficiently, seem altogether more sharable—among other reasons, because new films are quickly and widely circulated. And, partly because virtually the entire body of accomplishment in film can be consulted in the present (in film libraries, of which the most celebrated is the Cinémathèque Française), most film-makers are more knowledgeable about the entire history of their art than most theatre directors are about even the very recent past of theirs.

The key word in most discussions of cinema is "possibility." There is a merely classifying use of the word, as in Panofsky's engaging judgment that "within their self-imposed limitations the early Disney films . . . represent, as it were, a chemically pure distillation of cinematic possibilities." But behind this relatively neutral usage lurks a more polemical sense of cinema's possibilities, in which what is regularly intimated is the obsolescence of theatre and its supersession by films.

Thus, Panofsky describes the mediation of the camera eye as opening "up a world of possibility of which the stage can never dream." Already in 1924, Artaud declared that motion pictures had made the theatre obsolete. Movies "possess a sort of virtual power which probes into the mind and uncovers undreamt-of possibilities . . . When this art's exhilaration has been blended in the right proportions with the psychic ingredient it commands, it will leave the theatre far behind and we will relegate the latter to the attic of our memories." (When sound came in, though, Artaud became disenchanted with films and returned to theatre.)

Meyerhold, facing the challenge head on, thought the only hope for theatre lay in a wholesale emulation of the cinema. "Let us 'cinematify' the theatre," he urged, meaning that the staging of plays should be "industrialized," theatres must accommodate audiences in the tens of thousands rather than in the hundreds. Meyerhold also seemed to find some relief in the idea that the coming of sound signaled the downfall of movies. Believing that the international appeal of films depended entirely on the fact that the screen actors (unlike theatre actors) didn't have to speak any particular language, he was unable to imagine in 1930 that technology (dubbing, subtitling) could solve the problem.

Is cinema the successor, the rival, or the revivifyer of the theatre?

Sociologically, it is certainly the rival—one of many. Whether it is theatre's successor depends partly on how people understand and use the decline of theatre as an art form. One can't be sure that theatre is not in a state of irreversible decline, spurts of local vitality notwithstanding. And art forms *have* been abandoned (though not necessarily because they become "obsolete").

But why should theatre be rendered obsolete by movies?

Predictions of obsolescence amount to declaring that a something has one particular task (which another something may do as well or better). But has theatre one particular task or aptitude? One which cinema is better able to perform?

Those who predict the demise of the theatre, assuming that cinema has engulfed its function, tend to impute a relation between films and theatre reminiscent of what was once said about photography and painting. If the painter's job really had been no more than fabricating likenesses, then the invention of the camera might indeed have made painting obsolete. But painting is hardly just "pictures," any more than cinema is just theatre democratized and made available to the masses (because it can be reproduced and distributed in portable standardized units).

In the naïve tale of photography and painting, painting was reprieved when it claimed a new task: abstraction. As the superior realism of photography was supposed to have liberated painting, allowing it to go abstract, cinema's superior power to represent (not merely to stimulate) the imagination may appear to have similarly emboldened the theatre, inviting the gradual obliteration of the conventional "plot."

This was how it was supposed to be, but not how it in fact turned out. Actually, painting and photography evidence parallel development rather than a rivalry or a supersession. And, at an uneven rate, so do theatre and film. The possibilities for theatre that lie in going beyond psychological realism, thereby achieving greater abstractness, are equally germane to the future of narrative films. Conversely, the idea of movies as witness to real life, testimony rather than invention or artifice, the treatment of collective historical situations rather than the depiction of imaginary personal "dramas," seems equally relevant to theatre. Alongside documentary films and their sophisticated heir, *cinéma-vérité*, one can place the new documentary theatre, the so-called "theatre of fact," exemplified in plays by Hochhuth, in Weiss' *The Investigation*, in Peter Brook's recent projects for a production called *US* with the Royal Shakespeare company in London.

Despite Panofsky's strictures, there seems no reason for theatre and film not to exchange with each other, as they have been doing right along.

The influence of the theatre upon films in the early years of cinema history is well known. According to Kracauer, the distinctive lighting of *Dr. Caligari* (and of many German films of the early 1920's) can be traced to an experiment with lighting that Max Reinhardt made shortly before on the stage in his production of Sorge's *The Beggar*. Even in this period, however, the impact was reciprocal. The accomplishments of the "expressionist film" were immediately absorbed by the expressionist theatre. Stimulated by the cinematic technique of the "iris-in," stage lighting took to singling out a lone player or some segment of the scene, masking out the rest of the stage. Rotating sets tried to approximate the instantaneous displacement of the camera eye. (More recently, reports have come of ingenious lighting techniques used by the Gorky Theatre in Leningrad, directed since 1956 by Georgy Tovstonogov, which allow for incredibly rapid scene changes taking place behind a horizontal curtain of light.)

Today traffic seems, with few exceptions, entirely one way: film to theatre. Particularly in France and in Central and Eastern Europe, the staging of many plays is inspired by the movies. The aim of adapting neo-cinematic devices for the stage (I exclude the outright use of films within the theatre production) seems mainly to tighten up the theatrical experience, to approximate the cinema's absolute control of the flow and location of the audience's attention. But the conception can be even more directly cinematic. An example is Josef Svoboda's production of *The Insect Play* by the Čapek brothers at the Czech National Theatre in Prague (recently seen in London), which frankly attempted to install a mediated vision upon the stage, equivalent to the discontinuous intensifications of the camera eye. According to a London critic's account, "the set consisted of two huge, faceted mirrors slung at an angle to the stage, so that they reflect whatever happens there defracted as if through a decanter stopper or the colossally magnified eye of a fly. Any figure placed at the base of their angle becomes multiplied from floor to proscenium; further out, and you find yourself viewing it not only face to face but from overhead, the vantage point of a camera slung to a bird or a helicopter."

––––––

Marinetti was perhaps the first to propose the use of films as one element in a theatre experience. Writing between 1910 and 1914, he envisaged the theatre as a final synthesis of all the arts; and as such it had to draw in the newest art form, movies. No doubt the cinema also recommended itself for inclusion because of the priority Marinetti gave to existing forms of popular entertainment, such as the variety theatre and the *café chantant*. (He called his projected total art form "the Futurist Variety Theatre.") And at that time scarcely anyone considered cinema anything but a vulgar art.

After World War I, similar ideas appear frequently. In the total-theatre projects of the Bauhaus group in the 1920's (Gropius, Piscator, etc.) film had an important place. Meyerhold insisted on its use in the theatre, describing his program as fulfilling Wagner's once "wholly utopian" proposals to "use all means available from the other arts." Alban Berg specified that a silent film of the developing story was to be projected in the middle of Act 2 of his opera *Lulu*. By now, the employment of film in theatre has a fairly long history which includes the "living newspaper" of the 1930's, "epic theatre," and Happenings. This year marked the introduction of a film sequence into Broadway-level theatre. In two successful musicals, London's *Come Spy with Me* and New York's *Superman*, both parodic in tone, the action is interrupted to lower a screen and run off a movie showing the pop-art hero's exploits.

But thus far the use of film within live theatre events has tended to be stereotyped. Film is often employed as *document*, supportive of or redundant to the live stage events (as in Brecht's productions in East Berlin). Its other principal use is as *hallucinant*; recent examples are Bob Whitman's Happenings, and a new kind of nightclub situation, the mixed-media discothèque (Andy Warhol's The Plastic Inevitable, Murray the K's World). From the point of view of theatre, the interpolation of film into the theatre experience may be enlarging. But in terms of what cinema is capable of, it seems a reductive, monotonous use of film.

What Panofsky perhaps could not have realized when he wrote his essay is that much more than the "nature" of a specific art "medium" is at stake. The relation between film and theatre involves not simply a static definition of the two arts, but sensitivity to the possible course of their radicalization.

Every interesting aesthetic tendency now is a species of radicalism. The question each artist must ask is: What is *my* radicalism, the one dictated by *my* gifts and temperament? This doesn't mean all contemporary artists believe that art progresses. A radical position isn't necessarily a forward-looking position.

Consider the two principal radical positions in the arts today. One recommends the breaking down of distinctions between genres; the arts would eventuate in one art, consisting of many different kinds of behavior going on at the same time, a vast behavioral magma or synesthesia. The other position recommends the maintaining and clarifying of barriers between the arts, by the intensification of what each art distinctively is; painting must use only those means which pertain to painting, music only those which are musical, novels those which pertain to the novel and to no other literary form, etc. The two positions are, in a sense, irreconcilable—except that both are invoked to support the perennial modern quest for the definitive art form.

An art may be proposed as definitive because it is considered the most rigorous or most fundamental. For these reasons, Schopenhauer suggested and Pater asserted that all art aspires to the condition of music. More recently, the thesis that all the arts are leading toward one art has been advanced by enthusiasts of the cinema. The candidacy of film is founded on its being both so exact and, potentially, so complex a combination of music, literature, and the image.

Or, an art may be proposed as definitive because it is held to be most inclusive. This is the basis of the destiny for theatre held out by Wagner, Marinetti, Artaud, Cage—all of whom envisage theatre as a total art, potentially conscripting all the arts into its service. And as the ideas of synesthesia continue to proliferate among painters, sculptors, architects, and composers, theatre remains the favored candidate for the role of summative art. In this conception, theatre's role must disparage the claims of cinema. Partisans of theatre would argue that while music, painting, dance, cinema, and utterance can all converge on a "stage," the film object can only become bigger (multiple screens, 360 degree projection, etc.) or longer in duration or internally more articulated and complex. Theatre can be anything, everything; in the end, films can only be more of what they specifically (that is to say, cinematically) are.

Underlying the more grandiose apocalyptic expectations for both arts is a common animus. In 1923 Béla Balázs, anticipating in great detail the thesis of Marshall McLuhan, described movies as the herald of a new "visual culture" which will give us back our bodies, and particularly our faces, which have been rendered illegible, soulless, unexpressive by the centuries-old ascendancy of "print." An animus against literature, against the printing press and its "culture of concepts," also informs most interesting thinking about the theatre in our time.

No definition or characterization of theatre and cinema can be taken for granted—not even the apparently self-evident observation that both cinema and theatre are temporal arts. In theatre and cinema, like music (and unlike painting), everything is *not* present all at once. But there are significant developments today pointing up the atemporal aspect of these forms. The allure of mixed-media forms in theatre suggests not only a more elongated and more complex "drama" (like Wagnerian opera) but also a more compact theatre experience which approaches the condition of painting. This prospect of compactness is broached by Marinetti; he calls it simultaneity, a leading notion of Futurist aesthetics. As the final synthesis of all the arts, theatre "would use the new twentieth century devices of electricity and the cinema; this would enable plays to be extremely short, since all these technical means would enable the theatrical synthesis to be achieved in the shortest possible space of time, as all the elements could be presented simultaneously."

The source of the idea of art as an act of violence pervading cinema and theatre is the aesthetics of Futurism and of Surrealism; its principal texts are, for theatre, the writings of Artaud and, for cinema, two films of Luis Buñuel, *L'Age d'Or* and *Un Chien Andalou*. (More recent examples: the early plays of Ionesco, at least as conceived; the "cinema of cruelty" of Hitchcock, Clouzot, Franju, Robert Aldrich, Polanski; work by the Living Theatre; some of the neo-cinematic light shows in experimental theatres and discothèques; the sound of late Cage and LaMonte Young.) The relation of art to an audience understood to be passive, inert, surfeited, can only be assault. Art becomes identical with aggression.

However understandable and valuable this theory of art as an assault on the audience is today (like the complementary notion of art as ritual), one must continue to question it, particularly in the theatre. For it can become as much a convention as anything else and end, like all theatrical conventions, by reinforcing rather than challenging the deadness of the audience. (As Wagner's ideology of a total theatre played its role in confirming the philistinism of German culture.)

Moreover, the depth of the assault must be assessed honestly. In the theatre, this means not "diluting" Artaud. Artaud's writings express the demand for a totally open (therefore flayed, self-cruel) consciousness of which theatre would be one adjunct or instrument. No work in the theatre has yet amounted to this. Thus, Peter Brook has astutely and forthrightly disclaimed that his company's work in the "Theatre of Cruelty," which culminated in his celebrated production of *Marat/Sade*, is genuinely Artaudian. It is Artaudian, he says, in a trivial sense only. (Trivial from Artaud's point of view, not from ours.)

For some time, all useful ideas in art have been extremely sophisticated. Take, for example, the idea that everything is what it is and not another thing: a painting is a painting; sculpture is sculpture; a poem is a poem, not prose. Or the complementary idea: a painting can be "literary" or sculptural, a poem can be prose, theatre can emulate and incorporate cinema, cinema can be theatrical.

We need a new idea. It will probably be a very simple one. Will we be able to recognize it?

(1966)

Bergman's Persona

ONE impulse is to take Bergman's masterpiece for granted. Since 1960 at least, with the breakthrough into new narrative forms propagated with most notoriety (if not greatest distinction) by *Last Year in Marienbad*, film audiences have continued to be educated by the elliptical and complex. As Resnais' imagination was subsequently to surpass itself in *Muriel*, a succession of ever more difficult and accomplished films have turned up in recent years. But such good fortune releases nobody who cares about films from acclaiming work as original and triumphant as *Persona*. It is depressing that this film has received only a fraction of the attention it deserves since it opened in New York, London, and Paris.

To be sure, some of the paltriness of the critics' reaction may be more a response to the signature that *Persona* carries than to the film itself. That signature has come to mean a prodigal, tirelessly productive career; a rather facile, often merely beautiful, by now (it seemed) almost oversize body of work; a lavishly inventive, sensual, yet melodramatic talent, employed with what appeared to be a certain complacency, and prone to embarrassing displays of intellectual bad taste. From the Fellini of the North, exacting filmgoers could hardly be blamed for not expecting, ever, a truly great film. But *Persona* happily forces one to put aside such dismissive preconceptions about its author.

The rest of the neglect of *Persona* may be set down to emotional squeamishness; the film, like much of Bergman's recent work, bears an almost defiling charge of personal agony. This is particularly true of *The Silence*—most accomplished, by far, of the films Bergman has made before this one. And *Persona* draws liberally on the themes and schematic cast established in *The Silence*. (The principal characters in both films are two women bound together in a passionate agonized relationship, one of whom has a pitiably neglected small son. Both films take up the themes of the scandal of the erotic; the polarities of violence and powerlessness, reason and unreason, language and silence, the intelligible and the unintelligible.) But Bergman's new film ventures at least as much beyond *The Silence* as that film is an advance, in its emotional power and subtlety, over all his previous work.

That achievement gives, for the present moment, the measure of a work which is undeniably "difficult." *Persona* is bound to trouble, perplex, and frustrate most filmgoers—at least as much as *Marienbad* did in its day. Or so one would suppose. But, heaping imperturbability upon indifference, critical reaction to *Persona* has shied away from associating anything very baffling with the film. The critics have allowed, mildly, that the latest Bergman is unnecessarily obscure. Some add that this time he's overdone the mood of unremitting bleakness. It's intimated that with this film he has ventured out of his depth, exchanging art for artiness. But the difficulties and rewards of *Persona* are much more formidable than such banal objections would suggest.

Of course, evidence of these difficulties is available anyway—even in the absence of more pertinent controversy. Why else all the discrepancies and just plain misrepresentations in the accounts given by critics of what actually happens during the film? Like *Marienbad*, *Persona* seems defiantly obscure. Its general look has nothing of the built-in, abstract evocativeness of the château in Resnais' film; the space and furnishings of *Persona* are anti-romantic, cool, mundane, clinical (in one sense, literally so), and bourgeois-modern. But no less of a mystery is lodged in this setting. Actions and dialogue are given which the viewer is bound to find puzzling, being unable to decipher whether certain scenes take place in the past, present, or future; and whether certain images and episodes belong to reality or fantasy.

One common approach to a film presenting difficulties of this now familiar sort is to treat such distinctions as irrelevant and rule that the film is actually all of one piece. This usually means situating the action of the film in a merely (or wholly) mental universe. But this approach only covers over the difficulty, it seems to me. *Within* the structure of what is shown, the elements continue being related to each other in the ways that originally suggested to the viewer that some events were realistic while others were visionary (whether fantasy, dream, hallucination, or extra-worldly visitation). Causal connections observed in one portion of the film are still being flouted in another part; the film still gives several equally persuasive but mutually exclusive explanations of the same event. These discordant internal relations only get transposed, intact, but not reconciled, when the whole film is relocated in the mind. I should argue that it is no more helpful to describe *Persona* as a wholly subjective film—an action taking place within a single character's head—than it was (how easy to see that now) in elucidating *Marienbad*, a film whose disregard for conventional chronology and a clearly delineated border between fantasy and reality could scarcely have constituted more of a provocation than *Persona*.

But neither is it any sounder to approach this film in search of an objective narrative, ignoring the fact that *Persona* is strewn with signs that cancel each other. Even the most skillful attempt to arrange a single, plausible anecdote out of the film must leave out or contradict some of its key sections, images, and procedures. Attempted less skillfully, it has led to the flat, impoverished, and partly inaccurate account of Bergman's film promulgated by most reviewers and critics.

According to this account, *Persona* is a psychological chamber drama which chronicles the relation between two women. One is a successful actress, evidently in her mid-thirties, named Elizabeth Vogler (Liv Ullmann), now suffering from an enigmatic mental collapse whose chief symptoms are muteness and a near-catatonic lassitude. The other is the pretty young nurse of twenty-five named Alma (Bibi Andersson) charged with caring for Elizabeth—first at the mental hospital and then at the beach cottage loaned to them for this purpose by the woman psychiatrist at the hospital who is Elizabeth's doctor and Alma's supervisor. What happens in the course of the film, according to the critics' consensus, is that, through some mysterious process, the two women exchange identities. The ostensibly stronger one, Alma, becomes weaker, gradually assuming the problems and confusions of her patient, while the sick woman felled by despair (or psychosis) eventually regains her power of speech and returns to her former life. (We don't see this exchange consummated. What is shown at the end of *Persona* looks like an agonized stalemate. But it was reported that the film, until shortly before it was released, contained a brief closing scene that showed Elizabeth on the stage again, apparently completely recovered. From this, presumably, the viewer could infer that the nurse was now mute and had taken on the burden of Elizabeth's despair.)

Proceeding from this constructed version, half "story" and half "meaning," critics have read off a number of further meanings. Some regard the transaction between Elizabeth and Alma as illustrating an impersonal law that operates intermittently in human affairs; no ultimate responsibility pertains to either of them. Others posit a conscious cannibalism of the innocent Alma by the actress—and thus read the film as a parable of the predatory, demonic energies of the artist, incorrigibly scavenging life for raw material.* Other critics move quickly to an even more general plane, extracting from *Persona* a diagnosis of the contemporary dissociation of personality, a demonstration of the inevitable failure of good will and trust, and predictable correct views on such matters as the alienated affluent society, the nature of madness, psychiatry and its limitations, the American war on Vietnam, the Western legacy of sexual guilt, and the Six Million. (Then the critics often go on, as Michel Cournot did several months ago in *Le Nouvel Observateur*, to chide Bergman for this vulgar didacticism which they have imputed to him.)

But even when turned into a story, I think, this prevailing account of *Persona* grossly oversimplifies and misrepresents. True, Alma does seem to grow progressively more insecure, more vulnerable; in the course of the film she is reduced to fits of hysteria, cruelty, anxiety, childish dependence, and (probably) delusion. It's also true that Elizabeth gradually becomes

*For example, Richard Corliss in the Summer 1967 *Film Quarterly*: "Slowly Alma comes to understand that she is just another of Elizabeth's 'props.'" True, in the sense that Alma, after reading a letter Elizabeth writes to the psychiatrist does entertain this bitter idea of what Elizabeth is up to. Not true, though, in the sense that the viewer lacks the evidence for coming to any definite conclusions about what's really going on. Yet this is precisely what Corliss does assume, so that he can then go on to make a statement about Elizabeth which isn't backed up by anything said or shown in the film. "The actress had borne a child to help her 'live the part' of a mother, but was disgusted by the boy's determination to stay alive after the role was completed. Now she wants to toss Alma away like an old prompt book."

The same point about Elizabeth as an exemplar of the parasitical, unscrupulous energies of the artist is made by Vernon Young in his unfavorable notice of the film in the Summer 1967 *Hudson Review*. Both Corliss and Young point out that Elizabeth shares the same last name, Vogler, with the magician-artist in *The Magician*.

stronger, that is, more active, more responsive; though her change is far subtler and, until virtually the end, she still refuses to speak. But all this is hardly tantamount to the "exchange" of attributes and identities that critics have glibly spoken of. Nor is it established, as most critics have assumed, that Alma, however much she does come with pain and longing to identify herself with the actress, takes on Elizabeth's dilemmas, whatever those may be. (They're far from made clear.)

My own view is that the temptation to invent more story ought to be resisted. Take, for instance, the scene that starts with the abrupt presence of a middle-aged man wearing dark glasses (Gunnar Björnstrand) near the beach cottage where Elizabeth and Alma have been living in isolation. All we see is that he approaches Alma, addressing her and continuing to call her, despite her protests, by the name Elizabeth; that he tries to embrace her, ignoring her struggle to free herself; that throughout this scene Elizabeth's impassive face is never more than a few inches away; that Alma suddenly yields to his embraces, saying, "Yes, I am Elizabeth" (Elizabeth is still watching intently), and goes to bed with him amid a torrent of endearments. Then we see the two women together (shortly after?); they are alone, behaving as if nothing has happened. This sequence can be taken as illustrating Alma's growing identification with Elizabeth, and gauging the extent of the process by which Alma is learning (really? in her imagination?) to become Elizabeth. While Elizabeth has perhaps voluntarily renounced being an actress by becoming mute, Alma is involuntarily and painfully engaged in becoming that Elizabeth Vogler, the performer, who no longer exists. Still, nothing we see justifies describing this scene as a real event—something happening in the course of the plot on the same level as the initial removal of the two women to the beach cottage.* But neither can we be absolutely sure that this, or something like it, isn't taking place. After all,

* Which is what most critics have done with this scene: assume that it's a real event and insert it into the "action" of the film. Richard Corliss disposes of the matter, without a touch of uncertainty, thus: "When Elizabeth's blind husband visits, he mistakes Alma for his wife [and] they make love." But the only evidence for the husband being blind is that the man we see wears dark glasses—plus the critic's wish to find a "realistic" explanation for such implausible goings-on.

we do see it happening. (And it's the nature of cinema to confer on all events, without indications to the contrary, an equivalent degree of reality: everything shown on the screen is *there*, present.)

The difficulty of *Persona* stems from the fact that Bergman withholds the kind of clear signals for sorting out fantasies from reality offered, for example, by Buñuel in *Belle de Jour*. Buñuel puts in the clues; he wants the viewer to be able to decipher his film. The insufficiency of the clues Bergman has planted must be taken to indicate that he intends the film to remain partly encoded. The viewer can only move toward, but never achieve, certainty about the action. However, so far as the distinction between fantasy and reality is of any use in understanding *Persona*, I should argue that much more than the critics have allowed of what happens in and around the beach cottage is most plausibly understood as Alma's fantasy. One prime bit of evidence for this thesis is a sequence occurring soon after the two women arrive at the seaside. It's the sequence in which, after we have seen Elizabeth enter Alma's room and stand beside her and stroke her hair, we see Alma, pale, troubled, asking Elizabeth the next morning, "Did you come to my room last night?" and Elizabeth, slightly quizzical, anxious, shaking her head no. Now, there seems no reason to doubt Elizabeth's answer. The viewer isn't given any evidence of a malevolent plan on Elizabeth's part to undermine Alma's confidence in her own sanity; nor any evidence for doubting Elizabeth's memory or sanity in the ordinary sense. But if that is the case, two important points have been established early in the film. One is that Alma is hallucinating—and, presumably, will continue doing so. The other is that hallucinations or visions will appear on the screen with the same rhythms, the same look of objective reality as something "real." (However, some clues, too complex to describe here, are given in the lighting of certain scenes.) And once these points are granted, it seems highly plausible to take at least the scene with Elizabeth's husband as Alma's fantasy, as well as several scenes which depict a charged, trancelike physical contact between the two women.

But sorting out what is fantasy from what is real in *Persona* (i.e., what Alma imagines from what may be taken as really happening) is a minor achievement. And it quickly becomes a misleading one, unless subsumed under the larger issue of the form of exposition or narration employed by the film. As I have already suggested, *Persona* is constructed according to a form that resists being reduced to a story—say, the story about the relation (however ambiguous and abstract) between two women named Elizabeth and Alma, a patient and a nurse, a star and an ingenue, *alma* (soul) and *persona* (mask). Such reduction to a story means, in the end, a reduction of Bergman's film to the single dimension of psychology. Not that the psychological dimension isn't there. It is. But to understand *Persona*, the viewer must go beyond the psychological point of view.

This seems mandatory because Bergman allows the audience to interpret Elizabeth's mute condition in several different ways—as involuntary mental breakdown and as voluntary moral decision leading either toward a self-purification or toward suicide. But whatever the background of her condition, Bergman wishes to involve the viewer much more in the sheer fact of it than in its causes. In *Persona*, muteness is first of all a fact with a certain psychic and moral weight, a fact which initiates its own kind of psychic and moral causality upon an "other."

I am inclined to impute a privileged status to the speech made by the psychiatrist to Elizabeth before she departs with Alma to the beach cottage. The psychiatrist tells the silent, stony-faced Elizabeth that she has understood her case. She has grasped that Elizabeth wants to be sincere, not to play a role, not to lie; to make the inner and the outer come together. And that, having rejected suicide as a solution, she has decided to be mute. The psychiatrist concludes by advising Elizabeth to bide her time and live her experience through, predicting that eventually the actress will renounce her muteness and return to the world . . . But even if one treats this speech as setting forth a privileged view, it would be a mistake to take it as the key to *Persona*; or even to assume that the psychiatrist's thesis wholly explains Elizabeth's condition. (The doctor could be wrong, or, at the least, be simplifying the matter.) By placing this speech so early in the film (even earlier, a superficial account of Elizabeth's symptoms is addressed to Alma when the doctor first assigns her to the case), and by never referring explicitly to this "explanation" again, Bergman has, in effect, both taken account of psychology and dispensed with it. Without ruling out psychological explanation, he consigns to a relatively minor place any consideration of the role the actress's *motives* have in the action.

Persona takes a position beyond psychology—as it does, in an analogous sense, beyond eroticism. It certainly contains the materials of an erotic subject, such as the "visit" of Elizabeth's husband that ends with his going to bed with Alma while Elizabeth looks on. There is, above all, the connection between the two women themselves which, in its feverish proximity, its caresses, its sheer passionateness (avowed by Alma in word, gesture, and fantasy) could hardly fail, it would seem, to suggest a powerful, if largely inhibited, sexual involvement. But, in fact, what might be sexual in feeling is largely transposed into something beyond sexuality, beyond eroticism even. The most purely sexual episode in the film is the scene in which Alma, sitting across the room from Elizabeth, tells the story of an impromptu beach orgy; Alma speaks, transfixed, reliving the memory and at the same time consciously delivering up this shameful secret to Elizabeth as her greatest gift of love. Entirely through discourse and without any resort to images (through a flashback), a violent sexual atmosphere is generated. But this sexuality has nothing to do with the "present" of the film, and the relationship between the two women. In this respect, *Persona* makes a remarkable modification of the structure of *The Silence*. In the earlier film, the love-hate relationship between the two sisters projected an unmistakable sexual energy—particularly the feelings of the older sister (Ingrid Thulin). In *Persona*, Bergman has achieved a more interesting situation by delicately excising or transcending the possible sexual implications of the tie between the two women. It is a remarkable feat of moral and psychological poise. While maintaining the indeterminacy of the situation (from a psychological point of view), Bergman does not give the impression of evading the issue, and presents nothing that is psychologically improbable.

The advantages of keeping the psychological aspects of *Persona* indeterminate (while internally credible) are that Bergman can do many other things besides tell a story. Instead of a full-blown story, he presents something that is, in one sense, cruder and, in another, more abstract: a body of material, a subject. The function of the subject or material may be as much its opacity, its multiplicity, as the ease with which it yields itself to being incarnated in a determinate action or plot.

In a work constituted along these principles, the action would appear intermittent, porous, shot through intimations of absence, of what could not be univocally said. This doesn't mean that the narration has forfeited "sense." But it does mean that sense isn't necessarily tied to a determinate plot. Alternatively, there is the possibility of an extended narration composed of events that are not (wholly) explicated but are, nevertheless, possible and may even have taken place. The forward movement of such a narrative might be measured by reciprocal relations between its parts—e.g., displacements—rather than by ordinary realistic (mainly psychological) causality. There might exist what could be called a dormant plot. Still, critics have better things to do than ferret out the story line as if the author had—through mere clumsiness or error or frivolity or lack of craft—concealed it. In such narratives, it is a question not of a plot that has been mislaid but of one that has been (at least in part) annulled. That intention, whether conscious on the artist's part or merely implicit in the work, should be taken at face value and respected.

Take the matter of information. One tactic upheld by traditional narrative is to give "full" information (by which I mean all that is needed, according to the standard of relevance set up in the "world" proposed by the narrative), so that the ending of the viewing or reading experience coincides, ideally, with full satisfaction of one's desire to know, to understand what happened and why. (This is, of course, a highly manipulated quest for knowledge. The business of the artist is to convince his audience that what they haven't learned at the end they *can't* know, or shouldn't *care* about knowing.) In contrast, one of the salient features of new narratives is a deliberate, calculated frustration of the desire to know. Did anything happen last year at Marienbad? What did become of the girl in *L'Avventura*? Where is Alma going when she boards a bus alone toward the close of *Persona*?

Once it is conceived that the desire to know may be (in part) systematically thwarted, the old expectations about plotting no longer hold. Such films (or comparable works of prose fiction) can't be expected to supply many of the familiar satisfactions of traditional narrations, such as being "dramatic." At first it may seem that a plot still remains, only it's being related at an oblique, uncomfortable angle, where vision is obscured. Actually, the plot isn't there at all in the old sense; the point of these new works is not to tantalize but to involve the audience more directly in other matters, for instance, in the very processes of knowing and seeing. (An eminent precursor of this concept of narration is Flaubert; the persistent use of off-center detail in the descriptions in *Madame Bovary* is one instance of the method.)

The result of the new narration, then, is a tendency to de-dramatize. *Journey to Italy*, for example, tells what is ostensibly a story. But it is a story which proceeds by omissions. The audience is being haunted, as it were, by the sense of a lost or absent meaning to which even the artist himself has no access. The avowal of agnosticism on the artist's part may look like frivolity or contempt for the audience. Antonioni enraged many people by saying that he didn't know himself what happened to the missing girl in *L'Avventura*—whether she had, for instance, committed suicide or run away. But this attitude should be taken with the utmost seriousness. When the artist declares that he "knows" no more than the audience does, he is saying that all the meaning resides in the work itself, that there is nothing "behind" it. Such works seem to lack sense or meaning only to the extent that entrenched critical attitudes have established as a dictum for the narrative arts (cinema as well as prose literature) that meaning resides solely in this surplus of "reference" outside the work—to the "real world" or to the artist's "intention." But this is, at best, an arbitrary ruling. The meaning of a narration is not identical with a paraphrase of the values associated by an ideal audience with the "real-life" equivalents or sources of the plot elements, or with the attitudes projected by the artist toward these elements. Neither is meaning (whether in films, fiction, or theatre) a function of a determinate plot. Other kinds of narration are possible besides those based on a story, in which the fundamental problem is the treatment of the plot line and the construction of characters. For instance, the material can be treated as a *thematic resource*, one from which different (and perhaps concurrent) narrative structures are derived as variations. But inevitably, the formal mandates of such a construction must differ from those of a story (or even a set of parallel stories). The difference will probably appear most striking in the treatment of time.

A story involves the audience in what happens, how a situation comes out. Movement is decisively linear, whatever the meanderings and digressions. One moves from A to B, then to look forward to C, even as C (if the affair is satisfactorily managed) points one's interest in the direction of D. Each link in the chain is, so to speak, self-abolishing—once it has served its turn. In contrast, the development of a theme-and-variation narrative is much less linear. The linear movement can't be altogether suppressed, since the experience of the work remains an event in time (the time of viewing or reading). But this forward movement can be sharply qualified by a competing retrograde principle, which could take the form, say, of continual backward- and cross-references. Such a work would invite reexperiencing, multiple viewing. It would ask the spectator or reader ideally to position himself simultaneously at several different points in the narrative.

Such a demand, characteristic of theme-and-variation narratives, obviates the necessity of establishing a conventional chronological scheme. Instead, time may appear in the guise of a perpetual present; or events may form a conundrum which makes it impossible to distinguish exactly between past, present, and future. *Marienbad* and Robbe-Grillet's *L'Immortelle* are stringent examples of the latter procedure. In *Persona*, Bergman uses a mixed approach. While the treatment of time sequence in the body of the film seems roughly realistic or chronological, at the beginning and close of the film distinctions of "before" and "after" are drastically bleached out, almost indecipherable.

In my own view, the construction of *Persona* is best described in terms of this variations-on-a-theme form. The theme is that of *doubling*; the variations are those that follow from the leading possibilities of that theme (on both a formal and a psychological level) such as duplication, inversion, reciprocal exchange, unity and fission, and repetition. The action cannot be univocally paraphrased. It's correct to speak of *Persona* in terms of the fortunes of two characters named Elizabeth and Alma who are engaged in a desperate duel of identities. But it is equally pertinent to treat *Persona* as relating the duel between two mythical parts of a single self: the corrupted person who acts (Elizabeth) and the ingenuous soul (Alma) who founders in contact with corruption.

A sub-theme of doubling is the contrast between hiding and showing forth. The Latin word *persona*, from which the English "person" derives, means the mask worn by an actor. To be a person, then, is to possess a mask; and in *Persona*, both women wear masks. Elizabeth's mask is her muteness. Alma's mask is her health, her optimism, her normal life (she is engaged; she likes and is good at her work, etc.). But in the course of the film, both masks crack.

To summarize this drama by saying that the violence that the actress has done to herself is transferred to Alma is too simple. Violence and the sense of horror and impotence are, more truly, the residual experiences of consciousness subjected to an ordeal. By not just telling a "story" about the psychic ordeal of two women, Bergman is using that ordeal as a constituent element of his main theme. And that theme of doubling appears to be no less a formal idea than a psychological one. As I have already stressed, Bergman has withheld enough information about the story of the two women to make it impossible to determine clearly the main outlines, much less all, of what passes between them. Further, he has introduced a number of reflections about the nature of representation (the status of the image, of the word, of action, of the film medium itself). *Persona* is not just a representation of transactions between the two characters, Alma and Elizabeth, but a meditation on the film which is "about" them.

The most explicit parts of this meditation are the opening and closing sequences, in which Bergman tries to create the film as an object: a finite object, a made object, a fragile, perishable object, and therefore something existing in space as well as time.

Persona begins with darkness. Then two points of light gradually gain in brightness, until we see that they're the two carbons of the arc lamp; after this, a portion of the leader flashes by. Then follows a suite of rapid images, some barely identifiable—a chase scene from a slapstick silent film; an erect penis; a nail being hammered into the palm of a hand; a view from the rear of a stage of a heavily made-up actress declaiming to

the footlights and darkness beyond (we see this image soon
again and know that it's Elizabeth playing her last role, that
of Electra); the self-immolation of a Buddhist monk in South
Vietnam; assorted dead bodies in a morgue. All these images
go by very rapidly, mostly too fast to see; but gradually they
slow down, as if consenting to adjust to the duration in which
the viewer can comfortably perceive. Then follow the final set
of images—run off at normal speed. We see a thin, unhealthy-
looking boy around eleven lying prone under a sheet on a hospital cot against the wall of a bare room; the viewer at first is
bound to associate to the corpses just shown. But the boy stirs,
awkwardly kicks off the sheet, turns on his stomach, puts on a
pair of large round glasses, takes out a book, and begins to read.
Then we see before him an indecipherable blur, very faint, but
on its way to becoming an image, the larger-than-life but never
very distinct face of a beautiful woman. Slowly, tentatively, as
in a trance, the boy reaches up and begins to caress the image.
(The surface he touches suggests a movie screen, but also a
portrait and a mirror.)

Who is that boy? Most people have assumed he is Elizabeth's
son, because we learn later that she does have a son (whose
snapshot she tears up when her husband sends it to her in the
hospital) and because they think the face on the screen is the
actress's face. Actually, it isn't. Not only is the image far from
clear (this is obviously deliberate) but Bergman modulates the
image back and forth between Elizabeth's face and Alma's. If
only for this reason, it seems facile to assign the boy a literal
identity. Rather, I think, his identity is something we shouldn't
expect to know.

In any case, the boy is not seen again until the close of the
film when more briefly, after the action is finished, there is a
complementary montage of fragmented images, ending with
the child again reaching caressingly toward the huge blurry
blow-up of a woman's face. Then Bergman cuts to the shot of
the incandescent arc lamp, showing the reverse of the phenomenon which opens the film. The carbons begin to fade; slowly
the light goes out. The film dies, as it were, before our eyes. It
dies as an object or a thing does, declaring itself to be used up,
and thereby virtually independent of the volition of the maker.

Any account which leaves out or dismisses as incidental how *Persona* begins and ends hasn't been talking about the film that Bergman made. Far from being extraneous or pretentious, as many reviewers found it, the so-called frame of *Persona* is, it seems to me, a central statement of the motif of aesthetic self-reflexiveness that runs through the entire film. The element of self-reflexiveness in *Persona* is anything but an arbitrary concern, one superadded to the dramatic action. For one thing, it is the most explicit statement on the formal level of the theme of doubling or duplication present on a psychological level in the transactions between Alma and Elizabeth. The formal "doublings" in *Persona* are the largest extension of the theme of doubling which furnishes the material of the film.

Perhaps the most striking single episode, in which the formal and psychological resonances of the double theme are played out most starkly, is Alma's long description of Elizabeth's maternity and her relation to her son. This monologue is repeated twice in its entirety, the first time showing Elizabeth as she listens, the second time showing Alma as she speaks. The sequence ends spectacularly, with the close-up of a double or composite face, half Elizabeth's and half Alma's.

Here Bergman is pointing up the paradoxical promise of film—namely, that it always gives the illusion of a voyeuristic access to an untampered reality, a neutral view of things as they are. What is filmed is always, in some sense, a "document." But what contemporary film-makers more and more often show is the process of seeing itself, giving grounds or evidence for several different ways of seeing the same thing, which the viewer may entertain concurrently or successively.

Bergman's use of this idea in *Persona* is strikingly original, but the larger intention is a familiar one. In the ways that Bergman made his film self-reflexive, self-regarding, ultimately self-engorging, we should recognize not a private whim but the expression of a well-established tendency. For it is precisely the energy for this sort of "formalist" concern with the nature and paradoxes of the medium itself which was unleashed when the nineteenth-century formal structures of plot and characters (with their presumption of a much less complex reality than that envisaged by the contemporary consciousness) were demoted. What is commonly patronized as an overexquisite self-consciousness in contemporary art, leading to a species of auto-cannibalism, can be seen—less pejoratively—as the liberation of new energies of thought and sensibility.

This, for me, is the promise behind the familiar thesis that locates the difference between traditional and new cinema in the altered status of the camera. In the aesthetic of traditional films, the camera tried to remain unperceived, to efface itself before the spectacle it was rendering. In contrast, what counts as new cinema can be recognized, as Pasolini has remarked, by the "felt presence of the camera." (Needless to say, new cinema doesn't mean just cinema of the last decade. To cite only two predecessors, recall Vertov's *The Man with the Camera* [1929], with its Pirandellian playfulness with the contrast between film as a physical object and film as the live image, and Benjamin Christensen's *Häxan* [1921], with its leap back and forth between fiction and journalistic documentary.) But Bergman goes beyond Pasolini's criterion, inserting into the viewer's consciousness the felt present of the film as an object. This happens not only at the beginning and end but in the middle of *Persona*, when the image—a shot of Alma's horrified face—cracks, like a mirror, then burns. When the next scene begins immediately afterward (as if nothing had happened), the viewer has not only an almost indelible after-image of Alma's anguish but a sense of added shock, a formal-magical apprehension of the film, as if it had collapsed under the weight of registering such drastic suffering and then had been, as it were, magically reconstituted.

Bergman's intention, in the beginning and end of *Persona* and in this terrifying caesura in the middle, is quite different from—indeed, it is the romantic opposite of—Brecht's intention of alienating the audience by supplying continual reminders that what they are watching is theatre. Bergman seems only marginally concerned with the thought that it might be salutary for audiences to be reminded that they are watching a film (an artifact, something made), not reality. Rather, he is making a statement about the complexity of what can be represented, an assertion that the deep, unflinching knowledge of anything will in the end prove destructive. A character in Bergman's films who perceives something intensely eventually consumes what he knows, uses it up, is forced to move on to other things.

This principle of intensity at the root of Bergman's sensibility determines the specific ways in which he uses new narrative forms. Anything like the vivacity of Godard, the intellectual innocence of *Jules and Jim*, the lyricism of Bertolucci's *Before the Revolution* and Skolimowski's *Le Départ* are outside his range. Bergman's work is characterized by slowness, deliberateness of pacing—something like the heaviness of Flaubert. Hence, the excruciatingly unmodulated quality of *Persona* (and of *The Silence* before it), a quality only very superficially described as pessimism. It is not that Bergman is pessimistic about life and the human situation—as if it were a question of certain opinions—but rather that the quality of his sensibility, when he is faithful to it, has only a single subject: the depths in which consciousness drowns. If the maintenance of personality requires safeguarding the integrity of masks, and the truth about a person always means his unmasking, cracking the mask, then the truth about life as a whole is the shattering of the whole façade—behind which lies an absolute cruelty.

It is here, I think, that one must locate the ostensibly political allusions in *Persona*. Bergman's references to Vietnam and the Six Million are quite different from the references to the Algerian War, Vietnam, China in the films of Godard. Unlike Godard, Bergman is not a topical or historically oriented film-maker. Elizabeth watching a newsreel on TV of a bonze in Saigon immolating himself, or staring at the famous photograph of a little boy from the Warsaw Ghetto being led off to be slaughtered, are, for Bergman, above all, images of total violence, of unredeemed cruelty. They occur in *Persona* as images of what cannot be imaginatively encompassed or digested, rather than as occasions for right political and moral thoughts. In their function, these images don't differ from the earlier flashbacks of a palm into which a nail is being hammered or of the anonymous bodies in a morgue. History or politics enters *Persona* only in the form of pure violence. Bergman makes an "aesthetic" use of violence—far from ordinary left-liberal propaganda.

The subject of *Persona* is the violence of the spirit. If the two women violate each other, each can be said to have at least as profoundly violated herself. In the final parallel to this theme, the film itself seems to be violated—to emerge out of and descend back into the chaos of "cinema" and film-as-object.

———

Bergman's film, profoundly upsetting, at moments terrifying, relates the horror of the dissolution of personality: Alma crying out to Elizabeth at one point, "I'm not you!" And it depicts the complementary horror of the theft (whether voluntary or involuntary is left unclear) of personality, which mythically is rendered as vampirism: we see Elizabeth kissing Alma's neck; at one point, Alma sucks Elizabeth's blood. Of course, the theme of the vampiristic exchanges of personal substance needn't be treated as a horror story. Think of the very different emotional range of this material in Henry James' *The Sacred Fount*. The most obvious difference between James' treatment and Bergman's is in the degree of felt suffering that is represented. For all their undeniably disagreeable aura, the vampiristic exchanges between the characters in James' late novel are represented as partly voluntary and, in some obscure way, just. Bergman rigorously excludes the realm of justice (in which characters get what they "deserve"). The spectator is not furnished, from some reliable outside point of view, with any idea of the true moral standing of Elizabeth and Alma; their enmeshment is a given, not the result of some prior situation we are allowed to understand; the mood is one of desperation, in which all attributions of voluntariness seem superficial. All we are given is a set of compulsions or gravitations, in which the two women founder, exchanging "strength" and "weakness."

But perhaps the main difference between Bergman's and James' treatment of this theme derives from their contrasting position with respect to language. As long as discourse continues in the James novel, the texture of the person continues. The continuity of language constitutes a bridge over the abyss of the loss of personality, the foundering of the personality in absolute despair. But in *Persona*, it is precisely language—its continuity—which is put in question. (Bergman is the more modern artist, and cinema is the natural home of those who suspect language, a ready vehicle for the vast weight of suspicion lodged in the contemporary sensibility against "the word." As the purification of language has become the particular task of modernist poetry and of prose writers like Stein, Beckett, and Robbe-Grillet, much of the new cinema has become a vehicle for those wishing to demonstrate the futility and duplicities of language.) The theme had already appeared in *The Silence*, with the incomprehensible language into which the translator sister descends, unable to communicate with the old porter who attends her when at the end of the film she lies dying in the empty hotel in the imaginary garrison city. But Bergman does not take the theme beyond the fairly banal range of the "failure of communication" of the soul isolated in pain, and the "silence" of abandonment and death. In *Persona*, the theme of the burden and the failure of language is developed in a much more complex way.

Persona takes the form of a virtual monologue. Besides Alma, there are only two other speaking characters: the psychiatrist and Elizabeth's husband; they appear very briefly. For most of the film we are with the two women, in isolation at the beach—and only one of them, Alma, is talking, talking shyly but incessantly. Since the actress has renounced speech as some sort of contaminating activity, the nurse has moved in to demonstrate the harmlessness and utility of speech. Though the verbalization of the world in which Alma is engaged always has something uncanny about it, it is at the beginning a wholly generous act, conceived for the benefit of her patient. But this soon changes. The actress's silence becomes a provocation, a temptation, a trap. What Bergman unfolds is a situation reminiscent of Strindberg's one-act play *The Stronger*, a duel between two people, one of whom is aggressively silent. And, as in the Strindberg play, the one who talks, who spills her soul, turns out to be weaker than the one who keeps silent. For the quality of that silence alters continually, becoming more and more potent: the mute woman keeps changing. Each of Alma's gestures—of trustful affection, of envy, of hostility—is voided by Elizabeth's relentless silence.

Alma is also betrayed by speech itself. Language is presented as an instrument of fraud and cruelty (the glaring sounds of the newscast; Elizabeth's painful letter to the psychiatrist, which Alma reads); as an instrument of unmasking (the psychiatrist's explanation of why Elizabeth has "chosen" silence; Alma's excoriating portrait of the secrets of Elizabeth's motherhood); as an instrument of self-revelation (Alma's confessional narrative of the impromptu beach orgy); and as art and artifice (the lines of Electra Elizabeth is delivering on stage when she suddenly goes silent; the radio drama Alma switches on in Elizabeth's hospital room that makes the actress smile). *Persona* demonstrates the lack of an appropriate language, a language that is genuinely full. All that remains is a language of lacunae, appropriate to a narrative strung along a set of gaps in the "explanation." In *Persona* these absences of utterance become more potent than words: the person who places uncritical faith in words is brought down from relative composure and self-confidence to hysterical anguish.

Here, indeed, is the most powerful instance of the motif of exchange. The actress creates a void by her silence. The nurse, by speaking, falls into it—depleting herself. Sickened at the vertigo opened up by the absence of language, Alma at one point begs Elizabeth just to repeat nonsense words and phrases that she hurls at her. But during all the time at the shore, despite every kind of tact, cajoling, and finally frantic pleading by Alma, Elizabeth refuses (obstinately? cruelly? helplessly?) to speak. She has only two lapses. Once when Alma, in a fury, threatens her with a pot of scalding water, the terrified Elizabeth backs against the wall and screams, "No, don't hurt me!" For the moment Alma is triumphant; having made her point, she puts down the pot. But Elizabeth becomes entirely silent again, until late in the film—here, the time sequence is indeterminate—in a brief sequence in the bare hospital room, which shows Alma bending over Elizabeth's bed, begging the actress to say one word. Impassively, Elizabeth complies. The word is "Nothing."

Bergman's treatment of the theme of language in *Persona* also suggests a comparison with films of Godard, particularly *Deux ou Trois Choses* (the café scene). Another example is the recent short film, *Anticipation*, a story of anti-utopia, set in a future world extrapolated from our own which is ruled by the system of "spécialisation intégrale"; in this world there are two kinds of prostitutes, one representing physical love ("gestes sans paroles") and the other representing sentimental love ("paroles sans gestes"). Compared with Bergman's narrative context, the mode of science-fiction fantasy in which Godard has cast his theme permits him both a greater abstraction and the possibility of a resolution of the problem (the divorce between language and love, mind and body) posed so abstractly, so "aesthetically," in the film. At the end of *Anticipation*, the talking prostitute learns to make love and the interplanetary traveler's broken speech is mended; and the fourfold bleached-out color streams merge into full color. The mode of *Persona* is more complex, and far less abstract. There is no happy ending. At the close of the film, mask and person, speech and silence, actor and "soul" remain divided—however parasitically, even vampiristically, they are shown to be intertwined.

(1967)

Godard

"It may be true that one has to choose between ethics and aesthetics, but it is no less true that whichever one chooses, one will always find the other at the end of the road. For the very definition of the human condition should be in the *mise-en-scène* itself."

G ODARD'S work has been more passionately debated in recent years than that of any other contemporary film-maker. Though he has a good claim to being ranked as the greatest director, aside from Bresson, working actively in the cinema today, it's still common for intelligent people to be irritated and frustrated by his films, even to find them unbearable. Godard's films haven't yet been elevated to the status of classics or masterpieces—as have the best of Eisenstein, Griffith, Gance, Dreyer, Lang, Pabst, Renoir, Vigo, Welles, etc.; or, to take some nearer examples, *L'Avventura* and *Jules and Jim*. That is, his films aren't yet embalmed, immortal, unequivocally (and merely) "beautiful." They retain their youthful power to offend, to appear "ugly," irresponsible, frivolous, pretentious, empty. Film-makers and audiences are still learning from Godard's films, still quarreling with them.

Meanwhile Godard (partly by turning out a new film every few months) manages to keep nimbly ahead of the inexorable thrust of cultural canonization; extending old problems and abandoning or complicating old solutions—offending veteran admirers in numbers almost equal to the new ones he acquires. His thirteenth feature, *Deux ou Trois Choses que je sais d'elle* (1966), is perhaps the most austere and difficult of all his films. His fourteenth feature, *La Chinoise* (1967), opened in Paris last summer and took the first Special Jury Prize at the Venice Film Festival in September; but Godard didn't come from Paris to accept it (his first major film festival award) because he had just begun shooting his next film, *Weekend*, which was playing in Paris by January of this year.

To date, fifteen feature films have been completed and released, the first being the famous *À Bout de Souffle* (*Breathless*) in 1959. The succeeding films, in order, are:

Le Petit Soldat (1960)
Une Femme est une Femme (*A Woman Is a Woman*) (1961)

Vivre sa Vie (My Life to Live) (1962)
Les Carabiniers (1963)
Le Mépris (Contempt) (1963)
Bande à Part (Band of Outsiders) (1964)
Une Femme Mariée (A Married Woman) (1964)
Alphaville (1965)
Pierrot le Fou (1965)
Masculin Féminin (1966)
Made in U.S.A. (1966)

plus the last three I have already mentioned. In addition, five
shorts were made between 1954 and 1958, the most interesting
of these being the two from 1958, "Charlotte et son Jules" and
"Une Histoire d'Eau." There are also seven "sketches": the
first, "La Paresse," was one of the episodes in *Les Septs Péchés
Capitaux* (1961); the most recent three were all made in
1967—"Anticipation," in *Le Plus Vieux Métier du Monde*; a section of *Far From Vietnam*, the corporate film edited by Chris
Marker; and an episode in the still unreleased, Italian-produced
Gospel 70. Considering that Godard was born in 1930, and that
he has made all his films within the commercial cinema industry,
it's an astonishingly large body of work. Unfortunately, many of
the films have not been seen at all in the United States (among
the major gaps, *Pierrot le Fou* and *Deux ou Trois Choses*) or have
never been released for art-house distribution (like *Le Petit Soldat* and *Les Carabiniers*) or have been granted no more than
a brief, token run in New York City only. Though, of course,
not all the films are equally fine, these lacunae matter. Godard's work—unlike that of most film directors, whose artistic
development is much less personal and experimental—deserves,
ultimately demands, to be seen in its entirety. One of the most
modern aspects of Godard's artistry is that each of his films
derives its final value from its place in a larger enterprise, a life
work. Each film is, in some sense, a fragment—which, because
of the stylistic continuities of Godard's work, sheds light on
the others.

Indeed, practically no other director, with the exception of
Bresson, can match Godard's record of making *only* films that
are unmistakably and uncompromisingly their author's. (Contrast Godard on this score with two of his most gifted contemporaries: Resnais, who, after making the sublime *Muriel*, was
able to descend to *La Guerre est Finie*, and Truffaut, who could

follow *Jules and Jim* with *La Peau Douce*—for each director, only his fourth feature.) That Godard is indisputably the most influential director of his generation surely owes much to his having demonstrated himself incapable of adulterating his own sensibility, while still remaining manifestly unpredictable. One goes to a new film by Bresson fairly confident of being treated to another masterpiece. One goes to the latest Godard prepared to see something both achieved and chaotic, "work in progress" which resists easy admiration. The qualities that make Godard, unlike Bresson, a culture hero (as well as, like Bresson, one of the major artists of the age) are precisely his prodigal energies, his evident risk-taking, the quirky individualism of his mastery of a corporate, drastically commercialized art.

But Godard is not merely an intelligent iconoclast. He is a deliberate "destroyer" of cinema—hardly the first cinema has known, but certainly the most persistent and prolific and timely. His approach to established rules of film technique like the unobtrusive cut, consistency of point of view, and clear story line is comparable to Schoenberg's repudiation of the tonal language prevailing in music around 1910 when he entered his atonal period or to the challenge of the Cubists to such hallowed rules of painting as realistic figuration and three-dimensional pictorial space.

The great culture heroes of our time have shared two qualities: they have all been ascetics in some exemplary way, and also great destroyers. But this common profile has permitted two different, yet equally compelling attitudes toward "culture" itself. Some—like Duchamp, Wittgenstein, and Cage—bracket their art and thought with a disdainful attitude toward high culture and the past, or at least maintain an ironic posture of ignorance or incomprehension. Others—like Joyce, Picasso, Stravinsky, and Godard—exhibit a hypertrophy of appetite for culture (though often more avid for cultural debris than for museum-consecrated cultural achievements); they proceed by voraciously scavenging in culture, proclaiming that nothing is alien to their art.

From cultural appetite on this scale comes the creation of work that is on the order of a subjective compendium: casually encyclopedic, anthologizing, formally and thematically eclectic, and marked by a rapid turnover of styles and forms. Thus, one of the most striking features of Godard's work is its daring efforts at hybridization. Godard's insouciant mixtures of tonalities, themes, and narrative methods suggest something like the union of Brecht and Robbe-Grillet, Gene Kelly and Francis Ponge, Gertrude Stein and David Riesman, Orwell and Robert Rauschenberg, Boulez and Raymond Chandler, Hegel and rock 'n' roll. Techniques from literature, theatre, painting, and television mingle freely in his work, alongside witty, impertinent allusions to movie history itself. The elements often seem contradictory—as when (in the recent films) what Richard Roud calls "a fragmentation/collage method of narration"* drawn from advanced painting and poetry is combined with the bare, hard-staring, neo-realist aesthetic of television (cf. the interviews, filmed in frontal close-up and medium shot, in *A Married Woman*, *Masculine Feminine*, and *Deux ou Trois Choses*); or when Godard uses highly stylized visual compositions (such as the recurrent blues and reds in *A Woman Is a Woman*, *Contempt*, *Pierrot le Fou*, *La Chinoise*, and *Weekend*) at the same time that he seems eager to promote the look of improvisation and to conduct an unremitting search for the "natural" manifestations of personality before the truth-exacting eye of the camera. But, however jarring these mergers are in principle, the results Godard gets from them turn out to be something harmonious, plastically and ethically engaging, and emotionally tonic.

The consciously reflective—more precisely, reflexive—aspect of Godard's films is the key to their energies. His work constitutes a formidable meditation on the *possibilities* of cinema, which is to restate what I have already argued, that he enters the history of film as its first consciously destructive figure. Put otherwise, one might note that Godard is probably the first major director to enter the cinema on the level of commercial production with an explicitly critical intention. "I'm still as much of a critic as I ever was during the time of *Cahiers du Cinéma*," he has declared. (Godard wrote regularly for that magazine between 1956 and 1959, and still occasionally contributes to it.) "The only difference is that instead of writing criticism, I now

*In his excellent book *Godard* (New York: Doubleday and Co., 1968), the first full-length study of Godard in English.

film it." Elsewhere, he describes *Le Petit Soldat* as an "auto-critique," and that word, too, applies to all of Godard's films.

But the extent to which Godard's films speak in the first person, and contain elaborate and often humorous reflections on the cinema as a means, is not a private whim but one elaboration of a well-established tendency of the arts to become more self-conscious, more self-referring. Like every important body of work in the canon of modern culture, Godard's films are simply what they are and also events that push their audience to reconsider the meaning and scope of the art form of which they are instances; they're not only works of art, but meta-artistic activities aimed at reorganizing the audience's entire sensibility. Far from deploring the tendency, I believe that the most promising future of films as an art lies in this direction. But the manner in which films continue into the end of the twentieth century as a serious art, becoming more self-regarding and critical, still permits a great deal of variation. Godard's method is far removed from the solemn, exquisitely conscious, self-annihilating structures of Bergman's great film *Persona*. Godard's procedures are much more lighthearted, playful, often witty, sometimes flippant, sometimes just silly. Like any gifted polemicist (which Bergman is not), Godard has the courage to simplify himself. This simplistic quality in much of Godard's work is as much a kind of generosity toward his audience as an aggression against them; and, partly, just the overflow of an inexhaustibly vivacious sensibility.

The attitude that Godard brings to the film medium is often called, disparagingly, "literary." What's usually meant by this charge, as when Satie was accused of composing literary music or Magritte of making literary painting, is a preoccupation with ideas, with conceptualization, at the expense of the sensual integrity and emotional force of the work—more generally, the habit (a kind of bad taste, it's supposed) of violating the essential unity of a given art form by introducing alien elements into it. That Godard has boldly addressed the task of representing or embodying abstract ideas as no other film-maker has done before him is undeniable. Several films even include guest intellectual appearances: a fictional character falls in with a real philosopher (the heroine of *My Life to Live* interrogates Brice Parain in a café about language and sincerity; in *La Chinoise*, the Maoist girl disputes with Francis Jeanson on a train about the ethics of terrorism); a critic and film-maker delivers a speculative soliloquy (Roger Leenhardt on intelligence, ardent and compromising, in *A Married Woman*); a grand old man of film history has a chance to reinvent his own somewhat tarnished personal image (Fritz Lang as himself, a chorus figure meditating on German poetry, Homer, movie-making, and moral integrity, in *Contempt*). On their own, many of Godard's characters muse aphoristically to themselves or engage their friends on such topics as the difference between the Right and the Left, the nature of cinema, the mystery of language, and the spiritual void underlying the satisfactions of the consumer society. Moreover, Godard's films are not only idea-ridden, but many of his characters are ostentatiously literate. Indeed, from the numerous references to books, mentions of writers' names, and quotations and longer excerpts from literary texts scattered throughout his films, Godard gives the impression of being engaged in an unending agon with the very fact of literature— which he attempts to settle partially by incorporating literature and literary identities into his films. And, apart from his original use of it as a cinematic object, Godard is concerned with literature both as a model for film and as the revival and alternative to film. In interviews and in his own critical writings, the relation between cinema and literature is a recurrent theme. One of the differences Godard stresses is that literature exists "as art from the very start" but cinema doesn't. But he also notes a potent similarity between the two arts: that "we novelists and film-makers are condemned to an analysis of the world, of the real; painters and musicians aren't."

By treating cinema as above all an exercise in intelligence, Godard rules out any neat distinction between "literary" and "visual" (or cinematic) intelligence. If film is, in Godard's laconic definition, the "analysis" of something "with images and sounds," there can be no impropriety in making literature a subject for cinematic analysis. Alien to movies as this kind of material may seem, at least in such profusion, Godard would no doubt argue that books and other vehicles of cultural consciousness are part of the world; therefore they belong in films. Indeed, by putting on the same plane the fact that people read and think and go seriously to the movies and the fact that they cry and run and make love, Godard has disclosed a new vein of lyricism and pathos for cinema: in bookishness, in genuine cultural passion, in intellectual callowness, in the misery of someone strangling in his own thoughts. (An instance of Godard's original way with a more familiar subject, the poetry of loutish illiteracy, is the twelve-minute sequence in *Les Carabiniers* in which the soldiers unpack their picture-postcard trophies.) His point is that no material is inherently unassimilable. But what's required is that literature indeed undergo its transformation into material, just like anything else. All that can be given are literary extracts, shards of literature. In order to be absorbed by cinema, literature must be dismantled or broken into wayward units; then Godard can appropriate a portion of the intellectual "content" of any book (fiction or non-fiction), borrow from the public domain of culture any contrasting tone of voice (noble or vulgar), invoke in an instant any diagnosis of contemporary malaise that is thematically relevant to his narrative, no matter how inconsistent it may be with the psychological scope or mental competence of the characters as already established.

Thus, so far as Godard's films are "literary" in some sense, it seems clear that his alliance with literature is based on quite different interests from those which linked earlier experimental film-makers to the advanced writing of their time. If Godard envies literature, it is not so much for the formal innovations carried out in the twentieth century as for the heavy burden of explicit ideation accommodated within prose literary forms. Whatever notions Godard may have gotten from reading Faulkner or Beckett or Mayakovsky for formal inventions in cinema, his introduction of a pronounced literary taste (his own?) into his films serves mainly as a means for assuming a more public voice or elaborating more general statements. While the main tradition of avant-garde film-making has been a "poetic" cinema (films, like those made by the Surrealists in the 1920's and 1930's, inspired by the emancipation of modern poetry from storylike narrative and sequential discourse to the direct presentation and sensuous, polyvalent association of ideas and images), Godard has elaborated a largely anti-poetic cinema, one of whose chief literary models is the prose essay. Godard has even said: "I consider myself an essay writer. I write essays in the form of novels, or novels in the form of essays."

Notice that Godard has here made the novel interchangeable with film—apt in a way, since it is the tradition of the novel that weighs most heavily upon cinema, and the example of what the novel has recently become that spurs Godard.* "I've found an idea for a novel," mumbles the hero of *Pierrot le Fou* at one point, in partial self-mockery assuming the quavering voice of Michel Simon. "Not to write the life of a man, but only life, life itself. What there is between people, space . . . sound and colors. . . . There must be a way of achieving that; Joyce tried, but one must, must be able . . . to do better." Surely, Godard is here speaking for himself as a film-maker, and he appears confident that film can accomplish what literature cannot, literature's incapacity being partly due to the less favorable *critical* situation into which each important literary work is deposited. I have spoken of Godard's work as consciously destructive of old cinematic conventions. But this task of demolition is executed with the élan of someone working in an art form experienced as young, on the threshhold of its greatest development rather than at its end. Godard views the destruction of old rules as a constructive effort—in contrast to the received view of the current destiny of literature. As he has written, "literary critics often praise works like *Ulysses* or *Endgame* because they exhaust a certain genre, they close the doors on it. But in the cinema we are always praising works which *open* doors."

The relation to models offered by literature illuminates a major part of the history of cinema. Film, both protected and patronized by virtue of its dual status as mass entertainment and as art form, remains the last bastion of the values of the nineteenth-century novel and theatre—even to many of the same people who have found accessible and pleasurable such post-novels as

*Speaking historically, it would seem that modern literature has been much more heavily influenced by cinema than vice versa. But the matter of influence is complex. For example, the Czech director Vera Chytilova has said that her model for the diptych form of her brilliant first feature, *Something Else*, was the alternating narratives of *The Wild Palms*; but then a good case could be made out for the powerful influence of cinematic techniques upon Faulkner's mature methods of narrative construction. And Godard at one point, inspired by the same Faulkner book, wanted to have the two films he shot in the summer of 1966, *Made in U.S.A.* and *Deux ou Trois Choses*, projected together, with a reel of one alternating with a reel of the other.

Ulysses, Between the Acts, The Unnameable, Naked Lunch, and
Pale Fire, and the corrosively de-dramatized dramas of Beckett,
Pinter, and the Happenings. Hence, the standard criticism leveled against Godard is that his plots are undramatic, arbitrary,
often simply incoherent; and that his films generally are emotionally cold, static except for a busy surface of senseless movements, top-heavy with undramatized ideas, unnecessarily obscure. What his detractors don't grasp, of course, is that Godard
doesn't want to do what they reproach him for not doing. Thus,
audiences at first took the jump cuts in *Breathless* to be a sign
of amateurishness, or a perverse flouting of self-evident rules of
cinematic technique; actually, what looks as though the camera
had stopped inadvertently for a few seconds in the course of a
shot and then started up again was an effect Godard deliberately
obtained in the cutting room, by snipping pieces out of perfectly smooth takes. (If one sees *Breathless* today, however, the
once obtrusive cutting and the oddities of the hand-held camera are almost invisible, so widely imitated are these techniques
now.) No less deliberate is Godard's disregard for the formal
conventions of film narration based on the nineteenth-century
novel—cause-and-effect sequences of events, climactic scenes,
logical denouements. At the Cannes Film Festival several years
ago, Godard entered into debate with Georges Franju, one of
France's most talented and idiosyncratic senior film-makers.
"But surely, Monsieur Godard," the exasperated Franju is reported to have said, "you do at least acknowledge the necessity
of having a beginning, middle, and end in your films." "Certainly," Godard replied. "But not necessarily in that order."

Godard's insouciance seems to me quite justified. For what is
truly surprising is that film directors have not for some time, by
exploiting the fact that whatever is "shown" (and heard) in the
film experience is unremittingly *present,* made themselves more
independent of what are essentially novelistic notions of narrative. But, as I have indicated, until now the only well-understood
alternative has been to break completely with the formal structures of prose fiction, to dispense altogether with "story" and
"characters." This alternative, practiced entirely outside the
commercial cinema industries, resulted in the "abstract" film
or the "poetic" film based on the association of images. In contrast, Godard's method is still a narrative one, though divorced

from the literalism and reliance on psychological explanation
that most people associate with the serious novel. Because they
modify, rather than make a complete rupture with, the conventions of prose fiction underlying the main tradition of cinema,
Godard's films strike many as more puzzling than the forthright
"poetic" or "abstract" films of the official cinematic avant-garde.

Thus, it is precisely the presence, not the absence, of story in
Godard's films that gives rise to the standard criticism of them.
Unsatisfactory as his plots may be to many people, it would
hardly be correct to describe Godard's films as plotless—like,
say, Djiga Vertov's *The Man with the Camera*, the two silent
films of Buñuel (*L'Age d'Or*, *Un Chien Andalou*), or Kenneth
Anger's *Scorpio Rising*, films in which a story line has been completely discarded as the narrative framework. Like all ordinary
feature films, Godard's films show an interrelated group of
fictional characters located in a recognizable, consistent environment: in his case, usually contemporary and urban (Paris).
But while the sequence of events in a Godard film suggests a
fully articulated story, it doesn't add up to one; the audience is
presented with a narrative line that is partly erased or effaced
(the structural equivalent of the jump cut). Disregarding the
traditional novelist's rule of explaining things as fully as they
seem in need of explanation, Godard provides simplistic motives or frequently just leaves the motives unexplained; actions
are often opaque, and fail to issue into consequences; occasionally the dialogue itself is not entirely audible. (There are other
films, like Rossellini's *Journey to Italy* and Resnais' *Muriel*, that
employ a comparably "unrealistic" system of narration in which
the story is decomposed into disjunct objectified elements; but
Godard, the only director with a whole body of work along
these lines, has suggested more of the diverse routes for "abstracting" from an ostensibly realistic narrative than any other
director. It is important, too, to distinguish various structures
of abstracting—as, for instance, between the systematically "indeterminate" plot of Bergman's *Persona* and the "intermittent"
plots of Godard's films.)

Although Godard's narrative procedures apparently owe less
to cinematic models than to literary ones (at least, he never
mentions the avant-garde past of cinema in interviews and
statements but often mentions as models the work of Joyce,

Proust, and Faulkner), he has never attempted, nor does it seem conceivable that he will attempt in the future, a transposition into film of any of the serious works of contemporary post-novelistic fiction. On the contrary, like many directors, Godard prefers mediocre, even sub-literary material, finding that easier to dominate and transform by the *mise-en-scène*. "I don't really like telling a story," Godard has written, somewhat simplifying the matter. "I prefer to use a kind of tapestry, a background on which I can embroider my own ideas. But I generally do need a story. A conventional one serves as well, perhaps even best." Thus, Godard has ruthlessly described the novel on which his brilliant *Contempt* was based, Moravia's *Ghost at Noon*, as "a nice novel for a train journey, full of old-fashioned sentiments. But it is with this kind of novel that one can make the best films." Although *Contempt* stays close to Moravia's story, Godard's films usually show few traces of their literary origins. (At the other extreme and more typical is *Masculine Feminine*, which bears no recognizable relation to the stories by Maupassant, "La Femme de Paul" and "La Signe," from which Godard drew his original inspiration.)

Whether text or pretext, most of the novels that Godard has chosen as his point of departure are heavily plotted action stories. He has a particular fondness for American kitsch: *Made in U.S.A.* was based on *The Jugger* by Richard Stark, *Pierrot le Fou* on *Obsession* by Lionel White, and *Band of Outsiders* on Dolores Hitchens' *Fool's Gold*. Godard resorts to popular American narrative conventions as a fertile, solid base for his own anti-narrative inclinations. "The Americans know how to tell stories very well; the French not at all. Flaubert and Proust don't know how to narrate; they do something else." Although that something else is plainly what Godard is after too, he has discerned the utility of starting from crude narrative. One allusion to this strategy is the memorable dedication of *Breathless*: "To Monogram Pictures." (In its original version, *Breathless* had no credit titles whatever, and the first image of the film was preceded only by this terse salute to Hollywood's most prolific purveyors of low-budget, quickie action pictures during the 1940s and early 1950s.) Godard wasn't being impudent or flippant here—or only a little bit. Melodrama is one of the integral resources of his plotting. Think of the comic-strip quest of *Alphaville*; the gangster-movies romanticism of *Breathless*, *Band of Outsiders*, and *Made in U.S.A.*; the spy-thriller ambiance of *Le Petit Soldat* and *Pierrot le Fou*. Melodrama—which is characterized by the exaggeration, the frontality, the opaqueness of "action"—provides a framework for both intensifying and transcending traditional realistic procedures of serious film narrative, but in a way which isn't necessarily condemned (as the Surrealist films were) to seeming esoteric. By adapting familiar, second-hand, vulgar materials—popular myths of action and sexual glamour—Godard gains a considerable freedom to "abstract" without losing the possibility of a commercial theatre audience.

That such familiar materials do lend themselves to this kind of abstracting treatment—even contain the germ of it—had been amply demonstrated by one of the first great directors, Louis Feuillade, who worked in the debased form of the crime serial (*Fantômas*, *Les Vampires*, *Judex*, *Ti Minh*). Like the sub-literary model from which he drew, these serials (the greatest of which were done between 1913 and 1916) grant little to the standards of verisimilitude. Devoid of any concern for psychology, which was already beginning to make its appearance in films in the work of Griffith and De Mille, the story is populated by largely interchangeable characters and so crammed with incident that it can be followed only in a general way. But these are not the standards by which the films should be judged. What counts in Feuillade's serials is their formal and emotional values, which are produced by a subtle juxtaposition of the realistic and the highly improbable. The realism of the films lies in their look (Feuillade was one of the first European directors to do extensive location shooting); the implausibility comes from the wild nature of the actions inscribed on this physical space and the unnaturally speeded-up rhythms, formal symmetries, and repetitiveness of the action. In the Feuillade films, as in certain early Lang and early Hitchcock films, the director has carried the melodramatic narrative to absurd extremes, so that the action takes on a hallucinatory quality. Of course, this degree of abstraction of realistic material into the logic of fantasy requires a generous use of ellipsis. If time patterns and space patterns and the abstract rhythms of action are to predominate, the action itself must be "obscure." In one sense, such films clearly have stories—of the most direct, action-packed kind. But in another sense, that of the continuity and consistency and ultimate intelligibility of incidents, the story has no importance at all. The loss of the sparse intertitles on some of the Feuillade films which have survived in only a single print seems hardly to matter, just as the formidable impenetrability of the plots of Hawks' *The Big Sleep* and Aldrich's *Kiss Me Deadly* doesn't matter either, indeed seems quite satisfying. Such film narratives attain their emotional and aesthetic weight precisely through this incomprehensibility, as the "obscurity" of certain poets (Mallarmé, Roussel, Stevens, Empson) isn't a deficiency in their work but an important technical means for accumulating and compounding relevant emotions and for establishing different levels and units of "sense." The obscurity of Godard's plots (*Made in U.S.A.* ventures furthest in this direction) is equally functional, part of the program of abstracting his materials.

Yet at the same time, these materials being what they are, Godard retains some of the vivacity of his simplistic literary and film models. Even as he employs the narrative conventions of the Série Noire novels and the Hollywood thrillers, transposing them into abstract elements, Godard has responded to their casual, sensuous energy and has introduced some of that into his own work. One result is that most of his films give the impression of speed, verging sometimes on haste. By comparison, Feuillade's temperament seems more dogged. On a few essentially limited themes (like ingenuity, ruthlessness, physical grace), Feuillade's films present a seemingly inexhaustible number of formal variations. His choice of the open-ended serial form is thus entirely appropriate. After the twenty episodes of *Les Vampires*, nearly seven hours of projection time, it's clear there was no necessary end to the exploits of the stupendous Musidora and her gang of masked bandits, any more than the exquisitely matched struggle between arch-criminal and arch-detective in *Judex* need ever terminate. The rhythm of incident Feuillade establishes is subject to indefinitely prolonged repetition and embellishment, like a sexual fantasy elaborated in secret over a long period of time. Godard's films move to a quite different rhythm; they lack the unity of fantasy, along with its obsessional gravity and its tireless, somewhat mechanistic repetitiveness.

The difference may be accounted for by the fact that the hallucinatory, absurd, abstracted action tale, while a central resource for Godard, doesn't control the form of his films as it did for Feuillade. Although melodrama remains one term of Godard's sensibility, what has increasingly emerged as the opposing term is the resources of fact. The impulsive, dissociated tone of melodrama contrasts with the gravity and controlled indignation of the sociological exposé (note the recurrent theme of prostitution that appears in what is virtually Godard's first film, the short "Une Femme Coquette," which he made in 1955, and continues in *My Life to Live*, *A Married Woman*, *Deux ou Trois Choses*, and *Anticipation*) and the even cooler tones of straight documentary and quasi-sociology (in *Masculine Feminine*, *Deux ou Trois Choses*, *La Chinoise*).

Though Godard has toyed with the idea of the serial form, as in the end of *Band of Outsiders* (which promises a sequel, never made, relating further adventures of its hero and heroine in Latin America) and in the general conception of *Alphaville* (proposed as the latest adventure of a French serial hero, Lemmy Caution), Godard's films don't relate unequivocally to any single genre. The open-endedness of Godard's films doesn't mean the hyperexploitation of some particular genre, as in Feuillade, but the successive devouring of genres. The countertheme to the restless activity of the characters in Godard's films is an expressed dissatisfaction with the limits or stereotyping of "actions." Thus, in *Pierrot le Fou*, Marianne's being bored or fed up moves what there is of a plot; at one point, she says directly to the camera: "Let's leave the Jules Verne novel and go back to the *roman policier* with guns and so on." The emotional statement depicted in *A Woman Is a Woman* is summed up in the wish expressed by Belmondo's Alfredo and Anna Karina's Angela to be Gene Kelly and Cyd Charisse in a late 1940's Hollywood musical choreographed by Michael Kidd. Early in *Made in U.S.A.* Paula Nelson comments: "Blood and mystery already. I have the feeling of moving about in a Walt Disney film starring Humphrey Bogart. Therefore it must be a political film." But this remark measures the extent to which *Made in U.S.A.* both is and is not a political film. That Godard's characters occasionally look out of the "action" to locate themselves as actors in a film genre is only partly a piece of nostalgic first-person wit on the part of Godard the film-maker; mainly it's an ironic disavowal of commitment to any one genre or way of regarding an action.

If the organizing principle of Feuillade's films is serial repetitiveness and obsessional elaboration, that of Godard's is the juxtaposition of contrary elements of unpredictable length and explicitness. While Feuillade's work implicitly conceives art as the gratification and prolongation of fantasy, Godard's work implies a quite different function for art: sensory and conceptual dislocation. Each of Godard's films is a totality that undermines itself, a de-totalized totality (to borrow Sartre's phrase).

Instead of a narration unified by the coherence of events (a "plot") and a consistent tone (comic, serious, oneiric, affectless, or whatever), the narrative of Godard's films is regularly broken or segmented by the incoherence of events and by abrupt shifts in tone and level of discourse. Events appear to the spectator partly as converging toward a story, partly as a succession of independent tableaux.

The most obvious way Godard segments the forward-moving sequence of narration into tableaux is by explicitly theatricalizing some of his material, once more laying to rest the lively prejudice that there is an essential incompatibility between the means of theatre and those of film. The conventions of the Hollywood musical, with songs and stage performances interrupting the story, supply one precedent for Godard—inspiring the general conception of *A Woman Is a Woman*, the dance trio in the café in *Band of Outsiders*, the song sequences and Vietnam protest skit performed outdoors in *Pierrot le Fou*, the singing telephone call in *Weekend*. His other model is, of course, the non-realistic and didactic theatre expounded by Brecht. An aspect of Godard Brechtianizing is his distinctive style of constructing political micro-entertainments: in *La Chinoise*, the home political theatre-piece acting out the American aggression in Vietnam; or the Feiffer dialogue of the two ham radio operators that opens *Deux ou Trois Choses*. But the more profound influence of Brecht resides in those formal devices Godard uses to counteract ordinary plot development and complicate the emotional involvement of the audience. One device is the direct-to-camera declarations by the characters in many films, notably

Deux ou Trois Choses, *Made in U.S.A.*, and *La Chinoise*. ("One should speak as if one were quoting the truth," says Marina Vlady at the beginning of *Deux ou Trois Choses*, quoting Brecht. "The actors must quote.") Another frequently used technique derived from Brecht is the dissection of the film narrative into short sequences: in *My Life to Live*, in addition, Godard puts on the screen prefatory synopses to each scene which describe the action to follow. The action of *Les Carabiniers* is broken into short brutal sections introduced by long titles, most of which represent cards sent home by Ulysses and Michelangelo; the titles are handwritten, which makes them a little harder to read and brings home to the movie audience the fact that it is being asked to read. Another, simpler device is the relatively arbitrary subdivision of action into numbered sequences, as when the credits of *Masculine Feminine* announce a film consisting of "fifteen precise actions" (*quinze faits précis*). A minimal device is the ironic, pseudo-quantitative statement of something, as in *A Married Woman*, with the brief monologue of Charlotte's little son explaining how to do an unspecified something in exactly ten steps: or in *Pierrot le Fou*, when Ferdinand's voice announces at the beginning of a scene: "Chapter Eight. We cross France." Another example: the very title of one film, *Deux ou Trois Choses*—the lady about whom surely more than two or three things are known being the city of Paris. And, in support of these tropes of the rhetoric of disorientation, Godard practices many specifically sensorial techniques that serve to fragment the cinematic narrative. In fact, most of the familiar elements of Godard's visual and aural stylistics—rapid cutting, the use of unmatched shots, flash shots, the alternation of sunny takes with gray ones, the counterpoint of prefabricated images (signs, paintings, billboards, picture postcards, posters), the discontinuous music—function in this way.

Apart from the general strategy of "theatre," perhaps Godard's most striking application of the dissociative principle is his treatment of ideas. Certainly ideas are not developed in Godard's films systematically, as they might be in a book. They aren't meant to be. In contrast to their role in Brechtian theatre, ideas are chiefly formal elements in Godard's films, units of sensory and emotional stimulation. They function at least as much to dissociate and fragment as they do to indicate or illuminate the "meaning" of the action. Often the ideas, rendered in blocks of words, lie at a tangent to the action. Nana's reflections on sincerity and language in *My Life to Live*, Bruno's observations about truth and action in *Le Petit Soldat*, the articulate self-consciousness of Charlotte in *A Married Woman* and of Juliette in *Deux ou Trois Choses*, Lemmy Caution's startling aptitude for cultivated literary allusions in *Alphaville* are not functions of the realistic psychology of these characters. (Perhaps the only one of Godard's intellectually reflective protagonists who still seems "in character" when ruminating is Ferdinand in *Pierrot le Fou*.) Although Godard proposes film discourse as constantly open to ideas, ideas are only one element in a narrative form which posits an intentionally ambiguous, open, playful relation of *all* the parts to the total scheme.

Godard's fondness for interpolating literary "texts" in the action, which I have already mentioned, is one of the main variants on the presence of ideas in his films. Among the many instances: the Mayakovsky poem recited by the girl about to be executed by a firing squad in *Les Carabiniers*; the excerpt from the Poe story read aloud in the next-to-last episode in *My Life to Live*; the lines from Dante, Hölderlin, and Brecht that Lang quotes in *Contempt*; the oration from Saint-Just by a character dressed as Saint-Just in *Weekend*; the passage from Elie Faure's *History of Art* read aloud by Ferdinand to his young daughter in *Pierrot le Fou*; the lines from *Romeo and Juliet* in French translation dictated by the English teacher in *Band of Outsiders*; the scene from Racine's *Bérénice* rehearsed by Charlotte and her lover in *A Married Woman*; the quote from Fritz Lang read aloud by Camille in *Contempt*; the passages from Mao declaimed by the FLN agent in *Le Petit Soldat*; the antiphonal recitations from the little red book in *La Chinoise*. Usually someone makes an announcement before beginning to declaim, or can be seen taking up a book and reading from it. Sometimes, though, these obvious signals for the advent of a text are lacking—as with the excerpts from *Bouvard and Pécuchet* spoken by two custom-ers in a café in *Deux ou Trois Choses*, or the long extract from *Death on the Installment Plan* delivered by the maid ("Madame Celine") in *A Married Woman*. (Although usually literary, the text may be a film: like the excerpt from Dreyer's *Jeanne d'Arc* that Nana watches in *My Life to Live*, or a minute of film shot by Godard in Sweden, reputed to be a parody of Bergman's *The Silence*, that Paul and the two girls see in *Masculine Feminine*.) These texts introduce psychologically dissonant elements into the action; they supply rhythmical variety (temporarily slowing down the action); they interrupt the action and offer ambiguous comment on it; and they also vary and extend the point of view represented in the film. The spectator is almost bound to be misled if he regards these texts simply, either as opinions of characters in the film or as samples of some unified point of view advocated by the film which presumably is dear to the director. More likely, just the opposite is or comes to be the case. Aided by "ideas" and "texts," Godard's film narratives tend to consume the points of view presented in them. Even the political ideas expressed in Godard's work—part Marxist and part anarchist in one canonical style of the postwar French intelligentsia—are subject to this rule.

Like the ideas, which function partly as divisive elements, the fragments of cultural lore embedded in Godard's films serve in part as a form of mystification and a means for refracting emotional energy. (In *Le Petit Soldat*, for instance, when Bruno says of Veronica the first time he sees her that she reminds him of a Giraudoux heroine, and later wonders whether her eyes are Renoir gray or Velázquez gray, the main impact of these references is their unverifiability by the audience.) Inevitably, Godard broaches the menace of the bastardization of culture, a theme most broadly stated in *Contempt* in the figure of the American producer with his booklet of proverbs. And, laden as his films are with furnishings of high culture, it's perhaps inevitable that Godard should also invoke the project of laying down the burden of culture—as Ferdinand does in *Pierrot le Fou* when he abandons his life in Paris for the romantic journey southward carrying only a book of old comics. In *Weekend*, Godard posits against the petty barbarism of the car-owning urban bourgeoisie the possibly cleansing violence of a rebarbarized youth, imagined as a hippy-style liberation army roaming the countryside whose principal delights seem to be contemplation, pillage, jazz, and cannibalism. The theme of cultural disburdenment is treated most fully and ironically in *La Chinoise*. One sequence shows the young cultural revolutionaries purging their shelves of all their books but the little red one. Another brief sequence shows just a blackboard at first, filled with the neatly listed names of several dozen stars of Western culture from Plato to Shakespeare to Sartre; these are then erased one by one, thoughtfully, with Brecht the last to go. The five pro-Chinese students who live together want to have only one point of view, that of Chairman Mao; but Godard shows, without insulting anyone's intelligence, how chimerical and inadequate to reality (and yet how appealing) this hope actually is. For all his native radicalism of temperament, Godard himself still appears a partisan of that other cultural revolution, ours, which enjoins the artist-thinker to maintain a multiplicity of points of view on any material.

All the devices Godard employs to keep shifting the point of view within a film can be looked at another way—as adjuncts to a positive strategy, that of overlaying a number of narrative voices, for effectively bridging the difference between first-person and third-person narration. Thus *Alphaville* opens with three samples of first-person discourse: first, a prefatory statement spoken off-camera by Godard, then a declaration by the computer-ruler Alpha 60, and only then the usual soliloquizing voice, that of the secret-agent hero, shown grimly driving his big car into the city of the future. Instead of, or in addition to, using "titles" between scenes as narrative signals (for example: *My Life to Live*, *A Married Woman*), Godard seems now more to favor installing a narrative voice in the film. This voice may belong to the main character: Bruno's musings in *Le Petit Soldat*, Charlotte's free associating subtext in *A Married Woman*, Paul's commentary in *Masculine Feminine*. It may be the director's, as in *Band of Outsiders* and "Le Grand Escroc," the sketch from *Les Plus Belles Escroqueries du Monde* (1963). What's most interesting is when there are two voices, as in *Deux ou Trois Choses*, throughout which both Godard (whispering) and the heroine comment on the action. *Band of Outsiders* introduces the notion of a narrative intelligence which can "open a parenthesis" in the action and directly address the audience, explaining what Franz, Odile, and Arthur are really feeling at that moment; the narrator can intervene or comment ironically on the action or on the very fact of seeing a movie. (Fifteen minutes into the film, Godard off-camera says, "For the late-comers, what's happened so far is . . .") Thereby two different but concurrent times are established in the film—the time of the action shown, and the time of the narrator's reflection on what's shown—in a way which allows free passage back and forth between the first-person narration and the third-person presentation of the action.

Although the narrating voice already has a major role in some of his earliest work (for instance, the virtuoso comic monologue of the last of the pre-*Breathless* shorts, *Une Histoire d'Eau*), Godard continues to extend and complicate the task of oral narration, arriving at such recent refinements as the beginning of *Deux ou Trois Choses*, when from off-camera he introduces his leading actress, Marina Vlady, by name and then describes her as the character she will play. Such procedures tend, of course, to reinforce the self-reflexive and self-referring aspect of Godard's films, for the ultimate narrative presence is simply the fact of cinema itself; from which it follows that, for the sake of truth, the cinematic medium must be made to manifest itself before the spectator. Godard's methods for doing this range from the frequent ploy of having an actor make rapid playful asides to the camera (i.e., to the audience) in mid-action, to the use of a bad take—Anna Karina fumbles a line, asks if it's all right, then repeats the line—in *A Woman Is a Woman*. *Les Carabiniers* only gets underway after we hear first some coughing and shuffling and an instruction by someone, perhaps the composer or a sound technician, on the set. In *La Chinoise*, Godard makes the point about its being a movie by, among other devices, flashing the clapper board on the screen from time to time, and by briefly cutting to Raoul Coutard, the cameraman on this as on most of Godard's films, seated behind his apparatus. But then one immediately imagines some underling holding another clapper while that scene was shot, and someone else who had to be there behind another camera to photograph Coutard. It's impossible ever to penetrate behind the final veil and experience cinema unmediated by cinema.

I have argued that one consequence of Godard's disregard for the aesthetic rule of having a fixed point of view is that he dissolves the distinction between first-person and third-person narration. But perhaps it would be more accurate to say that Godard proposes a new conception of point of view, thereby staking out the possibility of making films in the first person.

By this, I don't mean simply that his films are subjective or personal; so is the work of many other directors, particularly the cinematic avant-garde and underground. I mean something stricter, which may indicate the originality of his achievement: namely, the way in which Godard, especially in his recent films, has built up a narrative presence, that of the film-maker, who is the central *structural* element in the cinematic narrative. This first-person film-maker isn't an actual character within the film. That is, he is not to be seen on the screen (except in the episode in *Far from Vietnam*, which shows only Godard at a camera talking, intercut with snippets from *La Chinoise*), though he is heard from time to time and one is increasingly aware of his presence just off-camera. But this off-screen persona is not a lucid, authorial intelligence, like the detached observer-figure of many novels cast in the first person. The ultimate first person in Godard's movies, his particular vision of the film-maker, is the person responsible for the film who stands outside it as a mind beset by more complex, fluctuating concerns than any single film can represent or incarnate. The most profound drama of a Godard film arises from the clash between this restless, wider consciousness of the director and the determinate, limited argument of the particular film he's engaged in making. Therefore each film is, simultaneously, a creative activity and a destructive one. The director virtually uses up his models, his sources, his ideas, his latest moral and artistic enthusiasms—and the shape of the film consists of various means for letting the audience know that's what is happening. This dialectic has reached its furthest development so far in *Deux ou Trois Choses*, which is more radically a first-person film than any Godard has made.

The advantage of the first-person mode for cinema is presumably that it vastly augments the liberty of the film-maker while at the same time providing incentives for greater formal rigor— the same goals espoused by all the serious post-novelists of this century. Thus Gide has Édouard, the author-protagonist of *The Counterfeiters*, condemn all previous novels because their contours are "defined," so that, however perfect, what they contain is "captive and lifeless." He wanted to write a novel that would "run freely" because he'd chosen "not to foresee its windings." But the liberation of the novel turned out to consist in writing a novel about writing a novel: presenting "literature" within literature. In a different context, Brecht discovered "theatre" within theatre. Godard has discovered "cinema" within cinema. However loose or spontaneous-looking or personally self-expressive his films may appear, what must be appreciated is that Godard subscribes to a severely alienated conception of his art: a cinema that eats cinema. Each film is an ambiguous event that must be simultaneously promulgated and destroyed. Godard's most explicit statement of this theme is the painful monologue of self-interrogation which was his contribution to *Far from Vietnam*. Perhaps his wittiest statement of this theme is a scene in *Les Carabiniers* (similar to the end of an early Mack Sennett two-reeler, *Mabel's Dramatic Career*) in which Michelangelo takes time off from the war to visit a movie theatre, apparently for the first time, since he reacts as audiences did sixty years ago when movies first began to be shown. He follows the movements of the actors on the screen with his whole body, ducks under the seat when a train appears, and at last, driven wild by the sight of a girl taking a bath in the film within a film, bolts from his seat and rushes up to the stage. After first standing on tiptoe to try to look into the tub, then feeling tentatively for the girl along the surface of the screen, he finally tries to grab her—ripping away part of the screen within the screen, and revealing the girl and the bathroom to be a projection on a filthy wall. Cinema, as Godard says in *Le Grand Escroc*, "is the most beautiful fraud in the world."

Though all his distinctive devices serve the fundamental aim of breaking up the narrative or varying the perspective, Godard doesn't aim at a systematic variation of points of view. Sometimes, to be sure, he does elaborate a strong plastic conception— like the intricate visual patterns of the couplings of Charlotte with her lover and her husband in *A Married Woman*; and the brilliant formal metaphor of the monochromatic photography in three "political colors" in *Anticipation*. Still, Godard's work characteristically lacks formal rigor, a quality preeminent in all the work of Bresson and Jean-Marie Straub and in the best films of Welles and Resnais.

The jump cuts in *Breathless*, for instance, are not part of any strict overall rhythmic scheme, an observation that's confirmed by Godard's account of their rationale. "I discovered in *Breathless* that when a discussion between two people became boring and tedious one could just as well cut between the speeches. I tried it once, and it went very well, so I did the same thing right through the film." Godard may be exaggerating the casualness of his attitude in the cutting room, but his reliance upon intuition on the set is well known. For no film has a full shooting script been prepared in advance, and many films have been improvised day by day throughout large parts of the shooting; in the recent films shot with direct sound, Godard has the actors wear tiny earphones so that while they are on camera he can speak to each of them privately, feeding them their lines or posing questions which they're to answer (direct-to-camera interviews). And, though he generally uses professional actors, Godard has been increasingly open to incorporating accidental presences. (Examples: in *Deux ou Trois Choses*, Godard, off camera, interviewing a young girl who worked in the beauty parlor which he'd taken over for a day of filming; Samuel Fuller talking, as himself, to Ferdinand, played by Belmondo, at a party at the beginning of *Pierrot le Fou*, because Fuller, an American director Godard admires, happened to be in Paris at the time and was visiting Godard on the set.) When using direct sound, Godard also generally keeps any natural or casual noises picked up on the soundtrack, even those unrelated to the action. While the results of this permissiveness are not interesting in every case, some of Godard's happiest effects have been last-minute inventions or the result of accident. The church bells tolling when Nana dies in *My Life to Live* just happened to go off, to everyone's surprise, during the shooting. The stunning scene in negative in *Alphaville* turned out that way because at the last moment Coutard told Godard there wasn't enough equipment on the set to light the scene properly (it was night); Godard decided to go ahead anyway. Godard has said that the spectacular ending of *Pierrot le Fou*, Ferdinand's suicide by self-dynamiting, "was invented on the spot, unlike the beginning, which was organized. It's a sort of Happening, but one that was controlled and dominated. Two days before I began I had nothing, absolutely nothing. Oh well, I did have the book. And a certain number of locations." Godard's conviction that it is possible to absorb chance, using it as an additional tool for developing new structures, extends beyond making only minimal preparations for a film and keeping the conditions of shooting flexible to the editing itself. "Sometimes I have shots that were badly filmed, because I lacked time or money," Godard has said. "Putting them together creates a different impression; I don't reject this; on the contrary, I try to do my best to bring out this new idea."

Godard's openness to the aleatoric miracle is supported by his predilection for shooting on location. In his work to date—features, shorts, and sketches all included—only his third feature, *A Woman Is a Woman*, was shot in a studio; the rest were done in "found" locations. (The small hotel room in which *Charlotte et son Jules* takes place was where Godard was then living; the apartment in *Deux ou Trois Choses* belonged to a friend; and the apartment in *La Chinoise* is where Godard lives now.) Indeed, one of the most brilliant and haunting aspects of Godard's science-fiction fables—the sketch from *RoGoPaG* (1962), "Le Nouveau Monde," *Alphaville*, and *Anticipation*—is that they were filmed entirely in unretouched sites and buildings existing around the Paris of the mid-1960's like Orly Airport and the Hotel Scribe and the new Electricity Board building. This, of course, is exactly Godard's point. The fables about the future are at the same time essays about today. The streak of movie-educated fantasy that runs strong through Godard's work is always qualified by the ideal of documentary truth.

From Godard's penchant for improvisation, for incorporating accidents, and for location shooting, one might infer a lineage from the neo-realist aesthetic made famous by Italian films of the last twenty-five years, starting with Visconti's *Ossessione* and *La Terra Trema* and reaching its apogee in the postwar films of Rossellini and the recent debut of Olmi. But Godard, although a fervent admirer of Rossellini, is not even a neo-neo-realist, and hardly aims to expel the artifice from art. What he seeks is to conflate the traditional polarities of spontaneous mobile thinking and finished work, of the casual jotting and the fully premeditated statement. Spontaneity, casualness, lifelikeness are not values in themselves for Godard, who is rather interested in the *convergence* of spontaneity with the emotional discipline of abstraction (the dissolution of "subject matter"). Naturally, the results are far from tidy. Although Godard achieved the basis of his distinctive style very quickly (by 1958), the restlessness of his temperament and his intellectual voracity impel him to adopt an essentially exploratory posture in relation to film-making, in which he may answer a problem raised but not resolved in one film by starting on another. Still, viewed as a whole, Godard's work is much closer in problems and scope to the work of a radical purist and formalist in film like Bresson than to the work of the neo-realists—even though the relation with Bresson must also be drawn largely in terms of contrasts.

Bresson also achieved his mature style very quickly, but his career has throughout consisted of thoroughly premeditated, independent works conceived within the limits of his personal aesthetic of concision and intensity. (Born in 1910, Bresson has made eight feature films, the first in 1943 and the most recent in 1967.) Bresson's art is characterized by a pure, lyric quality, by a naturally elevated tone, and by a carefully constructed unity. He has said, in an interview conducted by Godard (*Cahiers du Cinéma* #178, May 1966), that for him "improvisation is at the base of creation in the cinema." But the look of a Bresson film is surely the antithesis of improvisation. In the finished film, a shot must be both autonomous and necessary; which means that there's only one ideally correct way of composing each shot (though it may be arrived at quite intuitively) and of editing the shots into a narrative. For all their great energy, Bresson's films project an air of formal deliberateness, of having been organized according to a relentless, subtly calculated rhythm which required their having had everything inessential cut from them. Given his austere aesthetic, it seems apt that Bresson's characteristic subject is a person either literally imprisoned or locked within an excruciating dilemma. Indeed, if one does accept narrative and tonal unity as a primary standard for film, Bresson's asceticism—his maximal use of minimal materials, the meditative "closed" quality of his films—seems to be the only truly rigorous procedure.

Godard's work exemplifies an aesthetic (and, no doubt, a temperament and sensibility) the opposite of Bresson's. The moral energy informing Godard's film-making, while no less powerful than Bresson's, leads to a quite different asceticism: the labor of endless self-questioning, which becomes a constitutive element in the artwork. "More and more with each film," he said in 1965, "it seems to me the greatest problem in filming is to decide where and why to begin a shot and why to end it."

The point is that Godard cannot envisage anything but arbitrary solutions to his problem. While each shot is autonomous, no amount of thinking can make it necessary. Since film for Godard is preeminently an open structure, the distinction between what's essential and inessential in any given film becomes senseless. Just as no absolute, immanent standards can be discovered for determining the composition, duration, and place of a shot, there can be no truly sound reason for excluding anything from a film. This view of film as an assemblage rather than a unity lies behind the seemingly facile characterizations Godard has made of many of his recent films. "*Pierrot le Fou* isn't really a film, it's an attempt at cinema." About *Deux ou Trois Choses*: "In sum, it's not a film, it's an attempt at a film and is presented as such." *A Married Woman* is described in the main titles: "Fragments of a Film Shot in 1964"; and *La Chinoise* is subtitled "A Film in the Process of Being Made." In claiming to offer no more than "efforts" or "attempts," Godard acknowledges the structural openness or arbitrariness of his work. Each film remains a fragment in the sense that its possibilities of elaboration can never be used up. For granted the acceptability, even desirability, of the method of juxtaposition ("I prefer simply putting things side by side"), which assembles contrary elements without reconciling them, there can indeed be no internally necessary end to a Godard film, as there is to a Bresson film. Every film must either seem broken off abruptly or else ended arbitrarily—often by the violent death in the last reel of one or more of the main characters, as in *Breathless*, *Le Petit Soldat*, *My Life to Live*, *Les Carabiniers*, *Contempt*, *Masculine Feminine*, and *Pierrot le Fou*.

Predictably, Godard has supported these views by pressing the relationship (rather than the distinction) between "art" and "life." Godard claims never to have had the feeling as he worked, which he thinks a novelist must have, "that I am differentiating between life and creation." The familiar mythical terrain is occupied once again: "cinema is somewhere between art and life." Of *Pierrot le Fou*, Godard has written: "Life is the subject, with 'Scope and color as its attributes. . . . Life on its own as I would like to capture it, using pan shots on nature, *plans fixes* on death, brief shots, long takes, soft and loud sounds, the movements of Anna and Jean-Paul. In short, life filling the screen as a tap fills a bathtub that is simultaneously emptying at the same rate." This, Godard claims, is how he differs from Bresson, who, when shooting a film, has "an idea of the world" that he is "trying to put on the screen or, which comes to the same thing, an idea of the cinema" he's trying "to apply to the world." For a director like Bresson, "cinema and the world are moulds to be filled, while in *Pierrot* there is neither mould nor matter."

Of course Godard's films aren't bathtubs; and Godard harbors his complex sentiments about the world and his art to the same extent and in much the same way as Bresson. But despite Godard's lapse into a disingenuous rhetoric, the contrast with Bresson stands. For Bresson, who was originally a painter, it is the austerity and rigor of cinematic means which make this art (though very few movies) valuable to him. For Godard, it's the fact that cinema is so loose, promiscuous, and accommodating a medium which gives movies, even many inferior ones, their authority and promise. Film can mix forms, techniques, points of view; it can't be identified with any single leading ingredient. Indeed, what the film-maker must show is that nothing is excluded. "One can put everything in a film," says Godard. "One must put everything in a film."

A film is conceived of as a living organism: not so much an object as a presence or an encounter—a fully historical or contemporary event, whose destiny it is to be transcended by future events. Seeking to create a cinema which inhabits the real present, Godard regularly puts into his films references to current political crises: Algeria, de Gaulle's domestic politics, Angola, the Vietnam war. (Each of his last four features includes a scene in which the main characters denounce the American aggression in Vietnam, and Godard has declared that until that war ends he'll put such a sequence into every film he makes.) The films may include even more casual references and off-the-cuff sentiments—a dig at André Malraux; a compliment to Henri Langlois, director of the Cinémathèque Française; an attack on irresponsible projectionists who show 1:66 films in Cinemascope ratio; or a plug for the unreleased movie of a fellow director and friend. Godard welcomes the opportunity to use the cinema topically, "journalistically." Using the interview style of *cinéma-vérité* and TV documentary, he can canvas characters for their opinions about the pill or the significance of Bob

Dylan. Journalism can provide the basis for a film: Godard, who writes the scripts for all his movies, lists "Documentation from 'Où en est la prostitution?' by Marcel Sacotte" as a source for *My Life to Live*; the story of *Deux ou Trois Choses* was suggested by a feature story, published in *Le Nouvel Observateur*, about housewives in new low-income apartment projects becoming part-time prostitutes to augment the family income.

As photography, cinema has always been an art which records temporality; but up to now this has been an inadvertent aspect of feature fiction films. Godard is the first major director who deliberately incorporates certain contingent aspects of the particular social moment when he's shooting a film—sometimes making these the frame of the film. Thus, the frame of *Masculine Feminine* is a report on the situation of French youth during three politically critical months of winter 1965, between the first presidential election and the run-off; and *La Chinoise* analyzes the faction of Communist students in Paris inspired by the Maoist cultural revolution in the summer of 1967. But of course Godard does not intend to supply facts in a literal sense, the sense which denies the relevance of imagination and fantasy. In his view, "you can start either with fiction or documentary. But whichever you start with, you will inevitably find the other." Perhaps the most interesting development of his point is not the films which have the form of reportage but those which have the form of fables. The timeless universal war which is the subject of *Les Carabiniers* is illustrated by World War II documentary footage, and the squalor in which the mythic protagonists (Michelangelo, Ulysses, Cleopatra, Venus) live is concretely France today. *Alphaville* is, in Godard's words, "a fable on a realistic ground," because the intergalactic city is also, literally, Paris now.

Unworried by the issue of impurity—there are no materials unusable for film—Godard is, nevertheless, involved in an extremely purist venture: the attempt to devise a structure for films which speaks in a purer present tense. His effort is to make movies which live in the actual present, and not to tell something from the past, relate something that's already taken place. In this, of course, Godard is following a direction already taken in literature. Fiction, until recently, was the art of the past. Events told in an epic or novel are, when the reader starts the book, already (as it were) in the past. But in much of the new fiction, events pass before us as if in a present coexisting with the time of the narrative voice (more accurately, with the time in which the reader is being addressed by the narrative voice). Events exist, therefore, in the present—at least as much of the present as the reader himself inhabits. It is for this reason that such writers as Beckett, Stein, Burroughs, and Robbe-Grillet prefer actually to use the present tense, or its equivalent. (Another strategy: to make the distinction between past, present, and future time within the narration an explicit conundrum, and an insoluble one—as, for example, in certain tales of Borges and Landolfi and in *Pale Fire*.) But if the development is feasible for literature, it would seem even more apt for film to make a comparable move since, in a way, film narration knows *only* the present tense. (Everything shown is equally present, no matter when it takes place.) For film to exploit its natural liberty what was necessary was to have a much looser, less literal attachment to telling a "story." A story in the traditional sense—something that's already taken place—is replaced by a segmented situation in which the suppression of certain explicative connections between scenes creates the impression of an action continually beginning anew, unfolding in the present tense.

And, of necessity, this present tense must appear as a somewhat behaviorist, external, anti-psychological view of the human situation. For psychological understanding depends on holding in mind simultaneously the dimensions of past, present, and future. To see someone psychologically is to lay out temporal coordinates in which he is situated. An art which aims at the present tense cannot aspire to this kind of "depth" or innerness in the portrayal of human beings. The lesson is already clear from the work of Stein and Beckett; Godard demonstrates it for film.

Godard explicitly alludes to this choice only once, in connection with *My Life to Live*, which, he says, he "built . . . in tableaux to accentuate the theatrical side of the film. Besides, this division corresponded to the external view of things which best allowed me to give a feeling of what was going on inside. In other words, a contrary procedure to that used by Bresson in *Pickpocket*, in which the drama is seen from within. How can one render the 'inside'? I think, by staying prudently outside." But though there are obvious advantages to staying "outside"—flexibility of form, freedom from superimposed limiting solutions—the choice is not so clear-cut as Godard suggests. Perhaps one never goes "inside" in the sense Godard attributes to Bresson—a procedure considerably different from the reading off of motives and summing up of a character's interior life promoted by nineteenth-century novelistic realism. Indeed, by those standards, Bresson is himself considerably "outside" his characters; for instance, more involved in their somatic presence, the rhythm of their movements, the heavy weight of inexpressible feeling which they bear.

Still, Godard is right in saying that, compared with Bresson, he is "outside." One way he stays outside is by constantly shifting the point of view from which the film is told, by the juxtaposition of contrasting narrative elements: realistic alongside implausible aspects of the story, written signs interposed between images, "texts" recited aloud interrupting dialogue, static interviews as against rapid actions, interpolation of a narrator's voice explaining or commenting on the action, and so forth. A second way is by his rendering of "things" in a strenuously neutralized fashion, in contrast with Bresson's thoroughly intimate vision of things as objects used, disputed, loved, ignored, and worn out by people. Things in Bresson's films, whether a spoon, a chair, a piece of bread, a pair of shoes, are always marked by their human use. The point is *how* they are used—whether skillfully (as the prisoner uses his spoon in *Un Condamné à Mort*, and the heroine of *Mouchette* uses the saucepan and bowls to make breakfast coffee) or clumsily. In Godard's films, things display a wholly alienated character. Characteristically, they are used with indifference, neither skillfully nor clumsily; they are simply there. "Objects exist," Godard has written, "and if one pays more attention to them than to people, it is precisely because they exist more than these people. Dead objects are still alive. Living people are often already dead." Whether things can be the occasion for visual gags (like the suspended egg in *A Woman Is a Woman*, and the movie posters in the warehouse in *Made in U.S.A.*) or can introduce an element of great plastic beauty (as do the Pongeist studies in *Deux ou Trois Choses* of the burning end of a cigarette and of bubbles separating and coming together on the surface of a hot cup of coffee), they always occur in a context of, and serve to reinforce, emotional dissociation. The most noticeable form of Godard's dissociated rendering of things is his ambivalent immersion in the allure of pop imagery and his only partly ironic display of the symbolic currency of urban capitalism—pinball machines, boxes of detergent, fast cars, neon signs, billboards, fashion magazines. By extension, this fascination with alienated things dictates the settings of most of Godard's films: highways, airports, anonymous hotel rooms or soulless modern apartments, brightly lit modernized cafés, movie theatres. The furniture and settings of Godard's films are the landscape of alienation—whether he is displaying the pathos in the mundane facticity of the actual life of dislocated, urban persons such as petty hoodlums, discontented housewives, left-wing students, prostitutes (the everyday present) or presenting anti-utopian fantasies about the cruel future.

A universe experienced as fundamentally dehumanized or dissociated is also one conducive to rapid "associating" from one ingredient in it to another. Again, the contrast can be made with Bresson's attitude, which is rigorously non-associative and therefore concerned with the depth in any situation; in a Bresson film there are certain organically derived and mutually relevant exchanges of personal energy that flourish or exhaust themselves (either way, unifying the narrative and supplying it with an organic terminus). For Godard, there are no genuinely organic connections. In the landscape of pain, only three strictly unrelated responses of real interest are possible; violent action, the probe of "ideas," and the transcendence of sudden, arbitrary, romantic love. But each of these possibilities is understood to be revocable, or artificial. They are not acts of personal fulfillment; not so much solutions as dissolutions of a problem. It has been noted that many of Godard's films project a masochistic view of women, verging on misogyny, and an indefatigable romanticism about "the couple." It's an odd but rather familiar combination of attitudes. Such contradictions are psychological or ethical analogues to Godard's fundamental formal presuppositions. In work conceived of as open-ended, associative, composed of "fragments," constructed by the (partly aleatoric) juxtaposition of contrary elements, any principle of action or any decisive emotional resolution is bound to be an artifice (from an ethical point of view) or ambivalent (from a psychological point of view).

Each film is a provisional network of emotional and intellectual impasses. With the probable exception of his view on Vietnam, there is no attitude Godard incorporates in his films that is not simultaneously being bracketed, and therefore criticized, by a dramatization of the gap between the elegance and seductiveness of ideas and the brutish or lyrical opaqueness of the human condition. The same sense of impasse characterizes Godard's moral judgments. For all the use made of the metaphor and the fact of prostitution to sum up contemporary miseries, Godard's films can't be said to be "against" prostitution and "for" pleasure and liberty in the unequivocal sense that Bresson's films directly extol love, honesty, courage, and dignity and deplore cruelty and cowardice.

From Godard's perspective, Bresson's work is bound to appear "rhetorical," whereas Godard is bent on destroying rhetoric by a lavish use of irony—the familiar outcome when a restless, somewhat dissociated intelligence struggles to cancel an irrepressible romanticism and tendency to moralize. In many of his films Godard deliberately seeks the framework of parody, of irony as contradiction. For instance, *A Woman Is a Woman* proceeds by putting an ostensibly serious theme (a woman frustrated both as wife and as would-be mother) in an ironically sentimental framework. "The subject of *A Woman Is a Woman*," Godard has said, "is a character who succeeds in resolving a certain situation, but I conceived this subject within the framework of a neo-realistic musical: an *absolute contradiction*, but that is precisely why I wanted to make the film." Another example is the lyrical treatment of a rather nasty scheme of amateur gangsterism in *Band of Outsiders*, complete with the high irony of the "happy ending" in which Odile sails away with Franz to Latin America for further romantic adventures. Another example: the nomenclature of *Alphaville*, a film in which Godard takes up some of his most serious themes, is a collection of comic-strip identities (characters have names like Lemmy Caution, the hero of a famous series of French thrillers; Harry Dickson; Professor Leonard Nosferatu, alias von Braun; Professor Jeckyll) and the lead is played by Eddie Constantine, the expatriate American actor whose mug has been a cliché of

'B' French detective films for two decades; indeed, Godard's original title for the film was "Tarzan versus IBM." Still another example: the film Godard decided to make on the double theme of the Ben Barka and Kennedy murders, *Made in U.S.A.*, was conceived as a parodic remake of *The Big Sleep* (which had been revived at an art house in Paris in the summer of 1966), with Bogart's role of the trench-coated detective embroiled in an insoluble mystery now played by Anna Karina. The danger of such lavish use of irony is that ideas will be expressed at their point of self-caricature, and emotions only when they are mutilated. Irony intensifies what is already a considerable limitation on the emotions in the films that results from the insistence on the pure presentness of cinema narration, in which situations with less deep affect will be disproportionately represented—at the expense of vividly depicted states of grief, rage, profound erotic longing and fulfillment, and physical pain. Thus, while Bresson, at his almost unvarying best, is able to convey deep emotions without ever being sentimental, Godard, at his less effective, devises turns of plot that appear either hardhearted or sentimental (at the same time seeming emotionally flat).

Godard "straight" seems to me more successful—whether in the rare pathos he has allowed in *Masculine Feminine*, or in the hard coolness of such directly passionate films as *Les Carabiniers*, *Contempt*, *Pierrot le Fou*, and *Weekend*. This coolness is a pervasive quality of Godard's work. For all their violence of incident and sexual matter-of-factness, the films have a muted, detached relation to the grotesque and painful as well as to the seriously erotic. People are sometimes tortured and often die in Godard's films, but almost casually. (He has a particular predilection for automobile accidents: the end of *Contempt*, the wreck in *Pierrot le Fou*, the landscape of affectless highway carnage in *Weekend*.) And people are rarely shown making love, though if they are, what interests Godard isn't the sensual communion but what sex reveals "about the spaces between people." The orgiastic moments come when young people dance together or sing or play games or run—people run beautifully in Godard movies—not when they make love.

"Cinema is emotion," says Samuel Fuller in *Pierrot le Fou*, a thought one surmises that Godard shares. But emotion, for

Godard, always comes accompanied by some decoration of wit, some transmuting of feeling that he clearly puts at the center of the art-making process. This accounts for part of Godard's pre-occupation with language, both heard and seen on the screen. Language functions as a means of emotional distancing from the action. The pictorial element is emotional, immediate; but words (including signs, texts, stories, sayings, recitations, interviews) have a lower temperature. While images invite the spectator to identify with what is seen, the presence of words makes the spectator into a critic.

But Godard's Brechtian use of language is only one aspect of the matter. Much as Godard owes to Brecht, his treatment of language is more complex and equivocal and relates rather to the efforts of certain painters who use words actively to undermine the image, to rebuke it, to render it opaque and unintelligible. It's not simply that Godard gives language a place that no other film director has before him. (Compare the verbosity of Godard's films with Bresson's verbal severity and austerity of dialogue.) He sees nothing in the film medium that prevents one of the subjects of cinema from being language itself—as language has become the very subject of much contemporary poetry and, in a metaphoric sense, of some important painting, such as that of Jasper Johns. But it seems that language can become the subject of cinema only at that point when a film-maker is obsessed by the problematic character of language—as Godard so evidently is. What other directors have regarded mainly as an adjunct of greater "realism" (the advantage of sound films as compared with silents) becomes in Godard's hands a virtually autonomous, sometimes subversive instrument.

I have already noted the varied ways in which Godard uses language as speech—not only as dialogue, but as monologue, as recited discourse, including quotation, and in off-screen comment and interrogation. Language is as well an important visual or plastic element in his films. Sometimes the screen is entirely filled with a printed text or lettering, which becomes the substitute for or counterpoint to a pictorial image. (Just a few examples: the stylishly elliptical credits that open each film; the postcard messages from the two soldiers in *Les Carabiniers*; the billboards, posters, record sleeves, and magazine ads in *My Life to Live*, *A Married Woman*, and *Masculine Feminine*;

the pages from Ferdinand's journal, only part of which can be read, in *Pierrot le Fou*; the conversation with book covers in *A Woman Is a Woman*; the cover of the paperback series "*Idées*" used thematically in *Deux ou Trois Choses*; the Maoist slogans on the apartment walls in *La Chinoise*.) Not only does Godard not regard cinema as essentially moving photographs; for him, the fact that movies, which purport to be a pictorial medium, admit of language, precisely gives cinema its superior range and freedom compared with other art forms. Pictorial or photographic elements are in a sense only the raw materials of Godard's cinema; the transformative ingredient is language. Thus, to cavil at Godard for the talkiness of his films is to misunderstand his materials and his intentions. It is almost as if the pictorial image had a static quality, too close to "art," that Godard wants to infect with the blight of words. In *La Chinoise*, a sign on the wall of the student Maoist commune reads: "One must replace vague ideas with clear images." But that's only one side of the issue, as Godard knows. Sometimes images are too clear, too simple. (*La Chinoise* is Godard's sympathetic, witty treatment of the arch-romantic wish to make oneself entirely simple, altogether clear.) The highly permutated dialectic between image and language is far from stable. As he declares in his own voice at the beginning of *Alphaville*: "Some things in life are too complex for oral transmission. So we make fiction out of them, to make them universal." But again, it's clear that making things universal can bring oversimplification, which must be combated by the concreteness and ambiguity of words.

Godard has always been fascinated by the opaqueness and coerciveness of language, and a recurrent feature of the film narratives is some sort of deformation of speech. At perhaps its most innocent but still oppressive stage, speech can become hysterical monologue, as in *Charlotte et son Jules* and *Une Histoire d'Eau*. Speech can become halting and incomplete, as in Godard's early use of interview passages—in *Le Grand Escroc*, and in *Breathless*, where Patricia interviews a novelist (played by the director J.-P. Melville) at Orly Airport. Speech can become repetitive, as in the hallucinatory doubling of the dialogue by the quadrilingual translator in *Contempt* and, in *Band of Outsiders*, the English teacher's oddly intense repetitions of end phrases during her dictation. There are several instances of the outright dehumanization of speech—like the slow-motion croaking of the computer Alpha 60 and the mechanized impoverished speech of its catatonic human subjects in *Alphaville*; and the "broken" speech of the traveler in *Anticipation*. The dialogue may be out of step with the action, as in the antiphonal commentary in *Pierrot le Fou*; or simply fail to make sense, as in the account of "the death of logic" following a nuclear explosion over Paris in *Le Nouveau Monde*. Sometimes Godard prevents speech from being completely understood—as in the first scene in *My Life to Live*, and with the sonically harsh, partly unintelligible tape of the voice of "Richard Po—" in *Made in U.S.A.*, and in the long erotic confession at the opening of *Weekend*. Complementing these mutilations of speech and language are the many explicit discussions of language-as-a-problem in Godard's films. The puzzle about how it's possible to make moral or intellectual sense by speaking, owing to the betrayal of consciousness by language, is debated in *My Life to Live* and *A Married Woman*; the mystery of "translating" from one language to another is a theme in *Contempt* and *Band of Outsiders*; the language of the future is a subject of speculation by Guillaume and Véronique in *La Chinoise* (words will be spoken as if they were sounds and matter); the nonsensical underside of language is demonstrated in the exchange in the café between Marianne, the laborer, and the bartender in *Made in U.S.A.*; and the effort to purify language of philosophical and cultural dissociation is the explicit, main theme of *Alphaville* and *Anticipation*, the success of an individual's efforts to do this providing the dramatic resolution of both films.

At this moment in Godard's work, the problem of language appears to have become his leading motif. Behind their obtrusive verbosity, Godard's films are haunted by the duplicity and banality of language. Insofar as there is a "voice" speaking in all his films, it is one that questions all voices. Language is the widest context in which Godard's recurrent theme of prostitution must be located. Beyond its direct sociological interest for Godard, prostitution is his extended metaphor for the fate of language, that is, of consciousness itself. The coalescing of the two themes is clearest in the science-fiction nightmare of *Anticipation*: in an airport hotel some time in the future (that is, now), travelers have the choice of two kinds of temporary sexual companions, someone who makes bodily love without speaking or someone who can recite the words of love but can't take part in any physical embrace. This schizophrenia of the flesh and the soul is the menace that inspires Godard's preoccupation with language, and confers on him the painful, self-interrogatory terms of his restless art. As Natasha declares at the end of *Alphaville*, "There are words I don't know." But it's that painful knowledge, according to Godard's controlling narrative myth, that marks the beginning of her redemption; and—by an extension of the same goal—the redemption of art itself.

(February 1968)

III

What's Happening in America (1966)

[What follows is a response to a questionnaire sent out by the editors of *Partisan Review* in the summer of 1966 to a number of people. The questionnaire began: "There is a good deal of anxiety about the direction of American life. In fact, there is reason to fear that America may be entering a moral and political crisis." After more along these lines of understatement, contributors were invited to organize their replies around seven specific questions: 1. Does it matter who is in the White House? Or is there something in our system which would force any President to act as Johnson is acting? 2. How serious is the problem of inflation? The problem of poverty? 3. What is the meaning of the split between the Administration and the American intellectuals? 4. Is white America committed to granting equality to the American Negro? 5. Where do you think our foreign policies are likely to lead us? 6. What, in general, do you think is likely to happen in America? 7. Do you think any promise is to be found in the activities of young people today?

My own response, reprinted below, appeared in the Winter 1967 issue of the magazine, along with contributions from Martin Duberman, Michael Harrington, Tom Hayden, Nat Hentoff, H. Stuart Hughes, Paul Jacobs, Tom Kahn, Leon H. Keyserling, Robert Lowell, Jack Ludwig, Jack Newfield, Harold Rosenberg, Richard H. Rovere, Richard Schlatter, and Diana Trilling.]

E VERYTHING that one feels about this country is, or ought to be, conditioned by the awareness of American *power*: of America as the arch-imperium of the planet, holding man's biological as well as his historical future in its King Kong paws. Today's America, with Ronald Reagan the new daddy of California and John Wayne chawing spareribs in the White House, is pretty much the same Yahooland that Mencken was describing. The main difference is that what's happening in America matters so much more in the late 1960's than it did in the 1920's. Then, if one had tough innards, one might jeer, sometimes affectionately, at American barbarism and find American innocence somewhat endearing. Both the barbarism and the innocence are lethal, outsized today.

First of all, then, American power is indecent in its scale. But also the quality of American life is an insult to the possibilities of human growth; and the pollution of American space, with gadgetry and cars and TV and box architecture, brutalizes the senses, making gray neurotics of most of us, and perverse spiritual athletes and strident self-transcenders of the best of us.

Gertrude Stein said that America is the oldest country in the world. Certainly, it's the most conservative. It has the most to lose by change (sixty percent of the world's wealth owned by a country containing six percent of the world's population). Americans know their backs are against the wall: "they" want to take all that away from "us." And, I think, America deserves to have it taken away.

Three facts about this country.

America was founded on a genocide, on the unquestioned assumption of the right of white Europeans to exterminate a resident, technologically backward, colored population in order to take over the continent.

America had not only the most brutal system of slavery in modern times but a unique juridical system (compared with other slaveries, say in Latin America and the British colonies) which did not, in a single respect, recognize slaves as persons.

As a country—as distinct from a colony—America was created mainly by the surplus poor of Europe, reinforced by a small group who were just *Europamüde*, tired of Europe (a literary catchword of the 1840s). Yet even the poorest knew both a "culture," largely invented by his social betters and administered from above, and a "nature" that had been pacified for centuries. These people arrived in a country where the indigenous culture was simply the enemy and was in process of being ruthlessly annihilated, and where nature, too, was the enemy, a pristine force, unmodified by civilization, that is, by human wants, which had to be defeated. After America was "won," it was filled up by new generations of the poor and built up according to the tawdry fantasy of the good life that culturally deprived, uprooted people might have at the beginning of the industrial era. And the country looks it.

Foreigners extol the American "energy," attributing to it both our unparalleled economic prosperity and the splendid vivacity of our arts and entertainments. But surely this is energy bad at its source and for which we pay too high a price, a hypernatural and humanly disproportionate dynamism that flays everyone's nerves raw. Basically it is the energy of violence, of free-floating resentment and anxiety unleashed by chronic cultural dislocations which must be, for the most part, ferociously sublimated. This energy has mainly been sublimated into crude materialism and acquisitiveness. Into hectic philanthropy. Into benighted moral crusades, the most spectacular of which was Prohibition. Into an awesome talent for uglifying countryside and cities. Into the loquacity and torment of a minority of gadflies: artists, prophets, muckrakers, cranks, and nuts. And into self-punishing neuroses. But the naked violence keeps breaking through, throwing everything into question.

Needless to say, America is not the only violent, ugly, and unhappy country on this earth. Again, it is a matter of scale. Only three million Indians lived here when the white man arrived, rifle in hand, for his fresh start. Today American hegemony menaces the lives not of three million but of countless millions who, like the Indians, have never even *heard* of the "United States of America," much less of its mythical empire, the "free world." American policy is still powered by the fantasy of Manifest Destiny, though the limits were once set by the borders of the continent, whereas today America's destiny embraces the entire world. There are still more hordes of redskins to be mowed down before virtue triumphs; as the classic Western movies explain, the only good Red is a dead Red. This may sound like an exaggeration to those who live in the special and more finely modulated atmosphere of New York and its environs. Cross the Hudson. You find out that not just *some* Americans but virtually all Americans feel that way.

Of course, these people don't know what they're saying, literally. But that's no excuse. That, in fact, is what makes it all possible. The unquenchable American moralism and the American faith in violence are not just twin symptoms of some character neurosis taking the form of a protracted adolescence, which presages an eventual maturity. They constitute a full-grown, firmly installed national psychosis, founded, as are all psychoses, on the efficacious denial of reality. So far it's worked. Except for portions of the South a hundred years ago, America has never known war. A taxi driver said to me on the day that could have been Armageddon, when America and Russia were on collision course off the shores of Cuba: "Me, I'm not worried. I served in the last one, and now I'm over draft age. They can't get me again. But I'm all for letting 'em have it right now. What are we waiting for? Let's get it over with." Since wars always happen Over There, and we always win, why not drop the bomb? If all it takes is pushing a button, even better. For America is that curious hybrid—an apocalyptic country and a valetudinarian country. The average citizen may harbor the fantasies of John Wayne, but he as often has the temperament of Jane Austen's Mr. Woodhouse.

To answer, briefly, some of the questions:

1. I do *not* think that Johnson is forced by "our system" to act as he is acting: for instance, in Vietnam, where each evening he personally chooses the bombing targets for the next day's missions. But I think there is something awfully wrong with a *de facto* system which allows the President virtually unlimited discretion in pursuing an immoral and imprudent foreign policy, so that the strenuous opposition of, say, the Chairman of the Senate Foreign Relations Committee counts for exactly nothing. The *de jure* system vests the power to make war in the Congress—with the exception, apparently, of imperialist ventures and genocidal expeditions. These are best left undeclared.

However, I don't mean to suggest that Johnson's foreign policy is the whim of a clique which has seized control, escalated the power of the Chief Executive, castrated the Congress, and manipulated public opinion. Johnson is, alas, all too representative. As Kennedy was not. If there is a conspiracy, it is (or was) that of the more enlightened national leaders hitherto largely selected by the Eastern-seaboard plutocracy. They engineered the precarious acquiescence to liberal goals that has prevailed in this country for over a generation—a superficial consensus made possible by the strongly apolitical character of a decentralized electorate mainly preoccupied with local issues. If the Bill of Rights were put to a national referendum as a new piece of legislation, it would meet the same fate as New York City's Civilian Review Board. Most of the people in this country believe what Goldwater believes, and always have. But most of them don't know it. Let's hope they don't find out.

4. I do not think white America is committed to granting equality to the American Negro. So committed are only a minority of white Americans, mostly educated and affluent, few of whom have had any prolonged social contact with Negroes. This is a passionately racist country; it will continue to be so in the foreseeable future.

5. I think that this administration's foreign policies are likely to lead to more wars and to wider wars. Our main hope, and the chief restraint on American bellicosity and paranoia, lies in the fatigue and depoliticization of Western Europe, the lively fear of America and of another world war in Russia and the Eastern European countries, and the corruption and unreliability of our client states in the Third World. It's hard to lead a holy war without allies. But America is just crazy enough to try to do it.

6. The meaning of the split between the Administration and the intellectuals? Simply that our leaders are genuine yahoos, with all the exhibitionist traits of their kind, and that liberal intellectuals (whose deepest loyalties are to an international fraternity of the reasonable) are not *that* blind. At this point, moreover, they have nothing to lose by proclaiming their discontent and frustration. But it's well to remember that liberal intellectuals, like Jews, tend to have a classical theory of politics, in which the state has a monopoly of power; hoping that those in positions of authority may prove to be enlightened men, wielding power justly, they are natural, if cautious, allies of the "establishment." As the Russian Jews knew they had at least a chance with the Czar's officials but none at all with marauding Cossacks and drunken peasants (Milton Himmelfarb has pointed this out), liberal intellectuals more naturally expect to influence the "decisions" of administrators than they do the volatile "feelings" of masses. Only when it becomes clear that, in fact, the government itself is being staffed by Cossacks and peasants, can a rupture like the present one take place. When (and if) the man in the White House who paws people and scratches his balls in public is replaced by the man who dislikes being touched and finds Yevtushenko "an interesting fellow," American intellectuals won't be so disheartened. The vast majority of them are not revolutionaries, wouldn't know how to be if they tried. Mostly a salaried professoriat, they're as much at home in the system when it functions a little better than it does right now as anyone else.

7. A somewhat longer comment on this last question.

Yes, I do find much promise in the activities of young people. About the only promise one can find anywhere in this country today is in the way some young people are carrying on, making a fuss. I include both their renewed interest in politics (as protest and as community action, rather than as theory) and the way they dance, dress, wear their hair, riot, make love. I also include the homage they pay to Oriental thought and rituals. And I include, not least of all, their interest in taking drugs—despite the unspeakable vulgarization of this project by Leary and others.

A year ago Leslie Fiedler, in a remarkably wrongheaded and interesting essay titled "The New Mutants," called attention to the fact that the new style of young people indicated a deliberate blurring of sexual differences, signaling the creation of a new breed of youthful androgens. The longhaired pop groups with their mass teenage following and the tiny elite of turned-on kids from Berkeley to the East Village were both lumped together as representatives of the "post-humanist" era now upon us, in which we witness a "radical metamorphosis of the Western male," a "revolt against masculinity," even "a rejection of conventional male potency." For Fiedler, this new turn in personal mores, diagnosed as illustrating a "programmatic espousal of an anti-puritanical mode of existence," is something to deplore. (Though sometimes, in his characteristic have-it-both-ways manner, Fiedler seemed to be vicariously relishing this development, *mainly* he appeared to be lamenting it.) But why, he never made explicit. I think it is because he is sure such a mode of existence undercuts radical politics, and its moral visions, altogether. Being radical in the older sense (some version of Marxism or socialism or anarchism) meant to be attached still to traditional "puritan" values of work, sobriety, achievement, and family-founding. Fiedler suggests, as have Philip Rahv and Irving Howe and Malcolm Muggeridge among others, that the new style of youth must be, at bottom, apolitical, and their revolutionary spirit a species of infantilism. The fact that the same kid joins SNCC or boards a Polaris submarine or agrees with Conor Cruise O'Brien *and* smokes pot and is bisexual and adores the Supremes is seen as a contradiction, a kind of ethical fraud or intellectual weak-mindedness.

I don't believe this to be so. The depolarizing of the sexes, to mention the element that Fiedler observes with such fascination, is the natural, and desirable, next stage of the sexual revolution (its dissolution, perhaps) which has moved beyond the idea of sex as a damaged but discrete zone of human activity, beyond the discovery that "society" represses the free expression of sexuality (by fomenting guilt), to the discovery that the way we live and the ordinarily available options of character repress almost entirely the deep experience of pleasure, and the possibility of self-knowledge. "Sexual freedom" is a shallow, outmoded slogan. What, who is being liberated? For older people, the sexual revolution is an idea that remains meaningful. One can be for it or against it; if one is for it, the idea remains confined within the norms of Freudianism and its derivatives. But Freud *was* a puritan, or "a fink," as one of Fiedler's students distressingly blurted out. So was Marx. It is right that young people see beyond Freud and Marx. Let the professors be the caretakers of this indeed precious legacy, and discharge all the obligations of piety. No need for dismay if the kids don't continue to pay the old dissenter-gods obeisance.

It seems to me obtuse, though understandable, to patronize the new kind of radicalism, which is post-Freudian and post-Marxist. For this radicalism is as much an experience as an idea. Without the personal experience, if one is looking in from the outside, it does look messy and almost pointless. It's easy to be put off by the youngsters throwing themselves around with their eyes closed to the near-deafening music of the discothèques (unless you're dancing, too), by the longhaired marchers carrying flowers and temple bells as often as "Get Out of Vietnam" placards, by the inarticulateness of a Mario Savio. One is also aware of the high casualty rate among this gifted, visionary minority among the young, the tremendous cost in personal suffering and in mental strain. The fakers, the slobs, and the merely flipped-out are plentiful among them. But the complex desires of the best of them: to engage and to "drop out"; to be beautiful to look at and touch as well as to be good; to be loving and quiet as well as militant and effective—these desires make sense in our present situation. To sympathize, of course, you have to be convinced that things in America really are as desperately bad as I have indicated. This is hard to see; the desperateness of things is obscured by the comforts and liberties that America does offer. Most people, understandably, don't really believe things are that bad. That's why, for them, the antics of this youth can be no more than a startling item in the passing parade of cultural fashions, to be appraised with a friendly but essentially weary and knowing look. The sorrowful look that says: I was a radical, too, when I was young. When are these kids going to grow up and realize what we had to realize, that things never are going to be really different, except maybe worse?

From my own experience and observation, I can testify that there is a profound concordance between the sexual revolution, redefined, and the political revolution, redefined. That being a socialist and taking certain drugs (in a fully serious spirit: as a technique for exploring one's consciousness, not as an anodyne or a crutch) are not incompatible, that there is no incompatibility between the exploration of inner space and the rectification of social space. What some of the kids understand is that it's the whole character structure of modern American man, and his imitators, that needs rehauling. (Old folks like Paul Goodman and Edgar Z. Friedenberg have, of course, been suggesting this for a long time.) That rehauling includes Western "masculinity," too. They believe that some socialist remodeling of institutions and the ascendance, through electoral means or otherwise, of better leaders won't really change anything. And they are right.

Neither do I dare deride the turn toward the East (or more generally, to the wisdoms of the non-white world) on the part of a tiny group of young people—however uninformed and jejune the adherence usually is. (But then, nothing could be more ignorant than Fiedler's insinuation that Oriental modes of thought are "feminine" and passive," which is the reason the demasculinized kids are drawn to them.) Why shouldn't they look for wisdom elsewhere? If America *is* the culmination of Western white civilization, as everyone from the Left to the Right declares, then there must be something terribly wrong with Western white civilization. This is a painful truth; few of us want to go that far. It's easier, much easier, to accuse the kids, to reproach them for being "non-participants in the past" and "drop-outs from history." But it isn't real history Fiedler is referring to with such solicitude. It's just *our* history, which he claims is identical with "the tradition of the human," the tradition of "reason" itself. Of course, it's hard to assess life on this planet from a genuinely world-historical perspective; the effort induces vertigo and seems like an invitation to suicide. But from a world-historical perspective, that local history which some young people are repudiating (with their fondness for dirty words, their peyote, their macrobiotic rice, their Dadaist art, etc.) looks a good deal less pleasing and less self-evidently worthy of perpetuation. The truth is that Mozart, Pascal, Boolean algebra, Shakespeare, parliamentary government, baroque churches, Newton, the emancipation of women, Kant, Marx, and Balanchine ballets don't redeem what this particular civilization has wrought upon the world. The white race *is* the cancer of human history; it is the white race and it alone— its ideologies and inventions—which eradicates autonomous civilizations wherever it spreads, which has upset the ecological balance of the planet, which now threatens the very existence of life itself. What the Mongol hordes threaten is far less frightening than the damage that Western "Faustian" man, with his idealism, his magnificent art, his sense of intellectual adventure, his world-devouring energies for conquest, has already done, and further threatens to do.

This is what some of the kids sense, though few of them could put it in words. Again, I believe them to be right. I'm not arguing that they're going to prevail, or even that they're likely to change much of anything in this country. But a few of them may save their own souls. America is a fine country for inflaming people, from Emerson and Thoreau to Mailer and Burroughs and Leó Szilárd and John Cage and Judith and Julian Beck, with the project of trying to save their own souls. Salvation becomes almost a mundane, inevitable goal when things are so bad, really intolerable.

One last comparison, which I hope won't seem farfetched. The Jews left the ghetto in the early nineteenth century, thus becoming a people doomed to disappear. But one of the by-products of their fateful absorption into the modern world was an incredible burst of creativity in the arts, science, and secular scholarship—the relocation of a powerful but frustrated spiritual energy. These innovating artists and intellectuals were not alienated Jews, as is said so often, but people who were alienated *as* Jews.

I'm scarcely more hopeful for America than I am for the Jews. This is a doomed country, it seems to me; I only pray that, when America founders, it doesn't drag the rest of the planet down, too. But one should notice that, during its long elephantine agony, America is also producing its subtlest minority genera- tion of the decent and sensitive, young people who are alienated *as* Americans. They are not drawn to the stale truths of their sad elders (though these are truths). More of their elders should be listening to them.

(1966)

Trip to Hanoi

THOUGH I have been and am passionately opposed to the American aggression in Vietnam, I accepted the unexpected invitation to go to Hanoi that came in mid-April with the pretty firm idea that I wouldn't write about the trip upon my return. Being neither a journalist nor a political activist (though a veteran signer of petitions and anti-war demonstrator) nor an Asian specialist, but rather a stubbornly unspecialized writer who has so far been largely unable to incorporate into either novels or essays my evolving radical political convictions and sense of moral dilemma at being a citizen of the American empire, I doubted that my account of such a trip could add anything new to the already eloquent opposition to the war. And contributing to the anti-war polemic seemed to me the only worthwhile reason for an American to be writing about Vietnam now.

Perhaps the difficulty started there, with the lack of a purpose that really justified in my own mind my being invited to North Vietnam. Had I brought some clear intentions about the usefulness (to me or to anyone else) of my visit, I probably would have found it easier to sort out and assimilate what I saw. If occasionally I could have reminded myself that I was a writer and Vietnam was "material," I might have fended off some of the confusions that beset me. As it was, the first days of my stay were profoundly discouraging, with most of my energies going toward trying to keep my gloom within tolerable limits. But now that I'm back, and since returning want after all to write about North Vietnam, I don't regret that early decision. By denying myself a role that could have shielded me from my ignorance and spared me a lot of personal discomfort, I unwittingly assisted what discoveries I eventually did make during the trip.

Of course, it wasn't only this original refusal to envisage the trip as a professional task that opened the way to my confusion. In part, my bewilderment was direct and unavoidable: the honest reflex of being culturally dislocated. Also, I should mention that few Americans who visit Hanoi at this time go alone, the usual practice being, for the convenience of the Vietnamese, to assemble groups of sometimes two, usually three, four, or

five people who often don't know each other before the trip.
I traveled to North Vietnam as one of three. And I had met
neither of the two other Americans in whose company I made
the trip—Andrew Kopkind, the journalist, and Robert Greenblatt, a mathematician from Cornell now working full time for
the anti-war movement—before our rendezvous in Cambodia
in late April. Yet this trip involves unremitting and not wholly
voluntary proximity, the kind befitting a romance or a dangerous emergency, lasting without pause for at least a month. (We
were invited for two weeks. It took us ten days, because of
delays and missed connections, to go from New York via Paris
and Phnom Penh to Hanoi, and just under a week to make
the return trip.) Naturally, the situation with my companions
claimed a sizable part of the attention that, had I traveled alone,
would have gone to the Vietnamese: sometimes in the form of
an obligation, most often as a pleasure. There was the practical
necessity of learning to live amicably and intelligently with two
strangers in circumstances of instant intimacy, strangers even if,
or perhaps especially since, they were people already known to
me by reputation and, in the case of Andy Kopkind, by his writing, which I admired. We were further drawn together by being
in what was to all three of us an alien part of the world (neither
Bob Greenblatt nor I had ever been to Asia before; Andy Kopkind had made one trip five years ago, visiting Saigon, Bangkok,
the Philippines, and Japan), and meeting no one whose native
language was English (except a U.S.I.S. official and an American
journalist in Laos, where we were stuck for four days on our way
"in," and four American college students sponsored by S.D.S.
who arrived in Hanoi at the beginning of our second week).
All this added together, it seems inevitable that we spent a great
deal of time talking—gratefully, often feverishly—to each other.

   Still, I don't mean to suggest that these elements of my situation account for the wistfully negative tone of my early impressions of Vietnam. The serious explanation for that I would
locate not in the distractions and pressures of being one of an
arbitrarily assembled yet inseparable trio in a new land, but
in the demands and limitations of the approach to Vietnam I
myself was capable of. Made miserable and angry for four years
by knowledge of the excruciating suffering of the Vietnamese
people at the hands of my government, now that I was actually

there and being plied with gifts and flowers and rhetoric and tea and seemingly exaggerated kindness, I didn't *feel* any more than I already had ten thousand miles away. But being in Hanoi was far more mysterious, more puzzling intellectually, than I expected. I found that I couldn't avoid worrying and wondering how well I understood the Vietnamese, and they me and my country.

Yet this problem I posed for myself, frustrating as it proved, was perhaps the most important and fruitful one, at least to me. For it was not information (at least in the ordinary sense) that I'd come to find. Like anyone who cared about Vietnam in the last years, I already knew a great deal; and I could not hope to collect more or significantly better information in a mere two weeks than was already available. Ranging from the early reports in *The New York Times* by Harrison Salisbury of his visit in December and January of 1965–66 (later expanded into a book, *Behind the Lines—Hanoi*) and *The Other Side*, the book written jointly by Staughton Lynd and Tom Hayden, the first Americans from the anti-war movement to visit North Vietnam, to the analyses of Philippe Devillers and Jean Lacouture in the French press, to the recent articles by Mary McCarthy which I've been reading since my return to the United States, a multiple account has accumulated which conveys in vivid detail how Hanoi and large parts of North Vietnam appear to a sympathetic or at least reasonably objective outsider looking on. Anyone who wants to can get information on the achievements of the country since the French left in 1954: the expansion of medical services, the reorganization of education, the creation of a modest industrial base, and the beginnings of diversified agriculture. Even easier to obtain are the facts about the years of merciless bombing by the United States of all the population centers of North Vietnam—with the exception of downtown Hanoi (which has, however, been doused with "anti-personnel" or fragmentation bombs, those that don't harm buildings but only kill people)—and the destruction of virtually all the new schools and hospitals and factories built since 1954, as well as most bridges, theatres, pagodas, and Catholic churches and cathedrals. In my own case, several years of reading and of viewing newsreels had furnished a large portfolio of miscellaneous images of Vietnam: napalmed corpses, live citizens on bicycles, the hamlets of thatched huts, the razed cities like Nam Dinh and Phu Ly, the cylindrical, one-person bomb shelters spaced along the sidewalks of Hanoi, the thick yellow straw hats worn by schoolchildren as protection against fragmentation bombs. (Indelible horrors, pictorial and statistical, supplied by courtesy of television and *The New York Times* and *Life*, without one's even having to bestir oneself to consult the frankly partisan books of Wilfred Burchett or the documentation assembled by the Russell Foundation's International War Crimes Tribunal.) But the confrontation with the originals of these images didn't prove to be a simple experience; actually to see and touch them produced an effect both exhilarating and numbing. Matching concrete reality with mental image was at best a mechanical or merely additive process, while prying new facts from the Vietnamese officials and ordinary citizens I was meeting was a task for which I'm not particularly well equipped. Unless I could effect in myself some change of awareness, of consciousness, it would scarcely matter that I'd actually been to Vietnam. But that was exactly what was so hard, since I had only my own culture-bound, disoriented sensibility for an instrument.

Indeed, the problem was that Vietnam had become so much a fact of my consciousness as an American that I was having enormous difficulty getting it outside my head. The first experience of being there absurdly resembled meeting a favorite movie star, one who for years has played a role in one's fantasy life, and finding the actual person so much smaller, less vivid, less erotically charged, and mainly different. Most convincing were the experiences that were least real, like the evening of our arrival. I was nervous throughout the flight in the small International Control Commission plane that had belatedly taken off from Vientiane; and landing in Hanoi's Gia Lam airport at night several hours later, I was mainly relieved just to be alive and on the ground, and hardly bothered that I knew neither where I was nor whom I was with. Hugging my flowers, I crossed the dark landing area, trying to keep straight the names of the four smiling men from the Peace Committee who had come to meet us. And if our flight and landing had the quality of a hallucination, the rest of that night seemed like one vast back projection, the overvivid extensions and foreshortenings of time, scale, and movement. First, there were either the

few minutes or the hour spent waiting for our luggage in the
bleak airport building, awkwardly chatting with the Vietnamese. Then, when we were distributed in three cars and started
into the darkness, there was the rhythm of the ride into Hanoi.
A little way from the airport, the cars lurched down a bumpy
dirt road onto the narrow, shuddering pontoon bridge over
the Red River that has replaced the bombed-out iron one, and
inched across that; but once on the other side, the cars seemed
to go too fast and, entering Hanoi, passing through dim streets,
opened a rude swathe in the stream of indistinguishable figures
on bicycles, until we halted in front of our hotel. Its name,
Thong Nhat, means Reunification, someone said: a huge building, and indeterminate in style. A dozen people were sitting
about the very plain lobby, mostly non-Orientals but at that
point otherwise unidentifiable. After we were taken upstairs
and shown to our large rooms, there was a late supper for us
in a stark, deserted dining room with rows of propeller fans
slowly turning overhead. "Our" Vietnamese waited for us in
the lobby. When we joined them, we asked if, late as it was,
they would mind going out with us for a walk. So out we went,
weak with excitement. Along the streets, now almost empty
of people, we passed clusters of trucks parked between tents
which, they told us, sheltered all-night "mobile workshops" or
"dispersed factories." We went as far as the Mot Cot pagoda in
the Petit Lac, and lingering there, heard some—to me, barely
intelligible—tales of ancient Vietnamese history. Once back in
the hotel lobby, Oanh, evidently the leader of the group from
the Peace Committee, gently urged us to go to bed. People in
Hanoi, he explained, rise and eat breakfast very early (since the
bombing started, most stores open at 5 A.M. and close a few
hours later), and they would be coming by for us at 8 A.M. the
next day, which happened to be Buddha's birthday, to take us
to a pagoda. I remember reluctantly saying good night to the
Vietnamese and to my two companions; in my room, spending
a quarter of an hour trying to cope with the high vault of white
mosquito netting covering the bed; and finally sinking into a
difficult, agitated, but happy sleep.

Of course, North Vietnam was unreal that first night. But it
continued to seem unreal, or at least incomprehensible, for days
afterwards. To be sure, that initial haunting vision of wartime

Hanoi at night was corrected by more mundane daytime experiences. The Thong Nhat Hotel shrank to ordinary size (one could even visualize it in its former incarnation, the Metropole of French colonial days); individuals of varying age and character emerged out of the silent collective traffic of bicyclists and pedestrians; and the Petit Lac and the nearby tree-shaded streets became places of daily resort, where we walked casually, without our guides, whenever it wasn't too hot and one or two or all three of us had a spare hour. Though so far from and so unlike the only cities I knew, those of America and Europe, Hanoi quickly gained an eerie familiarity. Yet when I was honest with myself I had to admit that the place was simply too foreign, that I really understood nothing at all, except at a "distance."

In his brilliant episode in the film *Far from Vietnam*, Godard reflects (as we hear his voice, we see him sitting behind an idle movie camera) that it would be good if we each made a Vietnam inside ourselves, especially if we cannot actually go there (Godard had wanted to shoot his episode in North Vietnam, but was denied a visa). Godard's point—a variant on Che's maxim that, in order to crack the American hegemony, revolutionaries have the duty to create "two, three, many Vietnams"— had seemed to me exactly right. What I'd been creating and enduring for the last four years was a Vietnam inside my head, under my skin, in the pit of my stomach. But the Vietnam I'd been thinking about for years was scarcely filled out at all. It was really only the mold into which the American seal was cutting. My problem was not to try to feel more inside myself. My problem was that I (luckier than Godard) was now actually in Vietnam for a brief time, yet somehow was unable to make the full intellectual and emotional connections that my political and moral solidarity with Vietnam implied.

The most economical way, I think, of conveying these early difficulties is to transcribe from journal entries I made during the first week after our arrival on the third of May.

MAY 5

The cultural difference is the hardest thing to estimate, to overcome. A difference of manners, style, therefore of substance. (And how much of what I'm struck by is Asian, how much specifically Vietnamese, I am unlikely to find out on my first trip to Asia.) Clearly, they have a different way here of treating the guest, the stranger, the foreigner, not to mention the enemy. Also, I'm convinced, the Vietnamese have a different relation to language. The difference can't just be due to the fact that my sentences, already slowed down and simplified, more often than not have to be mediated by a translator. For even when I'm in conversation with someone who speaks English or French, it seems to me we're both talking baby talk.

To all this add the constraint of being reduced to the status of a child: scheduled, led about, explained to, fussed over, pampered, kept under benign surveillance. Not only a child individually but, even more exasperating, one of a group of children. The four Vietnamese from the Peace Committee who are seeing us around act as our nurses, our teachers. I try to discover the differences between each of them, but can't; and I worry that they don't see what's different or special about me. All too often I catch myself trying to please them, to make a good impression—to get the best mark of the class. I present myself as an intelligent, well-mannered, cooperative, uncomplicated person. So not only do I feel like a rather corrupt child but, being neither a child nor in fact as simple and easy to know as the way I'm coming on would indicate, I feel somewhat of a fraud. (It's no extenuation that this open, legible person is perhaps who I would like to be.)

Maybe, if I'm cheating, with the best intentions, trying to make it easier for them, they're doing the same for us. Is that why, though I know they must be different from each other, I can't get beyond the surface markings? Oanh has the most personal authority, walks and sits with that charming "American" slouch, and sometimes seems moody or distracted. (We've learned that his wife has been ill ever since she was captured and tortured for a year by the French in the early 1950's; and he has several small children.) Hieu alternates between boyishness—he giggles—and the pointed composure of a junior bureaucrat. Phan has the most affable manners; he usually seems out of breath when he talks, which he loves doing; he's also one of the very few plump Vietnamese I've seen. Toan generally looks eager and slightly intimidated, and never speaks unless you ask him a question. But what else? Phan is the oldest, I think.

Today we learned, to our great surprise, that Oahn is forty-six. It doesn't help that every Vietnamese (especially the men, who rarely go bald or even gray) looks at least ten years younger than he is.

What makes it especially hard to see people as individuals is that everybody here seems to talk in the same style and to have the same things to say. This impression is reinforced by the exact repetition of the ritual of hospitality at each place we visit. A bare room, a low table, wooden chairs, perhaps a couch. We all shake hands, then sit around the table, which holds several plates of overripe green bananas, Vietnamese cigarettes, damp cookies, a dish of paper-wrapped candies made in China, cups for tea. We are introduced. They tell us their names. We shake hands again. Pause. The spokesman of their group, wherever we are visiting (a factory, a school, a government ministry, a museum), gazes at us benignly, smiles, "*Cac ban* . . ." ("Friends . . ."). He has started his speech of welcome. Someone comes through a curtain and begins serving tea.

MAY 6

Of course, I'm not sorry to have come. Being in Hanoi is at the very least a duty, for me an important act of personal and political affirmation. What I'm not yet reconciled to is that it's also a piece of political theatre. They are playing their roles, we (I) must play ours (mine). The heaviness of it all comes from the fact that the script is written entirely by them; and they're directing the play, too. Though this is how it has to be—it's their country, their life-and-death struggle, while we are volunteers, extras, figurants who retain the option of getting off the stage and sitting safely in the audience—it makes my acts here appear to me largely dutiful, and the whole performance a little sad.

We have a role: American friends of the Vietnamese struggle. (About forty Americans in some way connected with the anti-war movement in the States have made this trip before us.) The trip to Hanoi is a kind of reward or patronage. We are being given a treat, being thanked for our unsolicited efforts; and then we are to return home with a reinforced sense of solidarity, to continue our separate ways of opposing the current American policy.

There is, of course, an exquisite politeness in this corporate identity. We are not asked, separately or collectively, to say why we merit this trip. Our being recommended (by Americans who were invited earlier and retain the confidence of the Vietnamese) and our willingness to come (all this way, at our own expense, and facing the risk of prosecution when we return to the States) seem to put Bob's, Andy's, and my efforts on the same level. Nobody here poses questions about what we specifically do for the anti-war movement, or asks us to justify the quality of our activities; it seems to be assumed that we each do what we can. Though our Vietnamese hosts evidently know we are not Communists, and indeed seem to have no illusions about the American Communist Party—"We know our Communist friends in the United States are not in great number," a government official remarked dryly—nobody inquires into our political beliefs. We are *cac ban* all.

Everybody says, "We know the American people are our friends. Only the present American government is our enemy." A journalist we met commended our efforts to "safeguard the freedom and prestige of the United States." Though I honor the nobility of this attitude, I'm exasperated by their naïveté. Do they really believe what they're saying? Don't they understand anything about America? Part of me can't help regarding them as children—beautiful, patient, heroic, martyred, stubborn children. And I know that I'm not a child, though the theatre of this visit requires that I play the role of one. The same shy, tender smile appears on the face of the soldier we pass in the park, the elderly Buddhist scholar, and the waitress in the hotel dining room as on the faces of the children lined up to greet us at the evacuated primary school we visited today just outside Hanoi; and we're smiling at them like that, too. We get little presents and souvenirs wherever we go, and at the end of each visit Bob distributes a handful of anti-war buttons (how lucky that he thought to bring a bagful of them). The most impressive of his random collection are the jumbo blue and white buttons from last October's March on the Pentagon, which we save for special occasions. How could we not be moved at the moment we are pinning on their tiny red and gold badges while they are adorning themselves with our big anti-war buttons? How could we not also be in bad faith?

The root of my bad faith: that I long for the three-dimensional, textured, "adult" world in which I live in America—even as I go about my (their) business in this two-dimensional world of the ethical fairy tale where I am paying a visit, and in which I do believe.

Part of the role (theirs and mine) is the stylizing of language: speaking mostly in simple declarative sentences, making all discourse either expository or interrogative. Everything is on one level here. All the words belong to the same vocabulary: struggle, bombings, friend, aggressor, imperialist, patriot, victory, brother, freedom, unity, peace. Though my strong impulse is to resist their flattening out of language, I've realized that I must talk this way—with moderation—if I'm to say anything that's useful to them. That even includes using the more loaded local epithets like "the puppet troops" (for the forces of the Saigon government) and "the American movement" (they mean *us!*). Luckily, I'm already comfortable with some of the key words. Within the last year, back in the States, I had started saying "the Front" (instead of Viet Cong) and "black people" (instead of Negroes) and "liberated zones" (for territory controlled by the National Liberation Front). But I'm far from getting it right, from their point of view. I notice that when I say "Marxism," it's usually rendered by our translator as "Marxism-Leninism." And while they may speak of "the socialist camp," it's hardly possible for me to say anything other than "Communist countries."

It's not that I judge their words to be false. For once, I think, the political and moral reality is as simple as the Communist rhetoric would have it. The French *were* "the French colonialists"; the Americans *are* "imperialist aggressors"; the Thieu-Ky regime *is* a "puppet government." Then what finicky private standard or bad vibrations make me balk? Is it just the old conviction of the inadequacy of that language, to which I was first introduced during my precociously political childhood when I read *PM* and Corliss Lamont and the Webbs on Russia, and later, by the time I was a junior at North Hollywood High School, worked in the Wallace campaign and attended screenings of Eisenstein films at the American-Soviet Friendship Society? But surely neither the philistine fraud on the American CP nor the special pathos of fellow-traveling in the 1940's is relevant here: North Vietnam, spring 1968. Yet how difficult it is, once words have been betrayed, to take them seriously again.

Only within the last two years (and that very much because of the impact of the Vietnam war) have I been able to pronounce the words "capitalism" and "imperialism" again. For more than fifteen years, though capitalism and imperialism hardly ceased to be facts in the world, the words themselves had seemed to me simply unusable, dead, dishonest (because a tool in the hands of dishonest people). A great deal is involved in these recent linguistic decisions: a new connection with my historical memory, my aesthetic sensibility, my very idea of the future. That I've begun to use some elements of Marxist or neo-Marxist language again seems almost a miracle, an unexpected remission of historical muteness, a new chance to address problems that I'd renounced ever understanding.

Still, when I hear these tag words here, spoken by the Vietnamese, I can't help experiencing them as elements of an *official* language, and they become again an alien way of talking. I'm not referring now to the truth of this language (the realities that the words point to), which I do acknowledge, but to the context and range of sensibility it presupposes. What's painfully exposed for me, by the way the Vietnamese talk, is the gap between ethics and aesthetics. As far as I can tell, the Vietnamese possess—even within the terribly austere and materially deprived existence they are forced to lead now—a lively, even passionate aesthetic sense. More than once, for instance, people have quite unaffectedly expressed their indignation and sadness at the disfigurement of the *beauty* of the Vietnamese countryside by the American bombing. Someone even commented on the "many beautiful names," like Cedar Falls and Junction City, that the Americans have given their "savage operations in the south." But the leading way of thinking and speaking in Vietnam is unreservedly moralistic. (I suspect this is quite natural to the Vietnamese, a cultural trait that precedes any grafting on of the moralizing framework of Communist language.) And perhaps it's the general tendency of aesthetic consciousness, when developed, to make judgments more complex and more highly qualified, while it's in the very nature of moral consciousness to be simplifying, even simplistic, and to sound—in translation at least—stiff and old-fashioned. There's a committee here (someone had left a piece of stationery in the hotel lobby) for maintaining contact with South Vietnamese intellectuals, called

"Committee of Struggle Against U.S. Imperialists and Henchmen's Persecution of Intellectuals in South Vietnam." Henchmen! But aren't they? In today's Vietnam News Agency bulletin the American soldiers are called "cruel thugs." Although again the quaintness of phrase makes me smile, that is just what they are—from the vantage point of helpless peasants being napalmed by swooping diving metal birds. Still, quite apart from the quaintness of particular words, such language does make me uncomfortable. Whether because I am laggard or maybe just dissociated, I both assent to the unreserved moral judgment and shy away from it, too. I believe they are right. At the same time, nothing here can make me forget that events are much more complicated than the Vietnamese represent them. But exactly what complexities would I have them acknowledge? Isn't it enough that their struggle is, objectively, just? Can they ever afford subtleties when they need to mobilize every bit of energy to continue standing up to the American Goliath? . . . Whatever I conclude, it seems to me I end up patronizing them.

Perhaps all I'm expressing is the difference between being an actor (them) and being a spectator (me). But that's a big difference, and I don't see how I can bridge it. My sense of solidarity with the Vietnamese, however genuine and felt, is a moral abstraction developed (and meant to be lived out) at a great distance from them. Since my arrival in Hanoi, I must maintain that sense of solidarity alongside new unexpected feelings which indicate that, unhappily, it will always remain a moral abstraction. For me—a spectator?—it's monochromatic here, and I feel oppressed by that.

MAY 7

Now, I think, I really understand—for the first time—the difference between history and psychology. It's the world of psychology that I miss. (What I meant yesterday by the "adult" world.) They live exclusively in the world of history.

And not only in history, but in a monothematic history that people allude to in more or less the same terms wherever we go. Today we got it in full, during a long, guided tour of the Historical Museum: four thousand years of continuous history, more than two thousand years of being overrun by foreign aggressors. The first successful Vietnamese uprising against foreign rule, in A.D. 40, was led by two women generals, the Trung sisters. That was over a thousand years before Joan of Arc, our woman guide at the museum added, as if to indicate we hadn't registered the proper surprise at the idea of a woman general. And you also have two of them, I joked back. She smiled slightly, then went on: "The tradition of the two sisters remains until now. In the present struggle many ladies have shown themselves worthwhile." No pleasantry, that. Oanh, who we've learned is one of the leading composers in North Vietnam, has written a song about the two sisters, and many temples in Hanoi and nearby are dedicated to them. . . . As the Vietnamese understand their history, it consists essentially of one scenario, which has been played out over and over again. Particular historical identities dissolve into instructive equivalences. The Americans = the French (who first entered Vietnam in 1787 with missionaries, and officially invaded the country in 1858) = the Japanese (in World War II) = the "Northern feudalists" (our guide's usual way of referring to the millennia of invading Chinese, I suppose out of politeness to the nominal ally of today). The general who repelled the Chinese invasion of 1075–76, Ly Thuong Kiet, was a poet as well and used his poems to rouse the Vietnamese people to take up arms—just like Ho Chi Minh, the guide pointed out. She told us the generals who defended the country against three invasions by "the Mongols" (another euphemism for the Chinese?) in the thirteenth century—in 1257, 1284–85, and 1287–88—originated the basic techniques of guerrilla warfare that General Giap successfully employed against the French between 1946 and 1954 and now uses against the Americans. In one room, examining a terrain map of the battle site, we learned that the turning point in a struggle against an invasion by two hundred thousand Manchu dynasty troops in 1789 was a surprise Tet offensive. As she relates, with the aid of maps and dioramas, the great sea battles on the Bach Dang River in 938 and 1288 which successfully terminated other wars of resistance, I detect unmistakable parallels to the strategies used at Dien Bien Phu. (The other night we saw an hour film on the Dien Bien Phu campaign, part original footage and part reconstruction. Today, by the way, is the anniversary of that victory, though I've seen no signs in Hanoi of any festivities.)

My first reaction to the didactically positive way the Vietnamese have of recounting their history is to find it simple-minded ("childish" again). I have to remind myself that historical understanding can have other purposes than the ones I take for granted: objectivity and completeness. This is history for use—for survival, to be precise—and it is an entirely *felt* history, not the preserve of detached intellectual concern. The past continues in the form of the present, and the present extends backwards in time. I see that there's nothing arbitrary or merely quaint (as I'd thought) in the standard epithet for Americans which I've seen on billboards and wall posters: *giac My xan luoc*, "pirate American aggressors." The very first foreign invaders were pirates. So the Chinese, the French, the Japanese, now the Americans, and anybody else who invades Vietnam will always be pirates, too.

Even more than the Jews, the Vietnamese seem to suffer from an appalling lack of variety in their collective existence. History is one long martyrdom: in the case of Vietnam, the chain of episodes of victimization at the hands of great powers. And one of their proudest boasts is that people here have succeeded in retaining "Vietnamese characteristics, though we live close to the Chinese superpower and were under complete French domination for eighty years," in the words of our guide today. Perhaps only a martyr people, one which has managed to survive against crushing odds, develops so acute and personal a historical concern. And this extraordinarily vivid sense of history—of living simultaneously in the past, the present, and the future—must be one of the great sources of Vietnamese strength.

But the decision to survive at all costs in suffering obviously imposes its own aesthetic, its own peculiar and (to people not consciously driven by the imperative of survival) maddening sensibility. The Vietnamese historical sense, being, above all, a sense of the sameness of history, is reflected, naturally, in the sameness of what they say—what they feel we ought to listen to. I've become aware here of how greatly prized, and taken for granted, the value of *variety* is in Western culture. In Vietnam, apparently something doesn't become less valuable or useful because it has been done (or said) before. On the contrary, repetition confers value on something. It is a positive moral style. Hence, the capsule summaries of Vietnamese history we get from most people we visit, almost as much a part of the ritual as the tea and green bananas and expressions of friendship for the American people whom we're supposed to represent.

But further, these speeches of historical recital that we hear almost daily are just one symptom of the general predilection of the Vietnamese for putting all information into a historical narrative. I've noticed that when we're discussing or asking questions about the country today, each account given to us is formulated around a pivotal date: usually either August 1945 (victory of the Vietnamese revolution, the founding of the state by Ho Chi Minh) or 1954 (expulsion of the French colonialists) or 1965 (beginning of "the escalation," as they call the American bombing). Everything is either before or after something else.

Their framework is chronological. Mine is both chronological and geographical. I am continually reaching toward cross-cultural comparisons, and these are the context of most of my questions. But because they don't share this context, they seem mildly puzzled by many things I ask. How hard it was yesterday, for instance, to get the affable, French-educated Minister of Higher Education, Professor Ta Quang Buu, to explore the differences between the French lycée curriculum used until 1954 and the program the Vietnamese have devised to replace it. Though he heard my question, for a while he simply didn't see the point of it. All he wanted was to out-line the Vietnamese system (kindergarten plus ten grades), report how few schools of any kind existed before 1954 and how many have been opened since (except for a good medical school inherited from the French, almost all university-level facilities have had to be developed from scratch), cite figures on rising literacy, tell how increasing numbers of teachers have been trained and young people given access to higher educa-tion and older people enrolled in adult-education courses since that date. The same thing happened when we talked to the Minister of Public Health, Dr. Pham Ngoc Thach, in his office in Hanoi, and when we met the young doctor of the tiny hamlet of Vy Ban in Hoa Binh province. After explaining that most of the Vietnamese population had no medical services of any kind under the French, they were eager to tell us how many hospitals and infirmaries have been built and how many doctors have been trained and to describe the programs undertaken since 1954 that have brought malaria under control and virtually eliminated opium addiction, but were quite taken aback when we wanted to know whether Vietnamese medicine was entirely Western in orientation or whether, as we suspected, Western techniques were mixed with Chinese methods such as herbal medicines and acupuncture. They must find us dilettantish, and may even regard such questions as a means of refusing full emotional solidarity with the unity and urgency of their struggle. Perhaps. It's still true that since Andy, Bob, and I don't share a history with the Vietnamese the historical view does narrow our understanding. To gain insight into what the Vietnamese are trying to build we must relate what they tell us to knowledge and perspectives we already have. But what we know, of course, is just what they don't know. And so most of our questions are a kind of rudeness, to which they respond with unfailing courtesy and patience, but sometimes obtusely.

MAY 8

Judging from these first days, I think it's hopeless. There is a barrier I can't cross. I'm overcome by how exotic the Vietnamese are—impossible for us to understand them, clearly impossible for them to understand us. No, I'm hedging here. The truth is: I feel I *can* in fact understand them (if not relate to them, except on their simplistic terms). But it seems to me that while my consciousness does include theirs, or could, theirs could never include mine. They may be nobler, more heroic, more generous than I am, but I have more on my mind than they do—probably just what precludes my ever being that virtuous. Despite my admiration for the Vietnamese and my shame over the deeds of my country, I still feel like someone from a "big" culture visiting a "little" culture. My consciousness, reared in that "big" culture, is a creature with many organs, accustomed to being fed by a stream of cultural goods, and infected by irony. While I don't think I'm lacking in moral seriousness, I shrink from having my seriousness ironed out; I know I'd feel reduced if there were no place for its contradictions and paradoxes, not to mention its diversions and distractions. Thus, the gluttonous habits of my consciousness prevent me from being at home with what I most admire, and—for all my raging against America—firmly unite me to what I condemn. "American friend" indeed!

Of course, I *could* live in Vietnam, or an ethical society like this one—but not without the loss of a big part of myself. Though I believe incorporation into such a society will greatly improve the lives of most people in the world (and therefore support the advent of such societies), I imagine it will in many ways impoverish mine. I live in an unethical society that coarsens the sensibilities and thwarts the capacities for goodness of most people but makes available for minority consumption an astonishing array of intellectual and aesthetic pleasures. Those who don't enjoy (in both senses) my pleasures have every right, from their side, to regard my consciousness as spoiled, corrupt, decadent. I, from my side, can't deny the immense richness of these pleasures, or my addiction to them. What came to mind this afternoon was the sentence of Talleyrand that Bertolucci used as the motto of his sad, beautiful film: "He who has not lived before the revolution has never known the sweetness of life." I told Andy, who knows the film, what I'd been thinking, and he confessed to similar feelings. We were walking along in a quarter of Hanoi far from the hotel and, like truants, began talking—nostalgically?—about San Francisco rock groups and *The New York Review of Books.*

Does all this mental appetitiveness and lust for variety disqualify me from entering, at least partially, into the singular reality of North Vietnam? I suspect it does, that it already has, as indicated by my baffled, frustrated reactions to the Vietnamese so far. Maybe I'm only fit to share a people's revolutionary aspirations at a comfortable distance from them and their struggle—one more volunteer in the armchair army of bourgeois intellectuals with radical sympathies in the head. Before I give up, though, I must make sure I've read these feelings correctly. My impulse is to follow the old, severe rule: if you can't put your life where your head (heart) is, then what you think (feel) is a fraud. But it's premature to talk of fraud and hypocrisy. If the test is whether I can put my life (even imaginatively) in Vietnam, the time to take it isn't now but when I have a somewhat less meager grasp of the country.

Even if I fail the test of being able to identify myself with the Vietnamese, what have I actually proven? Perhaps I haven't experienced the constraints, real or imaginary, of ethical—or revolutionary—societies in general, only of this one. Maybe I'm only saying I find something uncongenial about North

Vietnam. . . . And yet I do like the Vietnamese, respond to them, feel good with them, sometimes really happy here. Doesn't it all come down to the absurd complaint—the complaint of a real child, me—that people here aren't making it easier for me to perceive them, the wish that the Vietnamese "show" themselves to me clearly so that I can't find them opaque, simple-minded, naïve? Now I'm back where I started. The sense of the barrier between them and me. My not understanding them, their not understanding me. No judgments now (at least none I really believe).

MAY 9

How odd to feel estranged from Vietnam here, when Vietnam has been present in my thoughts every day in America. But if the Vietnam I've carried around like a wound in my heart and mind is not invalidated by what I see in Hanoi, it doesn't seem particularly related to this place at this time either. Having arrived after March 31, we are not under bombardment, though along with everyone else in Hanoi we take shelter at least once a day when the American reconnaissance planes come over. Where civilians are being slaughtered, villages burned, and crops poisoned, we aren't permitted to go. (Not for reasons of military security, since earlier American visitors were taken to areas under bombardment, but out of concern for our safety: where there's American bombing now, it goes on almost round the clock. The average daily tonnage of bombs being dropped on North Vietnam since March 31, though confined to the area below the 19th parallel, *exceeds* the daily average unloaded on the whole country before the "limited bombing pause.") We see only a handsome, evenly impoverished, clean Asian city; we see charming, dignified people living amid bleak material scarcity and the most rigorous demands on their energies and patience. The leveled towns and villages in the countryside to which we drive on short trips already constitute a tableau from the past, a thoroughly *accepted* environment in which people go on functioning, working toward their victory, making their revolution. I wasn't prepared for all this calm. Thinking about Vietnam in America, it seems natural to dwell on destruction and suffering. But not here. In Vietnam, there is also a peaceful, fiercely industrious present with which a visitor must be connected; and I'm not. I want their victory. But I don't understand their revolution.

It's all around me, of course, but I feel I'm in a glass box. We're supposed to be learning about it through the "activities" Oanh & Co. have set up in consultation with us since our arrival. In principle, we wanted to see anything and everything, and that's what's happening—though individual interests are swiftly catered to. (It was at my request that we spent an afternoon watching a movie being shot at the principal film studio in Hanoi; because Bob wanted to meet some mathematicians, a meeting with six math professors from the University of Hanoi was arranged, to which we all ended up going.) We are truly seeing and doing a great deal: at least one visit or meeting is planned for every morning and afternoon, and often in the evening as well, though we have an hour and a half each for lunch and dinner and are encouraged to rest after lunch until three o'clock, when the worst heat of the day is over. In other words, we're in the hands of skilled bureaucrats specializing in relations with foreigners. (Yes, even Oanh—whom I like more and more. Especially he.) All right, I see the inevitability of that. Who else could possibly take charge of us? But even within that framework, shouldn't we be able to go beyond it? I don't think I can. I'm obsessed by the protocol of our situation, which leaves me unable to believe I'm seeing a genuine sample of what this country is like. That suggests the trip isn't going to teach me something usable about revolutionary societies, as I'd assumed it would—unless I count getting so shaken up, as I was yesterday, that I question my right to profess a radical politics at all.

But perhaps there isn't much an American radical *can* learn from the Vietnamese revolution, because the Vietnamese themselves are too alien, in contrast to the considerable amount I think one can learn from the Cuban revolution, because—especially from this perspective—the Cubans are pretty much like us. Though it's probably an error, I can't help comparing the Vietnamese with the Cuban revolution: that is, my experience of it during a three-month stay in Cuba in 1960, plus accounts of how it has developed from friends who've visited more recently. (I probably won't understand anything here until I put Cuba out of my mind. But I can't ignore an experience that seems to me comparable to this one which I felt I did

understand and do have imaginative access to.) And almost all
my comparisons turn out favorable to the Cubans, unfavorable
to the Vietnamese—by the standard of what's useful, instructive, imitable, relevant to American radicalism.

Take, for instance, the populist manners of the Cuban revolution. The Cubans, as I remember well, are informal, impulsive,
easily intimate, and manic, even marathon talkers. These may
not always be virtues, but they seem so in the context of a successful, entrenched revolutionary society. In Vietnam, everything seems formal, measured, controlled, planned. I long for
someone to be indiscreet here. To talk about his personal life,
his emotions. To be carried away by "feeling." Instead, everyone is exquisitely polite, yet somehow bland. It fits with the
impression Vietnam gives of being an almost sexless culture,
from all that I've observed, and from the evidence of the three
movies I've seen so far in Hanoi this week and the novel I read
last night in English translation. (Hieu confirmed, when I asked
him, that there is no kissing in Vietnamese plays and films; obviously there's none in the streets or parks. I haven't seen people
touching each other even in a casual way.) As Cuba has proved,
a country doesn't have to adopt the puritan style when it goes
Communist. And, probably, the Vietnamese attitudes toward
sex and the expression of private feeling formed part of this
culture long before the advent of revolutionary Marxist idealism. Nevertheless, they do discomfort a Western neo-radical like
myself for whom revolution means not only creating political
and economic justice but releasing and validating personal (as
well as social) energies of all kinds, including erotic ones. And
this *is* what revolution has meant in Cuba—despite waves of
interference mainly by old-style orthodox Communist bureaucrats, who have been contested by Fidel precisely on this point.

I can't help contrasting the casual egalitarianism I observed
among Cubans, whatever their rank or degree of responsibility,
with the strongly hierarchical features of this society. No one is
in the least servile here, but people know their place. While the
deference I notice given to some by others is always graceful,
there is clearly the feeling that certain people are more important or valuable than others and deserve a bigger share of the
pitifully few comforts available. Hence, the store to which we
were taken the third day to get tire sandals and have us each

fitted for a pair of Vietnamese trousers. Hieu and Phan told us, with an almost proprietary pride, that this was a special store, reserved for foreigners (diplomatic personnel, guests) and important government people. I thought they should recognize that the existence of such facilities is "un-Communist." But maybe I'm showing here how "American" I am.

I'm troubled, too, by the meals at the Thong Nhat. While every lunch and dinner consists of several delicious meat and fish courses (we're eating only Vietnamese food) and whenever we eat everything in one of the large serving bowls a waitress instantly appears to put another one on our table, ninety-nine percent of the Vietnamese will have rice and bean curd for dinner tonight and are lucky to eat meat or fish once a month. Of course I haven't said anything. They'd probably be mystified, even insulted, if I suggested that we shouldn't be eating so much more than the average citizen's rations. It's well known that lavish and (what would be to us) self-sacrificing hospitality to guests is a staple of Oriental culture. Do I really expect them to violate their own sense of decorum? Still, it bothers me. . . . It also exasperates me that we're driven even very short distances; the Peace Committee has rented two cars, in fact—Volgas—that wait with their drivers in front of the hotel whenever we're due to go anywhere. The office of the NLF delegation in Hanoi, which we visited the other day, was all of two blocks from the hotel. And some of our destinations proved to be no more than fifteen or twenty blocks away. Why don't they let us walk, as Bob, Andy, and I have agreed among ourselves we'd feel more comfortable doing? Do they have a rule: only the best for the guests? But that kind of politeness, it seems to me, could well be abolished in a Communist society. Or must we go by car because they think we're weak, effete foreigners (Westerners? Americans?) who also need to be reminded to get out of the sun? It disquiets me to think that Vietnamese might regard walking as beneath our dignity (as official guests, celebrities, or something). Whatever their reason, there's no budging them on this. We roll through the crowded streets in our big ugly black cars—the chauffeurs blasting away on their horns to make people on foot and on bicycles watch out, give way. . . . Best, of course, would be if they would lend us, or let us rent, bicycles. But though we've dropped hints to Oanh more than once, it's clear they don't or won't take the request seriously. When we broach it, are they at least amused? Or do they just think we're being silly or impolite or dumb?

All I seem to have figured out about this place is that it's a very complex self that an American brings to Hanoi. At least this American! I sometimes have the miserable feeling that my being here (I won't speak for Andy and Bob) is a big waste of our Vietnamese hosts' time. Oanh should be spending these days writing music. Phan could reread Molière (he taught literature before he started working full-time for the Peace Committee) or visit his teenage daughters, who have been evacuated to the countryside. Hieu, whose profession turns out to be journalism, could be usefully composing articles in the dreadful prose of the North Vietnamese press. Only Toan, who apparently has some clerical job, might lose out; tagging along with the three others to entertain and keep busy the overgrown obtuse foreign guests is probably more amusing than that. What do the Vietnamese imagine is happening to us here? Do they grasp when we understand and when we don't? I'm thinking particularly of Oanh, who is obviously very shrewd and has traveled a lot in Europe, but also of all the smiling people who talk to us, flatter us ("We know your struggle is hard," someone said today), explain things to us. I fear they don't know the difference. They are simply too generous, too credulous.

But I'm also drawn to that kindly credulity. I like how people stare, often gape at us wherever we go in Hanoi. I feel they are enjoying us, that it's a pleasant experience for them to see us. I asked Oanh today if he thought people in the streets realized that we are Americans. He said that most wouldn't. Then who do they think we are, I asked. Probably Russians, was his answer; and indeed, several people have called out *tovarich* and some other Russian word at us. Most people, though, don't say anything in our direction. They stare calmly, point, then discuss us with their neighbors. Hieu says the comment most frequently made about us when we stroll or go to the movies is—delivered with good-natured amazement—how tall we are.

I go out for walks more often by myself now, whenever it's not too hot—trying to relate to the looks people give me, enjoying the ambiguities of my identity, protected by the fact that I don't speak Vietnamese and can only look back and smile. I'm no longer even surprised, as I first was, at how comfortable I am walking alone, even when I get lost in obscure neighborhoods far from the hotel. Though I'm aware of the possibility of an unpleasant incident occurring when I'm in another part of the city, unable to explain who I am or even read signs, I still feel entirely safe. There must be very few foreigners in Hanoi—except within a few blocks of the Thong Nhat, I've seen no one on the streets who isn't Vietnamese; yet here I walk unescorted among these people as if I had a perfect right to be prowling around Hanoi and to expect them all, down to the last old man squatting by the curb selling wooden flutes, to understand that and to ignore me in their amiable way. The impression of civility and lack of violence Hanoi gives is astounding, not just in comparison with any big American city but with Phnom Penh and Vientiane as well. People here are animated, plainly gregarious, but notably unquarrelsome among themselves. Even when the streets are most crowded, there's scarcely any strident noise. Though I see many small but not too well-nourished children and babies, I've yet to hear one cry.

Perhaps I feel so secure because I don't take the Vietnamese altogether seriously as "real people," according to the grim view popular where I come from that "real people" are dangerous, volatile; one is never altogether safe with them. I hope it's not that. I know I wouldn't prefer the Vietnamese to be mean or ill-tempered. But as much as I love the deep, sweet silence of Hanoi, I do miss among the Vietnamese a certain element of abrasiveness, a bigger—it doesn't have to be louder—range in their feelings.

For instance, it seems to me a defect that the North Vietnamese aren't good enough haters. How else to explain the odd fact that they actually appear to be quite fond of America? One of the recurrent themes of Dr. Thach's conversation with us was his fervent admiration for America's eminence in technology and science. (This from a cabinet minister of the country being ravaged by the cruelly perfect weapons produced by that very science and technology.) And I suspect that the extent to which the Vietnamese are so interested in and well informed about American politics—as I learned answering some questions put to me in the last days about the Nebraska primary, about Lindsay's influence in Harlem, and about American student

radicalism—isn't mere expediency, part of the policy of knowing your enemy, but springs from just plain fascination with
the United States. The government and professional people
here who have radios listen regularly to the Voice of America
and, to be sure, chuckle away at the American version of the
war: this week, it's the VOA's denial that any serious military
engagements are taking place in Saigon. But at the same time
they seem quite respectful of American political processes and
even a little sympathetic to the problems America faces as the
leading world power. Poets read us verses about "your Walt
Whitman" and "your Edgar Allan Poe." At the Writers Union
tonight someone asked me if I knew Arthur Miller and flushed
with shy pleasure when I said I did and could pass on to him
the copy of the Vietnamese translation of *Death of a Salesman*
I'd just been shown. "Tell us about your Norman Mailer," a
young novelist asked me, and then apologized because Mailer
hasn't yet been translated into Vietnamese. And they all wanted
to know what kind of books I write, and made me promise
to send them copies when I got back to the States. "We are
very interested in American literature," someone repeated. Few
translations of fiction are being published in Hanoi now, but
one of the few this year was an anthology of American short stories: Mark Twain, Jack London, Hemingway, Dorothy Parker,
plus some of the "progressive" writers from the 1930's favored
in Eastern Europe. When I mentioned that Americans didn't
consider Howard Fast and Albert Maltz in the same class as
most others in the collection, one Vietnamese writer assured
me they knew that. The trouble was that they actually had very
few books—their main library, at the University of Hanoi, was
bombed—and most of the volumes of American literature in
Hanoi are the choices, and editions, of the Foreign Languages
Press in Moscow. "In socialist countries with whom we have
normal relations, we can't find modern American writers," he
added with a laugh. Another writer who was listening to our
conversation grinned.

    Of course, I'm delighted to learn that some Vietnamese are
not unaware that belonging to the "socialist camp" has its
disadvantages—among them, cultural isolation and intellectual provincialism. But it's also sad to think of them carrying
the burden of that awareness as well, when they're so acutely

conscious of Vietnam as an isolated, provincial country in its own right. Doctors, writers, academics we've talked to speak of feeling desperately cut off. As one professor said, after describing the growth of the science faculties since 1954: "But we still fail to grasp the main tendencies of work going on in the rest of the world. The material we receive is late and not adequate." For all their pride in the progress made since the French were expelled, people often mention to us, apologetically, what a "backward" country Vietnam still is. And then I realize how aware they are that we come from the world's most "advanced" country; their respect for the United States is there, whether voiced or not.

It's at these moments that I also feel like the visitor from America, though in another way. It must be because I'm so American after all, too profoundly a citizen of the nation that thinks itself the greatest in everything, that I feel actually embarrassed by the modest (if proud) self-affirmation of citizens of a small, weak nation. Their cordial interest in America is so evidently sincere that it would be boorish not to respond to it. Yet somehow it chills me, for it seems a little indecent. I'm aware now how their unexpectedly complex, yet ingenuous, relation to the United States overlays every situation between individual Vietnamese and Bob, Andy, and me. But I don't have the insight or the moral authority to strip us down to our "real" situation, beyond pathos. My political sympathies being what they are, perhaps there's no way for me or someone like me to be here except in some stereotyped capacity (as an "American friend"), no way to avoid being either self-effacing or passive or sentimental or patronizing—just as there's no way for Americans, myself included, not to measure a good six inches taller than the average Vietnamese.

There are pages more of the same in the first half of the journal I kept during my stay, interspersed with pages and pages of detailed notes on each of our visits and encounters. The strictly reportorial body of my journal, full of factual information and physical descriptions and summaries of conversations, conveys an attitude of intense, uncomplicatedly attentive concentration. But the subjective interludes, which I have partly transcribed, convey something else—the callowness and stinginess of my response.

It wasn't that I'd expected to feel at ease in North Vietnam, or to find the Vietnamese as a people exactly like Europeans and Americans. But neither had I expected to be so baffled, so mistrustful of my experiences there—and unable to subdue the backlash of my ignorance. My understanding of the country was limited to Vietnam's election as the target of what's most ugly in America: the principle of "will," the self-righteous taste for violence, the insensate prestige of technological solutions to human problems. I had some knowledge of the style of American will, from living at various times in the Southwest, in California, in the Midwest, in New England, and in recent years in New York, and from observing its impact on Western Europe during the last decade. What I didn't understand, hadn't even a clue to, was the nature of Vietnamese will—its styles, its range, its nuances. Breton has distinguished two forms of the will in authentic revolutionary struggle: "revolutionary patience" and "the cry." But these can't be confronted without grasping something of the specific quality of a people—just what I was finding so difficult in North Vietnam. Whether I concluded that my limitations, or theirs, were being exposed by my inability to have a satisfactory contact with the Vietnamese, the impasse was the same. By around the fifth day, as the extracts from my journal indicate, I was ready to give up—on myself, which meant on the Vietnamese as well.

And then, suddenly, my experience started changing. The psychic cramp with which I was afflicted in the early part of my stay began to ease and the Vietnamese as real people, and North Vietnam as a real place, came into view.

The first sign was that I became more comfortable in talking to people: not only to Oanh, our chief guide—I talked to him more than to any other Vietnamese during my stay—but also to a militia girl or factory worker or schoolteacher or doctor or village leader whom we'd spend an hour with and never see again. I became less preoccupied with the constrictions of their language (a great deal of which I knew must be put down to that "abstractness" or "vagueness" of speech remarked on by Western visitors to every Oriental country) and with the reduction of my own resources of expression, and more sensitive to distinctions in the way the Vietnamese talked. For a start, I could distinguish between a propagandistic level of language (which still may convey the truth, but nevertheless sounds oppressive and wrong) and a merely simple kind of language. I learned, too, to pay more rather than less attention to whatever was constantly reiterated, and discovered the standard words and phrases to be richer than I'd thought.

Take, for instance, the notion of respect. "We respect your Norman Morrison" was a phrase often used in the ceremonial speeches of greeting made to us at each of our visits in Hanoi and in the countryside. We learned that Oanh had written a popular "Song to Emily"—Norman Morrison's youngest daughter, whom he took along with him when he went to immolate himself in front of the Pentagon. At the Writers Union, someone chanted for us a beautiful poem (which I'd read beforehand in English and French translation) called "The Flame of Morrison." Truck drivers taking supplies along the perilous route down to the 17th parallel are likely to have a picture of Norman Morrison pasted on their sun visors, perhaps alongside a photograph of Nguyen Van Troi, the Saigonese youth who was executed several years ago for plotting to assassinate McNamara during his visit to South Vietnam. At first a visitor is likely to be both moved by this cult of Norman Morrison and made uncomfortable by it. Although the emotion of individuals is plainly unfeigned, it seems excessive, sentimental, and redolent of the hagiography of exemplary cardboard heroes that has been a regular feature of Stalinist and Maoist culture. But after the twentieth time that Norman Morrison's name was invoked (often shyly, always affectionately, with an evident desire to be friendly and gracious to *us*, who were Americans), I started understanding the very specific relation the Vietnamese have with Norman Morrison. The Vietnamese believe that the life of a people, its very will, is nourished and sustained by heroes. And Norman Morrison really is a hero, in a precise sense. (The Vietnamese don't, as I suspected at first, overestimate the actual impact of his sacrifice upon the conscience of America; far more than its practical efficacy, what matters to them is the moral success of his deed, its *completeness* as an act of self-transcendence.) Therefore, they're speaking quite accurately when they declare their "respect" for him and when they call him, as they often do, their "benefactor." Norman Morrison has become genuinely important for the Vietnamese, so much so that they can't comprehend that he mightn't be an equally important aliment of consciousness to us, three of their "American friends."

That very definition of us as friends, initially a source of some embarrassment and malaise, now seemed—another sign of the change in me—more comprehensible. Whereas at first I'd felt both moved, sometimes to tears, and constrained by the friendliness shown to us, eventually I could simply appreciate it, becoming more genuine and flexible in my own response. I surely had no grounds for suspecting the Vietnamese of duplicity, or for dismissing their attitude as naïve. Since, after all, I was a friend, why was it naïve or gullible of them to know that? Instead of being so amazed at their ability to transcend their situation as America's victims and our identity as citizens of the enemy nation, I began to imagine concretely how it was indeed possible for the Vietnamese, at this moment in their history, to welcome American citizens as friends. It was important, I realized, not to be abashed by all the small gifts and flowers thrust on us wherever we went. I'd minded that we weren't allowed to pay for anything during our stay—not even the numerous books I asked for or the cables I sent my son in New York every few days to let him know I was all right (despite my insistence that at least I be allowed to pay for these). Gradually, I could see it was just stingy of me to resist, or feel oppressed by, the material generosity of our hosts.

But the change didn't consist only in my becoming a more graceful recipient of Vietnamese generosity, a better audience for their elaborate courtesy. Here, too, there was something further to be understood; and through more contact with people in Vietnam, I discovered their politeness to be quite unlike "ours," and not only because there was so much more of it. In America and Europe, being polite (whether in large or small doses) always carries a latent hint of insincerity, a mild imputation of coercion. For us, politeness means conventions of amiable behavior people have agreed to practice, whether or not they "really" feel like it, because their "real" feelings aren't consistently civil or generous enough to guarantee a working social order. By definition, politeness is never truly honest; it testifies to the disparity between social behavior and authentic feeling. Perhaps this disparity, accepted in this part of the world as an article of faith concerning the human condition, is what gives us our taste for irony. Irony becomes essential as a mode of indicating the truth, a whole life-truth: namely, that we both mean and don't mean what we're saying or doing. I had originally been disconcerted by the absence of irony among the Vietnamese. But if I could renounce, at least imaginatively, my conviction of the inevitability of irony, the Vietnamese suddenly looked far less undecipherable. Their language didn't seem quite so imprisoning and simplistic, either. (For the development of ironic truths, one needs lots of words. Without irony, not so many words are required.)

The Vietnamese operate by another notion of civility than the one we're accustomed to, and that implies a shift in the meaning of honesty and sincerity. Honesty as it is understood in Vietnam bears little resemblance to the sense of honesty that has been elevated by secular Western culture virtually above all other values. In Vietnam, honesty and sincerity are functions of the dignity of the individual. A Vietnamese, by being sincere, reinforces and enhances his personal dignity. In this society, being sincere often means precisely forfeiting one's claim to dignity, to an attractive appearance; it means the willingness to be shameless. The difference is acute. This culture subscribes to an empirical or descriptive notion of sincerity, which measures whether a man is sincere by how fully and accurately his words mirror his hidden thoughts and feelings. The Vietnamese have a normative or prescriptive notion of sincerity. While our aim is to make the right alignment—correspondence—between one's words and behavior and one's inner life (on the assumption that the truth voiced by the speaker is ethically neutral, or rather is rendered ethically neutral or even praiseworthy by the speaker's willingness to avow it), theirs is to construct an appropriate relation between the speaker's words and behavior and his social identity. Sincerity, in Vietnam, means behaving in a manner *worthy* of one's role; sincerity is a mode of ethical aspiration.

Thus, it's off the point to speculate whether the warmth of Pham Van Dong during the hour conversation Bob, Andy, and I had with him in the late afternoon of May 16 was sincere in our sense, or whether the Prime Minister "really" wanted to embrace us as we left his office, before walking us out the front door and across the gravel driveway to our waiting cars. He was sincere in the Vietnamese sense: his behavior was attractive, it was becoming, it intended good. Nor is it quite right to ask whether the Vietnamese "really" hate the Americans, even though they say they don't; or to wonder why they don't hate Americans, if indeed they do not. One basic unit of Vietnamese culture is the extraordinary, beautiful gesture. But gesture mustn't be interpreted in our sense—something put on, theatrical. The gestures a Vietnamese makes aren't a performance external to his real personality. By means of gestures, those acts brought off according to whatever standards he affirms, his self is consti- tuted. And in certain cases, personality can be wholly redefined by a single, unique gesture: for a person to do something finer than he ever has done may promote him, without residue, to a new level on which such acts are regularly possible. (In Viet- nam, moral ambition is a truth—an already confirmed reality— in a way it isn't among us, because of our psychological criteria of "the typical" and "the consistent." This contrast sheds light on the quite different role political and moral exhortation plays in a society like Vietnam. Much of the discourse we would dismiss as propagandistic or manipulative possesses a depth for the Vietnamese to which we are insensitive.)

Vietnam—at least in its official view of itself—may strike the secular Western eye as a society tremendously overextended ethically, that is, psychologically. But such a judgment depends entirely on our current, modest standards of how much virtue human beings are capable of. And Vietnam is, in many ways, an affront to these standards. I remember feeling just so af- fronted when, during the first afternoon of a two-day drive into mountainous Hoa Binh province north of Hanoi, we stopped briefly somewhere in the countryside to visit the grave of an American pilot. As we got out of our cars and walked off the road about fifty yards through the high grass, Oanh told us that it was the pilot of an F-105 brought down by a farmer with a rifle about a year ago. The pilot had failed to eject and crashed with his plane on this very spot; some villagers recov- ered his body from the wreckage. Coming into a clearing, we saw not a simple grave but an elevated mound decorated with chunks of the plane's engine and a crumpled piece of wing, like a Chamberlain sculpture, and with flowers, and topped by a wooden marker on which was written the pilot's name and the date of his death. I stood there some minutes feeling haunted, barely able to comprehend that initial act of burial, astonished by the look of the site and the evidence that it was still being looked after. And afterwards, when the vice-chairman of the province's administrative council, who was traveling in my car, explained that the pilot had been buried, and in "a coffin of good wood," so that his family in America could come after the war and take his body home, I felt almost undone. What is one to make of this amazing act? How could these people, who have had spouses and parents and children murdered by this pilot and his comrades (the load of one F-105, four canisters of CBU's, kills every unsheltered living creature within an area of one square kilometer), quietly take up their shovels and tastefully arrange his grave? What did they feel? Did they realize that whatever his objective guilt, he, just as much as their dead, was a precious, irreplaceable human being who should not have died? Could they pity him? Did they forgive him? But maybe these questions are misleading. What's likely is that the villagers thought burying the pilot was a beautiful (they would probably say "humane") thing to do—a standard that both overrides and transforms their personal feelings, so far as these might enter the matter.

Such transpersonal gestures are hard for a visitor to credit on their own terms. Certainly, I wasn't entirely able to put aside my own habitual understanding of how people function. Throughout the two weeks, I was continually tempted to frame psychological questions about the Vietnamese—all the while knowing how loaded such questions are with arbitrary, Western ethical assumptions. If it even makes sense to inquire, for instance, what "ego" is for the Vietnamese, I could observe that it doesn't take many of the expressive forms familiar to us. People in North Vietnam seem astonishingly calm, and though they talk of little else but the war, their discourse is singularly unmarked by hate. Even when they use the melodramatic Communist language of denunciation, it comes out sounding dutiful and a little flat. They talk of atrocities, the marrow of their history, with an almost gentle sorrow, and still with amazement. Can these things really have happened, their manner says. Did the French really disembowel that row of handcuffed plantation workers who had gone on strike, as the photograph we saw in the Revolutionary Museum shows? How can the Americans not be *ashamed* of what they're doing here? was the unspoken question that echoed throughout our tour of another, smaller "museum" in Hanoi devoted to a display of the various genocidal weapons used by the Americans on North Vietnam in the last three years. Indeed, I think, they don't quite understand—which, after all, is just the failure of understanding one might expect to find in a culture built on shame that's currently under attack by a culture whose energies come from deploying huge increments of guilt.

That Vietnam is a culture founded on shame probably accounts for much of what one sees (and does not see) there in the range of people's expressiveness. And my formation in a culture founded on guilt is surely one reason I found it hard to understand them. I would guess that guilt-cultures are typically prone to intellectual doubt and moral convolutedness, so that, from the point of view of guilt, all cultures founded on shame are indeed "naïve." The relation to moral demands tends to be much less ambivalently felt in shame-cultures, and collective action and the existence of public standards have an inherent validity they do not possess for us.

Prominent among these public standards in Vietnam is decorum—more generally, the concern for maintaining in all exchanges between people an exacting moral tone. I might have imagined this concern to be simply Asian if I hadn't already seen something of Cambodians and Laotians, in contrast with whom the Vietnamese are much more dignified and reserved, even prudish in their manner, and also more discreet in their dress. No matter how fiercely hot it gets, nowhere does one see in Vietnam (as one does throughout Cambodia and Laos) a man in shorts or without a shirt. Everyone is neatly, if shabbily, dressed from neck to ankles—women as well as men wear long trousers—and great value is placed on being clean. The pride of people in Na Phon when they showed us their two-stall brick and cement public latrine, the first such facility in the hamlet and completed just a day earlier, had to do with more than hygiene or convenience. The new latrine was a kind of moral victory. "All the water of the Eastern Sea could not wash away the dirt left by the enemy" is a saying that dates from one of the innumerable Vietnamese struggles against the Chinese, a war which began in 1418 and ended victoriously in 1427. No doubt the North Vietnamese regard with a similar anguish the three years of American assault: once again, and most horrendously, their country has been defiled. The moral metaphor of cleanliness and dirt is, of course, found almost universally, in all cultures; still, I felt it to be especially strong in Vietnam. Its strength is strikingly expressed in the eighteenth-century epic *Kieu*, the most famous work of Vietnamese literature. (The poem is studied in detail in the schools and recited often on the radio; practically every Vietnamese knows long passages from it by heart.) When the story begins, the heroine, Kieu, is a young girl. A young man sees her, falls in love with her, secretly, and patiently courts her, but family duties suddenly call him away before he can explain. Believing herself abandoned and faced by a family crisis of her own, Kieu sells herself as a concubine to a rich man, to save her father from debtors' prison. Only after twenty years of mistreatment and degradation, in which she ends up in a brothel and from there escapes to become a bonze, is Kieu able to return home, where she meets again the man she loved. He asks her to marry him. In the long final scene, which takes place on their wedding night, Kieu tells her husband that, although she loves him deeply and has never enjoyed sexual relations with any other man, their marriage can't be consummated. He protests that her unfortunate life during their long separation means nothing to him; but she insists that she is not clean. Precisely as they love each other, she argues, they must make this sacrifice. Eventually, out of respect and love for her, he agrees. The poem ends with a description of the harmony and joy of their married life. To a Western sensibility, such a happy ending is hardly happy at all. We would rather have Kieu die of tuberculosis in the arms of her true love, just after they are reunited, than award them a lifetime together of renunciation. But to the Vietnamese, even today, the resolution of the story is both satisfying and just. What may appear to us as their being "closed," secretive, or unexpressive, I think, is partly that they are a remarkably fastidious people.

Needless to say, the standards of today are not the same as those proposed in *Kieu*. Sexual self-control, however, is still much admired. In present-day Vietnam, women and men work, eat, fight, and sleep together without raising any issue of sexual temptation. By now the Vietnamese understand that Westerners don't have the same standards of sexual propriety. Oanh, when he told me that it's very unusual for Vietnamese husbands and wives to be unfaithful to each other, even in circumstances of

lengthy separation caused by war, said he knew marital fidelity
was "not common" in the West. With an edge of self-mockery,
he mentioned how shocked he was on one of his first trips
to Europe—it was to Russia—to hear people at parties telling
"indecent" jokes to each other. Now, he assured me, it bothers
him less. With their incorrigible politeness, the Vietnamese
have concluded that we arrange such matters differently. Thus,
whenever Andy Kopkind, Bob Greenblatt, and I traveled in
the countryside, no matter how primitive and small the sleeping accommodations, we were always given separate rooms (or
something that passed for rooms); but on one of these trips,
when we were accompanied by a nurse because Bob had become slightly ill in Hanoi the day before our departure, I noticed that the young, pretty nurse slept in the same room as our
guides and drivers, who were all men. . . . Sexual self-discipline,
I imagine, must be taken for granted in Vietnam. It's only a
single aspect of the general demand made on the individual to
maintain his dignity and to put himself at the disposal of others
for the common good. In contrast to Laos and Cambodia, with
their "Indian" or "southern" atmosphere that derives from an
eclectic blend of Hindu and Buddhist influences, Vietnam
presents the paradox of a country sharing the same severely
tropical climate but living by the classical values—hard work,
discipline, seriousness—of a country with a temperate or cold
climate. This "northern" atmosphere is undoubtedly the legacy
of those hordes of "Northern feudalists." (I also gathered that
it is more attenuated in the southern region of the country.
People in Hanoi describe the Saigonese as more easygoing,
more emotional, more charming, but also less honest and sexually looser—in short, the conventional northern clichés about
southerners.)

Thus, while the exacting demands the Vietnamese make
upon themselves, in their present form, are undoubtedly reinforced by the paramilitary ethos of a left-revolutionary society
under invasion, their basic form has deep historical roots, particularly in the Confucian as distinct from the Buddhist strands
in Vietnamese culture. In some societies, notably Chinese, these
two traditions have been experienced as sharply antagonistic.
But in Vietnam, I suspect, they have not. Most Vietnamese,
of course, apart from a large Catholic minority, are Buddhists.

Even though we saw mostly old people praying in the pagodas, a good deal of domestic ritual still takes place (we saw altars in many homes); beyond that, there appears to be a considerable secular continuity with Buddhist values. Nevertheless, whatever in Vietnam persists of the Buddhist ethos—with its fatalism, its intellectual playfulness, its stress on charity—seems quite compatible with the ethos of discipline characteristic of Confucianism. The behavior of the Vietnamese reflects the Confucian idea that both the body politic and an individual's well-being depend on cultivating the rules of appropriate and just behavior. Also intact is the Confucian view expressed by Hsün Tzu: "All rules of decorum and righteousness are the product of the acquired virtue of the sage and not the products of the nature of man." This Confucian idea of a people's dependence on its sages partly explains the veneration felt by the Vietnamese for Ho Chi Minh, their sage-poet-leader. But only partly. As indeed the Vietnamese often insist, their regard for Ho has nothing in common with the mindless adulation surrounding Mao today. Ho's birthday is mainly an annual occasion for the North Vietnamese to show their good taste, the delicacy of their feeling toward him. "We love and respect our leader," commented the monthly journal *Hoc Tap* on Ho's birthday last year, "but we do not deify him." Far from treating him like the usual bigger-than-life, heroic, all-wise leader, people I met spoke of Ho as if they knew him personally, and what fascinates and stirs them is their sense of him as a real man. Humorous anecdotes illustrating his modesty and shyness are legion. People find him charming, even a little eccentric. And they are moved when they speak of him, reminiscing about his years of privation in exile and his sufferings in Chinese jails throughout the 1930's, and worrying over his physical frailty. *Bac Ho*, Uncle Ho, is no special title, with Orwellian Big Brother overtones, but ordinary courtesy; a Vietnamese of any age addresses someone of an older generation to whom he's not related as "Uncle" or "Aunt." (Swedish has the same usage, except that *tant* and *farbror* are used only by children or young people to address adults who are strangers, and wouldn't be said by a middle-aged person to a seventy-year-old.) The feeling for Ho Chi Minh, an intimate affection and gratitude, is only the apex of the feeling that exists between people in a small, beleaguered nation who are able to regard each other as members of one big family. Indeed, almost all the virtues admired by the Vietnamese—such as frugality, loyalty, self-sacrifice, and sexual fidelity—have, as their basic supporting metaphor, the authority of family life. Here is still another feature pointing back to Confucianism—as distinct from Buddhism, which attaches the highest prestige to monastic separation from society and the renunciation of family ties—and away from the austerity and "puritanism" of Vietnamese culture considered as something relatively new, the graft of revolutionary ideology. (Considered as "Marxist-Leninist *thought*," Vietnamese Communism seems conveniently vague and outstandingly platitudinous.) Though a visitor is tempted to attribute the extraordinary discipline of the country in large measure to the influence of Communist ideology, it's probably the other way around: that the influence of Communist moral demands derived its authority from the indigenous Vietnamese respect for a highly moralized social and personal order.

But I am making the Vietnamese sound more solemn than they are, when actually what is particularly noticeable is the grace with which these ends are pursued. In conversation, the Vietnamese are low-keyed; even in public meetings, they are laconic and not particularly hortatory. It is hard to recognize the passionate consciousness when it lacks the signs of passion as we know them—such as agitation and pathos. One realizes that these are people living through the most exalted moment of their consciousness, the climax of more than a quarter of a century of continuous struggle. They have already beaten the French against incredible odds. (The French first brought napalm to Vietnam. Between 1950 and 1954, eighty percent of the French budget for the war was paid for by the United States.) Now, even more incredibly, they've demonstrated they can endure whatever punishment the Americans can inflict on them, and still cohere and prosper as a people, while in the South the National Liberation Front is steadily extending its support and control of territory. Yet most of the time this mood of exaltation has to be inferred by the sympathetic observer—not because the Vietnamese are unemotional, but because of their habitual emotional tact, a cultural principle of the conservation of emotional energy. We were told that in heavily bombed places in the countryside it's common for the farmers to take their coffins with them each day when they go to the rice fields, so that if someone dies, he can be buried right then while the others continue working. In the evacuated schools, children pack up their personal belongings and bedding before they leave the dormitory hut each morning for classes and pile the tiny bundles neatly in the nearest dirt shelter, in case there is a bombing raid during the day and the hut burns down; each evening they take their bundles out of the shelter, unpack them, and set up the dormitory again. . . . More than once, observing the incredible matter-of-factness of the Vietnamese, I thought of the Jews' more wasteful and more brilliant style of meeting their historical destiny of chronic suffering and struggle. One advantage of the Vietnamese over the Jews as a martyr people, perhaps, is simply that of any culture dominated by the peasant type over a culture that has crystallized into an urban bourgeoisie. Unlike the Jews, the Vietnamese belong to a culture whose various psychic types have not yet reached a high degree of articulation (forcing them to reflect upon *each other*). It is also the advantage of having a history, albeit mainly of cruel persecution, that is anchored to a land with which people identify themselves, rather than simply (and, therefore, complicatedly) to an "identity."

The Jews' manner of experiencing their suffering was direct, emotional, persuasive. It ran the gamut from stark declamation to ironic self-mockery. It attempted to engage the sympathy of others. At the same time, it projected a despair over the difficulties of engaging others. The source of the Jewish stubbornness, of their miraculous talent for survival, is their surrender to a complex kind of pessimism. Perhaps something like the Jewish (and also "Western") style of overt expressive suffering was what I unconsciously expected to find when I came to Vietnam. That would explain why at first I took for opaqueness and naïveté the quite different way the Vietnamese have of experiencing a comparably tragic history.

It took me a while, for instance, to realize that the Vietnamese were genuinely constrained by a kind of modesty about showing us the unspeakable sufferings they have endured. Even when describing the American atrocities, they hastened to emphasize—almost as if it would be bad taste not to—that the full horror of America's war on Vietnam couldn't be seen anywhere in the North. For that, they said, one must see "what is happening to our brothers in the South." We heard the statistics of civilian casualties since February 7, 1965: sixty percent of all people killed are women and children; twenty percent of those killed and seriously wounded are elderly people. We were taken to see towns where formerly no fewer than twenty thousand and as many as eighty thousand people lived, in which not a single building was standing. We saw photographs of bodies riddled with pellets from fragmentation bombs or charred by incendiary weapons (besides napalm, the Americans also drop white phosphorus, Thermit, and magnesium on the Vietnamese). We met briefly with some forlorn victims of "the escalation," among them a girl of twenty-four whose husband and mother-in-law and children had been killed in a single raid, and an elderly Mother Superior and two young nuns who were the only survivors of the bombing of a Catholic convent located just south of Hanoi. Nevertheless, our North Vietnamese hosts seemed anything but eager to ply us with atrocities. They seemed more pleased to tell us, as we visited ruin after ruin, when there had been no casualties—as was the case when the new 170-bed hospital outside of Hoa Binh City was destroyed. (The hospital had been evacuated just before the first raid in September 1967; it was bombed several times afterwards and of course has never been reoccupied.) The impression the Vietnamese prefer to give, and do, is of a peaceful, viable, optimistic society. Ho Chi Minh has even given, in a speech after August 1945, a five-point recipe "for making life optimistic": each person must (1) be good in politics, (2) be able to draw or paint, (3) know music, (4) practice some sport, and (5) know at least one foreign language. Thus, by optimism among the Vietnamese, I mean not only their implacable conviction that they are going to win, but their espousal of optimism as a form of understanding, the emphasis placed throughout the whole society on continuous improvement.

Indeed, one of the most striking aspects of Vietnam is the positiveness of their approach to almost any problem. As Professor Buu, the Minister of Higher Education, remarked without a trace of irony: "The Americans have taught us a lot. For instance, we see that what's necessary for education is not beautiful buildings, like the brand-new Polytechnic School in Hanoi which we had to abandon in 1965 with the start of the escalation. When we went into the jungle and built the de-centralized schools, education improved. We'd like better food and more colorful clothes, of course, but in these three years we've learned one can do many things without them. We don't regard them as fundamental, though very important all the same." Among the advantages, he said, in having been forced to evacuate the colleges of Hanoi into the countryside were that the college students had to put up their new school buildings themselves and learn how to grow their own food (every evacuated school or factory forms a new community and is asked not to be parasitic on the nearest village but to become self-sufficient on the level of a subsistence economy). Through these ordeals, "a new man" is being formed. Somehow, incredibly, the Vietnamese appreciate the assets of their situation, particularly its effect on character. When Ho Chi Minh said that bombing heightens the "spirit" of people, he meant more than a stiffening of morale. There is the belief that the war has effected a permanent improvement in the moral level of people. For instance, for a family to be uprooted and have all its possessions destroyed (many families have relics going back ten centuries) has always been considered in Vietnam the worst possible fate, but now that just this has happened to so many tens of thousands of families, people have discovered the positive advantages of being stripped of everything: that one becomes more generous, less attached to "things." (This is the theme of a movie I saw, *The Forest of Miss Thom*, in which at the end, to facilitate the repair of a truck route after bombing, an old peasant volunteers to cut down the two trees he has spent his whole life growing.) The bombing has also been, for instance, an occasion for developing people's poise and articulateness and administrative talents. Each village or hamlet, through an elected team, does its own reporting on the bombing; in Hanoi and Haiphong, several residents from each street are delegated to make out detailed reports. I remember, on our inspection of the bombed areas of Hanoi, receiving such a report from the leader of the "investigation team" of Quan Than Street (two kilometers from our hotel), an elderly uneducated worker who, since he was elected to this job by his neighbors, had learned a whole new set of skills. The war has made people cleverer and also democratized the use of intelligence, since everybody has essentially the same task: protecting the country, repelling the aggressors. Throughout North Vietnam, self-help plus cooperation has become the regular form of social and economic life. This may sound like the conventional code of a socialist economy applied in an underdeveloped country. But North Vietnam is not just one more small, economically backward member of the Third World, afflicted with the standard handicaps of an overspecialized economy (imposed by colonial rule), illiteracy, disease, and hard-to-assimilate tribal peoples culturally anterior to the majority population. (Vietnam has sixty "ethnic minorities.") It is a country that has literally been gashed and poisoned and leveled by steel, toxic chemicals, and fire. Under these circumstances, self-sufficiency would hardly be enough—were it not for the remarkable ability of the Vietnamese somehow to nourish themselves on disaster.

People there put it much more simply: it's just a question of being sufficiently ingenious. The overwhelming superiority of the United States in manpower, weapons, and resources and the extent of the devastation already wrought on their country pose a definite "problem," as the Vietnamese often said, but one they fully expect to solve by their unlimited and "creative" devotion to work. Everywhere we went, we saw evidence of the tremendous output of toil needed to keep North Vietnam going. Work is, as it were, evenly distributed over the whole surface of the country—like the huge wooden crates lying, unguarded, on the edges of sidewalks on many streets in Hanoi ("our evacuated warehouses," Oanh said) and on country roads, or the piles of tools and other material left in the open alongside the railroad tracks so that repair of the track can start within minutes after a bombing. Nevertheless, willing as the Vietnamese are to rebuild the country inch by inch with shovel and hammer, they have a rather elegant sense of priorities. For instance, it was usual for the craters blasted in rice fields by the B-52's to be filled in by the farmers within days after the raid. But we saw several craters, made by 2,000- and 3,000-pound bombs, so big it had been judged that the time and labor needed to fill them would be prohibitive; these had been converted into fish-breeding ponds. Though the on-going and endless work of repairing bomb-damaged sites and facilities or constructing new, better-protected ones consumes most of their energies now, the Vietnamese think a great deal about the future. Mindful of their postwar need for people with sophisticated skills, the Vietnamese have not mobilized teachers and professors or any of the 200,000 students in colleges and vocational schools; indeed, the number of students enrolled in programs of higher education has steadily risen since 1965. Architects have already drawn up plans for the completely new cities (including Hanoi, which the North Vietnamese fully expect to be razed before the Americans finally withdraw) that must be built after the war.

A visitor may conclude that this work, for all its ingenuity, is mainly conservative in purpose—the means whereby the society can survive—and only secondarily expresses a revolutionary vision—the instrument of a society bent on radical change. But the two purposes, I think, cannot be separated. The war seems to have democratized North Vietnam more profoundly, and radically, than any of the socialist economic reforms undertaken between 1954 and 1965. For instance, the war has broken down one of the few strong articulations in Vietnamese society: between the city and the country. (Peasants still make up eighty percent of the North Vietnamese population.) When the American bombing started, over a million and a half people left Hanoi, Haiphong, and other smaller cities and scattered throughout the countryside, where they have been living now for several years; the population of Hanoi alone dropped from around one million before 1965 to less than 200,000. And this migration, several Vietnamese told me, has already effected a marked change in manners and sensibility, both among peasants who have had to absorb a colony of motley refugees with urban habits and tastes, and among people from Hanoi or Haiphong, many of whom knew nothing about the starkly primitive conditions of daily existence that still prevail in the villages and hamlets but find themselves thriving psychically on physical austerity and the community-mindedness of rural life.

The war has also democratized the society by destroying most of the modest physical means as well as restricting the social space Vietnam had at its disposal for differentiated kinds of production (I include everything from industry to the arts). Thus, more and more people are working at all kinds of activities at the same level—with their bare hands. Each small, low building in the complexes of evacuated schools that have been

set up throughout the countryside had to be made in the simplest way: mud walls and a straw roof. All those kilometers of
neat trenches connecting and leading away from every building,
to get the children out in case of attack, had to be painstakingly dug out of the red clay. The omnipresent bomb shelters—
throughout Hanoi, in each village and hamlet, at intervals on
the side of every road, in every tilled field—had to be put up,
one by one, by people living nearby, in their spare time. (Since
1965, the Vietnamese have dug more than 50,000 kilometers of
trenches and constructed, for a population of 17,000,000, more
than 21,000,000 bomb shelters.) Late one night, on our way
back to Hanoi from a trip to the north, we visited a decentralized factory housed in crude sheds at the foot of a mountain.
While several hundred women and young boys were operating
the machines by the light of kerosene lamps, a dozen men using
only hammers were widening the walls of a small adjacent cave
to make a shelter safe from bombing for the biggest machinery.
Almost everything in North Vietnam has to be done manually,
with a minimum of tools. Time enough to wonder what the
vaunted aid from Russia and China amounts to: however much
there is of it, it's scarcely enough. The country is pitifully lacking in such elementary hospital equipment as sterilizers and
X-ray machines, in typewriters, in basic tools like lathes and
pneumatic drills and welding machines; there seem to be plenty
of bicycles and quite a few transistor radios, but books of all
kinds, paper, pens, phonographs, clocks, and cameras are very
scarce; the most modest consumer goods are virtually nonexistent. Clothing, too, exists only in a limited supply. A Vietnamese is lucky if he owns two sets of clothes and one pair of shoes;
rationing allows each person six meters of cotton fabric a year.
(The cotton comes in only a few colors and most garments are
almost identically cut: black trousers and white blouses for the
women; tan, gray, or beige trousers and tan or white shirts for
the men. Ties are never worn, and jackets only rarely.) Even the
clothes of very high officials are frayed, dully stained, shiny from
repeated washings. Dr. Thach, cousin of the former puppet emperor Bao Dai and, before throwing in his lot with the revolution, one of the richest landowners in Vietnam, mentioned that
he hasn't had any new clothes in two years. Food is very short,
too, though no one starves. Industrial workers get a monthly

ration of 24 kilos of rice; everyone else, including the highest
government officials, gets 13.5 kilos a month.

Lacking almost everything, the Vietnamese are forced to put
everything they do have to use, sometimes multiple use. Part
of this ingenuity is traditional; for example, the Vietnamese
make an astonishing number of things out of bamboo—houses,
bridges, irrigation devices, scaffolding, carrying poles, cups,
tobacco pipes, furniture. But there are many new inventions.
Thus, American planes have become virtual mines in the sky.
(The supply is still far from cut off. During our stay in Hanoi,
the Vietnamese bagged a dozen of the unmanned reconnaissance planes that have been flying over several times a day since
March 31; and they get more planes below the 19th parallel,
where the air attack is more intense now than at any time before
the "limited bombing pause.") Each plane that's shot down
is methodically taken apart. The tires are cut up to make the
rubber sandals that most people wear. Any component of the
engine that's still intact is modified to be reused as part of a
truck motor. The body of the plane is dismantled, and the metal
is melted down to be made into tools, small machine parts, surgical instruments, wire, spokes for bicycle wheels, combs, ashtrays, and of course the famous numbered rings given as presents to visitors. Every last nut, bolt, and screw from the plane is
used. The same holds for anything else the Americans drop. In
several hamlets we visited, the bell hanging from a tree which
summoned people to meetings or sounded the air-raid alert was
the casing of an unexploded bomb. Being shown through the
infirmary of a Thai hamlet, we saw that the protective canopy
of the operating room, relocated, since the bombing, in a rock
grotto, was a flare parachute.

In these circumstances, the notion of a "people's war" is no
mere propagandistic slogan but takes on a real concreteness, as
does that favorite hope of modern social planners, decentral-
ization. A people's war means the total, voluntary, generous
mobilization of every able-bodied person in the country, so that
everyone is available for any task. It also means the division of
the country into an indefinite number of small, self-sufficient
communities which can survive isolation, make decisions, and
continue contributing to production. People on a *local* level
are expected, for instance, to solve any kind of problem put to
them as the aftermath of enemy bombing.

To observe in some of its day-to-day functioning a society based on the principle of total use is particularly impressive to someone who comes from a society based on maximal waste. An unholy dialectic is at work here, in which the big wasteful society dumps its garbage, its partly unemployable proletarian conscripts, its poisons, and its bombs upon a small, virtually defenseless, frugal society whose citizens, those fortunate enough to survive, then go about picking up the debris, out of which they fashion materials for daily use and self-defense.

The principle of total use applies not only to things but to thoughts as well, and grasping this helped me to stop mechanically chafing at the intellectual flatness of Vietnamese discourse. As each material object must be made to go a long way, so must each idea. Vietnamese leaders specialize in an economical, laconic wisdom. Take the saying of Ho, repeated to us often: "Nothing is more precious than independence and liberty." Not until I'd heard the quote many many times did I actually consider it. But when I did, I thought, yes, it really does say a great deal. One could indeed, as the Vietnamese have, live spiritually from that simple sentence for a long time. The Vietnamese regard Ho not as a thinker but as a man of action; his words are for use. The same standard applies to the iconography of the Vietnamese struggle, which is hardly outstanding for either visual or ideological subtlety. (Of course, the utilitarian principle doesn't work equally well in all contexts, as evidenced by the rather low level of Vietnamese visual art, with the exception of posters. In contrast to the poor development not only of painting but of film, prose fiction, and dance as well, poetry and theatre seemed to me the only arts in a sophisticated condition, as arts, in Vietnam now.) The principle of getting maximal use from everything may partly explain why there are still quite a few pictures of Stalin in North Vietnam, hanging on the wall in some but hardly all government offices, factories, and schools. Stalin is the traditional figure on the right in the tintype pantheon Marx-Engels-Lenin-Stalin, and the Vietnamese lack both time and incentive for symbolic controversy. The composition of that quartet represents a form of politeness to the leading country and titular head of the "socialist camp" which was installed when the present government came to power in 1954. People in North Vietnam are perfectly well aware that the picture is out of date in 1968, and many North Vietnamese appeared to me to have grave reservations about the Soviet Union's domestic and foreign policies, even the character of its people. (Ho Chi Minh, whose picture is rarely to be seen in public buildings, pointedly refused the Lenin Prize a few years ago.) But whatever the Vietnamese, especially in Hanoi, might think, or even express privately, about the Russians—that they are collaborating with the Americans, that they don't genuinely back Vietnam's struggle, that they've abandoned the ideals of genuine Communism and of world revolution, that they're prone to be drunks and boors—does not yet invalidate the old icon. It remains, at least for the present, as a polite tribute to the *idea* of unity and solidarity among the Communist countries.

It's all part of the Vietnamese style, which seems guided by an almost principled avoidance of "heaviness," of making more complications than are necessary. No one can fail to credit the Vietnamese with subtlety in planning large-scale actions, as evidenced in the fabulous strategic sense of General Giap. But directness and plainness remain the rule when it comes to expressing something or making a gesture, and not out of any deeper artfulness. It was my impression that the Vietnamese, as a culture, genuinely believe that life is simple. They also believe, incredible as it may seem considering their present situation, that life is full of joy. Joy is to be discerned behind what is already so remarkable: the ease and total lack of self-pity with which people worked a backbreaking number of hours, or daily faced the possibility of their own death and the death of those they love. The phenomena of existential agony, of alienation, just don't appear among the Vietnamese—probably in part because they lack our kind of "ego" and our endowment of free-floating guilt. Of course, it's hard for a visitor to take all this at face value. I spent much of my early time in Vietnam wondering what lay "behind" the Vietnamese's apparent psychic equilibrium. The kind of seriousness—identified, Confucian-style, with unselfishness—that is deeply ingrained in Vietnamese culture is something which visitors from the Western capitalist world, equipped with their tools of psychological debunking, can hardly recognize, much less fully credit. Right away, the delicate build of the Vietnamese and their sheer physical gracefulness can set a gawky, big-boned American on edge. The Vietnamese behave with an unfaltering personal dignity that we tend to find suspect, either naïve or sham. And they appear so singularly and straightforwardly involved with the virtue of courage, and with the ideal of a noble, brave life. We live in an age marked by the discrediting of the heroic effort; hence, the awareness most people in this society have of their lives, whether they are appalled by it or not, as stale and flat. But in Vietnam one is confronted by a whole people possessed by a belief in what Lawrence called "the subtle, lifelong validity of the heroic impulse." Educated urban Americans, imbued with a sense of the decline of the heroic spirit, must find it especially difficult to perceive what animates the Vietnamese, to correlate the "known" historical dossier of their long, patient struggle to liberate their country with what can really be "believed" about people.

Ultimately, the difficulty encountered visiting North Vietnam reflects the crisis of credulity that is endemic in Western post-industrial society. Not only do the Vietnamese have virtues that thoughtful people in this part of the world simply don't believe in any more. They also mix virtues that we consider incompatible. For instance, we think war to be by its very nature "dehumanizing." But North Vietnam is simultaneously a martial society, completely mobilized for armed struggle, and a deeply civil society which places great value on gentleness and the demands of the heart. One of the more astonishing instances of Vietnamese concern for the heart, related to me by Phan, is the treatment accorded the thousands of prostitutes rounded up after the liberation of Hanoi from the French in 1954. They were put in charge of the Women's Union, which set up rehabilitation centers for them in the countryside, where they first passed months being elaborately pampered. Fairy tales were read to them; they were taught children's games and sent out to play. "That," Phan explained, "was to restore their innocence and give them faith again in man. You see, they had seen such a terrible side of human nature. The only way for them to forget that was to become little children again." Only after this period of mothering were they taught to read and write, instructed in a trade by which they could support themselves, and given dowries to improve their chances of eventually marrying. There seems no doubt that people who can think up such therapy really have a different moral imagination than we have. And as the quality of Vietnamese love differs from ours, so does the nature of their hate. Of course, the Vietnamese hate the Americans in some sense—but not as Americans would, if we had been subjected to equivalent punishment at the hands of a superior power. The North Vietnamese genuinely care about the welfare of the hundreds of captured American pilots and give them bigger rations than the Vietnamese population gets, "because they're bigger than we are," as a Vietnamese army officer told me, "and they're used to more meat than we are." People in North Vietnam really do believe in the goodness of man ("People in every country are good," Ho said in 1945, "only the governments are bad"), and in the perennial possibility of rehabilitating the morally fallen, among whom they include implacable enemies, even the Americans. In spite of all the stiff words disseminated by the Vietnamese, it's impossible not to be convinced by the genuineness of these concerns.

Still, apart from the general problem of credulity a Western visitor brings to a society like Vietnam, one may be doubly wary of any deeply positive reaction to the Vietnamese. The moment one begins to be affected by the moral beauty of the Vietnamese, not to mention their physical grace, a derisive inner voice starts calling it phony sentimentality. Understandably, one fears succumbing to that cut-rate sympathy for places like Vietnam which, lacking any real historical or psychological understanding, becomes another instance of the ideology of primitivism. The revolutionary politics of many people in capitalist countries is only a new guise for the old conservative culture-criticism: posing against overcomplex, hypocritical, devitalized, urban society choking on affluence the idea of a simple people living the simple life in a decentralized, uncoercive, passionate society with modest material means. As eighteenth-century *philosophes* pictured such a pastoral ideal in the Pacific islands or among the American Indians, and German romantic poets supposed it to have existed in ancient Greece, late twentieth-century intellectuals in New York and Paris are likely to locate it in the exotic revolutionary societies of the Third World. If some of what I've written evokes the very cliché of the Western left-wing intellectual idealizing an agrarian revolution that I was so set on not being, I must reply that a cliché is a cliché, truth is truth, and direct experience is—well—something one repudiates at one's peril. In the end I can only avow that, armed with these very self-suspicions, I found, through direct experience, North Vietnam to be a place which, in many respects, *deserves* to be idealized.

But, having stated my admiration for the Vietnamese (people, society) as bluntly and vulnerably as I can, I should emphasize that none of this amounts to a claim that North Vietnam is a model of a just state. One has only to recall the more notorious crimes committed by the present government: for example, the persecution of the Trotskyist faction and the execution of its leaders in 1946, and the forcible collectivization of agriculture in 1956, the brutalities and injustices of which high officials have recently admitted. Still, a foreigner should try to avoid padding out the lamentable facts with a reflex reaction to words. Upon learning that in North Vietnam today everyone belongs to at least one "organization" (usually several), a non-Communist visitor is likely to assume that the Vietnamese must be regimented and deprived of personal liberty. With the rise to dominance of the ideology of the bourgeoisie in the last two centuries, people in Europe and America have learned to associate membership in public organizations with becoming "depersonalized," and to identify achievement of the most valuable human goals with the autonomy of private life. But this apparently isn't how the threat of depersonalization arises in Vietnam; there, people rather experience themselves as dehumanized or depersonalized when they are not bound to each other in regular forms of collectivity. Again, a visitor of the independent Left will probably wince each time the Vietnamese mention "the Party." (The 1946 constitution does allow for a plurality of political groupings, and there is a Socialist Party and a Democratic Party, both of which publish weekly newspapers and have some representation in the government. But *Lao Dong*, the Workers Party, with nearly a hundred members on its Central Committee, is "the Party"; it runs the country, and the candidates it proposes are overwhelmingly favored by the electoral system.) But the preference for government by a single party of newly independent countries which have never known multi-party democracy is a fact that merits a more discriminating response than automatic disapproval. Several Vietnamese I met themselves brought up the dangers of single-party rule and claimed that in spite of these dangers the Workers Party had proved it deserves to hold power by being responsive to the concrete local demands of people. For the Vietnamese, "the Party" simply means the effective leadership of the country—from Ho Chi Minh, founder of the independent nation and of the Party (in 1930), to the young cadre just out of the Party School who comes to a village under bombardment to show its inhabitants how to build shelters or volunteers to live in the high mountains, among the Meo or Muong minorities, and teach them how to read and write. Of course, this conception of the Party as a vast corps of skilled, ethically impeccable, mostly unpaid public servants, tutoring and working alongside people in all their activities, sharing their hardships, doesn't exempt the Vietnamese system from terrible abuses. But neither does it preclude the possibility that the present system functions humanely, with genuine substantive democracy, much of the time.

In any case, I noticed that the word "democracy" was frequently invoked in Vietnam, far more often than in any other Communist country I've visited, including Cuba. The Vietnamese claim that democracy has deep roots in their culture, specifically in the customs of a fiercely independent peasantry. ("The law of the king must be subordinate to the law of the village," runs an old proverb.) Even in the past, Dr. Thach said, the form of the regime—kings and mandarins—was authoritarian, but its content—the traditions of village life—was democratic. Whether or not this account stands up to objective scrutiny, it's interesting that the Vietnamese *think* it true that their country is, and always has been, democratic. North Vietnam is the only Communist country I know in which people regularly praise the United States for being, after all and despite everything, "a great democracy." (As I've suggested, the Vietnamese don't show a very advanced command of Marxist thinking and critical analysis.) All this, myth as well as reality, must be taken into consideration when evaluating the nature of public institutions in North Vietnam and their role in promoting or discouraging individuality. The life of an institution cannot be appraised by examining a blueprint of its structure; run under the auspices of different feelings, similar structures can have a quite different quality. For instance, when love enters into the substance of social relations, the connection of people to a single party need not be dehumanizing. Though it's second nature for me to suspect the government of a Communist country of being oppressive and rigid, if not worse, most of my preconceptions about the misuses of state power in North Vietnam were really an abstraction. Against that abstract suspiciousness I must set (and be overruled by) what I actually saw when I was there—that the North Vietnamese genuinely love and admire their leaders; and, even more inconceivable to us, that the government loves the people. I remember the poignant, intimate tones in Pham Van Dong's voice as he described the sufferings the Vietnamese have endured in the last quarter of a century and their heroism, decency, and essential innocence. Seeing for the first time in my life a prime minister praising the moral character of his country's people with tears in his eyes has modified my ideas about the conceivable relations between rulers and ruled, and given me a more complex reaction to what I would ordinarily dismiss as mere propaganda.

For while no dearth of propaganda is put out by the North Vietnamese, what makes one despair is that this propaganda conveys so poorly, insensitively, and unconvincingly the most admirable qualities of the society built since 1954. Anyone who consults the publications about North Vietnam (on education, public health, the new role of women, literature, war crimes, etc.) issued in English and French by the Foreign Languages Press in Hanoi will not only get virtually nothing of the delicate texture of North Vietnamese society but be positively misled by the bombastic, shrill, and overly general character of these texts. Toward the close of my stay I mentioned to several government people that foreigners, reading these books and press releases, couldn't possibly form an idea of what North Vietnam is like, and explained my general impression that their revolution is being betrayed by its language. Though the Vietnamese I talked to seemed aware of the problem—they indicated I wasn't the first foreign visitor to tell them this—I felt they're far from knowing how to solve it. (I learned that Pham Van Dong had made a speech three years ago criticizing "the disease of rhetoric" that he charged was rife among the political cadres and appealing for an "improvement" of the Vietnamese language. But the only concrete advice he gave was that people spend less time talking about politics and more time reading classical Vietnamese literature.)

Can North Vietnam really be such an exceptional place? That's a question I have no way of answering. But I do know that North Vietnam, while definitely no Shangri-La, is a truly remarkable country; that the North Vietnamese is an extraordinary human being, and in ways not accounted for by the well-known fact that any keen struggle, a really desperate crisis, usually brings out the best (if not the worst) in people and promotes a euphoria of comradeship. What is admirable in the Vietnamese goes deeper than that. The Vietnamese are "whole" human beings, not "split" as we are. Inevitably, such people are likely to give outsiders the impression of great "simplicity." But while the Vietnamese are stripped down, they are hardly simple in any sense that grants us the right to patronize them.

It is *not* simple to be able to love calmly, to trust without ambivalence, to hope without self-mockery, to act courageously, to perform arduous tasks with unlimited resources of energy. In this society, a few people are able just faintly to imagine all these as achievable goals—though only in their private life. But in Vietnam the very distinction taken for granted here between the public and the private has not been strongly developed. This indistinct separation between public and private among the Vietnamese also informs their pragmatic, verbally and conceptually meager style of making their revolution. By way of contrast, the acute sense of the discontinuity of private and public in the West may partly explain the amount of talk, often very interesting talk, that accompanies every revolutionary gesture.* In our society, talk is perhaps the most intricately developed expression of private individuality. Conducted at this high pitch of development, talking becomes a double-edged activity: both an aggressive act and an attempted embrace. Thus talk often testifies to the poverty of inhibition of our feelings; it flourishes as a substitute for more organic connections between people. (When people really love, or are genuinely in touch with themselves, they tend to shut up.) But Vietnam is a culture in which people have not got the final devastating point about

---

* What brings about genuine revolutionary change is the shared experience of revolutionary *feelings*—not rhetoric, not the discovery of social injustice, not even intelligent analysis, and not any action considered in itself. And one can indeed "talk" revolutions away, by a disproportion between consciousness and verbalization, on the one hand, and the amount of practical *will*, on the other.

talking, have not gauged the subtle, ambivalent resources of language—because they don't experience as we do the isolation of a "private self." Talk is still a rather plain instrumentality for them, a less important means of being connected with their environment than direct feeling, love.

The absence of the sharp distinction between public and private spheres also allows the Vietnamese a relation to their country that must seem exotic to us. It is open to the Vietnamese to love their country passionately, every inch of it. One can't exaggerate the fervor of their patriotic passion and their intense attachment to particular places. Most people, I noticed, volunteer quickly where they are from, with a special melancholy if they were born in the South and have therefore been prevented from returning there for many years. And I remember Oanh describing his childhood on his uncle's fishing boat in Ha Long Bay, a famous resort area during the French colonial period. (Oanh recalled the excitement he felt as a small boy in the late 1920's when Paulette Goddard spent a holiday there.) But when Oanh had gone on for a while about the splendors of the rock formations in the bay, now heavily bombed, he stopped, almost apologetically, to say something like: Of course your Rocky Mountains must be very beautiful, too.

But is it possible to feel like that about America now? That was something I often debated with the Vietnamese. They assured me that I must love America just as much as they love Vietnam. It's my patriotism that makes me oppose my country's

---

(Hence the failure of the recent revolution in France. The French students talked—and very beautifully, too—instead of reorganizing the administration of the captured universities. Their staging of street demonstrations and confrontations with the police was conceived as a rhetorical or symbolic, rather than a practical, act; it too was a kind of talking.)

In our society, "idealistic" tends to mean "disorganized"; "militant" tends to mean merely "emotional." Most of the people in Europe and the Americas who are quite vociferous in their denunciations of the society in which they live are profoundly confused and thoughtless not only about what they would prefer instead but about any plan for actually taking power, so radical change might be effected. Indeed, revolution in the Western capitalist countries seems, more often than not, to be an activity expressly designed never to succeed. For many people, it is an *a*social activity, a form of action designed for the assertion of individuality against the body politic. It is the ritual activity of outsiders, rather than of people united by a passionate bond to their country.

foreign policy; I want to preserve the honor of the country I cherish above all others. There was some truth in what they said: all Americans—alas—believe that America is special, or ought to be. But I knew I didn't feel the positive emotion that Vietnamese attributed to me. Outrage and disappointment, yes. Love, no. Putting it in the baby language they and I shared (which I'd become rather skillful at), I explained: it's hard to love America right now, because of the violence which America is exporting all over the world; and given that the interests of humanity come before those of any particular people, a decent American today must be an internationalist first and a patriot second. Once at the Writers Union, when I had made this point (and not for the first time, so my voice may have been a little plaintive), a young poet answered me soothingly in English: "We are patriots, but in a happy way. You have more suffering in your patriotism." Sometimes they seemed to understand, but more often they didn't. Perhaps the difficulty is that, as I've already mentioned, they're quite fond of America themselves. People in Vietnam appear to take for granted that the United States *is* in many ways the greatest country in the world: the richest, the most advanced technologically, the most alive culturally, the most powerful, even the most free. They are not only endlessly curious about America—Oanh said several times how much he longs to visit the States as soon as the war is over—but genuinely admiring. I have described earlier the avidity of the poets and novelists for American literature. Pham Van Dong mentioned respectfully "your Declaration of Independence," from which Ho Chi Minh quoted when he declared the independence of Vietnam from the French on September 2, 1945. Hoang Tung, the editor of the principal daily paper, *Nhan Dan*, spoke of his "love" for the United States and praised to us "your tradition of freedom" which makes possible such creative political acts as the sit-in and the teach-in. The United States, he said, disposes of possibilities of good unmatched by any other country in the world.

If their view of the United States seemed at first improbable, then innocent and touching, the emotion the Vietnamese have for their own country seemed utterly alien, and even dangerous. But by the end of my visit I began to feel less estranged. Discovering the essential purity of their own patriotism showed me that such an emotion need not be identical with chauvinism. (How sensitive the Vietnamese are to the difference was clear in the only slightly concealed distaste of people I met in Hanoi for recent developments in China, like the cult of Mao and the cultural revolution.) If the Vietnamese could make such distinctions, so could I. Of course, I knew perfectly well why the attitude the Vietnamese expected of me was in fact so difficult. Ever since World War II, the rhetoric of patriotism in the United States has been in the hands of reactionaries and yahoos; by monopolizing it, they have succeeded in rendering the idea of loving America synonymous with bigotry, provincialism, and selfishness. But perhaps one shouldn't give up so easily. When the chairman of the Writers Union, Dang Thai Mai, said in his speech of welcome to Bob, Andy, and myself, "You are the very picture of the genuine American," why should I have slightly flinched? If what I feel is that flag-waving Legionnaires and Irish cops and small-town car salesmen who will vote for George Wallace are the genuine Americans, not I—which I fear part of me does feel—isn't that cowardly, shallow, and simply untrue? Why should I (we) not think of myself (ourselves) as a genuine American? With a little more purity of vision—but one would have to close the seepage of private despair into public grievances—maybe an intelligent American who cares for the other ninety-six percent of the human population and for the bio-ecological future of the planet could love America, too. Probably no serious radical movement has any future in America unless it can revalidate the tarnished idea of patriotism. One of my thoughts in the closing days of my stay in North Vietnam was that I would like to try.

Unfortunately, the first test of my vow came much sooner than I expected, almost immediately, in the first hours after leaving Hanoi the evening of May 17, and I failed right off. I wish something could be arranged to insure a proper "coming down" for visitors to North Vietnam in the first days after their departure. Unprepared, the ex-guest of the Democratic Republic of North Vietnam is in for a series of brutal assaults. Thirty minutes out of Hanoi, it was the spectacle of the drunken Polish members of the International Control Commission sitting around a table in the forward part of the plane dealing out a deck of pornographic playing cards. As we made our first touchdown, in the small airfield of Vientiane, it was seeing the landing area crowded with planes marked Air America (the C.I.A.'s private airline) which leave daily from here to drop napalm on villages in Northern Laos held by the Pathet Lao. Then came the taxi ride into Vientiane itself, River City U.S.A. (as Andy dubbed it), sordid outpost of the American empire. Servile, aggressive Laotian pedi-cab drivers trying to hustle a fare, an elderly lady tourist or a freaked-out hippie or an American soldier, weaved in and out of Cadillacs driven by American businessmen and Laotian government personnel. We passed the movie theatres showing skin flicks for the GI's, the "American" bars, the strip joints, stores selling paperbacks and picture magazines that could have been transplanted directly from Times Square, the American Embassy, Air France, signs for the weekly meeting of the Rotary Club. In the lobby of the Lane Xang, the one "modern" hotel in Vientiane, we bought copies of *Newsweek* and *Time* to catch up on what had been going on, during our absence of two weeks, in our world. Minutes later, Bob, Andy, and I were sitting on benches covered with thick red plastic in the hotel's air-conditioned cocktail lounge, getting drunk, soaking up Muzak, and poring helplessly, incredulously, and eagerly through the magazines. We began cracking hysterical jokes, with Andy further amplifying on his running gag about the Lone Ranger and Tonto that had been Bob's and my delight since the beginning of the trip—only it wasn't funny now. We debated going out and buying some grass (what else could one do here?) but decided against it, mainly because we were reluctant to go into the street and get even more depressed. By midnight we were all feeling positively sick. When dawn came four insomniac hours later, I could see out the window of my room across the flat, almost dry Mekong River. The river bed is an unguarded frontier, for what lies on the far side is Thailand, another, much more important American colony, home of the bases from which most planes take off daily to bomb the country we had just left. . . . And so on, out and out, further away from North Vietnam.

Due to one of the misadventures typical of the ICC flights, we had already spent four days in Vientiane before we went to Hanoi, staying at this very hotel, walking all over the town we'd just driven through. And though we had been jolted by its sordidness then, it seemed now that we couldn't have taken its full measure. And yet, of course, it had all been there before, and we'd seen it. In contrast to her subtler dealings with Western Europe, America exports to Southeast Asia only the most degraded aspects of her culture. And in that part of the world there is no dressing up or concealing the visible signs of American might. Though it could be helpful anyway to abstain from *Time* and *Newsweek* for at least ten days after a visit to North Vietnam, an American must brace himself for a big cultural shock—reverse cultural dislocation, I suppose—when the first environment he sees after leaving Hanoi is a place like Vientiane.

Remembering the intimations I'd had in North Vietnam of the possibility of loving my own country, I wanted very much not to react crudely, moralistically, not to slip back into the old posture of alienation. And after a while the keenest part of my outrage did subside. For the anger an American is likely to direct toward the emblems of his country's imperial dominance isn't founded simply upon their inherent repulsiveness, which permits no reaction other than aversion, but rather upon the despairing conviction that American power in its present form and guided by its present purposes is *invincible*. But this may not be, probably isn't, the case. The Vietnamese, for one, don't think so. And their wilder judgments do, by this time, have a claim to be taken seriously. After all, who—expect the Vietnamese themselves—would have predicted on February 7, 1965, that this small, poor nation could hold out against the awesome cruelty and thoroughness of American military force? But they have. Three years ago, enlightened world opinion pitied the Vietnamese, knowing that they couldn't possibly stand up to the United States; and the slogan of people protesting against the war was "Peace in Vietnam." Three years later, "Victory for Vietnam" is the only credible slogan. The Vietnamese don't want anybody's pity, as people in Hanoi told me; they want solidarity. The "tragedy" is Johnson's and the American government's, for continuing the war, Hoang Tung said. "There are many difficulties until the war ends," he added, "but we remain optimistic." For the Vietnamese, their victory is a "necessary fact."

The consequences for Vietnam of the eventual defeat of the

American invasion are not hard to envisage. They will consist, for the most part, in unqualified improvements over the present situation: cessation of all bombing, withdrawal of American troops from the South, the collapse of the Thieu-Ky government, and the accession to power of a government dominated by the National Liberation Front, which some day, but not in the near future (according to the present leadership of the NLF), will unite with the Hanoi government so that at long last the divided country will be reunified. But one can only speculate about the consequences of this defeat for the United States. It could be a turning point in our national history, for good or bad. Or it could mean virtually nothing—just the liquidation of a bad investment that leaves the military-industrial establishment free for other adventures with more favorable odds. To believe that things in America could move either way doesn't seem to me overly optimistic. But then, if there's at least some hope for America, 1968 would be the wrong time for people in this country who look toward radical change to lose heart.

As Hegel said, the problem of history is the problem of consciousness. The interior journey I made during my recent stay in Hanoi made the truth of this grandiose maxim sharp and concrete for me. There, in North Vietnam, what was ostensibly a somewhat passive experience of historical education became, as I think now it had to, an active confrontation with the limits of my own thinking.

The Vietnam that, before my trip to Hanoi, I supposed myself imaginatively connected with, proved when I was there to have lacked reality. During these last years, Vietnam has been stationed inside my consciousness as a quintessential image of the suffering and heroism of "the weak." But it was really America "the strong" that obsessed me—the contours of American power, of American cruelty, of American self-righteousness. In order eventually to encounter what was there in Vietnam, I had to forget about America; even more ambitiously, to push against the boundaries of the overall Western sensibility from which my American one derives. But I always knew I hadn't made more than a brief, amateurish foray into the Vietnamese reality. And anything really serious I'd gotten from my trip would return me to my starting point: the dilemmas of being an American, an unaffiliated radical American, an American writer.

For in the end, of course, an American has no way of incorporating Vietnam into his consciousness. It can glow in the remote distance like a navigator's star, it can be the seat of geological tremors that make the political ground shake under our own feet. But the virtues of the Vietnamese are certainly not directly emulatable by Americans; they're even hard to describe plausibly. And the revolution that remains to be made in this country must be made in American terms, not those of Asian peasant society. Radical Americans have profited from the war in Vietnam, profited from having a clear-cut moral issue on which to mobilize discontent and expose the camouflaged contradictions in the system. Beyond isolated private disenchantment or despair over America's betrayal of its ideals, Vietnam offered the key to a systematic criticism of America. In this scheme of use, Vietnam becomes an ideal Other. But such a status only makes Vietnam, already so alien culturally, even further removed from this country. Hence the task awaiting any sympathetic person who goes there: to understand what one is nevertheless barred from understanding. When American radicals visit North Vietnam, all things are thrown into question—their necessarily American attitudes to Communism, to revolution, to patriotism, to violence, to language, to courtesy, to eros, not to mention the more general Western features of their identity. I can testify that, at the very least, the world seems much bigger since I went to North Vietnam than it did before.

I came back from Hanoi considerably chastened. Life here looks both uglier and more promising. To describe what is promising, it's perhaps imprudent to invoke the promiscuous ideal of revolution. Still, it would be a mistake to underestimate the amount of diffuse yearning for radical change pulsing through this society. Increasing numbers of people do realize that we must have a more generous, more humane way of being with each other; and great, probably convulsive, social changes are needed to create these psychic changes. To prepare intelligently for radical change requires not only lucid and truthful social analysis: for instance, understanding better the realities of the distribution of political and economic power in the world which have secured for America its present hegemony. An equally relevant weapon is the analysis of psychic geography and history: for instance, getting more perspective on the human type that gradually became ascendant in the West from the time of the Reformation to the industrial revolution to modern post-industrial society. Almost everyone would agree that this isn't the only way human beings could have evolved, but very few people in Europe and America really, organically *believe* that there is any other way for a person to be or can *imagine* what they might be like. How can they when, after all, that's what they are, more or less? It's hard to step over one's own feet.

And yet, I think, the path isn't altogether blocked. Of course, most people are unlikely to come to a direct awareness of how local is the human type they embody, and even less likely to appreciate how arbitrary, drastically impoverished, and in urgent need of replacement it is. But they do know something else: that they are unhappy and that their lives are cramped and savorless and embittered. If that discontent isn't channeled off to be repaired by the kind of psycho-therapeutic awareness which robs it of social and political, of historical, dimension, the wide prevalence of unfocused unhappiness in modern Western culture could be the beginning of *real* knowledge—by which I mean the knowing that leads simultaneously to action and to self-transcendence, the knowing that would lead to a new version of human nature in this part of the world.

Ordinarily, changes in the human type (which is to say, in the quality of human relations) evolve very slowly, almost imperceptibly. Unfortunately, the exigencies of modern history being what they are, we can't be content to wait for the course of natural deliverance. There may not be enough time, given this society's strong taste for self-destructiveness. And even if Western man refrains from blowing himself up, his continuing as he is makes it so awfully hard, perhaps soon intolerably so, on the rest of the world—that is, most of the world, the more than two billion people who are neither white nor rich nor as expansionist as we are. Just possibly, the process of recasting the particular historical form of our human nature prevalent in Europe and America can be hurried a little, by more people becoming aware of capacities for sentiments and behavior that this culture's values have obscured and slandered.

An event that makes new feelings conscious is always the most important experience a person can have. These days, it's a pressing moral imperative as well. I was very lucky, I think: my ignorance, my empathic talents, and the habit of being dissatisfied with myself worked together to allow just such an experience by the end of my trip to North Vietnam in May. (Though the new feelings that were revealed to me are undoubtedly quite old in a historical sense, I personally had never experienced them before, or been able to name them, or been hitherto capable of believing in them.) Now, once again, I am far from Vietnam, trying to make these feelings live here in an appropriate and authentic form. That sounds difficult. Still, I doubt that what's required is a great effort of "holding on." In and by itself, such an experience is transformative. It is indelible.

I recognized a limited analogy to my present state in Paris in early July when, talking to acquaintances who had been on the barricades in May, I discovered they don't really accept the failure of their revolution. The reason for their lack of "realism," I think, is that they're still possessed by the new feelings revealed to them during those weeks—those precious weeks in which vast numbers of ordinarily suspicious, cynical urban people, workers and students, behaved with an unprecedented generosity and warmth and spontaneity toward each other. In a way, then, the young veterans of the barricades are right in not altogether acknowledging their defeat, in being unable fully to believe that things have returned to pre-May normality, if not worse. Actually it is they who are being realistic. Someone who has enjoyed new feelings of that kind—a reprieve, however brief, from the inhibitions on love and trust this society enforces—is never the same again. In him, the "revolution" has just started, and it continues. So I discover that what happened to me in North Vietnam did not end with my return to America, but is still going on.

(June–July 1968)

ON PHOTOGRAPHY

For Nicole Stéphane

It all started with one essay—about some of the problems, aesthetic and moral, posed by the omnipresence of photographed images; but the more I thought about what photographs are, the more complex and suggestive they became. So one generated another, and that one (to my bemusement) another, and so on—a progress of essays, about the meaning and career of photographs—until I'd gone far enough so that the argument sketched in the first essay, documented and digressed from in the succeeding essays, could be recapitulated and extended in a more theoretical way; and could stop.

The essays were first published (in a slightly different form) in *The New York Review of Books*, and probably would never have been written were it not for the encouragement given by its editors, my friends Robert Silvers and Barbara Epstein, to my obsession with photography. I am grateful to them, and to my friend Don Eric Levine, for much patient advice and unstinting help.

S. S.
May 1977

Contents

In Plato's Cave

HUMANKIND lingers unregenerately in Plato's cave, still reveling, its age-old habit, in mere images of the truth. But being educated by photographs is not like being educated by older, more artisanal images. For one thing, there are a great many more images around, claiming our attention. The inventory started in 1839 and since then just about everything has been photographed, or so it seems. This very insatiability of the photographing eye changes the terms of confinement in the cave, our world. In teaching us a new visual code, photographs alter and enlarge our notions of what is worth looking at and what we have a right to observe. They are a grammar and, even more importantly, an ethics of seeing. Finally, the most grandiose result of the photographic enterprise is to give us the sense that we can hold the whole world in our heads—as an anthology of images.

To collect photographs is to collect the world. Movies and television programs light up walls, flicker, and go out; but with still photographs the image is also an object, lightweight, cheap to produce, easy to carry about, accumulate, store. In Godard's *Les Carabiniers* (1963), two sluggish lumpen-peasants are lured into joining the King's Army by the promise that they will be able to loot, rape, kill, or do whatever else they please to the enemy, and get rich. But the suitcase of booty that Michel-Ange and Ulysse triumphantly bring home, years later, to their wives turns out to contain only picture postcards, hundreds of them, of Monuments, Department Stores, Mammals, Wonders of Nature, Methods of Transport, Works of Art, and other classified treasures from around the globe. Godard's gag vividly parodies the equivocal magic of the photographic image. Photographs are perhaps the most mysterious of all the objects that make up, and thicken, the environment we recognize as modern. Photographs really are experience captured, and the camera is the ideal arm of consciousness in its acquisitive mood.

To photograph is to appropriate the thing photographed. It means putting oneself into a certain relation to the world that feels like knowledge—and, therefore, like power. A now notorious first fall into alienation, habituating people to abstract the world into printed words, is supposed to have engendered that

529

surplus of Faustian energy and psychic damage needed to build modern, inorganic societies. But print seems a less treacherous form of leaching out the world, of turning it into a mental object, than photographic images, which now provide most of the knowledge people have about the look of the past and the reach of the present. What is written about a person or an event is frankly an interpretation, as are handmade visual statements, like paintings and drawings. Photographed images do not seem to be statements about the world so much as pieces of it, miniatures of reality that anyone can make or acquire.

Photographs, which fiddle with the scale of the world, themselves get reduced, blown up, cropped, retouched, doctored, tricked out. They age, plagued by the usual ills of paper objects; they disappear; they become valuable, and get bought and sold; they are reproduced. Photographs, which package the world, seem to invite packaging. They are stuck in albums, framed and set on tables, tacked on walls, projected as slides. Newspapers and magazines feature them; cops alphabetize them; museums exhibit them; publishers compile them.

For many decades the book has been the most influential way of arranging (and usually miniaturizing) photographs, thereby guaranteeing them longevity, if not immortality—photographs are fragile objects, easily torn or mislaid—and a wider public. The photograph in a book is, obviously, the image of an image. But since it is, to begin with, a printed, smooth object, a photograph loses much less of its essential quality when reproduced in a book than a painting does. Still, the book is not a wholly satisfactory scheme for putting groups of photographs into general circulation. The sequence in which the photographs are to be looked at is proposed by the order of pages, but nothing holds readers to the recommended order or indicates the amount of time to be spent on each photograph. Chris Marker's film, *Si j'avais quatre dromadaires* (1966), a brilliantly orchestrated meditation on photographs of all sorts and themes, suggests a subtler and more rigorous way of packaging (and enlarging) still photographs. Both the order and the exact time for looking at each photograph are imposed; and there is a gain in visual legibility and emotional impact. But photographs transcribed in a film cease to be collectable objects, as they still are when served up in books.

Photographs furnish evidence. Something we hear about, but doubt, seems proven when we're shown a photograph of it. In one version of its utility, the camera record incriminates. Starting with their use by the Paris police in the murderous roundup of Communards in June 1871, photographs became a useful tool of modern states in the surveillance and control of their increasingly mobile populations. In another version of its utility, the camera record justifies. A photograph passes for incontrovertible proof that a given thing happened. The picture may distort; but there is always a presumption that something exists, or did exist, which is like what's in the picture. Whatever the limitations (through amateurism) or pretensions (through artistry) of the individual photographer, a photograph—any photograph—seems to have a more innocent, and therefore more accurate, relation to visible reality than do other mimetic objects. Virtuosi of the noble image like Alfred Stieglitz and Paul Strand, composing mighty, unforgettable photographs decade after decade, still want, first of all, to show something "out there," just like the Polaroid owner for whom photographs are a handy, fast form of note-taking, or the shutterbug with a Brownie who takes snapshots as souvenirs of daily life.

While a painting or a prose description can never be other than a narrowly selective interpretation, a photograph can be treated as a narrowly selective transparency. But despite the presumption of veracity that gives all photographs authority, interest, seductiveness, the work that photographers do is no generic exception to the usually shady commerce between art and truth. Even when photographers are most concerned with mirroring reality, they are still haunted by tacit imperatives of taste and conscience. The immensely gifted members of the Farm Security Administration photographic project of the late 1930s (among them Walker Evans, Dorothea Lange, Ben Shahn, Russell Lee) would take dozens of frontal pictures of one of their sharecropper subjects until satisfied that they had gotten just the right look on film—the precise expression on the subject's face that supported their own notions about poverty, light, dignity, texture, exploitation, and geometry. In deciding how a picture should look, in preferring one exposure to another, photographers are always imposing standards on their subjects. Although there is a sense in which the camera does indeed capture reality, not just interpret it, photographs are as much an interpretation of the world as paintings and drawings are. Those occasions when the taking of photographs is relatively undiscriminating, promiscuous, or self-effacing do not lessen the didacticism of the whole enterprise. This very passivity—and ubiquity—of the photographic record is photography's "message," its aggression.

Images which idealize (like most fashion and animal photography) are no less aggressive than work which makes a virtue of plainness (like class pictures, still lifes of the bleaker sort, and mug shots). There is an aggression implicit in every use of the camera. This is as evident in the 1840s and 1850s, photography's glorious first two decades, as in all the succeeding decades, during which technology made possible an ever increasing spread of that mentality which looks at the world as a set of potential photographs. Even for such early masters as David Octavius Hill and Julia Margaret Cameron who used the camera as a means of getting painterly images, the point of taking photographs was a vast departure from the aims of painters. From its start, photography implied the capture of the largest possible number of subjects. Painting never had so imperial a scope. The subsequent industrialization of camera technology only carried out a promise inherent in photography from its very beginning: to democratize all experiences by translating them into images.

That age when taking photographs required a cumbersome and expensive contraption—the toy of the clever, the wealthy, and the obsessed—seems remote indeed from the era of sleek pocket cameras that invite anyone to take pictures. The first cameras, made in France and England in the early 1840s, had only inventors and buffs to operate them. Since there were then no professional photographers, there could not be amateurs either, and taking photographs had no clear social use; it was a gratuitous, that is, an artistic activity, though with few pretensions to being an art. It was only with its industrialization that photography came into its own as art. As industrialization provided social uses for the operations of the photographer, so the reaction against these uses reinforced the self-consciousness of photography-as-art.

Recently, photography has become almost as widely practiced an amusement as sex and dancing—which means that, like every mass art form, photography is not practiced by most people as an art. It is mainly a social rite, a defense against anxiety, and a tool of power.

Memorializing the achievements of individuals considered as members of families (as well as of other groups) is the earliest popular use of photography. For at least a century, the wedding photograph has been as much a part of the ceremony as the prescribed verbal formulas. Cameras go with family life. According to a sociological study done in France, most households have a camera, but a household with children is twice as likely to have at least one camera as a household in which there are no children. Not to take pictures of one's children, particularly when they are small, is a sign of parental indifference, just as not turning up for one's graduation picture is a gesture of adolescent rebellion.

Through photographs, each family constructs a portrait-chronicle of itself—a portable kit of images that bears witness to its connectedness. It hardly matters what activities are photographed so long as photographs get taken and are cherished. Photography becomes a rite of family life just when, in the industrializing countries of Europe and America, the very institution of the family starts undergoing radical surgery. As that claustrophobic unit, the nuclear family, was being carved out of a much larger family aggregate, photography came along to memorialize, to restate symbolically, the imperiled continuity and vanishing extendedness of family life. Those ghostly traces, photographs, supply the token presence of the dispersed relatives. A family's photograph album is generally about the extended family—and, often, is all that remains of it.

As photographs give people an imaginary possession of a past that is unreal, they also help people to take possession of space in which they are insecure. Thus, photography develops in tandem with one of the most characteristic of modern activities: tourism. For the first time in history, large numbers of people regularly travel out of their habitual environments for short periods of time. It seems positively unnatural to travel for pleasure without taking a camera along. Photographs will offer indisputable evidence that the trip was made, that the program was carried out, that fun was had. Photographs document sequences of consumption carried on outside the view of family, friends, neighbors. But dependence on the camera, as the device that makes real what one is experiencing, doesn't fade when people travel more. Taking photographs fills the same need for the cosmopolitans accumulating photograph-trophies of their boat trip up the Albert Nile or their fourteen days in China as it does for lower-middle-class vacationers taking snapshots of the Eiffel Tower or Niagara Falls.

A way of certifying experience, taking photographs is also a way of refusing it—by limiting experience to a search for the photogenic, by converting experience into an image, a souvenir. Travel becomes a strategy for accumulating photographs. The very activity of taking pictures is soothing, and assuages general feelings of disorientation that are likely to be exacerbated by travel. Most tourists feel compelled to put the camera between themselves and whatever is remarkable that they encounter. Unsure of other responses, they take a picture. This gives shape to experience: stop, take a photograph, and move on. The method especially appeals to people handicapped by a ruthless work ethic—Germans, Japanese, and Americans. Using a camera appeases the anxiety which the work-driven feel about not working when they are on vacation and supposed to be having fun. They have something to do that is like a friendly imitation of work: they can take pictures.

People robbed of their past seem to make the most fervent picture takers, at home and abroad. Everyone who lives in an industrialized society is obliged gradually to give up the past, but in certain countries, such as the United States and Japan, the break with the past has been particularly traumatic. In the early 1970s, the fable of the brash American tourist of the 1950s and 1960s, rich with dollars and Babbittry, was replaced by the mystery of the group-minded Japanese tourist, newly released from his island prison by the miracle of overvalued yen, who is generally armed with two cameras, one on each hip.

Photography has become one of the principal devices for experiencing something, for giving an appearance of participation. One full-page ad shows a small group of people standing pressed together, peering out of the photograph, all but one looking stunned, excited, upset. The one who wears a different expression holds a camera to his eye; he seems self-possessed, is almost smiling. While the others are passive, clearly alarmed spectators, having a camera has transformed one person into something active, a voyeur: only he has mastered the situation. What do these people see? We don't know. And it doesn't matter. It is an Event: something worth seeing—and therefore worth photographing. The ad copy, white letters across the dark lower third of the photograph like news coming over a teletype machine, consists of just six words: ". . . Prague . . . Woodstock . . . Vietnam . . . Sapporo . . . Londonderry . . . LEICA." Crushed hopes, youth antics, colonial wars, and winter sports are alike—are equalized by the camera. Taking photographs has set up a chronic voyeuristic relation to the world which levels the meaning of all events.

A photograph is not just the result of an encounter between an event and a photographer; picture-taking is an event in itself, and one with ever more peremptory rights—to interfere with, to invade, or to ignore whatever is going on. Our very sense of situation is now articulated by the camera's interventions. The omnipresence of cameras persuasively suggests that time consists of interesting events, events worth photographing. This, in turn, makes it easy to feel that any event, once underway, and whatever its moral character, should be allowed to complete itself—so that something else can be brought into the world, the photograph. After the event has ended, the picture will still exist, conferring on the event a kind of immortality (and importance) it would never otherwise have enjoyed. While real people are out there killing themselves or other real people, the photographer stays behind his or her camera, creating a tiny element of another world: the image-world that bids to outlast us all.

Photographing is essentially an act of non-intervention. Part of the horror of such memorable coups of contemporary photojournalism as the pictures of a Vietnamese bonze reaching for the gasoline can, of a Bengali guerrilla in the act of bayoneting a trussed-up collaborator, comes from the awareness of how plausible it has become, in situations where the photographer has the choice between a photograph and a life, to choose the photograph. The person who intervenes cannot record; the person who is recording cannot intervene. Dziga Vertov's great

film, *Man with a Movie Camera* (1929), gives the ideal image of
the photographer as someone in perpetual movement, someone moving through a panorama of disparate events with such
agility and speed that any intervention is out of the question.
Hitchcock's *Rear Window* (1954) gives the complementary
image: the photographer played by James Stewart has an intensified relation to one event, through his camera, precisely because he has a broken leg and is confined to a wheelchair; being
temporarily immobilized prevents him from acting on what he
sees, and makes it even more important to take pictures. Even
if incompatible with intervention in a physical sense, using a
camera is still a form of participation. Although the camera is
an observation station, the act of photographing is more than
passive observing. Like sexual voyeurism, it is a way of at least
tacitly, often explicitly, encouraging whatever is going on to
keep on happening. To take a picture is to have an interest in
things as they are, in the status quo remaining unchanged (at
least for as long as it takes to get a "good" picture), to be in
complicity with whatever makes a subject interesting, worth
photographing—including, when that is the interest, another
person's pain or misfortune.

"I always thought of photography as a naughty thing to do—
that was one of my favorite things about it," Diane Arbus wrote,
"and when I first did it I felt very perverse." Being a professional
photographer can be thought of as naughty, to use Arbus's pop
word, if the photographer seeks out subjects considered to be
disreputable, taboo, marginal. But naughty subjects are harder
to find these days. And what exactly is the perverse aspect of
picture-taking? If professional photographers often have sexual
fantasies when they are behind the camera, perhaps the perver-
sion lies in the fact that these fantasies are both plausible and
so inappropriate. In *Blowup* (1966), Antonioni has the fashion
photographer hovering convulsively over Verushka's body with
his camera clicking. Naughtiness, indeed! In fact, using a camera is not a very good way of getting at someone sexually. Between photographer and subject, there has to be distance. The
camera doesn't rape, or even possess, though it may presume,
intrude, trespass, distort, exploit, and, at the farthest reach of
metaphor, assassinate—all activities that, unlike the sexual push

and shove, can be conducted from a distance, and with some detachment.

There is a much stronger sexual fantasy in Michael Powell's extraordinary movie *Peeping Tom* (1960), which is not about a Peeping Tom but about a psychopath who kills women with a weapon concealed in his camera, while photographing them. Not once does he touch his subjects. He doesn't desire their bodies; he wants their presence in the form of filmed images— those showing them experiencing their own death—which he screens at home for his solitary pleasure. The movie assumes connections between impotence and aggression, professional- ized looking and cruelty, which point to the central fantasy connected with the camera. The camera as phallus is, at most, a flimsy variant of the inescapable metaphor that everyone un- selfconsciously employs. However hazy our awareness of this fantasy, it is named without subtlety whenever we talk about "loading" and "aiming" a camera, about "shooting" a film.

The old-fashioned camera was clumsier and harder to reload than a brown Bess musket. The modern camera is trying to be a ray gun. One ad reads:

> The Yashica Electro-35 GT is the spaceage camera your family will love. Take beautiful pictures day or night. Automatically. Without any nonsense. Just aim, focus and shoot. The GT's computer brain and electronic shutter will do the rest.

Like a car, a camera is sold as a predatory weapon—one that's as automated as possible, ready to spring. Popular taste ex- pects an easy, an invisible technology. Manufacturers reassure their customers that taking pictures demands no skill or expert knowledge, that the machine is all-knowing, and responds to the slightest pressure of the will. It's as simple as turning the ignition key or pulling the trigger.

Like guns and cars, cameras are fantasy-machines whose use is addictive. However, despite the extravagances of ordinary language and advertising, they are not lethal. In the hyperbole that markets cars like guns, there is at least this much truth: except in wartime, cars kill more people than guns do. The camera/gun does not kill, so the ominous metaphor seems to be all bluff—like a man's fantasy of having a gun, knife, or tool between his legs. Still, there is something predatory in the act of taking a picture. To photograph people is to violate them, by seeing them as they never see themselves, by having knowledge of them they can never have; it turns people into objects that can be symbolically possessed. Just as the camera is a sublimation of the gun, to photograph someone is a sublimated murder—a soft murder, appropriate to a sad, frightened time.

Eventually, people might learn to act out more of their aggressions with cameras and fewer with guns, with the price being an even more image-choked world. One situation where people are switching from bullets to film is the photographic safari that is replacing the gun safari in East Africa. The hunters have Hasselblads instead of Winchesters; instead of looking through a telescopic sight to aim a rifle, they look through a viewfinder to frame a picture. In end-of-the-century London, Samuel Butler complained that "there is a photographer in every bush, going about like a roaring lion seeking whom he may devour." The photographer is now charging real beasts, beleaguered and too rare to kill. Guns have metamorphosed into cameras in this earnest comedy, the ecology safari, because nature has ceased to be what it always had been—what people needed protection from. Now nature—tamed, endangered, mortal—needs to be protected from people. When we are afraid, we shoot. But when we are nostalgic, we take pictures.

It is a nostalgic time right now, and photographs actively promote nostalgia. Photography is an elegiac art, a twilight art. Most subjects photographed are, just by virtue of being photographed, touched with pathos. An ugly or grotesque subject may be moving because it has been dignified by the attention of the photographer. A beautiful subject can be the object of rueful feelings, because it has aged or decayed or no longer exists. All photographs are *memento mori*. To take a photograph is to participate in another person's (or thing's) mortality, vulnerability, mutability. Precisely by slicing out this moment and freezing it, all photographs testify to time's relentless melt.

Cameras began duplicating the world at that moment when the human landscape started to undergo a vertiginous rate of change: while an untold number of forms of biological and social life are being destroyed in a brief span of time, a device is available to record what is disappearing. The moody, intricately textured Paris of Atget and Brassaï is mostly gone. Like the dead relatives and friends preserved in the family album, whose presence in photographs exorcises some of the anxiety and remorse prompted by their disappearance, so the photographs of neighborhoods now torn down, rural places disfigured and made barren, supply our pocket relation to the past.

A photograph is both a pseudo-presence and a token of absence. Like a wood fire in a room, photographs—especially those of people, of distant landscapes and faraway cities, of the vanished past—are incitements to reverie. The sense of the unattainable that can be evoked by photographs feeds directly into the erotic feelings of those for whom desirability is enhanced by distance. The lover's photograph hidden in a married woman's wallet, the poster photograph of a rock star tacked up over an adolescent's bed, the campaign-button image of a politician's face pinned on a voter's coat, the snapshots of a cabdriver's children clipped to the visor—all such talismanic uses of photographs express a feeling both sentimental and implicitly magical: they are attempts to contact or lay claim to another reality.

Photographs can abet desire in the most direct, utilitarian way—as when someone collects photographs of anonymous examples of the desirable as an aid to masturbation. The matter is more complex when photographs are used to stimulate the moral impulse. Desire has no history—at least, it is experienced in each instance as all foreground, immediacy. It is aroused by archetypes and is, in that sense, abstract. But moral feelings are embedded in history, whose personae are concrete, whose situations are always specific. Thus, almost opposite rules hold true for the use of the photograph to awaken desire and to awaken conscience. The images that mobilize conscience are always linked to a given historical situation. The more general they are, the less likely they are to be effective.

A photograph that brings news of some unsuspected zone of misery cannot make a dent in public opinion unless there is an appropriate context of feeling and attitude. The photographs Mathew Brady and his colleagues took of the horrors of the battlefields did not make people any less keen to go on with the Civil War. The photographs of ill-clad, skeletal prisoners held at Andersonville inflamed Northern public opinion—against the South. (The effect of the Andersonville photographs must have been partly due to the very novelty, at that time, of seeing photographs.) The political understanding that many Americans came to in the 1960s would allow them, looking at the photographs Dorothea Lange took of Nisei on the West Coast being transported to internment camps in 1942, to recognize their subject for what it was—a crime committed by the government against a large group of American citizens. Few people who saw those photographs in the 1940s could have had so unequivocal a reaction; the grounds for such a judgment were covered over by the pro-war consensus. Photographs cannot create a moral position, but they can reinforce one—and can help build a nascent one.

Photographs may be more memorable than moving images, because they are a neat slice of time, not a flow. Television is a stream of underselected images, each of which cancels its predecessor. Each still photograph is a privileged moment, turned into a slim object that one can keep and look at again. Photographs like the one that made the front page of most newspapers in the world in 1972—a naked South Vietnamese child just sprayed by American napalm, running down a highway toward the camera, her arms open, screaming with pain—probably did more to increase the public revulsion against the war than a hundred hours of televised barbarities.

One would like to imagine that the American public would not have been so unanimous in its acquiescence to the Korean War if it had been confronted with photographic evidence of the devastation of Korea, an ecocide and genocide in some respects even more thorough than those inflicted on Vietnam a decade later. But the supposition is trivial. The public did not see such photographs because there was, ideologically, no space for them. No one brought back photographs of daily life in Pyongyang, to show that the enemy had a human face, as Felix Greene and Marc Riboud brought back photographs of Hanoi. Americans did have access to photographs of the suffering of the Vietnamese (many of which came from military sources and were taken with quite a different use in mind) because journalists felt backed in their efforts to obtain those photographs, the event having been defined by a significant number of people as a savage colonialist war. The Korean War was understood differently—as part of the just struggle of the Free World against the Soviet Union and China—and, given that characterization, photographs of the cruelty of unlimited American firepower would have been irrelevant.

Though an event has come to mean, precisely, something worth photographing, it is still ideology (in the broadest sense) that determines what constitutes an event. There can be no evidence, photographic or otherwise, of an event until the event itself has been named and characterized. And it is never photographic evidence which can construct—more properly, identify—events; the contribution of photography always follows the naming of the event. What determines the possibility of being affected morally by photographs is the existence of a relevant political consciousness. Without a politics, photographs of the slaughter-bench of history will most likely be experienced as, simply, unreal or as a demoralizing emotional blow.

The quality of feeling, including moral outrage, that people can muster in response to photographs of the oppressed, the exploited, the starving, and the massacred also depends on the degree of their familiarity with these images. Don McCullin's photographs of emaciated Biafrans in the early 1970s had less impact for some people than Werner Bischof's photographs of Indian famine victims in the early 1950s because those images had become banal, and the photographs of Tuareg families dying of starvation in the sub-Sahara that appeared in magazines everywhere in 1973 must have seemed to many like an unbearable replay of a now familiar atrocity exhibition.

Photographs shock insofar as they show something novel. Unfortunately, the ante keeps getting raised—partly through the very proliferation of such images of horror. One's first encounter with the photographic inventory of ultimate horror is a kind of revelation, the prototypically modern revelation: a negative epiphany. For me, it was photographs of Bergen-Belsen and Dachau which I came across by chance in a bookstore in Santa Monica in July 1945. Nothing I have seen—in photographs or in real life—ever cut me as sharply, deeply, instantaneously. Indeed, it seems plausible to me to divide my life into two parts, before I saw those photographs (I was twelve) and after, though it was several years before I understood fully what they were about. What good was served by seeing them? They were only photographs—of an event I had scarcely heard of and could do nothing to affect, of suffering I could hardly imagine and could do nothing to relieve. When I looked at those photographs, something broke. Some limit had been reached, and not only that of horror; I felt irrevocably grieved, wounded, but a part of my feelings started to tighten; something went dead; something is still crying.

To suffer is one thing; another thing is living with the photographed images of suffering, which does not necessarily strengthen conscience and the ability to be compassionate. It can also corrupt them. Once one has seen such images, one has started down the road of seeing more—and more. Images transfix. Images anesthetize. An event known through photographs certainly becomes more real than it would have been if one had never seen the photographs—think of the Vietnam War. (For a counter-example, think of the Gulag Archipelago, of which we have no photographs.) But after repeated exposure to images it also becomes less real.

The same law holds for evil as for pornography. The shock of photographed atrocities wears off with repeated viewings, just as the surprise and bemusement felt the first time one sees a pornographic movie wear off after one sees a few more. The sense of taboo which makes us indignant and sorrowful is not much sturdier than the sense of taboo that regulates the definition of what is obscene. And both have been sorely tried in recent years. The vast photographic catalogue of misery and injustice throughout the world has given everyone a certain familiarity with atrocity, making the horrible seem more ordinary—making it appear familiar, remote ("it's only a photograph"), inevitable. At the time of the first photographs of the Nazi camps, there was nothing banal about these images. After thirty years, a saturation point may have been reached. In these last decades, "concerned" photography has done at least as much to deaden conscience as to arouse it.

The ethical content of photographs is fragile. With the possible exception of photographs of those horrors, like the Nazi camps, that have gained the status of ethical reference points, most photographs do not keep their emotional charge. A photograph of 1900 that was affecting then because of its subject would, today, be more likely to move us because it is a photograph taken in 1900. The particular qualities and intentions of photographs tend to be swallowed up in the generalized pathos of time past. Aesthetic distance seems built into the very experience of looking at photographs, if not right away, then certainly with the passage of time. Time eventually positions most photographs, even the most amateurish, at the level of art.

The industrialization of photography permitted its rapid absorption into rational—that is, bureaucratic—ways of running society. No longer toy images, photographs became part of the general furniture of the environment—touchstones and confirmations of that reductive approach to reality which is considered realistic. Photographs were enrolled in the service of important institutions of control, notably the family and the police, as symbolic objects and as pieces of information. Thus, in the bureaucratic cataloguing of the world, many important documents are not valid unless they have, affixed to them, a photograph-token of the citizen's face.

The "realistic" view of the world compatible with bureaucracy redefines knowledge—as techniques and information. Photographs are valued because they give information. They tell one what there is; they make an inventory. To spies, meteorologists, coroners, archaeologists, and other information professionals, their value is inestimable. But in the situations in which most people use photographs, their value as information is of the same order as fiction. The information that photographs can give starts to seem very important at that moment in cultural history when everyone is thought to have a right to something called news. Photographs were seen as a way of giving information to people who do not take easily to reading. The *Daily News* still calls itself "New York's Picture Newspaper," its bid for populist identity. At the opposite end of the scale, *Le Monde*, a newspaper designed for skilled, well-informed readers, runs no photographs at all. The presumption is that, for such readers, a photograph could only illustrate the analysis contained in an article.

A new sense of the notion of information has been constructed around the photographic image. The photograph is a thin slice of space as well as time. In a world ruled by photographic images, all borders ("framing") seem arbitrary. Anything can be separated, can be made discontinuous, from

anything else: all that is necessary is to frame the subject differently. (Conversely, anything can be made adjacent to anything
else.) Photography reinforces a nominalist view of social reality
as consisting of small units of an apparently infinite number—as
the number of photographs that could be taken of anything is
unlimited. Through photographs, the world becomes a series
of unrelated, freestanding particles; and history, past and present, a set of anecdotes and *faits divers*. The camera makes reality atomic, manageable, and opaque. It is a view of the world
which denies interconnectedness, continuity, but which confers
on each moment the character of a mystery. Any photograph
has multiple meanings; indeed, to see something in the form
of a photograph is to encounter a potential object of fascination. The ultimate wisdom of the photographic image is to say:
"There is the surface. Now think—or rather feel, intuit—what
is beyond it, what the reality must be like if it looks this way."
Photographs, which cannot themselves explain anything, are
inexhaustible invitations to deduction, speculation, and fantasy.

Photography implies that we know about the world if we
accept it as the camera records it. But this is the opposite of
understanding, which starts from *not* accepting the world as it
looks. All possibility of understanding is rooted in the ability to
say no. Strictly speaking, one never understands anything from a
photograph. Of course, photographs fill in blanks in our mental
pictures of the present and the past: for example, Jacob Riis's
images of New York squalor in the 1880s are sharply instructive
to those unaware that urban poverty in late-nineteenth-century
America was really that Dickensian. Nevertheless, the camera's
rendering of reality must always hide more than it discloses. As
Brecht points out, a photograph of the Krupp works reveals
virtually nothing about that organization. In contrast to the
amorous relation, which is based on how something looks, understanding is based on how it functions. And functioning takes
place in time, and must be explained in time. Only that which
narrates can make us understand.

The limit of photographic knowledge of the world is that,
while it can goad conscience, it can, finally, never be ethical or
political knowledge. The knowledge gained through still photographs will always be some kind of sentimentalism, whether
cynical or humanist. It will be a knowledge at bargain prices—a

semblance of knowledge, a semblance of wisdom; as the act of taking pictures is a semblance of appropriation, a semblance of rape. The very muteness of what is, hypothetically, comprehensible in photographs is what constitutes their attraction and provocativeness. The omnipresence of photographs has an incalculable effect on our ethical sensibility. By furnishing this already crowded world with a duplicate one of images, photography makes us feel that the world is more available than it really is.

Needing to have reality confirmed and experience enhanced by photographs is an aesthetic consumerism to which everyone is now addicted. Industrial societies turn their citizens into image-junkies; it is the most irresistible form of mental pollution. Poignant longings for beauty, for an end to probing below the surface, for a redemption and celebration of the body of the world—all these elements of erotic feeling are affirmed in the pleasure we take in photographs. But other, less liberating feelings are expressed as well. It would not be wrong to speak of people having a *compulsion* to photograph: to turn experience itself into a way of seeing. Ultimately, having an experience becomes identical with taking a photograph of it, and participating in a public event comes more and more to be equivalent to looking at it in photographed form. That most logical of nineteenth-century aesthetes, Mallarmé, said that everything in the world exists in order to end in a book. Today everything exists to end in a photograph.

America, Seen Through
Photographs, Darkly

As Walt Whitman gazed down the democratic vistas of culture, he tried to see beyond the difference between beauty and ugliness, importance and triviality. It seemed to him servile or snobbish to make any discriminations of value, except the most generous ones. Great claims were made for candor by our boldest, most delirious prophet of cultural revolution. Nobody would fret about beauty and ugliness, he implied, who was accepting a sufficiently large embrace of the real, of the inclusiveness and vitality of actual American experience. All facts, even mean ones, are incandescent in Whitman's America—that ideal space, made real by history, where "as they emit themselves facts are showered with light."

The Great American Cultural Revolution heralded in the preface to the first edition of *Leaves of Grass* (1855) didn't break out, which has disappointed many but surprised none. One great poet alone cannot change the moral weather; even when the poet has millions of Red Guards at his disposal, it is still not easy. Like every seer of cultural revolution, Whitman thought he discerned art already being overtaken, and demystified, by reality. "The United States themselves are essentially the greatest poem." But when no cultural revolution occurred, and the greatest of poems seemed less great in days of Empire than it had under the Republic, only other artists took seriously Whitman's program of populist transcendence, of the democratic transvaluation of beauty and ugliness, importance and triviality. Far from having been themselves demystified by reality, the American arts—notably photography—now aspired to do the demystifying.

In photography's early decades, photographs were expected to be idealized images. This is still the aim of most amateur photographers, for whom a beautiful photograph is a photograph of something beautiful, like a woman, a sunset. In 1915 Edward Steichen photographed a milk bottle on a tenement fire escape, an early example of a quite different idea of the beautiful photograph. And since the 1920s, ambitious professionals, those whose work gets into museums, have steadily drifted away from lyrical subjects, conscientiously exploring plain, tawdry, or even vapid material. In recent decades, photography has succeeded in somewhat revising, for everybody, the definitions of what is beautiful and ugly—along the lines that Whitman had proposed. If (in Whitman's words) "each precise object or condition or combination or process exhibits a beauty," it becomes superficial to single out some things as beautiful and others as not. If "all that a person does or thinks is of consequence," it becomes arbitrary to treat some moment in life as important and most as trivial.

To photograph is to confer importance. There is probably no subject that cannot be beautified; moreover, there is no way to suppress the tendency inherent in all photographs to accord value to their subjects. But the meaning of value itself can be altered—as it has been in the contemporary culture of the photographic image which is a parody of Whitman's evangel. In the mansions of pre-democratic culture, someone who gets photographed is a celebrity. In the open fields of American experience, as catalogued with passion by Whitman and as sized up with a shrug by Warhol, everybody is a celebrity. No moment is more important than any other moment; no person is more interesting than any other person.

The epigraph for a book of Walker Evans's photographs published by the Museum of Modern Art is a passage from Whitman that sounds the theme of American photography's most prestigious quest:

> I do not doubt but the majesty & beauty of the world are latent in any iota of the world . . . I do not doubt there is far more in trivialities, insects, vulgar persons, slaves, dwarfs, weeds, rejected refuse, than I have supposed. . . .

Whitman thought he was not abolishing beauty but generalizing it. So, for generations, did the most gifted American photographers, in their polemical pursuit of the trivial and the vulgar. But among American photographers who have matured since World War II, the Whitmanesque mandate to record in its entirety the extravagant candors of actual American experience has gone sour. In photographing dwarfs, you don't get majesty & beauty. You get dwarfs.

Starting from the images reproduced and consecrated in the sumptuous magazine *Camera Work* that Alfred Stieglitz published from 1903 to 1917 and exhibited in the gallery he ran in New York from 1905 to 1917 at 291 Fifth Avenue (first called the Little Gallery of the Photo-Secession, later simply "291")—magazine and gallery constituting the most ambitious forum of Whitmanesque judgments—American photography has moved from affirmation to erosion to, finally, a parody of Whitman's program. In this history the most edifying figure is Walker Evans. He was the last great photographer to work seriously and assuredly in a mood deriving from Whitman's euphoric humanism, summing up what had gone on before (for instance, Lewis Hine's stunning photographs of immigrants and workers), anticipating much of the cooler, ruder, bleaker photography that has been done since—as in the prescient series of "secret" photographs of anonymous New York subway riders that Evans took with a concealed camera between 1939 and 1941. But Evans broke with the heroic mode in which the Whitmanesque vision had been propagandized by Stieglitz and his disciples, who had condescended to Hine. Evans found Stieglitz's work arty.

Like Whitman, Stieglitz saw no contradiction between making art an instrument of identification with the community and aggrandizing the artist as a heroic, romantic, self-expressing ego. In his florid, brilliant book of essays, *Port of New York* (1924), Paul Rosenfeld hailed Stieglitz as one "of the great affirmers of life. There is no matter in all the world so homely, trite, and humble that through it this man of the black box and chemical bath cannot express himself entire." Photographing, and thereby redeeming the homely, trite, and humble is also an ingenious means of individual expression. "The photographer," Rosenfeld writes of Stieglitz, "has cast the artist's net wider into the material world than any man before him or alongside him." Photography is a kind of overstatement, a heroic copulation with the material world. Like Hine, Evans sought a more impersonal kind of affirmation, a noble reticence, a lucid understatement. Neither in the impersonal architectural still lifes of American façades and inventories of rooms that he loved to make, nor in the exacting portraits of Southern sharecroppers he took in the late 1930s (published in the book done with James Agee, *Let Us Now Praise Famous Men*), was Evans trying to express himself.

Even without the heroic inflection, Evans's project still

descends from Whitman's: the leveling of discriminations between the beautiful and the ugly, the important and the trivial.
Each thing or person photographed becomes—a photograph;
and becomes, therefore, morally equivalent to any other of
his photographs. Evans's camera brought out the same formal
beauty in the exteriors of Victorian houses in Boston in the
early 1930s as in the store buildings on main streets in Alabama
towns in 1936. But this was a leveling up, not down. Evans
wanted his photographs to be "literate, authoritative, transcendent." The moral universe of the 1930s being no longer ours,
these adjectives are barely credible today. Nobody demands that
photography be literate. Nobody can imagine how it could be
authoritative. Nobody understands how anything, least of all a
photograph, could be transcendent.

Whitman preached empathy, concord in discord, oneness in
diversity. Psychic intercourse with everything, everybody—plus
sensual union (when he could get it)—is the giddy trip that
is proposed explicitly, over and over and over, in the prefaces
and the poems. This longing to proposition the whole world
also dictated his poetry's form and tone. Whitman's poems are
a psychic technology for chanting the reader into a new state
of being (a microcosm of the "new order" envisaged for the
polity); they are functional, like mantras—ways of transmitting
charges of energy. The repetition, the bombastic cadence, the
run-on lines, and the pushy diction are a rush of secular afflatus,
meant to get readers psychically airborne, to boost them up to
that height where they can identify with the past and with the
community of American desire. But this message of identification with other Americans is foreign to our temperament now.

The last sigh of the Whitmanesque erotic embrace of the nation,
but universalized and stripped of all demands, was heard in the
"Family of Man" exhibit organized in 1955 by Edward Steichen,
Stieglitz's contemporary and co-founder of Photo-Secession.
Five hundred and three photographs by two hundred and
seventy-three photographers from sixty-eight countries were
supposed to converge—to prove that humanity is "one" and
that human beings, for all their flaws and villainies, are attractive creatures. The people in the photographs were of all races,
ages, classes, physical types. Many of them had exceptionally

beautiful bodies; some had beautiful faces. As Whitman urged the readers of his poems to identify with him and with America, Steichen set up the show to make it possible for each viewer to identify with a great many of the people depicted and, potentially, with the subject of every photograph: citizens of World Photography all.

It was not until seventeen years later that photography again attracted such crowds at the Museum of Modern Art: for the retrospective given Diane Arbus's work in 1972. In the Arbus show, a hundred and twelve photographs all taken by one person and all similar—that is, everyone in them looks (in some sense) the same—imposed a feeling exactly contrary to the reassuring warmth of Steichen's material. Instead of people whose appearance pleases, representative folk doing their human thing, the Arbus show lined up assorted monsters and borderline cases—most of them ugly; wearing grotesque or unflattering clothing; in dismal or barren surroundings—who have paused to pose and, often, to gaze frankly, confidentially at the viewer. Arbus's work does not invite viewers to identify with the pariahs and miserable-looking people she photographed. Humanity is not "one."

The Arbus photographs convey the anti-humanist message which people of good will in the 1970s are eager to be troubled by, just as they wished, in the 1950s, to be consoled and distracted by a sentimental humanism. There is not as much difference between these messages as one might suppose. The Steichen show was an up and the Arbus show was a down, but either experience serves equally well to rule out a historical understanding of reality.

Steichen's choice of photographs assumes a human condition or a human nature shared by everybody. By purporting to show that individuals are born, work, laugh, and die everywhere in the same way, "The Family of Man" denies the determining weight of history—of genuine and historically embedded differences, injustices, and conflicts. Arbus's photographs undercut politics just as decisively, by suggesting a world in which everybody is an alien, hopelessly isolated, immobilized in mechanical, crippled identities and relationships. The pious uplift of Steichen's photograph anthology and the cool dejection of the Arbus retrospective both render history and politics irrelevant.

One does so by universalizing the human condition, into joy; the other by atomizing it, into horror.

The most striking aspect of Arbus's work is that she seems to have enrolled in one of art photography's most vigorous enterprises—concentrating on victims, on the unfortunate— but without the compassionate purpose that such a project is expected to serve. Her work shows people who are pathetic, pitiable, as well as repulsive, but it does not arouse any compassionate feelings. For what would be more correctly described as their dissociated point of view, the photographs have been praised for their candor and for an unsentimental empathy with their subjects. What is actually their aggressiveness toward the public has been treated as a moral accomplishment: that the photographs don't allow the viewer to be distant from the subject. More plausibly, Arbus's photographs—with their acceptance of the appalling—suggest a naïveté which is both coy and sinister, for it is based on distance, on privilege, on a feeling that what the viewer is asked to look at is really *other*. Buñuel, when asked once why he made movies, said that it was "to show that this is not the best of all possible worlds." Arbus took photographs to show something simpler—that there is another world.

The other world is to be found, as usual, inside this one. Avowedly interested only in photographing people who "looked strange," Arbus found plenty of material close to home. New York, with its drag balls and welfare hotels, was rich with freaks. There was also a carnival in Maryland, where Arbus found a human pincushion, a hermaphrodite with a dog, a tattooed man, and an albino sword-swallower; nudist camps in New Jersey and in Pennsylvania; Disneyland and a Hollywood set, for their dead or fake landscapes without people; and the unidentified mental hospital where she took some of her last, and most disturbing, photographs. And there was always daily life, with its endless supply of oddities—if one has the eye to see them. The camera has the power to catch so-called normal people in such a way as to make them look abnormal. The photographer chooses oddity, chases it, frames it, develops it, titles it.

"You see someone on the street," Arbus wrote, "and essentially what you notice about them is the flaw." The insistent sameness of Arbus's work, however far she ranges from her prototypical subjects, shows that her sensibility, armed with a camera, could insinuate anguish, kinkiness, mental illness with any subject. Two photographs are of crying babies; the babies look disturbed, crazy. Resembling or having something in common with someone else is a recurrent source of the ominous, according to the characteristic norms of Arbus's dissociated way of seeing. It may be two girls (not sisters) wearing identical raincoats whom Arbus photographed together in Central Park; or the twins and triplets who appear in several pictures. Many photographs point with oppressive wonder to the fact that two people form a couple; and every couple is an odd couple: straight or gay, black or white, in an old-age home or in a junior high. People looked eccentric because they didn't wear clothes, like nudists; or because they did, like the waitress in the nudist camp who's wearing an apron. Anybody Arbus photographed was a freak—a boy waiting to march in a pro-war parade, wearing his straw boater and his "Bomb Hanoi" button; the King and Queen of a Senior Citizens Dance; a thirtyish suburban couple sprawled in their lawn chairs; a widow sitting alone in her cluttered bedroom. In "A Jewish giant at home with his parents in the Bronx, NY, 1970," the parents look like midgets, as wrong-sized as the enormous son hunched over them under their low living-room ceiling.

The authority of Arbus's photographs derives from the contrast between their lacerating subject matter and their calm, matter-of-fact attentiveness. This quality of attention—the attention paid by the photographer, the attention paid by the subject to the act of being photographed—creates the moral theater of Arbus's straight-on, contemplative portraits. Far from spying on freaks and pariahs, catching them unawares, the photographer has gotten to know them, reassured them—so that they posed for her as calmly and stiffly as any Victorian notable sat for a studio portrait by Julia Margaret Cameron. A large part of the mystery of Arbus's photographs lies in what they suggest about how her subjects felt after consenting to be photographed. Do they see themselves, the viewer wonders, like *that*? Do they know how grotesque they are? It seems as if they don't.

The subject of Arbus's photographs is, to borrow the stately Hegelian label, "the unhappy consciousness." But most characters in Arbus's Grand Guignol appear not to know that they are ugly. Arbus photographs people in various degrees of unconscious or unaware relation to their pain, their ugliness. This necessarily limits what kinds of horrors she might have been drawn to photograph: it excludes sufferers who presumably know they are suffering, like victims of accidents, wars, famines, and political persecutions. Arbus would never have taken pictures of accidents, events that break into a life; she specialized in slow-motion private smashups, most of which had been going on since the subject's birth.

Though most viewers are ready to imagine that these people, the citizens of the sexual underworld as well as the genetic freaks, are unhappy, few of the pictures actually show emotional distress. The photographs of deviates and real freaks do not accent their pain but, rather, their detachment and autonomy. The female impersonators in their dressing rooms, the Mexican dwarf in his Manhattan hotel room, the Russian midgets in a living room on 100th Street, and their kin are mostly shown as cheerful, self-accepting, matter-of-fact. Pain is more legible in the portraits of the normals: the quarreling elderly couple on a park bench, the New Orleans lady bartender at home with a souvenir dog, the boy in Central Park clenching his toy hand grenade.

Brassaï denounced photographers who try to trap their subjects off-guard, in the erroneous belief that something special will be revealed about them.* In the world colonized by Arbus, subjects are always revealing themselves. There is no decisive moment. Arbus's view that self-revelation is a continuous, evenly distributed process is another way of maintaining the Whitmanesque imperative: treat all moments as of equal consequence. Like Brassaï, Arbus wanted her subjects to be as fully conscious as possible, aware of the act in which they were participating. Instead of trying to coax her subjects into a natural or typical position, they are encouraged to be awkward—that is, to pose. (Thereby, the revelation of self gets identified with

---

*Not an error, really. There is something on people's faces when they don't know they are being observed that never appears when they do. If we did not know how Walker Evans took his subway photographs (riding the New York subways for hundreds of hours, standing, with the lens of his camera peering between two buttons of his topcoat), it would be obvious from the pictures themselves that the seated passengers, although photographed close and frontally, didn't know they were being photographed; their expressions are private ones, not those they would offer to the camera.

what is strange, odd, askew.) Standing or sitting stiffly makes them seem like images of themselves.

Most Arbus pictures have the subjects looking straight into the camera. This often makes them look even odder, almost deranged. Compare the 1912 photograph by Lartigue of a woman in a plumed hat and veil ("Racecourse at Nice") with Arbus's "Woman with a Veil on Fifth Avenue, NYC, 1968." Apart from the characteristic ugliness of Arbus's subject (Lartigue's subject is, just as characteristically, beautiful), what makes the woman in Arbus's photograph strange is the bold unselfconsciousness of her pose. If the Lartigue woman looked back, she might appear almost as strange.

In the normal rhetoric of the photographic portrait, facing the camera signifies solemnity, frankness, the disclosure of the subject's essence. That is why frontality seems right for ceremonial pictures (like weddings, graduations) but less apt for photographs used on billboards to advertise political candidates. (For politicians the three-quarter gaze is more common: a gaze that soars rather than confronts, suggesting instead of the relation to the viewer, to the present, the more ennobling abstract relation to the future.) What makes Arbus's use of the frontal pose so arresting is that her subjects are often people one would not expect to surrender themselves so amiably and ingenuously to the camera. Thus, in Arbus's photographs, frontality also implies in the most vivid way the subject's cooperation. To get these people to pose, the photographer has had to gain their confidence, has had to become "friends" with them.

Perhaps the scariest scene in Tod Browning's film *Freaks* (1932) is the wedding banquet, when pinheads, bearded women, Siamese twins, and living torsos dance and sing their acceptance of the wicked normal-sized Cleopatra, who has just married the gullible midget hero. "One of us! One of us! One of us!" they chant as a loving cup is passed around the table from mouth to mouth to be finally presented to the nauseated bride by an exuberant dwarf. Arbus had a perhaps oversimple view of the charm and hypocrisy and discomfort of fraternizing with freaks. Following the elation of discovery, there was the thrill of having won their confidence, of not being afraid of them, of having mastered one's aversion. Photographing freaks "had a terrific excitement for me," Arbus explained. "I just used to adore them."

Diane Arbus's photographs were already famous to people who follow photography when she killed herself in 1971; but, as with Sylvia Plath, the attention her work has attracted since her death is of another order—a kind of apotheosis. The fact of her suicide seems to guarantee that her work is sincere, not voyeuristic, that it is compassionate, not cold. Her suicide also seems to make the photographs more devastating, as if it proved the photographs to have been dangerous to her.

She herself suggested the possibility. "Everything is so superb and breathtaking. I am creeping forward on my belly like they do in war movies." While photography is normally an omnipotent viewing from a distance, there is one situation in which people do get killed for taking pictures: when they photograph people killing each other. Only war photography combines voyeurism and danger. Combat photographers can't avoid participating in the lethal activity they record; they even wear military uniforms, though without rank badges. To discover (through photographing) that life is "really a melodrama," to understand the camera as a weapon of aggression, implies there will be casualties. "I'm sure there are limits," she wrote. "God knows, when the troops start advancing on you, you do approach that stricken feeling where you perfectly well can get killed." Arbus's words in retrospect describe a kind of combat death: having trespassed certain limits, she fell in a psychic ambush, a casualty of her own candor and curiosity.

In the old romance of the artist, any person who has the temerity to spend a season in hell risks not getting out alive or coming back psychically damaged. The heroic avant-gardism of French literature in the late nineteenth and early twentieth centuries furnishes a memorable pantheon of artists who fail to survive their trips to hell. Still, there is a large difference between the activity of a photographer, which is always willed, and the activity of a writer, which may not be. One has the right to, may feel compelled to, give voice to one's own pain—which is, in any case, one's own property. One volunteers to seek out the pain of others.

Thus, what is finally most troubling in Arbus's photographs is not their subject at all but the cumulative impression of the photographer's consciousness: the sense that what is presented is precisely a private vision, something voluntary. Arbus was not a poet delving into her entrails to relate her own pain but a photographer venturing out into the world to *collect* images that are painful. And for pain sought rather than just felt, there may be a less than obvious explanation. According to Reich, the masochist's taste for pain does not spring from a love of pain but from the hope of procuring, by means of pain, a strong sensation; those handicapped by emotional or sensory analgesia only prefer pain to not feeling anything at all. But there is another explanation of why people seek pain, diametrically opposed to Reich's, that also seems pertinent: that they seek it not to feel more but to feel less.

Insofar as looking at Arbus's photographs is, undeniably, an ordeal, they are typical of the kind of art popular among sophisticated urban people right now: art that is a self-willed test of hardness. Her photographs offer an occasion to demonstrate that life's horror can be faced without squeamishness. The photographer once had to say to herself, Okay, I can accept that; the viewer is invited to make the same declaration.

Arbus's work is a good instance of a leading tendency of high art in capitalist countries: to suppress, or at least reduce, moral and sensory queasiness. Much of modern art is devoted to lowering the threshold of what is terrible. By getting us used to what, formerly, we could not bear to see or hear, because it was too shocking, painful, or embarrassing, art changes morals—that body of psychic custom and public sanctions that draws a vague boundary between what is emotionally and spontaneously intolerable and what is not. The gradual suppression of queasiness does bring us closer to a rather formal truth—that of the arbitrariness of the taboos constructed by art and morals. But our ability to stomach this rising grotesqueness in images (moving and still) and in print has a stiff price. In the long run, it works out not as a liberation of but as a subtraction from the self: a pseudo-familiarity with the horrible reinforces alienation, making one less able to react in real life. What happens to people's feelings on first exposure to today's neighborhood pornographic film or to tonight's televised atrocity is not so different from what happens when they first look at Arbus's photographs.

The photographs make a compassionate response feel irrelevant. The point is not to be upset, to be able to confront the horrible with equanimity. But this look that is not (mainly) compassionate is a special, modern ethical construction: not hardhearted, certainly not cynical, but simply (or falsely) naïve. To the painful nightmarish reality out there, Arbus applied such adjectives as "terrific," "interesting," "incredible," "fantastic," "sensational"—the childlike wonder of the pop mentality. The camera—according to her deliberately naïve image of the photographer's quest—is a device that captures it all, that seduces subjects into disclosing their secrets, that broadens experience. To photograph people, according to Arbus, is necessarily "cruel," "mean." The important thing is not to blink.

"Photography was a license to go wherever I wanted and to do what I wanted to do," Arbus wrote. The camera is a kind of passport that annihilates moral boundaries and social inhibitions, freeing the photographer from any responsibility toward the people photographed. The whole point of photographing people is that you are not intervening in their lives, only visiting them. The photographer is supertourist, an extension of the anthropologist, visiting natives and bringing back news of their exotic doings and strange gear. The photographer is always trying to colonize new experiences or find new ways to look at familiar subjects—to fight against boredom. For boredom is just the reverse side of fascination: both depend on being outside rather than inside a situation, and one leads to the other. "The Chinese have a theory that you pass through boredom into fascination," Arbus noted. Photographing an appalling underworld (and a desolate, plastic overworld), she had no intention of entering into the horror experienced by the denizens of those worlds. They are to remain exotic, hence "terrific." Her view is always from the outside.

"I'm very little drawn to photographing people that are known or even subjects that are known," Arbus wrote. "They fascinate me when I've barely heard of them." However drawn she was to the maimed and the ugly, it would never have occurred to Arbus to photograph Thalidomide babies or napalm victims— public horrors, deformities with sentimental or ethical associations. Arbus was not interested in ethical journalism. She chose subjects that she could believe were found, just lying about, without any values attached to them. They are necessarily ahistorical subjects, private rather than public pathology, secret lives rather than open ones.

For Arbus, the camera photographs the unknown. But unknown to whom? Unknown to someone who is protected, who has been schooled in moralistic and in prudent responses. Like Nathanael West, another artist fascinated by the deformed and mutilated, Arbus came from a verbally skilled, compulsively health-minded, indignation-prone, well-to-do Jewish family, for whom minority sexual tastes lived way below the threshold of awareness and risk-taking was despised as another goyish craziness. "One of the things I felt I suffered from as a kid," Arbus wrote, "was that I never felt adversity. I was confined in a sense of unreality. . . . And the sense of being immune was, ludicrous as it seems, a painful one." Feeling much the same discontent, West in 1927 took a job as a night clerk in a seedy Manhattan hotel. Arbus's way of procuring experience, and thereby acquiring a sense of reality, was the camera. By experience was meant, if not material adversity, at least psychological adversity—the shock of immersion in experiences that cannot be beautified, the encounter with what is taboo, perverse, evil.

Arbus's interest in freaks expresses a desire to violate her own innocence, to undermine her sense of being privileged, to vent her frustration at being safe. Apart from West, the 1930s yield few examples of this kind of distress. More typically, it is the sensibility of someone educated and middle-class who came of age between 1945 and 1955—a sensibility that was to flourish precisely in the 1960s.

The decade of Arbus's serious work coincides with, and is very much of, the sixties, the decade in which freaks went public, and became a safe, approved subject of art. What in the 1930s was treated with anguish—as in *Miss Lonelyhearts* and *The Day of the Locust*—would in the 1960s be treated in a perfectly deadpan way, or with positive relish (in the films of Fellini, Arrabal, Jodorowsky, in underground comics, in rock spectacles). At the beginning of the sixties, the thriving Freak Show at Coney Island was outlawed; the pressure is on to raze the Times Square turf of drag queens and hustlers and cover it with skyscrapers. As the inhabitants of deviant underworlds are evicted from their restricted territories—banned as unseemly, a public nuisance, obscene, or just unprofitable—they increasingly come to infiltrate consciousness as the subject matter of art, acquiring a certain diffuse legitimacy and metaphoric proximity which creates all the more distance.

Who could have better appreciated the truth of freaks than someone like Arbus, who was by profession a fashion photographer—a fabricator of the cosmetic lie that masks the intractable inequalities of birth and class and physical appearance. But unlike Warhol, who spent many years as a commercial artist, Arbus did not make her serious work out of promoting and kidding the aesthetic of glamour to which she had been apprenticed, but turned her back on it entirely. Arbus's work is reactive—reactive against gentility, against what is approved. It was her way of saying fuck *Vogue*, fuck fashion, fuck what's pretty. This challenge takes two not wholly compatible forms. One is a revolt against the Jews' hyper-developed moral sensibility. The other revolt, itself hotly moralistic, turns against the success world. The moralist's subversion advances life as a failure as the antidote to life as a success. The aesthete's subversion, which the sixties was to make peculiarly its own, advances life as a horror show as the antidote to life as a bore.

Most of Arbus's work lies within the Warhol aesthetic, that is, defines itself in relation to the twin poles of boringness and freakishness; but it doesn't have the Warhol style. Arbus had neither Warhol's narcissism and genius for publicity nor the self-protective blandness with which he insulates himself from the freaky nor his sentimentality. It is unlikely that Warhol, who comes from a working-class family, ever felt any of the ambivalence toward success which afflicted the children of the Jewish upper middle classes in the 1960s. To someone raised a Catholic, like Warhol (and virtually everyone in his gang), a fascination with evil comes much more genuinely than it does to someone from a Jewish background. Compared with Warhol, Arbus seems strikingly vulnerable, innocent—and certainly more pessimistic. Her Dantesque vision of the city (and the suburbs) has no reserves of irony. Although much of Arbus's material is the same as that depicted in, say, Warhol's *Chelsea Girls* (1966), her photographs never play with horror, milking it for laughs; they offer no opening to mockery, and no possibility of finding freaks endearing, as do the films of Warhol and Paul Morrissey. For Arbus, both freaks and Middle America were equally exotic: a boy marching in a pro-war parade and a Levit-town housewife were as alien as a dwarf or a transvestite; lower-middle-class suburbia was as remote as Times Square, lunatic asylums, and gay bars. Arbus's work expressed her turn against what was public (as she experienced it), conventional, safe, reas-suring—and boring—in favor of what was private, hidden, ugly, dangerous, and fascinating. These contrasts, now, seem almost quaint. What is safe no longer monopolizes public imagery. The freakish is no longer a private zone, difficult of access. People who are bizarre, in sexual disgrace, emotionally vacant are seen daily on the newsstands, on TV, in the subways. Hobbesian man roams the streets, quite visible, with glitter in his hair.

Sophisticated in the familiar modernist way—choosing awk-wardness, naïveté, sincerity over the slickness and artificiality of high art and high commerce—Arbus said that the photographer she felt closest to was Weegee, whose brutal pictures of crime and accident victims were a staple of the tabloids in the 1940s. Weegee's photographs are indeed upsetting, his sensibility is urban, but the similarity between his work and Arbus's ends there. However eager she was to disavow standard elements of photographic sophistication such as composition, Arbus was not unsophisticated. And there is nothing journalistic about her motives for taking pictures. What may seem journalistic, even sensational, in Arbus's photographs places them, rather, in the main tradition of Surrealist art—their taste for the grotesque, their professed innocence with respect to their subjects, their claim that all subjects are merely *objets trouvés.*

"I would never choose a subject for what it meant to me when I think of it," Arbus wrote, a dogged exponent of the Surrealist bluff. Presumably, viewers are not supposed to judge the people she photographs. Of course, we do. And the very range of Arbus's subjects itself constitutes a judgment. Brassaï, who photographed people like those who interested Arbus—see his "La Môme Bijou" of 1932—also did tender cityscapes, por-traits of famous artists. Lewis Hine's "Mental Institution, New Jersey, 1924" could be a late Arbus photograph (except that the pair of Mongoloid children posing on the lawn are pho-tographed in profile rather than frontally); the Chicago street portraits Walker Evans took in 1946 are Arbus material, as are a number of photographs by Robert Frank. The difference is in the range of other subjects, other emotions that Hine, Brassaï, Evans, and Frank photographed. Arbus is an *auteur* in the most limiting sense, as special a case in the history of photography as is Giorgio Morandi, who spent a half century doing still lifes of bottles, in the history of modern European painting. She does not, like most ambitious photographers, play the field of subject matter—even a little. On the contrary, all her subjects are equivalent. And making equivalences between freaks, mad people, suburban couples, and nudists is a very powerful judgment, one in complicity with a recognizable political mood shared by many educated, left-liberal Americans. The subjects of Arbus's photographs are all members of the same family, inhabitants of a single village. Only, as it happens, the idiot village is America. Instead of showing identity between things which are different (Whitman's democratic vista), everybody is shown to look the same.

Succeeding the more buoyant hopes for America has come a bitter, sad embrace of experience. There is a particular melancholy in the American photographic project. But the melancholy was already latent in the heyday of Whitmanesque affirmation, as represented by Stieglitz and his Photo-Secession circle. Stieglitz, pledged to redeem the world with his camera, was still shocked by modern material civilization. He photographed New York in the 1910s in an almost quixotic spirit—camera/lance against skyscraper/windmill. Paul Rosenfeld described Stieglitz's efforts as a "perpetual affirmation." The Whitmanesque appetites have turned pious: the photographer now patronizes reality. One needs a camera to show patterns in that "dull and marvelous opacity called the United States."

Obviously, a mission as rotten with doubt about America—even at its most optimistic—was bound to get deflated fairly soon, as post–World War I America committed itself more boldly to big business and consumerism. Photographers with less ego and magnetism than Stieglitz gradually gave up the struggle. They might continue to practice the atomistic visual stenography inspired by Whitman. But, without Whitman's delirious powers of synthesis, what they documented was discontinuity, detritus, loneliness, greed, sterility. Stieglitz, using photography to challenge the materialist civilization, was, in

Rosenfeld's words, "the man who believed that a spiritual America existed somewhere, that America was not the grave of the Occident." The implicit intent of Frank and Arbus, and of many of their contemporaries and juniors, is to show that America *is* the grave of the Occident.

Since photography cut loose from the Whitmanesque affirmation—since it has ceased to understand how photographs could aim at being literate, authoritative, transcendent—the best of American photography (and much else in American culture) has given itself over to the consolations of Surrealism, and America has been discovered as the quintessential Surrealist country. It is obviously too easy to say that America is just a freak show, a wasteland—the cut-rate pessimism typical of the reduction of the real to the surreal. But the American partiality to myths of redemption and damnation remains one of the most energizing, most seductive aspects of our national culture. What we have left of Whitman's discredited dream of cultural revolution are paper ghosts and a sharp-eyed witty program of despair.

Melancholy Objects

PHOTOGRAPHY has the unappealing reputation of being the most realistic, therefore facile, of the mimetic arts. In fact, it is the one art that has managed to carry out the grandiose, century-old threats of a Surrealist takeover of the modern sensibility, while most of the pedigreed candidates have dropped out of the race.

Painting was handicapped from the start by being a fine art, with each object a unique, handmade original. A further liability was the exceptional technical virtuosity of those painters usually included in the Surrealist canon, who seldom imagined the canvas as other than figurative. Their paintings looked sleekly calculated, complacently well made, undialectical. They kept a long, prudent distance from Surrealism's contentious idea of blurring the lines between art and so-called life, between objects and events, between the intended and the unintentional, between pros and amateurs, between the noble and the tawdry, between craftsmanship and lucky blunders. The result was that Surrealism in painting amounted to little more than the contents of a meagerly stocked dream world: a few witty fantasies, mostly wet dreams and agoraphobic nightmares. (Only when its libertarian rhetoric helped to nudge Jackson Pollock and others into a new kind of irreverent abstraction did the Surrealist mandate for painters finally seem to make wide creative sense.) Poetry, the other art to which the early Surrealists were particularly devoted, has yielded almost equally disappointing results. The arts in which Surrealism has come into its own are prose fiction (as content, mainly, but much more abundant and more complex thematically than that claimed by painting), theater, the arts of assemblage, and—most triumphantly—photography.

That photography is the only art that is natively surreal does not mean, however, that it shares the destinies of the official Surrealist movement. On the contrary. Those photographers (many of them ex-painters) consciously influenced by Surrealism count almost as little today as the nineteenth-century "pictorial" photographers who copied the look of Beaux-Arts painting. Even the loveliest *trouvailles* of the 1920s—the solarized photographs and Rayographs of Man Ray, the photograms of László Moholy-Nagy, the multiple-exposure studies of

563

Bragaglia, the photomontages of John Heartfield and Alexander Rodchenko—are regarded as marginal exploits in the history of photography. The photographers who concentrated on interfering with the supposedly superficial realism of the photograph were those who most narrowly conveyed photography's surreal properties. The Surrealist legacy for photography came to seem trivial as the Surrealist repertoire of fantasies and props was rapidly absorbed into high fashion in the 1930s, and Surrealist photography offered mainly a mannered style of portraiture, recognizable by its use of the same decorative conventions introduced by Surrealism in other arts, particularly painting, theater, and advertising. The mainstream of photographic activity has shown that a Surrealist manipulation or theatricalization of the real is unnecessary, if not actually redundant. Surrealism lies at the heart of the photographic enterprise: in the very creation of a duplicate world, of a reality in the second degree, narrower but more dramatic than the one perceived by natural vision. The less doctored, the less patently crafted, the more naïve—the more authoritative the photograph was likely to be.

Surrealism has always courted accidents, welcomed the uninvited, flattered disorderly presences. What could be more surreal than an object which virtually produces itself, and with a minimum of effort? An object whose beauty, fantastic disclosures, emotional weight are likely to be further enhanced by any accidents that might befall it? It is photography that has best shown how to juxtapose the sewing machine and the umbrella, whose fortuitous encounter was hailed by a great Surrealist poet as an epitome of the beautiful.

Unlike the fine-art objects of pre-democratic eras, photographs don't seem deeply beholden to the intentions of an artist. Rather, they owe their existence to a loose cooperation (quasi-magical, quasi-accidental) between photographer and subject—mediated by an ever simpler and more automated machine, which is tireless, and which even when capricious can produce a result that is interesting and never entirely wrong. (The sales pitch for the first Kodak, in 1888, was: "You press the button, we do the rest." The purchaser was guaranteed that the picture would be "without any mistake.") In the fairy tale of photography the magic box insures veracity and banishes error, compensates for inexperience and rewards innocence.

The myth is tenderly parodied in a 1928 silent film, *The Cameraman*, which has an inept dreamy Buster Keaton vainly struggling with his dilapidated apparatus, knocking out windows and doors whenever he picks up his tripod, never managing to take one decent picture, yet finally getting some great footage (a photojournalist scoop of a tong war in New York's Chinatown)—by inadvertence. It is the hero's pet monkey who loads the camera with film and operates it part of the time.

The error of the Surrealist militants was to imagine the surreal to be something universal, that is, a matter of psychology, whereas it turns out to be what is most local, ethnic, class-bound, dated. Thus, the earliest surreal photographs come from the 1850s, when photographers first went out prowling the streets of London, Paris, and New York, looking for their unposed slice of life. These photographs, concrete, particular, anecdotal (except that the anecdote has been effaced)—moments of lost time, of vanished customs—seem far mo surreal to us now than any photograph rendered abstract a poetic by superimposition, underprinting, solarization, the like. Believing that the images they sought came from unconscious, whose contents they assumed as loyal Freu to be timeless as well as universal, the Surrealists mis stood what was most brutally moving, irrational, unassir mysterious—time itself. What renders a photograph s its irrefutable pathos as a message from time past, and creteness of its intimations about social class.

Surrealism is a bourgeois disaffection; that it' thought it universal is only one of the signs that ir bourgeois. As an aesthetics that yearns to be a poli' ism opts for the underdog, for the rights of a dise unofficial reality. But the scandals flattered by S thetics generally turned out to be just those hor obscured by the bourgeois social order: sex and which the early Surrealists placed at the summit (reality they sought to rehabilitate, was itself part of social station. While it seemed to flourish lu treme ends of the scale, both the lower classes being regarded as naturally libertine, middle- to toil to make their sexual revolution. Class mystery: the inexhaustible glamour of the rich and powerful, the opaque degradation of the poor and outcast.

The view of reality as an exotic prize to be tracked down and captured by the diligent hunter-with-a-camera has informed photography from the beginning, and marks the confluence of the Surrealist counter-culture and middle-class social adventurism. Photography has always been fascinated by social heights and lower depths. Documentarists (as distinct from courtiers with cameras) prefer the latter. For more than a century, photographers have been hovering about the oppressed, in attendance at scenes of violence—with a spectacularly good conscience. Social misery has inspired the comfortably-off with the urge to take pictures, the gentlest of predations, in order to document a hidden reality, that is, a reality hidden from them.

Gazing on other people's reality with curiosity, with detachment, with professionalism, the ubiquitous photographer operates as if that activity transcends class interests, as if its perspective is universal. In fact, photography first comes into its own as an extension of the eye of the middle-class *flâneur*, whose sensibility was so accurately charted by Baudelaire. The photographer is an armed version of the solitary walker reconnoitering, stalking, cruising the urban inferno, the voyeuristic stroller who discovers the city as a landscape of voluptuous extremes. Adept of the joys of watching, connoisseur of empathy, the *flâneur* finds the world "picturesque." The findings of Baudelaire's *flâneur* are variously exemplified by the candid snapshots taken in the 1890s by Paul Martin in London streets and at the seaside and by Arnold Genthe in San Francisco's Chinatown (both using a concealed camera), by Atget's twilight Paris of shabby streets and decaying trades, by the dramas of sex and loneliness depicted in Brassaï's book *Paris de nuit* (1933), by the image of the city as a theater of disaster in Weegee's *Naked City* (1945). The *flâneur* is not attracted to the city's official realities but to its dark seamy corners, its neglected populations—an unofficial reality behind the façade of bourgeois life that the photographer "apprehends," as a detective apprehends a criminal.

Returning to *The Cameraman*: a tong war among poor Chinese makes an ideal subject. It is completely exotic, therefore worth photographing. Part of what assures the success of the cameraman's film is that he doesn't understand his subject at all. (As played by Buster Keaton, he doesn't even understand that his life is in danger.) The perennial surreal subject is *How the Other Half Lives*, to cite the innocently explicit title that Jacob Riis gave to the book of photographs of the New York poor that he brought out in 1890. Photography conceived as social documentation was an instrument of that essentially middle-class attitude, both zealous and merely tolerant, both curious and indifferent, called humanism—which found slums the most enthralling of decors. Contemporary photographers have, of course, learned to dig in and limit their subject. Instead of the chutzpa of "the other half," we get, say, *East 100th Street* (Bruce Davidson's book of Harlem photographs published in 1970). The justification is still the same, that picture-taking serves a high purpose: uncovering a hidden truth, conserving a vanishing past. (The hidden truth is, moreover, often identified with the vanishing past. Between 1874 and 1886, prosperous Londoners could subscribe to the Society for Photographing the Relics of Old London.)

Starting as artists of the urban sensibility, photographers quickly became aware that nature is as exotic as the city, rustics as picturesque as city slum dwellers. In 1897 Sir Benjamin Stone, rich industrialist and conservative MP from Birmingham, founded the National Photographic Record Association with the aim of documenting traditional English ceremonies and rural festivals which were dying out. "Every village," Stone wrote, "has a history which might be preserved by means of the camera." For a wellborn photographer of the late nineteenth century like the bookish Count Giuseppe Primoli, the street life of the underprivileged was at least as interesting as the pastimes of his fellow aristocrats: compare Primoli's photographs of King Victor Emmanuel's wedding with his photographs of the Naples poor. It required the social immobility of a photographer of genius who happened to be a small child, Jacques-Henri Lartigue, to confine subject matter to the outlandish habits of the photographer's own family and class. But essentially the camera makes everyone a tourist in other people's reality, and eventually in one's own.

Perhaps the earliest model of the sustained look downward are the thirty-six photographs in *Street Life in London* (1877–78) taken by the British traveler and photographer John Thomson.

But for each photographer specializing in the poor, many more go after a wider range of exotic reality. Thomson himself had a model career of this kind. Before turning to the poor of his own country, he had already been to see the heathen, a sojourn which resulted in his four-volume *Illustrations of China and Its People* (1873–74). And following his book on the street life of the London poor, he turned to the indoor life of the London rich: it was Thomson who, around 1880, pioneered the vogue of at-home photographic portraiture.

From the beginning, professional photography typically meant the broader kind of class tourism, with most photographers combining surveys of social abjection with portraits of celebrities or commodities (high fashion, advertising) or studies of the nude. Many of the exemplary photographic careers of this century (like those of Edward Steichen, Bill Brandt, Henri Cartier-Bresson, Richard Avedon) proceed by abrupt changes in the social level and ethical importance of subject matter. Perhaps the most dramatic break is that between the pre-war and the post-war work of Bill Brandt. To have gone from the tough-minded photographs of Depression squalor in northern England to his stylish celebrity portraits and semi-abstract nudes of the last decades seems a long journey indeed. But there is nothing particularly idiosyncratic, or perhaps even inconsistent, in these contrasts. Traveling between degraded and glamorous realities is part of the very momentum of the photographic enterprise, unless the photographer is locked into an extremely private obsession (like the thing Lewis Carroll had for little girls or Diane Arbus had for the Halloween crowd).

Poverty is no more surreal than wealth; a body clad in filthy rags is not more surreal than a principessa dressed for a ball or a pristine nude. What is surreal is the distance imposed, and bridged, by the photograph: the social distance and the distance in time. Seen from the middle-class perspective of photography, celebrities are as intriguing as pariahs. Photographers need not have an ironic, intelligent attitude toward their stereotyped material. Pious, respectful fascination may do just as well, especially with the most conventional subjects.

Nothing could be farther from, say, the subtleties of Avedon than the work of Ghitta Carell, Hungarian-born photographer of the celebrities of the Mussolini era. But her portraits now look as eccentric as Avedon's, and far more surreal than Cecil Beaton's Surrealist-influenced photographs from the same period. By setting his subjects—see the photographs he took of Edith Sitwell in 1927, of Cocteau in 1936—in fanciful, luxurious decors, Beaton turns them into overexplicit, unconvincing effigies. But Carell's innocent complicity with the wish of her Italian generals and aristocrats and actors to appear static, poised, glamorous exposes a hard, accurate truth about them. The photographer's reverence has made them interesting; time has made them harmless, all too human.

Some photographers set up as scientists, others as moralists. The scientists make an inventory of the world; the moralists concentrate on hard cases. An example of photography-as-science is the project August Sander began in 1911: a photographic catalogue of the German people. In contrast to George Grosz's drawings, which summed up the spirit and variety of social types in Weimar Germany through caricature, Sander's "archetype pictures" (as he called them) imply a pseudo-scientific neutrality similar to that claimed by the covertly partisan typological sciences that sprang up in the nineteenth century like phrenology, criminology, psychiatry, and eugenics. It was not so much that Sander chose individuals for their representative character as that he assumed, correctly, that the camera cannot help but reveal faces as social masks. Each person photographed was a sign of a certain trade, class, or profession. All his subjects are representative, equally representative, of a given social reality—their own.

Sander's look is not unkind; it is permissive, unjudging. Compare his 1930 photograph "Circus People" with Diane Arbus's studies of circus people or with the portraits of demimonde characters by Lisette Model. People face Sander's camera, as they do in Model's and Arbus's photographs, but their gaze is not intimate, revealing. Sander was not looking for secrets; he was observing the typical. Society contains no mystery. Like Eadweard Muybridge, whose photographic studies in the 1880s managed to dispel misconceptions about what everybody had always seen (how horses gallop, how people move) because he had subdivided the subject's movements into a precise and lengthy enough sequence of shots, Sander aimed to shed light on the social order by atomizing it, into an indefinite number of social types. It doesn't seem surprising that in 1934, five years after its publication, the Nazis impounded the unsold copies of Sander's book *Antlitz der Zeit (The Face of Our Time)* and destroyed the printing blocks, thus bringing his national-portrait project to an abrupt end. (Sander, who stayed in Germany throughout the Nazi period, switched to landscape photography.) The charge was that Sander's project was anti-social. What might well have seemed anti-social to Nazis was his idea of the photographer as an impassive census-taker, the completeness of whose record would render all commentary, or even judgment, superfluous.

Unlike most photography with a documentary intention, enthralled either by the poor and unfamiliar, as preeminently photographable subjects, or by celebrities, Sander's social sample is unusually, conscientiously broad. He includes bureaucrats and peasants, servants and society ladies, factory workers and industrialists, soldiers and gypsies, actors and clerks. But such variety does not rule out class condescension. Sander's eclectic style gives him away. Some photographs are casual, fluent, naturalistic; others are naïve and awkward. The many posed photographs taken against a flat white background are a cross between superb mug shots and old-fashioned studio portraits. Unselfconsciously, Sander adjusted his style to the social rank of the person he was photographing. Professionals and the rich tend to be photographed indoors, without props. They speak for themselves. Laborers and derelicts are usually photographed in a setting (often outdoors) which locates them, which speaks for them—as if they could not be assumed to have the kinds of separate identities normally achieved in the middle and upper classes.

In Sander's work everybody is in place, nobody is lost or cramped or off-center. A cretin is photographed in exactly the same dispassionate way as a bricklayer, a legless World War I veteran like a healthy young soldier in uniform, scowling Communist students like smiling Nazis, a captain of industry like an opera singer. "It is not my intention either to criticize or describe these people," Sander said. While one might have expected that he would have claimed not to have criticized his subjects, by photographing them, it is interesting that he thought he hadn't described them either. Sander's complicity with everybody also means a distance from everybody. His complicity with his subjects is not naïve (like Carell's) but nihilistic. Despite its class realism, it is one of the most truly abstract bodies of work in the history of photography.

It is hard to imagine an American attempting an equivalent of Sander's comprehensive taxonomy. The great photographic portraits of America—like Walker Evans's *American Photographs* (1938) and Robert Frank's *The Americans* (1959)—have been deliberately random, while continuing to reflect the traditional relish of documentary photography for the poor and the dispossessed, the nation's forgotten citizens. And the most ambitious collective photographic project ever undertaken in this country, by the Farm Security Administration in 1935, under the direction of Roy Emerson Stryker, was concerned exclusively with "low-income groups."* The FSA project, conceived as "a pictorial documentation of our rural areas and rural problems" (Stryker's words), was unabashedly propagandistic, with Stryker coaching his team about the attitude they were to take toward their problem subject. The purpose of the project was to demonstrate the value of the people photographed. Thereby, it implicitly defined its point of view: that of middle-class people who needed to be convinced that the poor were really poor, and that the poor were dignified. It is instructive to compare the FSA photographs with those by Sander. Though the poor do not lack dignity in Sander's photographs, it is not because of any compassionate intentions. They have dignity by juxtaposition, because they are looked at in the same cool way as everybody else.

American photography was rarely so detached. For an approach reminiscent of Sander's, one must look to people who

---

*Though that changed, as is indicated in a memo from Stryker to his staff in 1942, when the new morale needs of World War II made the poor too downbeat a subject. "*We must have at once*: pictures of men, women and children who appear as if they really believed in the U.S. Get people with a little spirit. Too many in our file now paint the U.S. as an old person's home and that just about everybody is too old to work and too malnourished to care much what happens. . . . We particularly need young men and women who work in our factories. . . . Housewives in their kitchen or in their yard picking flowers. More contented-looking old couples. . . ."

documented a dying or superseded part of America—like Adam Clark Vroman, who photographed Indians in Arizona and New Mexico between 1895 and 1904. Vroman's handsome photographs are unexpressive, uncondescending, unsentimental. Their mood is the very opposite of the FSA photographs: they are not moving, they are not idiomatic, they do not invite sympathy. They make no propaganda for the Indians. Sander didn't know he was photographing a disappearing world. Vroman did. He also knew that there was no saving the world that he was recording.

Photography in Europe was largely guided by notions of the picturesque (i.e., the poor, the foreign, the time-worn), the important (i.e., the rich, the famous), and the beautiful. Photographs tended to praise or to aim at neutrality. Americans, less convinced of the permanence of any basic social arrangements, experts on the "reality" and inevitability of change, have more often made photography partisan. Pictures got taken not only to show what should be admired but to reveal what needs to be confronted, deplored—and fixed up. American photography implies a more summary, less stable connection with history; and a relation to geographic and social reality that is both more hopeful and more predatory.

The hopeful side is exemplified in the well-known use of photographs in America to awaken conscience. At the beginning of the century Lewis Hine was appointed staff photographer to the National Child Labor Committee, and his photographs of children working in cotton mills, beet fields, and coal mines did influence legislators to make child labor illegal. During the New Deal, Stryker's FSA project (Stryker was a pupil of Hine's) brought back information about migrant workers and sharecroppers to Washington, so that bureaucrats could figure out how to help them. But even at its most moralistic, documentary photography was also imperious in another sense. Both Thomson's detached traveler's report and the impassioned muckraking of Riis or Hine reflect the urge to appropriate an alien reality. And no reality is exempt from appropriation, neither one that is scandalous (and should be corrected) nor one that is merely beautiful (or could be made so by the camera). Ideally, the photographer was able to make the two realities cognate, as illustrated by the title of an interview with Hine in 1920, "Treating Labor Artistically."

The predatory side of photography is at the heart of the alliance, evident earlier in the United States than anywhere else, between photography and tourism. After the opening of the West in 1869 by the completion of the transcontinental railroad came the colonization through photography. The case of the American Indians is the most brutal. Discreet, serious amateurs like Vroman had been operating since the end of the Civil War. They were the vanguard of an army of tourists who arrived by the end of the century, eager for "a good shot" of Indian life. The tourists invaded the Indians' privacy, photographing holy objects and the sacred dances and places, if necessary paying the Indians to pose and getting them to revise their ceremonies to provide more photogenic material.

But the native ceremony that is changed when the tourist hordes come sweeping down is not so different from a scandal in the inner city that is corrected after someone photographs it. Insofar as the muckrakers got results, they too altered what they photographed; indeed, photographing something became a routine part of the procedure for altering it. The danger was of a token change—limited to the narrowest reading of the photograph's subject. The particular New York slum, Mulberry Bend, that Riis photographed in the late 1880s was subsequently torn down and its inhabitants rehoused by order of Theodore Roosevelt, then state governor, while other, equally dreadful slums were left standing.

The photographer both loots and preserves, denounces and consecrates. Photography expresses the American impatience with reality, the taste for activities whose instrumentality is a machine. "Speed is at the bottom of it all," as Hart Crane said (writing about Stieglitz in 1923), "the hundredth of a second caught so precisely that the motion is continued from the picture indefinitely: the moment made eternal." Faced with the awesome spread and alienness of a newly settled continent, people wielded cameras as a way of taking possession of the places they visited. Kodak put signs at the entrances of many towns listing what to photograph. Signs marked the places in national parks where visitors should stand with their cameras.

Sander is at home in his own country. American photographers

are often on the road, overcome with disrespectful wonder at
what their country offers in the way of surreal surprises. Moralists
and conscienceless despoilers, children and foreigners in their
own land, they will get something down that is disappearing—
and, often, hasten its disappearance by photographing it. To
take, like Sander, specimen after specimen, seeking an ideally
complete inventory, presupposes that society can be envisaged
as a comprehensible totality. European photographers have assumed that society has something of the stability of nature.
Nature in America has always been suspect, on the defensive,
cannibalized by progress. In America, every specimen becomes
a relic.

The American landscape has always seemed too varied, immense, mysterious, fugitive to lend itself to scientism. "He
doesn't *know*, he can't *say*, before the facts," Henry James wrote
in *The American Scene* (1907),

> and he doesn't even want to know or to say; the facts themselves
> loom, before the understanding, in too large a mass for a mere
> mouthful: it is as if the syllables were too numerous to make a
> legible word. The *il*legible word, accordingly, the great inscru-
> table answer to questions, hangs in the vast American sky, to his
> imagination, as something fantastic and *abracadabrant*, belong-
> ing to no known language, and it is under this convenient ensign
> that he travels and considers and contemplates, and, to the best
> of his ability, enjoys.

Americans feel the reality of their country to be so stupendous,
and mutable, that it would be the rankest presumption to approach it in a classifying, scientific way. One could get at it
indirectly, by subterfuge—breaking it off into strange fragments
that could somehow, by synecdoche, be taken for the whole.

American photographers (like American writers) posit something ineffable in the national reality—something, possibly, that
has never been seen before. Jack Kerouac begins his introduction to Robert Frank's book *The Americans*:

> That crazy feeling in America when the sun is hot on the streets
> and music comes out of the jukebox or from a nearby funeral,
> that's what Robert Frank has captured in these tremendous pho-
> tographs taken as he travelled on the road around practically
> forty-eight states in an old used car (on Guggenheim Fellowship)
> and with the agility, mystery, genius, sadness and strange secrecy

of a shadow photographed scenes that have never been seen on film. . . . After seeing these pictures you end up finally not knowing any more whether a jukebox is sadder than a coffin.

Any inventory of America is inevitably anti-scientific, a delirious "abracadabrant" confusion of objects, in which jukeboxes resemble coffins. James at least managed to make the wry judgment that "this particular effect of the scale of things is the only effect that, throughout the land, is not directly adverse to joy." For Kerouac—for the main tradition of American photography— the prevailing mood is sadness. Behind the ritualized claims of American photographers to be looking around, at random, without preconceptions—lighting on subjects, phlegmatically recording them—is a mournful vision of loss.

The effectiveness of photography's statement of loss depends on its steadily enlarging the familiar iconography of mystery, mortality, transience. More traditional ghosts are summoned up by some older American photographers, such as Clarence John Laughlin, a self-avowed exponent of "extreme romanticism" who began in the mid-1930s photographing decaying plantation houses of the lower Mississippi, funerary monuments in Louisiana's swamp burial grounds, Victorian interiors in Milwaukee and Chicago; but the method works as well on subjects which do not, so conventionally, reek of the past, as in a Laughlin photograph from 1962, "Spectre of Coca-Cola." In addition to romanticism (extreme or not) about the past, photography offers instant romanticism about the present. In America, the photographer is not simply the person who records the past but the one who invents it. As Berenice Abbott writes: "The photographer is the contemporary being par excellence; through his eyes the now becomes past."

Returning to New York from Paris in 1929, after the years of apprenticeship with Man Ray and her discovery (and rescue) of the then barely known work of Eugène Atget, Abbott set about recording the city. In the preface to her book of photographs that came out in 1939, *Changing New York*, she explains: "If I had never left America, I would never have wanted to photograph New York. But when I saw it with fresh eyes, I knew it was *my* country, something I had to set down in photographs." Abbott's purpose ("I wanted to record it before it changed completely") sounds like that of Atget, who spent the years between 1898 and his death in 1927 patiently, furtively documenting a small-scale, time-worn Paris that was vanishing. But Abbott is setting down something even more fantastic: the ceaseless replacement of the new. The New York of the thirties was very different from Paris: "not so much beauty and tradition as native fantasia emerging from accelerated greed." Abbott's book is aptly titled, for she is not so much memorializing the past as simply documenting ten years of the chronic self-destruct quality of American experience, in which even the recent past is constantly being used up, swept away, torn down, thrown out, traded in. Fewer and fewer Americans possess objects that have a patina, old furniture, grandparents' pots and pans—the used things, warm with generations of human touch, that Rilke celebrated in *The Duino Elegies* as being essential to a human landscape. Instead, we have our paper phantoms, transistorized landscapes. A featherweight portable museum.

Photographs, which turn the past into a consumable object, are a short cut. Any collection of photographs is an exercise in Surrealist montage and the Surrealist abbreviation of history. As Kurt Schwitters and, more recently, Bruce Conner and Ed Kienholz have made brilliant objects, tableaux, environments out of refuse, we now make a history out of our detritus. And some virtue, of a civic kind appropriate to a democratic society, is attached to the practice. The true modernism is not austerity but a garbage-strewn plenitude—the willful travesty of Whitman's magnanimous dream. Influenced by the photographers and the pop artists, architects like Robert Venturi learn from Las Vegas and find Times Square a congenial successor to the Piazza San Marco; and Reyner Banham lauds Los Angeles's "instant architecture and instant townscape" for its gift of freedom, of a good life impossible amid the beauties and squalors of the European city—extolling the liberation offered by a society whose consciousness is built, *ad hoc*, out of scraps and junk. America, that surreal country, is full of found objects. Our junk has become art. Our junk has become history.

Photographs are, of course, artifacts. But their appeal is that they also seem, in a world littered with photographic relics, to have the status of found objects—unpremeditated slices of the world. Thus, they trade simultaneously on the prestige of art and the magic of the real. They are clouds of fantasy and pellets of information. Photography has become the quintessential art of affluent, wasteful, restless societies—an indispensable tool of the new mass culture that took shape here after the Civil War, and conquered Europe only after World War II, although its values had gained a foothold among the well-off as early as the 1850s when, according to the splenetic description of Baudelaire, "our squalid society" became narcissistically entranced by Daguerre's "cheap method of disseminating a loathing for history."

The Surrealist purchase on history also implies an undertow of melancholy as well as a surface voracity and impertinence. At the very beginning of photography, the late 1830s, William H. Fox Talbot noted the camera's special aptitude for recording "the injuries of time." Fox Talbot was talking about what happens to buildings and monuments. For us, the more interesting abrasions are not of stone but of flesh. Through photographs we follow in the most intimate, troubling way the reality of how people age. To look at an old photograph of oneself, of anyone one has known, or of a much photographed public person is to feel, first of all: how much *younger* I (she, he) was then. Photography is the inventory of mortality. A touch of the finger now suffices to invest a moment with posthumous irony. Photographs show people being so irrefutably *there* and at a specific age in their lives; group together people and things which a moment later have already disbanded, changed, continued along the course of their independent destinies. One's reaction to the photographs Roman Vishniac took in 1938 of daily life in the ghettos of Poland is overwhelmingly affected by the knowledge of how soon all these people were to perish. To the solitary stroller, all the faces in the stereotyped photographs cupped behind glass and affixed to tombstones in the cemeteries of Latin countries seem to contain a portent of their death. Photographs state the innocence, the vulnerability of lives heading toward their own destruction, and this link between photography and death haunts all photographs of people. Some working-class Berliners in Robert Siodmak's film *Menschen am Sonntag* (1929) are having their pictures taken at the end of a Sunday outing. One by one they step before the itinerant photographer's black box—grin, look anxious, clown, stare. The movie camera lingers in close-up to let us savor the mobility of each face; then we see the face frozen in the last of its expressions, embalmed in a still. The photographs shock, in the flow of the movie—transmuting, in an instant, present into past, life into death. And one of the most disquieting films ever made, Chris Marker's *La Jetée* (1963), is the tale of a man who foresees his own death, narrated entirely with still photographs.

As the fascination that photographs exercise is a reminder of death, it is also an invitation to sentimentality. Photographs turn the past into an object of tender regard, scrambling moral distinctions and disarming historical judgments by the generalized pathos of looking at time past. One recent book arranges in alphabetical order the photographs of an incongruous group of celebrities as babies or children. Stalin and Gertrude Stein, who face outward from opposite pages, look equally solemn and huggable; Elvis Presley and Proust, another pair of youthful page-mates, slightly resemble each other; Hubert Humphrey (age 3) and Aldous Huxley (age 8), side by side, have in common that both already display the forceful exaggerations of character for which they were to be known as adults. No picture in the book is without interest and charm, given what we know (including, in most cases, photographs) of the famous creatures those children were to become. For this and similar ventures in Surrealist irony, naïve snapshots or the most conventional studio portraits are most effective: such pictures seem even more odd, moving, premonitory.

Rehabilitating old photographs, by finding new contexts for them, has become a major book industry. A photograph is only a fragment, and with the passage of time its moorings come unstuck. It drifts away into a soft abstract pastness, open to any kind of reading (or matching to other photographs). A photograph could also be described as a quotation, which makes a book of photographs like a book of quotations. And an increasingly common way of presenting photographs in book form is to match photographs themselves with quotes.

One example: Bob Adelman's *Down Home* (1972), a portrait of a rural Alabama county, one of the poorest in the nation, taken over a five-year period in the 1960s. Illustrating the continuing predilection of documentary photography for losers, Adelman's book descends from *Let Us Now Praise Famous Men*, whose point was precisely that its subjects were not famous, but forgotten. But Walker Evans's photographs were accompanied by eloquent prose written (sometimes overwritten) by James Agee, which aimed to deepen the reader's empathy with the sharecroppers' lives. No one presumes to speak for Adelman's subjects. (It is characteristic of the liberal sympathies which inform his book that it purports to have no point of view at all—that is, to be an entirely impartial, non-empathic look at its subjects.) *Down Home* could be considered a version in miniature, county-wide, of August Sander's project: to compile an objective photographic record of a people. But these specimens talk, which lends a weight to these unpretentious photographs that they would not have on their own. Paired with their words, their photographs characterize the citizens of Wilcox County as people obliged to defend or exhibit their territory; suggest that these lives are, in a literal sense, a series of positions or poses.

Another example: Michael Lesy's *Wisconsin Death Trip* (1973), which also constructs, with the aid of photographs, a portrait of a rural county—but the time is the past, between 1890 and 1910, years of severe recession and economic hardship, and Jackson County is reconstructed by means of found objects dating from those decades. These consist of a selection of photographs taken by Charles Van Schaick, the county seat's leading commercial photographer, some three thousand of whose glass negatives are stored in the State Historical Society of Wisconsin; and quotations from period sources, mainly local newspapers and the records of the county insane asylum, and fiction about the Midwest. The quotations have nothing to do with the photographs but are correlated with them in an aleatoric, intuitive way, as words and sounds by John Cage are matched at the time of performance with the dance movements already choreographed by Merce Cunningham.

The people photographed in *Down Home* are the authors of the declarations we read on the facing pages. White and black, poor and well-off talk, exhibiting contrasting views (particularly on matters of class and race). But whereas the statements that go with Adelman's photographs contradict each other, the texts that Lesy has collected all say the same thing: that an astonishing number of people in turn-of-the-century America were bent on hanging themselves in barns, throwing their children into wells, cutting their spouses' throats, taking off their clothes on Main Street, burning their neighbors' crops, and sundry other acts likely to land them in jail or the loony bin. In case anyone was thinking that it was Vietnam and all the domestic funk and nastiness of the past decade which had made America a country of darkening hopes, Lesy argues that the dream had collapsed by the end of the last century—not in the inhuman cities but in the farming communities; that the whole country has been crazy, and for a long time. Of course, *Wisconsin Death Trip* doesn't actually prove anything. The force of its historical argument is the force of collage. To Van Schaick's disturbing, handsomely time-eroded photographs Lesy could have matched other texts from the period—love letters, diaries—to give another, perhaps less desperate impression. His book is rousing, fashionably pessimistic polemic, and totally whimsical as history.

A number of American authors, most notably Sherwood Anderson, have written as polemically about the miseries of small-town life at roughly the time covered by Lesy's book. But although works of photo-fiction like *Wisconsin Death Trip* explain less than many stories and novels, they persuade more now, because they have the authority of a document. Photographs—and quotations—seem, because they are taken to be pieces of reality, more authentic than extended literary narratives. The only prose that seems credible to more and more readers is not the fine writing of someone like Agee, but the raw record—edited or unedited talk into tape recorders; fragments or the integral texts of sub-literary documents (court records, letters, diaries, psychiatric case histories, etc.); self-deprecatingly sloppy, often paranoid first-person reportage. There is a rancorous suspicion in America of whatever seems literary, not to mention a growing reluctance on the part of young people to read anything, even subtitles in foreign movies and copy on a record sleeve, which partly accounts for the new appetite for books of few words and many photographs. (Of course, photography itself increasingly reflects the prestige of the rough, the self-disparaging, the offhand, the undisciplined—the "anti-photograph.")

"All of the men and women the writer had ever known had become grotesques," Anderson says in the prologue to *Winesburg, Ohio* (1919), the title of which was originally supposed to be *The Book of the Grotesque*. He goes on: "The grotesques were not all horrible. Some were amusing, some almost beautiful. . . ." Surrealism is the art of generalizing the grotesque and then discovering nuances (and charms) in *that*. No activity is better equipped to exercise the Surrealist way of looking than photography, and eventually we look at all photographs surrealistically. People are ransacking their attics and the archives of city and state historical societies for old photographs; ever more obscure or forgotten photographers are being rediscovered. Books of photography pile higher and higher—measuring the lost past (hence, the promotion of amateur photography), taking the temperature of the present. Photographs furnish instant history, instant sociology, instant participation. But there is something remarkably anodyne about these new forms of packaging reality. The Surrealist strategy, which promised a new and exciting vantage point for the radical criticism of modern culture, has devolved into an easy irony that democratizes all evidence, that equates its scatter of evidence with history. Surrealism can only deliver a reactionary judgment; can make out of history only an accumulation of oddities, a joke, a death trip.

The taste for quotations (and for the juxtaposition of incongruous quotations) is a Surrealist taste. Thus, Walter Benjamin—whose Surrealist sensibility is the most profound of anyone's on record—was a passionate collector of quotations. In her magisterial essay on Benjamin, Hannah Arendt recounts that "nothing was more characteristic of him in the thirties than the little notebooks with black covers which he always carried with him and in which he tirelessly entered in the form of quotations what daily living and reading netted him in the way of 'pearls' and 'coral.' On occasion he read from them aloud, showed them around like items from a choice and precious collection." Though collecting quotations could be considered as merely an ironic mimetism—victimless collecting, as it were—this should not be taken to mean that Benjamin disapproved of, or did not indulge in, the real thing. For it was Benjamin's conviction that reality itself invited—and vindicated—the once heedless, inevitably destructive ministrations of the collector. In a world that is well on its way to becoming one vast quarry, the collector becomes someone engaged in a pious work of salvage. The course of modern history having already sapped the traditions and shattered the living wholes in which precious objects once found their place, the collector may now in good conscience go about excavating the choicer, more emblematic fragments.

The past itself, as historical change continues to accelerate, has become the most surreal of subjects—making it possible, as Benjamin said, to see a new beauty in what is vanishing. From the start, photographers not only set themselves the task of recording a disappearing world but were so employed by those hastening its disappearance. (As early as 1842, that indefatigable improver of French architectural treasures, Viollet-le-Duc, commissioned a series of daguerreotypes of Notre Dame before beginning his restoration of the cathedral.) "To renew the old world," Benjamin wrote, "that is the collector's deepest desire when he is driven to acquire new things." But the old world cannot be renewed—certainly not by quotations; and this is the rueful, quixotic aspect of the photographic enterprise.

Benjamin's ideas are worth mentioning because he was photography's most original and important critic—despite (and because of) the inner contradiction in his account of photography which follows from the challenge posed by his Surrealist sensibility to his Marxist/Brechtian principles—and because Benjamin's own ideal project reads like a sublimated version of the photographer's activity. This project was a work of literary criticism that was to consist entirely of quotations, and would thereby be devoid of anything that might betray empathy. A disavowal of empathy, a disdain for message-mongering, a claim to be invisible—these are strategies endorsed by most professional photographers. The history of photography discloses a long tradition of ambivalence about its capacity for partisanship: the taking of sides is felt to undermine its perennial assumption that all subjects have validity and interest. But what in Benjamin is an excruciating idea of fastidiousness, meant to permit the mute past to speak in its own voice, with all its unresolvable complexity, becomes—when generalized, in photography—the cumulative de-creation of the past (in the very act of preserving it), the fabrication of a new, parallel reality that makes the past immediate while underscoring its comic or tragic ineffectuality, that invests the specificity of the past with an unlimited irony, that transforms the present into the past and the past into pastness.

Like the collector, the photographer is animated by a passion that, even when it appears to be for the present, is linked to a sense of the past. But while traditional arts of historical consciousness attempt to put the past in order, distinguishing the innovative from the retrograde, the central from the marginal, the relevant from the irrelevant or merely interesting, the photographer's approach—like that of the collector—is unsystematic, indeed anti-systematic. The photographer's ardor for a subject has no essential relation to its content or value, that which makes a subject classifiable. It is, above all, an affirmation of the subject's thereness; its rightness (the rightness of a look on a face, of the arrangement of a group of objects), which is the equivalent of the collector's standard of genuineness; its quiddity—whatever qualities make it unique. The professional photographer's preeminently willful, avid gaze is one that not only resists the traditional classification and evaluation of subjects but seeks consciously to defy and subvert them. For this reason, its approach to subject matter is a good deal less aleatoric than is generally claimed.

In principle, photography executes the Surrealist mandate to adopt an uncompromisingly egalitarian attitude toward subject matter. (Everything is "real.") In fact, it has—like mainstream Surrealist taste itself—evinced an inveterate fondness for trash, eyesores, rejects, peeling surfaces, odd stuff, kitsch. Thus, Atget specialized in the marginal beauties of jerry-built wheeled vehicles, gaudy or fantastic window displays, the raffish art of shop signs and carousels, ornate porticoes, curious door knockers and wrought-iron grilles, stucco ornaments on the façades of run-down houses. The photographer—and the consumer of photographs—follows in the footsteps of the ragpicker, who was one of Baudelaire's favorite figures for the modern poet:

> Everything that the big city threw away, everything it lost, everything it despised, everything it crushed underfoot, he catalogues and collects. . . . He sorts things out and makes a wise choice; he collects, like a miser guarding a treasure, the refuse which will assume the shape of useful or gratifying objects between the jaws of the goddess of Industry.

Bleak factory buildings and billboard-cluttered avenues look as beautiful, through the camera's eye, as churches and pastoral landscapes. More beautiful, by modern taste. Recall that it was Breton and other Surrealists who invented the secondhand store as a temple of vanguard taste and upgraded visits to flea markets into a mode of aesthetic pilgrimage. The Surrealist ragpicker's acuity was directed to finding beautiful what other people found ugly or without interest and relevance—bric-a-brac, naïve or pop objects, urban debris.

As the structuring of a prose fiction, a painting, a film by means of quotations—think of Borges, of Kitaj, of Godard—is a specialized example of Surrealist taste, so the increasingly common practice of putting up photographs on living-room and bedroom walls, where formerly hung reproductions of paintings, is an index of the wide diffusion of Surrealist taste. For photographs themselves satisfy many of the criteria for Surrealist approbation, being ubiquitous, cheap, unprepossessing objects. A painting is commissioned or bought; a photograph is found (in albums and drawers), cut out (of newspapers and magazines), or easily taken oneself. And the objects that are photographs not only proliferate in a way that paintings don't but are, in a certain sense, aesthetically indestructible. Leonardo's "The Last Supper" in Milan hardly looks better now; it looks terrible. Photographs, when they get scrofulous, tarnished, stained, cracked, faded still look good; do often look better. (In this, as in other ways, the art that photography does resemble is architecture, whose works are subject to the same inexorable promotion through the passage of time; many buildings, and not only the Parthenon, probably look better as ruins.)

What is true of photographs is true of the world seen photographically. Photography extends the eighteenth-century literati's discovery of the beauty of ruins into a genuinely popular taste. And it extends that beauty beyond the romantics' ruins, such as those glamorous forms of decrepitude photographed by Laughlin, to the modernists' ruins—reality itself. The photographer is willy-nilly engaged in the enterprise of antiquing reality, and photographs are themselves instant antiques. The photograph offers a modern counterpart of that characteristically romantic architectural genre, the artificial ruin: the ruin which is created in order to deepen the historical character of a landscape, to make nature suggestive—suggestive of the past.

The contingency of photographs confirms that everything is perishable; the arbitrariness of photographic evidence indicates that reality is fundamentally unclassifiable. Reality is summed up in an array of casual fragments—an endlessly alluring, poignantly reductive way of dealing with the world. Illustrating that partly jubilant, partly condescending relation to reality that is the rallying point of Surrealism, the photographer's insistence that everything is real also implies that the real is not enough. By proclaiming a fundamental discontent with reality, Surrealism bespeaks a posture of alienation which has now become a general attitude in those parts of the world which are politically powerful, industrialized, and camera-wielding. Why else would reality ever be thought of as insufficient, flat, overordered, shallowly rational? In the past, a discontent with reality expressed itself as a longing for *another* world. In modern society, a discontent with reality expresses itself forcefully and most hauntingly by the longing to reproduce *this* one. As if only by looking at reality in the form of an object—through the fix of the photograph—is it really real, that is, surreal.

Photography inevitably entails a certain patronizing of reality. From being "out there," the world comes to be "inside" photographs. Our heads are becoming like those magic boxes that Joseph Cornell filled with incongruous small objects whose provenance was a France he never once visited. Or like a hoard of old movie stills, of which Cornell amassed a vast collection, in the same Surrealist spirit: as nostalgia-provoking relics of the original movie experience, as means of a token possession of the beauty of actors. But the relation of a still photograph to a film is intrinsically misleading. To quote from a movie is not the same as quoting from a book. Whereas the reading time of a book is up to the reader, the viewing time of a film is set by the filmmaker and the images are perceived only as fast or as slowly as the editing permits. Thus, a still, which allows one to linger over a single moment as long as one likes, contradicts the very form of film, as a set of photographs that freezes moments in a life or a society contradicts their form, which is a process, a flow in time. The photographed world stands in the same, essentially inaccurate relation to the real world as stills do to movies. Life is not about significant details, illuminated by a flash, fixed forever. Photographs are.

The lure of photographs, their hold on us, is that they offer at one and the same time a connoisseur's relation *to* the world and a promiscuous acceptance *of* the world. For this connoisseur's relation to the world is, through the evolution of the modernist revolt against traditional aesthetic norms, deeply implicated in the promotion of kitsch standards of taste. Though some photographs, considered as individual objects, have the bite and sweet gravity of important works of art, the proliferation of photographs is ultimately an affirmation of kitsch. Photography's ultra-mobile gaze flatters the viewer, creating a false sense of ubiquity, a deceptive mastery of experience. Surrealists, who aspire to be cultural radicals, even revolutionaries, have often been under the well-intentioned illusion that they could be, indeed should be, Marxists. But Surrealist aestheticism is too suffused with irony to be compatible with the twentieth century's most seductive form of moralism. Marx reproached philosophy for only trying to understand the world rather than trying to change it. Photographers, operating within the terms of the Surrealist sensibility, suggest the vanity of even trying to understand the world and instead propose that we collect it.

The Heroism of Vision

NOBODY ever discovered ugliness through photographs. But many, through photographs, have discovered beauty. Except for those situations in which the camera is used to document, or to mark social rites, what moves people to take photographs is finding something beautiful. (The name under which Fox Talbot patented the photograph in 1841 was the calotype: from *kalos*, beautiful.) Nobody exclaims, "Isn't that ugly! I must take a photograph of it." Even if someone did say that, all it would mean is: "I find that ugly thing . . . beautiful."

It is common for those who have glimpsed something beautiful to express regret at not having been able to photograph it. So successful has been the camera's role in beautifying the world that photographs, rather than the world, have become the standard of the beautiful. House-proud hosts may well pull out photographs of the place to show visitors how really splendid it is. We learn to see ourselves photographically: to regard oneself as attractive is, precisely, to judge that one would look good in a photograph. Photographs create the beautiful and—over generations of picture-taking—use it up. Certain glories of nature, for example, have been all but abandoned to the indefatigable attentions of amateur camera buffs. The image-surfeited are likely to find sunsets corny; they now look, alas, too much like photographs.

Many people are anxious when they're about to be photographed: not because they fear, as primitives do, being violated but because they fear the camera's disapproval. People want the idealized image: a photograph of themselves looking their best. They feel rebuked when the camera doesn't return an image of themselves as more attractive than they really are. But few are lucky enough to be "photogenic"—that is, to look better in photographs (even when not made up or flattered by the lighting) than in real life. That photographs are often praised for their candor, their honesty, indicates that most photographs, of course, are *not* candid. A decade after Fox Talbot's negative-positive process had begun replacing the daguerreotype (the first practicable photographic process) in the mid-1840s, a German photographer invented the first technique for retouching the negative. His two versions of the same portrait—one

587

retouched, the other not—astounded crowds at the Exposition Universelle held in Paris in 1855 (the second world fair, and the first with a photography exhibit). The news that the camera could lie made getting photographed much more popular.

The consequences of lying have to be more central for photography than they ever can be for painting, because the flat, usually rectangular images which are photographs make a claim to be true that paintings can never make. A fake painting (one whose attribution is false) falsifies the history of art. A fake photograph (one which has been retouched or tampered with, or whose caption is false) falsifies reality. The history of photography could be recapitulated as the struggle between two different imperatives: beautification, which comes from the fine arts, and truth-telling, which is measured not only by a notion of value-free truth, a legacy from the sciences, but by a moralized ideal of truth-telling, adapted from nineteenth-century literary models and from the (then) new profession of independent journalism. Like the post-romantic novelist and the reporter, the photographer was supposed to unmask hypocrisy and combat ignorance. This was a task which painting was too slow and cumbersome a procedure to take on, no matter how many nineteenth-century painters shared Millet's belief that *le beau c'est le vrai*. Astute observers noticed that there was something naked about the truth a photograph conveyed, even when its maker did not mean to pry. In *The House of the Seven Gables* (1851) Hawthorne has the young photographer, Holgrave, remark about the daguerreotype portrait that "while we give it credit only for depicting the merest surface, it actually brings out the secret character with a truth that no painter would ever venture upon, even could he detect it."

Freed from the necessity of having to make narrow choices (as painters did) about what images were worth contemplating, because of the rapidity with which cameras recorded anything, photographers made seeing into a new kind of project: as if seeing itself, pursued with sufficient avidity and single-mindedness, could indeed reconcile the claims of truth and the need to find the world beautiful. Once an object of wonder because of its capacity to render reality faithfully as well as despised at first for its base accuracy, the camera has ended by effecting a tremendous promotion of the value of appearances. Appearances as the camera records them. Photographs do not simply render reality—realistically. It is reality which is scrutinized, and evaluated, for its fidelity to photographs. "In my view," the foremost ideologue of literary realism, Zola, declared in 1901 after fifteen years of amateur picture-taking, "you cannot claim to have really seen something until you have photographed it." Instead of just recording reality, photographs have become the norm for the way things appear to us, thereby changing the very idea of reality, and of realism.

The earliest photographers talked as if the camera were a copying machine; as if, while people operate cameras, it is the camera that sees. The invention of photography was welcomed as a means of easing the burden of ever accumulating information and sense impressions. In his book of photographs *The Pencil of Nature* (1844–46) Fox Talbot relates that the idea of photography came to him in 1833, on the Italian Journey that had become obligatory for Englishmen of inherited wealth like himself, while making some sketches of the landscape at Lake Como. Drawing with the help of a camera obscura, a device which projected the image but did not fix it, he was led to reflect, he says, "on the inimitable beauty of the pictures of nature's painting which the glass lens of the camera throws upon the paper" and to wonder "if it were possible to cause these natural images to imprint themselves durably." The camera suggested itself to Fox Talbot as a new form of notation whose allure was precisely that it was impersonal—because it recorded a "natural" image; that is, an image which comes into being "by the agency of Light alone, without any aid whatever from the artist's pencil."

The photographer was thought to be an acute but noninterfering observer—a scribe, not a poet. But as people quickly discovered that nobody takes the same picture of the same thing, the supposition that cameras furnish an impersonal, objective image yielded to the fact that photographs are evidence not only of what's there but of what an individual sees, not just a record but an evaluation of the world.* It became clear that there was not just a simple, unitary activity called seeing

*The restriction of photography to impersonal seeing has of course continued to have its advocates. Among the Surrealists, photography was thought to be liberating to the extent that it transcended mere personal expression: Breton starts his essay of 1920 on Max Ernst by calling the practice of automatic

(recorded by, aided by cameras) but "photographic seeing,"
which was both a new way for people to see and a new activity
for them to perform.

A Frenchman with a daguerreotype camera was already roaming the Pacific in 1841, the same year that the first volume of *Ex-
cursions daguerriennes: Vues et monuments les plus remarquables
du globe* was published in Paris. The 1850s was the great age of
photographic Orientalism: Maxime Du Camp, making a Grand
Tour of the Middle East with Flaubert between 1849 and 1851,
centered his picture-taking activity on attractions like the Colossus of Abu Simbel and the Temple of Baalbek, not the daily
life of fellahin. Soon, however, travelers with cameras annexed
a wider subject matter than famous sites and works of art. Photographic seeing meant an aptitude for discovering beauty in
what everybody sees but neglects as too ordinary. Photographers were supposed to do more than just see the world as it
is, including its already acclaimed marvels; they were to create
interest, by new visual decisions.

There is a peculiar heroism abroad in the world since the invention of cameras: the heroism of vision. Photography opened
up a new model of freelance activity—allowing each person
to display a certain unique, avid sensibility. Photographers departed on their cultural and class and scientific safaris, searching
for striking images. They would entrap the world, whatever the
cost in patience and discomfort, by this active, acquisitive, evaluating, gratuitous modality of vision. Alfred Stieglitz proudly
reports that he had stood three hours during a blizzard on
February 22, 1893, "awaiting the proper moment" to take his
celebrated picture, "Fifth Avenue, Winter." The proper moment is when one can see things (especially what everyone has

---

writing "a true photography of thought," the camera being regarded as "a blind
instrument" whose superiority in "the imitation of appearances" had "dealt a
mortal blow to the old modes of expression, in painting as well as poetry." In
the opposing aesthetic camp, the Bauhaus theoreticians took a not dissimilar
view, treating photography as a branch of design, like architecture—creative
but impersonal, unencumbered by such vanities as the painterly surface, the
personal touch. In his book *Painting, Photography, Film* (1925) Moholy-Nagy
praises the camera for imposing "the hygiene of the optical," which will eventually "abolish that pictorial and imaginative association pattern . . . which has
been stamped upon our vision by great individual painters."

already seen) in a fresh way. The quest became the photographer's trademark in the popular imagination. By the 1920s the photographer had become a modern hero, like the aviator and the anthropologist—without necessarily having to leave home. Readers of the popular press were invited to join "our photographer" on a "journey of discovery," visiting such new realms as "the world from above," "the world under the magnifying glass," "the beauties of every day," "the unseen universe," "the miracle of light," "the beauty of machines," the picture that can be "found in the street."

Everyday life apotheosized, and the kind of beauty that only the camera reveals—a corner of material reality that the eye doesn't see at all or can't normally isolate; or the overview, as from a plane—these are the main targets of the photographer's conquest. For a while the close-up seemed to be photography's most original method of seeing. Photographers found that as they more narrowly cropped reality, magnificent forms appeared. In the early 1840s the versatile, ingenious Fox Talbot not only composed photographs in the genres taken over from painting—portrait, domestic scene, townscape, landscape, still life—but also trained his camera on a seashell, on the wings of a butterfly (enlarged with the aid of a solar microscope), on a portion of two rows of books in his study. But his subjects are still recognizably a shell, butterfly wings, books. When ordinary seeing was further violated—and the object isolated from its surroundings, rendering it abstract—new conventions about what was beautiful took hold. What is beautiful became just what the eye can't (or doesn't) see: that fracturing, dislocating vision that only the camera supplies.

In 1915 Paul Strand took a photograph which he titled "Abstract Patterns Made by Bowls." In 1917 Strand turned to close-ups of machine forms, and throughout the twenties did close-up nature studies. The new procedure—its heyday was between 1920 and 1935—seemed to promise unlimited visual delights. It worked with equally stunning effect on homely objects, on the nude (a subject one might have supposed to be virtually exhausted by painters), on the tiny cosmologies of nature. Photography seemed to have found its grandiose role, as the bridge between art and science; and painters were admonished to learn from the beauties of microphotographs and aerial views

in Moholy-Nagy's book *Von Material zur Architektur*, published by the Bauhaus in 1928 and translated into English as *The
New Vision*. It was the same year as the appearance of one of the
first photographic best-sellers, a book by Albert Renger-Patzsch
entitled *Die Welt ist schön (The World Is Beautiful)*, which consisted of one hundred photographs, mostly close-ups, whose
subjects range from a colocasia leaf to a potter's hands. Painting
never made so shameless a promise to prove the world beautiful.

The abstracting eye—represented with particular brilliance in
the period between the two world wars by some of the work of
Strand, as well as of Edward Weston and Minor White—seems
to have been possible only after the discoveries made by modernist painters and sculptors. Strand and Weston, who both
acknowledge a similarity between their ways of seeing and those
of Kandinsky and Brancusi, may have been attracted to the hard
edge of Cubist style in reaction to the softness of Stieglitz's images. But it is just as true that the influence flowed the other
way. In 1909, in his magazine *Camera Work*, Stieglitz notes the
undeniable influence of photography on painting, although he
cites only the Impressionists—whose style of "blurred definition" inspired his own.* And Moholy-Nagy in *The New Vision*
correctly points out that "the technique and spirit of photography directly or indirectly influenced Cubism." But for all the
ways in which, from the 1840s on, painters and photographers
have mutually influenced and pillaged each other, their procedures are fundamentally opposed. The painter constructs, the
photographer discloses. That is, the identification of the subject
of a photograph always dominates our perception of it—as it

*The large influence that photography exercised upon the Impressionists is a
commonplace of art history. Indeed, it is not much of an exaggeration to say,
as Stieglitz does, that "the impressionist painters adhere to a style of composition that is strictly photographic." The camera's translation of reality into highly
polarized areas of light and dark, the free or arbitrary cropping of the image in
photographs, the indifference of photographers to making space, particularly
background space, intelligible—these were the main inspiration for the Impressionist painters' professions of scientific interest in the properties of light, for
their experiments in flattened perspective and unfamiliar angles and decentralized forms that are sliced off by the picture's edge. ("They depict life in scraps
and fragments," as Stieglitz observed in 1909.) A historical detail: the very first
Impressionist exhibition, in April 1874, was held in Nadar's photography studio
on the Boulevard des Capucines in Paris.

does not, necessarily, in a painting. The subject of Weston's "Cabbage Leaf," taken in 1931, looks like a fall of gathered cloth; a title is needed to identify it. Thus, the image makes its point in two ways. The form is pleasing, and it is (surprise!) the form of a cabbage leaf. If it were gathered cloth, it wouldn't be so beautiful. We already know that beauty, from the fine arts. Hence the formal qualities of style—the central issue in painting—are, at most, of secondary importance in photography, while what a photograph is *of* is always of primary importance. The assumption underlying all uses of photography, that each photograph is a piece of the world, means that we don't know how to react to a photograph (if the image is visually ambiguous: say, too closely seen or too distant) until we know *what* piece of the world it is. What looks like a bare coronet—the famous photograph taken by Harold Edgerton in 1936—becomes far more interesting when we find out it is a splash of milk.

Photography is commonly regarded as an instrument for knowing things. When Thoreau said, "You can't say more than you see," he took for granted that sight had pride of place among the senses. But when, several generations later, Thoreau's dictum is quoted by Paul Strand to praise photography, it resonates with a different meaning. Cameras did not simply make it possible to apprehend more by seeing (through microphotography and teledetection). They changed seeing itself, by fostering the idea of seeing for seeing's sake. Thoreau still lived in a polysensual world, though one in which observation had already begun to acquire the stature of a moral duty. He was talking about a seeing not cut off from the other senses, and about seeing in context (the context he called Nature), that is, a seeing linked to certain presuppositions about what he thought was worth seeing. When Strand quotes Thoreau, he assumes another attitude toward the sensorium: the didactic cultivation of perception, independent of notions about what is worth perceiving, which animates all modernist movements in the arts.

The most influential version of this attitude is to be found in painting, the art which photography encroached on remorselessly and plagiarized from enthusiastically from its beginnings, and with which it still coexists in febrile rivalry. According to the usual account, what photography did was to usurp the painter's task of providing images that accurately transcribe reality. For this "the painter should be deeply grateful," insists Weston, viewing this usurpation, as have many photographers before and since, as in fact a liberation. By taking over the task of realistic picturing hitherto monopolized by painting, photography freed painting for its great modernist vocation—abstraction. But photography's impact on painting was not as clear-cut as that. For, as photography was entering the scene, painting was already, on its own, beginning its long retreat from realistic representation—Turner was born in 1775, Fox Talbot in 1800— and the territory photography came to occupy with such rapid and complete success would probably have been depopulated anyway. (The instability of nineteenth-century painting's strictly representational achievements is most clearly demonstrated by the fate of portraiture, which came more and more to be about painting itself rather than about sitters—and eventually ceased to interest most ambitious painters, with such notable recent exceptions as Francis Bacon and Warhol, who borrow lavishly from photographic imagery.)

The other important aspect of the relation between painting and photography omitted in the standard account is that the frontiers of the new territory acquired by photography immediately started expanding, as some photographers refused to be confined to turning out those ultra-realistic triumphs with which painters could not compete. Thus, of the two famous inventors of photography, Daguerre never conceived of going beyond the naturalist painter's range of representation, while Fox Talbot immediately grasped the camera's ability to isolate forms which normally escape the naked eye and which painting had never recorded. Gradually photographers joined in the pursuit of more abstract images, professing scruples reminiscent of the modernist painters' dismissal of the mimetic as mere picturing. Painting's revenge, if you will. The claim made by many professional photographers to do something quite different from recording reality is the clearest index of the immense counter-influence that painting has had on photography. But however much photographers have come to share some of the same attitudes about the inherent value of perception exercised for perception's sake and the (relative) unimportance of subject matter which have dominated advanced painting for more than a century, their applications of these attitudes cannot duplicate those of painting. For it is in the nature of a photograph that it can never entirely transcend its subject, as a painting can. Nor can a photograph ever transcend the visual itself, which is in some sense the ultimate aim of modernist painting.

The version of the modernist attitude most relevant to photography is not to be found in painting—even as it was then (at the time of its conquest, or liberation, by photography), certainly as it is now. Except for such marginal phenomena as Super Realism, a revival of Photo-Realism which is not content with merely imitating photographs but aims to show that painting can achieve an even greater illusion of verisimilitude, painting is still largely ruled by a suspicion of what Duchamp called the merely retinal. The ethos of photography—that of schooling us (in Moholy-Nagy's phrase) in "intensive seeing"— seems closer to that of modernist poetry than that of painting. As painting has become more and more conceptual, poetry (since Apollinaire, Eliot, Pound, and William Carlos Williams) has more and more defined itself as concerned with the visual. ("No truth but in things," as Williams declared.) Poetry's commitment to concreteness and to the autonomy of the poem's language parallels photography's commitment to pure seeing. Both imply discontinuity, disarticulated forms and compensatory unity: wrenching things from their context (to see them in a fresh way), bringing things together elliptically, according to the imperious but often arbitrary demands of subjectivity.

While most people taking photographs are only seconding received notions of the beautiful, ambitious professionals usually think they are challenging them. According to heroic modernists like Weston, the photographer's venture is elitist, prophetic, subversive, revelatory. Photographers claimed to be performing the Blakean task of cleansing the senses, "revealing to others the living world around them," as Weston described his own work, "showing to them what their own unseeing eyes had missed."

Although Weston (like Strand) also claimed to be indifferent to the question of whether photography is an art, his demands on photography still contained all the romantic assumptions about the photographer as Artist. By the century's second decade, certain photographers had confidently appropriated the rhetoric of a vanguard art: armed with cameras, they were doing rude battle with conformist sensibilities, busy fulfilling Pound's summons to Make It New. Photography, not "soft, gutless painting," says Weston with virile disdain, is best equipped to "bore into the spirit of today." Between 1930 and 1932 Weston's diaries or *Daybooks* are full of effusive premonitions of impending change and declarations of the importance of the visual shock therapy that photographers were administering. "Old ideals are crashing on all sides, and the precise uncompromising camera vision is, and will be more so, a world force in the revaluation of life."

Weston's notion of the photographer's agon shares many themes with the heroic vitalism of the 1920s popularized by D. H. Lawrence: affirmation of the sensual life, rage at bourgeois sexual hypocrisy, self-righteous defense of egotism in the service of one's spiritual vocation, manly appeals for a union with nature. (Weston calls photography "a way of self-development, a means to discover and identify oneself with all the manifestations of basic forms—with nature, the source.") But while Lawrence wanted to restore the wholeness of sensory appreciation, the photographer—even one whose passions seem so reminiscent of Lawrence's—necessarily insists on the preeminence of one sense: sight. And, contrary to what Weston asserts, the habit of photographic seeing—of looking at reality as an array of potential photographs—creates estrangement from, rather than union with, nature.

Photographic seeing, when one examines its claims, turns out to be mainly the practice of a kind of dissociative seeing, a subjective habit which is reinforced by the objective discrepancies between the way that the camera and the human eye focus and judge perspective. These discrepancies were much remarked by the public in the early days of picture-taking. Once they began to think photographically, people stopped talking about photographic distortion, as it was called. (Now, as William Ivins, Jr., has pointed out, they actually hunt for that distortion.) Thus, one of the perennial successes of photography has been its strategy of turning living beings into things, things into living beings. The peppers Weston photographed in 1929 and 1930 are voluptuous in a way that his female nudes rarely are. Both the nudes and the pepper are photographed for the play of forms—but the body is characteristically shown bent over upon itself, all the extremities cropped, with the flesh rendered as opaque as normal lighting and focus allow, thus decreasing its sensuality and heightening the abstractness of the body's form; the pepper is viewed close-up but in its entirety, the skin polished or oiled, and the result is a discovery of the erotic suggestiveness of an ostensibly neutral form, a heightening of its seeming palpability.

It was the beauty of forms in industrial and scientific photography that dazzled the Bauhaus designers, and, indeed, the camera has recorded few images more interesting formally than those taken by metallurgists and crystallographers. But the Bauhaus approach to photography has not prevailed. No one now considers the beauty revealed in photographs to be epitomized by scientific microphotography. In the main tradition of the beautiful in photography, beauty requires the imprint of a human decision: that *this* would make a good photograph, and that the good picture would make some comment. It proved more important to reveal the elegant form of a toilet bowl, the subject of a series of pictures Weston did in Mexico in 1925, than the poetic magnitude of a snowflake or a coal fossil.

For Weston, beauty itself was subversive—as seemed confirmed when some people were scandalized by his ambitious nudes. (In fact, it was Weston—followed by André Kertész and Bill Brandt—who made nude photography respectable.) Now photographers are more likely to emphasize the ordinary humanity of their revelations. Though photographers have not ceased to look for beauty, photography is no longer thought to create, under the aegis of beauty, a psychic breakthrough. Ambitious modernists, like Weston and Cartier-Bresson, who understand photography as a genuinely new way of seeing (precise, intelligent, even scientific), have been challenged by photographers of a later generation, like Robert Frank, who want a camera eye that is not piercing but democratic, who don't claim to be setting new standards for seeing. Weston's assertion that "photography has opened the blinds to a new world vision" seems typical of the overoxygenated hopes of modernism in all the arts during the first third of the century—hopes since abandoned. Although the camera did make a psychic revolution, it was hardly in the positive, romantic sense that Weston envisaged.

Insofar as photography does peel away the dry wrappers of habitual seeing, it creates another habit of seeing: both intense and cool, solicitous and detached; charmed by the insignificant detail, addicted to incongruity. But photographic seeing has to be constantly renewed with new shocks, whether of subject matter or technique, so as to produce the impression of violating ordinary vision. For, challenged by the revelations of photographers, seeing tends to accommodate to photographs. The avant-garde vision of Strand in the twenties, of Weston in the late twenties and early thirties, was quickly assimilated. Their rigorous close-up studies of plants, shells, leaves, time-withered trees, kelp, driftwood, eroded rocks, pelicans' wings, gnarled cypress roots, and gnarled workers' hands have become clichés of a merely photographic way of seeing. What it once took a very intelligent eye to see, anyone can see now. Instructed by photographs, everyone is able to visualize that once purely literary conceit, the geography of the body: for example, photographing a pregnant woman so that her body looks like a hillock, a hillock so that it looks like the body of a pregnant woman.

Increased familiarity does not entirely explain why certain conventions of beauty get used up while others remain. The attrition is moral as well as perceptual. Strand and Weston could hardly have imagined how these notions of beauty could become so banal, yet it seems inevitable once one insists—as Weston did—on so bland an ideal of beauty as perfection. Whereas the painter, according to Weston, has always "tried to improve nature by self-imposition," the photographer has "proved that nature offers an endless number of perfect 'compositions,'—order everywhere." Behind the modernist's belligerent stance of aesthetic purism lay an astonishingly generous acceptance of the world. For Weston, who spent most of his photographic life on the California coast near Carmel, the Walden of the 1920s, it was relatively easy to find beauty and order, while for Aaron Siskind, a photographer of the generation after Strand and a New Yorker, who began his career by taking architectural photographs and genre photographs of city people, the question is one of creating order. "When I make a photograph," Siskind writes, "I want it to be an altogether new object, complete and self-contained, whose basic condition is order." For Cartier-Bresson, to take photographs is "to find the structure of the world—to revel in the pure pleasure of form," to disclose that "in all this chaos, there is order." (It may well be impossible to talk about the perfection of the world without sounding unctuous.) But displaying the perfection of the world was too sentimental, too ahistorical a notion of beauty to sustain photography. It seems inevitable that Weston, more committed than Strand ever was to abstraction, to the discovery of forms, produced a much narrower body of work than Strand did. Thus Weston never felt moved to do socially conscious photography and, except for the period between 1923 and 1927 that he spent in Mexico, shunned cities. Strand, like Cartier-Bresson, was attracted to the picturesque desolations and damages of urban life. But even far from nature, both Strand and Cartier-Bresson (one could also cite Walker Evans) still photograph with the same fastidious eye that discerns order everywhere.

The view of Stieglitz and Strand and Weston—that photographs should be, first of all, beautiful (that is, beautifully composed)—seems thin now, too obtuse to the truth of disorder: even as the optimism about science and technology which lay behind the Bauhaus view of photography seems almost pernicious. Weston's images, however admirable, however beautiful, have become less interesting to many people, while those taken by the mid-nineteenth-century English and French primitive photographers and by Atget, for example, enthrall more than ever. The judgment of Atget as "not a fine technician" that Weston entered in his *Daybooks* perfectly reflects the coherence of Weston's view and his distance from contemporary taste. "Halation destroyed much, and the color correction not good," Weston notes; "his instinct for subject matter was keen, but his recording weak,—his construction inexcusable . . . so often one feels he missed the real thing." Contemporary taste faults Weston, with his devotion to the perfect print, rather than Atget and the other masters of photography's demotic tradition. Imperfect technique has come to be appreciated precisely because it breaks the sedate equation of Nature and Beauty. Nature has become more a subject for nostalgia and indignation than an object of contemplation, as marked by the distance of taste which separates both the majestic landscapes of Ansel Adams (Weston's best-known disciple) and the last important body of photographs in the Bauhaus tradition, Andreas Feininger's *The Anatomy of Nature* (1965), from current photographic imagery of nature defiled.

As these formalist ideals of beauty seem, in retrospect, linked to a certain historical mood, optimism about the modern age (the new vision, the new era), so the decline of the standards of photographic purity represented by both Weston and the Bauhaus school has accompanied the moral letdown experienced in recent decades. In the present historical mood of disenchantment one can make less and less sense out of the formalist's notion of timeless beauty. Darker, time-bound models of beauty have become prominent, inspiring a reevaluation of the photography of the past; and, in an apparent revulsion against the Beautiful, recent generations of photographers prefer to show disorder, prefer to distill an anecdote, more often than not a disturbing one, rather than isolate an ultimately reassuring "simplified form" (Weston's phrase). But notwithstanding the declared aims of indiscreet, unposed, often harsh photography to reveal truth, not beauty, photography still beautifies. Indeed, the most enduring triumph of photography has been its aptitude for discovering beauty in the humble, the inane, the decrepit. At the very least, the real has a pathos. And that pathos is—beauty. (The beauty of the poor, for example.)

Weston's celebrated photograph of one of his fiercely loved sons, "Torso of Neil," 1925, seems beautiful because of the shapeliness of its subject and because of its bold composition and subtle lighting—a beauty that is the result of skill and taste. Jacob Riis's crude flashlit photographs taken between 1887 and 1890 seem beautiful because of the force of their subject, grimy shapeless New York slum-dwellers of indeterminate age, and because of the rightness of their "wrong" framing and the blunt contrasts produced by the lack of control over tonal values—a beauty that is the result of amateurism or inadvertence. The evaluation of photographs is always shot through with such aesthetic double standards. Initially judged by the norms of painting, which assume conscious design and the elimination of non-essentials, the distinctive achievements of photographic seeing were until quite recently thought to be identical with the work of that relatively small number of photographers who, through reflection and effort, managed to transcend the camera's mechanical nature to meet the standards of art. But it is now clear that there is no inherent conflict between the mechanical or naïve use of the camera and formal beauty of a very high order, no kind of photograph in which such beauty could not turn out to be present: an unassuming functional snapshot may be as visually interesting, as eloquent, as beautiful as the most acclaimed fine-art photographs. This democratizing of formal standards is the logical counterpart to photography's democratizing of the notion of beauty. Traditionally associated with exemplary models (the representative art of the classical Greeks showed only youth, the body in its perfection), beauty has been revealed by photographs as existing everywhere. Along with people who pretty themselves for the camera, the unattractive and the disaffected have been assigned their beauty.

For photographers there is, finally, no difference—no greater aesthetic advantage—between the effort to embellish the world and the counter-effort to rip off its mask. Even those photographers who disdained retouching their portraits—a mark of honor for ambitious portrait photographers from Nadar on—tended to protect the sitter in certain ways from the camera's too revealing gaze. And one of the typical endeavors of portrait photographers, professionally protective toward famous faces (like Garbo's) which really are ideal, is the search for "real" faces, generally sought among the anonymous, the poor, the socially defenseless, the aged, the insane—people indifferent to (or powerless to protest) the camera's aggressions. Two portraits that Strand did in 1916 of urban casualties, "Blind Woman" and "Man," are among the first results of this search conducted in close-up. In the worst years of the German depression Helmar Lerski made a whole compendium of distressing faces, published under the title *Köpfe des Alltags (Everyday Faces)* in 1931. The paid models for what Lerski called his "objective character studies"—with their rude revelations of over-enlarged pores, wrinkles, skin blemishes—were out-of-work servants procured from an employment exchange, beggars, street sweepers, vendors, and washerwomen.

The camera can be lenient; it is also expert at being cruel. But its cruelty only produces another kind of beauty, according to the surrealist preferences which rule photographic taste. Thus, while fashion photography is based on the fact that something can be more beautiful in a photograph than in real life, it is not surprising that some photographers who serve fashion are also drawn to the non-photogenic. There is a perfect complementarity between Avedon's fashion photography, which flatters, and the work in which he comes on as The One Who Refuses to Flatter—for example, the elegant, ruthless portraits Avedon did in 1972 of his dying father. The traditional function of portrait painting, to embellish or idealize the subject, remains the aim of everyday and of commercial photography, but it has had a much more limited career in photography considered as an art. Generally speaking, the honors have gone to the Cordelias.

As the vehicle of a certain reaction against the conventionally beautiful, photography has served to enlarge vastly our notion of what is aesthetically pleasing. Sometimes this reaction is in the name of truth. Sometimes it is in the name of sophistication or of prettier lies: thus, fashion photography has been developing, over more than a decade, a repertoire of paroxysmic gestures that shows the unmistakable influence of Surrealism. ("Beauty will be *convulsive*," Breton wrote, "or it will not be at all.") Even the most compassionate photojournalism is under pressure to satisfy simultaneously two sorts of expectations, those arising from our largely surrealist way of looking at all photographs, and those created by our belief that some photographs give real and important information about the world. The photographs that W. Eugene Smith took in the late 1960s in the Japanese fishing village of Minamata, most of whose inhabitants are crippled and slowly dying of mercury poisoning, move us because they document a suffering which arouses our indignation—and distance us because they are superb photographs of Agony, conforming to surrealist standards of beauty. Smith's photograph of a dying youth writhing on his mother's lap is a Pietà for the world of plague victims which Artaud invokes as the true subject of modern dramaturgy; indeed, the whole series of photographs are possible images for Artaud's Theater of Cruelty.

Because each photograph is only a fragment, its moral and emotional weight depends on where it is inserted. A photograph changes according to the context in which it is seen: thus Smith's Minamata photographs will seem different on a contact sheet, in a gallery, in a political demonstration, in a police file, in a photographic magazine, in a general news magazine, in a book, on a living-room wall. Each of these situations suggests a different use for the photographs but none can secure their meaning. As Wittgenstein argued for words, that the meaning *is* the use—so for each photograph. And it is in this way that the presence and proliferation of all photographs contributes to the erosion of the very notion of meaning, to that parceling out of the truth into relative truths which is taken for granted by the modern liberal consciousness.

Socially concerned photographers assume that their work can convey some kind of stable meaning, can reveal truth. But partly because the photograph is, always, an object in a context, this meaning is bound to drain away; that is, the context which shapes whatever immediate—in particular, political—uses the photograph may have is inevitably succeeded by contexts in which such uses are weakened and become progressively less relevant. One of the central characteristics of photography is that process by which original uses are modified, eventually supplanted by subsequent uses—most notably, by the discourse of art into which any photograph can be absorbed. And, being images themselves, some photographs right from the start refer us to other images as well as to life. The photograph that the Bolivian authorities transmitted to the world press in October 1967 of Che Guevara's body, laid out in a stable on a stretcher on top of a cement trough, surrounded by a Bolivian colonel, a U.S. intelligence agent, and several journalists and soldiers, not only summed up the bitter realities of contemporary Latin American history but had some inadvertent resemblance, as John Berger has pointed out, to Mantegna's "The Dead Christ" and Rembrandt's "The Anatomy Lesson of Professor Tulp." What is compelling about the photograph partly derives from what it shares, as a composition, with these paintings. Indeed, the very extent to which that photograph is unforgettable indicates its potential for being depoliticized, for becoming a timeless image.

The best writing on photography has been by moralists—Marxists or would-be Marxists—hooked on photographs but troubled by the way photography inexorably beautifies. As Walter Benjamin observed in 1934, in an address delivered in Paris at the Institute for the Study of Fascism, the camera

is now incapable of photographing a tenement or a rubbish-heap
without transfiguring it. Not to mention a river dam or an electric
cable factory: in front of these, photography can only say, 'How
beautiful.' . . . It has succeeded in turning abject poverty itself,
by handling it in a modish, technically perfect way, into an object
of enjoyment.

Moralists who love photographs always hope that words will
save the picture. (The opposite approach to that of the museum
curator who, in order to turn a photojournalist's work into
art, shows the photographs without their original captions.)
Thus, Benjamin thought that the right caption beneath a picture could "rescue it from the ravages of modishness and confer
upon it a revolutionary use value." He urged that writers start
taking photographs, to show the way.

Socially concerned writers have not taken to cameras, but
they are often enlisted, or volunteer, to spell out the truth to
which photographs testify—as James Agee did in the texts he
wrote to accompany Walker Evans's photographs in *Let Us Now
Praise Famous Men*, or as John Berger did in his essay on the
photograph of the dead Che Guevara, this essay being in effect
an extended caption, one that attempts to firm up the political
associations and moral meaning of a photograph that Berger
found too satisfying aesthetically, too suggestive iconographi-
cally. Godard and Gorin's short film *A Letter to Jane* (1972)
amounts to a kind of counter-caption to a photograph—a mor-
dant criticism of a photograph of Jane Fonda taken during a
visit to North Vietnam. (The film is also a model lesson on
how to read any photograph, how to decipher the un-innocent
nature of a photograph's framing, angle, focus.) What the
photograph—it shows Fonda listening with an expression of
distress and compassion as an unidentified Vietnamese describes the ravages of American bombing—meant when it was
published in the French picture magazine *L'Express* in some
ways reverses the meaning it had for the North Vietnamese,
who released it. But even more decisive than how the photograph was changed by its new setting is how its revolutionary use-value to the North Vietnamese was sabotaged by what
L'Express furnished as a caption. "This photograph, like any
photograph," Godard and Gorin point out, "is physically mute.
It talks through the mouth of the text written beneath it." In

fact, words do speak louder than pictures. Captions do tend to override the evidence of our eyes; but no caption can permanently restrict or secure a picture's meaning.

What the moralists are demanding from a photograph is that it do what no photograph can ever do—speak. The caption is the missing voice, and it is expected to speak for truth. But even an entirely accurate caption is only one interpretation, necessarily a limiting one, of the photograph to which it is attached. And the caption-glove slips on and off so easily. It cannot prevent any argument or moral plea which a photograph (or set of photographs) is intended to support from being undermined by the plurality of meanings that every photograph carries, or from being qualified by the acquisitive mentality implicit in all picture-taking—and picture-collecting—and by the aesthetic relation to their subjects which all photographs inevitably propose. Even those photographs which speak so laceratingly of a specific historical moment also give us vicarious possession of their subjects under the aspect of a kind of eternity: the beautiful. The photograph of Che Guevara is finally . . . beautiful, as was the man. So are the people of Minamata. So is the small Jewish boy photographed in 1943 during a round-up in the Warsaw Ghetto, his arms raised, solemn with terror—whose picture the mute heroine of Bergman's *Persona* has brought with her to the mental hospital to meditate on, as a photo-souvenir of the essence of tragedy.

In a consumer society, even the most well-intentioned and properly captioned work of photographers issues in the discovery of beauty. The lovely composition and elegant perspective of Lewis Hine's photographs of exploited children in turn-of-the-century American mills and mines easily outlast the relevance of their subject matter. Protected middle-class inhabitants of the more affluent corners of the world—those regions where most photographs are taken and consumed—learn about the world's horrors mainly through the camera: photographs can and do distress. But the aestheticizing tendency of photography is such that the medium which conveys distress ends by neutralizing it. Cameras miniaturize experience, transform history into spectacle. As much as they create sympathy, photographs cut sympathy, distance the emotions. Photography's realism creates a confusion about the real which is (in the long run) analgesic morally as well as (both in the long and in the short run) sensorially stimulating. Hence, it clears our eyes. This is the fresh vision everyone has been talking about.

Whatever the moral claims made on behalf of photography, its main effect is to convert the world into a department store or museum-without-walls in which every subject is depreciated into an article of consumption, promoted into an item for aesthetic appreciation. Through the camera people become customers or tourists of reality—of *Réalités*, as the name of the French photo-magazine suggests, for reality is understood as plural, fascinating, and up for grabs. Bringing the exotic near, rendering the familiar and homely exotic, photographs make the entire world available as an object of appraisal. For photographers who are not confined to projecting their own obsessions, there are arresting moments, beautiful subjects everywhere. The most heterogeneous subjects are then brought together in the fictive unity offered by the ideology of humanism. Thus, according to one critic, the greatness of Paul Strand's pictures from the last period of his life—when he turned from the brilliant discoveries of the abstracting eye to the touristic, world-anthologizing tasks of photography—consists in the fact that "his people, whether Bowery derelict, Mexican peon, New England farmer, Italian peasant, French artisan, Breton or Hebrides fisherman, Egyptian fellahin, the village idiot or the great Picasso, are all touched by the same heroic quality—humanity." What is this humanity? It is a quality things have in common when they are viewed as photographs.

The urge to take photographs is in principle an indiscriminate one, for the practice of photography is now identified with the idea that everything in the world could be made interesting through the camera. But this quality of being interesting, like that of manifesting humanity, is an empty one. The photographic purchase on the world, with its limitless production of notes on reality, makes everything homologous. Photography is no less reductive when it is being reportorial than when it reveals beautiful forms. By disclosing the thingness of human beings, the humanness of things, photography transforms reality into a tautology. When Cartier-Bresson goes to China, he shows that there are people in China, and that they are Chinese.

Photographs are often invoked as an aid to understanding and tolerance. In humanist jargon, the highest vocation of photography is to explain man to man. But photographs do not explain; they acknowledge. Robert Frank was only being honest when he declared that "to produce an authentic contemporary document, the visual impact should be such as will nullify explanation." If photographs are messages, the message is both transparent and mysterious. "A photograph is a secret about a secret," as Arbus observed. "The more it tells you the less you know." Despite the illusion of giving understanding, what seeing through photographs really invites is an acquisitive relation to the world that nourishes aesthetic awareness and promotes emotional detachment.

The force of a photograph is that it keeps open to scrutiny instants which the normal flow of time immediately replaces. This freezing of time—the insolent, poignant stasis of each photograph—has produced new and more inclusive canons of beauty. But the truths that can be rendered in a dissociated moment, however significant or decisive, have a very narrow relation to the needs of understanding. Contrary to what is suggested by the humanist claims made for photography, the camera's ability to transform reality into something beautiful derives from its relative weakness as a means of conveying truth. The reason that humanism has become the reigning ideology of ambitious professional photographers—displacing formalist justifications of their quest for beauty—is that it masks the confusions about truth and beauty underlying the photographic enterprise.

Photographic Evangels

L IKE other steadily aggrandizing enterprises, photography
has inspired its leading practitioners with a need to explain,
again and again, what they are doing and why it is valuable.
The era in which photography was widely attacked (as parrici-
dal with respect to painting, predatory with respect to people)
was a brief one. Painting of course did not expire in 1839, as
one French painter hastily predicted; the finicky soon ceased
to dismiss photography as menial copying; and by 1854 a great
painter, Delacroix, graciously declared how much he regretted
that such an admirable invention came so late. Nothing is more
acceptable today than the photographic recycling of reality,
acceptable as an everyday activity and as a branch of high art.
Yet something about photography still keeps the first-rate professionals defensive and hortatory: virtually every important
photographer right up to the present has written manifestoes
and credos expounding photography's moral and aesthetic mission. And photographers give the most contradictory accounts
of what kind of knowledge they possess and what kind of art
they practice.

The disconcerting ease with which photographs can be taken,
the inevitable even when inadvertent authority of the camera's
results, suggest a very tenuous relation to knowing. No one
would dispute that photography gave a tremendous boost to
the cognitive claims of sight, because—through close-up and
remote sensing—it so greatly enlarged the realm of the visible.
But about the ways in which any subject within the range of un-
aided vision is further known through a photograph or the extent to which, in order to get a good photograph, people need
to know anything about what they are photographing, there is
no agreement. Picture-taking has been interpreted in two entirely different ways: either as a lucid and precise act of knowing,
of conscious intelligence, or as a pre-intellectual, intuitive mode
of encounter. Thus Nadar, speaking of his respectful, expressive
pictures of Baudelaire, Doré, Michelet, Hugo, Berlioz, Nerval,
Gautier, Sand, Delacroix, and other famous friends, said "the
portrait I do best is of the person I know best," while Avedon
has observed that most of his good portraits are of people he
met for the first time when photographing them.

In this century, the older generation of photographers described photography as a heroic effort of attention, an ascetic discipline, a mystic receptivity to the world which requires that the photographer pass through a cloud of unknowing. According to Minor White, "the state of mind of the photographer while creating is a blank . . . when looking for pictures. . . . The photographer projects himself into everything he sees, identifying himself with everything in order to know it and to feel it better." Cartier-Bresson has likened himself to a Zen archer, who must *become* the target so as to be able to hit it; "thinking should be done beforehand and afterwards," he says, "never while actually taking a photograph." Thought is regarded as clouding the transparency of the photographer's consciousness, and as infringing on the autonomy of what is being photographed. Determined to prove that photographs could—and when they are good, always do—transcend literalness, many serious photographers have made of photography a noetic paradox. Photography is advanced as a form of knowing without knowing: a way of outwitting the world, instead of making a frontal attack on it.

But even when ambitious professionals disparage thinking—suspicion of the intellect being a recurrent theme in photographic apologetics—they usually want to assert how rigorous this permissive visualizing needs to be. "A photograph is not an accident—it is a concept," Ansel Adams insists. "The 'machine-gun' approach to photography—by which many negatives are made with the hope that one will be good—is fatal to serious results." To take a good photograph, runs the common claim, one must already see it. That is, the image must exist in the photographer's mind at or before the moment when the negative is exposed. Justifying photography has for the most part precluded admitting that the scattershot method, especially as used by someone experienced, may yield a thoroughly satisfactory result. But despite their reluctance to say so, most photographers have always had—with good reason—an almost superstitious confidence in the lucky accident.

Lately, the secret is becoming avowable. As the defense of photography enters its present, retrospective phase, there is an increasing diffidence in claims about the alert, knowing state of mind that accomplished picture-taking presumes. The anti-intellectual declarations of photographers, commonplaces of modernist thinking in the arts, have prepared the way for the gradual tilt of serious photography toward a skeptical investigation of its own powers, a commonplace of modernist practice in the arts. Photography as knowledge is succeeded by photography as—photography. In sharp reaction against any ideal of authoritative representation, the most influential of the younger American photographers reject any ambition to pre-visualize the image and conceive their work as showing how different things look when photographed.

Where the claims of knowledge falter, the claims of creativity take up the slack. As if to refute the fact that many superb pictures are by photographers devoid of any serious or interesting intentions, the insistence that picture-taking is first of all the focusing of a temperament, only secondarily of a machine, has always been one of the main themes of the defense of photography. This is the theme stated so eloquently in the finest essay ever written in praise of photography, Paul Rosenfeld's chapter on Stieglitz in *Port of New York*. By using "his machinery"—as Rosenfeld puts it—"unmechanically," Stieglitz shows that the camera not only "gave him an opportunity of expressing himself" but supplied images with a wider and "more delicate" gamut "than the hand can draw." Similarly, Weston insists over and over that photography is a supreme opportunity for self-expression, far superior to that offered by painting. For photography to compete with painting means invoking originality as an important standard for appraising a photographer's work, originality being equated with the stamp of a unique, forceful sensibility. What is exciting "are photographs that say something in a new manner," Harry Callahan writes, "*not* for the sake of being different, but because the individual is different and the individual expresses himself." For Ansel Adams "a great photograph" has to be "a full expression of what one feels about what is being photographed in the deepest sense and is, thereby, a true expression of what one feels about life in its entirety."

That there is a difference between photography conceived as "true expression" and photography conceived (as it more commonly is) as faithful recording is evident; though most accounts of photography's mission attempt to paper over the difference, it is implicit in the starkly polarized terms that photographers employ to dramatize what they do. As modern forms of the quest for self-expression commonly do, photography recapitulates both of the traditional ways of radically opposing self and world. Photography is seen as an acute manifestation of the individualized "I," the homeless private self astray in an overwhelming world—mastering reality by a fast visual anthologizing of it. Or photography is seen as a means of finding a place in the world (still experienced as overwhelming, alien) by being able to relate to it with detachment—bypassing the interfering, insolent claims of the self. But between the defense of photography as a superior means of self-expression and the praise of photography as a superior way of putting the self at reality's service there is not as much difference as might appear. Both presuppose that photography provides a unique system of disclosures: that it shows us reality as we had *not* seen it before.

This revelatory character of photography generally goes by the polemical name of realism. From Fox Talbot's view that the camera produces "natural images" to Berenice Abbott's denunciation of "pictorial" photography to Cartier-Bresson's warning that "the thing to be feared most is the artificially contrived," most of the contradictory declarations of photographers converge on pious avowals of respect for things-as-they-are. For a medium so often considered to be merely realistic, one would think photographers would not have to go on as they do, exhorting each other to stick to realism. But the exhortations continue—another instance of the need photographers have for making something mysterious and urgent of the process by which they appropriate the world.

To insist, as Abbott does, that realism is the very essence of photography does not, as it might seem, establish the superiority of one particular procedure or standard; does not necessarily mean that photo-documents (Abbott's word) are better than pictorial photographs.* Photography's commitment to realism can accommodate any style, any approach to subject matter.

*The original meaning of pictorial was, of course, the positive one popularized by the most famous of the nineteenth-century art photographers, Henry Peach Robinson, in his book *Pictorial Effect in Photography* (1869). "His system was to flatter everything," Abbott says in a manifesto she wrote in 1951, "Photography at the Crossroads." Praising Nadar, Brady, Atget, and Hine as masters of the photo-document, Abbott dismisses Stieglitz as Robinson's heir, founder of a "super-pictorial school" in which, once again, "subjectivity predominated."

Sometimes it will be defined more narrowly, as the making of images which resemble, and inform us about, the world. Interpreted more broadly, echoing the distrust of mere likeness which has inspired painting for more than a century, photographic realism can be—is more and more—defined not as what is "really" there but as what I "really" perceive. While all modern forms of art claim some privileged relation to reality, the claim seems particularly justified in the case of photography. Yet photography has not, finally, been any more immune than painting has to the most characteristic modern doubts about any straightforward relation to reality—the inability to take for granted the world as observed. Even Abbott cannot help assuming a change in the very nature of reality: that it needs the selective, more acute eye of the camera, there being simply much more of it than ever before. "Today, we are confronted with reality on the vastest scale mankind has known," she declares, and this puts "a greater responsibility on the photographer."

All that photography's program of realism actually implies is the belief that reality is hidden. And, being hidden, is something to be unveiled. Whatever the camera records is a disclosure—whether it is imperceptible, fleeting parts of movement, an order that natural vision is incapable of perceiving or a "heightened reality" (Moholy-Nagy's phrase), or simply the elliptical way of seeing. What Stieglitz describes as his "patient waiting for the moment of equilibrium" makes the same assumption about the essential hiddenness of the real as Robert Frank's waiting for the moment of revealing disequilibrium, to catch reality off-guard, in what he calls the "in-between moments."

Just to show something, anything, in the photographic view is to show that it is hidden. But it is not necessary for photographers to point up the mystery with exotic or exceptionally striking subjects. When Dorothea Lange urges her colleagues to concentrate on "the familiar," it is with the understanding that the familiar, rendered by a sensitive use of the camera, will thereby become mysterious. Photography's commitment to realism does not limit photography to certain subjects, as more real than others, but rather illustrates the formalist understanding of what goes on in every work of art: reality is, in Viktor Shklovsky's word, de-familiarized. What is being urged is an aggressive relation to all subjects. Armed with their machines, photographers are to make an assault on reality—which is perceived as recalcitrant, as only deceptively available, as unreal. "The pictures have a reality for me that the people don't," Avedon has declared. "It is through the photographs that I know them." To claim that photography must be realistic is not incompatible with opening up an even wider gap between image and reality, in which the mysteriously acquired knowledge (and the enhancement of reality) supplied by photographs presumes a prior alienation from or devaluation of reality.

As photographers describe it, picture-taking is both a limitless technique for appropriating the objective world and an unavoidably solipsistic expression of the singular self. Photographs depict realities that already exist, though only the camera can disclose them. And they depict an individual temperament, discovering itself through the camera's cropping of reality. For Moholy-Nagy the genius of photography lies in its ability to render "an objective portrait: the individual to be photographed so that the photographic result shall not be encumbered with subjective intention." For Lange every portrait of another person is a "self-portrait" of the photographer, as for Minor White—promoting "self-discovery through a camera"—landscape photographs are really "inner landscapes." The two ideals are antithetical. Insofar as photography is (or should be) about the world, the photographer counts for little, but insofar as it is the instrument of intrepid, questing subjectivity, the photographer is all.

Moholy-Nagy's demand for the photographer's self-effacement follows from his appreciation of how edifying photography is: it retains and upgrades our powers of observation, it brings about "a psychological transformation of our eyesight." (In an essay published in 1936, he says that photography creates or enlarges eight distinct varieties of seeing: abstract, exact, rapid, slow, intensified, penetrative, simultaneous, and distorted.) But self-effacement is also the demand behind quite different, anti-scientific approaches to photography, such as that expressed in Robert Frank's credo: "There is one thing the photograph must contain, the humanity of the moment." In both views the photographer is proposed as a kind of ideal observer—for Moholy-Nagy, seeing with the detachment of a researcher; for Frank, seeing "simply, as through the eyes of the man in the street."

One attraction of any view of the photographer as ideal

observer—whether impersonal (Moholy-Nagy) or friendly (Frank)—is that it implicitly denies that picture-taking is in any way an aggressive act. That it can be so described makes most professionals extremely defensive. Cartier-Bresson and Avedon are among the very few to have talked honestly (if ruefully) about the exploitative aspect of the photographer's activities. Usually photographers feel obliged to protest photography's innocence, claiming that the predatory attitude is incompatible with a good picture, and hoping that a more affirmative vocabulary will put over their point. One of the more memorable examples of such verbiage is Ansel Adams's description of the camera as an "instrument of love and revelation"; Adams also urges that we stop saying that we "take" a picture and always say we "make" one. Stieglitz's name for the cloud studies he did in the late 1920s—"Equivalents," that is, statements of his inner feelings—is another, soberer instance of the persistent effort of photographers to feature the benevolent character of picture-taking and discount its predatory implications. What talented photographers do cannot of course be characterized either as simply predatory or as simply, and essentially, benevolent. Photography is the paradigm of an inherently equivocal connection between self and world—its version of the ideology of realism sometimes dictating an effacement of the self in relation to the world, sometimes authorizing an aggressive relation to the world which celebrates the self. One side or the other of the connection is always being rediscovered and championed.

An important result of the coexistence of these two ideals—assault on reality and submission to reality—is a recurrent ambivalence toward photography's *means*. Whatever the claims for photography as a form of personal expression on a par with painting, it remains true that its originality is inextricably linked to the powers of the machine: no one can deny the informativeness and formal beauty of many photographs made possible by the steady growth of these powers, like Harold Edgerton's high-speed photographs of a bullet hitting its target, of the swirls and eddies of a tennis stroke, or Lennart Nilsson's endoscopic photographs of the interior of the human body. But as cameras get ever more sophisticated, more automated, more acute, some photographers are tempted to disarm themselves or to suggest that they are really not armed, and prefer to submit themselves to the limits imposed by a pre-modern camera technology—a cruder, less high-powered machine being thought to give more interesting or expressive results, to leave more room for the creative accident. Not using fancy equipment has been a point of honor for many photographers—including Weston, Brandt, Evans, Cartier-Bresson, Frank—some sticking with a battered camera of simple design and slow lens that they acquired early in their careers, some continuing to make their contact prints with nothing more elaborate than a few trays, a bottle of developer, and a bottle of hypo solution.

The camera is indeed the instrument of "fast seeing," as one confident modernist, Alvin Langdon Coburn, declared in 1918, echoing the Futurist apotheosis of machines and speed. Photography's present mood of doubt can be gauged by Cartier-Bresson's recent statement that it may be *too* fast. The cult of the future (of faster and faster seeing) alternates with the wish to return to a more artisanal, purer past—when images still had a handmade quality, an aura. This nostalgia for some pristine state of the photographic enterprise underlies the current enthusiasm for daguerreotypes, stereograph cards, photographic *cartes de visite*, family snapshots, the work of forgotten nineteenth- and early-twentieth-century provincial and commercial photographers.

But the reluctance to use the newest high-powered equipment is not the only or indeed the most interesting way in which photographers express their attraction to photography's past. The primitivist hankerings that inform current photographic taste are actually being aided by the ceaseless innovativeness of camera technology. For many of these advances not only enlarge the camera's powers but also recapitulate—in a more ingenious, less cumbersome form—earlier, discarded possibilities of the medium. Thus, the development of photography hinges on the replacement of the daguerreotype process, direct positives on metal plates, by the positive-negative process, whereby from an original (negative) an unlimited number of prints (positives) can be made. (Although invented simultaneously in the late 1830s, it was Daguerre's government-supported invention, announced in 1839 with great publicity, rather than Fox Talbot's positive-negative process, that was the first photographic process in general use.) But now the camera could be said to be turning back upon itself. The Polaroid camera revives the principle of the daguerreotype camera: each print is a unique object. The hologram (a three-dimensional image created with laser light) could be considered as a variant on the heliogram—the first, cameraless photographs made in the 1820s by Nicéphore Niépce. And the increasingly popular use of the camera to produce slides—images which cannot be displayed permanently or stored in wallets and albums, but can only be projected on walls or on paper (as aids for drawing)—goes back even further into the camera's pre-history, for it amounts to using the photographic camera to do the work of the camera obscura.

"History is pushing us to the brink of a realistic age," according to Abbott, who summons photographers to make the jump themselves. But while photographers are perpetually urging each other to be bolder, a doubt persists about the value of realism which keeps them oscillating between simplicity and irony, between insisting on control and cultivating the unexpected, between the eagerness to take advantage of the complex evolution of the medium and the wish to reinvent photography from scratch. Photographers seem to need periodically to resist their own knowingness and to remystify what they do.

Questions about knowledge are not, historically, photography's first line of defense. The earliest controversies center on the question whether photography's fidelity to appearances and dependence on a machine did not prevent it from being a fine art—as distinct from a merely practical art, an arm of science, and a trade. (That photographs give useful and often startling kinds of information was obvious from the beginning. Photographers only started worrying about what they knew, and what kind of knowledge in a deeper sense a photograph supplies, *after* photography was accepted as an art.) For about a century the defense of photography was identical with the struggle to establish it as a fine art. Against the charge that photography was a soulless, mechanical copying of reality, photographers asserted that it was a vanguard revolt against ordinary standards of seeing, no less worthy an art than painting.

Now photographers are choosier about the claims they make. Since photography has become so entirely respectable as a branch of the fine arts, they no longer seek the shelter that the notion of art has intermittently given the photographic enterprise. For all the important American photographers who have proudly identified their work with the aims of art (like Stieglitz, White, Siskind, Callahan, Lange, Laughlin), there are many more who disavow the question itself. Whether or not the camera's "results come under the category of Art is irrelevant," Strand wrote in the 1920s; and Moholy-Nagy declared it "quite unimportant whether photography produces 'art' or not." Photographers who came to maturity in the 1940s or later are bolder, openly snubbing art, equating art with artiness. They generally claim to be finding, recording, impartially observing, witnessing, exploring themselves—anything but making works of art. At first, it was photography's commitment to realism that placed it in a permanently ambivalent relation to art; now it is its modernist heritage. The fact that important photographers are no longer willing to debate whether photography is or is not a fine art, except to proclaim that their work is *not* involved with art, shows the extent to which they simply take for granted the concept of art imposed by the triumph of modernism: the better the art, the more subversive it is of the traditional aims of art. And modernist taste has welcomed this unpretentious activity that can be consumed, almost in spite of itself, as high art.

Even in the nineteenth century, when photography was thought to be so evidently in need of defense as a fine art, the line of defense was far from stable. Julia Margaret Cameron's claim that photography qualifies as an art because, like painting, it seeks the beautiful was succeeded by Henry Peach Robinson's Wildean claim that photography is an art because it can lie. In the early twentieth century Alvin Langdon Coburn's praise of photography as "the most modern of the arts," because it is a fast, impersonal way of seeing, competed with Weston's praise of photography as a new means of individual visual creation. In recent decades the notion of art has been exhausted as an instrument of polemic; indeed, a good part of the immense prestige that photography has acquired as an art form comes from its declared ambivalence toward being an art. When photographers now deny that they are making works of art, it is because they think they are doing something better than that. Their disclaimers tell us more about the harried status of any notion of art than about whether photography is or isn't one.

Despite the efforts of contemporary photographers to exorcise the specter of art, something lingers. For instance, when professionals object to having their photographs printed to the edge of the page in books or magazines, they are invoking the model inherited from another art: as paintings are put in frames, photographs should be framed in white space. Another instance: many photographers continue to prefer black-and-white images, which are felt to be more tactful, more decorous than color—or less voyeuristic and less sentimental or crudely lifelike. But the real basis for this preference is, once again, an implicit comparison with painting. In the introduction to his book of photographs *The Decisive Moment* (1952), Cartier-Bresson justified his unwillingness to use color by citing technical limitations: the slow speed of color film, which reduces the depth of focus. But with the rapid progress in color-film technology during the last two decades, making possible all the tonal subtlety and high resolution one might desire, Cartier-Bresson has had to shift his ground, and now proposes that photographers renounce color as a matter of principle. In Cartier-Bresson's version of that persistent myth according to which—following the camera's invention—a division of territory took place between photography and painting, color belongs to painting. He enjoins photographers to resist temptation and keep up their side of the bargain.

Those still involved in defining photography as an art are always trying to hold some line. But it is impossible to hold the line: any attempt to restrict photography to certain subjects or certain techniques, however fruitful these have proved to be, is bound to be challenged and to collapse. For it is in the very nature of photography that it be a promiscuous form of seeing, and, in talented hands, an infallible medium of creation. (As John Szarkowski observes, "a skillful photographer can photograph anything well.") Hence, its longstanding quarrel with art, which (until recently) meant the results of a discriminating or purified way of seeing, and a medium of creation governed by standards that make genuine achievement a rarity. Understandably, photographers have been reluctant to give up the attempt to define more narrowly what good photography is. The history of photography is punctuated by a series of dualistic controversies—such as the straight print versus the doctored print, pictorial photography versus documentary photography—each of which is a different form of the debate about photography's relation to art: how close it can get while still retaining its claim to unlimited visual acquisition. Recently, it has become common to maintain that all these controversies are now outmoded, which suggests that the debate has been settled. But it is unlikely that the defense of photography as art will ever completely subside. As long as photography is not only a voracious way of seeing but one which needs to claim that it is a special, distinctive way, photographers will continue to take shelter (if only covertly) in the defiled but still prestigious precincts of art.

Photographers who suppose they are getting away from the pretensions of art as exemplified in painting by taking pictures remind us of those Abstract Expressionist painters who imagined they were getting away from art, or Art, by the act of painting (that is, by treating the canvas as a field of action rather than as an object). And much of the prestige that photography has recently acquired as an art is based on the convergence of its claims with those of more recent painting and sculpture.* The seemingly insatiable appetite for photography in the 1970s expresses more than the pleasure of discovering and exploring a relatively neglected art form; it derives much of its fervor from the desire to reaffirm the dismissal of abstract art which was one of the messages of the pop taste of the 1960s. Paying more and more attention to photographs is a great relief to sensibilities tired of, or eager to avoid, the mental exertions demanded by abstract art. Classical modernist painting presupposes highly developed skills of looking, and a familiarity with other art and with certain notions about the history of art. Photography, like pop art, reassures viewers that art isn't hard; it seems to be more about subjects than about art.

Photography is the most successful vehicle of modernist taste

*The claims of photography are, of course, much older. For the now familiar practice that substitutes encounter for fabrication, found objects or situations for made (or made-up) ones, decision for effort, the prototype is photography's instant art through the mediation of a machine. It was photography that first put into circulation the idea of an art that is produced not by pregnancy and childbirth but by a blind date (Duchamp's theory of "rendez-vous"). But professional photographers are much less secure than their Duchamp-influenced contemporaries in the established fine arts, and generally hasten to point out that a moment's decision presupposes a long training of sensibility, of the eye, and to insist that the effortlessness of picture-taking does not make the photographer any less of an artificer than a painter.

in its pop version, with its zeal for debunking the high culture of the past (focusing on shards, junk, odd stuff; excluding nothing); its conscientious courting of vulgarity; its affection for kitsch; its skill in reconciling avant-garde ambitions with the rewards of commercialism; its pseudo-radical patronizing of art as reactionary, elitist, snobbish, insincere, artificial, out of touch with the broad truths of everyday life; its transformation of art into cultural document. At the same time, photography has gradually acquired all the anxieties and self-consciousness of a classic modernist art. Many professionals are now worried that this populist strategy is being carried too far, and that the public will forget that photography is, after all, a noble and exalted activity—in short, an art. For the modernist promotion of naïve art always contains a joker: that one continue to honor its hidden claim to sophistication.

It cannot be a coincidence that just about the time that photographers stopped discussing whether photography is an art, it was acclaimed as one by the general public and photography entered, in force, into the museum. The museum's naturalization of photography as art is the conclusive victory of the century-long campaign waged by modernist taste on behalf of an open-ended definition of art, photography offering a much more suitable terrain than painting for this effort. For the line between amateur and professional, primitive and sophisticated is not just harder to draw with photography than it is with painting—it has little meaning. Naïve or commercial or merely utilitarian photography is no different in kind from photography as practiced by the most gifted professionals: there are pictures taken by anonymous amateurs which are just as interesting, as complex formally, as representative of photography's characteristic powers as a Stieglitz or an Evans.

That all the different kinds of photography form one continuous and interdependent tradition is the once startling, now obvious-seeming assumption which underlies contemporary photographic taste and authorizes the indefinite expansion of that taste. To make this assumption only became plausible when photography was taken up by curators and historians and regularly exhibited in museums and art galleries. Photography's career in the museum does not reward any particular style;

rather, it presents photography as a collection of simultaneous intentions and styles which, however different, are not perceived as in any way contradictory. But while the operation has been a huge success with the public, the response of photography professionals is mixed. Even as they welcome photography's new legitimacy, many of them feel threatened when the most ambitious images are discussed in direct continuity with *all* sorts of images, from photojournalism to scientific photography to family snapshots—charging that this reduces photography to something trivial, vulgar, a mere craft.

The real problem with bringing functional photographs, photographs taken for a practical purpose, on commercial assignment, or as souvenirs, into the mainstream of photographic achievement is not that it demeans photography, considered as a fine art, but that the procedure contradicts the nature of most photographs. In most uses of the camera, the photograph's naïve or descriptive function is paramount. But when viewed in their new context, the museum or gallery, photographs cease to be "about" their subjects in the same direct or primary way; they become studies in the possibilities of photography. Photography's adoption by the museum makes photography itself seem problematic, in the way experienced only by a small number of self-conscious photographers whose work consists precisely in questioning the camera's ability to grasp reality. The eclectic museum collections reinforce the arbitrariness, the subjectivity of all photographs, including the most straightforwardly descriptive ones.

Putting on shows of photographs has become as featured a museum activity as mounting shows of individual painters. But a photographer is not like a painter, the role of the photographer being recessive in much of serious picture-taking and virtually irrelevant in all the ordinary uses. So far as we care about the subject photographed, we expect the photographer to be an extremely discreet presence. Thus, the very success of photojournalism lies in the difficulty of distinguishing one superior photographer's work from another's, except insofar as he or she has monopolized a particular subject. These photographs have their power as images (or copies) of the world, not of an individual artist's consciousness. And in the vast majority of photographs which get taken—for scientific and industrial purposes, by the press, by the military and the police, by families—any trace of the personal vision of whoever is behind the camera interferes with the primary demand on the photograph: that it record, diagnose, inform.

It makes sense that a painting is signed but a photograph is not (or it seems bad taste if it is). The very nature of photography implies an equivocal relation to the photographer as *auteur*; and the bigger and more varied the work done by a talented photographer, the more it seems to acquire a kind of corporate rather than individual authorship. Many of the published photographs by photography's greatest names seem like work that could have been done by another gifted professional of their period. It requires a formal conceit (like Todd Walker's solarized photographs or Duane Michals's narrative-sequence photographs) or a thematic obsession (like Eakins with the male nude or Laughlin with the Old South) to make work easily recognizable. For photographers who don't so limit themselves, their body of work does not have the same integrity as does comparably varied work in other art forms. Even in those careers with the sharpest breaks of period and style—think of Picasso, of Stravinsky—one can perceive the unity of concerns that transcends these breaks and can (retrospectively) see the inner relation of one period to another. Knowing the whole body of work, one can see how the same composer could have written *Le Sacre du printemps*, the Dumbarton Oaks Concerto, and the late neo-Schoenbergian works; one recognizes Stravinsky's hand in all these compositions. But there is no internal evidence for identifying as the work of a single photographer (indeed, one of the most interesting and original of photographers) those studies of human and animal motion, the documents brought back from photo-expeditions in Central America, the government-sponsored camera surveys of Alaska and Yosemite, and the "Clouds" and "Trees" series. Even after knowing they were all taken by Muybridge, one still can't relate these series of pictures to each other (though each series has a coherent, recognizable style), any more than one could infer the way Atget photographed trees from the way he photographed Paris shop windows, or connect Roman Vishniac's pre-war portraits of Polish Jews with the scientific microphotographs he has been taking since 1945. In photography the subject matter always pushes through, with different subjects creating unbridgeable gaps between one period and another of a large body of work, confounding signature.

Indeed, the very presence of a coherent photographic style—think of the white backgrounds and flat lighting of Avedon's portraits, of the distinctive grisaille of Atget's Paris street studies—seems to imply unified material. And subject matter seems to have the largest part in shaping a viewer's preferences. Even when photographs are isolated from the practical context in which they may originally have been taken, and looked at as works of art, to prefer one photograph to another seldom means only that the photograph is judged to be superior formally; it almost always means—as in more casual kinds of looking—that the viewer prefers that kind of mood, or respects that intention, or is intrigued by (or feels nostalgic about) that subject. The formalist approaches to photography cannot account for the power of *what* has been photographed, and the way distance in time and cultural distance from the photograph increase our interest.

Still, it seems logical that contemporary photographic taste has taken a largely formalist direction. Although the natural or naïve status of subject matter in photography is more secure than in any other representational art, the very plurality of situations in which photographs are looked at complicates and eventually weakens the primacy of subject matter. The conflict of interest between objectivity and subjectivity, between demonstration and supposition, is unresolvable. While the authority of a photograph will always depend on the relation to a subject (that it is a photograph *of* something), all claims on behalf of photography as art must emphasize the subjectivity of seeing. There is an equivocation at the heart of all aesthetic evaluations of photographs; and this explains the chronic defensiveness and extreme mutability of photographic taste.

For a brief time—say, from Stieglitz through the reign of Weston—it appeared that a solid point of view had been erected with which to evaluate photographs: impeccable lighting, skill of composition, clarity of subject, precision of focus, perfection of print quality. But this position, generally thought of as Westonian—essentially technical criteria for what makes a photograph good—is now bankrupt. (Weston's deprecating appraisal of the great Atget as "not a fine technician" shows its limitations.) What position has replaced Weston's? A much more inclusive one, with criteria which shift the center of judgment from the individual photograph, considered as a finished object, to the photograph considered as an example of "photographic seeing." What is meant by photographic seeing would hardly exclude Weston's work but it would also include a large number of anonymous, unposed, crudely lit, asymmetrically composed photographs formerly dismissed for their lack of composition. The new position aims to liberate photography, as art, from the oppressive standards of technical perfection; to liberate photography from beauty, too. It opens up the possibility of a global taste, in which no subject (or absence of subject), no technique (or absence of technique) disqualifies a photograph.

While in principle all subjects are worthy pretexts for exercising the photographic way of seeing, the convention has arisen that photographic seeing is clearest in offbeat or trivial subject matter. Subjects are chosen because they are boring or banal. Because we are indifferent to them, they best show up the ability of the camera to "see." When Irving Penn, known for his handsome photographs of celebrities and food for fashion magazines and ad agencies, was given a show at the Museum of Modern Art in 1975, it was for a series of close-ups of cigarette butts. "One might guess," commented the director of the museum's Department of Photography, John Szarkowski, "that [Penn] has only rarely enjoyed more than a cursory interest in the nominal subjects of his pictures." Writing about another photographer, Szarkowski commends what can "be coaxed from subject matter" that is "profoundly banal." Photography's adoption by the museum is now firmly associated with those important modernist conceits: the "nominal subject" and the "profoundly banal." But this approach not only diminishes the importance of subject matter; it also loosens the photograph from its connection with a single photographer. The photographic way of seeing is far from exhaustively illustrated by the many one-photographer shows and retrospectives that museums now put on. To be legitimate as an art, photography must cultivate the notion of the photographer as *auteur* and of all photographs taken by the same photographer as constituting a body of work. These notions are easier to apply to some photographers than to others. They seem more applicable to, say, Man Ray, whose style and purposes straddle photographic and painterly norms, than to Steichen, whose work includes abstractions, portraits, ads for consumer goods, fashion photographs, and aerial reconnaissance photographs (taken during his military career in both world wars). But the meanings that a photograph acquires when seen as part of an individual body of work are not particularly to the point when the criterion is photographic seeing. Rather, such an approach must necessarily favor the new meanings that any one picture acquires when juxtaposed—in ideal anthologies, either on museum walls or in books—with the work of other photographers.

Such anthologies are meant to educate taste about photography in general; to teach a form of seeing which makes all subjects equivalent. When Szarkowski describes gas stations, empty living rooms, and other bleak subjects as "patterns of random facts in the service of [the photographer's] imagination," what he really means is that these subjects are ideal for the camera. The ostensibly formalist, neutral criteria of photographic seeing are in fact powerfully judgmental about subjects and about styles. The revaluation of naïve or casual nineteenth-century photographs, particularly those which were taken as humble records, is partly due to their sharp-focus style—a pedagogic corrective to the "pictorial" soft focus which, from Cameron to Stieglitz, was associated with photography's claim to be an art. Yet the standards of photographic seeing do not imply an unalterable commitment to sharp focus. Whenever serious photography is felt to have been purged of outmoded relations to art and to prettiness, it could just as well accommodate a taste for pictorial photography, for abstraction, for noble subjects rather than cigarette butts and gas stations and turned backs.

The language in which photographs are generally evaluated is extremely meager. Sometimes it is parasitical on the vocabulary of painting: composition, light, and so forth. More often it consists in the vaguest sorts of judgments, as when photographs are praised for being subtle, or interesting, or powerful, or complex, or simple, or—a favorite—deceptively simple.

The reason the language is poor is not fortuitous: say, the absence of a rich tradition of photographic criticism. It is something inherent in photography itself, whenever it is viewed as an art. Photography proposes a process of imagination and an appeal to taste quite different from that of painting (at least as traditionally conceived). Indeed, the difference between a good photograph and a bad photograph is not at all like the difference between a good and a bad painting. The norms of aesthetic evaluation worked out for painting depend on criteria of authenticity (and fakeness), and of craftsmanship—criteria that are more permissive or simply non-existent for photography. And while the tasks of connoisseurship in painting invariably presume the organic relation of a painting to an individual body of work with its own integrity, and to schools and iconographical traditions, in photography a large individual body of work does not necessarily have an inner stylistic coherence, and an individual photographer's relation to schools of photography is a much more superficial affair.

One criterion of evaluation which painting and photography do share is innovativeness; both paintings and photographs are often valued because they impose new formal schemes or changes in the visual language. Another criterion which they can share is the quality of presence, which Walter Benjamin considered the defining characteristic of the work of art. Benjamin thought that a photograph, being a mechanically reproduced object, could not have genuine presence. It could be argued, however, that the very situation which is now determinative of taste in photography, its exhibition in museums and galleries, has revealed that photographs do possess a kind of authenticity. Furthermore, although no photograph is an original in the sense that a painting always is, there is a large qualitative difference between what could be called originals—prints made from the original negative at the time (that is, at the same moment in the technological evolution of photography) that the picture was taken—and subsequent generations of the same photograph. (What most people know of the famous photographs—in books, newspapers, magazines, and so forth—are photographs of photographs; the originals, which one is likely to see only in a museum or a gallery, offer visual pleasures which are not reproducible.) The result of mechanical reproduction, Benjamin says, is to "put the copy of the original into situations which would be out of reach for the original itself." But to the extent that, say, a Giotto can still be said to possess an aura in the situation of museum display, where it too has been wrenched from its original context and, like the photograph, "meets the beholder halfway" (in the strictest sense of Benjamin's notion of the aura, it does not), to that extent an Atget photograph printed on the now unobtainable paper he used can also be said to possess an aura.

The real difference between the aura that a photograph can have and that of a painting lies in the different relation to time. The depredations of time tend to work against paintings. But part of the built-in interest of photographs, and a major source of their aesthetic value, is precisely the transformations that time works upon them, the way they escape the intentions of their makers. Given enough time, many photographs do acquire an aura. (The fact that color photographs don't age in the way black-and-white photographs do may partly explain the marginal status which color has had until very recently in serious photographic taste. The cold intimacy of color seems to seal off the photograph from patina.) For while paintings or poems do not get better, more attractive simply because they are older, all photographs are interesting as well as touching if they are old enough. It is not altogether wrong to say that there is no such thing as a bad photograph—only less interesting, less relevant, less mysterious ones. Photography's adoption by the museum only accelerates that process which time will bring about anyway: making all work valuable.

The role of the museum in forming contemporary photographic taste cannot be overestimated. Museums do not so much arbitrate what photographs are good or bad as offer new conditions for looking at all photographs. This procedure, which appears to be creating standards of evaluation, in fact abolishes them. The museum cannot be said to have created a secure canon for the photographic work of the past, as it has for painting. Even as it seems to be sponsoring a particular photographic taste, the museum is undermining the very idea of normative taste. Its role is to show that there are *no* fixed standards of evaluation, that there is *no* canonical tradition of work. Under the museum's attentions, the very idea of a canonical tradition is exposed as redundant.

What keeps photography's Great Tradition always in flux,

constantly being reshuffled, is not that photography is a new art and therefore somewhat insecure—this is part of what photographic taste is about. There is a more rapid sequence of rediscovery in photography than in any other art. Illustrating that law of taste given its definitive formulation by T. S. Eliot whereby each important new work necessarily alters our perception of the heritage of the past, new photographs change how we look at past photographs. (For example, Arbus's work has made it easier to appreciate the greatness of the work of Hine, another photographer devoted to portraying the opaque dignity of victims.) But the swings in contemporary photographic taste do not only reflect such coherent and sequential processes of reevaluation, whereby like enhances like. What they more commonly express is the complementarity and equal value of antithetical styles and themes.

For several decades American photography has been dominated by a reaction against "Westonism"—that is, against contemplative photography, photography considered as an independent visual exploration of the world with no evident social urgency. The technical perfection of Weston's photographs, the calculated beauties of White and Siskind, the poetic constructions of Frederick Sommer, the self-assured ironies of Cartier-Bresson—all these have been challenged by photography that is, at least programmatically, more naïve, more direct; that is hesitant, even awkward. But taste in photography is not that linear. Without any weakening of the current commitments to informal photography and to photography as social document, a perceptible revival of Weston is now taking place—as, with the passage of enough time, Weston's work no longer looks timeless; as, by the much broader definition of naïveté with which photographic taste operates, Weston's work also looks naïve.

Finally, there is no reason to exclude any photographer from the canon. Right now there are mini-revivals of such long-despised pictorialists from another era as Oscar Gustav Rejlander, Henry Peach Robinson, and Robert Demachy. As photography takes the whole world as its subject, there is room for every kind of taste. Literary taste does exclude: the success of the modernist movement in poetry elevated Donne but diminished Dryden. With literature, one can be eclectic up to a point, but one can't like everything. With photography, eclecticism has no limits. The plain photographs from the 1870s of abandoned children admitted to a London institution called Doctor Barnardo's Home (taken as "records") are as moving as David Octavius Hill's complex portraits of Scottish notables of the 1840s (taken as "art"). The clean look of Weston's classic modern style is not refuted by, say, Benno Friedman's ingenious recent revival of pictorial blurriness.

This is not to deny that each viewer likes the work of some photographers more than others: for example, most experienced viewers today prefer Atget to Weston. What it does mean is that, by the nature of photography, one is not really obliged to choose; and that preferences of that sort are, for the most part, merely reactive. Taste in photography tends to be, is perhaps necessarily, global, eclectic, permissive, which means that in the end it must deny the difference between good taste and bad taste. This is what makes all the attempts of photography polemicists to erect a canon seem ingenuous or ignorant. For there is something fake about all photographic controversies— and the attentions of the museum have played a crucial role in making this clear. The museum levels up all schools of photography. Indeed, it makes little sense even to speak of schools. In the history of painting, movements have a genuine life and function: painters are often much better understood in terms of the school or movement to which they belonged. But movements in the history of photography are fleeting, adventitious, sometimes merely perfunctory, and no first-rate photographer is better understood as a member of a group. (Think of Stieglitz and Photo-Secession, Weston and ƒ64, Renger-Patzsch and the New Objectivity, Walker Evans and the Farm Security Administration project, Cartier-Bresson and Magnum.) To group photographers in schools or movements seems to be a kind of misunderstanding, based (once again) on the irrepressible but invariably misleading analogy between photography and painting.

The leading role now played by museums in forming and clarifying the nature of photographic taste seems to mark a new stage from which photography cannot turn back. Accompanying its tendentious respect for the profoundly banal is the museum's diffusion of a historicist view, one that inexorably promotes the entire history of photography. Small wonder that photography critics and photographers seem anxious. Underlying many of the recent defenses of photography is the fear that photography is already a senile art, littered by spurious or dead movements; that the only task left is curatorship and historiography. (While prices skyrocket for photographs old and new.) It is not surprising that this demoralization should be felt at the moment of photography's greatest acceptance, for the true extent of photography's triumph as art, and over art, has not really been understood.

Photography entered the scene as an upstart activity, which seemed to encroach on and diminish an accredited art: painting. For Baudelaire, photography was painting's "mortal enemy"; but eventually a truce was worked out, according to which photography was held to be painting's liberator. Weston employed the most common formula for easing the defensiveness of painters when he wrote in 1930: "Photography has, or will eventually, negate much painting—for which the painter should be deeply grateful." Freed by photography from the drudgery of faithful representation, painting could pursue a higher task: abstraction.* Indeed, the most persistent idea in histories of photography and in photography criticism is this mythic pact concluded between painting and photography, which authorized both to pursue their separate but equally valid tasks, while creatively influencing each other. In fact, the legend falsifies much of the history of both painting and photography. The camera's way of fixing the appearance of the external world

---

*Valéry claimed that photography performed the same service for writing, by exposing the "illusory" claim of language to "convey the idea of a visual object with any degree of precision." But writers should not fear that photography "might ultimately restrict the importance of the art of writing and act as its substitute," Valéry says in "The Centenary of Photography" (1929). If photography "discourages us from describing," he argues,

we are thus reminded of the limits of language and are advised, as writers, to put our tools to a use more befitting their true nature. A literature would purify itself if it left to other modes of expression and production the tasks which they can perform far more effectively, and devoted itself to ends it alone can accomplish . . . one of which [is] the perfecting of language that constructs or expounds abstract thought, the other exploring all the variety of poetic patterns and resonances.

suggested new patterns of pictorial composition and new subjects to painters: creating a preference for the fragment, raising interest in glimpses of humble life, and in studies of fleeting motion and the effects of light. Painting did not so much turn to abstraction as adopt the camera's eye, becoming (to borrow Mario Praz's words) telescopic, microscopic, and photoscopic in structure. But painters have never stopped attempting to imitate the realistic effects of photography. And, far from confining itself to realistic representation and leaving abstraction to painters, photography has kept up with and absorbed all the anti-naturalistic conquests of painting.

More generally, this legend does not take into account the voraciousness of the photographic enterprise. In the transactions between painting and photography, photography has always had the upper hand. There is nothing surprising in the fact that painters from Delacroix and Turner to Picasso and Bacon have used photographs as visual aids, but no one expects photographers to get help from painting. Photographs may be incorporated or transcribed into the painting (or collage, or combine), but photography encapsulates art itself. The experience of looking at paintings may help us to look better at photographs. But photography has weakened our experience of painting. (In more than one sense, Baudelaire was right.) Nobody ever found a lithograph or an engraving of a painting—the popular older methods of mechanical reproduction—more

----

Valéry's argument is not convincing. Although a photograph may be said to record or show or present, it does not ever, properly speaking, "describe"; only language describes, which is an event in time. Valéry suggests opening a passport as "proof" of his argument: "the description scrawled there does not bear comparison with the snapshot stapled alongside it." But this is using description in the most debased, impoverished sense; there are passages in Dickens or Nabokov which describe a face or a part of the body better than any photograph. Nor does it argue for the inferior descriptive powers of literature to say, as Valéry does, that "the writer who depicts a landscape or a face, no matter how skillful he may be at his craft, will suggest as many different visions as he has readers." The same is true of a photograph.

As the still photograph is thought to have freed writers from the obligation of describing, movies are often held to have usurped the novelist's task of narrating or storytelling—thereby, some claim, freeing the novel for other, less realistic tasks. This version of the argument is more plausible, because movies are a temporal art. But it does not do justice to the relation between novels and films.

satisfying or more exciting than the painting. But photographs, which turn interesting details into autonomous compositions, which transform true colors into brilliant colors, provide new, irresistible satisfactions. The destiny of photography has taken it far beyond the role to which it was originally thought to be limited: to give more accurate reports on reality (including works of art). Photography is the reality; the real object is often experienced as a letdown. Photographs make normative an experience of art that is mediated, second-hand, intense in a different way. (To deplore that photographs of paintings have become substitutes for the paintings for many people is not to support any mystique of "the original" that addresses the viewer without mediation. Seeing is a complex act, and no great painting communicates its value and quality without some form of preparation and instruction. Moreover, the people who have a harder time seeing the original work of art after seeing the photographic copy are generally those who would have seen very little in the original.)

As most works of art (including photographs) are now known from photographic copies, photography—and the art activities derived from the model of photography, and the mode of taste derived from photographic taste—has decisively transformed the traditional fine arts and the traditional norms of taste, including the very idea of the work of art. Less and less does the work of art depend on being a unique object, an original made by an individual artist. Much of painting today aspires to the qualities of reproducible objects. Finally, photographs have become so much the leading visual experience that we now have works of art which are produced in order to be photographed. In much of conceptual art, in Christo's packaging of the landscape, in the earthworks of Walter De Maria and Robert Smithson, the artist's work is known principally by the photographic report of it in galleries and museums; sometimes the size is such that it can *only* be known in a photograph (or from an airplane). The photograph is not, even ostensibly, meant to lead us back to an original experience.

It was on the basis of this presumed truce between photography and painting that photography was—grudgingly at first, then enthusiastically—acknowledged as a fine art. But the very question of whether photography is or is not an art is essentially a misleading one. Although photography generates works that can be called art—it requires subjectivity, it can lie, it gives aesthetic pleasure—photography is not, to begin with, an art form at all. Like language, it is a medium in which works of art (among other things) are made. Out of language, one can make scientific discourse, bureaucratic memoranda, love letters, grocery lists, and Balzac's Paris. Out of photography, one can make passport pictures, weather photographs, pornographic pictures, X-rays, wedding pictures, and Atget's Paris. Photography is not an art like, say, painting and poetry. Although the activities of some photographers conform to the traditional notion of a fine art, the activity of exceptionally talented individuals producing discrete objects that have value in themselves, from the beginning photography has also lent itself to that notion of art which says that art is obsolete. The power of photography—and its centrality in present aesthetic concerns—is that it confirms both ideas of art. But the way in which photography renders art obsolete is, in the long run, stronger.

Painting and photography are not two potentially competitive systems for producing and reproducing images, which simply had to arrive at a proper division of territory to be reconciled. Photography is an enterprise of another order. Photography, though not an art form in itself, has the peculiar capacity to turn all its subjects into works of art. Superseding the issue of whether photography is or is not an art is the fact that photography heralds (and creates) new ambitions for the arts. It is the prototype of the characteristic direction taken in our time by both the modernist high arts and the commercial arts: the transformation of arts into meta-arts or media. (Such developments as film, TV, video, the tape-based music of Cage, Stockhausen, and Steve Reich are logical extensions of the model established by photography.) The traditional fine arts are elitist: their characteristic form is a single work, produced by an individual; they imply a hierarchy of subject matter in which some subjects are considered important, profound, noble, and others unimportant, trivial, base. The media are democratic: they weaken the role of the specialized producer or *auteur* (by using procedures based on chance, or mechanical techniques which anyone can learn; and by being corporate or collaborative efforts); they regard the whole world as material. The traditional fine arts rely on the distinction between authentic and fake, between original and copy, between good taste and bad taste; the media blur, if they do not abolish outright, these distinctions. The fine arts assume that certain experiences or subjects have a meaning. The media are essentially contentless (this is the truth behind Marshall McLuhan's celebrated remark about the message being the medium itself); their characteristic tone is ironic, or deadpan, or parodistic. It is inevitable that more and more art will be designed to end as photographs. A modernist would have to rewrite Pater's dictum that all art aspires to the condition of music. Now all art aspires to the condition of photography.

The Image-World

REALITY has always been interpreted through the reports given by images; and philosophers since Plato have tried to loosen our dependence on images by evoking the standard of an image-free way of apprehending the real. But when, in the mid-nineteenth century, the standard finally seemed attainable, the retreat of old religious and political illusions before the advance of humanistic and scientific thinking did not—as anticipated—create mass defections to the real. On the contrary, the new age of unbelief strengthened the allegiance to images. The credence that could no longer be given to realities understood *in the form of* images was now being given to realities understood *to be* images, illusions. In the preface to the second edition (1843) of *The Essence of Christianity*, Feuerbach observes about "our era" that it "prefers the image to the thing, the copy to the original, the representation to the reality, appearance to being"—while being aware of doing just that. And his premonitory complaint has been transformed in the twentieth century into a widely agreed-on diagnosis: that a society becomes "modern" when one of its chief activities is producing and consuming images, when images that have extraordinary powers to determine our demands upon reality and are themselves coveted substitutes for firsthand experience become indispensable to the health of the economy, the stability of the polity, and the pursuit of private happiness.

Feuerbach's words—he is writing a few years after the invention of the camera—seem, more specifically, a presentiment of the impact of photography. For the images that have virtually unlimited authority in a modern society are mainly photographic images; and the scope of that authority stems from the properties peculiar to images taken by cameras.

Such images are indeed able to usurp reality because first of all a photograph is not only an image (as a painting is an image), an interpretation of the real; it is also a trace, something directly stenciled off the real, like a footprint or a death mask. While a painting, even one that meets photographic standards of resemblance, is never more than the stating of an interpretation, a photograph is never less than the registering of an emanation (light waves reflected by objects)—a material vestige of its subject in a way that no painting can be. Between two fantasy alternatives, that Holbein the Younger had lived long enough to have painted Shakespeare or that a prototype of the camera had been invented early enough to have photographed him, most Bardolators would choose the photograph. This is not just because it would presumably show what Shakespeare really looked like, for even if the hypothetical photograph were faded, barely legible, a brownish shadow, we would probably still prefer it to another glorious Holbein. Having a photograph of Shakespeare would be like having a nail from the True Cross.

Most contemporary expressions of concern that an image-world is replacing the real one continue to echo, as Feuerbach did, the Platonic depreciation of the image: true insofar as it resembles something real, sham because it is no more than a resemblance. But this venerable naïve realism is somewhat beside the point in the era of photographic images, for its blunt contrast between the image ("copy") and the thing depicted (the "original")—which Plato repeatedly illustrates with the example of a painting—does not fit a photograph in so simple a way. Neither does the contrast help in understanding image-making at its origins, when it was a practical, magical activity, a means of appropriating or gaining power over something. The further back we go in history, as E. H. Gombrich has observed, the less sharp is the distinction between images and real things; in primitive societies, the thing and its image were simply two different, that is, physically distinct, manifestations of the same energy or spirit. Hence, the supposed efficacy of images in propitiating and gaining control over powerful presences. Those powers, those presences were present in *them*.

For defenders of the real from Plato to Feuerbach to equate image with mere appearance—that is, to presume that the image is absolutely distinct from the object depicted—is part of that process of desacralization which separates us irrevocably from the world of sacred times and places in which an image was taken to participate in the reality of the object depicted. What defines the originality of photography is that, at the very moment in the long, increasingly secular history of painting when secularism is entirely triumphant, it revives—in wholly secular terms—something like the primitive status of images. Our irrepressible feeling that the photographic process is something magical has a genuine basis. No one takes an easel painting to be in any sense co-substantial with its subject; it only represents or refers. But a photograph is not only like its subject, a homage to the subject. It is part of, an extension of that subject; and a potent means of acquiring it, of gaining control over it.

Photography is acquisition in several forms. In its simplest form, we have in a photograph surrogate possession of a cherished person or thing, a possession which gives photographs some of the character of unique objects. Through photographs, we also have a consumer's relation to events, both to events which are part of our experience and to those which are not—a distinction between types of experience that such habit-forming consumership blurs. A third form of acquisition is that, through image-making and image-duplicating machines, we can acquire something as information (rather than experience). Indeed, the importance of photographic images as the medium through which more and more events enter our experience is, finally, only a by-product of their effectiveness in furnishing knowledge dissociated from and independent of experience.

This is the most inclusive form of photographic acquisition. Through being photographed, something becomes part of a system of information, fitted into schemes of classification and storage which range from the crudely chronological order of snapshot sequences pasted in family albums to the dogged accumulations and meticulous filing needed for photography's uses in weather forecasting, astronomy, microbiology, geology, police work, medical training and diagnosis, military reconnaissance, and art history. Photographs do more than redefine the stuff of ordinary experience (people, things, events, whatever we see—albeit differently, often inattentively—with natural vision) and add vast amounts of material that we never see at all. Reality as such is redefined—as an item for exhibition, as a record for scrutiny, as a target for surveillance. The photographic exploration and duplication of the world fragments continuities and feeds the pieces into an interminable dossier, thereby providing possibilities of control that could not even be dreamed of under the earlier system of recording information: writing.

That photographic recording is always, potentially, a means of control was already recognized when such powers were in their infancy. In 1850, Delacroix noted in his *Journal* the success of some "experiments in photography" being made at Cambridge, where astronomers were photographing the sun and the moon and had managed to obtain a pinhead-size impression of the star Vega. He added the following "curious" observation:

> Since the light of the star which was daguerreotyped took twenty years to traverse the space separating it from the earth, the ray which was fixed on the plate had consequently left the celestial sphere a long time before Daguerre had discovered the process by means of which we have just gained control of this light.

Leaving behind such puny notions of control as Delacroix's, photography's progress has made ever more literal the senses in which a photograph gives control over the thing photographed. The technology that has already minimized the extent to which the distance separating photographer from subject affects the precision and magnitude of the image; provided ways to photograph things which are unimaginably small as well as those, like stars, which are unimaginably far; rendered picture-taking independent of light itself (infrared photography) and freed the picture-object from its confinement to two dimensions (holography); shrunk the interval between sighting the picture and holding it in one's hands (from the first Kodak, when it took weeks for a developed roll of film to be returned to the amateur photographer, to the Polaroid, which ejects the image in a few seconds); not only got images to move (cinema) but achieved their simultaneous recording and transmission (video)—this technology has made photography an incomparable tool for deciphering behavior, predicting it, and interfering with it.

   Photography has powers that no other image-system has ever enjoyed because, unlike the earlier ones, it is *not* dependent on an image maker. However carefully the photographer intervenes in setting up and guiding the image-making process, the process itself remains an optical-chemical (or electronic) one, the workings of which are automatic, the machinery for which will inevitably be modified to provide still more detailed and, therefore, more useful maps of the real. The mechanical genesis of these images, and the literalness of the powers they confer, amounts to a new relationship between image and reality. And if photography could also be said to restore the most primitive relationship—the partial identity of the image and object—the potency of the image is now experienced in a very different way. The primitive notion of the efficacy of images presumes that images possess the qualities of real things, but our inclination is to attribute to real things the qualities of an image.

As everyone knows, primitive people fear that the camera will rob them of some part of their being. In the memoir he published in 1900, at the end of a very long life, Nadar reports that Balzac had a similar "vague dread" of being photographed. His explanation, according to Nadar, was that

> every body in its natural state was made up of a series of ghostly images superimposed in layers to infinity, wrapped in infinitesimal films. . . . Man never having been able to create, that is to make something material from an apparition, from something impalpable, or to make from nothing, an object—each Daguerreian operation was therefore going to lay hold of, detach, and use up one of the layers of the body on which it focused.

It seems fitting for Balzac to have had this particular brand of trepidation—"Was Balzac's fear of the Daguerreotype real or feigned?" Nadar asks. "It was real . . ."—since the procedure of photography is a materializing, so to speak, of what is most original in his procedure as a novelist. The Balzacian operation was to magnify tiny details, as in a photographic enlargement, to juxtapose incongruous traits or items, as in a photographic layout: made expressive in this way, any one thing can be connected with everything else. For Balzac, the spirit of an entire milieu could be disclosed by a single material detail, however paltry or arbitrary-seeming. The whole of a life may be summed up in a momentary appearance.* And a change in appearances is

---

*I am drawing on the account of Balzac's realism in Erich Auerbach's *Mimesis*. The passage that Auerbach describes from the beginning of *Le Père Goriot* (1834)—Balzac is describing the dining room of the Vauquer pension at seven in the morning and the entry of Madame Vauquer—could hardly be more explicit (or proto-Proustian). "Her whole person," Balzac writes, "explains the pension, as the pension implies her person. . . . The short-statured woman's blowsy *embonpoint* is the product of the life here, as typhoid is the consequence of the exhalations of a hospital. Her knitted wool petticoat, which is longer than her outer skirt (made of an old dress), and whose wadding is escaping by the gaps in the splitting material, sums up the drawing-room, the dining room, the little garden, announces the cooking and gives an inkling of the boarders. When she is there, the spectacle is complete."

a change in the person, for he refused to posit any "real" person ensconced behind these appearances. Balzac's fanciful theory, expressed to Nadar, that a body is composed of an infinite series of "ghostly images," eerily parallels the supposedly realistic theory expressed in his novels, that a person is an aggregate of appearances, appearances which can be made to yield, by proper focusing, infinite layers of significance. To view reality as an endless set of situations which mirror each other, to extract analogies from the most dissimilar things, is to anticipate the characteristic form of perception stimulated by photographic images. Reality itself has started to be understood as a kind of writing, which has to be decoded—even as photographed images were themselves first compared to writing. (Niépce's name for the process whereby the image appears on the plate was heliography, sun-writing; Fox Talbot called the camera "the pencil of nature.")

The problem with Feuerbach's contrast of "original" with "copy" is its static definitions of reality and image. It assumes that what is real persists, unchanged and intact, while only images have changed: shored up by the most tenuous claims to credibility, they have somehow become more seductive. But the notions of image and reality are complementary. When the notion of reality changes, so does that of the image, and vice versa. "Our era" does not prefer images to real things out of perversity but partly in response to the ways in which the notion of what is real has been progressively complicated and weakened, one of the early ways being the criticism of reality as façade which arose among the enlightened middle classes in the last century. (This was of course the very opposite of the effect intended.) To reduce large parts of what has hitherto been regarded as real to mere fantasy, as Feuerbach did when he called religion "the dream of the human mind" and dismissed theological ideas as psychological projections; or to inflate the random and trivial details of everyday life into ciphers of hidden historical and psychological forces, as Balzac did in his encyclopedia of social reality in novel form—these are themselves ways of experiencing reality as a set of appearances, an image.

Few people in this society share the primitive dread of cameras that comes from thinking of the photograph as a material part of themselves. But some trace of the magic remains: for example, in our reluctance to tear up or throw away the photograph of a loved one, especially of someone dead or far away. To do so is a ruthless gesture of rejection. In *Jude the Obscure* it is Jude's discovery that Arabella has sold the maple frame with the photograph of himself in it which he gave her on their wedding day that signifies to Jude "the utter death of every sentiment in his wife" and is "the conclusive little stroke to demolish all sentiment in him." But the true modern primitivism is not to regard the image as a real thing; photographic images are hardly that real. Instead, reality has come to seem more and more like what we are shown by cameras. It is common now for people to insist about their experience of a violent event in which they were caught up—a plane crash, a shoot-out, a terrorist bombing—that "it seemed like a movie." This is said, other descriptions seeming insufficient, in order to explain how real it was. While many people in non-industrialized countries still feel apprehensive when being photographed, divining it to be some kind of trespass, an act of disrespect, a sublimated looting of the personality or the culture, people in industrialized countries seek to have their photographs taken—feel that they are images, and are made real by photographs.

A steadily more complex sense of the real creates its own compensatory fervors and simplifications, the most addictive of which is picture-taking. It is as if photographers, responding to an increasingly depleted sense of reality, were looking for a transfusion—traveling to new experiences, refreshing the old ones. Their ubiquitous activities amount to the most radical, and the safest, version of mobility. The urge to have new experiences is translated into the urge to take photographs: experience seeking a crisis-proof form.

As the taking of photographs seems almost obligatory to those who travel about, the passionate collecting of them has special appeal for those confined—either by choice, incapacity, or coercion—to indoor space. Photograph collections can be used to make a substitute world, keyed to exalting or consoling or tantalizing images. A photograph can be the starting point of a romance (Hardy's Jude had already fallen in love with Sue Bridehead's photograph before he met her), but it is more common for the erotic relation to be not only created by but understood as limited to the photographs. In Cocteau's *Les Enfants Terribles*, the narcissistic brother and sister share their bedroom, their "secret room," with images of boxers, movie stars, and murderers. Isolating themselves in their lair to live out their private legend, the two adolescents put up these photographs, a private pantheon. On one wall of cell No. 426 in Fresnes Prison in the early 1940s Jean Genet pasted the photographs of twenty criminals he had clipped from newspapers, twenty faces in which he discerned "the sacred sign of the monster," and in their honor wrote *Our Lady of the Flowers*; they served as his muses, his models, his erotic talismans. "They watch over my little routines," writes Genet—conflating reverie, masturbation, and writing—and "are all the family I have and my only friends." For stay-at-homes, prisoners, and the self-imprisoned, to live among the photographs of glamorous strangers is a sentimental response to isolation and an insolent challenge to it.

J. G. Ballard's novel *Crash* (1973) describes a more specialized collecting of photographs in the service of sexual obsession: photographs of car accidents which the narrator's friend Vaughan collects while preparing to stage his own death in a car crash. The acting out of his erotic vision of car death is anticipated and the fantasy itself further eroticized by the repeated perusal of these photographs. At one end of the spectrum, photographs are objective data; at the other end, they are items of psychological science fiction. And as in even the most dreadful, or neutral-seeming, reality a sexual imperative can be found, so even the most banal photograph-document can mutate into an emblem of desire. The mug shot is a clue to a detective, an erotic fetish to a fellow thief. To Hofrat Behrens, in *The Magic Mountain*, the pulmonary X-rays of his patients are diagnostic tools. To Hans Castorp, serving an indefinite sentence in Behrens's TB sanatorium, and made lovesick by the enigmatic, unattainable Clavdia Chauchat, "Clavdia's X-ray portrait, showing not her face, but the delicate bony structure of the upper half of her body, and the organs of the thoracic cavity, surrounded by the pale, ghostlike envelope of flesh," is the most precious of trophies. The "transparent portrait" is a far more intimate vestige of his beloved than the Hofrat's painting of Clavdia, that "exterior portrait," which Hans had once gazed at with such longing.

Photographs are a way of imprisoning reality, understood as recalcitrant, inaccessible; of making it stand still. Or they enlarge a reality that is felt to be shrunk, hollowed out, perishable, remote. One can't possess reality, one can possess (and be possessed by) images—as, according to Proust, most ambitious of voluntary prisoners, one can't possess the present but one can possess the past. Nothing could be more unlike the self-sacrificial travail of an artist like Proust than the effortlessness of picture-taking, which must be the sole activity resulting in accredited works of art in which a single movement, a touch of the finger, produces a complete work. While the Proustian labors presuppose that reality is distant, photography implies instant access to the real. But the results of this practice of instant access are another way of creating distance. To possess the world in the form of images is, precisely, to reexperience the unreality and remoteness of the real.

The strategy of Proust's realism presumes distance from what is normally experienced as real, the present, in order to reanimate what is usually available only in a remote and shadowy form, the past—which is where the present becomes in his sense real, that is, something that can be possessed. In this effort photographs were of no help. Whenever Proust mentions photographs, he does so disparagingly: as a synonym for a shallow, too exclusively visual, merely voluntary relation to the past, whose yield is insignificant compared with the deep discoveries to be made by responding to cues given by all the senses—the technique he called "involuntary memory." One can't imagine the Overture to *Swann's Way* ending with the narrator's coming across a snapshot of the parish church at Combray and the savoring of *that* visual crumb, instead of the taste of the humble madeleine dipped in tea, making an entire part of his past spring into view. But this is not because a photograph cannot evoke memories (it can, depending on the quality of the viewer rather than of the photograph) but because of what Proust makes clear about his own demands upon imaginative recall, that it be not just extensive and accurate but give the texture and essence of things. And by considering photographs only so far as he could use them, as an instrument of memory, Proust somewhat misconstrues what photographs are: not so much an instrument of memory as an invention of it or a replacement.

It is not reality that photographs make immediately accessible, but images. For example, now all adults can know exactly how they and their parents and grandparents looked as children—a knowledge not available to anyone before the invention of cameras, not even to that tiny minority among whom it was customary to commission paintings of their children. Most of these portraits were less informative than any snapshot. And even the very wealthy usually owned just one portrait of themselves or any of their forebears as children, that is, an image of one moment of childhood, whereas it is common to have many photographs of oneself, the camera offering the possibility of possessing a complete record, at all ages. The point of the standard portraits in the bourgeois household of the eighteenth and nineteenth centuries was to confirm an ideal of the sitter (proclaiming social standing, embellishing personal appearance); given this purpose, it is clear why their owners did not feel the need to have more than one. What the photograph-record confirms is, more modestly, simply that the subject exists; therefore, one can never have too many.

The fear that a subject's uniqueness was leveled by being photographed was never so frequently expressed as in the 1850s, the years when portrait photography gave the first example of how cameras could create instant fashions and durable industries. In Melville's *Pierre*, published at the start of the decade, the hero, another fevered champion of voluntary isolation,

> considered with what infinite readiness now, the most faithful portrait of any one could be taken by the Daguerreotype, whereas in former times a faithful portrait was only within the power of the moneyed, or mental aristocrats of the earth. How natural then the inference, that instead of, as in old times, immortalizing a genius, a portrait now only *dayalized* a dunce. Besides, when every body has his portrait published, true distinction lies in not having yours published at all.

But if photographs demean, paintings distort in the opposite way: they make grandiose. Melville's intuition is that all forms of portraiture in the business civilization are compromised; at least, so it appears to Pierre, a paragon of alienated sensibility. Just as a photograph is too little in a mass society, a painting is too much. The nature of a painting, Pierre observes, makes it

better entitled to reverence than the man; inasmuch as nothing
belittling can be imagined concerning the portrait, whereas many
unavoidably belittling things can be fancied as touching the man.

Even if such ironies can be considered to have been dissolved
by the completeness of photography's triumph, the main difference between a painting and a photograph in the matter of
portraiture still holds. Paintings invariably sum up; photographs
usually do not. Photographic images are pieces of evidence in
an ongoing biography or history. And one photograph, unlike
one painting, implies that there will be others.

"Ever—the Human Document to keep the present and the
future in touch with the past," said Lewis Hine. But what photography supplies is not only a record of the past but a new way
of dealing with the present, as the effects of the countless billions of contemporary photograph-documents attest. While old
photographs fill out our mental image of the past, the photographs being taken now transform what is present into a mental
image, like the past. Cameras establish an inferential relation to
the present (reality is known by its traces), provide an instantly
retroactive view of experience. Photographs give mock forms of
possession: of the past, the present, even the future. In Nabokov's *Invitation to a Beheading* (1938), the prisoner Cincinnatus
is shown the "photohoroscope" of a child cast by the sinister
M'sieur Pierre: an album of photographs of little Emmie as an
infant, then a small child, then pre-pubescent, as she is now,
then—by retouching and using photographs of her mother—of
Emmie the adolescent, the bride, the thirty-year-old, concluding with a photograph at age forty, Emmie on her deathbed.
A "parody of the work of time" is what Nabokov calls this exemplary artifact; it is also a parody of the work of photography.

Photography, which has so many narcissistic uses, is also a powerful instrument for depersonalizing our relation to the world;
and the two uses are complementary. Like a pair of binoculars
with no right or wrong end, the camera makes exotic things
near, intimate; and familiar things small, abstract, strange,
much farther away. It offers, in one easy, habit-forming activity,
both participation and alienation in our own lives and those of
others—allowing us to participate, while confirming alienation.

War and photography now seem inseparable, and plane crashes and other horrific accidents always attract people with cameras. A society which makes it normative to aspire never to experience privation, failure, misery, pain, dread disease, and in which death itself is regarded not as natural and inevitable but as a cruel, unmerited disaster, creates a tremendous curiosity about these events—a curiosity that is partly satisfied through picture-taking. The feeling of being exempt from calamity stimulates interest in looking at painful pictures, and looking at them suggests and strengthens the feeling that one is exempt. Partly it is because one is "here," not "there," and partly it is the character of inevitability that all events acquire when they are transmuted into images. In the real world, something *is* happening and no one knows what is *going* to happen. In the image-world, it *has* happened, and it *will* forever happen in that way.

Knowing a great deal about what is in the world (art, catastrophe, the beauties of nature) through photographic images, people are frequently disappointed, surprised, unmoved when they see the real thing. For photographic images tend to subtract feeling from something we experience at first hand and the feelings they do arouse are, largely, not those we have in real life. Often something disturbs us more in photographed form than it does when we actually experience it. In a hospital in Shanghai in 1973, watching a factory worker with advanced ulcers have nine-tenths of his stomach removed under acupuncture anesthesia, I managed to follow the three-hour procedure (the first operation I'd ever observed) without queasiness, never once feeling the need to look away. In a movie theater in Paris a year later, the less gory operation in Antonioni's China documentary *Chung Kuo* made me flinch at the first cut of the scalpel and avert my eyes several times during the sequence. One is vulnerable to disturbing events in the form of photographic images in a way that one is not to the real thing. That vulnerability is part of the distinctive passivity of someone who is a spectator twice over, spectator of events already shaped, first by the participants and second by the image maker. For the real operation I had to get scrubbed, don a surgical gown, then stand alongside the busy surgeons and nurses with my roles to play: inhibited adult, well-mannered guest, respectful witness. The movie operation precludes not only this modest participation but whatever is active in spectatorship. In the operating room, I am the one who changes focus, who makes the close-ups and the medium shots. In the theater, Antonioni has already chosen what parts of the operation I can watch; the camera looks for me—and obliges me to look, leaving as my only option not to look. Further, the movie condenses something that takes hours to a few minutes, leaving only interesting parts presented in an interesting way, that is, with the intent to stir or shock. The dramatic is dramatized, by the didactics of layout and montage. We turn the page in a photo-magazine, a new sequence starts in a movie, making a contrast that is sharper than the contrast between successive events in real time.

Nothing could be more instructive about the meaning of photography for us—as, among other things, a method of hyping up the real—than the attacks on Antonioni's film in the Chinese press in early 1974. They make a negative catalogue of all the devices of modern photography, still and film.* While for us photography is intimately connected with discontinuous ways of seeing (the point is precisely to see the whole by means of a part—an arresting detail, a striking way of cropping), in China it is connected only with continuity. Not only are there proper subjects for the camera, those which are positive, inspirational (exemplary activities, smiling people, bright weather), and orderly, but there are proper ways of photographing, which derive from notions about the moral order of space that preclude the very idea of photographic seeing. Thus Antonioni was reproached for photographing things that were old, or

---

*See *A Vicious Motive, Despicable Tricks—A Criticism of Antonioni's Anti-China Film "China"* (Peking: Foreign Languages Press, 1974), an eighteen-page pamphlet (unsigned) which reproduces an article that appeared in the paper *Renminh Ribao* on January 30, 1974; and "Repudiating Antonioni's Anti-China Film," *Peking Review,* No. 8 (February 22, 1974), which supplies abridged versions of three other articles published that month. The aim of these articles is not, of course, to expound a view of photography—their interest on that score is inadvertent—but to construct a model ideological enemy, as in other mass educational campaigns staged during this period. Given this purpose, it was as unnecessary for the tens of millions mobilized in the meetings held in schools, factories, army units, and communes around the country to "Criticize Antonioni's Anti-China Film" to have actually seen *Chung Kuo* as it was for the participants in the "Criticize Lin Piao and Confucius" campaign of 1976 to have read a text of Confucius.

old-fashioned—"he sought out and took dilapidated walls and blackboard newspapers discarded long ago"; paying "no attention to big and small tractors working in the fields, [he] chose only a donkey pulling a stone roller"—and for showing undecorous moments—"he disgustingly filmed people blowing their noses and going to the latrine"—and undisciplined movement—"instead of taking shots of pupils in the classroom in our factory-run primary school, he filmed the children running out of the classroom after a class." And he was accused of denigrating the right subjects by his way of photographing them: by using "dim and dreary colors" and hiding people in "dark shadows"; by treating the same subject with a variety of shots—"there are sometimes long-shots, sometimes close-ups, sometimes from the front, and sometimes from behind"—that is, for not showing things from the point of view of a single, ideally placed observer; by using high and low angles—"The camera was intentionally turned on this magnificent modern bridge from very bad angles in order to make it appear crooked and tottering"; and by not taking enough full shots—"He racked his brain to get such close-ups in an attempt to distort the people's image and uglify their spiritual outlook."

Besides the mass-produced photographic iconography of revered leaders, revolutionary kitsch, and cultural treasures, one often sees photographs of a private sort in China. Many people possess pictures of their loved ones, tacked to the wall or stuck under the glass on top of the dresser or office desk. A large number of these are the sort of snapshots taken here at family gatherings and on trips; but none is a candid photograph, not even of the kind that the most unsophisticated camera user in this society finds normal—a baby crawling on the floor, someone in mid-gesture. Sports photographs show the team as a group, or only the most stylized balletic moments of play: generally, what people do with the camera is assemble for it, then line up in a row or two. There is no interest in catching a subject in movement. This is, one supposes, partly because of certain old conventions of decorum in conduct and imagery. And it is the characteristic visual taste of those at the first stage of camera culture, when the image is defined as something that can be stolen from its owner; thus, Antonioni was reproached for "forcibly taking shots against people's wishes," like "a thief." Possession of a camera does not license intrusion, as it does in this society whether people like it or not. (The good manners of a camera culture dictate that one is supposed to pretend not to notice when one is being photographed by a stranger in a public place as long as the photographer stays at a discreet distance—that is, one is supposed neither to forbid the picture-taking nor to start posing.) Unlike here, where we pose where we can and yield when we must, in China taking pictures is always a ritual; it always involves posing and, necessarily, consent. Someone who "deliberately stalked people who were unaware of his intention to film them" was depriving people and things of their right to pose, in order to look their best.

Antonioni devoted nearly all of the sequence in *Chung Kuo* about Peking's Tien An Men Square, the country's foremost goal of political pilgrimage, to the pilgrims waiting to be photographed. The interest to Antonioni of showing Chinese performing that elementary rite, having a trip documented by the camera, is evident: the photograph and being photographed are favorite contemporary subjects for the camera. To his critics, the desire of visitors to Tien An Men Square for a photograph souvenir

> is a reflection of their deep revolutionary feelings. But with bad intentions, Antonioni, instead of showing this reality, took shots only of people's clothing, movement, and expressions: here, someone's ruffled hair; there, people peering, their eyes dazzled by the sun; one moment, their sleeves; another, their trousers. . . .

The Chinese resist the photographic dismemberment of reality. Close-ups are not used. Even the postcards of antiquities and works of art sold in museums do not show part of something; the object is always photographed straight on, centered, evenly lit, and in its entirety.

We find the Chinese naïve for not perceiving the beauty of the cracked peeling door, the picturesqueness of disorder, the force of the odd angle and the significant detail, the poetry of the turned back. We have a modern notion of embellishment—beauty is not inherent in anything; it is to be found, by another way of seeing—as well as a wider notion of meaning, which photography's many uses illustrate and powerfully reinforce. The more numerous the variations of something, the richer its possibilities of meaning: thus, more is said with photographs in the West than in China today. Apart from whatever is true about *Chung Kuo* as an item of ideological merchandise (and the Chinese are not wrong in finding the film condescending), Antonioni's images simply mean *more* than any images the Chinese release of themselves. The Chinese don't want photographs to mean very much or to be very interesting. They do not want to see the world from an unusual angle, to discover new subjects. Photographs are supposed to display what has already been described. Photography for us is a double-edged instrument for producing clichés (the French word that means both trite expression and photographic negative) and for serving up "fresh" views. For the Chinese authorities, there are only clichés—which they consider not to be clichés but "correct" views.

In China today, only two realities are acknowledged. We see reality as hopelessly and interestingly plural. In China, what is defined as an issue for debate is one about which there are "two lines," a right one and a wrong one. Our society proposes a spectrum of discontinuous choices and perceptions. Theirs is constructed around a single, ideal observer; and photographs contribute their bit to the Great Monologue. For us, there are dispersed, interchangeable "points of view"; photography is a polylogue. The current Chinese ideology defines reality as a historical process structured by recurrent dualisms with clearly outlined, morally colored meanings; the past, for the most part, is simply judged as bad. For us, there are historical processes with awesomely complex and sometimes contradictory meanings; and arts which draw much of their value from our consciousness of time as history, like photography. (This is why the passing of time adds to the aesthetic value of photographs, and the scars of time make objects more rather than less enticing to photographers.) With the idea of history, we certify our interest in knowing the greatest number of things. The only use the Chinese are allowed to make of their history is didactic: their interest in history is narrow, moralistic, deforming, uncurious. Hence, photography in our sense has no place in their society.

The limits placed on photography in China only reflect the character of their society, a society unified by an ideology of stark, unremitting conflict. Our unlimited use of photographic images not only reflects but gives shape to this society, one unified by the denial of conflict. Our very notion of the world—the

capitalist twentieth century's "one world"—is like a photographic overview. The world is "one" not because it is united
but because a tour of its diverse contents does not reveal conflict but only an even more astounding diversity. This spurious
unity of the world is affected by translating its contents into
images. Images are always compatible, or can be made compatible, even when the realities they depict are not.

Photography does not simply reproduce the real, it recycles
it—a key procedure of a modern society. In the form of photographic images, things and events are put to new uses, assigned
new meanings, which go beyond the distinctions between the
beautiful and the ugly, the true and the false, the useful and the
useless, good taste and bad. Photography is one of the chief
means for producing that quality ascribed to things and situations which erases these distinctions: "the interesting." What
makes something interesting is that it can be seen to be like,
or analogous to, something else. There is an art and there are
fashions of seeing things in order to make them interesting; and
to supply this art, these fashions, there is a steady recycling of
the artifacts and tastes of the past. Clichés, recycled, become
meta-clichés. The photographic recycling makes clichés out of
unique objects, distinctive and vivid artifacts out of clichés.
Images of real things are interlayered with images of images.
The Chinese circumscribe the uses of photography so that there
are no layers or strata of images, and all images reinforce and
reiterate each other.* We make of photography a means by

* The Chinese concern for the reiterative function of images (and of words)
inspires the distributing of additional images, photographs that depict scenes in
which, clearly, no photographer could have been present; and the continuing
use of such photographs suggests how slender is the population's understanding of what photographic images and picture-taking imply. In his book *Chinese
Shadows*, Simon Leys gives an example from the "Movement to Emulate Lei
Feng," a mass campaign of the mid-1960s to inculcate the ideals of Maoist
citizenship built around the apotheosis of an Unknown Citizen, a conscript
named Lei Feng who died at twenty in a banal accident. Lei Feng Exhibitions
organized in the large cities included "photographic documents, such as 'Lei
Feng helping an old woman to cross the street,' 'Lei Feng secretly [sic] doing
his comrade's washing,' 'Lei Feng giving his lunch to a comrade who forgot
his lunch box,' and so forth," with, apparently, nobody questioning "the providential presence of a photographer during the various incidents in the life of
that humble, hitherto unknown soldier." In China, what makes an image true
is that it is good for people to see it.

which, precisely, anything can be said, any purpose served. What in reality is discrete, images join. In the form of a photograph the explosion of an A-bomb can be used to advertise a safe.

To us, the difference between the photographer as an individual eye and the photographer as an objective recorder seems fundamental, the difference often regarded, mistakenly, as separating photography as art from photography as document. But both are logical extensions of what photography means: note-taking on, potentially, everything in the world, from every possible angle. The same Nadar who took the most authoritative celebrity portraits of his time and did the first photo-interviews was also the first photographer to take aerial views; and when he performed "the Daguerreian operation" on Paris from a balloon in 1855 he immediately grasped the future benefit of photography to warmakers.

Two attitudes underlie this presumption that anything in the world is material for the camera. One finds that there is beauty or at least interest in everything, seen with an acute enough eye. (And the aestheticizing of reality that makes everything, anything, available to the camera is what also permits the co-opting of any photograph, even one of an utterly practical sort, as art.) The other treats everything as the object of some present or future use, as matter for estimates, decisions, and predictions. According to one attitude, there is nothing that should not be *seen*; according to the other, there is nothing that should not be *recorded*. Cameras implement an aesthetic view of reality by being a machine-toy that extends to everyone the possibility of making disinterested judgments about importance, interest, beauty. ("*That* would make a good picture.") Cameras implement the instrumental view of reality by gathering information that enables us to make a more accurate and much quicker response to whatever is going on. The response may of course be either repressive or benevolent: military reconnaissance photographs help snuff out lives, X-rays help save them.

Though these two attitudes, the aesthetic and the instrumental, seem to produce contradictory and even incompatible feelings about people and situations, that is the altogether characteristic contradiction of attitude which members of a society that divorces public from private are expected to share in and live with. And there is perhaps no activity which prepares us so well to live with these contradictory attitudes as does picture-taking, which lends itself so brilliantly to both. On the one hand, cameras arm vision in the service of power—of the state, of industry, of science. On the other hand, cameras make vision expressive in that mythical space known as private life. In China, where no space is left over from politics and moralism for expressions of aesthetic sensibility, only some things are to be photographed and only in certain ways. For us, as we become further detached from politics, there is more and more free space to fill up with exercises of sensibility such as cameras afford. One of the effects of the newer camera technology (video, instant movies) has been to turn even more of what is done with cameras in private to narcissistic uses—that is, to self-surveillance. But such currently popular uses of image-feedback in the bedroom, the therapy session, and the weekend conference seem far less momentous than video's potential as a tool for surveillance in public places. Presumably, the Chinese will eventually make the same instrumental uses of photography that we do, except, perhaps, this one. Our inclination to treat character as equivalent to behavior makes more acceptable a widespread public installation of the mechanized regard from the outside provided by cameras. China's far more repressive standards of order require not only monitoring behavior but changing hearts; there, surveillance is internalized to a degree without precedent, which suggests a more limited future in their society for the camera as a means of surveillance.

China offers the model of one kind of dictatorship, whose master idea is "the good," in which the most unsparing limits are placed on all forms of expression, including images. The future may offer another kind of dictatorship, whose master idea is "the interesting," in which images of all sorts, stereotyped and eccentric, proliferate. Something like this is suggested in Nabokov's *Invitation to a Beheading*. Its portrait of a model totalitarian state contains only one, omnipresent art: photography—and the friendly photographer who hovers around the hero's death cell turns out, at the end of the novel, to be the headsman. And there seems no way (short of undergoing a vast historical amnesia, as in China) of limiting the proliferation of photographic images. The only question is whether the function of the image-world created by cameras could be other than it is. The present function is clear enough, if one considers in what contexts photographic images are seen, what dependencies they create, what antagonisms they pacify—that is, what institutions they buttress, whose needs they really serve.

A capitalist society requires a culture based on images. It needs to furnish vast amounts of entertainment in order to stimulate buying and anesthetize the injuries of class, race, and sex. And it needs to gather unlimited amounts of information, the better to exploit natural resources, increase productivity, keep order, make war, give jobs to bureaucrats. The camera's twin capacities, to subjectivize reality and to objectify it, ideally serve these needs and strengthen them. Cameras define reality in the two ways essential to the workings of an advanced industrial society: as a spectacle (for masses) and as an object of surveillance (for rulers). The production of images also furnishes a ruling ideology. Social change is replaced by a change in images. The freedom to consume a plurality of images and goods is equated with freedom itself. The narrowing of free political choice to free economic consumption requires the unlimited production and consumption of images.

The final reason for the need to photograph everything lies in the very logic of consumption itself. To consume means to burn, to use up—and, therefore, to need to be replenished. As we make images and consume them, we need still more images; and still more. But images are not a treasure for which the world must be ransacked; they are precisely what is at hand wherever the eye falls. The possession of a camera can inspire something akin to lust. And like all credible forms of lust, it cannot be satisfied: first, because the possibilities of photography are infinite; and, second, because the project is finally self-devouring. The attempts by photographers to bolster up a depleted sense of reality contribute to the depletion. Our oppressive sense of the transience of everything is more acute since cameras gave us the means to "fix" the fleeting moment. We consume images at an ever faster rate and, as Balzac suspected cameras used up layers of the body, images consume reality. Cameras are the antidote and the disease, a means of appropriating reality and a means of making it obsolete.

The powers of photography have in effect de-Platonized our understanding of reality, making it less and less plausible to reflect upon our experience according to the distinction between images and things, between copies and originals. It suited Plato's derogatory attitude toward images to liken them to shadows—transitory, minimally informative, immaterial, impotent co-presences of the real things which cast them. But the force of photographic images comes from their being material realities in their own right, richly informative deposits left in the wake of whatever emitted them, potent means for turning the tables on reality—for turning *it* into a shadow. Images are more real than anyone could have supposed. And just because they are an unlimited resource, one that cannot be exhausted by consumerist waste, there is all the more reason to apply the conservationist remedy. If there can be a better way for the real world to include the one of images, it will require an ecology not only of real things but of images as well.

A Brief Anthology of Quotations
[HOMAGE TO W. B.]

I longed to arrest all beauty that came before me, and at length
the longing has been satisfied.

—Julia Margaret Cameron

I long to have such a memorial of every being dear to me in the
world. It is not merely the likeness which is precious in such
cases—but the association and the sense of nearness involved in
the thing . . . the fact of the *very shadow of the person* lying there
fixed forever! It is the very sanctification of portraits I think—
and it is not at all monstrous in me to say, what my brothers
cry out against so vehemently, that I would rather have such a
memorial of one I dearly loved, than the noblest artist's work
ever produced.

—Elizabeth Barrett
(1843, letter to Mary Russell Mitford)

Your photography is a record of your living, for anyone who
really sees. You may see and be affected by other people's ways,
you may even use them to find your own, but you will have
eventually to free yourself of them. That is what Nietzsche
meant when he said, "I have just read Schopenhauer, now I
have to get rid of him." He knew how insidious other people's
ways could be, particularly those which have the forcefulness
of profound experience, if you let them get between you and
your own vision.

—Paul Strand

That the outer man is a picture of the inner, and the face an
expression and revelation of the whole character, is a presumption likely enough in itself, and therefore a safe one to go on;
borne out as it is by the fact that people are always anxious to
see anyone who has made himself famous. . . . Photography . . .
offers the most complete satisfaction of our curiosity.

—Schopenhauer

To experience a thing as beautiful means: to experience it necessarily wrongly.

—Nietzsche

Now, for an absurdly small sum, we may become familiar not only with every famous locality in the world, but also with almost every man of note in Europe. The ubiquity of the photographer is something wonderful. All of us have seen the Alps and know Chamonix and the Mer de Glace by heart, though we have never braved the horrors of the Channel. . . . We have crossed the Andes, ascended Tenerife, entered Japan, "done" Niagara and the Thousand Isles, drunk delight of battle with our peers (at shop windows), sat at the councils of the mighty, grown familiar with kings, emperors and queens, prima donnas, pets of the ballet, and "well graced actors." Ghosts have we seen and have not trembled; stood before royalty and have not uncovered; and looked, in short, through a three-inch lens at every single pomp and vanity of this wicked but beautiful world.

—"D.P.," columnist in *Once a Week*
[London], June 1, 1861

It has quite justly been said of Atget that he photographed [deserted Paris streets] like scenes of crime. The scene of a crime, too, is deserted; it is photographed for the purpose of establishing evidence. With Atget, photographs become standard evidence for historical occurrences, and acquire a hidden political significance.

—Walter Benjamin

If I could tell the story in words, I wouldn't need to lug a camera.

—Lewis Hine

I went to Marseille. A small allowance enabled me to get along, and I worked with enjoyment. I had just discovered the Leica. It became the extension of my eye, and I have never been separated from it since I found it. I prowled the streets all day, feeling very strung-up and ready to pounce, determined to "trap" life—to preserve life in the act of living. Above all, I craved to

seize the whole essence, in the confines of one single photograph, of some situation that was in the process of unrolling
itself before my eyes.

—Henri Cartier-Bresson

It's hard to tell where you leave off
and the camera begins.

A Minolta 35mm SLR makes it almost effortless to capture the
world around you. Or express the world within you. It feels
comfortable in your hands. Your fingers fall into place naturally.
Everything works so smoothly that the camera becomes a part
of you. You never have to take your eye from the viewfinder
to make adjustments. So you can concentrate on creating the
picture. . . . And you're free to probe the limits of your imagination with a Minolta. More than 40 lenses in the superbly crafted
Rokkor-X and Minolta/Celtic systems let you bridge distances
or capture a spectacular "fisheye" panorama . . .

MINOLTA
When you are the camera and the camera is you
—advertisement (1976)

I photograph what I do not wish to paint and I paint what I
cannot photograph.

—Man Ray

Only with effort can the camera be forced to lie: basically it is
an honest medium: so the photographer is much more likely to
approach nature in a spirit of inquiry, of communion, instead of
with the saucy swagger of self-dubbed "artists." And contemporary vision, the new life, is based on honest approach to all
problems, be they morals or art. False fronts to buildings, false
standards in morals, subterfuges and mummery of all kinds,
must be, will be scrapped.

—Edward Weston

I attempt, through much of my work, to animate all things—
even so-called "inanimate" objects—with the spirit of man. I
have come, by degrees, to realize that this extremely animistic
projection rises, ultimately, from my profound fear and disquiet

over the accelerating mechanization of man's life; and the resulting attempts to stamp out individuality in all the spheres of
man's activity—this whole process being one of the dominant
expressions of our military-industrial society. . . . The creative
photographer sets free the *human contents* of objects; and imparts humanity to the inhuman world around him.

—Clarence John Laughlin

You can photograph anything now.

—Robert Frank

I always prefer to work in the studio. It isolates people from
their environment. They become in a sense . . . symbolic of
themselves. I often feel that people come to me to be photographed as they would go to a doctor or a fortune teller—to
find out how they are. So they're dependent on me. I have to
engage them. Otherwise there's nothing to photograph. The
concentration has to come from me and involve them. Sometimes the force of it grows so strong that sounds in the studio
go unheard. Time stops. We share a brief, intense intimacy.
But it's unearned. It has no past . . . no future. And when the
sitting is over—when the picture is done—there's nothing left
except the photograph . . . the photograph and a kind of embarrassment. They leave . . . and I don't know them. I've hardly
heard what they've said. If I meet them a week later in a room
somewhere, I expect they won't recognize me. Because I don't
feel I was really there. At least the part of me that was . . . is now
in the photograph. And the photographs have a reality for me
that the people don't. It's through the photographs that I know
them. Maybe it's in the nature of being a photographer. I'm
never really implicated. I don't have to have any real knowledge.
It's all a question of recognitions.

—Richard Avedon

The daguerreotype is not merely an instrument which serves to
draw nature . . . [it] gives her the power to reproduce herself.
—Louis Daguerre (1838, from a notice
circulated to attract investors)

The creations of man or nature never have more grandeur than in an Ansel Adams photograph, and his image can seize the viewer with more force than the natural object from which it was made.

> —advertisement for a book of
> photographs by Adams (1974)

**This Polaroid SX-70 photograph is part of
the collection of the Museum of Modern Art.**
The work is by Lucas Samaras, one of America's foremost artists. It is part of one of the world's most important collections. It was produced using the finest instant photographic system in the world, the Polaroid SX-70 Land camera. That same camera is owned by millions. A camera of extraordinary quality and versatility capable of exposures from 10.4 inches to infinity. . . . Samaras' work of art from the SX-70, a work of art in itself.

> —advertisement (1977)

Most of my photographs are compassionate, gentle, and personal. They tend to let the viewer see himself. They tend not to preach. And they tend not to pose as art.

> —Bruce Davidson

New forms in art are created by the canonization of peripheral forms.

> —Viktor Shklovsky

. . . a new industry has arisen which contributes not a little to confirming stupidity in its faith and to ruining what might have remained of the divine in the French genius. The idolatrous crowd postulates an ideal worthy of itself and appropriate to its nature—that is perfectly understandable. As far as painting and sculpture are concerned, the current credo of the sophisticated public, above all in France . . . is this: "I believe in Nature, and I believe only in Nature (there are good reasons for that). I believe that Art is, and cannot be other than, the exact reproduction of Nature. . . . Thus an industry that could give us a result identical to Nature would be the absolute of art." A vengeful God has granted the wishes of this multitude. Daguerre was his Messiah. And now the public says to itself: "Since photography gives us every guarantee of exactitude that we could desire (they really believe that, the idiots!), then photography and Art are the same thing." From that moment our squalid society rushed, Narcissus to a man, to gaze at its trivial image on a scrap of metal. . . . Some democratic writer ought to have seen here a cheap method of disseminating a loathing for history and for painting among the people. . . .

—Baudelaire

Life itself is not the reality. We are the ones who put life into stones and pebbles.

—Frederick Sommer

The young artist has recorded, stone by stone, the cathedrals of Strasbourg and Rheims in over a hundred different prints. Thanks to him we have climbed all the steeples . . . what we never could have discovered through our own eyes, he has seen for us . . . one might think the saintly artists of the Middle Ages had foreseen the daguerreotype in placing on high their statues and stone carvings where birds alone circling the spires could marvel at their detail and perfection. . . . The entire cathedral is reconstructed, layer on layer, in wonderful effects of sunlight, shadows, and rain. M. Le Secq, too, has built his monument.

—H. de Lacretelle,
in *La Lumière*, March 20, 1852

The need to bring things spatially and humanly "nearer" is almost an obsession today, as is the tendency to negate the unique or ephemeral quality of a given event by reproducing it photographically. There is an ever-growing compulsion to reproduce the object photographically, in close-up. . . .

—Walter Benjamin

It is no accident that the photographer becomes a photographer any more than the lion tamer becomes a lion tamer.

—Dorothea Lange

If I were just curious, it would be very hard to say to someone, "I want to come to your house and have you talk to me and tell me the story of your life." I mean people are going to say,

"You're crazy." Plus they're going to keep mighty guarded. But the camera is a kind of license. A lot of people, they want to be paid that much attention and that's a reasonable kind of attention to be paid.

—Diane Arbus

. . . Suddenly a small boy dropped to the ground next to me. I realized then that the police were not firing warning shots. They were shooting into the crowd. More children fell. . . . I began taking pictures of the little boy who was dying next to me. Blood poured from his mouth and some children knelt next to him and tried to stop the flow of blood. Then some children shouted they were going to kill me. . . . I begged them to leave me alone. I said I was a reporter and was there to record what happened. A young girl hit me on the head with a rock. I was dazed, but still on my feet. Then they saw reason and some led me away. All the time helicopters circled overhead and there was the sound of shooting. It was like a dream. A dream I will never forget.

—from the account by Alf Khumalo, a black
reporter on the *Johannesburg Sunday Times*,
of the outbreak of riots in Soweto, South Africa,
published in *The Observer* [London],
Sunday, June 20, 1976

Photography is the only "language" understood in all parts of the world, and bridging all nations and cultures, it links the family of man. Independent of political influence—where people are free—it reflects truthfully life and events, allows us to share in the hopes and despair of others, and illuminates political and social conditions. We become the eye-witnesses of the humanity and inhumanity of mankind . . .

—Helmut Gernsheim
(*Creative Photography* [1962])

Photography is a system of visual editing. At bottom, it is a matter of surrounding with a frame a portion of one's cone of vision, while standing in the right place at the right time. Like chess, or writing, it is a matter of choosing from among given possibilities, but in the case of photography the number of possibilities is not finite but infinite.

—John Szarkowski

Sometimes I would set up the camera in a corner of the room, sit some distance away from it with a remote control in my hand, and watch our people while Mr. Caldwell talked with them. It might be an hour before their faces or gestures gave us what we were trying to express, but the instant it occurred the scene was imprisoned on a sheet of film before they knew what had happened.

—Margaret Bourke-White

The picture of Mayor William Gaynor of New York at the moment of being shot by an assassin in 1910. The Mayor was about to board a ship to go on holiday in Europe as an American newspaper photographer arrived. He asked the Mayor to pose for a picture and as he raised his camera two shots were fired from the crowd. In the midst of this confusion the photographer remained calm and his picture of the blood-spattered Mayor lurching into the arms of an aide has become part of photographic history.

—a caption in *"Click"*:
A Pictorial History of the Photograph (1974)

I have been photographing our toilet, that glossy enameled receptacle of extraordinary beauty. . . . Here was every sensuous curve of the "human figure divine" but minus the imperfections. Never did the Greeks reach a more significant consummation to their culture, and it somehow reminded me, forward movement of finely progressing contours, of the Victory of Samothrace.

—Edward Weston

Good taste at this time in a technical democracy ends up to be nothing more than taste prejudice. If all that art does is create good or bad taste, then it has failed completely. In the question of taste analysis, it is just as easy to express good or bad taste in the kind of refrigerator, carpet or armchair that you have in your home. What good camera artists are trying to do now is to raise art beyond the level of mere taste. Camera Art must be completely devoid of logic. The logic vacuum must be there so that the viewer applies his own logic to it and the work, in fact, makes itself before the viewer's eyes. So that it becomes a direct reflection of the viewer's consciousness, logic, morals, ethics and taste. The work should act as a feedback mechanism to the viewer's own working model of himself.

—Les Levine ("Camera Art,"
in *Studio International*, July/August 1975)

Women and men—it's an impossible subject, because there can be no answers. We can find only bits and pieces of clues. And this small portfolio is just the crudest sketches of what it's all about. Maybe, today, we're planting the seeds of more honest relationships between women and men.

—Duane Michals

"Why do people keep photographs?"

"Why? Goodness knows! Why do people keep things—junk—trash, bits and pieces. They do—that's all there is to it!"

"Up to a point I agree with you. Some people keep things. Some people throw everything away as soon as they have done with it. That, yes, it is a matter of temperament. But I speak now especially of photographs. Why do people keep, in particular, *photographs*?"

"As I say, because they just don't throw things away. Or else because it reminds them—"

Poirot pounced on the words.

"Exactly. *It reminds them.* Now again we ask—why? *Why* does a woman keep a photograph of herself when young? And I say that the first reason is, essentially, vanity. She has been a pretty girl and she keeps a photograph of herself to remind her of what a pretty girl she was. It encourages her when her mirror tells her unpalatable things. She says, perhaps, to a friend, 'That was me when I was eighteen . . .' and she sighs . . . You agree?"

"Yes—yes, I should say that's true enough."

"Then that is reason No. 1. Vanity. Now reason No. 2. Sentiment."

"That's the same thing?"

"No, no, not quite. Because this leads you to preserve, not only your own photograph but that of someone else . . . A picture of your married daughter—when she was a child sitting on a hearthrug with tulle round her. . . . Very embarrassing to the subject sometimes, but mothers like to do it. And sons and daughters often keep pictures of their mothers, especially, say, if their mother died young. 'This was my mother as a girl.'"

"I'm beginning to see what you're driving at, Poirot."

"And there is, possibly, a *third* category. Not vanity, not sentiment, not love—perhaps *hate*—what do you say?"

"Hate?"

"Yes. To keep a desire for revenge alive. Someone who has injured you—you might keep a photograph to remind you, might you not?"

—from Agatha Christie's
Mrs. McGinty's Dead (1951)

Previously, at dawn that day, a commission assigned to the task had discovered the corpse of Antonio Conselheiro. It was lying in one of the huts next to the arbor. After a shallow layer of earth had been removed, the body appeared wrapped in a sorry shroud—a filthy sheet—over which pious hands had strewn a few withered flowers. There, resting upon a reed mat, were the last remains of the "notorious and barbarous agitator". . . . They carefully disinterred the body, precious relic that it was— the sole prize, the only spoils of war this conflict had to offer!— taking the greatest of precautions to see that it did not fall apart. . . . They photographed it afterward and drew up an affidavit in due form, certifying its identity; for the entire nation must be thoroughly convinced that at last this terrible foe had been done away with.

—from Euclides da Cunha's
Rebellion in the Backlands (1902)

Men still kill one another, they have not yet understood how they live, why they live; politicians fail to observe that the earth is an entity, yet television (Telehor) has been invented: the "Far Seer"—tomorrow we shall be able to look into the heart of our fellow-man, be everywhere and yet be alone; illustrated books, newspapers, magazines are printed—in millions. The unambiguousness of the real, the truth in the everyday situation is there for all classes. **The *hygiene of the optical*, the health of the visible is slowly filtering through.**

—László Moholy-Nagy (1925)

As I progressed further with my project, it became obvious that it was really unimportant where I chose to photograph. The particular place simply provided an excuse to produce work. . . . you can only see what you are ready to see—what mirrors your mind at that particular time.

—George Tice

I photograph to find out what something will look like photographed.

—Garry Winogrand

The Guggenheim trips were like elaborate treasure hunts, with false clues mixed among the genuine ones. We were always being directed by friends to their own favorite sights or views or formations. Sometimes these tips paid off with real Weston prizes; sometimes the recommended item proved to be a dud . . . and we drove for miles with no payoffs. By that time, I had reached the point of taking no pleasure in scenery that didn't call Edward's camera out, so he didn't risk much when he settled back against the seat saying, "I'm not asleep—just resting my eyes"; he knew my eyes were at his service, and that the moment anything with a "Weston" look appeared, I would stop the car and wake him up.

—Charis Weston (quoted in Ben Maddow,
Edward Weston: Fifty Years [1973])

**Polaroid's SX-70. It won't let you stop.
Suddenly you see a picture everywhere you look. . . .**
Now you press the red electric button. Whirr . . . whoosh . . . and there it is. You watch your picture come to life, growing more vivid, more detailed, until minutes later you have a print as real as life. Soon you're taking rapid-fire shots—as fast as every 1.5 seconds!—as you search for new angles or make copies on the spot. The SX-70 becomes like a part of you, as it slips through life effortlessly. . . .

—advertisement (1975)

. . . we *regard* the photograph, the picture on our wall, as the object itself (the man, landscape, and so on) depicted there.

This need not have been so. We could easily imagine people who did not have this relation to such pictures. Who, for example, would be repelled by photographs, because a face without colour and even perhaps a face in reduced proportions struck them as inhuman.

—Wittgenstein

Is it an instant picture of . . .

the destructive test of an axle?
the proliferation of a virus?
a forgettable lab setup?
the scene of the crime?
the eye of a green turtle?
the divisional sales chart?
chromosomal aberrations?
page 173 of Gray's Anatomy?
an electrocardiogram read-out?
a line conversion of half-tone art?
the three-millionth 8¢ Eisenhower stamp?
a hairline fracture of the fourth vertebra?
a copy of that irreplaceable 35mm slide?
your new diode, magnified 13 times?
a metallograph of vanadium steel?
reduced type for mechanicals?
an enlarged lymph node?
the electrophoresis results?
the world's worst malocclusion?
the world's best-corrected malocclusion?

As you can see from the list . . . there's no limit to the kind of material that people need to record. Fortunately, as you can see from the list of Polaroid Land cameras below, there's almost no limit to the kind of photographic records you can get. And, since you get them on the spot, if anything's missing, you can re-shoot on the spot. . . .

—advertisement (1976)

An object that tells of the loss, destruction, disappearance of objects. Does not speak of itself. Tells of others. Will it include them?

—Jasper Johns

Belfast, Northern Ireland—The people of Belfast are buying picture postcards of their city's torment by the hundreds. The most popular shows a boy throwing a stone at a British armored car. . . . other cards show burned-out homes, troops in battle positions on city streets and children at play amid smoking rubble. Each card sells for approximately 25 cents in the three Gardener's shops.

"Even at that price, people have been buying them in bundles of five or six at a time," said Rose Lehane, manager of one shop. Mrs. Lehane said that nearly 1,000 cards were sold in four days.

Since Belfast has few tourists, she said, most of the buyers are local people, mostly young men who want them as "souvenirs."

Neil Shawcross, a Belfast man, bought two complete sets of the cards, explaining, "I think they're interesting mementoes of the times and I want my two children to have them when they grow up."

"The cards are good for people," said Alan Gardener, a director of the chain. "Too many people in Belfast try to cope with the situation here by closing their eyes and pretending it doesn't exist. Maybe something like this will jar them into seeing again."

"We have lost a lot of money through the troubles, with our stores being bombed and burned down," Mr. Gardener added. "If we can get a bit of money back from the troubles, well and good."

—from *The New York Times*, October 29, 1974
("Postcards of Belfast Strife Are Best-Sellers There")

Photography is a tool for dealing with things everybody knows about but isn't attending to. My photographs are intended to represent something you don't see.

—Emmet Gowin

The camera is a fluid way of encountering that other reality.

—Jerry N. Uelsmann

Oswiecim, Poland—Nearly 30 years after Auschwitz concentration camp was closed down, the underlying horror of the place
seems diminished by the souvenir stands, Pepsi-Cola signs and
the tourist-attraction atmosphere.

Despite chilling autumn rain, thousands of Poles and some
foreigners visit Auschwitz every day. Most are modishly dressed
and obviously too young to remember World War II.

They troop through the former prison barracks, gas chambers
and crematoria, looking with interest at such gruesome displays
as an enormous showcase filled with some of the human hair
the S.S. used to make into cloth. . . . At the souvenir stands,
visitors can buy a selection of Auschwitz lapel pins in Polish
and German, or picture postcards showing gas chambers and
crematoria, or even souvenir Auschwitz ballpoint pens which,
when held up to the light, reveal similar pictures.

—from *The New York Times*,
November 3, 1974 ("At Auschwitz,
a Discordant Atmosphere of Tourism")

The media have substituted themselves for the older world.
Even if we should wish to recover that older world we can do
it only by an intensive study of the ways in which the media
have swallowed it.

—Marshall McLuhan

. . . Many of the visitors were from the countryside, and some,
unfamiliar with city ways, spread out newspapers on the asphalt
on the other side of the palace moat, unwrapped their home-
cooking and chopsticks and sat there eating and chatting while
the crowds sidestepped. The Japanese addiction to snapshots
rose to fever pitch under the impetus of the august backdrop of
the palace gardens. Judging by the steady clicking of the shut-
ters, not only everybody present but also every leaf and blade of
grass must now be recorded on film, in all their aspects.

—from *The New York Times*, May 3, 1977
("Japan Enjoys 3 Holidays of 'Golden Week'
by Taking a 7-Day Vacation from Work")

I'm always mentally photographing everything as practice.
—Minor White

The daguerreotypes of all things are preserved . . . the imprints
of all that has existed live, spread out through the diverse zones
of infinite space.

—Ernest Renan

These people live again in print as intensely as when their images were captured on the old dry plates of sixty years ago. . . .
I am walking in their alleys, standing in their rooms and sheds
and workshops, looking in and out of their windows. And they
in turn seem to be aware of me.

—Ansel Adams (from the Preface to
Jacob A. Riis: Photographer & Citizen [1974])

Thus in the photographic camera we have the most reliable aid
to a beginning of objective vision. Everyone will be compelled
to see that which is optically true, is explicable in its own terms,
is objective, before he can arrive at any possible subjective position. This will abolish that pictorial and imaginative association
pattern which has remained unsuperseded for centuries and
which has been stamped upon our vision by great individual
painters.

   We have—through a hundred years of photography and two
decades of film—been enormously enriched in this respect. **We
may say that we see the world with entirely different eyes.**
Nevertheless, the total result to date amounts to little more
than a visual encyclopaedic achievement. This is not enough.
We wish to **produce** systematically, since it is important for life
that we create *new relationships.*

—László Moholy-Nagy (1925)

Any one who knows what the worth of family affection is
among the lower classes, and who has seen the array of little
portraits stuck over a labourer's fireplace . . . will perhaps feel
with me that in counteracting the tendencies, social and industrial, which every day are sapping the healthier family affections,
the sixpenny photograph is doing more for the poor than all the
philanthropists in the world.

—*Macmillan's Magazine* [London], September 1871

Who, in his opinion, would buy an instant movie camera? Dr. Land said he expects the housewife to be a good prospect. "All she has to do is point the camera, press the shutter release and in minutes relive her child's cute moment, or perhaps, birthday party. Then, there is the large number of people who prefer pictures to equipment. Golf and tennis fans can evaluate their swings in instant replay; industry, schools and other areas where instant replay coupled with easy-to-use equipment would be helpful. . . . Polavision's boundaries are as wide as your imagination. There is no end to the uses that will be found for this and future Polavision cameras."

—from *The New York Times*, May 8, 1977
("A Preview of Polaroid's New Instant Movies")

Most modern reproducers of life, even including the camera, really repudiate it. We gulp down evil, choke at good.

—Wallace Stevens

The war had thrust me, as a soldier, into the heart of a mechanical atmosphere. Here I discovered the beauty of the fragment. I sensed a new reality in the detail of a machine, in the common object. I tried to find the plastic value of these fragments of our modern life. I rediscovered them on the screen in the close-ups of objects which impressed and influenced me.

—Fernand Léger (1923)

575.20 **fields of photography**

> aerophotography, aerial photography
> astrophotography
> candid photography
> chromophotography
> chronophotography
> cinematography
> cinephotomicrography
> cystophotography
> heliophotography
> infrared photography
> macrophotography
> microphotography
> miniature photography

    phonophotography
    photogrammetry
    photomicrography
    photospectroheliography
    phototopography
    phototypography
    phototypy
    pyrophotography
    radiography
    radiophotography
    sculptography
    skiagraphy
    spectroheliography
    spectrophotography
    stroboscopic photography
    telephotography
    uranophotography
    X-ray photography

              —from *Roget's International Thesaurus,*
                                 Third Edition

The weight of words. The shock of photos.
                        —*Paris-Match*, advertisement

June 4, 1857. —Saw today, at the Hôtel Drouot, the first sale of photographs. Everything is becoming black in this century, and photography seems like the black clothing of things.

          .   .   .

November 15, 1861.—I sometimes think the day will come when all modern nations will adore a sort of American god, a god who will have been someone who lived as a human being and about whom much will have been written in the popular press: images of this god will be set up in the churches, not as the imagination of each individual painter may fancy him, not floating on a Veronica cloth, but fixed once and for all by photography. Yes, I foresee a photographed god, wearing spectacles.
        —from the *Journal* of Edmond and Jules de Goncourt

In the spring of 1921, two automatic photographic machines, recently invented abroad, were installed in Prague, which reproduced six or ten or more exposures of the same person on a single print.

When I took such a series of photographs to Kafka I said light-heartedly: "For a couple of krone one can have oneself photographed from every angle. The apparatus is a mechanical *Know-Thyself*."

"You mean to say, the *Mistake-Thyself*," said Kafka, with a faint smile.

I protested: "What do you mean? The camera cannot lie!"

"Who told you that?" Kafka leaned his head toward his shoulder. "Photography concentrates one's eye on the superficial. For that reason it obscures the hidden life which glimmers through the outlines of things like a play of light and shade. One can't catch that even with the sharpest lens. One has to grope for it by feeling. . . . This automatic camera doesn't multiply men's eyes but only gives a fantastically simplified fly eye's view."

—from Gustav Janouch's *Conversations with Kafka*

Life appears always fully present along the epidermis of his body: vitality ready to be squeezed forth entire in fixing the instant, in recording a brief weary smile, a twitch of the hand, the fugitive pour of sun through clouds. And not a tool, save the camera, is capable of registering such complex ephemeral responses, and expressing the full majesty of the moment. No hand can express it, for the reason that the mind cannot retain the unmutated truth of a moment sufficiently long to permit the slow fingers to notate large masses of related detail. The impressionists tried in vain to achieve the notation. For, consciously or unconsciously, what they were striving to demonstrate with their effects of light was the truth of moments; impressionism has ever sought to fix the wonder of the here, the now. But the momentary effects of lighting escaped them while they were busy analyzing; and their "impression" remains usually a series of impressions superimposed one upon the other. Stieglitz was better guided. He went directly to the instrument made for him.

—Paul Rosenfeld

The camera is my tool. Through it I give a reason to everything around me.

—André Kertész

*A double leveling down, or a method of leveling down
which double-crosses itself*

With the daguerreotype everyone will be able to have their portrait taken—formerly it was only the prominent; and at the same time everything is being done to make us all look exactly the same—so that we shall only need one portrait.

—Kierkegaard (1854)

Make picture of kaleidoscope.

—William H. Fox Talbot
(ms. note dated February 18, 1839)

ILLNESS AS METAPHOR

For Robert Silvers

ILLNESS is the night-side of life, a more onerous citizenship. Everyone who is born holds dual citizenship, in the kingdom of the well and in the kingdom of the sick. Although we all prefer to use only the good passport, sooner or later each of us is obliged, at least for a spell, to identify ourselves as citizens of that other place.

I want to describe, not what it is really like to emigrate to the kingdom of the ill and live there, but the punitive or sentimental fantasies concocted about that situation: not real geography, but stereotypes of national character. My subject is not physical illness itself but the uses of illness as a figure or metaphor. My point is that illness is *not* a metaphor, and that the most truthful way of regarding illness—and the healthiest way of being ill—is one most purified of, most resistant to, metaphoric thinking. Yet it is hardly possible to take up one's residence in the kingdom of the ill unprejudiced by the lurid metaphors with which it has been landscaped. It is toward an elucidation of those metaphors, and a liberation from them, that I dedicate this inquiry.

I

Two diseases have been spectacularly, and similarly, encumbered by the trappings of metaphor: tuberculosis and cancer.

The fantasies inspired by TB in the last century, by cancer now, are responses to a disease thought to be intractable and capricious—that is, a disease not understood—in an era in which medicine's central premise is that all diseases can be cured. Such a disease is, by definition, mysterious. For as long as its cause was not understood and the ministrations of doctors remained so ineffective, TB was thought to be an insidious, implacable theft of a life. Now it is cancer's turn to be the disease that doesn't knock before it enters, cancer that fills the role of an illness experienced as a ruthless, secret invasion—a role it will keep until, one day, its etiology becomes as clear and its treatment as effective as those of TB have become.

Although the way in which disease mystifies is set against a backdrop of new expectations, the disease itself (once TB, cancer today) arouses thoroughly old-fashioned kinds of dread. Any disease that is treated as a mystery and acutely enough feared will be felt to be morally, if not literally, contagious. Thus, a surprisingly large number of people with cancer find themselves being shunned by relatives and friends and are the object of practices of decontamination by members of their household, as if cancer, like TB, were an infectious disease. Contact with someone afflicted with a disease regarded as a mysterious malevolency inevitably feels like a trespass; worse, like the violation of a taboo. The very names of such diseases are felt to have a magic power. In Stendhal's *Armance* (1827), the hero's mother refuses to say "tuberculosis," for fear that pronouncing the word will hasten the course of her son's malady. And Karl Menninger has observed (in *The Vital Balance*) that "the very word 'cancer' is said to kill some patients who would not have succumbed (so quickly) to the malignancy from which they suffer." This observation is offered in support of anti-intellectual pieties and a facile compassion all too triumphant in contemporary medicine and psychiatry. "Patients who consult us because of their suffering and their distress and their disability," he continues, "have every right to resent being plastered with a damning index tab." Dr. Menninger recommends that physicians generally abandon "names" and "labels" ("our function is to help these people, not to further afflict them")—which would mean, in effect, increasing secretiveness and medical paternalism. It is not naming as such that is pejorative or damning, but the name "cancer." As long as a particular disease is treated as an evil, invincible predator, not just a disease, most people with cancer will indeed be demoralized by learning what disease they have. The solution is hardly to stop telling cancer patients the truth, but to rectify the conception of the disease, to de-mythicize it.

When, not so many decades ago, learning that one had TB was tantamount to hearing a sentence of death—as today, in the popular imagination, cancer equals death—it was common to conceal the identity of their disease from tuberculars and, after they died, from their children. Even with patients informed about their disease, doctors and family were reluctant to talk freely. "Verbally I don't learn anything definite," Kafka wrote to a friend in April 1924 from the sanatorium where he died two months later, "since in discussing tuberculosis . . . everybody drops into a shy, evasive, glassy-eyed manner of speech." Conventions of concealment with cancer are even more strenuous. In France and Italy it is still the rule for doctors to communicate a cancer diagnosis to the patient's family but not to the patient; doctors consider that the truth will be intolerable to all but exceptionally mature and intelligent patients. (A leading French oncologist has told me that fewer than a tenth of his patients know they have cancer.) In America—in part because of the doctors' fear of malpractice suits—there is now much more candor with patients, but the country's largest cancer hospital mails routine communications and bills to outpatients in envelopes that do not reveal the sender, on the assumption that the illness may be a secret from their families. Since getting cancer can be a scandal that jeopardizes one's love life, one's chance of promotion, even one's job, patients who know what they have tend to be extremely prudish, if not outright secretive, about their disease. And a federal law, the 1966 Freedom of Information Act, cites "treatment for cancer" in a clause exempting from disclosure matters whose disclosure "would be an unwarranted invasion of personal privacy." It is the only disease mentioned.

All this lying to and by cancer patients is a measure of how much harder it has become in advanced industrial societies to come to terms with death. As death is now an offensively meaningless event, so that disease widely considered a synonym for death is experienced as something to hide. The policy of equivocating about the nature of their disease with cancer patients reflects the conviction that dying people are best spared the news that they are dying, and that the good death is the sudden one, best of all if it happens while we're unconscious or asleep. Yet the modern denial of death does not explain the extent of the lying and the wish to be lied to; it does not touch the deepest dread. Someone who has had a coronary is at least as likely to die of another one within a few years as someone with cancer is likely to die soon from cancer. But no one thinks of concealing the truth from a cardiac patient: there is nothing shameful about a heart attack. Cancer patients are lied to, not just because the disease is (or is thought to be) a death sentence, but because it is felt to be obscene—in the original meaning of that word: ill-omened, abominable, repugnant to the senses. Cardiac disease implies a weakness, trouble, failure that is mechanical; there is no disgrace, nothing of the taboo that once

surrounded people afflicted with TB and still surrounds those
who have cancer. The metaphors attached to TB and to cancer
imply living processes of a particularly resonant and horrid kind.

2

Throughout most of their history, the metaphoric uses of TB
and cancer crisscross and overlap. The *Oxford English Dictionary* records "consumption" in use as a synonym for pulmonary tuberculosis as early as 1398.* (John of Trevisa: "Whan
the blode is made thynne, soo folowyth consumpcyon and
wastyng.") But the pre-modern understanding of cancer also
invokes the notion of consumption. The OED gives as the early
figurative definition of cancer: "Anything that frets, corrodes,
corrupts, or consumes slowly and secretly." (Thomas Paynell in
1528: "A canker is a melancolye impostume, eatynge partes of
the bodye.") The earliest literal definition of cancer is a growth,
lump, or protuberance, and the disease's name—from the
Greek *karkínos* and the Latin *cancer*, both meaning crab—was
inspired, according to Galen, by the resemblance of an external
tumor's swollen veins to a crab's legs; not, as many people think,
because a metastatic disease crawls or creeps like a crab. But
etymology indicates that tuberculosis was also once considered
a type of abnormal extrusion: the word tuberculosis—from the
Latin *tūberculum*, the diminutive of *tūber*, bump, swelling—
means a morbid swelling, protuberance, projection, or growth.[†]
Rudolf Virchow, who founded the science of cellular pathology
in the 1850s, thought of the tubercle as a tumor.

   Thus, from late antiquity until quite recently, tuberculosis

---

*Godefroy's *Dictionnaire de l'ancienne langue française* cites Bernard de Gordon's *Pratiqum* (1495): "*Tisis, c'est ung ulcere du polmon qui consume tout le
corp.*"

[†] The same etymology is given in the standard French dictionaries. "*La tuber-
cule*" was introduced in the sixteenth century by Ambroise Paré from the Latin
tūberculum, meaning "*petite bosse*" (little lump). In Diderot's *Encyclopédie*, the
entry on tuberculosis (1765) cites the definition given by the English physician
Richard Morton in his *Phthisiologia* (1689): "*des petits tumeurs qui paraissent
sur la surface du corps.*" In French, all tiny surface tumors were once called
"*tubercules*"; the word became limited to what we identify as TB only after
Koch's discovery of the tubercle bacillus.

was—typologically—cancer. And cancer was described, like TB, as a process in which the body was consumed. The modern conceptions of the two diseases could not be set until the advent of cellular pathology. Only with the microscope was it possible to grasp the distinctiveness of cancer, as a type of cellular activity, and to understand that the disease did not always take the form of an external or even palpable tumor. (Before the mid-nineteenth century, nobody could have identified leukemia as a form of cancer.) And it was not possible definitively to separate cancer from TB until after 1882, when tuberculosis was discovered to be a bacterial infection. Such advances in medical thinking enabled the leading metaphors of the two diseases to become truly distinct and, for the most part, contrasting. The modern fantasy about cancer could then begin to take shape—a fantasy which from the 1920s on would inherit most of the problems dramatized by the fantasies about TB, but with the two diseases and their symptoms conceived in quite different, almost opposing, ways.

TB is understood as a disease of one organ, the lungs, while cancer is understood as a disease that can turn up in any organ and whose outreach is the whole body.

TB is understood as a disease of extreme contrasts: white pallor and red flush, hyperactivity alternating with languidness. The spasmodic course of the disease is illustrated by what is thought of as the prototypical TB symptom, coughing. The sufferer is wracked by coughs, then sinks back, recovers breath, breathes normally; then coughs again. Cancer is a disease of growth (sometimes visible; more characteristically, inside), of abnormal, ultimately lethal growth that is measured, incessant, steady. Although there may be periods in which tumor growth is arrested (remissions), cancer produces no contrasts like the oxymorons of behavior—febrile activity, passionate resignation—thought to be typical of TB. The tubercular is pallid some of the time; the pallor of the cancer patient is unchanging.

TB makes the body transparent. The X-rays which are the standard diagnostic tool permit one, often for the first time, to see one's insides—to become transparent to oneself. While TB is understood to be, from early on, rich in visible symptoms (progressive emaciation, coughing, languidness, fever), and can be suddenly and dramatically revealed (the blood on the handkerchief), in cancer the main symptoms are thought to be, characteristically, invisible—until the last stage, when it is too late. The disease, often discovered by chance or through a routine medical checkup, can be far advanced without exhibiting any appreciable symptoms. One has an opaque body that must be taken to a specialist to find out if it contains cancer. What the patient cannot perceive, the specialist will determine by analyzing tissues taken from the body. TB patients may see their X-rays or even possess them: the patients at the sanatorium in *The Magic Mountain* carry theirs around in their breast pockets. Cancer patients don't look at their biopsies.

TB was—still is—thought to produce spells of euphoria, increased appetite, exacerbated sexual desire. Part of the regimen for patients in *The Magic Mountain* is a second breakfast, eaten with gusto. Cancer is thought to cripple vitality, make eating an ordeal, deaden desire. Having TB was imagined to be an aphrodisiac, and to confer extraordinary powers of seduction. Cancer is considered to be de-sexualizing. But it is characteristic of TB that many of its symptoms are deceptive—liveliness that comes from enervation, rosy cheeks that look like a sign of health but come from fever—and an upsurge of vitality may be a sign of approaching death. (Such gushes of energy will generally be self-destructive, and may be destructive of others: recall the Old West legend of Doc Holliday, the tubercular gunfighter released from moral restraints by the ravages of his disease.) Cancer has only true symptoms.

TB is disintegration, febrilization, dematerialization; it is a disease of liquids—the body turning to phlegm and mucus and sputum and, finally, blood—and of air, of the need for better air. Cancer is degeneration, the body tissues turning to something hard. Alice James, writing in her journal a year before she died from cancer in 1892, speaks of "this unholy granite substance in my breast." But this lump is alive, a fetus with its own will. Novalis, in an entry written around 1798 for his encyclopedia project, defines cancer, along with gangrene, as "full-fledged *parasites*—they grow, are engendered, engender, have their structure, secrete, eat." Cancer is a demonic pregnancy. St. Jerome must have been thinking of cancer when he wrote: "The one there with his swollen belly is pregnant with his own death" ("*Alius tumenti aqualiculo mortem parturit*"). Though the course of both diseases is emaciating, losing weight from TB is understood very differently from losing weight from cancer. In TB, the person is "consumed," burned up. In cancer, the patient is "invaded" by alien cells, which multiply, causing an atrophy or blockage of bodily functions. The cancer patient "shrivels" (Alice James's word) or "shrinks" (Wilhelm Reich's word).

TB is a disease of time; it speeds up life, highlights it, spiritualizes it. In both English and French, consumption "gallops." Cancer has stages rather than gaits; it is (eventually) "terminal." Cancer works slowly, insidiously: the standard euphemism in obituaries is that someone has "died after a long illness." Every characterization of cancer describes it as slow, and so it was first used metaphorically. "The word of hem crepith as a kankir," Wyclif wrote in 1382 (translating a phrase in II Timothy 2:17); and among the earliest figurative uses of cancer are as a metaphor for "idleness" and "sloth."* Metaphorically, cancer is not so much a disease of time as a disease or pathology of space. Its principal metaphors refer to topography (cancer "spreads" or "proliferates" or is "diffused"; tumors are surgically "excised"), and its most dreaded consequence, short of death, is the mutilation or amputation of part of the body.

TB is often imagined as a disease of poverty and deprivation— of thin garments, thin bodies, unheated rooms, poor hygiene, inadequate food. The poverty may not be as literal as Mimi's garret in *La Bohème*; the tubercular Marguerite Gautier in *La Dame aux camélias* lives in luxury, but inside she is a waif. In contrast, cancer is a disease of middle-class life, a disease associated with affluence, with excess. Rich countries have the highest cancer rates, and the rising incidence of the disease is seen as resulting, in part, from a diet rich in fat and proteins and from the toxic effluvia of the industrial economy that creates affluence. The treatment of TB is identified with the stimulation of appetite, cancer treatment with nausea and the loss of appetite. The undernourished nourishing themselves—alas, to no avail. The overnourished, unable to eat.

The TB patient was thought to be helped, even cured, by a change in environment. There was a notion that TB was a

---

*As cited in the OED, which gives as an early figurative use of "canker": "that pestilent and most infectious canker, idlenesse"—T. Palfreyman, 1564. And of "cancer" (which replaced "canker" around 1700): "Sloth is a Cancer, eating up that Time Princes should cultivate for Things sublime"—Edmund Ken, 1711.

wet disease, a disease of humid and dank cities. The inside of the body became damp ("moisture in the lungs" was a favored locution) and had to be dried out. Doctors advised travel to high, dry places—the mountains, the desert. But no change of surroundings is thought to help the cancer patient. The fight is all inside one's own body. It may be, is increasingly thought to be, something in the environment that has caused the cancer. But once cancer is present, it cannot be reversed or diminished by a move to a better (that is, less carcinogenic) environment.

TB is thought to be relatively painless. Cancer is thought to be, invariably, excruciatingly painful. TB is thought to provide an easy death, while cancer is the spectacularly wretched one. For over a hundred years TB remained the preferred way of giving death a meaning—an edifying, refined disease. Nineteenth-century literature is stocked with descriptions of almost symptomless, unfrightened, beatific deaths from TB, particularly of young people, such as Little Eva in *Uncle Tom's Cabin* and Dombey's son Paul in *Dombey and Son* and Smike in *Nicholas Nickleby*, where Dickens described TB as the "dread disease" which "refines" death

> of its grosser aspect . . . in which the struggle between soul and body is so gradual, quiet, and solemn, and the result so sure, that day by day, and grain by grain, the mortal part wastes and withers away, so that the spirit grows light and sanguine with its lightening load. . . .*

Contrast these ennobling, placid TB deaths with the ignoble, agonizing cancer deaths of Eugene Gant's father in Thomas Wolfe's *Of Time and the River* and of the sister in Bergman's film *Cries and Whispers.* The dying tubercular is pictured as made more beautiful and more soulful; the person dying of cancer is portrayed as robbed of all capacities of self-transcendence, humiliated by fear and agony.

----

*Nearly a century later, in his edition of Katherine Mansfield's posthumously published *Journal,* John Middleton Murry uses similar language to describe Mansfield on the last day of her life. "I have never seen, nor shall I ever see, any one so beautiful as she was on that day; it was as though the exquisite perfection which was always hers had taken possession of her completely. To use her own words, the last grain of 'sediment,' the last 'traces of earthly degradation,' were departed for ever. But she had lost her life to save it."

These are contrasts drawn from the popular mythology of both diseases. Of course, many tuberculars died in terrible pain, and some people die of cancer feeling little or no pain to the end; the poor and the rich both get TB and cancer; and not everyone who has TB coughs. But the mythology persists. It is not just because pulmonary tuberculosis is the most common form of TB that most people think of TB, in contrast to cancer, as a disease of one organ. It is because the myths about TB do not fit the brain, larynx, kidneys, long bones, and other sites where the tubercle bacillus can also settle, but do have a close fit with the traditional imagery (breath, life) associated with the lungs.

While TB takes on qualities assigned to the lungs, which are part of the upper, spiritualized body, cancer is notorious for attacking parts of the body (colon, bladder, rectum, breast, cervix, prostate, testicles) that are embarrassing to acknowledge. Having a tumor generally arouses some feelings of shame, but in the hierarchy of the body's organs, lung cancer is felt to be less shameful than rectal cancer. And one non-tumor form of cancer now turns up in commercial fiction in the role once monopolized by TB, as the romantic disease which cuts off a young life. (The heroine of Erich Segal's *Love Story* dies of leukemia—the "white" or TB-like form of the disease, for which no mutilating surgery can be proposed—not of stomach or breast cancer.) A disease of the lungs is, metaphorically, a disease of the soul.* Cancer, as a disease that can strike anywhere, is a disease of the body. Far from revealing anything spiritual, it reveals that the body is, all too woefully, just the body.

Such fantasies flourish because TB and cancer are thought to be much more than diseases that usually are (or were) fatal. They are identified with death itself. In *Nicholas Nickleby*, Dickens apostrophized TB as the

---

* The Goncourt brothers, in their novel *Madame Gervaisais* (1869), called TB "this illness of the lofty and noble parts of the human being," contrasting it with "the diseases of the crude, base organs of the body, which clog and soil the patient's mind. . . ." In Mann's early story "Tristan," the young wife has tuberculosis of the trachea: ". . . the trachea, and not the lungs, thank God! But it is a question whether, if it had been the lungs, the new patient could have looked any more pure and ethereal, any remoter from the concerns of this world, than she did now as she leaned back pale and weary in her chaste white-enamelled arm-chair, beside her robust husband, and listened to the conversation."

disease in which death and life are so strangely blended, that
death takes the glow and hue of life, and life the gaunt and grisly
form of death; disease which medicine never cured, wealth never
warded off, or poverty could boast exemption from. . . .

And Kafka wrote to Max Brod in October 1917 that he had
"come to think that tuberculosis . . . is no special disease, or
not a disease that deserves a special name, but only the germ of
death itself, intensified. . . ." Cancer inspires similar speculations.
Georg Groddeck, whose remarkable views on cancer in *The
Book of the It* (1923) anticipate those of Wilhelm Reich, wrote:

Of all the theories put forward in connection with cancer, only
one has in my opinion survived the passage of time, namely, that
cancer leads through definite stages to death. I mean by that that
what is not fatal is not cancer. From that you may conclude that
I hold out no hope of a new method of curing cancer . . . [only]
the many cases of so-called cancer. . . .

For all the progress in treating cancer, many people still subscribe to Groddeck's equation: cancer = death. But the metaphors surrounding TB and cancer reveal much about the idea
of the morbid, and how it has evolved from the nineteenth
century (when TB was the most common cause of death) to our
time (when cancer is the most dreaded disease). The Romantics
moralized death in a new way: with the TB death, which dissolved the gross body, etherealized the personality, expanded
consciousness. It was equally possible, through fantasies about
TB, to aestheticize death. Thoreau, who had TB, wrote in 1852:
"Death and disease are often beautiful, like . . . the hectic glow
of consumption." Nobody conceives of cancer the way TB was
thought of—as a decorative, often lyrical death. Cancer is a rare
and still scandalous subject for poetry; and it seems unimaginable to aestheticize the disease.

3

The most striking similarity between the myths of TB and of
cancer is that both are, or were, understood as diseases of passion. Fever in TB was a sign of an inward burning: the tubercular is someone "consumed" by ardor, that ardor leading to

the dissolution of the body. The use of metaphors drawn from TB to describe love—the image of a "diseased" love, of a passion that "consumes"—long antedates the Romantic movement.* Starting with the Romantics, the image was inverted, and TB was conceived as a variant of the disease of love. In a heartbreaking letter of November 1, 1820 from Naples, Keats, forever separated from Fanny Brawne, wrote, "If I had any chance of recovery [from tuberculosis], this passion would kill me." As a character in *The Magic Mountain* explains: "Symptoms of disease are nothing but a disguised manifestation of the power of love; and all disease is only love transformed."

As once TB was thought to come from too much passion, afflicting the reckless and sensual, today many people believe that cancer is a disease of insufficient passion, afflicting those who are sexually repressed, inhibited, unspontaneous, incapable of expressing anger. These seemingly opposite diagnoses are actually not so different versions of the same view (and deserve, in my opinion, the same amount of credence). For both psychological accounts of a disease stress the insufficiency or the balking of vital energies. As much as TB was celebrated as a disease of passion, it was also regarded as a disease of repression. The high-minded hero of Gide's *The Immoralist* contracts TB (paralleling what Gide perceived to be his own story) because he has repressed his true sexual nature; when Michel accepts Life, he recovers. With this scenario, today Michel would have to get cancer.

As cancer is now imagined to be the wages of repression, so TB was once explained as the ravages of frustration. What is called a liberated sexual life is believed by some people today to stave off cancer, for virtually the same reason that sex was often prescribed to tuberculars as a therapy. In *The Wings of the Dove*, Milly Theale's doctor advises a love affair as a cure for her TB; and it is when she discovers that her duplicitous suitor, Merton Densher, is secretly engaged to her friend Kate Croy that she dies. And in his letter of November 1820, Keats exclaimed: "My dear Brown, I should have had her when I was in health, and I should have remained well."

---

*As in Act II, Scene 2 of Sir George Etherege's play *The Man of Mode* (1676): "When love grows diseas'd, the best thing we can do is to put it to a violent death; I cannot endure the torture of a lingring and consumptive passion."

According to the mythology of TB, there is generally some passionate feeling which provokes, which expresses itself in, a bout of TB. But the passions must be thwarted, the hopes blighted. And the passion, although usually love, could be a political or moral passion. At the end of Turgenev's *On the Eve* (1860), Insarov, the young Bulgarian revolutionary-in-exile who is the hero of the novel, realizes that he can't return to Bulgaria. In a hotel in Venice, he sickens with longing and frustration, gets TB, and dies.

According to the mythology of cancer, it is generally a steady repression of feeling that causes the disease. In the earlier, more optimistic form of this fantasy, the repressed feelings were sexual; now, in a notable shift, the repression of violent feelings is imagined to cause cancer. The thwarted passion that killed Insarov was idealism. The passion that people think will give them cancer if they don't discharge it is rage. There are no modern Insarovs. Instead, there are cancerphobes like Norman Mailer, who recently explained that had he not stabbed his wife (and acted out "a murderous nest of feeling") he would have gotten cancer and "been dead in a few years himself." It is the same fantasy that was once attached to TB, but in rather a nastier version.

The source for much of the current fancy that associates cancer with the repression of passion is Wilhelm Reich, who defined cancer as "a disease following emotional resignation—a bio-energetic shrinking, a giving up of hope." Reich illustrated his influential theory with Freud's cancer, which he thought began when Freud, naturally passionate and "very unhappily married," yielded to resignation:

> He lived a very calm, quiet, decent family life, but there is little doubt that he was very much dissatisfied genitally. Both his resignation and his cancer were evidence of that. Freud had to give up, as a person. He had to give up his personal pleasures, his personal delights, in his middle years. . . . if my view of cancer is correct, you just give up, you resign—and, then, you shrink.

Tolstoy's "The Death of Ivan Ilyich" is often cited as a case history of the link between cancer and characterological resignation. But the same theory has been applied to TB by Groddeck, who defined TB as

the pining to die away. The desire must die away, then, the desire
for the in and out, the up and down of erotic love, which is symbolized in breathing. And with the desire the lungs die away. . . .
the body dies away. . . .*

As do accounts of cancer today, the typical accounts of TB
in the nineteenth century all feature resignation as the cause
of the disease. They also show how, as the disease advances,
one *becomes* resigned—Mimi and Camille die because of their
renunciation of love, beatified by resignation. Robert Louis
Stevenson's autobiographical essay "Ordered South," written in
1874, describes the stages whereby the tubercular is "tenderly
weaned from the passion of life," and an ostentatious resignation is characteristic of the rapid decline of tuberculars as
reported at length in fiction. In *Uncle Tom's Cabin*, Little Eva
dies with preternatural serenity, announcing to her father a few
weeks before the end: "My strength fades away every day, and
I know I must go." All we learn of Milly Theale's death in *The
Wings of the Dove* is that "she turned her face to the wall." TB
was represented as the prototypical passive death. Often it was
a kind of suicide. In Joyce's "The Dead," Michael Furey stands
in the rain in Gretta Conroy's garden the night before she leaves
for the convent school; she implores him to go home; "he said
he did not want to live" and a week later he dies.

TB sufferers may be represented as passionate but are, more
characteristically, deficient in vitality, in life force. (As in the contemporary updating of this fantasy, the cancer-prone are those
who are not sufficiently sensual or in touch with their anger.)
This is how those two famously tough-minded observers, the
Goncourt brothers, explain the TB of their friend Murger (the
author of *Scènes de la vie de Bohème*): he is dying "for want of
vitality with which to withstand suffering." Michael Furey was
"very delicate," as Gretta Conroy explains to her "stout, tallish,"
virile, suddenly jealous husband. TB is celebrated as the disease
of born victims, of sensitive, passive people who are not quite
life-loving enough to survive. (What is hinted at by the yearning

* The passage continues: ". . . because desire increases during the illness, because
the guilt of the ever-repeated symbolic dissipation of semen in the sputum is
continually growing greater, . . . because the It allows pulmonary disease to
bring beauty to the eyes and cheek, alluring poisons!"

but almost somnolent belles of Pre-Raphaelite art is made explicit in the emaciated, hollow-eyed, tubercular girls depicted by Edvard Munch.) And while the standard representation of a death from TB places the emphasis on the perfected sublimation of feeling, the recurrent figure of the tubercular courtesan indicates that TB was also thought to make the sufferer sexy.

Like all really successful metaphors, the metaphor of TB was rich enough to provide for two contradictory applications. It described the death of someone (like a child) thought to be too "good" to be sexual: the assertion of an angelic psychology. It was also a way of describing sexual feelings—while lifting the responsibility for libertinism, which is blamed on a state of objective, physiological decadence or deliquescence. It was both a way of describing sensuality and promoting the claims of passion and a way of describing repression and advertising the claims of sublimation, the disease inducing both a "numbness of spirit" (Robert Louis Stevenson's words) and a suffusion of higher feelings. Above all, it was a way of affirming the value of being more conscious, more complex psychologically. Health becomes banal, even vulgar.

4

It seems that having TB had already acquired the associations of being romantic by the mid-eighteenth century. In Act I, Scene I of Oliver Goldsmith's satire on life in the provinces, *She Stoops to Conquer* (1773), Mr. Hardcastle is mildly remonstrating with Mrs. Hardcastle about how much she spoils her loutish son by a former marriage, Tony Lumpkin:

MRS. H.: And am I to blame? The poor boy was always too sickly to do any good. A school would be his death. When he comes to be a little stronger, who knows what a year or two's Latin may do for him?

MR. H.: Latin for him! A cat and fiddle. No, no, the ale-house and the stable are the only schools he'll ever go to.

MRS. H.: Well, we must not snub the poor boy now, for I believe we shan't have him long among us. Any body that looks in his face may see he's consumptive.

MR. H.: Ay, if growing too fat be one of the symptoms.

MRS. H.: He coughs sometimes.

MR. H.: Yes, when his liquor goes the wrong way.

MRS. H.: I'm actually afraid of his lungs.

MR. H.: And truly so am I; for he sometimes whoops like a speaking trumpet—[TONY *hallooing behind the Scenes*]—O there he goes—A very consumptive figure, truly.

This exchange suggests that the fantasy about TB was already a received idea, for Mrs. Hardcastle is nothing but an anthology of clichés of the smart London world to which she aspires, and which was the audience of Goldsmith's play.* Goldsmith presumes that the TB myth is already widely disseminated—TB being, as it were, the anti-gout. For snobs and parvenus and social climbers, TB was one index of being genteel, delicate, sensitive. With the new mobility (social and geographical) made possible in the eighteenth century, worth and station are not given; they must be asserted. They were asserted through new notions about clothes ("fashion") and new attitudes toward illness. Both clothes (the outer garment of the body) and illness (a kind of interior décor of the body) became tropes for new attitudes toward the self.

Shelley wrote on July 27, 1820 to Keats, commiserating as one TB sufferer to another, that he has learned "that you continue to wear a consumptive appearance." This was no mere turn of phrase. Consumption was understood as a manner of appearing, and that appearance became a staple of nineteenth-century manners. It became rude to eat heartily. It was glamorous to look sickly. "Chopin was tubercular at a time when good health was not chic," Camille Saint-Saëns wrote in 1913. "It was fashionable to be pale and drained; Princess Belgiojoso strolled along the boulevards . . . pale as death in person." Saint-Saëns was right to connect an artist, Chopin, with the most celebrated *femme fatale* of the period, who did a great deal to popularize

---

*Goldsmith, who was trained as a doctor and practiced medicine for a while, had other clichés about TB. In his essay "On Education" (1759) Goldsmith wrote that a diet lightly salted, sugared, and seasoned "corrects any consumptive habits, not unfrequently found amongst the children of city parents." Consumption is viewed as a habit, a disposition (if not an affectation), a weakness that must be strengthened and to which city people are more disposed.

the tubercular look. The TB-influenced idea of the body was a new model for aristocratic looks—at a moment when aristocracy stops being a matter of power, and starts being mainly a matter of image. ("One can never be too rich. One can never be too thin," the Duchess of Windsor once said.) Indeed, the romanticizing of TB is the first widespread example of that distinctively modern activity, promoting the self as an image. The tubercular look had to be considered attractive once it came to be considered a mark of distinction, of breeding. "I cough continually!" Marie Bashkirtsev wrote in the once widely read *Journal*, which was published, after her death at twenty-four, in 1887. "But for a wonder, far from making me look ugly, this gives me an air of languor that is very becoming." What was once the fashion for aristocratic *femmes fatales* and aspiring young artists became, eventually, the province of fashion as such. Twentieth-century women's fashions (with their cult of thinness) are the last stronghold of the metaphors associated with the romanticizing of TB in the late eighteenth and early nineteenth centuries.

Many of the literary and erotic attitudes known as "romantic agony" derive from tuberculosis and its transformations through metaphor. Agony became romantic in a stylized account of the disease's preliminary symptoms (for example, debility is transformed into languor) and the actual agony was simply suppressed. Wan, hollow-chested young women and pallid, rachitic young men vied with each other as candidates for this mostly (at that time) incurable, disabling, really awful disease. "When I was young," wrote Théophile Gautier, "I could not have accepted as a lyrical poet anyone weighing more than ninety-nine pounds." (Note that Gautier says lyrical poet, apparently resigned to the fact that novelists had to be made of coarser and bulkier stuff.) Gradually, the tubercular look, which symbolized an appealing vulnerability, a superior sensitivity, became more and more the ideal look for women—while great men of the mid- and late nineteenth century grew fat, founded industrial empires, wrote hundreds of novels, made wars, and plundered continents.

One might reasonably suppose that this romanticization of TB was merely literary transfiguration of the disease, and that in the era of its great depredations TB was probably thought to be disgusting—as cancer is now. Surely everyone in the nineteenth century knew about, for example, the stench in the breath of the consumptive person. (Describing their visit to the dying Murger, the Goncourts note "the odor of rotting flesh in his bedroom.") Yet all the evidence indicates that the cult of TB was not simply an invention of romantic poets and opera librettists but a widespread attitude, and that the person dying (young) of TB really was perceived as a romantic personality. One must suppose that the reality of this terrible disease was no match for important new ideas, particularly about individuality. It is with TB that the idea of individual illness was articulated, along with the idea that people are made more conscious as they confront their deaths, and in the images that collected around the disease one can see emerging a modern idea of individuality that has taken in the twentieth century a more aggressive, if no less narcissistic, form. Sickness was a way of making people "interesting"—which is how "romantic" was originally defined. (Schlegel, in his essay "On the Study of Greek Poetry" [1795], offers "the interesting" as the ideal of modern—that is, romantic—poetry.) "The ideal of perfect health," Novalis wrote in a fragment from the period 1799–1800, "is only scientifically interesting"; what is really interesting is sickness, "which belongs to individualizing." This idea—of how interesting the sick are—was given its boldest and most ambivalent formulation by Nietzsche in *The Will to Power* and other writings, and though Nietzsche rarely mentioned a specific illness, those famous judgments about individual weakness and cultural exhaustion or decadence incorporate and extend many of the clichés about TB.

The romantic treatment of death asserts that people were made singular, made more interesting, by their illnesses. "I look pale," said Byron, looking into the mirror. "I should like to die of a consumption." Why? asked his tubercular friend Tom Moore, who was visiting Byron in Patras in February 1828. "Because the ladies would all say, 'Look at that poor Byron, how interesting he looks in dying.'" Perhaps the main gift to sensibility made by the Romantics is not the aesthetics of cruelty and the beauty of the morbid (as Mario Praz suggested in his famous book), or even the demand for unlimited personal liberty, but the nihilistic and sentimental idea of "the interesting."

Sadness made one "interesting." It was a mark of refinement, of sensibility, to be sad. That is, to be powerless. In Stendhal's *Armance*, the anxious mother is reassured by the doctor that Octave is not, after all, suffering from tuberculosis but only from that "dissatisfied and critical melancholy characteristic of young people of his generation and position." Sadness and tuberculosis became synonymous. The Swiss writer Henri Amiel, himself tubercular, wrote in 1852 in his *Journal intime*:

> Sky draped in gray, pleated by subtle shading, mists trailing on the distant mountains; nature despairing, leaves falling on all sides like the lost illusions of youth under the tears of incurable grief. . . . The fir tree, alone in its vigor, green, stoical in the midst of this universal tuberculosis.

But it takes a sensitive person to feel such sadness; or, by implication, to contract tuberculosis. The myth of TB constitutes the next-to-last episode in the long career of the ancient idea of melancholy—which was the artist's disease, according to the theory of the four humours. The melancholy character—or the tubercular—was a superior one: sensitive, creative, a being apart. Keats and Shelley may have suffered atrociously from the disease. But Shelley consoled Keats that "this consumption is a disease particularly fond of people who write such good verses as you have done. . . ." So well established was the cliché which connected TB and creativity that at the end of the century one critic suggested that it was the progressive disappearance of TB which accounted for the current decline of literature and the arts.

But the myth of TB provided more than an account of creativity. It supplied an important model of bohemian life, lived with or without the vocation of the artist. The TB sufferer was a dropout, a wanderer in endless search of the healthy place. Starting in the early nineteenth century, TB became a new reason for exile, for a life that was mainly traveling. (Neither travel nor isolation in a sanatorium was a form of treatment for TB before then.) There were special places thought to be good for tuberculars: in the early nineteenth century, Italy; then, islands in the Mediterranean or the South Pacific; in the twentieth century, the mountains, the desert—all landscapes that had themselves been successively romanticized. Keats was advised by his doctors to move to Rome; Chopin tried the islands of the western Mediterranean; Robert Louis Stevenson chose a Pacific exile; D. H. Lawrence roamed over half the globe.* The Romantics invented invalidism as a pretext for leisure, and for dismissing bourgeois obligations in order to live only for one's art. It was a way of retiring from the world without having to take responsibility for the decision—the story of *The Magic Mountain*. After passing his exams and before taking up his job in a Hamburg ship-building firm, young Hans Castorp makes a three-week visit to his tubercular cousin in the sanatorium at Davos. Just before Hans "goes down," the doctor diagnoses a spot on his lungs. He stays on the mountain for the next seven years.

By validating so many possibly subversive longings and turning them into cultural pieties, the TB myth survived irrefutable human experience and accumulating medical knowledge for nearly two hundred years. Although there was a certain reaction against the Romantic cult of the disease in the second half of the last century, TB retained most of its romantic attributes—as the sign of a superior nature, as a becoming frailty—through the end of the century and well into ours. It is still the sensitive young artist's disease in O'Neill's *Long Day's Journey into Night*. Kafka's letters are a compendium of speculations about the meaning of tuberculosis, as is *The Magic Mountain*, published in 1924, the year Kafka died. Much of the irony of *The Magic Mountain* turns on Hans Castorp, the stolid burgher, getting TB, the artist's disease—for Mann's novel is a late,

---

*"By a curious irony," Stevenson wrote, "the places to which we are sent when health deserts us are often singularly beautiful . . . [and] I daresay the sick man is not very inconsolable when he receives sentence of banishment, and is inclined to regard his ill-health as not the least fortunate accident of his life." But the experience of such enforced banishment, as Stevenson went on to describe it, was something less agreeable. The tubercular cannot enjoy his good fortune: "the world is disenchanted for him."

Katherine Mansfield wrote: "I seem to spend half of my life arriving at strange hotels. . . . The strange door shuts upon the stranger, and then I slip down in the sheets. Waiting for the shadows to come out of the corners and spin their slow, slow web over the Ugliest Wallpaper of All. . . . The man in the room next to mine has the same complaint as I. When I wake in the night I hear him turning. And then he coughs. And after a silence I cough. And he coughs again. This goes on for a long time. Until I feel we are like two roosters calling each other at false dawns. From far-away hidden farms."

self-conscious commentary on the myth of TB. But the novel still reflects the myth: the burgher *is* indeed spiritually refined by his disease. To die of TB was still mysterious and (often) edifying, and remained so until practically nobody in Western Europe and North America died of it any more. Although the incidence of the disease began to decline precipitously after 1900 because of improved hygiene, the mortality rate among those who contracted it remained high; the power of the myth was dispelled only when proper treatment was finally developed, with the discovery of streptomycin in 1944 and the introduction of isoniazid in 1952.

If it is still difficult to imagine how the reality of such a dreadful disease could be transformed so preposterously, it may help to consider our own era's comparable act of distortion, under the pressure of the need to express romantic attitudes about the self. The object of distortion is not, of course, cancer—a disease which nobody has managed to glamorize (though it fulfills some of the functions as a metaphor that TB did in the nineteenth century). In the twentieth century, the repellent, harrowing disease that is made the index of a superior sensitivity, the vehicle of "spiritual" feelings and "critical" discontent, is insanity.

The fancies associated with tuberculosis and insanity have many parallels. With both illnesses, there is confinement. Sufferers are sent to a "sanatorium" (the common word for a clinic for tuberculars and the most common euphemism for an insane asylum). Once put away, the patient enters a duplicate world with special rules. Like TB, insanity is a kind of exile. The metaphor of the psychic voyage is an extension of the romantic idea of travel that was associated with tuberculosis. To be cured, the patient has to be taken out of his or her daily routine. It is not an accident that the most common metaphor for an extreme psychological experience viewed positively—whether produced by drugs or by becoming psychotic—is a trip.

In the twentieth century the cluster of metaphors and attitudes formerly attached to TB split up and are parceled out to two diseases. Some features of TB go to insanity: the notion of the sufferer as a hectic, reckless creature of passionate extremes, someone too sensitive to bear the horrors of the vulgar, everyday world. Other features of TB go to cancer—the agonies that can't be romanticized. Not TB but insanity is the current vehicle of our secular myth of self-transcendence. The romantic view is that illness exacerbates consciousness. Once that illness was TB; now it is insanity that is thought to bring consciousness to a state of paroxysmic enlightenment. The romanticizing of madness reflects in the most vehement way the contemporary prestige of irrational or rude (spontaneous) behavior (acting-out), of that very passionateness whose repression was once imagined to cause TB, and is now thought to cause cancer.

5

In "Death in Venice," passion brings about the collapse of all that has made Gustav von Aschenbach singular—his reason, his inhibitions, his fastidiousness. And disease further reduces him. At the end of the story, Aschenbach is just another cholera victim, his last degradation being to succumb to the disease afflicting so many in Venice at that moment. When in *The Magic Mountain* Hans Castorp is discovered to have tuberculosis, it is a promotion. His illness will make Hans become more singular, will make him more intelligent than he was before. In one fiction, disease (cholera) is the penalty for a secret love; in the other, disease (TB) is its expression. Cholera is the kind of fatality that, in retrospect, has simplified a complex self, reducing it to sick environment. The disease that individualizes, that sets a person in relief against the environment, is tuberculosis.

What once made TB seem so "interesting"—or, as it was usually put, romantic—also made it a curse and a source of special dread. In contrast to the great epidemic diseases of the past (bubonic plague, typhus, cholera), which strike each person as a member of an afflicted community, TB was understood as a disease that isolates one from the community. However steep its incidence in a population, TB—like cancer today—always seemed to be a mysterious disease of individuals, a deadly arrow that could strike anyone, that singled out its victims one by one.

As after a cholera death, it used to be common practice to burn the clothes and other effects of someone who died of TB. "Those brutal Italians have nearly finished their monstrous business," Keats's companion Joseph Severn wrote from Rome on March 6, 1821, two weeks after Keats died in the little room on the Piazza di Spagna. "They have burned all the furniture—and are now scraping the walls—making new windows—new doors—and even a new floor." But TB was frightening, not only as a contagion, like cholera, but as a seemingly arbitrary, uncommunicable "taint." And people could believe that TB was inherited (think of the disease's recurrence in the families of Keats, the Brontës, Emerson, Thoreau, Trollope) and also believe that it revealed something singular about the person afflicted. In a similar way, the evidence that there are cancer-prone families and, possibly, a hereditary factor in cancer can be acknowledged without disturbing the belief that cancer is a disease that strikes each person, punitively, as an individual. No one asks "Why me?" who gets cholera or typhus. But "Why me?" (meaning "It's not fair") is the question of many who learn they have cancer.

However much TB was blamed on poverty and insalubrious surroundings, it was still thought that a certain inner disposition was needed in order to contract the disease. Doctors and laity believed in a TB character type—as now the belief in a cancer-prone character type, far from being confined to the back yard of folk superstition, passes for the most advanced medical thinking. In contrast to the modern bogey of the cancer-prone character—someone unemotional, inhibited, repressed—the TB-prone character that haunted imaginations in the nineteenth century was an amalgam of two different fantasies: someone both passionate and repressed.

That other notorious scourge among nineteenth-century diseases, syphilis, was at least not mysterious. Contracting syphilis was a predictable consequence, the consequence, usually, of having sex with a carrier of the disease. So, among all the guilt-embroidered fantasies about sexual pollution attached to syphilis, there was no place for a type of personality supposed to be especially susceptible to the disease (as was once imagined for TB and is now for cancer). The syphilitic personality type was someone who had the disease (Osvald in Ibsen's *Ghosts*, Adrian Leverkühn in *Doctor Faustus*), not someone who was likely to get it. In its role as scourge, syphilis implied a moral judgment (about off-limits sex, about prostitution) but not a

psychological one. TB, once so mysterious—as cancer is now—
suggested judgments of a deeper kind, both moral and psychological, about the ill.

The speculations of the ancient world made disease most often
an instrument of divine wrath. Judgment was meted out either
to a community (the plague in Book I of the *Iliad* that Apollo
inflicts on the Achaeans in punishment for Agamemnon's abduction of Chryses' daughter; the plague in *Oedipus* that strikes
Thebes because of the polluting presence of the royal sinner) or
to a single person (the stinking wound in Philoctetes' foot). The
diseases around which the modern fantasies have gathered—
TB, cancer—are viewed as forms of self-judgment, of self-
betrayal.

One's mind betrays one's body. "My head and lungs have
come to an agreement without my knowledge," Kafka said
about his TB in a letter to Max Brod in September 1917. Or
one's body betray's one's feelings, as in Mann's late novel *The
Black Swan*, whose aging heroine, youthfully in love with a
young man, takes as the return of her menses what is actually a
hemorrhage and the symptom of incurable cancer. The body's
treachery is thought to have its own inner logic. Freud was
"very beautiful . . . when he spoke," Wilhelm Reich reminisced.
"Then it hit him just here, in the mouth. And that is where my
interest in cancer began." That interest led Reich to propose his
version of the link between a mortal disease and the character
of those it humiliates.

In the pre-modern view of disease, the role of character was
confined to one's behavior after its onset. Like any extreme situation, dreaded illnesses bring out both people's worst and best.
The standard accounts of epidemics, however, are mainly of
the devastating effect of disease upon character. The weaker the
chronicler's preconception of disease as a punishment for wick-
edness, the more likely that the account will stress the moral
corruption made manifest by the disease's spread. Even if the
disease is not thought to be a judgment on the community, it
becomes one—retroactively—as it sets in motion an inexorable
collapse of morals and manners. Thucydides relates the ways in
which the plague that broke out in Athens in 430 B.C. spawned
disorder and lawlessness ("The pleasure of the moment took

the place both of honor and expedience") and corrupted language itself. And the whole point of Boccaccio's description in the first pages of the *Decameron* of the great plague of 1348 is how badly the citizens of Florence behaved.

In contrast to this disdainful knowledge of how most loyalties and loves shatter in the panic produced by epidemic disease, the accounts of modern diseases—where the judgment tends to fall on the individual rather than the society—seem exaggeratedly unaware of how poorly many people take the news that they are dying. Fatal illness has always been viewed as a test of moral character, but in the nineteenth century there is a great reluctance to let anybody flunk the test. And the virtuous only become more so as they slide toward death. This is standard achievement for TB deaths in fiction, and goes with the inveterate spiritualizing of TB and the sentimentalizing of its horrors. Tuberculosis provided a redemptive death for the fallen, like the young prostitute Fantine in *Les Misérables*, or a sacrificial death for the virtuous, like the heroine of Selma Lagerlöf's *The Phantom Chariot*. Even the ultra-virtuous, when dying of this disease, boost themselves to new moral heights. *Uncle Tom's Cabin*: Little Eva during her last days urges her father to become a serious Christian and free his slaves. *The Wings of the Dove*: after learning that her suitor is a fortune hunter, Milly Theale wills her fortune to him and dies. *Dombey and Son*: "From some hidden reason, very imperfectly understood by himself—if understood at all—[Paul] felt a gradually increasing impulse of affection, towards almost everything and everybody in the place."

For those characters treated less sentimentally, the disease is viewed as the occasion finally to behave well. At the least, the calamity of disease can clear the way for insight into lifelong self-deceptions and failures of character. The lies that muffle Ivan Ilyich's drawn-out agony—his cancer being unmentionable to his wife and children—reveal to him the lie of his whole life; when dying, he is, for the first time, in a state of truth. The sixty-year-old civil servant in Kurosawa's film *Ikiru* (1952) quits his job after learning he has terminal stomach cancer and, taking up the cause of a slum neighborhood, fights the bureaucracy he had served. With one year left to live, Watanabe wants to do something that is worthwhile, wants to redeem his mediocre life.

6

Disease occurs in the *Iliad* and the *Odyssey* as supernatural punishment, as demonic possession, and as the result of natural causes. For the Greeks, disease could be gratuitous or it could be deserved (for a personal fault, a collective transgression, or a crime of one's ancestors). With the advent of Christianity, which imposed more moralized notions of disease, as of everything else, a closer fit between disease and "victim" gradually evolved. The idea of disease as punishment yielded the idea that a disease could be a particularly appropriate and just punishment. Cresseid's leprosy in Henryson's *The Testament of Cresseid* and Madame de Merteuil's smallpox in *Les Liaisons dangereuses* show the true face of the beautiful liar—a most involuntary revelation.

In the nineteenth century, the notion that the disease fits the patient's character, as the punishment fits the sinner, was replaced by the notion that it expresses character. It is a product of will. "The will exhibits itself as organized body," wrote Schopenhauer, "and the presence of disease signifies that the will itself is sick." Recovery from a disease depends on the healthy will assuming "dictatorial power in order to subsume the rebellious forces" of the sick will. One generation earlier, a great physician, Bichat, had used a similar image, calling health "the silence of organs," disease "their revolt." Disease is the will speaking through the body, a language for dramatizing the mental: a form of self-expression. Groddeck described illness as "a symbol, a representation of something going on within, a drama staged by the It. . . ."*

According to the pre-modern ideal of a well-balanced character, expressiveness is supposed to be limited. Behavior is defined by its potentiality for excess. Thus, when Kant makes figurative use of cancers, it is as a metaphor for excess feeling. "Passions are cancer for pure practical reason and often incurable," Kant wrote in *Anthropologie* (1798). "The passions are . . .

---

*Kafka, after his TB was diagnosed in September 1917, wrote in his diary: ". . . the infection in your lungs is only a symbol," the symbol of an emotional "wound whose inflammation is called F[elice]. . . ." To Max Brod he wrote: "the illness is speaking for me because I have asked it to do so"; and to Felice: "Secretly I don't believe this illness to be tuberculosis, at least not primarily tuberculosis, but rather a sign of my general bankruptcy."

unfortunate moods that are pregnant with many evils," he added, evoking the ancient metaphoric connection between cancer and a pregnancy. When Kant compares passions (that is, extreme feelings) to cancers, he is of course using the pre-modern sense of the disease and a pre-Romantic evaluation of passion. Soon, turbulent feeling was to be viewed much more positively. "There is no one in the world less able to conceal his feelings than Émile," said Rousseau—meaning it as a compliment.

As excess feelings become positive, they are no longer analogized—in order to denigrate them—to a terrible disease. Instead, disease is seen as the vehicle of excess feeling. TB is the disease that makes manifest intense desire; that discloses, in spite of the reluctance of the individual, what the individual does not want to reveal. The contrast is no longer between moderate passions and excessive ones but between hidden passions and those which are brought into the open. Illness reveals desires of which the patient probably was unaware. Diseases—and patients—become subjects for decipherment. And these hidden passions are now considered a source of illness. "He who desires but acts not, breeds pestilence," Blake wrote: one of his defiant Proverbs of Hell.

The early Romantic sought superiority by desiring, and by desiring to desire, more intensely than others do. The inability to realize these ideals of vitality and perfect spontaneity was thought to make someone an ideal candidate for TB. Contemporary romanticism starts from the inverse principle—that it is others who desire intensely, and that it is oneself (the narratives are typically in the first person) who has little or no desire at all. There are precursors of the modern romantic egos of unfeeling in nineteenth-century Russian novels (Pechorin in Lermontov's *A Hero of Our Time*, Stavrogin in *The Possessed*); but they are still heroes—restless, bitter, self-destructive, tormented by their inability to feel. (Even their glum, merely self-absorbed descendants, Roquentin in Sartre's *Nausea* and Meursault in Camus's *The Stranger*, seem bewildered by their inability to feel.) The passive, affectless anti-hero who dominates contemporary American fiction is a creature of regular routines or unfeeling debauch; not self-destructive but prudent; not moody, dashing, cruel, just dissociated. The ideal candidate, according to contemporary mythology, for cancer.

Ceasing to consider disease as a punishment which fits the objective moral character, making it an expression of the inner
self, might seem less moralistic. But this view turns out to be
just as, or even more, moralistic and punitive. With the modern
diseases (once TB, now cancer), the romantic idea that the disease expresses the character is invariably extended to assert that
the character causes the disease—because it has not expressed
itself. Passion moves inward, striking and blighting the deepest
cellular recesses.

"The sick man himself creates his disease," Groddeck wrote;
"he is the cause of the disease and we need seek none other."
"Bacilli" heads Groddeck's list of mere "external causes"—
followed by "chills, overeating, overdrinking, work, and anything else." He insists that it is "because it is not pleasant to
look within ourselves" that doctors prefer to "attack the outer
causes with prophylaxis, disinfection, and so on," rather than
address the real, internal causes. In Karl Menninger's more recent formulation: "Illness is in part what the world has done
to a victim, but in a larger part it is what the victim has done
with his world, and with himself. . . ." Such preposterous and
dangerous views manage to put the onus of the disease on the
patient and not only weaken the patient's ability to understand
the range of plausible medical treatment but also, implicitly,
direct the patient away from such treatment. Cure is thought
to depend principally on the patient's already sorely tested or
enfeebled capacity for self-love. A year before her death in 1923,
Katherine Mansfield wrote in her *Journal*:

> A bad day. . . . horrible pains and so on, and weakness. I could do
> nothing. The weakness was not only physical. I *must heal my Self*
> before I will be well. . . . This must be done alone and at once. It
> is at the root of my not getting better. My mind is not *controlled*.

Mansfield not only thinks it was the "Self" which made her sick
but thinks that she has a chance of being cured of her hopelessly
advanced lung disease if she could heal that "Self."*

---

*Mansfield, wrote John Middleton Murry, "had come to the conviction
that her bodily health depended upon her spiritual condition. Her mind was
henceforth preoccupied with discovering some way to 'cure her soul'; and

Both the myth about TB and the current myth about cancer propose that one is responsible for one's disease. But the cancer imagery is far more punishing. Given the romantic values in use for judging character and disease, some glamour attaches to having a disease thought to come from being too full of passion. But there is mostly shame attached to a disease thought to stem from the repression of emotion—an opprobrium echoed in the views propagated by Groddeck and Reich, and the many writers influenced by them. The view of cancer as a disease of the failure of expressiveness condemns the cancer patient: expresses pity but also conveys contempt. Miss Gee, in Auden's poem from the 1930s, "passed by the loving couples" and "turned her head away." Then:

> Miss Gee knelt down in the side-aisle,
>   She knelt down on her knees;
> 'Lead me not into temptation
>   But make me a good girl, please.'
>
> The days and nights went by her
>   Like waves round a Cornish wreck;
> She bicycled down to the doctor
>   With her clothes buttoned up to her neck.
>
> She bicycled down to the doctor,
>   And rang the surgery bell;
> 'O, doctor, I've a pain inside me,
>   And I don't feel very well.'
>
> Doctor Thomas looked her over,
>   And then he looked some more;
> Walked over to his wash-basin,
>   Said, 'Why didn't you come before?'
>
> Doctor Thomas sat over his dinner,
>   Though his wife was waiting to ring,
> Rolling his bread into pellets;
>   Said, 'Cancer's a funny thing.

she eventually resolved, to my regret, to abandon her treatment and to live as though her grave physical illness were incidental, and even, so far as she could, as though it were non-existent."

'Nobody knows what the cause is,
  Though some pretend they do;
It's like some hidden assassin
  Waiting to strike at you.

'Childless women get it,
  And men when they retire;
It's as if there had to be some outlet
  For their foiled creative fire.' . . .

The tubercular could be an outlaw or a misfit; the cancer personality is regarded more simply, and with condescension, as one of life's losers. Napoleon, Ulysses S. Grant, Robert A. Taft, and Hubert Humphrey have all had their cancer diagnosed as the reaction to political defeat and the curtailing of their ambitions. And the cancer deaths of those harder to describe as losers, like Freud and Wittgenstein, have been diagnosed as the gruesome penalty exacted for a lifetime of instinctual renunciation. (Few remember that Rimbaud died of cancer.) In contrast, the disease that claimed the likes of Keats, Poe, Chekhov, Simone Weil, Emily Brontë, and Jean Vigo was as much an apotheosis as a verdict of failure.

7

Cancer is generally thought an inappropriate disease for a romantic character, in contrast to tuberculosis, perhaps because unromantic depression has supplanted the romantic notion of melancholy. "A fitful strain of melancholy," Poe wrote, "will ever be found inseparable from the perfection of the beautiful." Depression is melancholy minus its charms—the animation, the fits.

Supporting the theory about the emotional causes of cancer, there is a growing literature and body of research: and scarcely a week passes without a new article announcing to some general public or other the scientific link between cancer and painful feelings. Investigations are cited—most articles refer to the same ones—in which out of, say, several hundred cancer patients, two-thirds or three-fifths report being depressed or unsatisfied with their lives, and having suffered from the loss (through death or rejection or separation) of a parent, lover, spouse, or close friend. But it seems likely that of several hundred people who do *not* have cancer, most would also report depressing emotions and past traumas: this is called the human condition. And these case histories are recounted in a particularly forth-coming language of despair, of discontent about and obsessive preoccupation with the isolated self and its never altogether satisfactory "relationships," which bears the unmistakable stamp of our consumer culture. It is a language many Americans now use about themselves.*

Investigations carried out by a few doctors in the last cen-tury showed a high correlation between cancer and that era's complaints. In contrast to contemporary American cancer patients, who invariably report having feelings of isolation and loneliness since childhood, Victorian cancer patients described overcrowded lives, burdened with work and family obligations, and bereavements. These patients don't express discontent with their lives as such or speculate about the quality of its satisfactions and the possibility of a "meaningful relationship." Physicians found the causes or predisposing factors of their patients' cancers in grief, in worry (noted as most acute among businessmen and the mothers of large families), in straitened economic circumstances and sudden reversals of fortune, and in overwork—or, if the patients were successful writers or

*A study by Dr. Caroline Bedell Thomas of the Johns Hopkins University School of Medicine was thus summarized in one recent newspaper article ("Can Your Personality Kill You?"): "In brief, cancer victims are low-gear persons, seldom prey to outbursts of emotion. They have feelings of isolation from their parents dating back to childhood." Drs. Claus and Marjorie Bahnson at the Eastern Pennsylvania Psychiatric Institute have "charted a personality pattern of denial of hostility, depression and of memory of emotional depriva-tion in childhood" and "difficulty in maintaining close relationships." Dr. O. Carl Simonton, a radiologist in Fort Worth, Texas, who gives patients both radiation and psychotherapy, describes the cancer personality as someone with "a great tendency for self-pity and a markedly impaired ability to make and maintain meaningful relationships." Lawrence LeShan, a New York psycholo-gist and psychotherapist (*You Can Fight for Your Life: Emotional Factors in the Causation of Cancer* [1977]), claims that "there is a general type of personality configuration among the majority of cancer patients" and a world-view that cancer patients share and "which pre-dates the development of cancer." He divides "the basic emotional pattern of the cancer patient" into three parts:

politicians, in grief, rage, intellectual overexertion, the anxiety that accompanies ambition, and the stress of public life.*

Nineteenth-century cancer patients were thought to get the disease as the result of hyperactivity and hyperintensity. They seemed to be full of emotions that had to be damped down. As a prophylaxis against cancer, one English doctor urged his patients "to avoid overtaxing their strength, and to bear the ills of life with equanimity; above all things, not to 'give way' to any grief." Such stoic counsels have now been replaced by prescriptions for self-expression, from talking it out to the primal scream. In 1885, a Boston doctor advised "those who have apparently benign tumors in the breast of the advantage of being cheerful." Today, this would be regarded as encouraging the sort of emotional dissociation now thought to predispose people to cancer.

Popular accounts of the psychological aspects of cancer often cite old authorities, starting with Galen, who observed that "melancholy women" are more likely to get breast cancer than "sanguine women." But the meanings have changed. Galen (second century A.D.) meant by melancholy a physiological condition with complex characterological symptoms; we mean a mere mood. "Grief and anxiety," said the English surgeon Sir Astley Cooper in 1845, are among "the most frequent causes"

———————

"a childhood or adolescence marked by feelings of isolation," the loss of the "meaningful relationship" found in adulthood, and a subsequent "conviction that life holds no more hope." "The cancer patient," LeShan writes, "almost invariably is contemptuous of himself, and of his abilities and possibilities." Cancer patients are "empty of feeling and devoid of self."

*"Always much trouble and hard work" is a notation that occurs in many of the brief case histories in Herbert Snow's *Clinical Notes on Cancer* (1883). Snow was a surgeon in the Cancer Hospital in London, and most of the patients he saw were poor. A typical observation: "Of 140 cases of breast-cancer, 103 gave an account of previous mental trouble, hard work, or other debilitating agency. Of 187 uterine ditto, 91 showed a similar history." Doctors who saw patients who led more comfortable lives made other observations. The physician who treated Alexandre Dumas for cancer, G. von Schmitt, published a book on cancer in 1871 in which he listed "deep and sedentary study and pursuits, the feverish and anxious agitation of public life, the cares of ambition, frequent paroxysms of rage, violent grief" as "the principal causes" of the disease. Quoted in Samuel J. Kowal, M.D., "Emotions as a Cause of Cancer: 18th and 19th Century Contributions," *Review of Psychoanalysis*, 42, 3 (July 1955).

of breast cancer. But the nineteenth-century observations undermine rather than support late-twentieth-century notions—evoking a manic or manic-depressive character type almost the opposite of that forlorn, self-hating, emotionally inert creature, the contemporary cancer personality. As far as I know, no oncologist convinced of the efficacy of polychemotherapy and immunotherapy in treating patients has contributed to fictions about a specific cancer personality. Needless to say, the hypothesis that distress can affect immunological responsiveness (and, in some circumstances, lower immunity to disease) is hardly the same as—or constitutes evidence for—the view that emotions cause diseases, much less for the belief that specific emotions can produce specific diseases.

Recent conjecture about the modern cancer character type finds its true antecedent and counterpart in the literature on TB, where the same theory, put in similar terms, had long been in circulation. In his *Morbidus Anglicus* (1672), Gideon Harvey declared "melancholy" and "choler" to be "the sole cause" of TB (for which he used the metaphor term "corrosion"). In 1881, a year before Robert Koch published his paper announcing the discovery of the tubercle bacillus and demonstrating that it was the primary cause of the disease, a standard medical textbook gave as the causes of tuberculosis: hereditary disposition, unfavorable climate, sedentary indoor life, defective ventilation, deficiency of light, and "depressing emotions."* Though the entry had to be changed for the next edition, it took a long time for these notions to lose credibility. "I'm mentally ill, the disease of the lungs is nothing but an overflowing of my mental disease," Kafka wrote to Milena in 1920. Applied to TB, the theory that emotions cause diseases survived well into this century—until, finally, it was discovered how to cure the disease. The theory's fashionable current application—which relates cancer to emotional withdrawal and lack of self-confidence and confidence in the future—is likely to prove no more tenable than its application to tuberculosis.

————————

*August Flint and William H. Welch, *The Principles and Practice of Medicine* (fifth edition, 1881), cited in René and Jean Dubos, *The White Plague* (1952).

In the plague-ridden England of the late sixteenth and seventeenth centuries, according to the historian Keith Thomas, it was widely believed that "the happy man would not get plague." The fantasy that a happy state of mind would fend off disease probably flourished for all infectious diseases, before the nature of infection was understood. Theories that diseases are caused by mental states and can be cured by will power are always an index of how much is not understood about the physical terrain of a disease.

Moreover, there is a peculiarly modern predilection for psychological explanations of disease, as of everything else. Psychologizing seems to provide control over the experiences and events (like grave illnesses) over which people have in fact little or no control. Psychological understanding undermines the "reality" of a disease. That reality has to be explained. (It really means; or is a symbol of; or must be interpreted so.) For those who live neither with religious consolations about death nor with a sense of death (or of anything else) as natural, death is the obscene mystery, the ultimate affront, the thing that cannot be controlled. It can only be denied. A large part of the popularity and persuasiveness of psychology comes from its being a sublimated spiritualism: a secular, ostensibly scientific way of affirming the primacy of "spirit" over matter. That ineluctably material reality, disease, can be given a psychological explanation. Death itself can be considered, ultimately, a psychological phenomenon. Groddeck declared in *The Book of the It* (he was speaking of TB): "He alone will die who wishes to die, to whom life is intolerable." The promise of a temporary triumph over death is implicit in much of the psychological thinking that starts from Freud and Jung.

At the least, there is the promise of a triumph over illness. A "physical" illness becomes in a way less real—but, in compensation, more interesting—so far as it can be considered a "mental" one. Speculation throughout the modern period has tended steadily to enlarge the category of mental illness. Indeed, part of the denial of death in this culture is a vast expansion of the category of illness as such.

Illness expands by means of two hypotheses. The first is that every form of social deviation can be considered an illness. Thus, if criminal behavior can be considered an illness, then criminals are not to be condemned or punished but to be understood (as a doctor understands), treated, cured.* The second is that every illness can be considered psychologically. Illness is interpreted as, basically, a psychological event, and people are encouraged to believe that they get sick because they (unconsciously) want to, and that they can cure themselves by the mobilization of will; that they can choose not to die of the disease. These two hypotheses are complementary. As the first seems to relieve guilt, the second reinstates it. Psychological theories of illness are a powerful means of placing the blame on the ill. Patients who are instructed that they have, unwittingly, caused their disease are also being made to feel that they have deserved it.

8

Punitive notions of disease have a long history, and such notions are particularly active with cancer. There is the "fight" or "crusade" against cancer; cancer is the "killer" disease; people who have cancer are "cancer victims." Ostensibly, the illness is the culprit. But it is also the cancer patient who is made culpable. Widely believed psychological theories of disease assign to the luckless ill the ultimate responsibility both for falling ill and for getting well. And conventions of treating cancer as no mere disease but a demonic enemy make cancer not just a lethal disease but a shameful one.

Leprosy in its heyday aroused a similarly disproportionate sense of horror. In the Middle Ages, the leper was a social text in which corruption was made visible; an exemplum, an emblem of decay. Nothing is more punitive than to give a disease a meaning—that meaning being invariably a moralistic one. Any important disease whose causality is murky, and for which treatment is ineffectual, tends to be awash in significance. First, the

---

*An early statement of this view, now so much on the defensive, is in Samuel Butler's *Erewhon* (1872). Butler's way of suggesting that criminality was a disease, like TB, that was either hereditary or the result of an unwholesome environment was to point out the absurdity of condemning the sick. In Erewhon, those who murdered or stole are sympathetically treated as ill persons, while tuberculosis is punished as a crime.

subjects of deepest dread (corruption, decay, pollution, ano-
mie, weakness) are identified with the disease. The disease itself
becomes a metaphor. Then, in the name of the disease (that
is, using it as a metaphor), that horror is imposed on other
things. The disease becomes adjectival. Something is said to be
disease-like, meaning that it is disgusting or ugly. In French, a
moldering stone façade is still *lépreuse*.

Epidemic diseases were a common figure for social disorder.
From pestilence (bubonic plague) came "pestilent," whose figurative meaning, according to the *Oxford English Dictionary*,
is "injurious to religion, morals, or public peace—1513"; and
"pestilential," meaning "morally baneful or pernicious—1531."
Feelings about evil are projected onto a disease. And the disease
(so enriched with meanings) is projected onto the world.

In the past, such grandiloquent fantasies were regularly attached
to the epidemic diseases, diseases that were a collective calamity.
In the last two centuries, the diseases most often used as metaphors for evil were syphilis, tuberculosis, and cancer—all diseases imagined to be, preeminently, the diseases of individuals.

Syphilis was thought to be not only a horrible disease but a
demeaning, vulgar one. Anti-democrats used it to evoke the
desecrations of an egalitarian age. Baudelaire, in a note for his
never completed book on Belgium, wrote:

> We all have the republican spirit in our veins, like syphilis in our
> bones—we are democratized and venerealized.

In the sense of an infection that corrupts morally and debili-
tates physically, syphilis was to become a standard trope in late-
nineteenth- and early-twentieth-century anti-Semitic polemics.
In 1933 Wilhelm Reich argued that "the irrational fear of syphilis
was one of the major sources of National Socialism's political
views and its anti-Semitism." But although he perceived sexual
and political phobias being projected onto a disease in the grisly
harping on syphilis in *Mein Kampf*, it never occurred to Reich
how much was being projected in his own persistent use of cancer as a metaphor for the ills of the modern era. Indeed, cancer
can be stretched much further than syphilis can as a metaphor.

Syphilis was limited as a metaphor because the disease itself
was not regarded as mysterious; only awful. A tainted heredity

(Ibsen's *Ghosts*), the perils of sex (Charles-Louis Philippe's *Bubu de Montparnasse*, Mann's *Doctor Faustus*)—there was horror aplenty in syphilis. But no mystery. Its causality was clear, and understood to be singular. Syphilis was the grimmest of gifts, "transmitted" or "carried" by a sometimes ignorant sender to the unsuspecting receiver. In contrast, TB was regarded as a mysterious affliction, and a disease with myriad causes—just as today, while everyone acknowledges cancer to be an unsolved riddle, it is also generally agreed that cancer is multi-determined. A variety of factors—such as cancer-causing substances ("carcinogens") in the environment, genetic makeup, lowering of immuno-defenses (by previous illness or emotional trauma), characterological predisposition—are held responsible for the disease. And many researchers assert that cancer is not one but more than a hundred clinically distinct diseases, that each cancer has to be studied separately, and that what will eventually be developed is an array of cures, one for each of the different cancers.

The resemblance of current ideas about cancer's myriad causes to long-held but now discredited views about TB suggests the possibility that cancer may be one disease after all and that it may turn out, as TB did, to have a principal causal agent and be controllable by one program of treatment. Indeed, as Lewis Thomas has observed, all the diseases for which the issue of causation has been settled, and which can be prevented and cured, have turned out to have a simple physical cause—like the pneumococcus for pneumonia, the tubercle bacillus for tuberculosis, a single vitamin deficiency for pellagra—and it is far from unlikely that something comparable will eventually be isolated for cancer. The notion that a disease can be explained only by a variety of causes is precisely characteristic of thinking about diseases whose causation is *not* understood. And it is diseases thought to be multi-determined (that is, mysterious) that have the widest possibilities as metaphors for what is felt to be socially or morally wrong.

TB and cancer have been used to express not only (like syphilis) crude fantasies about contamination but also fairly complex feelings about strength and weakness, and about energy. For more than a century and a half, tuberculosis provided a

metaphoric equivalent for delicacy, sensitivity, sadness, powerlessness; while whatever seemed ruthless, implacable, predatory,
could be analogized to cancer. (Thus, Baudelaire in 1852, in his
essay "*L'École païenne*," observed: "A frenzied passion for art
is a canker that devours the rest. . . .") TB was an ambivalent
metaphor, both a scourge and an emblem of refinement. Cancer
was never viewed other than as a scourge; it was, metaphorically,
the barbarian within.

While syphilis was thought to be passively incurred, an entirely involuntary disaster, TB was once, and cancer is now,
thought to be a pathology of energy, a disease of the will. Concern about energy and feeling, fears about the havoc they wreak,
have been attached to both diseases. Getting TB was thought
to signify a defective vitality, or vitality misspent. "There
was a great want of vital power . . . and great constitutional
weakness"—so Dickens described little Paul in *Dombey and Son*.
The Victorian idea of TB as a disease of low energy (and heightened sensitivity) has its exact complement in the Reichian idea
of cancer as a disease of unexpressed energy (and anesthetized
feelings). In an era in which there seemed to be no inhibitions
on being productive, people were anxious about not having
enough energy. In our own era of destructive overproduction
by the economy and of increasing bureaucratic restraints on
the individual, there is both a fear of having too much energy
and an anxiety about energy not being allowed to be expressed.

Like Freud's scarcity-economics theory of "instincts," the fantasies about TB which arose in the last century (and lasted well
into ours) echo the attitudes of early capitalist accumulation.
One has a limited amount of energy, which must be properly
spent. (Having an orgasm, in nineteenth-century English slang,
was not "coming" but "spending.") Energy, like savings, can
be depleted, can run out or be used up, through reckless ex-
penditure. The body will start "consuming" itself, the patient
will "waste away."

The language used to describe cancer evokes a different
economic catastrophe: that of unregulated, abnormal, incoherent growth. The tumor has energy, not the patient; "it"
is out of control. Cancer cells, according to the textbook account, are cells that have shed the mechanism which "restrains"
growth. (The growth of normal cells is "self-limiting," due to a

mechanism called "contact inhibition.") Cells without inhibitions, cancer cells will continue to grow and extend over each other in a "chaotic" fashion, destroying the body's normal cells, architecture, and functions.

Early capitalism assumes the necessity of regulated spending, saving, accounting, discipline—an economy that depends on the rational limitation of desire. TB is described in images that sum up the negative behavior of nineteenth-century *homo economicus*: consumption; wasting; squandering of vitality. Advanced capitalism requires expansion, speculation, the creation of new needs (the problem of satisfaction and dissatisfaction); buying on credit; mobility—an economy that depends on the irrational indulgence of desire. Cancer is described in images that sum up the negative behaviors of twentieth-century *homo economicus*: abnormal growth; repression of energy, that is, refusal to consume or spend.

TB was understood, like insanity, to be a kind of one-sidedness: a failure of will or an overintensity. However much the disease was dreaded, TB always had pathos. Like the mental patient today, the tubercular was considered to be someone quintessentially vulnerable, and full of self-destructive whims. Nineteenth- and early-twentieth-century physicians addressed themselves to coaxing their tubercular patients back to health. Their prescription was the same as the enlightened one for mental patients today: cheerful surroundings, isolation from stress and family, healthy diet, exercise, rest.

The understanding of cancer supports quite different, avowedly brutal notions of treatment. (A common cancer hospital witticism, heard as often from doctors as from patients: "The treatment is worse than the disease.") There can be no question of pampering the patient. With the patient's body considered to be under attack ("invasion"), the only treatment is counterattack.

The controlling metaphors in descriptions of cancer are, in fact, drawn not from economics but from the language of warfare: every physician and every attentive patient is familiar with, if perhaps inured to, this military terminology. Thus, cancer cells do not simply multiply; they are "invasive." ("Malignant tumors invade even when they grow very slowly," as one textbook puts it.) Cancer cells "colonize" from the original tumor to far sites in the body, first setting up tiny outposts ("micrometastases") whose presence is assumed, though they cannot be detected. Rarely are the body's "defenses" vigorous enough to obliterate a tumor that has established its own blood supply and consists of billions of destructive cells. However "radical" the surgical intervention, however many "scans" are taken of the body landscape, most remissions are temporary; the prospects are that "tumor invasion" will continue, or that rogue cells will eventually regroup and mount a new assault on the organism.

Treatment also has a military flavor. Radiotherapy uses the metaphors of aerial warfare; patients are "bombarded" with toxic rays. And chemotherapy is chemical warfare, using poisons.* Treatment aims to "kill" cancer cells (without, it is hoped, killing the patient). Unpleasant side effects of treatment are advertised, indeed overadvertised. ("The agony of chemotherapy" is a standard phrase.) It is impossible to avoid damaging or destroying healthy cells (indeed, some methods used to treat cancer can cause cancer), but it is thought that nearly any damage to the body is justified if it saves the patient's life. Often, of course, it doesn't work. (As in: "We had to destroy Ben Suc in order to save it.") There is everything but the body count.

The military metaphor in medicine first came into wide use in the 1880s, with the identification of bacteria as agents of disease. Bacteria were said to "invade" or "infiltrate." But talk of siege and war to describe disease now has, with cancer, a striking literalness and authority. Not only is the clinical course

---

*Drugs of the nitrogen mustard type (so-called alkylating agents)—like cyclophosphamide (Cytoxan)—were the first generation of cancer drugs. Their use—with leukemia (which is characterized by an excessive production of immature white cells), then with other forms of cancer—was suggested by an inadvertent experiment with chemical warfare toward the end of World War II, when an American ship, loaded with nitrogen mustard gas, was blown up in the Naples harbor, and many of the sailors died of their lethally low white-cell and platelet counts (that is, of bone-marrow poisoning) rather than of burns or sea-water inhalation.

Chemotherapy and weaponry seem to go together, if only as a fancy. The first modern chemotherapy success was with syphilis: in 1910, Paul Ehrlich introduced an arsenic derivative, arsphenamine (Salvarsan), which was called "the magic bullet."

of the disease and its medical treatment thus described, but the disease itself is conceived as the enemy on which society wages war. More recently, the fight against cancer has sounded like a colonial war—with similarly vast appropriations of government money—and in a decade when colonial wars haven't gone too well, this militarized rhetoric seems to be backfiring. Pessimism among doctors about the efficacy of treatment is growing, in spite of the strong advances in chemotherapy and immunotherapy made since 1970. Reporters covering "the war on cancer" frequently caution the public to distinguish between official fictions and harsh facts; a few years ago, one science writer found American Cancer Society proclamations that cancer is curable and progress has been made "reminiscent of Vietnam optimism prior to the deluge." Still, it is one thing to be skeptical about the rhetoric that surrounds cancer, another to give support to many uninformed doctors who insist that no significant progress in treatment has been made, and that cancer is not really curable. The bromides of the American cancer establishment, tirelessly hailing the imminent victory over cancer; the professional pessimism of a large number of cancer specialists, talking like battle-weary officers mired down in an interminable colonial war—these are twin distortions in this military rhetoric about cancer.

Other distortions follow with the extension of cancer images in more grandiose schemes of warfare. As TB was represented as the spiritualizing of consciousness, cancer is understood as the overwhelming or obliterating of consciousness (by a mindless It). In TB, you are eating yourself up, being refined, getting down to the core, the real you. In cancer, non-intelligent ("primitive," "embryonic," "atavistic") cells are multiplying, and you are being replaced by the non-you. Immunologists class the body's cancer cells as "nonself."

It is worth noting that Reich, who did more than anyone else to disseminate the psychological theory of cancer, also found something equivalent to cancer in the biosphere.

> There is a deadly orgone energy. It is in the atmosphere. You can demonstrate it on devices such as the Geiger counter. It's a swampy quality. . . . Stagnant, deadly water which doesn't flow, doesn't metabolize. Cancer, too, is due to the stagnation of the flow of the life energy of the organism.

Reich's language has its own inimitable coherence. And more and more—as its metaphoric uses gain in credibility—cancer is felt to be what he thought it was, a cosmic disease, the emblem of all the destructive, alien powers to which the organism is host.

As TB was the disease of the sick self, cancer is the disease of the Other. Cancer proceeds by a science-fiction scenario: an invasion of "alien" or "mutant" cells, stronger than normal cells (*Invasion of the Body Snatchers*, *The Incredible Shrinking Man*, *The Blob*, *The Thing*). One standard science-fiction plot is mutation, either mutants arriving from outer space or accidental mutations among humans. Cancer could be described as a triumphant mutation, and mutation is now mainly an image for cancer. As a theory of the psychological genesis of cancer, the Reichian imagery of energy checked, not allowed to move outward, then turned back on itself, driving cells berserk, is already the stuff of science fiction. And Reich's image of death in the air—of deadly energy that registers on a Geiger counter—suggests how much the science-fiction images about cancer (a disease that comes from deadly rays, and is treated by deadly rays) echo the collective nightmare. The original fear about exposure to atomic radiation was genetic deformities in the next generation; that was replaced by another fear, as statistics started to show much higher cancer rates among Hiroshima and Nagasaki survivors and their descendants.

Cancer is a metaphor for what is most ferociously energetic; and these energies constitute the ultimate insult to natural order. In a science-fiction tale by Tommaso Landolfi, the spaceship is called "Cancerqueen." (It is hardly within the range of the tuberculosis metaphor that a writer could have imagined an intrepid vessel named "Consumptionqueen.") When not being explained away as something psychological, buried in the recesses of the self, cancer is being magnified and projected into a metaphor for the biggest enemy, the furthest goal. Thus, Nixon's bid to match Kennedy's promise to put Americans on the moon was, appropriately enough, the promise to "conquer" cancer. Both were science-fiction ventures. The equivalent of the legislation establishing the space program was the National Cancer Act of 1971, which did not envisage the near-to-hand decisions that could bring under control the industrial economy that pollutes—only the great destination: the cure.

TB was a disease in the service of a romantic view of the world. Cancer is now in the service of a simplistic view of the world that can turn paranoid. The disease is often experienced as a form of demonic possession—tumors are "malignant" or "benign," like forces—and many terrified cancer patients are disposed to seek out faith healers, to be exorcised. The main organized support for dangerous nostrums like Laetrile comes from far-right groups to whose politics of paranoia the fantasy of a miracle cure for cancer makes a serviceable addition, along with a belief in UFOs. (The John Birch Society distributes a forty-five-minute film called *World Without Cancer.*) For the more sophisticated, cancer signifies the rebellion of the injured ecosphere: Nature taking revenge on a wicked technocratic world. False hopes and simplified terrors are raised by crude statistics brandished for the general public, such as that 90 percent of all cancers are "environmentally caused," or that imprudent diet and tobacco smoking alone account for 75 percent of all cancer deaths. To the accompaniment of this numbers game (it is difficult to see how any statistics about "all cancers" or "all cancer deaths" could be defended), cigarettes, hair dyes, bacon, saccharine, hormone-fed poultry, pesticides, low-sulphur coal—a lengthening roll call of products we take for granted have been found to cause cancer. X-rays give cancer (the treatment meant to cure kills); so do emanations from the television set and the microwave oven and the fluorescent clock face. As with syphilis, an innocent or trivial act—or exposure—in the present can have dire consequences far in the future. It is also known that cancer rates are high for workers in a large number of industrial occupations. Though the exact processes of causation lying behind the statistics remain unknown, it seems clear that many cancers are preventable. But cancer is not just a disease ushered in by the Industrial Revolution (there was cancer in Arcadia) and certainly more than the sin of capitalism (within their more limited industrial capacities, the Russians pollute worse than we do). The widespread current view of cancer as a disease of industrial civilization is as unsound scientifically as the right-wing fantasy of a "world without cancer" (like a world without subversives). Both rest on the mistaken feeling that cancer is a distinctively "modern" disease.

The medieval experience of the plague was firmly tied to notions of moral pollution, and people invariably looked for a scapegoat external to the stricken community. (Massacres of Jews in unprecedented numbers took place everywhere in plague-stricken Europe of 1347–48, then stopped as soon as the plague receded.) With the modern diseases, the scapegoat is not so easily separated from the patient. But much as these diseases individualize, they also pick up some of the metaphors of epidemic diseases. (Diseases understood to be simply epidemic have become less useful as metaphors, as evidenced by the near-total historical amnesia about the influenza pandemic of 1918–19, in which more people died than in the four years of World War I.) Presently, it is as much a cliché to say that cancer is "environmentally" caused as it was—and still is—to say that it is caused by mismanaged emotions. TB was associated with pollution (Florence Nightingale thought it was "induced by the foul air of houses"), and now cancer is thought of as a disease of the contamination of the whole world. TB was "the white plague." With awareness of environmental pollution, people have started saying that there is an "epidemic" or "plague" of cancer.

9

Illnesses have always been used as metaphors to enliven charges that a society was corrupt or unjust. Traditional disease metaphors are principally a way of being vehement; they are, compared with the modern metaphors, relatively contentless. Shakespeare does many variations on a standard form of the metaphor, an infection in the "body politic"—making no distinction between a contagion, an infection, a sore, an abscess, an ulcer, and what we would call a tumor. For purposes of invective, diseases are of only two types: the painful but curable, and the possibly fatal. Particular diseases figure as examples of diseases in general; no disease has its own distinctive logic. Disease imagery is used to express concern for social order, and health is something everyone is presumed to know about. Such metaphors do not project the modern idea of a specific master illness, in which what is at issue is health itself.

Master illnesses like TB and cancer are more specifically polemical. They are used to propose new, critical standards of

individual health, and to express a sense of dissatisfaction with
society as such. Unlike the Elizabethan metaphors—which
complain of some general aberration or public calamity that is,
in consequence, dislocating to individuals—the modern metaphors suggest a profound disequilibrium between individual
and society, with society conceived as the individual's adversary. Disease metaphors are used to judge society not as out of
balance but as repressive. They turn up regularly in Romantic
rhetoric which opposes heart to head, spontaneity to reason,
nature to artifice, country to city.

When travel to a better climate was invented as a treatment
for TB in the early nineteenth century, the most contradictory
destinations were proposed. The south, mountains, deserts,
islands—their very diversity suggests what they have in common: the rejection of the city. In *La Traviata*, as soon as
Alfredo wins Violetta's love, he moves her from unhealthy
wicked Paris to the wholesome countryside: instant health follows. And Violetta's giving up on happiness is tantamount to
leaving the country and returning to the city—where her doom
is sealed, her TB returns, and she dies.

The metaphor of cancer expands the theme of the rejection
of the city. In *Lost Illusions*, in the section called "A Provincial
Celebrity in Paris," Balzac described Lucien de Rubempré after
a literary party:

> This evening he had seen things as they are. And instead of being
> seized with horror at the spectacle of that cancer in the very heart
> of Paris . . . he was intoxicated with the pleasure of being in such
> intellectually brilliant society. These remarkable men, with their
> dazzling armor of vice. . . .

Before the city was understood as, literally, a cancer-causing
(carcinogenic) environment, the city was seen as itself a
cancer—a place of abnormal, unnatural growth, and extravagant, devouring, armored passions.*

* In *The Living City* (1958), Frank Lloyd Wright compared the city of earlier
times, a healthy organism ("The city then was not malignant"), with the modern city. "To look at the cross-section of any plan of a big city is to look at the
section of a fibrous tumor." The sociologist Herbert Gans has called my attention to the importance of tuberculosis and the alleged or real threat of it in the
slum-clearing and "model tenement" movements of the late nineteenth and

Throughout the nineteenth century, disease metaphors become more virulent, preposterous, demagogic. And there is an increasing tendency to call any situation one disapproves of a disease. Disease, which could be considered as much a part of nature as is health, became the synonym of whatever was "unnatural." In *Les Misérables*, Hugo wrote:

> Monasticism, such as it existed in Spain and as it exists in Tibet, is for civilization a sort of tuberculosis. It cuts off life. Quite simply, it depopulates. Confinement, castration. It was a scourge in Europe.

Bichat in 1800 defined life as "the ensemble of functions which resists death." That contrast between life and death was to be transferred to a contrast between life and disease. Disease (now equated with death) is what opposes life.

In 1916, in "Socialism and Culture," Gramsci denounced

> the habit of thinking that culture is encyclopedic knowledge. . . . This form of culture serves to create that pale and broken-winded intellectualism . . . which has produced a whole crowd of boasters and daydreamers more harmful to a healthy social life than tuberculosis or syphilis microbes are to the body's beauty and health. . . .

In 1919, Mandelstam paid the following tribute to Pasternak:

> To read Pasternak's verse is to clear one's throat, to fortify one's breathing, to fill one's lungs; such poetry must be healthy, a cure for tuberculosis. No poetry is healthier at the present moment. It is like drinking *koumis* after canned American milk.

And Marinetti, denouncing Communism in 1920:

> Communism is the exasperation of the bureaucratic cancer that has always wasted humanity. A German cancer, a product of the characteristic German preparationism. Every pedantic preparation is anti-human. . . .

---

early twentieth centuries, the feeling being that slum housing "bred" TB. The shift from TB to cancer in planning and housing rhetoric had taken place by the 1950s. "Blight" (a virtual synonym for slum) is seen as a cancer that spreads insidiously, and the use of the term "invasion" to describe when the non-white and poor move into a middle-class neighborhood is as much a metaphor borrowed from cancer as from the military: the two discourses overlap.

It is for the same iniquity that the protofascist Italian writer attacks Communism and the future founder of the Italian Communist Party attacks a certain bourgeois idea of culture ("truly harmful, especially to the proletariat," Gramsci says)—for being artificial, pedantic, rigid, lifeless. Both TB and cancer have been regularly invoked to condemn repressive practices and ideals, repression being conceived of as an environment that deprives one of strength (TB) or of flexibility and spontaneity (cancer). Modern disease metaphors specify an ideal of society's well-being, analogized to physical health, that is as frequently anti-political as it is a call for a new political order.

Order is the oldest concern of political philosophy, and if it is plausible to compare the polis to an organism, then it is plausible to compare civil disorder to an illness. The classical formulations which analogize a political disorder to an illness—from Plato to, say, Hobbes—presuppose the classical medical (and political) idea of balance. Illness comes from imbalance. Treatment is aimed at restoring the right balance—in political terms, the right hierarchy. The prognosis is always, in principle, optimistic. Society, by definition, never catches a fatal disease.

When a disease image is used by Machiavelli, the presumption is that the disease can be cured. "Consumption," he wrote,

> in the commencement is easy to cure, and difficult to understand; but when it has neither been discovered in due time, nor treated upon a proper principle, it becomes easy to understand, and difficult to cure. The same thing happens in state affairs, by foreseeing them at a distance, which is only done by men of talents, the evils which might arise from them are soon cured; but when, from want of foresight, they are suffered to increase to such a height that they are perceptible to everyone, there is no longer any remedy.

Machiavelli invokes TB as a disease whose progress can be cut off, if it is detected at an early stage (when its symptoms are barely visible). Given proper foresight, the course of a disease is not irreversible; the same for disturbances in the body politic. Machiavelli offers an illness metaphor that is not so much about society as about statecraft (conceived as a therapeutic art): as prudence is needed to control serious diseases, so foresight is needed to control social crises. It is a metaphor about foresight, and a call to foresight.

In political philosophy's great tradition, the analogy between disease and civil disorder is proposed to encourage rulers to pursue a more rational policy. "Although nothing can be immortall, which mortals make," Hobbes wrote,

> yet, if men had the use of reason they pretend to, their Commonwealths might be secured, at least, from perishing by internal diseases. . . . Therefore when they come to be dissolved, not by externall violence, but intestine disorder, the fault is not in men, as they are the *Matter*; but as they are the *Makers*, and orderers of them.

Hobbes's view is anything but fatalistic. Rulers have the responsibility and the ability (through reason) to control disorder. For Hobbes, murder ("externall violence") is the only "natural" way for a society or institution to die. To perish from internal disorder—analogized to a disease—is suicide, something quite preventable; an act of will, or rather a failure of will (that is, of reason).

The disease metaphor was used in political philosophy to reinforce the call for a rational response. Machiavelli and Hobbes fixed on one part of medical wisdom, the importance of cutting off serious disease early, while it is relatively easy to control. The disease metaphor could also be used to encourage rulers to another kind of foresight. In 1708, Lord Shaftesbury wrote:

> There are certain humours in mankind which of necessity must have vent. The human mind and body are both of them naturally subject to commotions . . . as there are strange ferments in the blood, which in many bodies occasion an extraordinary discharge. . . . Should physicians endeavour absolutely to allay those ferments of the body, and strike in the humours which discover themselves in such eruptions, they might, instead of making a cure, bid fair perhaps to raise a plague, and turn a spring-ague or an autumn-surfeit into an epidemical malignant fever. They are certainly as ill physicians in the body politic who would needs be tampering with these mental eruptions, and, under the specious pretence of healing this itch of superstition and saving souls from the contagion of enthusiasm, should set all nature in an uproar, and turn a few innocent carbuncles into an inflammation and mortal gangrene.

Shaftesbury's point is that it is rational to tolerate a certain amount of irrationality ("superstition," "enthusiasm"), and that stern repressive measures are likely to aggravate disorder rather than cure it, turning a nuisance into a disaster. The body politic should not be overmedicalized; a remedy should not be sought for every disorder.

For Machiavelli, foresight; for Hobbes, reason; for Shaftesbury, tolerance—these are all ideas of how proper statecraft, conceived on a medical analogy, can prevent a fatal disorder. Society is presumed to be in basically good health; disease (disorder) is, in principle, always manageable.

In the modern period, the use of disease imagery in political rhetoric implies other, less lenient assumptions. The modern idea of revolution, based on an estimate of the unremitting bleakness of the existing political situation, shattered the old, optimistic use of disease metaphors. John Adams wrote in his diary, in December 1772:

> The Prospect before me . . . is very gloomy. My Country is in deep Distress, and has very little Ground of Hope. . . . The Body of the People seem to be worn out, by struggling, and Venality, Servility and Prostitution, eat and spread like a Cancer.

Political events started commonly to be defined as being unprecedented, radical; and eventually both civil disturbances and wars come to be understood as, really, revolutions. As might be expected, it was not with the American but with the French Revolution that disease metaphors in the modern sense came into their own—particularly in the conservative response to the French Revolution. In *Reflections on the Revolution in France* (1790), Edmund Burke contrasted older wars and civil disturbances with this one, which he considered to have a totally new character. Before, no matter what the disaster, "the organs . . . of the state, however shattered, existed." But, he addressed the French, "your present confusion, like a palsy, has attacked the fountain of life itself."

As classical theories of the polis have gone the way of the theories of the four humours, so a modern idea of politics has been complemented by a modern idea of disease. Disease equals death. Burke invoked a palsy (and "the living ulcer of a corroding memory"). The emphasis was soon to be on diseases that are loathsome and fatal. Such diseases are not to be managed or treated; they are to be attacked. In Hugo's novel about the French Revolution, *Quatre-vingt-treize* (1874), the revolutionary Gauvain, condemned to the guillotine, absolves the Revolution with all its bloodshed, including his own imminent execution,

> because it is a storm. A storm always knows what it is doing. . . . Civilization was in the grip of plague; this gale comes to the rescue. Perhaps it is not selective enough. Can it act otherwise? It is entrusted with the arduous task of sweeping away disease! In face of the horrible infection, I understand the fury of the blast.

It is hardly the last time that revolutionary violence would be justified on the grounds that society has a radical, horrible illness. The melodramatics of the disease metaphor in modern political discourse assume a punitive notion: of the disease not as a punishment but as a sign of evil, something to be punished.

Modern totalitarian movements, whether of the right or of the left, have been peculiarly—and revealingly—inclined to use disease imagery. The Nazis declared that someone of mixed "racial" origin was like a syphilitic. European Jewry was repeatedly analogized to syphilis, and to a cancer that must be excised. Disease metaphors were a staple of Bolshevik polemics, and Trotsky, the most gifted of all communist polemicists, used them with the greatest profusion—particularly after his banishment from the Soviet Union in 1929. Stalinism was called a cholera, a syphilis, and a cancer.* To use only fatal diseases for imagery in politics gives the metaphor a much more pointed character. Now, to liken a political event or situation to an illness is to impute guilt, to prescribe punishment.

---

*Cf. Isaac Deutscher, *The Prophet Outcast: Trotsky, 1929–1940* (1963): "'Certain measures,' Trotsky wrote to [Philip] Rahv [on March 21, 1938], 'are necessary for a struggle against incorrect theory, and others for fighting a cholera epidemic. Stalin is incomparably nearer to cholera than to a false theory. The struggle must be intense, truculent, merciless. An element of "fanaticism" . . . is salutary.'" And: "Trotsky spoke of the 'syphilis of Stalinism' or of the 'cancer that must be burned out of the labour movement with a hot iron.' . . ."

Notably, Solzhenitsyn's *Cancer Ward* contains virtually no uses of cancer as a metaphor—for Stalinism, or for anything else. Solzhenitsyn was not misrepresenting his novel when, hoping to get it published in the Soviet Union, he told the Board of the Union of Writers in 1967 that the title was not "some kind of symbol," as was being charged, and that "the subject is specifically and literally cancer."

This is particularly true of the use of cancer as a metaphor. It amounts to saying, first of all, that the event or situation is unqualifiedly and unredeemably wicked. It enormously ups the ante. Hitler, in his first political tract, an anti-Semitic diatribe written in September 1919, accused the Jews of producing "a racial tuberculosis among nations."* Tuberculosis still retained its prestige as the overdetermined, culpable illness of the nineteenth century. (Recall Hugo's comparison of monasticism with TB.) But the Nazis quickly modernized their rhetoric, and indeed the imagery of cancer was far more apt for their purposes. As was said in speeches about "the Jewish problem" throughout the 1930s, to treat a cancer, one must cut out much of the healthy tissue around it. The imagery of cancer for the Nazis prescribes "radical" treatment, in contrast to the "soft" treatment thought appropriate for TB—the difference between sanatoria (that is, exile) and surgery (that is, crematoria). (The Jews were also identified with, and became a metaphor for, city life—with Nazi rhetoric echoing all the Romantic clichés about cities as a debilitating, merely cerebral, morally contaminated, unhealthy environment.)

To describe a phenomenon as a cancer is an incitement to violence. The use of cancer in political discourse encourages fatalism and justifies "severe" measures—as well as strongly reinforcing the widespread notion that the disease is necessarily fatal. The concept of disease is never innocent. But it could be argued that the cancer metaphors are in themselves implicitly genocidal. No specific political view seems to have a monopoly on this metaphor. Trotsky called Stalinism the cancer of Marxism; in China in the last year, the Gang of Four have become, among other things, "the cancer of China." John Dean

---

* "[The Jew's] power is the power of money which in the form of interest effortlessly and interminably multiplies itself in his hands and forces upon nations that most dangerous of yokes. . . . Everything which makes men strive for higher things, whether religion, socialism, or democracy, is for him only a means to an end, to the satisfaction of a lust for money and domination. His activities produce a racial tuberculosis among nations. . . ." A late-nineteenth-century precursor of Nazi ideology, Julius Langbehn, called the Jews "only a passing pest and cholera." But in Hitler's TB image there is already something easily transferred to cancer: the idea that Jewish power "effortlessly and interminably multiplies."

explained Watergate to Nixon: "We have a cancer within—close to the Presidency—that's growing." The standard metaphor of Arab polemics—heard by Israelis on the radio every day for the last twenty years—is that Israel is "a cancer in the heart of the Arab world" or "the cancer of the Middle East," and an officer with the Christian Lebanese rightist forces besieging the Palestine refugee camp of Tal Zaatar in August 1976 called the camp "a cancer in the Lebanese body." The cancer metaphor seems hard to resist for those who wish to register indignation. Thus, Neal Ascherson wrote in 1969 that the Slansky Affair "was—is—a huge cancer in the body of the Czechoslovak state and nation"; Simon Leys, in *Chinese Shadows*, speaks of "the Maoist cancer that is gnawing away at the face of China"; D. H. Lawrence called masturbation "the deepest and most danger-ous cancer of our civilization"; and I once wrote, in the heat of despair over America's war on Vietnam, that "the white race is the cancer of human history."

But how to be morally severe in the late twentieth century? How, when there is so much to be severe about; how, when we have a sense of evil but no longer the religious or philosophical language to talk intelligently about evil. Trying to comprehend "radical" or "absolute" evil, we search for adequate metaphors. But the modern disease metaphors are all cheap shots. The people who have the real disease are also hardly helped by hearing their disease's name constantly being dropped as the epitome of evil. Only in the most limited sense is any historical event or problem like an illness. And the cancer metaphor is particularly crass. It is invariably an encouragement to simplify what is complex and an invitation to self-righteousness, if not to fanaticism.

It is instructive to compare the image of cancer with that of gangrene. With some of the same metaphoric properties as cancer—it starts from nothing; it spreads; it is disgusting—gangrene would seem to be laden with everything a polemi-cist would want. Indeed, it was used in one important moral polemic—against the French use of torture in Algeria in the 1950s; the title of the famous book exposing that torture was called *La Gangrène*. But there is a large difference between the cancer and the gangrene metaphors. First, causality is clear with gangrene. It is external (gangrene can develop from a scratch);

cancer is understood as mysterious, a disease with multiple causes, internal as well as external. Second, gangrene is not as all-encompassing a disaster. It leads often to amputation, less often to death; cancer is presumed to lead to death in most cases. Not gangrene—and not the plague (despite the notable attempts by writers as different as Artaud, Reich, and Camus to impose that as a metaphor for the dismal and the disastrous)— but cancer remains the most radical of disease metaphors. And just because it is so radical, it is particularly tendentious—a good metaphor for paranoids, for those who need to turn campaigns into crusades, for the fatalistic (cancer = death), and for those under the spell of ahistorical revolutionary optimism (the idea that only the most radical changes are desirable). As long as so much militaristic hyperbole attaches to the description and treatment of cancer, it is a particularly unapt metaphor for the peace-loving.

It is, of course, likely that the language about cancer will evolve in the coming years. It must change, decisively, when the disease is finally understood and the rate of cure becomes much higher. It is already changing, with the development of new forms of treatment. As chemotherapy is more and more supplanting radiation in the treatment of cancer patients, an effective form of treatment (already a supplementary treatment of proven use) seems likely to be found in some kind of immunotherapy. Concepts have started to shift in certain medical circles, where doctors are concentrating on the steep buildup of the body's immunological responses to cancer. As the language of treatment evolves from military metaphors of aggressive warfare to metaphors featuring the body's "natural defenses" (what is called the "immunodefensive system" can also—to break entirely with the military metaphor—be called the body's "immune competence"), cancer will be partly de-mythicized; and it may then be possible to compare something to a cancer without implying either a fatalistic diagnosis or a rousing call to fight by any means whatever a lethal, insidious enemy. Then perhaps it will be morally permissible, as it is not now, to use cancer as a metaphor.

But at that time, perhaps nobody will want any longer to compare anything awful to cancer. Since the interest of the metaphor is precisely that it refers to a disease so overlaid with mystification, so charged with the fantasy of inescapable fatality. Since our views about cancer, and the metaphors we have imposed on it, are so much a vehicle for the large insufficiencies of this culture, for our shallow attitude toward death, for our anxieties about feeling, for our reckless improvident responses to our real "problems of growth," for our inability to construct an advanced industrial society which properly regulates consumption, and for our justified fears of the increasingly violent course of history. The cancer metaphor will be made obsolete, I would predict, long before the problems it has reflected so persuasively will be resolved.

UNCOLLECTED ESSAYS

William Burroughs and the Novel

Among English-speaking writers, critics, and readers there exists a remarkable degree of consensus about the novel. According to this consensus, the novel is understood not so much as a work of art but as a mirror of reality. For most people, the interest of novels consists in what they are "about," which means the real-life local milieux in which they are situated. Thus, the principal standard applied to novels is how accurate, how pungent is the news they provide about character and about environments (both familiar and unfamiliar), and how wise is the "position" they espouse toward their material. So far as the novel has a serious purpose (something other than mere diversion, entertainment, escape), it is thought to be this: the responsible and intelligent dramatizing of psychological and social and ethical issues, and the supplying of information. Most novels written in England and America these days are reportorial in conception.*

The fact is, there does not exist in English any continuous formalist tradition of the novel—a tradition that maintains an alternative to the main tradition of realism. Despite many examples of work which is "experimental," the novel in England and America is extremely conservative. The beginnings or makings of an Anglo-American formalist tradition exist in the work of Joyce, Virginia Woolf, Beckett, Gertrude Stein, Laura Riding, Nathanael West, and John Dos Passos (who is usually grouped with naturalists like Farrell and Dreiser). In the 1920s and early 1930s, it seemed as if the practice of the long fiction we go on calling "the novel" for lack of a better name had been decisively renovated. Then, in the late 1930s, taste largely reverted to what had seemed to be rendered obsolete by the innovations of these writers. Since then, most critically respectable novels (I am not speaking of ordinary best sellers) are written as if these writers had never existed. The work of the early twentieth century experimental writers, now elevated

---

* This consensus must not be too narrowly interpreted. It does not mean naturalism—confinement to the laws of probability, and to mundane, prosaic, and quotidian slices of experience. Hence, the proliferation of satire and "black humor" in recent American literature does not signify a genuine challenge to the consensus about the novel I have described.

to the status of classics and studied respectfully in university classrooms, recedes into the past. Picasso is hardly a "modern" painter; a whole tradition has followed from him, and itself been superseded by several newer modernisms. But Joyce is still "modern," still in the vanguard; and a serious literary tradition issuing from Joyce's work, or any of the other writers I have mentioned, has not evolved. The English and American novel has, by and large, returned to the aesthetic premises of nineteenth century realism, in which the artist gives "form" to a certain "subject." According to this conception, the demands of the novel as an art form can only be considered as an adjunct to the novelist's job of telling the truth.

I should like to explore as a criterion for novels the concern for form itself. Obviously, I do not mean form in the gross sense according to which, say, we distinguish the standard novel told in the third person from first-person narrations such as the novel in letters or the novel in the guise of a diary. By form, I mean a structuring of the literary work analogous to, though not altogether like, the calculations that (traditionally) enter into the composition of music or the making of a painting. To be sure, it seems hard to imagine forms for the novel that would be wholly quantifiable, abstract—as they can be in music and painting. The primary use of language connects with something understood as lying outside language (so-called "reality"), and it seems unlikely that any employment of language in art would ever want wholly to disregard that connection. Nevertheless, that works of literature refer to "reality" in a cruder sense is not as such an obstacle to a formalist approach to the novel. That works of literature have "subjects" or tell "stories" can be regarded as one of the most interesting and decisive *formal* conventions of literary art.

The discovery of form, so defined, in the novel (which is tantamount to the discovery of the novel as an aesthetic *object*) is distinctly modern. It is, indeed, the hallmark of modernism in prose literature. Joyce, in *Ulysses*, was perhaps the first writer to envisage clearly a rigorous and extensive formal design in the novel. Proust must be cited for his notion of the "musical" structuring of memories (the task of narrating having been equated with the task of remembering). But, of course, there are predecessors. One is Laclos in *Les Liaisons Dangereuses* (1782). I cite this novel as the earliest I know of organized around the application and exfoliation of a single, controlling metaphor—namely, life (and particularly the emotions, eroticism) as war and a problem of military tactics. Henry James is another, much better known predecessor, for his notion (spelled out in the famous prefaces) of the well-formed novel as unified by the point of view or controlling consciousness of an observer situated within the story.

The alignment of these examples is meant to indicate that the choices are still open and underdeveloped. One idea discernible in many of the efforts to articulate complex forms for the novel is that of making the form, or structure, *visible*. This tendency in the novel parallels what has been taking place (much more rapidly) in architecture, painting, music, sculpture, and most other arts—the willingness to emphasize the artifice in art.* Against the old feeling that an artist's technique should be invisible (or at least inconspicuous), many of those who press the claims of "form" in literature insist on letting the scaffolding and traces of workmanship show. For instance, the writer may supply "footnotes," either of a scholarly or purely personal, idiosyncratic character, which stand as an appendix to the work. Examples: Beckett's *Watt*, Durrell's *Alexandria Quartet*, Burroughs' *Naked Lunch*. (It seems to have been the poets—T. S. Eliot in *The Waste Land*, Marianne Moore—who supplied the modern model for this device.) Another device is to present a text in which some of the words and phrases have been crossed out. Example: a recent short novel by the poet James Merrill, *The (Diblos) Notebook*.

But new forms of order tend, of course, to look like willful disorder. One of the prospects that has proved most attractive to contemporary artists is that of abolishing established formal hierarchies that have ordered the arts. In the new language of music (the twelve-tone row, etc.), the point is that one note is as privileged as any other. Certain contemporary paintings—for example, the striped canvases of Frank Stella, the "flags" of Jasper Johns—make the point that every part of the canvas has the

---

*Here, one might compare the conservatism of the contemporary American novel with the conservatism of academic film technique as taught in the United States—until recently. The principle was that film technique (camera work, etc.) should always be as inconspicuous as possible; it *serves* the story. Orson Welles in *Citizen Kane* (1941) was the first director in Hollywood during the period of sound films to insist on a deliberately artificial mode of story narration.

same weight, value, inflection, as any other part. Analogously, at least *one* direction for prose literature (as well as for films, which have been largely confined to novelistic story-telling*) would be to discard the traditional supremacy of the "story" or "plot."

Another new form of order proceeds by the cultivation of chance or casual means of composition. The discovery of chance as a valid element of literary composition seems to run counter to all established notions of literary formalism. But the aesthetic of chance can be viewed not just as a move toward disorder but as a shrewd means for achieving a greater abstractness in the art object. Randomness can be said to achieve many of the same aesthetic goals as the most rigid neo-mathematical planning. The element added by randomness is that the work of art becomes not only abstract but open-ended. The acceptance of random or casual decisions in constructing a work of art is, indeed, partly derived from the questioning of the very idea of a bounded, complete, self-sufficient work of art. Fundamental to the modernist aesthetic—which goes back to the Romantics—is the notion that there cannot be any complete work of art. In the early nineteenth century, Novalis prophesied the advent of a new literary art which would consist of either one "total book" or a series of fragments. He thought the latter more likely. The art of the fragment, which involves the demand for a fragmentary "speech," is designed not to *hinder* communication but to make it absolute. Explicating Novalis' prophecy, Maurice Blanchot has written:

> A discontinuous form is the only one suited to Romantic irony since it alone can make speech and silence coexist, as well as play and the serious, the need for declaration, even for the oracular, and the indecision of a thought at once unstable and divided; in the end a mind obliged to be both systematic and to hold system in horror.

* The fifty years of the cinema present us with something like a scrambled recapitulation of the more than two hundred year history of the novel. For instance, with Griffith, the cinema had its Samuel Richardson. The director of *Birth of a Nation* (1915), *Intolerance* (1916), *Broken Blossoms* (1919), *Way Down East* (1920), *One Exciting Night* (1922), and hundreds of other films, voiced many of the same moral conceptions and occupied an approximately similar position with respect to the development of the film art as the author of *Pamela* and *Clarissa* did with respect to the development of the novel.

Novalis' words were indeed prophetic, for the fragment, often of huge proportions, is an important literary form of our time. (Cf. Kafka's *The Trial* and *The Castle*; Gadda's *Quer pasticciaccio brutto de via Merulana*; Genet's *Notre Dame des Fleurs*; the narratives of Burroughs.)

Yet it would not be correct to argue that only the fragment, the truncated work or the unfinished book, suits the irony that pervades *our* romantic time. Another characteristic modern strategy must be mentioned: the deliberate use, partly ironic and partly serious, of banal or outmoded narrative forms. Many contemporary writers searching for revivifying forms for the novel have settled precisely on the most calcified, familiar, "closed" types of narration. (What is really banal becomes all the more available for original use.) One example is Burroughs' use of the science-fiction tale. Another example: the use of the "spy novel" in Thomas Pynchon's *V*, in which that genre's conventional patterns of suspense and peculiar behavior are filled with philosophical and historical mystification. (French film directors have employed the American gangster film and B-film format in a similar way, as in Truffaut's *Tirez sur le Pianiste*.)

There is perhaps no one recent book that exemplifies in a central way, as did Joyce's *Ulysses*, new possibilities for enlarging and complicating the forms of prose literature. But the writings of Burroughs have perhaps more priority than any other. Burroughs, who was born in 1914 in St. Louis, Missouri, published a pseudonymous novel of a conventional kind, *Junkie: Confessions of an Unredeemed Drug Addict*, in 1953, which he does not consider part of his work as a serious writer. But ever since the publication of *Naked Lunch* in 1962, he has been beyond a doubt the most controversial and the most interesting figure in American letters. (*Naked Lunch* was followed by *Nova Express* in 1964 and *The Soft Machine* in 1966. A fourth book, called *The Ticket That Exploded*, already brought out by the Olympia Press in Paris, has not yet been published in America.)

All of Burroughs' books are fragments, and that in several senses. He is writing a series of installments of a giant endless oeuvre. (Thus far, the first installment, *Naked Lunch*, seems most complex and powerful.) And, each one of the books consists of fragments; their length, development, and ordering follow no discernible sequence. "You can cut into *Naked Lunch* at any intersection point," Burroughs writes in the "Atrophied Preface" which is to be found at the end of the book. Elsewhere he has said: "The final form of *Naked Lunch* and the juxtaposition of sections were determined by the order in which material went—at random—to the printer." (It is perhaps worth noting that *The Soft Machine*, as originally published by the Olympia Press, is longer than the book of that title later brought out in America, and the material is in a different order.)

Clearly, one cannot read Burroughs' books as novels in the conventional sense. There is no "plot" (though there are shards of "stories"). And there are no "characters" (though there are "figures"). Of this aspect of his work, Burroughs has written in *Naked Lunch*, somewhat misleadingly:

> There is only one thing a writer can write about: *what is in front of his senses at the moment of writing*. . . . I am a recording instrument. . . . I do not presume to impose 'story' 'plot' 'continuity.' . . . Insofar as I succeed in *Direct* recording of certain areas of psychic process I may have limited function. . . . I am not an entertainer.

I call this account somewhat misleading because, although it may describe what Burroughs feels when he writes, it does not describe what he has written. Each of Burroughs' books is an oneiric enterprise. In *Naked Lunch*, a substructure of narrative, characterization, and place descriptions fades into "routines"—heightened fantastic projections of people, places, and actions on the one hand, and learned footnotes on drugs, diseases, and folkways on the other. But all is scarcely the chaos Burroughs might have us believe. The absence of a plot does not mean the absence of a narrative. Burroughs has arranged his narrative on a nonlinear principle—that of an indefinite number of variations and repetitions.

Most of Burroughs' admirers, most of those who are not put off by the unpleasantness of Burroughs' "material" or by the sheer difficulty of reading his books, vindicate him as a "satirist" of American life and the Americanization of the world situation—of our dehumanization by technology, sexual repression, overpolicing, and the threat of the Bomb. A related view takes Burroughs' recurrent themes of metamorphosis, instant orgies, and interplanetary invasions as demented and scrambled science fiction. While neither the intention of satire nor the recourse to science-fiction conventions can be denied or ought to be neglected, it seems to me that such readings hardly do justice to Burroughs' gift. The main interest of Burroughs' work is in the new and immensely powerful voice that he has set down. Strictly speaking, it is not a single voice, as in older literary endeavors, but a stream of fragmented and intercutting voices that derive from pulp magazines, disc-jockey patter, newspaper headlines, street obscenities, carney talk, scientific obfuscation, bureaucratic jargon, comic book and Hollywood movie dialogue. From *The Soft Machine*:

> We fold writers of all time in together and record radio programs, movie sound tracks, TV and juke box sounds all the words of the world stirring around in a cement mixer and pour in the resistance message "Calling partisans of all nations—Cut word lines—Shift linguals—Free doorways—Vibrate 'tourists'—Word falling—Photo falling—Break through in Gray Room."

Yet, in the end, the voices come together—to sound the most serious, urgent, and original note in American letters to be heard in many years.

Burroughs' work cannot be read as an example of "spontaneous prose." He is a conscious, extremely complex artist, who exhibits the confluence of two, seemingly opposed positions which have appeared in the search for rigorous forms appropriate to the "novel." One position is that the long, imaginative prose work has been constricted by being merely "literary," and that an infusion of techniques from other media (leading to an eventual synthesis of the arts) is overdue. The other position is that fiction's task is to purify itself and to perfect strictly literary means of expression, the means that are peculiar to literature (as distinct from entertainment, exhortation, and "communication").

With the first tendency we are dealing with an old mandate. The breakdown of rigid genre distinctions is one of the richest legacies of Romanticism. (This is Novalis' "total book," and Wagner's idea of "the art work of the future," which he called the *Gesamtkunstwerk*, the total-art-work.) In the novel, leaving aside the attraction which poetry has exercised from time to time, the alien art forms that have proved most alluring are painting and the cinema.

It was the attempt to reorganize fictional forms according to the forms of painting that inspired the art of Gertrude Stein, as she makes clear in her *Lectures in America* (1935) and in *The Autobiography of Alice B. Toklas*. The characteristic aesthetic of modern painting depends on emphasizing the painting as a physical object, as a flat surface; this constitutes a new evaluation of the difference between the flat "pictorial" space and "real" space. Stein is perhaps the only writer to work systematically on extending this aesthetic to prose literature, her search for "presentness" in narration being analogous to the modern painter's embrace of the flatness, the two-dimensionality of the canvas. (The possible exchanges between writing and painting have also been important to certain recent American poets, notably John Ashbery, Kenneth Koch, and Frank O'Hara.)

But more common as a model for new notions of writing than painting is the cinema. Writers as different as Ronald Firbank, Djuna Barnes (in *Nightwood*), Horace McCoy (in *They Shoot Horses, Don't They?*), and Faulkner (take, as only one example, his story "Red Leaves") adapted the principles of cinematic composition and pacing to literary narration and description. More recently, Robbe-Grillet (and many of the newer French novelists, such as Claude Ollier) have, as has often been noted, attempted a more radical emulation in fiction of cinema rhythms and camera movements.

With Burroughs, too, the evidence of cinematic models is everywhere. To be sure, Burroughs does allude to an inspiration from painting; he speaks of using a "collage technique." For some time, in association with the painter Brion Gysin, he has been writing by assembling strips of words chosen at random from disparate book, newspaper, and magazine texts. (A parallel could be drawn between "the cut-up method," the name Burroughs has given to his procedure, and the famous game and art technique invented by the Surrealists, *le cadavre exquis*.) But to call this technique "collage" fails to do justice to Burroughs' drastic involvement with the dimension of *time* in experience. In Burroughs' books, space travel is invariably rendered as vertiginous travel in time. A cinematic analogy, "montage," provides a closer analogy to Burroughs' technique than any that might be drawn from painting.

In *Naked Lunch*, he writes: ". . . cures past and future shuttle pictures through his spectral substance vibrating in silent winds of accelerated Time . . . Pick a shot . . . Any shot. . . ." Since *Naked Lunch*, the cinematic preoccupations have been reinforced and developed. In a recent interview in the *Paris Review*, Burroughs likened experience to a series of "reality photographs." And "the gray room," a recurrent image in *Nova Express*, is the photographic darkroom where the reality photographs are produced. "Implicit in *Nova Express*," said Burroughs, "is a theory that what we call reality is actually a movie. It's a film, what I call a biologic film."

The Soft Machine, too, can be described as a vision of the world controlled by the metaphor of reality as cinema. The book, whose title recalls H. G. Wells' *The Time Machine*, is a manual of what Burroughs describes as "basic training in time travel." It depicts a series of trips by man, the soft machine, through a disoriented world in which one has "learned to talk and think backward on all levels—This was done by running film and sound track backwards." As in *Naked Lunch* and *Nova Express*, many of the actions in *The Soft Machine* are actions seen and experienced as on film. Example:

> They walked through a city of black and white movies fading streets of thousand-run smoke faces. Figures of the world slow down to catatonic limestone. City blocks speed up out in photo flash. Hotel lobbies 1920 time fill with slow gray film fallout . . .

Events take place at "action stations." These might be called St. Louis or Mexico City or New York or Tangier, but that does not matter; all space has been converted into time. The principle of movement, or narration, is that the writer can "cut" (as the movies do) from one place to another at will and without transition. As Burroughs says in *Naked Lunch*:

> Why all this waste paper getting The People from one place to another? Perhaps to spare The Reader stress of sudden space shifts and keep him Gentle? And so a ticket is bought, a taxi called, a plane boarded. . . .
>
> I am not American Express. . . . If one of my people is seen in New York walking around in citizen clothes and next sentence Timbuktu putting down lad talk on a gazelle-eyed youth, we may assume that he (the party non-resident of Timbuktu) transported himself there by the usual methods of communication . . .

Needless to say, the recognition of cinematic metaphors in Burroughs' books does not exhaust their interest. But without an understanding of these (of their persistence and their variety), it is impossible to grasp what Burroughs is doing.

It might be noted that although Burroughs is writing an endless book in fragments or installments, anyone interested in reading him would be well advised not to begin with the later books. Although some of the cast (like "the Subliminal Kid," Doc Benway, "Mr. Bradley Mr. Martin") as well as key recurrent phrases (like "Word falling—Photo falling") continue from one book to the next, Burroughs' books have quite different degrees of explicitness. *Naked Lunch* and *Nova Express* are very reflective books. (Cf. the sections in *Nova Express* on "the silence" demanded of the reader, on the idea of "total emergency," and on "word units.") *The Soft Machine* and *The Ticket That Exploded* are considerably less explicit. Here, Burroughs seems to assume familiarity with his method and the justifications for it. Thus, despite its commitment to an "open form" based on the freedom of dreaming (including "retroactive dreaming") and on the discontinuities of movie narration, Burroughs' work is more rewarding when read in its present sequence, however arbitrary that may be.

A final question: If Burroughs is valuable as an artist, for his accomplishments within the sphere of art and for what these suggest about new forms for the novel, does that mean it would be inappropriate for us to concern ourselves with what he seems to be saying, in accents of the greatest urgency, about our world?

According to Robbe-Grillet, the demands of the novel as art and the demands laid on art to be both mirror and critique of reality are mutually exclusive. Robbe-Grillet quotes Heidegger, who says: "The human condition is *to be there*." What follows from this is a conception of literature which points to nothing beyond what is described, "nothing of what can traditionally be called a message." For Robbe-Grillet, man is a witness; and the novel, like any other art, is a pure creation, referring to nothing outside itself. Therefore, "the only possible commitment for the writer is literature." It is thus that Robbe-Grillet would dispose of the thorny relation between art and life, art and truth. There is none. Art owes nothing to life, or to truth.

But can matters be that simple? If so, there would be more credibility in the opposite thesis: that literature is not an art, and that the novelist's responsibility is precisely to life and to truth. It could be argued that it is precisely such over-simplifications of the issue that account for the hostile or impatient attitude toward novels shared by many intelligent people today. This hostility and condescension to the novel will not be dissolved until the old shibboleth of art versus life is laid to rest. I mean, specifically, the accusation that so far as the novel devotes itself to perfecting itself as art, it thereby loses contact with "reality" and with the edifying role that literature has played in the past. Essentially, this is the charge brought in 1915 by H. G. Wells against Henry James; it has regularly been levelled against "avant-garde" or "experimental" literature ever since. And it is given renewed currency by counter-statements such as Nabokov makes about his art. Nabokov regularly boasts that his books are "blessed by a total lack of social significance." They contain no "political 'message'"; they are "also mythproof." The only function proper to literature, Nabokov insists in the preface to *Lolita*, is to procure for the reader "pure aesthetic bliss."

Nevertheless, despite Nabokov's strictures, despite the contention of Robbe-Grillet's essays that art cannot be made to serve any "truth," the issue is more complicated than both the friends and the enemies of modernist literature are willing to admit.

This seems to me the final interest of Burroughs' work. Burroughs acknowledges no contradiction between the noncommunicative (purely expressive) aspects of his prose—in other words, its autonomy as art—and literature's moral or truth-telling function. If, for Robbe-Grillet, man is a witness, for Burroughs, man is a sufferer. Man is there, he suffers, he shares his anguish with others, he tries to influence others. In the *Paris Review* interview, Burroughs says:

> I do definitely mean what I say to be taken literally, yes, to make people aware of the true criminality of our times . . . All of my work is directed against those who are bent, through stupidity or design, on blowing up the planet or rendering it uninhabitable. Like the advertising people . . . I'm concerned with the precise manipulation of word and image to create an alteration in the reader's consciousness.

The notion of art as efficacious is something that no one would want to deny—not even Robbe-Grillet, whose critical theory asserts that he is not concerned with such matters but whose substantive wishes for literature imply that he is. Robbe-Grillet's proposal of a new direction for literature, a literature that disclaims "interiority," that challenges the prestige of the "tragic experience of life," plainly suggests that human beings would be better off without such conceptions. And the proposal itself (as well as Robbe-Grillet's body of work) aims to bring closer such an improved state of affairs.

But what is implicit in Robbe-Grillet's analysis must be made explicit. The persuasive, didactic, and regenerative functions of serious art are not separate from the way art functions as distraction, as entertainment, as autonomous play of the mind and senses. We need more exact ways of discussing *how* art alters consciousness.

(1966)

The Double Standard of Aging

"How old are you?" The person asking the question is anybody. The respondent is a woman, a woman "of a certain age," as the French say discreetly. That age might be anywhere from her early twenties to her late fifties. If the question is impersonal—routine information requested when she applies for a driver's license, a credit card, a passport—she will probably force herself to answer truthfully. Filling out a marriage license application, if her future husband is even slightly her junior, she may long to subtract a few years; probably she won't. Competing for a job, her chances often partly depend on being the "right age," and if hers isn't right, she will lie if she thinks she can get away with it. Making her first visit to a new doctor, perhaps feeling particularly vulnerable at the moment she's asked, she will probably hurry through the correct answer. But if the question is only what people call personal—if she's asked by a new friend, a casual acquaintance, a neighbor's child, a coworker in an office, store, factory—her response is harder to predict. She may side-step the question with a joke or refuse it with playful indignation. "Don't you know you're not supposed to ask a woman her age?" Or, hesitating a moment, embarrassed but defiant, she may tell the truth. Or she may lie. But neither truth, evasion, nor lie relieves the unpleasantness of that question. For a woman to be obliged to state her age, after "a certain age," is always a miniature ordeal.

If the question comes from a woman, she will feel less threatened than if it comes from a man. Other women are, after all, comrades in sharing the same potential for humiliation. She will be less arch, less coy. But she probably still dislikes answering and may not tell the truth. Bureaucratic formalities excepted, whoever asks a woman this question—after "a certain age"— is ignoring a taboo and possibly being impolite or downright hostile. Almost everyone acknowledges that once she passes an age that is, actually, quite young, a woman's exact age ceases to be a legitimate target of curiosity. After childhood the year of a woman's birth becomes her secret, her private property. It is something of a dirty secret. To answer truthfully is always indiscreet.

The discomfort a woman feels each time she tells her age is

quite independent of the anxious awareness of human mortality that everyone has, from time to time. There is a normal sense in which nobody, men and women alike, relishes growing older. After thirty-five any mention of one's age carries with it the reminder that one is probably closer to the end of one's life than to the beginning. There is nothing unreasonable in that anxiety. Nor is there any abnormality in the anguish and anger that people who are really old, in their seventies and eighties, feel about the implacable waning of their powers, physical and mental. Advanced age is undeniably a trial, however stoically it may be endured. It is a shipwreck, no matter with what courage elderly people insist on continuing the voyage. But the objective, sacred pain of old age is of another order than the subjective, profane pain of aging. Old age is a genuine ordeal, one that men and women undergo in a similar way. Growing older is mainly an ordeal of the imagination—a moral disease, a social pathology—intrinsic to which is the fact that it afflicts women much more than men. It is particularly women who experience growing older (everything that comes *before* one is actually old) with such distaste and even shame.

The emotional privileges this society confers upon youth stir up some anxiety about getting older in everybody. All modern urbanized societies—unlike tribal, rural societies—condescend to the values of maturity and heap honors on the joys of youth. This revaluation of the life cycle in favor of the young brilliantly serves a secular society whose idols are ever-increasing industrial productivity and the unlimited cannibalization of nature. Such a society must create a new sense of the rhythms of life in order to incite people to buy more, to consume and throw away faster. People let the direct awareness they have of their needs, of what really gives them pleasure, be overruled by commercialized *images* of happiness and personal well-being; and, in this imagery designed to stimulate ever more avid levels of consumption, the most popular metaphor for happiness is "youth." (I would insist that it is a metaphor, not a literal description. Youth is a metaphor for energy, restless mobility, appetite: for the state of "wanting.") This equating of well-being with youth makes everyone naggingly aware of exact age—one's own and that of other people. In primitive and pre-modern societies people attach much less importance to dates. When lives are divided into long periods with stable responsibilities and steady ideals (and hypocrisies), the exact number of years someone has lived becomes a trivial fact; there is hardly any reason to mention, even to know, the year in which one was born. Most people in nonindustrial societies are not sure exactly how old they are. People in industrial societies are haunted by numbers. They take an almost obsessional interest in keeping the score card of aging, convinced that anything above a low total is some kind of bad news. In an era in which people actually live longer and longer, what now amounts to the latter *two-thirds* of everyone's life is shadowed by a poignant apprehension of unremitting loss.

The prestige of youth afflicts everyone in this society to some degree. Men, too, are prone to periodic bouts of depression about aging—for instance, when feeling insecure or unfulfilled or insufficiently rewarded in their jobs. But men rarely panic about aging in the way women often do. Getting older is less profoundly wounding for a man, for in addition to the propaganda for youth that puts both men and women on the defensive as they age, there is a double standard about aging that denounces women with special severity. Society is much more permissive about aging in men, as it is more tolerant of the sexual infidelities of husbands. Men are "allowed" to age, without penalty, in several ways that women are not.

This society offers even fewer rewards for aging women than it does to men. Being physically attractive counts much more in a woman's life than in a man's, but beauty, identified, as it is for women, with youthfulness, does not stand up well to age. Exceptional mental powers can increase with age, but women are rarely encouraged to develop their minds above dilettante standards. Because the wisdom considered the special province of women is "eternal," an age-old, intuitive knowledge about the emotions to which a repertoire of facts, worldly experience, and the methods of rational analysis have nothing to contribute, living a long time does not promise women an increase in wisdom either. The private skills expected of women are exercised early and, with the exception of a talent for making love, are not the kind that enlarge with experience. "Masculinity" is identified with competence, autonomy, self-control—qualities which the disappearance of youth does not threaten. Competence in most of the activities expected from men, physical sports excepted, increases with age. "Femininity" is identified with incompetence, helplessness, passivity, noncompetitiveness, being nice. Age does not improve these qualities.

Middle-class men feel diminished by aging, even while still young, if they have not yet shown distinction in their careers or made a lot of money. (And any tendencies they have toward hypochondria will get worse in middle age, focusing with particular nervousness on the specter of heart attacks and the loss of virility.) Their aging crisis is linked to that terrible pressure on men to be "successful" that precisely defines their membership in the middle class. Women rarely feel anxious about their age because they haven't succeeded at something. The work that women do outside the home rarely counts as a form of achievement, only as a way of earning money; most employment available to women mainly exploits the training they have been receiving since early childhood to be servile, to be both supportive and parasitical, to be unadventurous. They can have menial, low-skilled jobs in light industries, which offer as feeble a criterion of success as housekeeping. They can be secretaries, clerks, sales personnel, maids, research assistants, waitresses, social workers, prostitutes, nurses, teachers, telephone operators— public transcriptions of the servicing and nurturing roles that women have in family life. Women fill very few executive posts, are rarely found suitable for large corporate or political responsibilities, and form only a tiny contingent in the liberal professions (apart from teaching). They are virtually barred from jobs that involve an expert, intimate relation with machines or an aggressive use of the body, or that carry any physical risk or sense of adventure. The jobs this society deems appropriate to women are auxiliary, "calm" activities that do not compete with, but aid, what men do. Besides being less well paid, most work women do has a lower ceiling of advancement and gives meager outlet to normal wishes to be powerful. All outstanding work by women in this society is voluntary; most women are too inhibited by the social disapproval attached to their being ambitious and aggressive. Inevitably, women are exempted from the dreary panic of middle-aged men whose "achievements" seem paltry, who feel stuck on the job ladder or fear being pushed off it by someone younger. But they are also denied most of the real satisfactions that men derive from work— satisfactions that often do increase with age.

The double standard about aging shows up most brutally in the conventions of sexual feeling, which presuppose a disparity between men and women that operates permanently to women's disadvantage. In the accepted course of events a woman anywhere from her late teens through her middle twenties can expect to attract a man more or less her own age. (Ideally, he should be at least slightly older.) They marry and raise a family. But if her husband starts an affair after some years of marriage, he customarily does so with a woman much younger than his wife. Suppose, when both husband and wife are already in their late forties or early fifties, they divorce. The husband has an excellent chance of getting married again, probably to a younger woman. His ex-wife finds it difficult to remarry. Attracting a second husband younger than herself is improbable; even to find someone her own age she has to be lucky, and she will probably have to settle for a man considerably older than herself, in his sixties or seventies. Women become sexually ineligible much earlier than men do. A man, even an ugly man, can remain eligible well into old age. He is an acceptable mate for a young, attractive woman. Women, even good-looking women, become ineligible (except as partners of very old men) at a much younger age.

Thus, for most women, aging means a humiliating process of gradual sexual disqualification. Since women are considered maximally eligible in early youth, after which their sexual value drops steadily, even young women feel themselves in a desperate race against the calendar. They are old as soon as they are no longer very young. In late adolescence some girls are already worrying about getting married. Boys and young men have little reason to anticipate trouble because of aging. What makes men desirable to women is by no means tied to youth. On the contrary, getting older tends (for several decades) to operate in men's favor, since their value as lovers and husbands is set more by what they do than how they look. Many men have more success romantically at forty than they did at twenty or twenty-five; fame, money, and, above all, power are sexually enhancing. (A woman who has won power in a competitive profession or business career is considered less, rather than more, desirable. Most men confess themselves intimidated or turned off sexually by such a woman, obviously because she is harder to treat as just a sexual "object.") As they age, men may start feeling anxious about actual sexual performance, worrying about a loss of sexual vigor or even impotence, but their sexual eligibility is not abridged simply by getting older. Men stay sexually possible as long as they can make love. Women are at a disadvantage because their sexual candidacy depends on meeting certain much stricter "conditions" related to looks and age.

Since women are imagined to have much more limited sexual lives than men do, a woman who has never married is pitied. She was not found acceptable, and it is assumed that her life continues to confirm her unacceptability. Her presumed lack of sexual opportunity is embarrassing. A man who remains a bachelor is judged much less crudely. It is assumed that he, at any age, still has a sexual life—or the chance of one. For men there is no destiny equivalent to the humiliating condition of being an old maid, a spinster. "Mr.," a cover from infancy to senility, precisely exempts men from the stigma that attaches to any woman, no longer young, who is still "Miss." (That women are divided into "Miss" and "Mrs.," which calls unrelenting attention to the situation of each woman with respect to marriage, reflects the belief that being single or married is much more decisive for a woman than it is for a man.)

For a woman who is no longer very young, there is certainly some relief when she has finally been able to marry. Marriage soothes the sharpest pain she feels about the passing years. But her anxiety never subsides completely, for she knows that should she re-enter the sexual market at a later date—because of divorce, or the death of her husband, or the need for erotic adventure—she must do so under a handicap far greater than any man of her age (*whatever* her age may be) and regardless of how good-looking she is. Her achievements, if she has a career, are no asset. The calendar is the final arbiter.

To be sure, the calendar is subject to some variations from country to country. In Spain, Portugal, and the Latin American countries, the age at which most women are ruled physically undesirable comes earlier than in the United States. In France it is somewhat later. French conventions of sexual feeling make a quasi-official place for the woman between thirty-five and forty-five. Her role is to initiate an inexperienced or timid young man, after which she is, of course, replaced by a young girl. (Colette's novella *Chéri* is the best-known account in fiction of such a love affair; biographies of Balzac relate a well-documented example from real life.) This sexual myth does make turning forty somewhat easier for French women. But there is no difference in any of these countries in the basic attitudes that disqualify women sexually much earlier than men.

Aging also varies according to social class. Poor people look old much earlier in their lives than do rich people. But anxiety about aging is certainly more common, and more acute, among middle-class and rich women than among working-class women. Economically disadvantaged women in this society are more fatalistic about aging; they can't afford to fight the cosmetic battle as long or as tenaciously. Indeed, nothing so clearly indicates the fictional nature of this crisis than the fact that women who keep their youthful appearance the longest—women who lead unstrenuous, physically sheltered lives, who eat balanced meals, who can afford good medical care, who have few or no children—are those who feel the defeat of age most keenly. Aging is much more a social judgment than a biological eventuality. Far more extensive than the hard sense of loss suffered during menopause (which, with increased longevity, tends to arrive later and later) is the depression about aging, which may not be set off by any real event in a woman's life, but is a recurrent state of "possession" of her imagination, ordained by society—that is, ordained by the way this society limits how women feel free to imagine themselves.

There is a model account of the aging crisis in Richard Strauss's sentimental-ironic opera *Der Rosenkavalier*, whose heroine is a wealthy and glamorous married woman who decides to renounce romance. After a night with her adoring young lover, the Marschallin has a sudden, unexpected confrontation with herself. It is toward the end of Act I; Octavian has just left. Alone in her bedroom she sits at her dressing table, as she does every morning. It is the daily ritual of self-appraisal practiced by every woman. She looks at herself and, appalled, begins to weep. Her youth is over. Note that the Marschallin does not discover, looking in the mirror, that she is ugly. She is as beautiful as ever. The Marschallin's discovery is moral—that is, it is a discovery of her imagination; it is nothing she actually *sees*. Nevertheless, her discovery is no less devastating. Bravely, she makes her painful, gallant decision. She will arrange for her beloved Octavian to fall in love with a girl his own age. She must be realistic. She is no longer eligible. She is now "the old Marschallin."

Strauss wrote the opera in 1910. Contemporary operagoers are rather shocked when they discover that the libretto indicates that the Marschallin is all of thirty-four years old; today the role is generally sung by a soprano well into her forties or in her fifties. Acted by an attractive singer of thirty-four, the Marschallin's sorrow would seem merely neurotic, or even ridiculous. Few women today think of themselves as old, wholly disqualified from romance, at thirty-four. The age of retirement has moved up, in line with the sharp rise in life expectancy for everybody in the last few generations. The *form* in which women experience their lives remains unchanged. A moment approaches inexorably when they must resign themselves to being "too old." And that moment is invariably—objectively— premature.

In earlier generations the renunciation came even sooner. Fifty years ago a woman of forty was not just aging but old, finished. No struggle was even possible. Today, the surrender to aging no longer has a fixed date. The aging crisis (I am speaking only of women in affluent countries) starts earlier but lasts longer; it is diffused over most of a woman's life. A woman hardly has to be anything like what would reasonably be considered old to worry about her age, to start lying (or being tempted to lie). The crises can come at any time. Their schedule depends on a blend of personal ("neurotic") vulnerability and the swing of social mores. Some women don't have their first crisis until thirty. No one escapes a sickening shock upon turning forty. Each birthday, but especially those ushering in a new decade—for round numbers have a special authority—sounds a new defeat. There is almost as much pain in the anticipation as in the reality. Twenty-nine has become a queasy age ever since the official end of youth crept forward, about a generation ago, to thirty. Being thirty-nine is also hard; a whole year in which to meditate in glum astonishment that one stands on the threshhold of middle age. The frontiers are arbitrary, but not any less vivid for that. Although a woman on her fortieth birthday is hardly different from what she was when she was still thirty-nine, the day seems like a turning point. But long before actually becoming a woman of forty, she has been steeling herself against the depression she will feel. One of the greatest tragedies of each woman's life is simply getting older; it is certainly the *longest* tragedy.

Aging is a movable doom. It is a crisis that never exhausts itself, because the anxiety is never really used up. Being a crisis of the imagination rather than of "real life," it has the habit of repeating itself again and again. The territory of aging (as opposed to actual old age) has no fixed boundaries. Up to a point it can be defined as one wants. Entering each decade—after the initial shock is absorbed—an endearing, desperate impulse of survival helps many women to stretch the boundaries to the decade following. In late adolescence thirty seems the end of life. At thirty, one pushes the sentence forward to forty. At forty, one still gives oneself ten more years.

I remember my closest friend in college sobbing on the day she turned twenty-one. "The best part of my life is over. I'm not young any more." She was a senior, nearing graduation. I was a precocious freshman, just sixteen. Mystified, I tried lamely to comfort her, saying that I didn't think twenty-one was *so* old. Actually, I didn't understand at all what could be demoralizing about turning twenty-one. To me, it meant only something good: being in charge of oneself, being free. At sixteen, I was too young to have noticed, and become confused by, the peculiarly loose, ambivalent way in which this society demands that one stop thinking of oneself as a girl and start thinking of oneself as a woman. (In America that demand can now be put off to the age of thirty, even beyond.) But even if I thought her distress was absurd, I must have been aware that it would not simply be absurd but quite unthinkable in a *boy* turning twenty-one. Only women worry about age with that degree of inanity and pathos. And, of course, as with all crises that are inauthentic and therefore repeat themselves compulsively (because the danger is largely fictive, a poison in the imagination), this friend of mine went on having the same crisis over and over, each time as if for the first time.

I also came to her thirtieth birthday party. A veteran of many love affairs, she had spent most of her twenties living abroad and had just returned to the United States. She had been good-looking when I first knew her; now she was beautiful. I teased her about the tears she had shed over being twenty-one. She laughed and claimed not to remember. But thirty, she said ruefully, that really is the end. Soon after, she married. My friend is now forty-four. While no longer what people call beautiful, she is striking-looking, charming, and vital. She teaches elementary school; her husband, who is twenty years older than she, is a part-time merchant seaman. They have one child, now nine years old. Sometimes, when her husband is away, she takes a lover. She told me recently that forty was the most upsetting birthday of all (I wasn't at that one), and although she has only a few years left, she means to enjoy them while they last. She has become one of those women who seize every excuse offered in any conversation for mentioning how old they really are, in a spirit of bravado compounded with self-pity that is not too different from the mood of women who regularly lie about their age. But she is actually fretting much less about aging than she was two decades ago. Having a child, and having one rather late, past the age of thirty, has certainly helped to reconcile her to her age. At fifty, I suspect, she will be ever more valiantly postponing the age of resignation.

My friend is one of the more fortunate, sturdier casualties of the aging crisis. Most women are not as spirited, nor as innocently comic in their suffering. But almost all women endure some version of this suffering: A recurrent seizure of the imagination that usually begins quite young, in which they project themselves into a calculation of loss. The rules of this society are cruel to women. Brought up to be never fully adult, women are deemed obsolete earlier than men. In fact most women don't become relatively free and expressive sexually until their thirties. (Women mature sexually this late, certainly much later than men, not for innate biological reasons but because this culture retards women. Denied most outlets for sexual energy permitted to men, it takes many women *that* long to wear out some of their inhibitions.) The time at which they start being disqualified as sexually attractive persons is just when they have grown up sexually. The double standard about aging cheats women of those years, between thirty-five and fifty, likely to be the best of their sexual life.

That women expect to be flattered often by men, and the

extent to which their self-confidence depends on this flattery, reflects how deeply women are psychologically weakened by this double standard. Added on to the pressure felt by everybody in this society to look young as long as possible are the values of "femininity," which specifically identify sexual attractiveness in women with youth. The desire to be the "right age" has a special urgency for a woman it never has for a man. A much greater part of her self-esteem and pleasure in life is threatened when she ceases to be young. Most men experience getting older with regret, apprehension. But most women experience it even more painfully: with shame. Aging is a man's destiny, something that must happen because he is a human being. For a woman, aging is not only her destiny. Because she is that more *narrowly* defined kind of human being, a woman, it is also her vulnerability.

To be a woman is to be an actress. Being feminine is a kind of theater, with its appropriate costumes, *décor*, lighting, and stylized gestures. From early childhood on, girls are trained to care in a pathologically exaggerated way about their appearance and are profoundly mutilated (to the extent of being unfitted for first-class adulthood) by the extent of the stress put on presenting themselves as physically attractive objects. Women look in the mirror more frequently than men do. It is, virtually, their duty to look at themselves—to look often. Indeed, a woman who is not narcissistic is considered unfeminine. And a woman who spends literally *most* of her time caring for, and making purchases to flatter, her physical appearance is not regarded in this society as what she is: a kind of moral idiot. She is thought to be quite normal and is envied by other women whose time is mostly used up at jobs or caring for large families. The display of narcissism goes on all the time. It is expected that women will disappear several times in an evening—at a restaurant, at a party, during a theater intermission, in the course of a social visit—simply to check their appearance, to see that nothing has gone wrong with their make-up and hairstyling, to make sure that their clothes are not spotted or too wrinkled or not hanging properly. It is even acceptable to perform this activity in public. At the table in a restaurant, over coffee, a woman opens a compact mirror and touches up her make-up and hair without embarrassment in front of her husband or her friends.

All this behavior, which is written off as normal "vanity" in women, would seem ludicrous in a man. Women are more vain than men because of the relentless pressure on women to maintain their appearance at a certain high standard. What makes the pressure even more burdensome is that there are actually several standards. Men present themselves as face-and-body, a physical whole. Women are split, as men are not, into a body and a face—each judged by somewhat different standards. What is important for a face is that it be beautiful. What is important for a body is two things, which may even be (depending on fashion and taste) somewhat incompatible: first, that it be desirable and, second, that it be beautiful. Men usually feel sexually attracted to women much more because of their bodies than their faces. The traits that arouse desire—such as fleshiness—don't always match those that fashion decrees as beautiful. (For instance, the ideal woman's body promoted in advertising in recent years is extremely thin: the kind of body that looks more desirable clothed than naked.) But women's concern with their appearance is not simply geared to arousing desire in men. It also aims at fabricating a certain image by which, as a more indirect way of arousing desire, women state their value. A woman's value lies in the way she *represents* herself, which is much more by her face than her body. In defiance of the laws of simple sexual attraction, women do not devote most of their attention to their bodies. The well-known "normal" narcissism that women display—the amount of time they spend before the mirror—is used primarily in caring for the face and hair.

Women do not simply have faces, as men do; they are identified with their faces. Men have a naturalistic relation to their faces. Certainly they care whether they are good-looking or not. They suffer over acne, protruding ears, tiny eyes; they hate getting bald. But there is a much wider latitude in what is esthetically acceptable in a man's face than what is in a woman's. A man's face is defined as something he basically doesn't need to tamper with; all he has to do is keep it clean. He can avail himself of the options for ornament supplied by nature: a beard, a mustache, longer or shorter hair. But he is not supposed to disguise himself. What he is "really" like is supposed to show. A man lives through his face; it records the progressive stages of his life. And since he doesn't tamper with his face, it is not separate from but is completed by his body—which is judged attractive by the impression it gives of virility and energy. By contrast, a woman's face is potentially separate from her body. She does not treat it naturalistically. A woman's face is the canvas upon which she paints a revised, corrected portrait of herself. One of the rules of this creation is that the face *not* show what she doesn't want it to show. Her face is an emblem, an icon, a flag. How she arranges her hair, the type of make-up she uses, the quality of her complexion—all these are signs, not of what she is "really" like, but of how she asks to be treated by others, especially men. They establish her status as an "object."

For the normal changes that age inscribes on every human face, women are much more heavily penalized than men. Even in early adolescence, girls are cautioned to protect their faces against wear and tear. Mothers tell their daughters (but never their sons): You look ugly when you cry. Stop worrying. Don't read too much. Crying, frowning, squinting, even laughing—all these human activities make "lines." The same usage of the face in men is judged quite positively. In a man's face lines are taken to be signs of "character." They indicate emotional strength, maturity—qualities far more esteemed in men than in women. (They show he has "lived.") Even scars are often not felt to be unattractive; they too can add "character" to a man's face. But lines of aging, any scar, even a small birthmark on a woman's face, are always regarded as unfortunate blemishes. In effect, people take character in men to be different from what constitutes character in women. A woman's character is thought to be innate, static—not the product of her experience, her years, her actions. A woman's face is prized so far as it remains unchanged by (or conceals the traces of) her emotions, her physical risk-taking. Ideally, it is supposed to be a mask—immutable, unmarked. The model woman's face is Garbo's. Because women are identified with their faces much more than men are, and the ideal woman's face is one that is "perfect," it seems a calamity when a woman has a disfiguring accident. A broken nose or a scar or a burn mark, no more than regrettable for a man, is a terrible psychological wound to a woman; objectively, it diminishes her value. (As is well known, most clients for plastic surgery are women.)

Both sexes aspire to a physical ideal, but what is expected of boys and what is expected of girls involves a very different moral relation to the self. Boys are encouraged to *develop* their bodies, to regard the body as an instrument to be improved. They invent their masculine selves largely through exercise and sport, which harden the body and strengthen competitive feelings; clothes are of only secondary help in making their bodies attractive. Girls are not particularly encouraged to develop their bodies through any activity, strenuous or not; and physical strength and endurance are hardly valued at all. The invention of the feminine self proceeds mainly through clothes and other signs that testify to the very effort of girls to look attractive, to their commitment to please. When boys become men, they may go on (especially if they have sedentary jobs) practicing a sport or doing exercises for a while. Mostly they leave their appearance alone, having been trained to accept more or less what nature has handed out to them. (Men may start doing exercises again in their forties to lose weight, but for reasons of health—there is an epidemic fear of heart attacks among the middle-aged in rich countries—not for cosmetic reasons.) As one of the norms of "femininity" in this society is being preoccupied with one's physical appearance, so "masculinity" means *not* caring very much about one's looks.

This society allows men to have a much more affirmative relation to their bodies than women have. Men are more "at home" in their bodies, whether they treat them casually or use them aggressively. A man's body is defined as a strong body. It contains no contradiction between what is felt to be attractive and what is practical. A woman's body, so far as it is considered attractive, is defined as a fragile, light body. (Thus, women worry more than men do about being overweight.) When they do exercises, women avoid the ones that develop the muscles, particularly those in the upper arms. Being "feminine" means looking physically weak, frail. Thus, the ideal woman's body is one that is not of much practical use in the hard work of this world, and one that must continually "be defended." Women do not develop their bodies, as men do. After a woman's body has reached its sexually acceptable form by late adolescence, most further development is viewed as negative. And it is thought irresponsible for women to do what is normal for men: simply leave their appearance alone. During early youth they are likely

to come as close as they ever will to the ideal image—slim figure, smooth firm skin, light musculature, graceful movements.
Their task is to try to maintain that image, unchanged, as long
as possible. Improvement as such is not the task. Women care
for their bodies—against toughening, coarsening, getting fat.
They *conserve* them. (Perhaps the fact that women in modern
societies tend to have a more conservative political outlook
than men originates in their profoundly conservative relation
to their bodies.)

In the life of women in this society the period of pride, of
natural honesty, of unself-conscious flourishing is brief. Once
past youth women are condemned to inventing (and maintaining) themselves against the inroads of age. Most of the physical qualities regarded as attractive in women deteriorate much
earlier in life than those defined as "male." Indeed, they perish
fairly soon in the normal sequence of body transformation. The
"feminine" is smooth, rounded, hairless, unlined, soft, unmus-
cled—the look of the very young; characteristics of the weak,
of the vulnerable; eunuch traits, as Germaine Greer has pointed
out. Actually, there are only a few years—late adolescence, early
twenties—in which this look is physiologically natural, in which
it can be had without touching-up and covering-up. After that,
women enlist in a quixotic enterprise, trying to close the gap
between the imagery put forth by society (concerning what is
attractive in a woman) and the evolving facts of nature.

Women have a more intimate relation to aging than men
do, simply because one of the accepted "women's" occupations is taking pains to keep one's face and body from showing
the signs of growing older. Women's sexual validity depends,
up to a certain point, on how well they stand off these natural
changes. After late adolescence women become the caretakers
of their bodies and faces, pursuing an essentially defensive strategy, a holding operation. A vast array of products in jars and
tubes, a branch of surgery, and armies of hairdressers, mas-
seuses, diet counselors, and other professionals exist to stave
off, or mask, developments that are entirely normal biologically.
Large amounts of women's energies are diverted into this passionate, corrupting effort to defeat nature: to maintain an ideal,
static appearance against the progress of age. The collapse of the
project is only a matter of time. Inevitably, a woman's physical

appearance develops beyond its youthful form. No matter how exotic the creams or how strict the diets, one cannot indefinitely keep the face unlined, the waist slim. Bearing children takes its toll: the torso becomes thicker; the skin is stretched. There is no way to keep certain lines from appearing, in one's mid-twenties, around the eyes and mouth. From about thirty on, the skin gradually loses its tonus. In women this perfectly natural process is regarded as a humiliating defeat, while nobody finds anything remarkably unattractive in the equivalent physical changes in men. Men are "allowed" to look older without sexual penalty.

Thus, the reason that women experience aging with more pain than men is not simply that they care more than men about how they look. Men also care about their looks and want to be attractive, but since the business of men is mainly being and doing, rather than appearing, the standards for appearance are much less exacting. The standards for what is attractive in a man are permissive; they conform to what is possible or "natural" to most men throughout most of their lives. The standards for women's appearance go against nature, and to come anywhere near approximating them takes considerable effort and time. Women must try to be beautiful. At the least, they are under heavy social pressure not to be ugly. A woman's fortunes depend, far more than a man's, on being at least "acceptable" looking. Men are not subject to this pressure. Good looks in a man is a bonus, not a psychological necessity for maintaining normal self-esteem.

Behind the fact that women are more severely penalized than men are for aging is the fact that people, in this culture at least, are simply less tolerant of ugliness in women than in men. An ugly woman is never merely repulsive. Ugliness in a woman is felt by everyone, men as well as women, to be faintly embarrassing. And many features or blemishes that count as ugly in a woman's face would be quite tolerable on the face of a man. This is not, I would insist, just because the esthetic standards for men and women are different. It is rather because the esthetic standards for women are much higher, and narrower, than those proposed for men.

Beauty, women's business in this society, is the theater of their enslavement. Only one standard of female beauty is sanctioned: the *girl*. The great advantage men have is that our culture allows two standards of male beauty: the *boy* and the *man*. The beauty of a boy resembles the beauty of a girl. In both sexes it is a fragile kind of beauty and flourishes naturally only in the early part of the life-cycle. Happily, men are able to accept themselves under another standard of good looks—heavier, rougher, more thickly built. A man does not grieve when he loses the smooth, unlined, hairless skin of a boy. For he has only exchanged one form of attractiveness for another: the darker skin of a man's face, roughened by daily shaving, showing the marks of emotion and the normal lines of age. There is no equivalent of this second standard for women. The single standard of beauty for women dictates that they must go on having clear skin. Every wrinkle, every line, every grey hair, is a defeat. No wonder that no boy minds becoming a man, while even the passage from girlhood to early womanhood is experienced by many women as their downfall, for all women are trained to want to continue looking like girls.

This is not to say there are no beautiful older women. But the standard of beauty in a woman of any age is how far she retains, or how she manages to simulate, the appearance of youth. The exceptional woman in her sixties who is beautiful certainly owes a large debt to her genes. Delayed aging, like good looks, tends to run in families. But nature rarely offers enough to meet this culture's standards. Most of the women who successfully delay the appearance of age are rich, with unlimited leisure to devote to nurturing along nature's gifts. Often they are actresses. (That is, highly paid professionals at doing what all women are taught to practice as amateurs.) Such women as Mae West, Dietrich, Stella Adler, Dolores Del Rio, do not challenge the rule about the relation between beauty and age in women. They are admired precisely because they *are* exceptions, because they have managed (at least so it seems in photographs) to outwit nature. Such miracles, exceptions made by nature (with the help of art and social privilege), only confirm the rule, because what makes these women seem beautiful to us is precisely that they do not look their real age. Society allows no place in our imagination for a beautiful old woman who does look like an old woman—a woman who might be like Picasso at the age of ninety, being photographed outdoors on his estate in the south of France, wearing only shorts and sandals. No one imagines such a woman exists. Even the special exceptions—Mae West & Co.—are always photographed indoors, cleverly lit, from the most flattering angle and fully, artfully clothed. The implication is they would not stand a closer scrutiny. The idea of an old woman in a bathing suit being attractive, or even just accept-able looking, is inconceivable. An older woman is, by definition, sexually repulsive—unless, in fact, she doesn't look old at all. The body of an old woman, unlike that of an old man, is always understood as a body that can no longer be shown, offered, unveiled. At best, it may appear in costume. People still feel un-easy, thinking about what they might see if her mask dropped, if she took off her clothes.

Thus, the point for women of dressing up, applying make-up, dyeing their hair, going on crash diets, and getting face-lifts is not just to be attractive. They are ways of defending them-selves against a profound level of disapproval directed toward women, a disapproval that can take the form of aversion. The double standard about aging converts the life of women into an inexorable march toward a condition in which they are not just unattractive, but disgusting. The profoundest terror of a woman's life is the moment represented in a statue by Rodin called *Old Age*: a naked old woman, seated, pathetically con-templates her flat, pendulous, ruined body. Aging in women is a process of becoming obscene sexually, for the flabby bosom, wrinkled neck, spotted hands, thinning white hair, waistless torso, and veined legs of an old woman are felt to be obscene. In our direst moments of the imagination, this transformation can take place with dismaying speed—as in the end of *Lost Horizon*, when the beautiful young girl is carried by her lover out of Shangri-La and, within minutes, turns into a withered, repulsive crone. There is no equivalent nightmare about men. This is why, however much a man may care about his appear-ance, that caring can never acquire the same desperateness it often does for women. When men dress according to fashion or now even use cosmetics, they do not expect from clothes and make-up what women do. A face-lotion or perfume or deodor-ant or hairspray, used by a man, is not part of a disguise. Men, as men, do not feel the need to disguise themselves to fend off morally disapproved signs of aging, to outwit premature sexual obsolescence, to cover up aging as obscenity. Men are not subject to the barely concealed revulsion expressed in this culture against the female body—except in its smooth, youthful, firm, odorless, blemish-free form.

One of the attitudes that punish women most severely is the visceral horror felt at aging female flesh. It reveals a radical fear of women installed deep in this culture, a demonology of women that has crystallized in such mythic caricatures as the vixen, the virago, the vamp, and the witch. Several centuries of witch-phobia, during which one of the cruelest extermination programs in Western history was carried out, suggest something of the extremity of this fear. That old women are repulsive is one of the most profound esthetic and erotic feelings in our culture. Women share it as much as men do. (Oppressors, as a rule, deny oppressed people their own "native" standards of beauty. And the oppressed end up being convinced that they *are* ugly.) How women are psychologically damaged by this misogynistic idea of what is beautiful parallels the way in which blacks have been deformed in a society that has up to now defined beautiful as white. Psychological tests made on young black children in the United States some years ago showed how early and how thoroughly they incorporate the white standard of good looks. Virtually all the children expressed fantasies that indicated they considered black people to be ugly, funny looking, dirty, brutish. A similar kind of self-hatred infects most women. Like men, they find old age in women "uglier" than old age in men.

This esthetic taboo functions, in sexual attitudes, as a racial taboo. In this society most people feel an involuntary recoil of the flesh when imagining a middle-aged woman making love with a young man—exactly as many whites flinch viscerally at the thought of a white woman in bed with a black man. The banal drama of a man of fifty who leaves a wife of forty-five for a girlfriend of twenty-eight contains no strictly sexual outrage, whatever sympathy people may have for the abandoned wife. On the contrary. Everyone "understands." Everyone knows that men like girls, that young women often want middle-aged men. But no one "understands" the reverse situation. A woman of forty-five who leaves a husband of fifty for a lover of twenty-eight is the makings of a social and sexual scandal at a deep level of feeling. No one takes exception to a romantic couple in which the man is twenty years or more the woman's senior. The movies pair Joanne Dru and John Wayne, Marilyn Monroe and Joseph Cotten, Audrey Hepburn and Cary Grant, Jane Fonda and Yves Montand, Catherine Deneuve and Marcello Mastroianni; as in actual life, these are perfectly plausible, appealing couples. When the age difference runs the other way, people are puzzled and embarrassed and simply shocked. (Remember Joan Crawford and Cliff Robertson in *Autumn Leaves*? But so troubling is this kind of love story that it rarely figures in the movies, and then only as the melancholy history of a failure.) The usual view of why a woman of forty and a boy of twenty, or a woman of fifty and a man of thirty, marry is that the man is seeking a mother, not a wife; no one believes the marriage will last. For a woman to respond erotically and romantically to a man who, in terms of his age, could be her father is considered normal. A man who falls in love with a woman who, however attractive she may be, is old enough to be his mother is thought to be extremely neurotic (victim of an "Oedipal fixation" is the fashionable tag), if not mildly contemptible.

The wider the gap in age between partners in a couple, the more obvious is the prejudice against women. When old men, such as Justice Douglas, Picasso, Strom Thurmond, Onassis, Chaplin, and Pablo Casals, take brides thirty, forty, fifty years younger than themselves, it strikes people as remarkable, perhaps an exaggeration—but still plausible. To explain such a match, people enviously attribute some special virility and charm to the man. Though he can't be handsome, he is famous; and his fame is understood as having boosted his attractiveness to women. People imagine that his young wife, respectful of her elderly husband's attainments, is happy to become his helper. For the man a late marriage is always good public relations. It adds to the impression that, despite his advanced age, he is still to be reckoned with; it is the sign of a continuing vitality presumed to be available as well to his art, business activity, or political career. But an elderly woman who married a young man would be greeted quite differently. She would have broken a fierce taboo, and she would get no credit for her courage. Far from being admired for her vitality, she would probably be condemned as predatory, willful, selfish, exhibitionistic. At the same time she would be pitied, since such a marriage would be taken as evidence that she was in her dotage. If she had a conventional career or were in business or held public office, she would quickly suffer from the current of disapproval. Her very credibility as a professional would decline, since people would suspect that her young husband might have an undue influence on her. Her "respectability" would certainly be compromised. Indeed, the well-known old women I can think of who dared such unions, if only at the end of their lives—George Eliot, Colette, Édith Piaf—have all belonged to that category of people, creative artists and entertainers, who have special license from society to behave scandalously. It is thought to be a scandal for a woman to ignore that she is old and therefore too ugly for a young man. Her looks and a certain physical condition determine a woman's desirability, not her talents or her needs. Women are not supposed to be "potent." A marriage between an old woman and a young man subverts the very ground rule of relations between the two sexes, that is: whatever the variety of appearances, men remain dominant. Their claims come first. Women are supposed to be the associates and companions of men, not their full equals—and never their superiors. Women are to remain in the state of a permanent "minority."

The convention that wives should be younger than their husbands powerfully enforces the "minority" status of women, since being senior in age always carries with it, in any relationship, a certain amount of power and authority. There are no laws on the matter, of course. The convention is obeyed because to do otherwise makes one feel as if one is doing something ugly or in bad taste. Everyone feels intuitively the esthetic rightness of a marriage in which the man is older than the woman, which means that any marriage in which the woman is older creates a dubious or less gratifying mental picture. Everyone is addicted to the visual pleasure that women give by meeting certain esthetic requirements from which men are exempted, which keeps women working at staying youthful-looking while men are left free to age. On a deeper level everyone finds the signs of old age in women esthetically offensive, which conditions one to feel automatically repelled by the prospect of an elderly woman marrying a much younger man. The situation in which women are kept minors for life is largely organized by such conformist, unreflective preferences. But taste is not free, and its judgments are never merely "natural." Rules of taste enforce structures of power. The revulsion against aging in women is the cutting edge of a whole set of oppressive structures (often masked as gallantries) that keep women in their place.

The ideal state proposed for women is docility, which means not being fully grown up. Most of what is cherished as typically "feminine" is simply behavior that is childish, immature, weak. To offer so low and demeaning a standard of fulfillment in itself constitutes oppression in an acute form—a sort of moral neo-colonialism. But women are not simply condescended to by the values that secure the dominance of men. They are repudiated. Perhaps because of having been their oppressors for so long, few men really *like* women (though they love individual women), and few men ever feel really comfortable or at ease in women's company. This malaise arises because relations between the two sexes are rife with hypocrisy, as men manage to love those they dominate and therefore don't respect. Oppressors always try to justify their privileges and brutalities by imagining that those they oppress belong to a lower order of civilization or are less than fully "human." Deprived of part of their ordinary human dignity, the oppressed take on certain "demonic" traits. The oppressions of large groups have to be anchored deep in the psyche, continually renewed by partly unconscious fears and taboos, by a sense of the obscene. Thus, women arouse not only desire and affection in men but aversion as well. Women are thoroughly domesticated familiars. But, at certain times and in certain situations, they become alien, untouchable. The aversion men feel, so much of which is covered over, is felt most frankly, with least inhibition, toward the type of woman who is most taboo "esthetically," a woman who has become—with the natural changes brought about by aging—obscene.

Nothing more clearly demonstrates the vulnerability of women than the special pain, confusion, and bad faith with which they experience getting older. And in the struggle that some women are waging on behalf of all women to be treated (and treat themselves) as full human beings—not "only" as women—one of the earliest results to be hoped for is that women become aware, indignantly aware, of the double standard about aging from which they suffer so harshly.

It is understandable that women often succumb to the temptation to lie about their age. Given society's double standard, to question a woman about her age is indeed often an aggressive act, a trap. Lying is an elementary means of self-defense, a way of scrambling out of the trap, at least temporarily. To expect a woman, after "a certain age," to tell exactly how old she is— when she has a chance, either through the generosity of nature or the cleverness of art, to pass for being somewhat younger than she actually is—is like expecting a landowner to admit that the estate he has put up for sale is actually worth less than the buyer is prepared to pay. The double standard about aging sets women up as property, as objects whose value depreciates rapidly with the march of the calendar.

The prejudices that mount against women as they grow older are an important arm of male privilege. It is the present unequal distribution of adult roles between the two sexes that gives men a freedom to age denied to women. Men actively administer the double standard about aging because the "masculine" role awards them the initiative in courtship. Men choose; women are chosen. So men choose younger women. But although this system of inequality is operated by men, it could not work if women themselves did not acquiesce in it. Women reinforce it powerfully with their complacency, with their anguish, with their lies.

Not only do women lie more than men do about their age but men forgive them for it, thereby confirming their own superiority. A man who lies about his age is thought to be weak, "unmanly." A woman who lies about her age is behaving in a quite acceptable, "feminine" way. Petty lying is viewed by men with indulgence, one of a number of patronizing allowances made for women. It has the same moral unimportance as the fact that women are often late for appointments. Women are not expected to be truthful, or punctual, or expert in handling and repairing machines, or frugal, or physically brave. They are expected to be second-class adults, whose natural state is that of a grateful dependence on men. And so they often are, since that is what they are brought up to be. So far as women heed the stereotypes of "feminine" behavior, they *cannot* behave as fully responsible, independent adults.

Most women share the contempt for women expressed in the

double standard about aging—to such a degree that they take their lack of self-respect for granted. Women have been accustomed so long to the protection of their masks, their smiles, their endearing lies. Without this protection, they know, they would be more vulnerable. But in protecting themselves as women, they betray themselves as adults. The model corruption in a woman's life is denying her age. She symbolically accedes to all those myths that furnish women with their imprisoning securities and privileges, that create their genuine oppression, that inspire their real discontent. Each time a woman lies about her age she becomes an accomplice in her own underdevelopment as a human being.

Women have another option. They can aspire to be wise, not merely nice; to be competent, not merely helpful; to be strong, not merely graceful; to be ambitious for themselves, not merely for themselves in relation to men and children. They can let themselves age naturally and without embarrassment, actively protesting and disobeying the conventions that stem from this society's double standard about aging. Instead of being girls, girls as long as possible, who then age humiliatingly into middle-aged women and then obscenely into old women, they can become women much earlier—and remain active adults, enjoying the long, erotic career of which women are capable, far longer. Women should allow their faces to show the lives they have lived. Women should tell the truth.

(1972)

The Third World of Women

*Note: The following text was written in July 1972 in response to a
questionnaire sent to me and five other women (including Simone
de Beauvoir and the Italian Communist deputy Rossana Ros-
sanda) by the editors of* Libre, *a new Spanish-language political
and literary quarterly with a loosely Marxist orientation, edited
in Paris, It was published in the October 1972 issue of* Libre, No.
3, *in a translation by the Spanish novelist Juan Goytisolo. Most
of the readers of* Libre *live in Latin America, which explains the
painstakingly explicit character of what I wrote. The nature of
the magazine's readership explains as well my freedom to assume,
when writing my answers, that a revolutionary socialist view of
the subject is, at the very least, something to contend with. In the
United States, where militant feminism is a livelier and much
more widely heard point of view right now than it is anywhere
else, discussion tends to be less and less explicit about the root questions, and rarely even alludes to the Marxist analysis. Nevertheless,
because the formulation of a political perspective is still everywhere
in its early stages, that seems to me to justify printing here what I
wrote for a quite different audience.*

A few paragraphs first, a sort of prologue, a response to a more
general question which you don't ask: *At what stage now is the
struggle for women's liberation?*

For thousands of years, practically everyone in the world assumed that it lay in the "nature" of the human species that some
people were superior (and should be masters) and other people
were inferior (and should be slaves). Only about a hundred
and fifty years ago did elements of the ruling classes begin to
suspect that slavery was not really, after all, "natural," and that
the undeniably servile and culturally underdeveloped character
of slaves could be explained by the very fact that these people
were slaves, were brought up to be slaves—instead of proving
that they deserved to be slaves.

Support for the emancipation of women stands today approximately where support for the emancipation of slaves stood
two centuries ago. Just as throughout the millennia of unquestioning acceptance of slavery, the age-old oppression of women
is justified by an appeal to presumed inequalities "natural" to

the species, the vast majority of people on this planet—women as well as men—remain convinced that women have a different "nature" than men, and that these "natural" differences make women inferior.

Educated people in urbanized countries, especially those who regard themselves as liberals or socialists, often deny they believe these differences make women inferior. That women differ from men, they argue, does not mean that women are not the equal of men. Their argument is as dishonest as the separate-but-equal argument once used to defend the legal segregation of the races in schools. For the specific content of these supposedly innate differences between women and men imply a scale of values in which the qualities assigned to women are clearly less estimable than those assigned to men. "Masculinity" is identified with competence, autonomy, self-control, ambition, risk-taking, independence, rationality; "femininity" is identified with incompetence, helplessness, irrationality, passivity, non-competitiveness, being nice. Women are trained for second-class adulthood, most of what is cherished as typically "feminine" behavior being simply behavior that is childish, servile, weak, immature. No wonder men balk at accepting women as their full equals. *Vive la différence* indeed!

Not expecting women to be truthful, or punctual, or expert in handling and repairing machines, or frugal, or muscular, or physically brave makes all women who are—exceptional. Every generation produces a few women of genius (or at least of irrepressible eccentricity) who win special status for themselves. But the historical visibility of the Trung sisters, Joan of Arc, Saint Theresa, Mademoiselle Maupin, George Eliot, Louise Michel, Harriet Tubman, Isabelle Eberhardt, Marie Curie, Rosa Luxemburg, Amelia Earhart, and the other of that small band, is understood to follow precisely from their possessing qualities that women do not normally have. Such women are credited with "masculine" energy, intelligence, willfulness, and courage. Examples of unusually capable and genuinely independent women do not shake the general presumption of women's inferiority, any more than the discovery (and favored treatment) of intellectually talented slaves made cultivated Roman slaveowners doubt the naturalness of slavery: the argument from "nature" is self-confirming. Individual lives which do not confirm the argument will always be taken as exceptions, thereby leaving the stereotypes intact.

Historically, or rather prehistorically, the oppression of women must have arisen out of certain practical arrangements to insure their special biological responsibility: childbearing. The elaborate forms of women's oppression—psychological, political, economic, cultural—all refer back to the biological division of labor. But the fact that women bear children while men do not hardly proves that women and men are fundamentally different. It rather indicates how slim is the basis in "nature" for the supposed difference—whereby women's reproductive physiology is converted into a life-vocation, with its appropriately narrow norms of character and temperament. But even physiological "nature" is not an immutable fact with unchanging consequences. It, too, is part of history—and evolves with history. If the whole difference between women and men ultimately rests on the fact that women are busy bearing children, then the circumstances in which that vocation is exercised have been severely modified: if "nature" has supplied the pretext for women's enslavement, then history now supplies the objective conditions for their social and psychological liberation. For it is just this importance of the physiological difference between women and men which is becoming obsolete.

The Industrial Revolution provided the material base for a reconsideration of slavery; when machines were invented that were more productive and efficient than unpaid labor, it became reasonable to free people from legal bondage to work. Now the Ecological Turning Point (increased longevity, plus the population explosion, plus the rapid depletion of natural resources) makes it not only possible but ultimately imperative that most women be freed from all but the most minimal relation to their biological responsibility. Once the reproductive destiny of women shrinks to two, one, or no pregnancies (with every likelihood that, for the first time in history, almost all children born will live to adulthood), the underlying rationale for the repressive definition of women as servile, domestic, primarily childrearing creatures collapses. As the Industrial Revolution encouraged people to rethink the "naturalness" of slavery, so the new ecological era which the planet entered in the middle of the twentieth century is enabling people to rethink the hitherto self-evident "femininity" of women. The "femininity" of women and the "masculinity" of men are morally defective and historically obsolete conceptions. The liberation of women seems to me as much a historical necessity as the abolition of slavery—like abolition, a hopeless-looking cause before it actually triumphs; even more momentous than abolition in its psychic and historical consequences.

But, anachronistic as their oppression may be, women will not be liberated without a hard struggle, a struggle that really does deserve the adjective "revolutionary." This revolution must be both radical and conservative. It is conservative in the sense that it will reject the ideology of unlimited growth (ever-increasing levels of productivity and consumption; the unlimited cannibalization of the environment)—an ideology shared with equal enthusiasm by the countries which call themselves capitalist and by those which aspire to communism. It is radical in the sense that it will challenge, and remake, the basically authoritarian moral habits common to both capitalist and communist countries. Liberating women is the most radical part of this new revolutionary process.

In opposition to the whole accredited modern tradition about revolution, I am arguing that what used to be called "the woman question" not only exists but exists independently of the issues generally posed by political radicals. Marx, Engels, Lenin, Trotsky, Luxemburg, and Gramsci held that the oppression of women was not a separate problem, but rather one to be absorbed by the class struggle and eventually resolved by the creation of socialism. I do not agree. The fact is, no government which claims to operate on part of Marx's legacy has rethought the condition of women. On the contrary, every communist country has been content with offering women merely liberal improvements in their situations—like increased access to education and jobs and divorces—while preserving intact the overwhelming monopoly of political power by man, and leaving unchanged the structures of repression that characterize private relations between the two sexes. But this striking failure of all countries where left-revolutionary governments have come to power to do anything "radical" for women should not be surprising. In none of the many edifying declarations made by the principal theorists of proletarian revolution in favor of emancipating women has the true complexity of the question ever been grasped. Marxists have not properly estimated the depth of sexism any more than, in setting out to defeat imperialism, they properly estimated the depths of racism.

Now, to the questions you do ask.

1. *What meaning does the idea of women's liberation have for you?*

One often hears now that the liberation of women cannot take place without the liberation of men. The cliché is true, up to a point. Women and men share the same ultimate aim: to gain genuine autonomy, which means participating in (and being let alone by) a society that is not based on alienation and repression. But the cliché is also dangerous, for it implicitly denies that there are stages in the struggle to liberate women. Like many clichés which are true, it disarms thought and pacifies rage. It encourages a passive and merely reformist view of the problem. (Thus, aptly enough, "the liberation of women equals the liberation of men" is the official slogan of the Swedish government's eminently superficial policies for securing equality for women within the framework of sophisticated liberal capitalism.)

To be sure, every human being in this imperfect world stands in need of liberation—masters as well as slaves, oppressors as well as the oppressed. But a just society cannot be accurately conceived, or fought for, in a unitary or universal way. Liberating a Thai peasant is not the same as liberating a white factory worker in Detroit. The oppression of women does not, in terms of fundamental structures, resemble the oppression of men.

Reasonable-sounding as the idea may be, it is simply not true that the liberation of men and the liberation of women are two parts of a reciprocal process. However much men too are deformed psychologically by sexist stereotypes, these stereotypes do confer undeniable privileges on them. Men have a greater range of behavior available to them than women have, and they have considerably more mobility in the world. (Simply consider the fact that in *most* places she might go in "the world," a woman alone risks rape or physical violence. Basically, a woman is only safe at "home" or when protected by a man.) In the most concrete way, in that he need not always be on guard against predatory assault, a man is always better off than a woman. Men (and women) are oppressed by other men. But all women are oppressed by all men.

The cliché that when women are liberated men will be liberated too shamelessly slides over the raw reality of male domination—as if this were an arrangement in fact arranged by nobody, which suits nobody, which works to nobody's advantage. In fact, the very opposite is true. The domination of men over women is to the advantage of men; the liberation of women will be at the expense of male privilege. Perhaps afterwards, in some happy sense, men will be liberated too— liberated from the tiresome obligation to be "masculine." But allowing oppressors to lay down their psychological burdens is quite another, secondary sense of liberation. The first priority is to liberate the oppressed. Never before in history have the claims of oppressed and oppressors turned out to be, on inspection, quite harmonious. It will not be true this time either.

All women live in an "imperialist" situation in which men are colonialists and women are natives. In so-called Third World countries, the situation of women with respect to men is tyrannically, brutally colonialist. In economically advanced countries (both capitalist and Communist) the situation of women is neo-colonialist: the segregation of women has been liberalized; the use of physical force against women has declined; men delegate some of their authority, their rule is less overtly institutionalized. But the same basic relations of inferiority and superiority, of powerlessness and power, of cultural underdevelopment and cultural privilege, prevail between women and men in all countries.

Any serious program for liberating women must start from the premise that liberation is not just about *equality* (the "liberal" idea). It is about *power*. Women cannot be liberated without reducing the power of men. Their liberation not only means changing consciousness and social structures in ways that will transfer to women much of the power monopolized by men. The nature of power itself will thereby change, since throughout history power has itself been defined in sexist terms—being identified with normative, supposedly innate masculine taste for aggressiveness and physical coercion, and with the ceremonies and prerogatives of all-male groupings in war, government, religion, sport, and commerce. Anything less than a change in who has power and what power is, is not liberation but pacification. Changes that are not profound buy off the resentment that threatens established authority. Ameliorating an unstable and too oppressive rule—as when old empires replace colonialist by neocolonialist forms of exploitation—actually serves to regenerate the existing forms of dominance.

To advocate that women make a common front with men to bring about their mutual liberation pulls a veil over the harsh realities of the power relations that determine all dialogue between the sexes. It is not for women to assume the task of liberating men, when they have first to liberate themselves—which means exploring the grounds of enmity, unsweetened for the moment by the dream of reconciliation. Women must change themselves; they must change each other, without worrying about how this will affect men. The consciousness of women will change only when they think about themselves, and forget about what is good for their men. Supposing that these changes can be undertaken in collaboration with men minimizes (and trivializes) the range and depths of women's struggle.

If women change, men will be forced to change. But these changes in men will not occur without considerable resistance. No ruling class ever ceded its real privileges without a struggle. The very structure of society is founded on male privilege, and men will not cede their privileges simply because doing so is more humane or just. Men may make concessions, reluctantly granting women more "civil rights." In most countries now, women can vote and attend institutions of higher education and are permitted to train for the professions. Within the next twenty years, they will get equal pay for equal work and be granted effective ownership of their own bodies (through easy access to contraceptives and the legalization of abortion). But these concessions, however desirable they may be, do not challenge the fundamental attitudes that maintain women as second-class citizens nor touch the root of male privileges.

A radical, as opposed to a liberal, change in the status of women will abolish the mystique of "nature." Women should work toward an end to *all* stereotyping of any kind, positive as well as negative, according to people's sexual identity. Changing the laws that discriminate against women in specific situations (with respect to suffrage, entering into contracts, access to education, and employment) is not enough. The forms of work, sexual customs, the idea of family life have to be altered; language itself, which crudely enshrines the ancient bias against women, cannot remain unaffected. For, however advanced our ideas, every time we speak we continue to affirm the superiority (activity) of men and the inferiority (passivity) of women. It is "grammatically correct" to assume that agents, active persons are men. Grammar, the ultimate arena of sexist brainwashing, conceals the very existence of women—except in special situations. Thus we *must* say "he" when we mean a person who might be of either sex. "Man" is the accepted way to refer to all human beings; "men" is the literary way of saying people. (As "men in dark times," a line from a poem by Brecht and the title of one of Hannah Arendt's books, means people in dark times. Indeed, of the ten people Arendt writes about in her brilliant, noble book two are women. But one, Isak Dinesen, adopted a male pseudonym and the other, Rosa Luxemburg, was, as the jacket copy comments coyly, "the manliest of them all!") The pronoun that substitutes for nouns like student, worker, citizen, artist, public official, athlete, industrialist is "he." Language is not, of course, the source of the prejudice that identifies "men" as the human race, and associates most human activities with men only. Language merely expresses the sexist order that has prevailed throughout history.

The women's movement has already made the sexist bias of grammar feel offensive to a vocal minority of women. Sensitizing increasing numbers of people to sexism in language—as most people have only recently become alert to racist clichés in language (and art)—is an important task. More generally, people must be helped to wake up to the profound misogyny expressed on all levels of human interchange, not just in laws but in the detail of everyday life: in forms of politeness and in the conventions (clothes, gestures, etc.) which polarize sexual identity, and in the flow of images (in art, news, and advertising) which perpetuate sexist stereotypes. These attitudes will change only when women free themselves from their "nature" and start creating and inhabiting another history.

2. *In the process of liberating women, do you give equal importance to economic liberation and to sexual liberation?*

The question seems to me to reveal the underlying weakness of the very concept of "liberation." Unless made more specific, "women's liberation" is an empty goal—and one which blurs the focus and dilutes the energy of women's struggle. I am not sure that the economic and the sexual are two different kinds of liberation. But suppose that they are or, at least, that they can be considered separately. Without more clarity about what women are being liberated from and for, it is meaningless to ask whether both liberations are equally important.

The notion of "economic liberation" can be used to cover up the real issues. That women have access to a wide variety of jobs outside the home for which they are properly paid is certainly a primary, unnegotiable demand. The key to women's psychological and cultural underdevelopment is the fact that most women do not support themselves—neither in the literal (economic) nor metaphoric (psychological, cultural) sense. But it is hardly enough for women to secure the *possibility* of earning money through the opening up of more jobs, through the creation of free facilities for the care of young children. Work must not be merely an option, an alternative to the still more common (and normative) "career" of housewife and mother. It must be *expected* that most women will work, that they will be economically independent (whether married or not) just as men are. Without work, women will never break the chains of dependence on men—the minimal prerequisite for their becoming fully adult. Unless they work, and their work is usually as valuable as their husbands', married women have not even the chance of gaining real power over their own lives which means the power to change their lives. The arts of psychological coercion and conciliation for which women are notorious— flattery, charm, wheedling, glamor, tears—are a servile substitute for real influence and autonomy.

Simply being able to work, however, hardly means that a woman is "liberated." Large numbers of women already do work, and of these a minority already earns wages that guarantee economic independence; yet most women who work remain as dependent as ever on men. The reason is that employment itself is organized along sexist lines. The colonialized status of women is confirmed and indeed strengthened by the sexist division of labor. Women do not participate gainfully in modern work on the same footing as men. They play a supportive, back-up role in the economy. What they do in "the world" tends to reproduce their image as "household" (serving and nurturing) creatures; they are considered unfit for large executive responsibilities. Thus, women cannot be said to be economically liberated until they perform *all* activities now performed by men, on the same terms (with respect to wages, standards of performance, exposure to risk) as men—thereby relinquishing the prerogatives of the fool, the child, and the servant. Their economic liberation is essential not merely to the psychological and moral well-being of individual women. Until they become important to the economy, not just as a reserve labor pool but because in large numbers they possess the major professional and executive skills, women have no means of exercising political power, which means gaining control of institutions and having an effective say in how society will change in the coming decades. Once again: liberation means *power*—or it hardly means anything at all.

The notion of "sexual liberation" seems to me even more suspect. The ancient double standard, which imputes to women less sexual energy and fewer sexual desires than men (and punishes them for behavior condoned in men), is clearly a way of keeping women in their place. But to demand for women the same privileges of sexual experimentation that men have is not enough, since the very conception of sexuality is an instrument of repression. Most sexual relationships act out the attitudes which oppress women and perpetuate male privilege. Merely to remove the onus placed on the sexual expressiveness of women is a hollow victory if the sexuality they become freer to enjoy remains the old one that converts women into objects. The mores of late, urban capitalist society have been for some time, as everyone has noticed, increasingly more "permissive," penalizing women much less than before for behaving like sexual beings outside the context of monogamous marriage. But this already "freer" sexuality mostly reflects a spurious idea of freedom: the right of each person, briefly, to exploit and dehumanize someone else.

Without a change in the very norms of sexuality, the liberation of women is a meaningless goal. Sex as such is not liberating for women. Neither is more sex.

The question is: *what* sexuality are women to be liberated to enjoy? The only sexual ethic liberating for women is one which challenges the primacy of genital heterosexuality. A non-repressive society, a society in which women are subjectively and objectively the genuine equals of men, will necessarily be an androgynous society. Why? Because the only other plausible terms on which the oppression of women could be ended are that men and women decide to live apart, and that is impossible. Separatism does remain plausible as a way of putting an end to the oppression of "colored" peoples by the white race. Conceivably, the different races originating in different parts of the planet could agree to live quite separately again (with the habits and mentalities of each strictly protected against all incursions of cultural as well as economic imperialism). But women and men will undoubtedly always cohabit. If, therefore, the answer to sexism—unlike racism—is not even conceivably separatism, then defending the distinct moral and aesthetic "traditions" of each sex (to preserve something equivalent to "cultural plurality") and attacking the single standard of intellectual excellence or rationality as male "cultural imperialism" (to revalidate the unknown and despised "women's culture") are misleading tactics in the struggle to liberate women.

The aim of struggle should not be to protect the differences between the two sexes but to undermine them. To create a nonrepressive relation between women and men means to erase as far as possible the conventional demarcation lines that have been set up between the two sexes, to reduce the tension between women and men that arises from "otherness." As everyone has noticed, there has been a lively tendency among young people in recent years to narrow and even confuse sex differences in clothes, hair styles, gestures, taste. But this first step toward depolarizing the sexes, partly coopted within capitalist forms of consumership as mere "style" (the commerce of unisex boutiques), will be denied its political implications unless the tendency takes root at a deeper level.

The more profound depolarization of the sexes must take place in the world of work and, increasingly, in sexual relations themselves. As "otherness" is reduced, some of the energy of sexual attraction between the sexes will decline. Women and men will certainly continue to make love and to pair off in couples. But women and men will no longer *primarily* define each other as potential sexual partners. In a nonrepressive non-sexist society, sexuality will in one sense have a more important role than it has today—because it will be more diffused. Homo-sexual choices will be as valid and respectable as heterosexual choices; both will grow out of a genuine bisexuality. (Exclu-sive homosexuality—which, like exclusive heterosexuality, is learned—would be much less common in a nonsexist society than it is at present.) But in such a society, sexuality will in another sense be less important than it is now—because sexual relations will no longer be hysterically craved as a substitute for genuine freedom and for so many other pleasures (intimacy, intensity, feeling of belonging, blasphemy) which this society frustrates.

3. *In your opinion, what is the relationship between the struggle for women's liberation and the class struggle? Do you believe the first must be subordinated to the second?*

I see little relation at present between the class struggle and the struggle to liberate women. The double content of mod-ern left-revolutionary politics—the overthrow of one class by another within a nation, and the freeing of colonialized peoples from imperialist control—is basically irrelevant to the struggle of women as women. Women are neither a class nor a nation. Politically radical women may well prefer to participate in exist-ing insurgent movements than to limit their energies, as they see it, to the struggle of women. But in doing so they should realize that, at the most, all that such multi-issue revolution-ary politics (like parliamentary party politics) offers women is reformist gains, the promise of formal "equality."

Which level of struggle should come first? I don't see how one can take a general position about that. The priorities of struggle vary from nation to nation, from historical moment to historical moment—and depend, within a given nation, on one's race and one's social class. It seems beyond question that the liberation of women in Vietnam has to be subordinated at the present time to the struggle for national liberation. In the affluent countries, however, the liberation of women is a much more immediately relevant issue—both in itself and for its use-fulness in radicalizing people for other forms of struggle. (For instance, to explore the nature of women's oppression helps one to understand the nature of imperialism. And the other way around.)

As I see it, the main point about the relationship of the struggle of women to what Marxist-oriented revolutionary movements define as the central struggle, the class struggle, is the following. To liberate women requires a cultural revolution that will attack attitudes and mental habits which otherwise could well survive the reconstruction of economic relationships that is the goal of the class struggle. The position of women could, conceivably, be scarcely affected by a change in class relationships. Because Marx and Engels were humanists, heirs of the Enlightenment, they denounced the oppression of women under capitalism. But the traditional "feminism" of Marx and his successors is not *logically* connected with the Marxist analysis. (Neither, I would argue, is Freud's coarse "antifeminism" *logically* connected with the basic ideas of psychoanalytic theory.) Socialism will not inevitably bring about the liberation of women. Nevertheless, only in a society that one calls, for want of a better name, socialist, would it be *possible* to invent and institutionalize forms of life that would liberate women. Therefore, though the struggle to build socialism and the cause of women's liberation are hardly identical, militant feminists do have a vested interest in the fortunes of a revolutionary socialist movement and good reason to be, if only tacitly, allies—as they have reason to be the enemies of all right-revolutionary (or fascist) movements, which always preach the reinforcement of male privilege and the subservience of women.

4. *Do you think the fact that the work of a housewife is unsalaried and has no exchange value on the labor market makes women a separate class existing apart from other economic classes? Do you view patriarchal oppression as a principal or secondary contradiction in modern society?*

No. The fact that "housework," which is defined as women's work, is physical and, unlike work done in the "world," unpaid, does not put women into a separate economic class. Women do not form a class any more than men do. Like men, women make up half the membership of every class. The wives, sisters, and daughters of rich men participate in the oppression of the poor; by virtue of their class membership rather than their sex, a minority of women oppress other women. If a label is needed, women could perhaps be considered a caste. But this is only an analogy. There is no suitable label to be borrowed from other vocabularies of social analysis. To suppose that women constitute a class makes no more sense than to suppose that blacks are a class. The human species is divided into two sexes (and "caste"-type relations based on sexual identity), as well as a plurality of races (with "caste"-type relations based mainly on color). The oppression of one class by another is only one form of oppression. The structures built around the existence of two sexes, like those built around the existence of many races, are irreducible to structures built around the existence of social classes—although, obviously, oppressions can and often do overlap.

I detect in this question a pious hope that the oppression of women could be blamed on a particular form of society, a particular set of class arrangements. But it can't. If socialism—at least as it exists so far—is not self-evidently the solution, neither is capitalism self-evidently the culprit. Women have always been treated as inferior, have always been marginal politically and culturally. The oppression of women constitutes the most fundamental type of repression in organized societies. That is, it is the most *ancient* form of oppression, pre-dating all oppression based on class, caste, and race. It is the most primitive form of hierarchy.

Because this is so I do not see how "patriarchal oppression" (your term) can be considered as any kind of contradiction, either principal or secondary. On the contrary, the structure of this society is precisely based on patriarchal oppression, the undoing of which will modify the most deeply rooted habits of friendship and love, the conceptions of work, the ability to wage war (which is profoundly nourished by sexist anxieties), and the mechanisms of power. The very nature of power in organized societies is founded on sexist models of conduct. Power is defined in terms of, and feeds on, machismo.

Modern industrial society certainly contains many contradictory structures and ideologies, but the struggle to liberate women cannot be expected to succeed, in my opinion, if it is mainly directed toward trying to aggravate and intensify already existing contradictions; the task is not so much to exploit a contradiction as to dislodge this most profoundly rooted of structures. The women's movement must lead to a critical assault on the very nature of the state—the millennial tyranny of patriarchal rule being the low-keyed model of the peculiarly modern tyranny of the fascist state.

I would maintain that fascism, far from being a political aberration whose greatest plausibility was confined to Europe and the interval between the two World Wars, is the *normal* condition of the modern state: the condition to which the governments of all industrially advanced countries tend. Fascism, in other words, is the natural development of the values of the patriarchal state applied to the conditions (and contradictions) of twentieth-century "mass" societies. Virginia Woolf was altogether correct when she declared in the late 1930s, in a remarkable tract called *Three Guineas*, that the fight to liberate women is a fight against fascism.

5. *It is often said that most salaried work in present day society is alienating. In spite of this, do you advise women to seek salaried employment as a means of liberation?*

However alienating most salaried work may be, for women it is still liberating to have a job, if only because it frees them from the confinement of domesticity and parasitism. But the commitment to work is only a first step, of course. Women will never be autonomous unless they participate in society's work on terms of complete equality. Women must break out of the ghettos of work in which they are isolated: jobs that continue to exploit their life-long training to be servile, to be both supportive and parasitical, to be unadventurous. For a woman to leave "home" to go out into "the world" and work rarely carries a full commitment to "the world," that is, achievement; in most cases, it is strictly understood to be just a way of earning money, of supplementing the family income. Women fill very few corporate or political posts, and contribute only a tiny contingent to the liberal professions (apart from teaching). Except in communist countries, they are virtually barred from jobs that involve an expert, intimate relation to machines or an aggressive use of the body, or that carry any physical danger or sense of adventure, or that directly compete with (instead of support) what men do. Besides being less well paid, most employment available to women has a low ceiling of advancement and gives meager outlet to normal wishes to be active and to make decisions.

The result of these prejudices is that virtually all outstanding work by women in capitalist countries has been voluntary, for few women can stand up to the disapproval unleashed when they deviate from the stereotypes of "feminine" submissiveness and illogicality. (Thus, it is disparaging to describe a woman as "ambitious" or "tough" or "intellectual"; and she will be called "castrating" for behavior that would be viewed, in a man, as normal or even commendable aggressiveness.)

Granted that almost all jobs available in modern societies could be described as alienating, I am more impressed by the double alienation from which women suffer—by being denied even those limited satisfactions that men can derive from work. By entering the world of work in its present forms, women have much to gain. They acquire skills, by which they can take care of themselves and organize themselves better. And they acquire a specific arena of struggle, in each job or profession, where they can press the demands for their liberation.

These demands must go beyond "equality" as that may be achieved between individuals in the work situations to which women are admitted. Far more important than getting the same pay for the same work (though that minimal "liberal" demand has not yet been met in *any* country in the world, including China) is breaking down the sex-stereotyping according to which the world of work is organized. Women must become surgeons, agronomists, lawyers, mechanics, soldiers, electricians, astronauts, factory executives, orchestra conductors, sound engineers, chess players, construction workers, pilots— and in numbers large enough so that their presence is no longer remarked. (When women become the vast majority doing a job formerly monopolized by men, as in the medical profession in the Soviet Union, the challenge to sex-stereotyping is much slighter. The result is that the hitherto "masculine" role of doctor has become a "feminine" role.)

As long as the system of sex segregation in work remains strong, most people—women as well as men—will continue to rationalize it by insisting that women lack the physical strength or the capacity for rational judgment or the emotional self-control to do many jobs. As that system weakens, women will get more competent. And when they are not merely tolerated in but *expected* to perform the jobs from which they are now barred, large numbers of women will in fact be able to do them.

When work becomes fully desegregated sexually, women will be better qualified to join with their co-workers who are men in questioning its fundamental terms, as presently defined. The bureaucratic style in which work in modern society is laid out must be redesigned to provide more democratic, decentralized ways of planning and making decisions. Most important of all, the very ideal of "productivity" (and consumership) must be challenged. The economy of affluent countries operates by a division of function that runs along sexual lines: men are defined as "producers" and tool-users, while women (and adolescents) are defined principally as "consumers." Unless this distinction is subverted, the full admission of women to the work men do will just double the ranks of that great army of psychologically alienated "producers" already drafted into the ecologically suicidal campaign of manufacturing unlimited amounts of goods (and waste).

The rethinking about work that inevitably must take place could well be done by the presently existing elites, and women may find that men have made the key decisions without them. The new structures of work to be devised in the next two decades (part of whose character will be determined by the need to have much *less* work of many kinds) could still perpetuate the sexist system intact—confining women to the role of parasitical, deferring helper. This can be prevented from happening only if women invade the world of work now, even while it is still "alienating," with a militant feminist consciousness.

6. *In what way do you envisage the struggle for women's liberation: (a) in the framework of a revolutionary/political organization or (b) exclusively in the women's movement?*

It is good news whenever a radical political organization supports the cause of women—particularly when the organization is one, like the Black Panthers, that had been notorious for its blatant sexism. But I am not optimistic about the long-term benefits of such support. The alliance seems more natural than it really is. Revolutionary struggle usually does tend to enfranchise women as historical agents and to override sexist stereotypes in a quick, dramatic way. Think of what women have done (have been "allowed" to do) in the Commune, the Russian revolution, the French and Italian resistance during World War II, the struggle to create the State of Israel, the Cuban revolution, the thirty years of Vietnamese liberation struggle, the

Palestinian guerrilla movement, the urban guerrilla movements in Latin America—in relation to what women were allowed to do (thought capable of doing) in each of these societies just before the start of armed struggle. But the enfranchisement is only temporary. After the struggle ends, whether in victory or defeat, women are inevitably demobilized rapidly and encouraged to return to their traditional, passive, ahistorical roles. (Later their participation will be ignored or glossed over by historians and ideologists—as, for instance, in France, where there is an astonishing silence today about the numerous fighters and martyrs of the Resistance who were women. If their deeds are told at all, they will be fitted into imagery that confirms the leadership of men, as in that eminently sexist recent Chinese film ostensibly made to honor and praise the women soldiers in Mao's army in the 1930s, *The Red Detachment of Women*.)

To break radically with sexual stereotypes, even if just temporarily seems to come easily to political radicals only when they engage in insurrection, in "people's war," in guerrilla struggle, or in underground resistance to foreign occupation. In situations that fall short of military-type urgency, the treatment of women in radical political organizations is in fact anything but exemplary. Despite their often-proclaimed feminist "views," the internal life of almost all radical organizations, in or out of power—from the official Communist parties to the new Left and semianarchist groups active since the 1960s—uncritically condones and promotes all sorts of sexist "habits."

Thus, the present wave of feminism was born out of the painful awakening of women in the largest radical student organization in America in the 1960s to the fact that they were being treated like second-class members. Women were never listened to with the same seriousness at meetings; it was always women members who were asked (or volunteered) to take the minutes, or to leave a meeting in progress to go into the kitchen to make coffee. Often chivalrously protected by their men comrades from police violence during demonstrations, they were invariable excluded from positions of leadership. To be sure, the complacent sexism of radical organizations has lessened somewhat, at least in America, precisely because of the protest these women made. At first only an isolated, ridiculed minority, they heralded a new level of consciousness on the part of many women—which, having started in America, is now belatedly spreading (though in a tamer and more limited way) to Western Europe. In the 1970s women seeking to liberate themselves and other women can find more allies than ever among radical men. But working within existing revolutionary organizations is not enough. At this point, it is not even central.

Now and for some time to come, I think, the primary role must be played by women's movements. However many radical men can now be counted as allies (and they are not *that* numerous), women have to conduct the main part of the struggle themselves. Women must form groups in each class, each occupation, each community, to sustain and encourage different levels of struggle and emerging consciousness. (For example: all-women professional collectives—of doctors who will treat only women patients, of lawyers and accountants who will handle only women clients—as well as all-women rock groups, farms, film-making crews, small businesses, and so forth.) Politically, women will not find a militant voice until they organize in groups which they lead—just as blacks did not find their true political militancy as long as they were represented mainly by integrated organizations, which meant, in practice, being led by benevolent, well-educated, liberal whites. One of the purposes of political action is to educate those who stage the action. At the present point of women's political underdevelopment, working with men (even sympathetic men) slows down the process by which women learn how to be politically mature.

Women have to learn, first of all, how to talk to each other. Like blacks (and other colonized peoples), women have trouble organizing, are not easily disposed to respect each other and to take each other seriously. They are used to leadership, support, and approval by men. It is therefore all the more important that they do learn to organize politically by themselves, and try to reach other women. Their mistakes are at least *their* mistakes.

More generally: people who favor women working for their liberation in concert with men tacitly deny the realities of women's oppression. Such a policy insures that all struggle on behalf of women will be moderate and, ultimately, cooptable. It is to arrange, in advance, that nothing "radical" will happen, that the consciousness of women will not change in a profound way. For integrated actions, those taken alongside of men, necessarily limit the freedom of women to think "radically." The sole chance women have to effect that deep change in their consciousness required for their liberation is by organizing separately. Consciousness changes only through confrontation, in situations in which appeasement is not possible.

Thus, there are certain activities that only all-women's groups can—or will want to—perform. Only groups composed entirely of women will be diversified enough in their tactics, and sufficiently "extreme." Women should lobby, demonstrate, march. They should take karate lessons. They should whistle at men in the streets, raid beauty parlors, picket toy manufacturers who produce sexist toys, convert in sizeable numbers to militant lesbianism, operate their own free psychiatric and abortion clinics, provide feminist divorce counselling, establish make-up withdrawal centers, adopt their mothers' family names as their last names, deface billboard advertising that insults women, disrupt public events by singing in honor of the docile wives of male celebrities and politicians, collect pledges to renounce alimony and giggling, bring law suits for defamation against the mass-circulation "women's magazines," conduct telephone harassment campaigns against male psychiatrists who have sexual relations with their women patients, organize beauty contests for men, put up feminist candidates for all public offices. Though no single action is necessary, the "extremist" acts are valuable in themselves, because they help women to raise their own consciousness. And, however much people claim to be shocked or put off by such acts, their rhetoric *does* have a positive effect upon the silent majority. Performed by even a small minority, this guerrilla theater forces millions to become defensive about hitherto barely-conscious sexist attitudes, accustoming them to the idea that these attitudes are at least not self-evident. (I do not exclude the utility of real guerrilla violence as well.)

Undeterred by the fear of confirming sexist cliches (e.g., women as creatures of emotion, incapable of being detached, objective), militant groups must commit themselves to behavior that does violate the stereotypes of femininity. A common way of reinforcing the political passivity of women has been to say they will be more effective and influential if they act with "dignity," if they don't violate decorum, if they remain charming. Women should show their contempt for this form of intimidation disguised as friendly advice. Women will be much more effective politically if they are rude, shrill, and—by sexist standards—"unattractive." They will be met with ridicule, which they should do more than bear stoically. They should, indeed, welcome it. Only when their acts are described as "ridiculous" and their demands are dismissed as "exaggerated" and "unreasonable" can militant women be sure they are on the right track.

7. And in this case, what will be the long-term and the short-term objectives?

The important difference is not between short-term and long-term objectives but, as I have already indicated, between objectives which are reformist (or liberal) and those which are radical. From suffrage onward, most of the objectives that women have sought have been reformist.

An example of the difference. To demand that women receive equal pay for equal work is reformist; to demand that women have access to all jobs and professions, without exception, is radical. The demand for equal wages does not attack the system of sexual stereotyping. Paying a woman the same wages a man gets *if* she holds the same job he does establishes a merely formal kind of equity. When roughly half the people doing every kind of job are women, when all forms of employment and public responsibility become fully coeducational, sexual stereotyping will end—not before.

In underlining this difference once again, I am not suggesting that the reformist gains are negligible. They are eminently worth struggling for—as evidenced by the fact that these demands are, for most people, too "radical." Most of the reformist demands are far from being granted. In that slow procession toward fulfilling the reformist demands, the Communist countries have taken a clear lead. Next, but well behind them in terms of the degree of "liberal" enlightenment of public policy, come the capitalist countries with a Protestant background, notably Sweden, Denmark, England, Holland, the United States, Canada, and New Zealand. Lagging far behind to the rear are those countries with a Catholic cultural base, like France, Italy, Spain, Portugal, Mexico, and the countries of Central and South America—where married women cannot buy and dispose of property without the signature of their husbands; and where the right to divorce, not to mention the legality of abortion, remains fiercely contested. And still further behind the Latin countries, almost out of sight, are the countries with a Moslem culture—where women are still subjected to ferociously strict forms of social segregation, economic exploitation, and sexual surveillance. . . .

Despite the cultural unevenness with which the situation of women is being ameliorated, I would predict that most of the reformist demands will be granted in most countries by the end of the century. My point is that then the struggle will have only begun. The granting of these demands can leave intact all the oppressive and patronizing attitudes that make women into second-class citizens. Women have to feel, and learn to express, their anger.

Women must start making concrete demands—first of all upon themselves and then upon men. For a start, women can note their acceptance of full adult status by symbolic acts, like not changing their last names when they marry. They can wean themselves from the enslaving concern with their personal appearance by which they consent to make themselves into objects. (By giving up make-up, and the reassuring ministrations of beauty parlors, they symbolically renounce the narcissism and vanity that are, insultingly, deemed normal in women.) They can refuse the rituals of male gallantry which dramatize their inferior position and convert it into a seduction. As often as not women should light men's cigarettes for them, carry their suitcases, and fix their flat tires. Even the trivial acts by which women ignore preassigned "feminine" roles have weight, helping to educate both women and men. They are the necessary prologue to any serious consideration on the part of women of the institutional framework for their liberation. This thinking must coincide with the creation of experimental institutions run by women, for women—living collectives, work collectives, schools, day-care centers, medical centers—which will embody the solidarity of women, their increasingly politicized consciousness and their practical strategies for outwitting the system of sexual stereotyping.

The liberation of women has both short-term and long-term political meaning. Changing the status of women is not only a political objective in itself but prepares for (as well as constitutes part of) that radical change in the structure of consciousness and society which is what I understand by revolutionary socialism. It is not simply that the liberation of women need not wait for the advent of socialism, so defined. It cannot wait.

I do not think socialism can triumph unless big victories for feminism have been won beforehand. The liberation of women is a necessary preparation for building a just society—not the other way around, as Marxists always claim. For if it does happen the other way around, women are likely to find their liberation a fraud. Should the transformation of society according to revolutionary socialism be undertaken without a prior militant independent women's movement, women will find that they have merely passed from the hegemony of one oppressive moral ethic to another.

8. *Do you consider that the family is an obstacle for the liberation of woman?*

Certainly the modern "nuclear family" operates to oppress women. And little consolation is to be had by considering other shapes that the family is known to have taken in the past and has today outside the societies of "European" type. Virtually *all* known forms of the family define women in ways that subordinate them to men—keeping them within the "home" while investing public power exclusively in the hands of men, who organize in all-male groups outside the family. In the chronology of human lives, the family is the first and psychologically the most irrefutable school for sexism. It is as small children, through the systematically contrasting ways in which girls and boys are treated (dressed, talked to, praised, punished), that the norms of dependency and narcissism are instilled in girls. Growing up, children learn the different expectations they may have for themselves from the models of mother and father: the fundamentally dissimilar geography of commitment that women and men make to family life.

The family is an institution organized around the exploitation of women as full-time inhabitants of the family's space. Hence, for women to work means relieving at least some part of their oppression. Working at a paid job, any job, a woman is no longer just a family creature. But she can still continue to be exploited, as a now part-time family creature still saddled with nearly full-time duties. Women who have gained the freedom to go out into "the world" but still have the responsibility for marketing, cooking, cleaning, and the children when they return from work have simply doubled their labor. This is the plight of almost all married working women in both capitalist and Communist countries. (The oppressiveness of women's double load is particularly stark in the Soviet Union: with more diversity in the jobs open to women than in, say, the United States; with its consumer-society style of life just getting underway; and with hardly any "service" facilities.) Even when the wife holds down a job that is as honorable or as physically tiring as her husband's, when they both come home it still seems natural to the husband (and usually to the wife) that he rest while she prepares the dinner and cleans up afterwards. Such exploitation will continue, even with the rising number of women entering the labor force, as long as their work so rarely challenges the notion of the "feminine" role.

Because most jobs that women get are conceived to be suited to their "feminine" aptitudes, most men and women experience no contradiction between that "woman's job" and the traditionally "feminine" arts (assistant, nurse, cook) that women are expected to exercise at home. Only when all sorts of jobs are filled by many women will it no longer seem natural to a husband to let his wife do all or most of the housework. What appear to be two quite different demands must be made jointly: that the range of employment no longer be determined along the lines of sexual identity, and that men share fully in the traditionally "feminine" work of domestic life. Both demands encounter intense resistance. Men find both demands embarrassing, threatening, though they seem to be made slightly less uncomfortable these days by the first than by the second—demonstrating that the grammar of family life (like language itself) is the most intense and stubborn fortress of sexist assumptions.

In an arrangement of family life which would not oppress women, men will take part in all domestic activities. (And women will be expected to give considerable time to "outside" obligations that have nothing to do with their families.) But the solution involves more than adjusting the degree of participation of men, the ideal being an equal sharing of all chores and responsibilities. These activities must themselves be re-thought. The family does not have to be a sealed-off molecule, all of whose activities belong to "it." Many domestic tasks would be more efficiently and pleasantly carried out in a communal space—as they were in premodern societies. There is no genuine benefit in each family having (if it could) its private babysitter or maid; that is, freelance women hired to share or take over a wife's unpaid, unofficial servant role. Similarly, there is no reason (besides selfishness and fear) for each family to have its own washing machine, car, dishwasher, television set, and so forth. While private human (mostly female) domestic service is disappearing, except for the extremely rich, as countries pass from premodern economies to industrialization and consumerism, private mechanical services proliferate. Most of the new mechanical servants and services whose acquisition by the "individual" family is the primary article of faith of the consumer society could well be the common property of groups of families—thus reducing unnecessary duplication of labor; restraining competition, acquisitiveness; lessening waste. Democratizing family tasks is one of the steps necessary to change the oppressive definitions of the role of wife and husband, mother and father. It will also help break down the walls constructed in all modern industrial societies that separate one tiny family from another, thereby putting such devastating psychological strains on the members of each family.

The modern "nuclear" family is a psychological and moral disaster. It is a prison of sexual repression, a playing-field of inconsistent moral laxity, a museum of possessiveness, a guilt-producing factory, and a school of selfishness. Yet despite the frightful price its members pay in anxiety and a backlog of murderous feelings, the modern family does allow some positive experiences. Particularly in capitalist society today, as Juliet Mitchell has pointed out, the family is often the only place where something approximating unalienated personal relations (of warmth, trust, dialogue, uncompetitiveness, loyalty, spontaneity, sexual pleasure, fun) are still permitted. It is no accident that one of the slogans of capitalist society, the form of society which promotes the greatest alienation in work and all communal bonds, is the sanctity of the family. (By the family is meant, though never said, the patriarchal "nuclear" family only.) Family life is the anachronistic reserve of exactly those "human-scale" values which industrial urban society destroys—but which it must somehow manage to conserve.

To survive, that is, to extract the maximum productivity and appetite for consumption from its citizenry, capitalism (and its cousin, Russian-style communism) must continue to grant a limited existence to the values of nonalienation. Thus it awards these values a privileged or protected status in an institution, the family, that is economically and politically innocuous. This is the ideological secret behind the very form of the modern nuclear family: a family unit too small in numbers, too stripped down, too confined in its living space (archetypally, the three- or four-room city apartment) to be viable as an economic unit or politically connected with sources of power. Early in the modern era, the home lost its ancient role as a site of altars and ritual; religious functions came to be entirely monopolized by "churches," whose activities the family members leave the house to attend as *individuals*. Since the late eighteenth century, the family has been forced to cede its right to educate (or not educate) its children to the centralized nation-state, which operates "public schools" that the children of each family are legally obliged to attend as *individuals*. The nuclear family, also known as the basic family, is the useless family—an ideal invention of urban industrial society. Its function is just that: to be useless, to be a refuge. Deprived of all economic, religious, and educational functions, the family exists solely as a source of emotional warmth in a cold world.

The glorification of the family is not only a piece of rank hypocrisy; it reveals an important structural contradiction in the ideology and workings of capitalist society. The ideological function of the modern family is manipulative—more accurately, self-manipulative. This does not mean we can dismiss what goes on in family life as entirely fraudulent. Genuine values are incarnated in the nuclear family. Indeed, were it not for even that poor form of family life that flourishes today, people would lead far more alienated lives than they already do. But the strategy will not work indefinitely. The contradiction between the values family life is charged with preserving and the values promoted by industrial mass society as a whole is, ultimately, an untenable one. Families are, in fact, less and less able to perform well this assigned task, the task which justifies the family in its modern form. The function of the family as ethical museum in industrial society is deteriorating; even there, "human-scale" values are leaking away. Industrial mass society stores the values of nonalienation in a safe place, an institution that is (by definition) apolitical. But no place is safe. The acids of the world "outside" are so strong that the family is becoming increasingly poisoned, more and more contaminated by society—which intrudes directly, for instance, in the homogenized voices of the television set in every living room.

To advocate "destroying" the family, because it is authoritarian, is a facile cliché. The vice of family life throughout history is not its authoritarianism, but that authority *per se* is founded on relations of ownership. Husbands "own" wives; parents "own" their children. (This is only one of the many similarities between the status of women and the status of children. Thus the sex whose members are *defined* as adult, and therefore as physically responsible for themselves, gallantly forces "women and children first" off sinking ships. In Spain, no married woman may hold a job, open a bank account, apply for a passport, or sign a contract without her husband's written permission—just like a child. Women, like children, have essentially the status of minors; they are wards of their husbands, as children are the wards of their parents.) Even the modern nuclear family in its liberalized Northern European and North American form is still based, though less blatantly so, on treating women and children as property.

The family based on ownership is the target: people should not be treated as property; adults should not be treated as minors. But some forms of authority make sense in family life. The question is what kind of authority, which depends on what the base of its legitimacy is. The restructuring of the family required for the emancipation of women means subtracting from the authority available to family arrangements one of its principal forms of legitimacy: the authority that men have over women. Although the family is the institution in which the oppression of women is originally incarnated, eliminating this oppression will not dissolve the family. Nor will a nonsexist family be without *any* idea of legitimate authority. When family arrangements are no longer a hierarchy dictated by sex roles, they will still have certain hierarchical features dictated by differences in age. A nonsexist family will not be completely unstructured, though it will be "open."

Precisely because the family is a singular institution—the only institution that modern society insists on defining as "private"—reconstructing the family is an extremely delicate project, and less amenable to the kind of advance planning for change that one can apply to other institutions. (What to do about schools, for instance, in order to make them nonsexist, as well as less authoritarian in other ways, is much clearer.) The reconstruction of family life must be part of the construction of new, but still small-scale, forms of community. This is where the women's movement can be particularly useful, by bringing into existence, within the context of today's society, alternative institutions that will pioneer the development of a new praxis of group life.

In any case, nothing can be done about the family by fiat. And, undoubtedly, some form of family life will continue. What is desirable is not to destroy the family, but to destroy the opposition (particularly entrenched in capitalist countries) between "home" and "the world." This opposition is decadent. It is oppressive to women (and children), and it stifles or drains off those communitarian—sororal and fraternal—feelings on which a new society could be built.

9. *What place do you give to the right to abortion on demand among the objectives of women's struggle?*

The legalization of abortion is a reformist demand—like the removal of the stigma on unwed mothers and so-called illegitimate children, and the establishment of free child-care facilities for working mothers—and as such, suspect. History shows that the anger of women, when channelled into pressing reformist demands only, is all too easily defused (as happened to the movement organized around suffrage in England and America once women were finally given the vote after World War I). Such reforms tend to narrow, and then abruptly disperse, militant energies. It also can be argued that they directly bolster the repressive system, by ameliorating some of its hardships. Contrary to what is felt with such passion, particularly in Latin countries, it's more plausible to suppose that gaining the right to have an abortion—like the right to divorce and to purchase contraceptives legally and cheaply—will help conserve the present system of marriage and the family. In this way, such reforms actually reinforce the power of men, indirectly confirming the licentious sexuality, exploitative of women, that is considered normal in this society.

These reforms do nevertheless correspond to the concrete, immediate needs of hundreds of millions of women—all but the rich and privileged. Ameliorating their condition can, given a proper theoretical consciousness in the women's movement, lead to other demands. Much of the value of struggling for goals of such limited, questionable political weight depends on where the struggle is taking place. As a rule, the harder the struggle is, the greater is the chance of politicizing it. Thus, to campaign for the legalizing of contraceptives and abortions has a larger political dimension in Italy or Argentina than it does in Norway or Australia. In itself, the right to abortion has no serious political content at all—despite its extreme desirability on humanitarian and ecological grounds. It becomes a valuable demand, however, when taken as a step in a chain of demands, and actions, which can mobilize and move forward the awareness of large numbers of women who have not yet begun to think consciously about their oppression. Nothing in the situation of women will be changed when any one of these rights is won. The fact that divorce is virtually impossible to get in Spain, while it is easy to get in Mexico, does not make the situation of women in Mexico substantially better than it is in Spain. But the struggle for these rights can be an important step in preparing for a more profound level of struggle.

10. *How do you, who are precisely a liberated woman, experience the attitude of men toward you?*

I would never describe myself as a liberated woman. Of course, things are never as simple as *that*. But I have always been a feminist.

When I was five years old, I day-dreamed about becoming a biochemist and winning the Nobel Prize. (I had just read a biography of Madame Curie.) I stuck with chemistry until the age of ten, when I decided I would become a doctor. At fifteen, I knew I was going to be a writer. That is to say: from the beginning it never even occurred to me that I might be prevented from doing things in "the world" because I was born female. Perhaps because I spent most of my sickly childhood reading and in my chemistry laboratory in the empty garage, growing up in a very provincial part of the United States with a family life so minimal that it could be described as subnuclear, I was curiously innocent of the very existence of a barrier. When, at fifteen, I left home to go to a university, and then took up various careers, the relations that I had with men in my professional life seemed to me, with some exceptions, cordial and untroubled. So I went on not knowing there was a problem. I didn't even know I was a feminist, so unfashionable was that point of view at the time, when I married at the age of seventeen and kept my own name; it seemed to me an equally "personal" act of principle on my part, when I divorced my husband seven years later, to have indignantly rejected my lawyer's automatic bid for alimony, even though I was broke, homeless, and jobless at that moment and I had a six-year-old child to support.

Now and then, people I met would allude to the supposed difficulties of being both independent and a woman; I was always surprised—and sometimes annoyed, because, I thought, they were being obtuse. The problem didn't exist for me— except in the envy and resentment I occasionally felt from other women, the educated, jobless, home stranded wives of the men with whom I worked. I was conscious of being an exception, but it hadn't ever seemed hard to be an exception; and I accepted the advantages I enjoyed as my right. I know better now.

My case is not uncommon. Not so paradoxically, the position of a "liberated" woman in a liberal society where the vast majority of women are *not* liberated can be embarrassingly easy. Granted a good dose of talent and a certain cheerful or merely dogged lack of self-consciousness, one can even escape (as I did) the initial obstacles and derision that are likely to afflict a woman who insists on autonomy. It will not seem so hard for such a woman to lead an independent life; she may even reap some professional advantages from being a woman, such as greater visibility. Her good fortune is like the good fortune of a few blacks in a liberal but still racist society. Every liberal grouping (whether political, professional or artistic) needs its token woman.

What I have learned in the last five years—helped by the women's movement—is to situate my own experience in a certain *political* perspective. My good fortune is really beside the point. What does it prove? Nothing.

Any already "liberated" woman who complacently accepts her privileged situation participates in the oppression of other women. I accuse the overwhelming majority of women with careers in the arts and sciences, in the liberal professions, and in politics of doing just that.

I have often been struck by how misogynistic most successful women are. They are eager to say how silly, boring, superficial, or tiresome they find other women, and how much they prefer the company of men. Like most men, who basically despise and patronize women, most "liberated" women don't like or respect other women. If they don't fear them as sexual rivals, they fear them as professional rivals—wishing to guard their special status as women admitted into largely all-male professional worlds. Most women who pass as being "liberated" are shameless Uncle Toms, eager to flatter their men colleagues, becoming their accomplices in putting down other, less accomplished women, dishonestly minimizing the difficulties they themselves have run into because of being women. The implication of their behavior is that all women can do what they have done, if only they would exert themselves; that the barriers put up by men are flimsy; that it is mainly women themselves who hold themselves back. This simply is not true.

The first responsibility of a "liberated" woman is to lead the fullest, freest, and most imaginative life she can. The second responsibility is her solidarity with other women. She may live and work and make love with men. But she has no right to represent her situation as simpler, or less suspect, or less full of compromises than it really is. Her good relations with men must not be bought at the price of betraying her sisters.

(1973)

Francis Bacon: "About Being in Pain"

A RETROSPECTIVE can be a cruel event. A painter's output suddenly looks even bigger—or it shrinks. Thus one main result of the large and loving retrospectives given Modigliani and Magritte was to make them seem overestimated. Having a lifetime of work assembled under one prestigious roof is the highest accolade, but it also invites the most devastating judgment: the work is now understood, understood all too well.

Bacon's art might seem to be particularly open to the risks of apotheosis. Generally, painters get retrospectives only after a number of works have been tested by familiarity, and the career has been sufficiently celebrated to be secured against sudden critical deflation, brutal reversals of taste. It is then ready to be transmuted into a "body of work." And there is something especially seductive—but even more often, retroactively, obvious-seeming—about work that really is a "body"; about an out-pouring of artifacts every one of which is so unmistakably stamped by a single imagination. Bacon is not only one of the best known but one of the most easily identifiable of contemporary painters. After seeing only two or three Bacons, one would have no problem in identifying almost *any* other painting he did as being by him.

But the obsessional coherence of Bacon's work does not mean that it is static. On the contrary. He is getting better and better. The period since the big retrospective held in Paris (at the Grand Palais) in the winter of 1971/72 has been one of bold development. Perhaps the most stunning work in the current retrospective in New York (at the Metropolitan Museum) is what Bacon has done since 1971 and the Paris retrospective.

A precocious talent, Bacon now has a long career behind him. Yet he has claimed that he was forty-five before he produced any painting of value. (Bacon was born in 1909, so that would be in 1954.) He has also claimed, in interviews, not to have started painting until the age of thirty. Actually, Bacon was doing drawings and watercolors in 1927 (during a year spent working in Paris) when he was eighteen; and he began to paint in late 1929 and showed his paintings publicly for the first time in 1930 (in his studio in London), at the age of twenty-one. Bacon is supposed to have destroyed all the paintings done before 1944. Bacon's taste for concealing his early work is not just an example of idle tampering with his biography. Rather these "falsifications" of the chronological record point to an important psychological and artistic truth: that Bacon is someone who was "falsely" precocious and is, in reality, a late developer.

Most artists cling indefatigably to all the work they have done, ever eager to justify it. Only exceptions like Ingmar Bergman and Bacon, having made in middle age, or later, such astonishing leaps into their own being, can afford the luxury of disavowing their early work. Bergman, for instance, has said that only when he reached his late thirties did he begin, just begin, to do something of value in films. (The dismissal is more interesting if one knows that Bergman was a *Wunderkind* who, by his late teens, was already a successful writer, film scenarist, and theater director; and what he dismisses as worthless now includes at least his first ten movies.) Most artists, writers, and film directors do their most original work when they are at the early/middle of their careers, and then settle down to imitating and systematizing themselves. Bacon, like Bergman, is one of those rare artists—often precocious, usually astoundingly prolific—who become really daring only in middle age and then continue to grow and to astonish. (It is interesting that such people tend, as Bergman and Bacon have, to remain preternaturally youthful-looking in middle age and beyond.)

Although Bacon has already received almost every kind of acclaim that a living painter can have, it does not seem as dangerous a situation for him to be in as it usually is. He is sufficiently cultivated, complex, and hidden as a human being to be able to defend himself. Bacon is one of the least provincial of important modern painters. It is almost startling to remember that he is English—and not just because one has stopped expecting truly major, ambitious, full-blooded work in any of the arts to come out of England. Bacon seems particularly supra-national, almost ideally European. He is probably lucky not to have been born either French or American, and thereby to have been burdened with that load of chauvinist self-consciousness that has gone with the self-definitions of Paris (before World War II) and now New York as The World Capital of Art. Residing for most of his creative life in a city—London—which has never been a serious contender for that title, Bacon has been spared some of the pressures to choose between mythicized Old World versus New World values (like sophistication vs. energy; literacy vs. innocence).

Despite all the recognition given to Bacon, many lesser talents have more influence in contemporary painting than he does. Bacon may be the only painter around who is "great" in the way that painters were traditionally; the only contemporary who has affiliations with the heroic figures of Western painting: Michelangelo, Titian, Rembrandt, Goya. This is the daring of Bacon's work. This is also its pathos, its impotence. Bacon's work seems so centered, so personal, so idiosyncratic, so powerful. It is as if he were already a classic. As the last of the traditional painters, Bacon is both absolutely central to contemporary painting (by virtue of the quality and integrity of his work) and marginal to it (by virtue of the work's authority, its completeness, its assuredness, its inwardness, its commitment to despair).

The principal modern way of looking at a painting is to situate it inside the history of painting, a history which is now more and more identified as the history of *thinking* about painting. It's as if being a (mere) painting were not enough. The main virtue of most modernist painting is its intelligence. It is obvious from Bacon's work that he is extremely intelligent. But Bacon's painting (unlike Duchamp's or, say, Jasper Johns's) is not "about" being intelligent. It is "about" being in pain.

The painter who felt self-confident enough in 1971, at the time of his Paris retrospective, to risk the hyperbole of declaring that "Duchamp has ruined American painting for a hundred years" will not be surprised if some American art-world professionals—trained to admire the flight from suffering into intelligence so brilliantly espoused by Duchamp—continue to treat his work a little condescendingly. But whatever the range of reactions, there can be no doubt that Bacon survives the ordeal of his current retrospective in New York, triumphantly.

(1975)

A Woman's Beauty:
Put-Down or Power Source?

FOR the Greeks, beauty was a virtue: a kind of excellence. Persons then were assumed to be what we now have to call—lamely, enviously—*whole* persons. If it did occur to the Greeks to distinguish between a person's "inside" and "outside," they still expected that inner beauty would be matched by beauty of the other kind. The well-born young Athenians who gathered around Socrates found it quite paradoxical that their hero was so intelligent, so brave, so honorable, so seductive—and so ugly. One of Socrates' main pedagogical acts was to be ugly—and teach those innocent, no doubt splendid-looking disciples of his how full of paradoxes life really was.

They may have resisted Socrates' lesson. We do not. Several thousand years later, we are more wary of the enchantments of beauty. Being beautiful no longer speaks, presumptively, for the worth of a whole person. We not only split off—with the greatest facility—the "inside" (character, intellect) from the "outside" (looks); but we are actually surprised when someone who is beautiful is also intelligent, talented, good.

It was principally the influence of Christianity that deprived beauty of the central place it had in classical ideals of human excellence. By limited excellence (*virtus* in Latin) to *moral* virtue only, Christianity set beauty adrift—as an alienated, arbitrary, superficial enchantment. And beauty has continued to lose prestige. For close to two centuries it has become a convention to attribute beauty to only one of the two sexes: the sex which, however Fair, is always Second. Associating beauty with women has put beauty even further on the defensive, morally.

A beautiful woman, we say in English. But a handsome man. "Handsome" is the masculine equivalent of—and refusal of—a compliment which has accumulated certain demeaning overtones, by being reserved for women only. That one can call a man "beautiful" in French and in Italian suggests that Catholic countries—unlike those countries shaped by the Protestant version of Christianity—still retain some vestiges of the pagan admiration for beauty. But the difference, if one exists, is of degree only. In every modern country that is Christian or post-Christian, women *are* the beautiful sex—to the detriment of the notion of beauty as well as of women.

To be called beautiful is thought to name something essential to women's character and concerns. (In contrast to men—whose essence is to be strong, or effective, or competent.) It does not take someone in the throes of advanced feminist awareness to perceive that the way women are taught to be involved with beauty encourages narcissism, reinforces dependence and immaturity. Everybody (women and men) knows that. For it is "everybody," a whole society, that has identified being feminine with caring about how one *looks*. (In contrast to being masculine—which is identified with caring about what one *is* and *does* and only secondarily, if at all, about how one looks.) Given these stereotypes, it is no wonder that beauty enjoys, at best, a rather mixed reputation.

It is not, of course, the desire to be beautiful that is wrong but the obligation to be—or to try. What is accepted by most women as a flattering idealization of their sex is a way of making women feel inferior to what they actually are—or normally grow to be. For the ideal of beauty is administered as a form of self-oppression. Women are taught to see their bodies in *parts*, and to evaluate each part separately. Breasts, feet, hips, waistline, neck, eyes, nose, complexion, hair, and so on—each in turn is submitted to an anxious, fretful, often despairing scrutiny. Even if some pass muster, some will always be found wanting. Nothing less than perfection will do.

In men, good looks is a whole, something taken in at a glance. It does not need to be confirmed by giving measurements of different regions of the body, nobody encourages a man to dissect his appearance, feature by feature. As for perfection, that is considered trivial—almost unmanly. Indeed, in the ideally good-looking man a small imperfection or blemish is considered positively desirable. According to one movie critic (a woman) who is a declared Robert Redford fan, it is having that cluster of skin-colored moles on one cheek that saves Redford from being merely a "pretty face." Think of the depreciation of women—as well as of beauty—that is implied in that judgment.

"The privileges of beauty are immense," said Cocteau. To be sure, beauty is a form of power. And deservedly so. What is lamentable is that it is the only form of power that most women are encouraged to seek. This power is always conceived in relation to men; it is not the power to do but the power to attract. It is a power that negates itself. For this power is not one that can be chosen freely—at least, not by women—or renounced without social censure.

To preen, for a woman, can never be just a pleasure. It is also a duty. It is her work. If a woman does real work—and even if she has clambered up to a leading position in politics, law, medicine, business, or whatever—she is always under pressure to confess that she still works at being attractive. But in so far as she is keeping up as one of the Fair Sex, she brings under suspicion her very capacity to be objective, professional, authoritative, thoughtful. Damned if they do—women are. And damned if they don't.

One could hardly ask for more important evidence of the dangers of considering persons as split between what is "inside" and what is "outside" than that interminable half-comic half-tragic tale, the oppression of women. How easy it is to start off by defining women as caretakers of their surfaces, and then to disparage them (or find them adorable) for being "superficial." It is a crude trap, and it has worked for too long. But to get out of the trap requires that women get some critical distance from that excellence and privilege which is beauty, enough distance to see how much beauty itself has been abridged in order to prop up the mythology of the "feminine." There should be a way of saving beauty *from* women—and *for* them.

                                                                    (1975)

Beauty: How Will It Change Next?

THE ideas which seem most expressive, and exercise the greatest powers of seduction, are basically self-contradictory. One such idea is freedom. Another is beauty, that over-rich brew of so many familiar opposites: the natural and the historical, the pristine and the artificial, the individualizing and the conformist—even the beautiful and the ugly.

Beauty, thought to be something intuitively apprehended (and appreciated), is associated with the natural. Yet it is overwhelmingly clear that beauty is an historical fact. Different cultures exhibit an astonishing spread of ideas about beauty. And it is among so-called primitive, or at any rate premodern, societies that beauty is most drastically linked to artifice. Depilation of body hair, body painting, ornamental scarring of the skin are among the tamer forms of basic dressing-up, while some cultures practice more ambitious mutilations—to get lips like saucers, cantilevered buttocks, crushed feet, and similar beauty ideals that we in turn find extravagantly, self-evidently ugly.

But all programs of beauty, even when they seem particularly perverse or tenacious, are inherently fragile. Any culture's ideal of beauty, however artificial or however natural, will be modified by contact with another culture; and, in cases of cultural rape, a society may precipitously lose confidence in its own standards of beauty—as the statistics on eyelid-straightening operations performed in Japan since World War II attest.

Another paradox. Beauty is always thought to be "given." But, at the same time, it is understood to be acquired. Beauty is something that needs to be taken care of, that must be watched over, that can be enhanced: through exercise, the right diet, lotions and creams. Something that can, within limits, be created or faked: through makeup, flattering clothes. (The last resort is, of course, surgery.) Beauty is the raw material for the arts of beautification, for what has become, in our time, the beauty "industry." Beauty is thought of both as a gift—that some people are born beautiful and others not passes for one of nature's (or God's) ruder injustices—and a mode of self-improvement. Physical attractiveness is regarded both as the natural condition of women and as a goal they have to work at, and diligently pursue, to distinguish themselves from other women.

And this suggests still another paradox. To be beautiful makes one singular, exceptional. But to be beautiful also means measuring up to a norm or rule ("fashion"). The paradox is partly eased when one remembers that beauty is one of those ideas—like truth, like freedom—that gets its meaning from its always being contrasted (if only tacitly) with an adversary, negative idea. But it would be naïve to suppose that the "ugly" is the only opposite implied by the "beautiful." Indeed, according to the very logic of fashion, the beautiful often has to seem—at first—ugly. The implicit opposite of the "beautiful" is rather the "common," the "vulgar."

In matters of beauty we are all born country bumpkins. We learn what is beautiful—which means that beauty can be, and is, taught. But it is hardly a teaching that promotes egalitarian feelings. Beauty is a class system, operating within the sexist code; its ruthless rating procedures and intractable encouragement to feelings of superiority and inferiority persist in spite of (and maybe because of) a striking amount of upward and downward mobility. Beauty is endless social climbing—rendered particularly arduous by the fact that, in our society, the terms that confer membership in the aristocracy of beauty keep changing. At the top of the hierarchy are "stars" who monopolize the right to launch a *new* insolent idea of beauty—which is then taken up and imitated by large numbers of people.

Some of the changes in the idea of beauty aren't real changes. Often, seemingly different standards of beauty in fact celebrate the same values. When most Europeans and Americans—including women—worked outdoors, very white skin was a *sine qua non* of feminine beauty. Now that most people work indoors, it's bronzed skin that is attractive. The apparent change of beauty ideal conceals a perfect continuity of standard. What is prized in both pallor and suntan is a skin color that is not associated with toil—that signifies luxury, privilege, leisure. Another example. It is not because of some arbitrary shift of "taste" that the ideal feminine figure has been getting progressively leaner (particularly in the hips) over the last century. Because all societies throughout history have been under the lash of scarcity, so that most people never had enough to eat, it was usually plumpness (or even obesity) that seemed beautiful. In unprecedentedly affluent modern Europe and North America, where for the first time in history most people eat too much, it is distinguished to be thin.

That many standards of the beautiful are attached to what sets off the "few" from the "many" does not mean, however, that all ideas of beauty in our society are equivalent or that there is no change of any interesting kind. Beauty, as we know it, flourishes according to the imperatives of the consumer society: that is, to create needs that didn't exist before.

In the early stages of consumerism, when only a relatively small number of people are solicited, the standards can remain provocatively high, snobbish. Beauty is associated with fragility, inaccessibility, glamour, elegance. But as the number of customers for those needs is steadily enlarged, it is inevitable that the standard come down a little. Now we have less aristocratic, less melancholy, less intimidating models of beauty.

Sarah Bernhardt, Greta Garbo, Marlene Dietrich were the most celebrated of the *princesses lointaines*; and it would be hard to overestimate the hypnotic authority that their languid, static poses and perfect faces had over whole generations. Nothing remotely like that degree of fealty and imaginative submission was given to those late (too late) representatives of their race: plastic princesses like Grace Kelly and Catherine Deneuve, who are, for *my* taste, simply too beautiful. (In the cases of Deneuve and Kelly, their stalled or abandoned careers as stars suggest that being *that* beautiful is, in our generation, something of a handicap. A borderline case: Faye Dunaway, whose career has already faltered over the problem. In order to make it as a star, Dunaway has to seek roles that hide how beautiful she is.)

We have today more "natural," "healthier," more varied ideas of beauty, which emphasize activity rather than languidness. (Though the activities—romantic courtship, sports, vacationing—are still identified with leisure rather than work.) Beauty is no longer ideal; it is individualized. Presumably, this change makes clients of the beautiful feel less anxiety about not meeting impossibly high standards. But even in its relatively more accessible form, as standards of beauty appear to be becoming more democratic, they are still propagated by "stars."

Fashion sets a standard that is, by definition, high, probably too high; otherwise it would not be compelling. Yet those standards are, we are told, accessible to everyone. But how far can beauty be democratized—without losing its authority as an idea, its allure as a paradox? Probably, all democratizations of beauty in our culture are spurious: just another turn of fashion's wheel. Thus, fashion both exalts perfection and ostentatiously de-emphasizes it. Even the "natural" is a form of theater; it takes a lot of artifice to look "natural." It is probably no easier to model oneself on Lauren Hutton than on Sarah Bernhardt.

That current notions of beauty are both natural and more theatrical follows from the role that beauty and the beauty "industry" play in the consumer society. In China, the model *anti*-consumer society, there is no ideology of beauty at all. In the Soviet Union, an example of a society in the early stages of transition to consumerism, the ideology of beauty is either nonexistent or retrograde. The Soviets' first attempts at "fashion" not only seem frumpy and unpoetic by our standards but—what may amount to the same thing—reflect old-style bourgeois stereotypes about femininity. Russians seem (to our eyes) remarkably unselfconscious about ugliness—particularly fat, as one concludes from the display of unembarrassed ample flesh on beaches. The self-consciousness will come, as the consumer society gets underway, and will probably mean a step backward—at least temporarily—from the more egalitarian situation of women (at least in job roles) that currently prevails in the U.S.S.R. But it will be a long time (how many generations of affluence?) before the Russians are ready for a fanciful approach to the idea of beauty, the one perfected in our own advanced consumer society.

Beauty is, of course, a myth. The question is, what sort of myth. In the past two centuries, it has been a myth imprisoning to women—because it is exclusively associated with *them*. The idea of beauty that we inherit was invented by men (to buttress their own claims to superior, less superficial virtues) and is still largely administered by men. It is a system from which men scrupulously have exempted themselves.

But that is beginning to change. The last ten years have been the decade in which male beauty has come out of the closet. The myth of beauty seems, once more, to be going coed. Now, standards of beauty are being applied to men as well as women—with men consenting to be treated and treating

themselves as sexual "objects," not just as virile hairy preda-
tors. To some extent, the recent tilt of beauty toward a single
standard (at least among the young) seems to render the myth
of beauty less reactionary—that is, less noxious for women.

To be sure, the taste for unisex beauty is not a truly radical
change. Beauty, as a notion, still remains stamped by allusions
to the "feminine"—even in the newly colonized androgynous
world of male beauty. Thus, David Bowie's beauty derives
from the extent to which he resembles—and comments on—
the beauty of Katharine Hepburn. But masculine narcissism
has other dimensions, another morality, other consequences
than feminine narcissism. Society does not define caring for
one's appearance as a duty for men. It can never be less than a
choice—not (as for women) an obligation that is regarded as
part of one's sexual identity.

At the moment when standards for men became more dandy-
ish, some women took up arms against the way the conventions
of beauty reinforce the image of women as indolent, smooth-
skinned, odorless, empty-headed, affable playthings. There was
a flurry of revolt against makeup. Some women stopped shaving their legs. Fewer and fewer younger women patronized
hairdressers. For women who decided that they did not have to
tamper with themselves, did not have to be works of art in order
to be beautiful, the beauty of women acquired a new, polemical
meaning—as a feminist slogan.

Feminists affirmed that "women are beautiful" in the same
defiant spirit that Afro-Americans proclaimed that "Black is
beautiful." Women were recovering a suppressed freedom with
respect to beauty, as Blacks were recovering a non-Caucasian
standard of beauty, one more "natural" to them.

Feminism—which has been rather rough on the traditional
hard sell of beauty to women, for all obvious and good reasons—
has pushed for a beauty that is more "natural." But that idea still
competes with other ideas of beauty that remain influential and
moving. It is no accident that the feminist critique surfaced in
a really effective and vivid way in the 1960s, a decade in which
the richest and most central notion was "style." (By the triumph
of "style" in the '60s I mean, of course, the validation of a
plurality of styles.) According to the new permissive standards,
ugly—freaky, eccentric—is beautiful. "Natural" is beautiful. But
so is "unnatural." Fantasy proliferates. Change is a constant.

Modifications of the idea of beauty succeed each other in an accelerating rhythm, so that it is fair to predict that no ideal of face or figure will last for a person's lifetime, or even get one through early adulthood without several major retoolings. (Anyone over thirty-five has already lived through several radical changes of beauty ideals: from the big breasts of the 1940s and early '50s to the boyish silhouette of the 1960s, from laboriously straightened hair to glorious Afros, etc.)

But perhaps more important than any specific recent change in the idea of beauty is the immense diffusion of awareness that beauty changes. What was once the specialized knowledge of anthropologists, historians of clothes, sociologists, and fashion professionals is now common knowledge. Everyone acknowledges the "relativity" of beauty: that different cultures construct beauty differently and that our own culture has a complex history of notions about the beautiful. Beauty is an idea that has entered the era of self-consciousness. Every idea of beauty that is proposed has as its sub-text that it will not last: that it is only a "fashion."

In a sense, we can't take beauty as seriously as we once did. But now we are free to play with it. Hence, the cannibalizing of styles from the past that now makes high fashion virtually synonymous with irony. Clothes become costumes. The once awkwardly received fact of the influence of homosexual taste is now matter-of-factly accepted. In the age of innocence, beauty is conceived as a fixed, real value. We come after the age of innocence.

Everything now conspires to undermine the old, static myth of beauty as something fixed. Expensively produced magazines that articulate and promote fashion contribute, inadvertently, to the demolition of the reactionary idea of beauty as much as do such sharp-eyed critics of the fashion industry as Blair Sabol. Both the cult of fashion and the feminist critique of it are undermining the stability of the beauty-myth. And increasing the beautiful. There seem to be more and more good-looking people around, in the societies touched by "fashion." The rapidity with which our ideas of beauty change is not just a by-product of the modern world's resources for ever quicker transmission of information. It itself produces a qualitative alteration in our idea of beauty, one that makes it less oppressive, more voluntary, and more of a turn-on.

Beauty continues to become more complicated, more self-conscious than ever and subject to chronic (if partly forced) change. Which—from the feminist point of view—may well be good news. And good news for esthetes and sensualists as well. It would seem that, for once, the interests of moralists (of the feminist persuasion) and esthetes coincide. Both have something to gain from the fact that it is now part of the *essence* of beauty that it change.

(1975)

CHRONOLOGY

NOTE ON THE TEXTS

NOTES

INDEX

Chronology

1933   Born Susan Lee Rosenblatt January 16 in New York City, first
            child of Mildred (Jacobson) Rosenblatt and Jasky (Jack)
            Rosenblatt. (Father, born 1906 on New York's Lower East
            Side, is owner of a fur-trading business, the Kung Chen
            Fur Corporation, with an office in New York but based in
            Tientsin, China; parents married in 1930. Both are in Tien-
            tsin when mother becomes pregnant and returns to U.S.)
            Mother returns to China; for the first five years of her life
            Sontag is cared for by a nanny, Rose McNulty and by other
            family members in New York and in Verona, New Jersey.

1936   Sister Judith born February 27 in New York.

1938   Father dies in China of tuberculosis on October 19. Mother
            returns to New York with father's body. Lives with mother
            and sister in Forest Hills, New York, and in Great Neck,
            New York.

1939   Develops symptoms of asthma; moves with family to Miami
            for a few months in the hope that this will be beneficial for
            her health. This having been counterproductive, the family
            returns to New York City. Begins first grade in September
            at P.S. 3 but is soon skipped to the third grade; later attends
            P.S. 144. A reader since age three, she continues to immerse
            herself in books. Mother works as a schoolteacher.

1943   Moves with family to a four-room bungalow in Tucson.
            Attends Mansfield Junior High. Discovers the Modern Li-
            brary editions in a bookstore in Tucson.

1946   Mother marries U.S. Army Air Forces captain Nathan Son-
            tag, who is recuperating from wounds in a military hospital
            in Arizona. Family moves to Sherman Oaks, a Los Angeles
            suburb. Agrees to mother's request to take her stepfather's
            name.

1947   Begins attending North Hollywood High School. Frequents
            Pickwick's bookstore, the symphony, and Evenings on the
            Roof, weekly performances of modern music in Los Ange-
            les in the 1940s, which was among the first places in the
            U.S. where composers such as Pierre Boulez and John Cage
            were played regularly. With a friend, visits Thomas Mann.

1948   Edits school newspaper *The Arcade* and literary magazine
            Vintage '48.

1949   Graduates from North Hollywood High in January. Attends
            University of California at Berkeley for one term. Forms
            close friendship with fellow student Harriet Sohmers.
            Transfers to University of Chicago in the fall; teachers in-
            clude Kenneth Burke, Joseph Schwab, Leo Strauss, and
            Richard McKeon.

1950   Audits class in a Freud course taught by Philip Rieff, eleven
            years her senior; afterwards he asks her to lunch. They
            marry ten days later and move off campus.

1951–52   After receiving BA, moves with Rieff first, briefly, to Wis-
            consin, and then to Boston where he has accepted a teach-
            ing position at Brandeis. Son David born September 28,
            1952, in Boston. They live at 29 Chauncy Street in Cam-
            bridge. Sontag forms friendship with Jacob Taubes, phi-
            losopher and scholar of Judaism, and his wife Susan Taubes;
            Susan Taubes will remain one of her closest friends.

1953   Enters graduate English program at University of Connecti-
            cut (Storrs), commuting from Cambridge, Massachusetts;
            also works there as a teaching assistant. Leaves without a
            degree.

1954   Takes graduate English courses at Harvard.

1955–56   After being told by Harry Levin, one of the leading fig-
            ures in the Harvard English department, that he does not
            "believe" in women graduate students, she asks the phi-
            losopher Morton White to allow her to enter the graduate
            program in philosophy at Harvard, which he does; teach-
            ers include theologian Paul Tillich. Appointed a Teaching
            Fellow.

1957   Receives MA in philosophy. Awarded fellowship at St.
            Anne's College, Oxford, by American Association of Uni-
            versity Women; travels to England alone (husband has
            accepted fellowship at Stanford, and moves to Palo Alto
            with David and Rose McNulty. She works on PhD disser-
            tation on "metaphysical presuppositions of ethics." Leaves
            Oxford, where her teachers have included A. J. Ayer and
            H.L.A. Hart, after a term; in December goes to Paris to
            attend the Sorbonne. Reunites with Harriet Sohmers, now

working at the Paris *Herald Tribune*. They live together for most of Sontag's remaining time in Paris. Engages in an acrimonious correspondence with Rieff and determines to divorce him.

1958   In Paris, moves in a circle largely of expatriate artists and writers, including the novelist Alfred Chester and playwright Maria Irene Fornés (with whom Sontag will live in New York between 1959 and 1963). Plays minor role in Pierre Kast's film *Le Bel Age*. Travels to Germany, Spain, and Greece with Sohmers. Returns to the United States in August and joins her husband and son, now living in Berkeley, and immediately asks Rieff for a divorce. The divorce is granted and Sontag is awarded custody of David. She accepts child support payments but refuses alimony.

1959   Moves to New York in January. Works briefly as an editor at *Commentary*. Philip Rieff's *Freud: The Mind of the Moralist* is published; Sontag had worked closely with him on the book; she will always claim to have been its coauthor, and Rieff to deny it. Begins lecturing in philosophy at Sarah Lawrence and CUNY.

1960   Begins teaching in the religion department of Columbia University (will continue there until 1964), including classes taught with Jacob Taubes. Sontag and Fornés spend most of the summer in Cuba, where Fornés was born. Begins to publish book reviews.

1961   Chapter from novel in progress (*The Benefactor*) published in *Provincetown Review*. Begins to become more involved in literary New York, one of her childhood ambitions.

1962   Continues to work on *The Benefactor* and to teach at Columbia. Philip Rieff unsuccessfully sues for full custody of David.

1963   Essay on Simone Weil published in first issue of *The New York Review of Books* in February. Publishes first contribution to *Partisan Review*, a review of Isaac Bashevis Singer's *The Slave*, in July. *The Benefactor* published by Farrar, Straus (the publisher of all her subsequent books) in October; establishes close working relationship with publisher Roger Straus. Her relationship with Irene Fornés comes to an end.

1964   Writes series of drama reviews for *Partisan Review*. Spends summer in Paris, where she writes "Notes on Camp,"

published in *Partisan Review*. Essay "Against Interpretation" appears in *Evergreen Review*. Becomes a member of
American PEN and begins to become more widely known
and written about.

1965   Publishes essays and reviews in *Mademoiselle*, *Book Week*,
Commentary, and *Partisan Review*. Receives grant from
Merrill Foundation. Begins to travel internationally with
far greater frequency. In August and September, visits Paul
and Jane Bowles in Tangier, where Alfred Chester is now
living. Spends an increasing amount of time in London
as well, and through her friendship there with the theater
director Peter Brook and the actress Irene Worth moves for
a time in the circle of English Gurdjieffians. On the basis of
this begins a novel tentatively titled *The Organization*, on
which she will work for several years but never finish. Does
some television work in the UK with the writer and director
Jonathan Miller, a close friend whom Sontag had met in
New York the previous year. Becomes involved for a time
with the painter Jasper Johns, and through him becomes
friendly with John Cage, the dancer Merce Cunningham,
and the art dealer Leo Castelli. Travels extensively in the
U.S. making speeches at university teach-ins and public ral-
lies in opposition to the war in Vietnam.

1966   Essay collection *Against Interpretation* published in January. Participates in February in "Read-In for Peace in Vietnam" at Town Hall, along with Norman Mailer, Robert
Lowell, and other writers. Her anti-Vietnam War activism becomes more intense. Wins George Polk Memorial
Award for Criticism and Guggenheim Fellowship. Becomes
friendly with the painter Joseph Cornell.

1967   Novel *Death Kit* appears in August. Publishes essays "The
Pornographic Imagination" (*Partisan Review*) and "The
Aesthetics of Silence" (*Aspen*). Serves as juror at Venice
Film Festival and on selection committee for New York
Film Festival, on which she will remain through the early
seventies.

1968   Her political activism widens. In May, signs a collective let-
ter to the *New York Times* protesting the police killing of a
Black Panther member in Oakland. Makes two-week visit to
North Vietnam the same month, accompanied by journalist
Andrew Kopkind and Cornell professor Robert Greenberg.

Publishes account of trip in *Esquire*; it is reprinted in book form as *Trip to Hanoi*. Makes film *Duet for Cannibals* in Sweden.

1969   Travels to Cuba; meets poet Heberto Padilla. Publishes "Some Thoughts on the Right Way (for us) to Love the Cuban Revolution" in *Ramparts* in April. *Duet for Cannibals* shown at Cannes Film Festival in May and subsequently at New York Film Festival. Writes regularly for *The New York Review of Books*. In the spring meets and falls in love with Carlotta Del Pezzo. Essay collection *Styles of Radical Will* published in October. Shocked by suicide in November of Susan Taubes.

1970   Makes second film, *Brother Carl*, in Sweden. Publishes screenplay of *Duet for Cannibals*. Relationship with Carlotta Del Pezzo ends in October.

1971   *Brother Carl* shown at Cannes. Signs public letter protesting the Cuban government's arrest and show trial of Heberto Padilla. Meets and becomes involved with the French actress and film producer Nicole Stéphane. Spends an increasing amount of time in Paris.

1972   *Brother Carl* opens in New York. Publishes essay "The Double Standard of Aging" in *Saturday Review* in September.

1973   Visits China, January–February. Publishes essays "The Third World of Women" (*Partisan Review*) and "Approaching Artaud" (*The New Yorker*). Shoots film *Promised Lands* in Israel during and immediately after the Yom Kippur War. First of series of essays on photography appears in *The New York Review of Books* in October. Continues to spend much of her time in Paris.

1974   Is more in Paris than in New York. Undertakes a number of film projects, none of which comes to fruition.

1975   Essay "Fascinating Fascism" appears in *The New York Review of Books* in February. Participates in televised symposium on feminism in Mexico City. Undergoes surgery in October after being diagnosed with Stage 4 metastatic breast cancer; receives recommendation for experimental program of chemotherapy and immunotherapy developed by French oncologist Lucien Israel. Receives Guggenheim fellowship.

1976   Moves back to New York, where she undergoes two
            and a half years of chemotherapy administered at Sloan-
            Kettering hospital. Continues to work on photography
            essays. Honored by American Academy and Institute of
            Arts and Letters and by Ingram Merrill Foundation. Pub-
            lishes an edition of *Antonin Artaud: Selected Writings*.

1977   Publishes *On Photography* in November. Becomes a fellow
            at the newly formed New York Institute for the Humani-
            ties at New York University. Her relationship with Nicole
            Stéphane ends. Starts to become close to the Russian poet
            Joseph Brodsky, with whom she becomes involved toward
            the end of the year.

1978   Receives National Book Critics Circle Award for *On Pho-
            tography*. Publishes *Illness as Metaphor* in June and story
            collection *I, etcetera* in November.

1979   Travels to Japan for three-week lecture tour, which marks
            the beginning of a fascination with that country that will
            endure for the rest of her life. Directs production of Piran-
            dello's *As You Desire Me* in Turin, Italy; production will play
            in Florence and Rome the following year.

1980   Makes trip to Eastern Europe, sponsored by United States
            Information Agency, in the spring with a group of writers
            including John Ashbery and Joyce Carol Oates; delivers talk
            at literary conference in Poland. Publishes *Under the Sign
            of Saturn* in October.

1981   Publishes first of a series of essays on dance in *New Per-
            formance*. Participates in "The Writer and Human Rights
            Congress" in October in Toronto.

1982   On February 6, at Town Hall in New York, at a public
            meeting in support of the Polish Solidarity movement,
            delivers speech ("Poland and Other Questions: Commu-
            nism and the Left") declaring that "communism is fascism
            with a human face," which marks her definitive break with
            the American Left. Sues *Soho News* for printing her Town
            Hall speech without permission. Publishes *A Susan Sontag
            Reader* and *A Barthes Reader*. Makes film *Unguided Tour*,
            based on her short story of the same name and starring
            Lucinda Childs, with whom Sontag is deeply involved, for
            Italian television.

1984   Appears in Nestor Almendros's film *Improper Conduct*, documentary about the Cuban government's imprisonment of homosexuals and others, and in French television series *Le Deuxième Sexe*.

1985   Directs production of Milan Kundera's *Jacques and His Master* at American Repertory Theater at Harvard.

1986   Story "The Way We Live Now" appears in *The New Yorker*. Serves on jury of film festival at East-West Center of University of Hawaii.

1987   Elected president of PEN (will serve until 1989). "Pilgrimage," memoir of early encounter with Thomas Mann, published in *The New Yorker* in December.

1988   Presides over PEN congress in Seoul, South Korea; leads protests against mistreatment of South Korean writers. "AIDS and Its Metaphors" published in *The New York Review of Books*. Provides the voice of Sarah Bernhardt for Edgardo Cozarinsky's documentary *Sarah*.

1989–90 Publishes *AIDS and Its Metaphors* in book form in January. As president of PEN, makes public statements condemning fatwa of Iranian government against Salman Rushdie. Begins writing novel *The Volcano Lover* during residency at the DAAD in Berlin. Contracts with first agent of her career, Andrew Wylie, and receives four-book advance from Farrar, Straus and Giroux. Buys a penthouse apartment in Chelsea in New York City; photographer Annie Leibovitz, with whom Sontag has become involved, moves into another penthouse in the same complex. Awarded fellowship from MacArthur Foundation in July. Returns to Berlin for another residency.

1991   "A Parsifal," text of short play written for theater director Robert Wilson, is published in exhibition catalogue *Robert Wilson's Vision*. *The Way We Live Now* published in book form. Play *Alice in Bed* produced in Bonn. Receives Elmer Holmes Bobst Award in Arts and Letters.

1992   *The Volcano Lover: A Romance* is published and becomes a bestseller. Edits *The Best American Essays 1992*. Receives Malaparte Prize in Italy.

1993   Awarded honorary degree by Harvard. Travels to Sarajevo in April; returns to direct production of Beckett's *Waiting for Godot*, which opens in August. "Godot Comes to Sarajevo" published in *The New York Review of Books* in October. (Will make eleven visits in all to the city, of which she is made an honorary citizen and where one of the central squares of the city is now named after her.) *Alice in Bed* is published; a production directed by Robert Wilson opens in Berlin.

1994   Receives Montblanc de la Culture award for her work in Sarajevo. Undertakes research on nineteenth-century Polish actress Helena Modjeska at Getty Institute in California for a new novel that will eventually become *In America*. Interviewed in July by Edward Hirsch for *The Paris Review*'s "Art of Fiction" series.

1995   Edits *Homo Poeticus*, a collection of the nonfiction of the Serbian writer Danilo Kiš.

1998   She is diagnosed with a uterine sarcoma, has surgery, and receives intense and dangerous chemotherapy. *Lady from the Sea*, adapted from Ibsen's play, has its world premiere in Italy, at the Teatro Comunale of Ferrara, in a production by Robert Wilson.

1999   Publishes op-ed "Why Are We in Kosovo?" in the *New York Times*. Appears in and contributes an essay to Leibovitz's book of photographs *Women*, a project she had proposed to the photographer. Is named Commandeur de l'Ordre des Arts et des Lettres by the French government.

2000   Publishes novel *In America*, which wins the National Book Award. Delivers speech "The Conscience of Words" in May in Jerusalem upon acceptance of the Jerusalem Prize.

2001   Publishes essay collection *Where the Stress Falls*. The brief response to the World Trade Center attack of September 11 that she publishes in *The New Yorker* stirs up a great deal of controversy.

2002   Delivers St. Jerome Lecture on Literary Translation, "The World as India," in London in June. Receives George Polk Award for Cultural Criticism for "Looking at War," excerpt from forthcoming book *Regarding the Pain of Others*, published in December in *The New Yorker*.

2003   Publishes *Regarding the Pain of Others*. Delivers speech "Literature Is Freedom" in Frankfurt in October, upon acceptance of the Peace Prize of the German Book Trade. Her speech is boycotted by Senator Daniel Coats, then the Bush administration's ambassador to Berlin. Receives the Prince of Asturias Award in Literature.

2004   Delivers "At the Same Time: The Novelist and Moral Reasoning," the first Nadine Gordimer Lecture, in Cape Town and Johannesburg in March. Publishes "Regarding the Torture of Others," in response to revelations of abuse by American soldiers at Abu Ghraib prison in Iraq, in *The New York Times Magazine* on May 23. Prepares tentative table of contents for collection ultimately edited by Paolo Dilonardo and Anne Jump and published in 2007 as *At the Same Time: Essays and Speeches*. In the spring is diagnosed with AML (Acute Myelogenous Leukemia). Receives a bone marrow transplant that summer—the only hope of saving her life—at the Fred Hutchinson Cancer Center/ University of Washington Hospital in Seattle. It fails. She is flown back to the Memorial Sloan-Kettering Cancer Center in Manhattan, where she had initially been treated. She dies there on December 28. She is buried at Cimetière Montparnasse in Paris.

Note on the Texts

This volume contains four books by Susan Sontag, *Against Interpretation* (1966), *Styles of Radical Will* (1969), *On Photography* (1977), and *Illness as Metaphor* (1978), along with six essays published during the same period but not collected by Sontag.

Against Interpretation and Other Essays was published, like all of Sontag's books, by Farrar, Straus & Giroux. It collects twenty-six essays that appeared originally in the publications listed below. The texts are in many cases significantly revised, in some instances only taking the original as a point of departure for new writing.

Against Interpretation: *Evergreen Review* 34, December 1964.

On Style: *Partisan Review* 32, Fall 1965.

The Artist as Exemplary Sufferer: *Second Coming* v.1 n.4, June 1962, as "Death and Art and the Utility of Despair."

Simone Weil: *The New York Review of Books*, Special Issue, 1963.

Camus' *Notebooks: The New York Review of Books*, September 26, 1963, as "The Ideal Husband."

Michel Leiris' *Manhood: The New York Review of Books*, March 5, 1964, as "Odd Man Out."

The Anthropologist as Hero: *The New York Review of Books*, November 28, 1963, as "A Hero of Our Time."

The Literary Criticism of Georg Lukács: *Book Week* (*The New York Herald Tribune*), May 10, 1964, as "Putting Up a Stiff Fight with Old Artillery."

Sartre's *Saint Genet: Partisan Review* 30, Spring 1963, as "The Flowers of Evil."

Nathalie Sarraute and the Novel: *Partisan Review* 30, Summer 1963, as "Is the Reader Necessary?"

Ionesco: *The New York Review of Books*, July 9, 1964, as "Ionesco: The Theater of the Banal."

Reflections on *The Deputy: Book Week* (*The New York Herald Tribune*), March 1, 1964, as "All the World's a Stage."

The Death of Tragedy: *Partisan Review* 30, Spring 1963.

Going to Theater, etc.: *Partisan Review* 31, Spring 1964 and Summer 1964, as "Going to Theater (and the Movies)."

Marat/Sade/Artaud: *Partisan Review* 32, Spring 1965.

Spiritual Style in the Films of Robert Bresson: *Seventh Art* v.2 n.3, Summer 1964.

Godard's *Vivre Sa Vie: Moviegoer* 2, Summer–Autumn 1964, as "On Godard's *Vivre Sa Vie*."

The Imagination of Disaster: *Commentary*, October 1965.

Jack Smith's *Flaming Creatures*: *The Nation*, April 13, 1964, as "A Feast for Open Eyes."

Resnais' *Muriel*: *Film Quarterly* v.17 n.2, Winter 1963–1964, as "*Muriel ou Le Temps d'un Retour*."

A Note on Novels and Film: *Supplement* (*Columbia Daily Spectator*), October 27, 1961, as "Some Notes on Antonioni and Others."

Piety Without Content: *Second Coming* v.1 n.3, March 1962.

Psychoanalysis and Norman O. Brown's *Life Against Death*: *Supplement* (*Columbia Daily Spectator*), April 28, 1961, as "Of Freud and the New Resurrection of the Flesh."

Happenings: An Art of Radical Juxtaposition: *Second Coming* v.1 n.6, January 1965, as "An Art of Radical Juxtaposition."

Notes on "Camp": *Partisan Review* 31, Fall 1964.

One Culture and the New Sensibility: *Mademoiselle*, April 1965, as "Opinion, Please—From New York: Susan Sontag."

The text used here is that of the first printing of the edition of 1966, with the exception of a significant revision that Sontag made to the prefatory matter for the first English edition (London: Eyre & Spottiswoode, 1967) and retained in all subsequent printings of the book. As published in the first edition, the first two paragraphs of "A Note and Some Acknowledgments" read as follows:

> The articles, reviews, and critical journalism collected here make up a good part of the criticism I have written in the last four years, and seem to me to express a developing but nonetheless cohesive point of view. What that point of view is I shall not attempt to summarize here, since that's what the more recent essays try to do.
>
> When I was rereading everything that I had written to decide what to include in this book, I was surprised at how little I disagreed with most of my opinions of two, three, and four years ago. (Some things dismayed me. But not as many as I had expected.) I realized, though, that many issues and themes that had engaged me seemed remote now, no doubt *because* I had written about them. Writing criticism has proved to be an act of intellectual disburdenment as much as of intellectual self-expression. I have the impression not so much of having, for myself, solved a certain number of alluring and troubling problems as of having used them up. I should perhaps explain that the assessment of this or that novel, film, play, or whatever, does not greatly interest me: I don't, ultimately, care about handing out grades to works of art (which is why I dislike and have mostly avoided the opportunity of writing about things

I don't admire); and I have no illusions about the likelihood that some of my specific appraisals are wrong, that I have, say, overestimated or underestimated the merit of certain works I have discussed because of a passionate interest in some problem raised by the work. Which is to say that, in the end, what I have been writing is not criticism at all, strictly speaking, but case studies for an aesthetic, a theory of my own sensibility. It was not (though I didn't always know it) the particular judgment about the particular work of art I was really after. I wanted to expose and clarify the assumptions underlying certain judgments and tastes. What might have been objects of criticism have been, instead, materials available for this task of theoretical clarification. I hope to persuade some of my readers of the urgency of this task; without attempting it, any challenge (in art and in critical discourse) to prevailing standards of taste falls into arbitrariness.

These paragraphs were subsequently deleted and replaced in the first English edition (under the title "Preface to the English Edition and Acknowledgements"), in the first American paperback edition (New York: Delta/Dell Publishing, 1967, under the title "Note to the Paperback Edition"), and in subsequent printings (as "A Note and Some Acknowledgments") by the four paragraphs included in the main text of this volume.

Styles of Radical Will was published in 1969 by Farrar, Straus & Giroux and drew on the sources listed below, with occasional revisions. The English edition (London: Secker & Warburg) was published the same year in an identical text.

The Aesthetics of Silence: *Aspen* 5–6, Fall–Winter 1967.

The Pornographic Imagination: *Partisan Review* 34, Spring 1967.

"Thinking Against Oneself": Reflections on Cioran: Introduction to *The Temptation to Exist* by E. M. Cioran, Quadrangle Books (Chicago), 1968.

Theatre and Film: *Tulane Drama Review* v.11 n.1, Fall 1969, as "Film and Theatre."

Bergman's *Persona: Sight and Sound* 36, Autumn 1967, as "*Persona*."

Godard: *Partisan Review* 35, Spring 1968, as "Going to the Movies: Godard."

What's Happening in America (1966): *Partisan Review* 34, Winter 1967, as Sontag's contribution to "What's Happening to America (A Symposium)."

Trip to Hanoi: *Trip to Hanoi* (New York: Farrar, Straus & Giroux, 1968).

On Photography was published in 1977 by Farrar, Straus & Giroux; an English edition, with identical text, was published the following year by Allen Lane. It is divided into six sections that had originally appeared in different form as five essays in *The New York Review of Books* as follows:

In Plato's Cave: October 18, 1973, as "Photography."

America, Seen Through Photographs, Darkly: April 18, 1974, as "Shooting America."

Melancholy Objects: April 18, 1974, as "Shooting America."

The Heroism of Vision: November 28, 1974, as "Photography: The Beauty Treatment."

Photographic Evangels: January 20, 1977, as "Photography in Search of Itself."

The Image-World: June 23, 1977, as "Photography Unlimited."

The book concludes with "A Brief Anthology of Quotations." With the printing of 1989, Sontag added two quotations to this section. The 1977 edition of *On Photography* is used here, with the added quotations from the 1989 printing.

Illness as Metaphor was published by Farrar, Straus & Giroux and by McGraw-Hill Ryerson (Toronto) in 1978. An English edition, with identical text, was published the following year by Allen Lane. It had originally appeared, in different form, in *The New York Review of Books* as "Illness as Metaphor" (January 26, 1978), "Images of Illness" (February 9, 1978), and "Disease as Political Metaphor" (February 23, 1978). The 1978 edition of *Illness as Metaphor* is used here.

Uncollected Essays. "William Burroughs and the Novel" is a revised version of a section from Sontag's lengthy contribution ("The Year's Developments in the Arts and Sciences: Literature") to *The Great Ideas Today 1966*, edited by Robert M. Hutchins and Mortimer J. Adler (Great Books Foundation). It was included in *Kunst und Antikunst: 24 literärische Analysen* (Reinbek bei Hamburg: Rowohlt, 1968), a German translation of twenty-four essays by Sontag drawn mostly from *Against Interpretation* and *L'Oeuvre parle* (Paris: Editions du Seuil, 1968), a French translation of nineteen Sontag essays. The text included here is from the revised typescript in the Susan Sontag Archive at the UCLA Library. The publication history of the other uncollected essays is as follows:

"The Double Standard of Aging": *The Saturday Review*, September 23, 1972.

"The Third World of Women": *Partisan Review* 40, Summer 1973.

"Francis Bacon: 'About Being in Pain'": *Vogue*, March 1975.

"A Woman's Beauty: Put-Down or Power Source?": *Vogue*, April 1975.

"Beauty: How Will It Change Next?": *Vogue*, May 1975.

This volume presents the texts of the original printings chosen for inclusion here, but it does not attempt to reproduce nontextual features of their typographic design. The texts are presented without change, except for the correction of typographical errors. Spelling, punctuation, and capitalization are often expressive features and are not altered, even when inconsistent or irregular. The following is a list of typographical errors corrected, cited by page and line number: 39.40, Wuoronin; 40.1, Burrough's; 60.26, Camus's; 64.3, narrative *L'Age*; 66.24, in not; 66.32, *Littérature*; 68.39, *Innomées*; 84.25, N.; 89.11, Theodore; 120.22, acknowedge; 125.1, theatre; 125.5, the *The*; 138.32, Robard; 160.16, have; 162.19, unnecessasy; 166.5, Alan; 166.6, Oldenberg; 167.4, multipled; 171.1, *Peché* (and *passim*); 197.29, possessses; 210.14, others'; 211.14–15, *That Mars*; 216.10, *Le Chien* (and *passim*); 216.21, Markopolous; 253.38, Dali (and *passim*); 261.11, *Salome*; 261.15, Lynn; 263.6, Feuil-liére; 270.36, *Windemere's*; 279.12, Joseph; 279.33, Siegfried Gidieon; 282.28, Buckminister; 283.1, unleased; 320.22, Louys' (and *passim*); 378.5, threatre; 379.4, *Der Dreigroschen Oper*; 386.35, Cinemathèque; 392.5, Bálacz,; 396.21, Ullman),; 405.10, etc.) But; 414.36, *A*; 425.17, (*Fantomas*,; 430.35, *Pecuchet*; 431.23, Velàsquez; 434.34, Edouard,; 438.16, *Cinèma*; 440.34, Cinemathèque; 441.1, 'Ou; 449.21, Vero-nique; 460.28, Leo Szilard; 585.37, illuminated a; 616.6, Niepce (and *passim*); 702.8, Emile,"; 720.39, tenament"; 742.21, read its; 770.31, Earhardt,; 784.1, result is of; 788.20–21, harrassment; 795.12, *pe se*; 797.8, woman's; 797.22, rights are; 797.38, occured; 808.16, Dierich; 808.17, *princesse*.

Notes

In the notes below, the reference numbers denote page and line of this volume (the line count includes headings). No note is made for material included in standard desk-reference books. Biographical information beyond that included in the Chronology may be found in Susan Sontag, *Reborn: Journals and Notebooks, 1947–1963*, ed. David Rieff (New York: Farrar, Straus & Giroux, 2008); Susan Sontag, *As Consciousness Is Harnessed to Flesh: Journals and Notebooks, 1964–1980*, ed. David Rieff (New York: Farrar, Straus & Giroux, 2012); David Rieff, *Swimming in a Sea of Death: A Son's Memoir* (New York: Simon & Schuster, 2008); Leland Poague, ed., *Conversations with Susan Sontag* (Jackson: University Press of Mississippi, 1995); Alice Kaplan, *Dreaming in French: The Paris Years of Jacqueline Bouvier Kennedy, Susan Sontag, and Angela Davis* (Chicago: University of Chicago Press, 2012); and Leland Poague and Kathy A. Parsons, *Susan Sontag: An Annotated Bibliography, 1948–1992* (New York: Garland Publishing, 2000).

AGAINST INTERPRETATION

12.30   Leto] Goddess in Greek mythology, who gave birth to the twins Apollo and Artemis after an adulterous union with Zeus.

12.31   Philo of Alexandria] Philo Judaeus (c. 20 B.C.E.–50 C.E.), Jewish philosopher who wrote in Greek, author of exegetical works on the Pentateuch.

13.23–24   as *manifest content*] In *The Interpretation of Dreams* (1900).

15.18–19   notes that Elia Kazan published] "Notebook for *A Streetcar Named Desire*," in *Directors on Directing*, ed. Toby Cole and Helen Krich Chinoy (1963). Kazan (1909–2003) had directed the inaugural Broadway production of Williams's play (1947) and its film adaptation (1951).

16.13–14   "Never trust the teller, trust the tale," said Lawrence] Cf. D. H. Lawrence, *Studies in Classic American Literature* (1923), ch. 2: "Never trust the artist. Trust the tale."

18.4–5   Cukor, Walsh, Hawks] American film directors George Cukor (1899–1983), Raoul Walsh (1887–1980), and Howard Hawks (1896–1977).

19.5   his two essays on Robbe-Grillet] "There Is No Robbe-Grillet School" (1958) and "The Last Word on Robbe-Grillet?" (1962), essays on French novelist, essayist, and filmmaker Alain Robbe-Grillet (1922–2008), author of *The Erasers* (1953), *The Voyeur* (1955), and *For a New Novel* (1963).

19.15–17   Manny Farber's film criticism . . . Jarrell's essay on Walt Whitman] American film critic and painter Manny Farber (1917–2008) was a regular reviewer for *The New Republic* and *The Nation*, among other publications;

the essay on Dickens by American critic and professor Dorothy van Ghent (1907–1967) was published in 1950 in *Sewanee Review*; "Walt Whitman: He Had His Nerve," essay by poet and critic Randall Jarrell (1914–1965), was published in *Kenyon Review* in 1952.

32.23–24   barbarity of war by Goya . . . *An American Tragedy*] Spanish artist Francisco de Goya y Lucientes (1746–1828) depicted wartime atrocities in his series of prints *The Disasters of War* (1810–14); *An American Tragedy* (1925), novel by American writer Theodore Dreiser (1871–1945), tells the story of a man convicted of murder and executed.

33.27   Raymond Bayer has written] In "The Essence of Rhythm," essay (1953) by French philosopher and Sorbonne professor Raymond Bayer (1898–1960), translated and included in the anthology *Reflections on Art* (1958), edited by Suzanne K. Langer.

34.9   William Earle] American philosopher, filmmaker, and photographer (1919–1988), who spent most of his academic career as a professor at Northwestern University.

37.33   justifiable *propter hoc*] That is, justifiable after the fact, from *post hoc ergo propter hoc*, Latin phrase meaning "after this, therefore because of this," used to describe a logical fallacy.

38.32–33   Radiguet's two novels] *The Devil in the Flesh* (1923) and the posthumously published *The Count's Ball* (1924), by the French writer Raymond Radiguet (1903–1923).

39.39–40.2   Merce Cunningham's "Winterbranch" . . . Ad Reinhardt] Dance (1964) by American choreographer Merce Cunningham (1919–2009), employing lights flashing at irregular intervals and a screeching soundtrack played at loud volume; American composer Charles Wuorinen (b. 1938), whose chamber concertos include Chamber Concerto for Cello and 10 Players (1963) and Chamber Concerto for Flute and 10 Players (1964); *Naked Lunch* (1959), novel by American writer William S. Burroughs (1914–1997); American artist Ad Reinhardt (1913–1967) completed numerous black canvases in the 1950s and 1960s that he regarded as the culmination of prior developments in painting.

40.18–19   Gertrude Stein's *Melanctha*] Long story written in 1905–6, the second narrative of Stein's book *Three Lives* (1909).

48.16   Rig-Veda] Sacred Hindu text, a collection of ancient Sanskrit hymns.

49.19   an American film star] Constance Dowling (1920–1969).

50.30   thesis of Denis de Rougemont] In *Love in the Western World* (1939; tr. 1956) by the Swiss philosopher and cultural historian Denis de Rougemont (1906–1985).

51.2–3   Catharist] Referring to the heterodox Christian sect also known as Albigensians, violently suppressed by the Roman Catholic Church in the first half of the thirteenth century.

60.12–13   Merleau-Ponty . . . *Temps Modernes*] With Jean-Paul Sartre, Simone de Beauvoir, and other intellectuals, French phenomenologist philosopher Maurice Merleau-Ponty (1908–1961) was a member of the original editorial committee of *Les Temps Modernes*, a journal with a Marxist orientation founded in 1945, and served as its political editor and editor-in-chief. In 1952, Albert Camus and Sartre engaged in a political and personal quarrel conducted largely in the pages of *Les Temps Modernes*, and the following year Merleau-Ponty resigned from the journal, taking issue with Sartre's support of Soviet communism. He went on to publish a lengthy attack on Sartre's politics in *Adventures of the Dialectic* (1955).

60.23   Lionel Abel spoke of him] In a review of Camus's essay collection *Resistance, Rebellion, and Death* (1960) by American critic, playwright, and translator Lionel Abel (1910–2001). Sontag reviewed Abel's book *Metatheatre* (1963); see "The Death of Tragedy," pp. 127–34 in this volume.

62.15   Raymond Aron] French philosopher, sociologist, and journalist (1905–1983), author of *The Century of Total War* (1951; tr. 1954), the anti-Marxist *The Opium of the Intellectuals* (1955; tr. 1957), *Peace and War* (1962, trans. 1966), and some forty other books.

62.35   Théâtre de l'Équipe] Theater company established by Camus in Algiers in 1937, the successor to the Théâtre du Travail, which he had founded two years earlier.

64.12–13   important prefatory essay, "Literature Considered as a Bullfight"] In Richard Howard's 1963 translation, this essay is entitled "The Autobiographer as *Torero*" and is placed as an afterword to *Manhood*.

64.23   Max Jacob] French poet, novelist, and painter (1876–1944).

65.23   Jouhandeau] Prolific French novelist and diarist Marcel Jouhandeau (1888–1979), whose twenty-eight volumes of published journals span nearly his entire life.

72.28–34   *Anthropologie Structurale . . . Elémentaires de la Parenté*] These works by Lévi-Strauss were published in English translation as follows: *Anthropologie structurale* (vol. I, 1958) as *Structural Anthropology* (1963); *Le Totémisme aujourd'hui* (1962) as *Totemism* (1963); *La Pensée sauvage* (1962) as *The Savage Mind* (1966); *Race et histoire* (1952) as *Race and History* (1952); *Les Structures élémentaires de la parenté* (1949) as *The Elementary Structures of Kinship* (1969); *Le Cru et le cuit* (1964), vol. I of the four-volume *Mythologiques* (1964–71) as *The Raw and the Cooked* (1969), vol. I of *Introduction to a Science of Mythology* (1969–81).

73.21   Paul Nizan] French novelist, critic, and journalist (1905–1940), author of *Aden Arabie* (1931), *Antoine Bloye* (1933) and *The Trojan Horse* (1935). He was a member of the French Communist Party, 1927–39, and a professor of philosophy at a Paris lycée, 1931–32.

77.6–7   writing about ancient Judaism or Confucian China] In later works by the German sociologist Max Weber (1864–1920), namely the essays written in

1917–19, posthumously collected and translated into English as *Ancient Judaism* (1952), and *Konfuzianismus und Taoismus* (1915, rev. 1920), published in English as *The Religion of China: Confucianism and Taoism* (1951).

77.7–9   a Frazer describing . . . Philippines] In *The Golden Bough* (1890–1915), a twelve-volume study by the British anthropologist James George Frazer (1854–1941).

78.33–34   *Essai sur Quelques Formes Primitives de Classification*] "De quelques formes primitives de classification," known in English translation (1963) as *Primitive Classification.*

78.34–35   *Essai sur le Don* (1924)] Known in English translation (1954) as *The Gift: Form and Function of Exchange in Archaic Societies.*

78.42   "*la pensée . . . pensée quantifiée.* "] So-called primitive thought is a form of quantified thought.

80.25   Mircea Eliade] Romanian-born historian of religion and novelist (1907–1986), whose books include *The Myth of the Eternal Return: Or, Cosmos and History* (1949), *Shamanism: Archaic Techniques of Ecstasy* (1951), and the novel *The Forbidden Forest* (1955).

81.11–12   Nathalie Sarraute . . . Michel Butor] Practitioners of the *nouveau roman* (new novel): Russian-born French novelist Nathalie Sarraute (1900–1999), see pp. 99–110 in this volume; Alain Robbe-Grillet, see note 19.5; French novelist and critic Michel Butor (b. 1926), author of *Passing Time* (1956) and *La Modification* (1957; published in English translation as *Second Thoughts*).

84.6   Béla Kun] Hungarian revolutionary and politician (1886–1938), founder (1918) of the Hungarian Communist Party and leader (March–August 1919) of the short-lived Hungarian Soviet Republic. Kun fled to Soviet Russia in 1920 and became a prominent figure in the Comintern. He was arrested in June 1937 during the Great Purge and shot in August 1938.

84.25   D. Ryazanoff] David Riazanov (1870–1938), Russian scholar who founded a prominent Soviet research center, the Marx-Engels Institute, and edited the collected writings of Marx and Engels. Accused of counterrevolutionary activity in 1931, Riazanov was expelled from the Communist Party and exiled to Saratov, a city on the Volga where he worked in a university library before being arrested in 1937. He was shot on January 21, 1938.

85.10–12   a minister in Imre Nagy's government . . . revolution] Lukács served as minister of culture in 1956 in the short-lived government of Imre Nagy (1896–1958), a Communist reformer who became prime minister of Hungary on October 24, 1956, following a popular uprising in Budapest. The Soviet Union sent troops to invade Hungary on November 4, 1956, and replaced Nagy's government with a regime led by János Kádár (1912–1989). Nagy was arrested on November 22 and hanged on June 16, 1958, after a secret trial.

86.7–8   Roger Martin du Gard] French novelist (1881–1958), winner of the Nobel Prize in Literature in 1937, author of the series of novels *The Thibaults* (1922–40).

87.11   Sir Herbert Read has praised him lavishly] In "Georg Lukács," essay (1957) by English critic and poet Herbert Read (1893–1968), which also cites Thomas Mann's praise of Lukács quoted at 87.12–13, published in a letter to the journal *Der Aufbau* in 1949.

87.13–16   George Steiner . . . Kazin] The first quote from George Steiner (b. 1929), American critic, academic, and fiction writer born to a Viennese Jewish family in Paris, is taken from "In Respect of Georg Lukács," essay published in *Encounter* in 1963; the second quote is from Steiner's introduction to Lukács's *Realism in Our Time* (1964), American title of English translation of *Die Gegenwartsbedeutung des kritischen Realismus* (1958). American critic Alfred Kazin (1915–1998) wrote the introduction to the edition (1964) of Lukács's *Studies in European Realism* (1948) that Sontag reviewed.

88.31   Benn] German poet Gottfried Benn (1886–1956).

88.40–89.2   ideas of the late Walter Benjamin . . . allegory] In *Ursprung des deutschen Trauerspiels*, submitted by the German-Jewish critic and philosopher Walter Benjamin (1892–1940) as a doctoral dissertation in 1925, and published in revised form in 1928; it did not appear in English translation, as *The Origin of German Tragic Drama*, until 1977.

89.9   German school] More commonly known as the Frankfurt School.

91.13–14   Lucien Goldmann . . . Malraux] In a lengthy chapter devoted to Malraux in *Towards a Sociology of the Novel* (1964, tr. 1975) by the Romanian-born French critic and philosopher Lucien Goldmann (1913–1970).

91.14–16   Benjamin . . . did not deal with any 20th century writers] Among the twentieth-century writers written about by Benjamin are Kafka ("Franz Kafka," 1934) and Brecht ("What Is Epic Theatre?" 1931, rev. 1939).

91.18   an important essay] "The Work of Art in the Age of Mechanical Reproduction" (1936).

95.21   Husserlian *epoché*] The act of suspending our natural attention toward the world, a key concept in the phenomenology of German philosopher Edmund Husserl (1859–1938).

99.39   Gian-Carlo Menotti . . . Bernard Buffet] Italian-born American composer Gian Carlo Menotti (1911–2007), whose popular operas include *The Medium* (1946) and *Amahl and the Night Visitors* (1951); popular and commercially successful French painter Bernard Buffet (1928–1999).

100.12   E. M. Cioran calls "destiny in lower case."] In "La Fin du roman" (1953), essay by the Romanian-born philosopher, essayist, and aphorist E. M. Cioran (1911–1995), translated in 1961 as "Beyond the Novel" and later included in *The Temptation to Exist* (1968). See Sontag's essay on Cioran, pp. 353–71 in this volume.

101.2   Machado de Assis, Svevo] Joaquim Maria Machado de Assis (1839–1908), Brazilian novelist whose many books include *Epitaph for a Small Winner* (1881) and *Dom Casmurro* (1899); Italo Svevo, pseudonym of Ettore Schmitz (1861–1928), Italian novelist, author of *Confessions of Zeno* (1923).

101.4   *Nightwood*] Novel (1936) by American writer Djuna Barnes (1892–1982).

102.27–28   Maurice Blanchot, Georges Bataille, and Pierre Klossowski] French writers Maurice Blanchot (1907–2003), author of *Thomas the Obscure* (1941, rev. 1950) and *Death Sentence* (1948); Georges Bataille (1897–1962), author of *Story of the Eye* (1928) and *Blue of Noon* (1935, pub. 1957); and Pierre Klossowski (1905–2001), author of the trilogy of novels *The Laws of Hospitality* (1954–60).

102.32   Claude Simon] French novelist (1913–2005), winner of the Nobel Prize in Literature in 1985, author of *The Grass* (1958) and *The Flanders Road* (1960).

112.8–9   Boris Vian's *The Empire Builders . . . Amédée*] Play (1959) by French playwright Boris Vian (1920–1959); Ionesco's first full-length play, *Amédée*, premiered in 1954.

112.34   *The Theatre and Its Double*] Collection of essays and letters on theater (1938) by French playwright and filmmaker Antonin Artaud (1896–1948), including two "Theater of Cruelty" manifestoes (1932, 1933). Artaud called for a radically new theater based on the staging of extreme bodily acts, the eschewal of a traditional script, and the use of stage effects that create an atmosphere of violent intensity. He founded the Theater of Cruelty in Paris in 1935, where he staged his adaptation of Shelley's *The Cenci*. Sontag was the editor of *Antonin Artaud: Selected Writings* (1976), to which she contributed an introduction; see also Sontag's discussion on p. 256, and her essay "Marat/Sade/Artaud," pp. 157–67 in this volume.

122.10   Harold Rosenberg] In "The Trial and Eichmann" (1961), essay for *Commentary* magazine by the American art critic and essayist Harold Rosenberg (1906–1978).

123.28   Erwin Piscator] German theatrical director (1893–1966), known for his commitment to political theater and innovative stage techniques; he was director of the Dramatic Workshop of the New School for Social Research in New York from 1939 to 1951, when he returned to Germany. His production of *The Deputy* was staged at the Freie Volksbühne Theater in West Berlin in 1963.

125.22   Peter Brook for his production of the play in Paris] Jorge Semprún's translation of Hochhuth's play, codirected by influential English theater director Peter Brook (b. 1925) and French director François Darbon (1915–1998), premiered in Paris in December 1963.

132.24   Jan Kott] Polish theater critic (1914–2001) best known for *Shakespeare Our Contemporary*, essays first published in book form in French translation in 1962, then in English in 1964.

132.29   *The Play of Daniel*] Thirteenth-century Latin liturgical drama, adapted by the New York Pro Musica ensemble led by Noah Greenberg (1919–1966) in 1958, featuring additional onstage narration by English poet W. H. Auden.

135.35   Franzblau] Abraham Franzblau (1901–1982), psychiatrist and author, whose books include *Religious Belief and Character Among Jewish Adolescents* (1934), *The Road to Sexual Maturity* (1954), and *A Sane and Happy Life* (1963).

137.40–138.3   Elia Kazan, well known to be . . . Miller and Kazan] Called before the House Un-American Activities Committee (HUAC) on April 10, 1952, Kazan testified that he had been a member of the American Communist Party from 1934 to 1936 while working with the Group Theatre in New York, and gave the names of eight of his colleagues who had also been Party members (the names were already known by the committee). Kazan had refused to name names at an earlier appearance before HUAC on January 14, 1952; he explained his decision to identify the Party members to Arthur Miller shortly before his April testimony.

138.29–30   WEVD soap opera] WEVD was a New York radio station founded in 1927 by Socialists; the letters "EVD" stand for American labor leader Eugene V. Debs (1855–1926). Much of its programming was in Yiddish, including serials.

141.20   *Dylan*] Play (1964) about the last years of Welsh poet Dylan Thomas by American playwright Sidney Michaels (1927–2011).

145.17–19   *Waiting for Lefty . . . The Crucible*] The American plays *Waiting for Lefty* (1935) by Clifford Odets (1906–1963), *Watch on the Rhine* (1941) by Lillian Hellmann (1905–1984), *Tomorrow the World* (1943) by James Gow (1907–1952) and Arnaud d'Usseau (1916–1990), *Deep Are the Roots* (1945) by James Gow and Arnaud d'Usseau, *The Crucible* (1953) by Arthur Miller.

145.26   Emmett Till] Emmett Till (1941–1955), a fourteen-year-old African American boy visiting Leflore County, Mississippi, from Chicago, was beaten and shot to death on August 28, 1955, after he allegedly whistled at a white woman. His murder and the acquittal on September 23 of Roy Bryant and J. W. Milan, the two white men charged with the crime (both of whom later admitted to a journalist that they had killed Till), attracted widespread public attention.

145.28   Medgar Evers] Medgar Evers (1925–1963), the field secretary of the Mississippi NAACP, 1954–63, who was shot outside his house in Jackson by a white supremacist.

145.29–30   dead children of Birmingham] Ku Klux Klansmen bombed the Sixteenth Street Baptist Church in Birmingham, Alabama, on September 15, 1963, killing Denise McNair, eleven; Cynthia Wesley, fourteen; Carole Robertson, fourteen; and Addie Mae Collins, fourteen.

148.2   Paddy Chayefsky] American playwright and screenwriter (1923–1981), author of *Marty* (teleplay, 1953; movie screenplay, 1955) and the screenplay for *The Americanization of Emily* (1964).

151.4   a small theater on East Fourth Street] The Writers' Theatre.

151.16   Ron Rice's *Flower Thief*] *The Flower Thief* (1960), film by experimental filmmaker Ron Rice (1935–1964), set in San Francisco.

151.18–19   Harry Langdon] American comic actor (1884–1944), a star of vaudeville and silent movies.

152.26   Margaret Dumont mother] American actress Margaret Dumont (1882–1965) often played society dowagers, starting with the Broadway production of George S. Kaufman's *The Cocoanuts* (1925) and continuing through several Marx Brothers movies, including *Duck Soup* (1933) and *A Day at the Races* (1937).

155.12   recent essay] "King Lear or Endgame" by Jan Kott (see note 132.24).

165.27–28   *Tel Quel*] Influential literary journal cofounded in Paris in 1960 by the French critic and novelist Philippe Sollers (b. 1936) and several other writers.

165.38   *Pour en Finir avec le Jugement de Dieu*] *To Have Done with the Judgment of God*, written for French radio shortly before Artaud's death.

166.12   final production of The Living Theater] The experimental theater company Living Theatre, founded in 1947 by Julian Beck (1925–1985) and Judith Malina (b. 1926) and profoundly influenced by the writings of Artaud, was evicted from its Manhattan performance space in 1963 because of nonpayment of taxes. For its final performance of *The Brig*, held in defiance of the eviction order, the audience entered the padlocked theater by climbing through the windows. The troupe continued to perform abroad, mostly in Europe, before basing itself once again in New York in 1984.

167.2–3   the critic who complained] English theater critic John Gross (1935–2011), in "1793 & All That," review of *Marat/Sade* in *Encounter*, November 1964.

173.39–174.1   Alexandre Astruc . . . "Le Camera-Stylo,"] "The Birth of a New Avant-Garde: The Camera-Pen" (1948), first published in the journal *L'Écran français*, by director and critic Alexandre Astruc (b. 1923).

175.38–39   *Le Vent Souffle où il Veut*] "The wind blows where it will," the words of Jesus to Nicodemus in John 3:8.

177.3   Berliner Ensemble] Theater company founded in East Berlin by Bertolt Brecht (1898–1956) and Helene Weigel (1900–1971) in 1949.

187.1   *Godard's* Vivre Sa Vie] The film was released in the United States as *My Life to Live*.

194.34   Brice Parain] French philosopher (1897–1971), one of Godard's teachers at the Sorbonne, author of *Researches into the Nature and Function of Language* (1942) and *Joseph* (1964).

195.6–7   the story of Dumas' Porthos] Porthos dies in *The Vicomte de Bragelonne*, but the immediate cause is a weakness in his legs.

198.7–34   VIVRE SA VIE . . . Sa Vie] Godard's text can be translated: "A film on prostitution that recounts how a young and pretty Parisian salesgirl gives her body but keeps her soul while she traverses like appearances a series of adventures which make known to her all possible profound human feelings and which have been filmed by Jean-Luc Godard and acted by Anna Karina *Vivre Sa Vie.*"

202.16–17   Inoshiro Honda . . . George Pal] Honda (1911–1993, real name Ishiro Honda), director of *Godzilla* (1954), *Rodan* (1956), *The Mysterians* (1957), *The H-Man* (1958), *Battle in Outer Space* (1959), *The Human Vapor* (1960), *Mothra* (1961), *Matango* (1963), and many other science fiction and fantasy films; Pal (1908–1980, born György Pál Marczincsak), producer of *When Worlds Collide* (1951), *The War of the Worlds* (1953), and *Conquest of Space* (1955), and director of *The Time Machine* (1960) and *Atlantis, the Lost Continent* (1961).

213.8–9   Sabbatai Zevi] Smyrna-born kabbalist (1626–1676) who declared himself the Messiah in 1648 and attracted a large following of believers throughout the Middle East, Europe, and North Africa. His movement weakened after he was forced to convert to Islam to save his life in Constantinople in 1666. He continued to assert messianic claims while observing the outward forms of Islam.

214.21–22   "thinking . . . Herman Kahn] *Thinking About the Unthinkable* (1962) by physicist Herman Kahn (1922–1983), and his *On Thermonuclear War* (1960) and *On Escalation* (1965), were controversial books on nuclear strategy.

215.1   *Jack Smith's*] Jack Smith (1932–1989), photographer, filmmaker, and performance artist, whose forty-five-minute *Flaming Creatures* (1963) is his only completed film.

215.29   police hostility] *Flaming Creatures* was seized by the New York Police Department during a raid on March 3, 1964, at a screening held by the Film-Makers' Cooperative at the New Bowery Theatre. The cooperative's director, Lithuanian-born American filmmaker Jonas Mekas (b. 1922), the projectionist, filmmaker Ken Jacobs (b. 1933), and the ticket-takers Jerry Sims and Florence Karpf, were arrested on obscenity charges for showing the film. *Flaming Creatures* was declared obscene in New York County Criminal Court on June 12, 1964, with the defendants receiving suspended sentences. Sontag testified for the defense during the trial.

215.37–38   New American Cinema . . . *Film Culture*] The New American Cinema group was founded in 1960 under the leadership of Jonas Mekas, dedicated to promoting independent and experimental film. It published a manifesto the following year in *Film Culture*, the journal Mekas edited, decrying the "false, polished, slick films" of the cinematic mainstream. Among the filmmakers associated with the group were Shirley Clarke (1919–1997), Stan Brakhage (1933–2003), Gregory Markopoulos (1928–1992), and Emile de Antonio (1919–1989).

220.10–11　*Muriel, ou Le Temps d'un retour*] *Muriel, or The Time of a Return.*

220.26　*le temps retrouvé*] French: time regained.

221.4　colons] French colonial settlers in Algeria, also known colloquially as *pieds noirs.*

225.20　*homme de gauche*] French: man of the Left.

230.2　Anthony Hope] English novelist (1863–1933), author of the popular adventure novel *The Prisoner of Zenda* (1894) and *The Dolly Dialogues* (1894).

230.39–231.1　Artaud's *La Coquille et le clergyman*] Film (1928) directed by Germaine Dulac, based on a scenario written by Artaud.

234.27　Morris Cohen . . . Sidney Hook] Russian-born American philosopher Morris Cohen (1880–1947), author of *Reason and Nature: An Essay on the Meaning of Scientific Method* (1931); American philosopher Sidney Hook (1902–1989), author of *Towards the Understanding of Karl Marx* (1933) and *The Hero in History* (1943).

236.17–18　essay of W. K. Clifford . . . famous reply of William James] "The Ethics of Belief" (1877), an essay by English mathematician William Kingdom Clifford (1845–1879), was attacked by William James in "The Will to Believe" (1896).

236.30　Maritain] French Catholic theologian Jacques Maritain (1882–1973), whose books include *Art and Scholasticism* (1920) and *Moral Philosophy* (1960).

236.32　Gabriel Marcel] French Christian existentialist philosopher and playwright (1889–1973).

236.32–33　letters exchanged . . . possible conversion] French writer Paul Claudel (1868–1955) tried unsuccessfully to convert Protestant French writer André Gide (1869–1951) to Catholicism, as recorded in their correspondence, published in 1949.

236.34　Newman . . . assent,"] See *The Grammar of Assent* (1870) by English Catholic cardinal and theologian John Henry Newman (1801–1890).

236.34　Lord Acton] John Emmerich Edward Dalberg-Acton, 1st Baron Acton (1834–1902), English Catholic philosopher and historian of science.

236.37　Pastor Niemöller] Martin Niemöller (1892–1984), German Protestant clergyman and theologian who opposed the Nazis and spent eight years in a concentration camp; president of the World Council of Churches, 1961–68.

237.29　Bultmann] German biblical scholar and theologian Rudolf Bultmann (1884–1976), author of *Theology of the New Testament* (1948–53).

237.32 Franz Rosenzweig] German-Jewish philosopher, theologian, and translator (1886–1929), author of *The Star of Redemption* (1921).

237.32 Gershom Scholem] German-Jewish scholar of Jewish mysticism and messianism (1897–1982), whose writings, such as *Major Trends in Jewish Mysticism* (1941) and *On the Kabbalah and Its Symbolism* (1965), brought about a renewal of interest in the Kabbalah.

238.35 as Günther Anders has shown] In *Kafka: Pro und Contra* (1951), by the German-Jewish philosopher and cultural critic Günther Anders (1902–1992).

239.36 Wilhelm Reich] Austrian-born psychoanalyst Wilhelm Reich (1897–1957), author of *Character Analysis* (1933), *The Mass Psychology of Fascism* (1933), *The Sexual Revolution* (1936), and other works.

241.18 Cabanis, and Enfantin] French physician and philosopher Pierre Cabanis (1757–1808); French social reformer Barthélemy Prosper Enfantin (1796–1864), leader of a Saint-Simonian community who advocated sexual freedom among its members.

241.21 *L'Histoire d'O*] Novel (1954) published under the pseudonym "Pauline Réage" by French writer Anne Desclos (1907–1998); she also published under the name "Dominique Aury."

242.30 the suppression of the Hungarian revolution] See note 85.11–12.

244.9 Ferenczi] Sándor Ferenczi (1873–1933), Hungarian psychoanalyst who collaborated with Freud.

248.20 *Voglio un bichiere di acqua*] Italian: I want a glass of water.

254.40 second volume of her memoirs] *La Force de l'âge* (1960), translated in 1962 as *The Prime of Life*, the second of four autobiographical books by de Beauvoir.

256.9 Polish *Life Is Beautiful*] Film (1957) directed by Polish director Tadeusz Makarczyński (1918–1987).

257.6 As Ruskin noted in 1880] In the essay "Fiction—Fair and Foul" by English writer John Ruskin (1819–1900).

257.7 *Guy Mannering*] Novel (1815) by Sir Walter Scott (1771–1832).

257.33 Tex Avery] American animator (1908–1980), creator of Bugs Bunny and Daffy Duck.

257.34 *Ubu Roi*] Play (1896) by French writer Alfred Jarry (1873–1907).

257.34 the Goon Show] Popular English radio comedy broadcast on the BBC, 1951–60, featuring among its comedians the British actors Spike Milligan (1918–2002), Harry Secombe (1921–2001), and Peter Sellers (1925–1980).

260.17   "One should either . . . of art."] All section epigraphs in this essay are taken from Oscar Wilde.

261.3   *Zuleika Dobson*] Novel (1911) by English novelist, essayist, and caricaturist Max Beerbohm (1872–1956).

261.5   Scopitone films] Short 16 mm films made to accompany song selections on specially equipped jukeboxes.

261.6   Brown Derby Restaurant] Restaurant on Wiltshire Boulevard in Los Angeles in the shape of a brown derby hat.

261.14   La Lupe] Stage name of Guadalupe Yoli (1939–1992), Cuban-born Latin pop singer.

261.15   Lynd Ward's novel in woodcuts, *Gods' Man*] Published in 1929, the first of six wordless novels in woodcuts by the American artist Lynd Ward (1905–1985).

261.19   Ronald Firbank . . . Ivy Compton-Burnett] English novelists who developed highly idiosyncratic styles: Ronald Firbank (1886–1926), author of *The Flower Beneath the Foot* (1923) and *Concerning the Eccentricities of Cardinal Pirelli* (1926), and Ivy Compton-Burnett (1884–1969), author of *A House and Its Head* (1935) and *Mother and Son* (1955).

262.6   major films of Louis Feuillade] Such as the serial films *Fantômas* (1913–14) and *Les Vampires* (1915–16), directed by French filmmaker Louis Feuillade (1873–1925).

262.15   Empson's phrase, "urban pastoral"] In *Some Versions of Pastoral* (1935) by English critic and poet William Empson (1906–1984).

263.25   Strawberry Hill] Estate of English writer and politician Horace Walpole (1717–1797), with gardens designed not to adhere to Continental standards of symmetry and formality but instead to appear more "natural."

264.1   *les précieux* in France] *Les Précieuses* (the precious ones), circle of writers associated with Madeleine de Scudéry (1607–1701), novelist, letter writer, and *salonnière*.

267.35   Maciste] Repeating character in Italian cinema, beginning with the silent epic *Cabiria* (1914), in which he figures as the heroic and loyal slave of a Roman patrician during the Third Punic War; in twenty-six silent sequels he became a more generalized hero characterized by superhuman strength and good-hearted simplicity. The character was revived in the 1960s in a series of films including *Maciste contro il vampiro* (1961) and *Maciste, l'eroe più grande del mondo* (1963).

268.17   Rudy Vallée] The singing style of Alexander Galloway, vocalist of the English jazz group The Temperance Seven in the 1950s and '60s, was reminiscent of the crooning of Rudy Vallée (1901–1986), popular singer and actor of the 1920s, '30s, and '40s.

268.28   Loïe Fuller] Innovative American dancer Loïe Fuller (1862–1928), who lived most of her adult life in Europe and became one of the most celebrated performers of the Belle Époque, as well as a pioneer in the use of lighting in performance.

271.31   *À Rebours*] *Against the Grain* (1884), novel by French writer J. K. Huysmans (1848–1907), whose protagonist is the author's alter ego, Des Esseintes.

271.31–32   *Marius the Epicurean*] Novel (1885) by Walter Pater (1839–1894).

274.31   Tishman Building] Forty-one-story skyscraper at 666 Fifth Avenue in New York City, built in 1957.

276.10–11   C. P. Snow in a famous lecture] *The Two Cultures and the Scientific Revolution* (1959) by the English scientist and novelist C. P. Snow (1905–1980), originally delivered as the Rede Lecture at Cambridge University in 1959.

279.31   C. S. Sherrington] English neurologist Charles Scott Sherrington (1857–1952), winner of the Nobel Prize in Physiology or Medicine in 1932, author of *Man on His Nature* (1940, rev. 1951).

279.33   Sigfried Giedion] Swiss architecture critic (1888–1968), author of *Mechanization Takes Command* (1948) and *The Eternal Present* (1964).

279.34   Gyorgy Kepes] Hungarian-born artist and designer (1906–2001), author of *Language of Vision* (1944) and *The New Landscape in Art and Science* (1956).

280.36–281.4   "while the new conditions . . . order."] From "Notes on Burroughs" by the Canadian media theorist and cultural critic Marshall McLuhan (1911–1980), first published in *The Nation*, December 28, 1964.

STYLES OF RADICAL WILL

294.16   Jacques Vaché] Vaché (1895–1919), who died of an opium overdose in Nantes, was a veteran of World War I whose personality and beliefs, expressed in a series of letters, powerfully influenced André Breton's views on life and art.

295.14   René Char] This statement by Char (1907–1988) can be found in his collection *À une sérénité crispée* (1951).

297.26–27   Cage's 4'33"] Musical composition (1952) by John Cage that instructs the instrumentalist or instrumentalists not to play their instruments for three designated time periods totaling four minutes and thirty-three seconds.

310.1   Krishnamurti] Jiddu Krishnamurti (1895–1986), Indian writer and teacher on mind, consciousness, meditation, and other subjects.

311.12–13   Francis Ponge] French poet (1899–1988) whose collections included *Le parti pris des choses* (1942), whose title has sometimes been translated as *The Voice of Things* or *Taking the Side of Things*.

311.19   Roussel's *Impressions of Africa*] Novel (1910), later adapted by Raymond Roussel (1877–1933), into a stage play. The book was generated, according to Roussel, by a complex system of word association explained in his posthumously published "How I Wrote Certain of My Books."

314.11   Gadda, Laura Riding] Carlo Emilio Gadda (1893–1973), Italian novelist and poet, author of the novel *Quer pasticciaccio brutto de via Merulana* (*That Awful Mess on the Via Merulana*, 1946); Riding (1901–1991), poet and fiction writer, author of the story collection *Progress of Stories* (1935).

320.22   *Trois filles de leur mère*] *Mother's Three Daughters*, posthumously published in 1926.

320.24   *The Image*] Novel (1956) published under the pseudonym Jean de Berg; the author was later identified as Catherine Robbe-Grillet (b. 1930).

320.34   *The Man Who Loved Children*] Novel (1940) by Christina Stead.

321.20   George P. Elliott] Fiction writer (1918–1980), author of *Parktilden Village* (1958) and *Among the Dangs* (1961).

321.21   Paul Goodman] Goodman (1911–1972) was the author of *Growing Up Absurd* (1960), *Compulsory Mis-Education* (1964), and many other works in a wide range of genres. Sontag's essay "On Paul Goodman" is included in *Under the Sign of Saturn* (1980).

322.18   Wayland Young] British politician and writer (1923–2009), 2nd Baron Kennet, author of *Eros Denied: Sex in Western Society* (1964).

324.35   Biely's *St. Petersburg*] Andrei Bely (1880–1934) published the first edition of *Petersburg* in 1913; a revised version appeared in 1922.

326.13   Jacques Rivière] Critic and memoirist (1886–1925) who edited the *Nouvelle Revue Française*, 1919–25.

331.5   "Pauline Réage"] See note 241.21.

331.6–7   Jean Paulhan] Writer, editor, and publisher (1884–1968).

331.24   "Jean de Berg"] See note 320.24.

332.40   well-known essay of Beauvoir] "Faut-il brûler Sade?" (1951–52), translated as "Must We Burn Sade?"

333.1   biography undertaken by Gilbert Lely] Lely (1904–1985), a French poet, published his *Life of the Marquis de Sade* in two volumes, 1952–57, and later revised it.

333.2   Klossowski] See note 102.27–28. Klossowski published *Sade My Neighbor* in 1947.

348.27   Mandiargues] Andre Pieyre de Mandiargues (1909–1991), author of *Blaze of Embers* (1959), *The Motorcycle* (1963), and other works.

357.4–6 *Précis . . . dans le Temps*] These works have been translated as *A Short History of Decay, All Gall Is Divided, The Temptation to Exist, History and Utopia*, and *The Fall into Time*.

365.16 Donoso Cortés . . . Eric Voegelin] Juan Donoso Cortés (1809–1853), Spanish writer and diplomat, author of *Catholicism, Liberalism, and Socialism Considered in Their Fundamental Principles* (1851); Voegelin (1901–1985), political philosopher who fled from Austria to the United States in 1938, author of the unfinished *Order and History*, of which five volumes were published from 1956 to 1987.

375.7 Forbes-Robertson] Johnston Forbes-Robertson (1853–1937) was considered the outstanding Hamlet of his time.

375.9 Helene Weigel] Weigel (1900–1971) was married to Bertolt Brecht and originated many roles in his plays, among them Mother Courage.

375.10 Berliner Ensemble] See note 177.2.

376.10 Siegfried Kracauer] Kracauer (1889–1966) published his *Theory of Film: The Redemption of Physical Reality* in 1960.

376.14–15 Flaherty . . . Ruspoli] Robert J. Flaherty (1884–1951), pioneering American documentary filmmaker whose films include *Nanook of the North* (1922), *Moana* (1926), and *Man of Aran* (1934); Jean Rouch (1917–2004), French filmmaker known for *Les maîtres fous* (1955), *Moi, un noir* (1958), *La Pyramide humaine* (1959), *Chronicle of a Summer* (1960), and other works; Chris Marker (1921–2012), French filmmaker and photographer whose films include *Letters from Siberia* (1957), *La jetée* (1962), and *Le joli mai* (1963); Mario Ruspoli (1925–1986), Italian-born documentary filmmaker whose works include *Les Inconnus de la terre* (1961) and *Regards sur la folie* (1962).

377.12–13 Theo van Doesburg] Dutch artist (1883–1931), founder of artistic group De Stijl.

377.18 Robert Breer] American filmmaker (1926–2011), creator of films including *Form Phases I–IV* (1952–56) and *A Man and His Dog Out for Air* (1957).

379.18–19 1904 Danish play] *Gertrud* (1906) was written by the Swedish playwright Hjalmar Söderberg (1869–1941).

381.17–18 Eisenstein . . . essay on Dickens] "Dickens, Griffith, and the Film Today" was published in 1944 and collected in English in the volume *Film Form: Essays in Film Theory* (1949).

381.34–35 Paradjanov's *Shadows of Our Forgotten Ancestors*] The last shot of Parajanov's 1964 film shows a window through whose panes a group of children are peering, with no clear indication of its relation to the shot that precedes it.

381.37 *Rope*] Hitchcock's 1948 film, based on a play by Patrick Hamilton, attempts to create the impression of continuous duration by linking together a series of ten long takes.

384.19   Harry Smith] Smith (1923–1991), an artist and musical archivist known for his collection of early recordings, *Anthology of American Folk Music* (1952); his films include *Heaven and Earth Magic*, repeatedly reedited into versions of various lengths.

388.34–35   *The Investigation . . . US*] Weiss's play (1965) drew on testimony from the trials of twenty-two former members of the Auschwitz camp administration held in Frankfurt in 1963–65; *US* (1966) explored responses to the Vietnam War.

389.27   *The Insect Play*] Play (1921) by Karel and Josef Čapek, sometimes known as *The Insect Comedy* or *The World We Live In*.

390.20   "living newspaper" of the 1930's] The Federal Theater Project produced a series of plays dramatizing contemporary issues, including *Triple-A Plowed Under* (1936), *Power* (1937), and *One-Third of a Nation* (1938). Congressional objection to the left-wing tendencies of these plays led to the closing of the Federal Theater Project in 1939.

390.23   *Come Spy with Me . . . Superman*] *Come Spy with Me* (1966), musical by Bryan Blackburn; *It's a Bird . . . It's a Plane . . . It's Superman* (1966), musical by Charles Strouse, Lee Adams, David Newman, and Robert Benton.

390.32–33   Andy Warhol's The Plastic Inevitable, Murray the K's World] Warhol's Plastic Inevitable, or Exploding Plastic Inevitable, was a series of multimedia events featuring the rock band the Velvet Underground, 1966–67; Murray the K's World was a discotheque located at Roosevelt Field on Long Island, established in April 1966 by the disc jockey Murray Kaufman (1922–1982).

392.5   Béla Balázs] Béla Balázs (1884–1949), Hungarian film theorist and poet.

403.12   *Journey to Italy*] Roberto Rossellini's *Viaggio in Italia*, generally shown in the U.S. as *Voyage to Italy*.

408.14–15   Benjamin Christensen's *Häxan*] Often shown in the U.S. as *Witchcraft Through the Ages*.

412.29   *Anticipation*] Godard's film is one of the six episodes of the omnibus film *The Oldest Profession* (1967).

417.5   David Riesman] American sociologist (1909–2002), author of *The Lonely Crowd* (1950).

417.11   Richard Roud] Roud (1929–1989), a founder and director of the New York Film Festival, 1963–87, was the author of *Godard* (1968), *Jean-Marie Straub* (1972), and *A Passion for Film* (1983).

419.1   Francis Jeanson] French journalist and philosopher (1922–2009); he was convicted in absentia and sentenced to ten years in prison in 1960 for his activities in support of the National Liberation Front during the Algerian War, and lived in exile until he was granted amnesty in 1966.

419.3 Roger Leenhardt] Leenhardt (1903–1985), French critic and filmmaker, was a founder of the important cinema club Objectif 49; his films included *Les Dernières vacances* (1948) and *Le Rendez-vous de minuit* (1961).

421.7 Michel Simon] Swiss actor (1895–1975), star of *La Chienne* (1931), *Boudu Saved from Drowning* (1932), *L'Atalante* (1934), and many other films.

424.12 *Ghost at Noon*] Moravia's novel *Contempt* was first published in the U.S. as *A Ghost at Noon*.

426.32 Musidora] Actress, born Jeanne Roques (1889–1957), who starred in Louis Feuillade's serials *Les Vampires* and *Judex*.

427.20 Lemmy Caution] Fictional FBI agent, later a private detective, created by Peter Cheyney in his novel *This Man Is Dangerous* (1936) and featured in nine subsequent books; the character was played in a series of seven French movies (1953–63) by Eddie Constantine prior to his portrayal of the role in Godard's *Alphaville* (1965).

428.34 Feiffer dialogue] In the manner of Jules Feiffer (b. 1929), cartoonist whose work appeared in *The Village Voice* and was collected in such volumes as *Sick Sick Sick* (1958) and *The Explainers* (1960).

429.10 Ulysses and Michelangelo] The peasant recruits who are the leading characters of *Les Carabiniers*.

435.35 Jean-Marie Straub] French filmmaker (b. 1933) who worked in collaboration with his wife Danièle Huillet (1936–2006); their films included *Nicht versöhnt* (1965) and *Chronicle of Anna Magdalena Bach* (1968).

437.29 Olmi] Ermanno Olmi (b. 1931), Italian filmmaker whose early documentary films were followed by *Time Stood Still* (1959), *Il Posto* (1961), *I Fidanzati* (1963), and other features.

442.12 Landolfi] See Sontag's note on p. 45 of this volume.

445.38 Harry Dickson] Protagonist, described as "the American Sherlock Holmes," of a long series of fantastic adventure novels chiefly written by the Belgian writer Jean Ray (1887–1964).

446.4 Ben Barka] The Moroccan politician Mehdi Ben Barka (1920–1965), leader of the left-wing National Union of Popular Forces, disappeared in Paris on October 29, 1965, and was killed shortly thereafter. His abduction and murder were the result of a plot involving high-ranking Moroccan security officials and members of the French foreign intelligence service, the Paris police, and the French underworld.

455.10–11 Jane Austen's Mr. Woodhouse] The self-absorbed, hypochondriac father of the heroine of *Emma* (1815).

456.36 Yevtushenko] Yevgeny Yevtushenko (b. 1933), Russian poet, best known for the long poem *Babi Yar* (1961).

457.10   Leary] Timothy Leary (1920–1996), Harvard professor who conducted extensive experiments with LSD and, after being fired by the university
in 1963, publicly promoted the use of psychedelics.

457.12   Leslie Fiedler] Literary critic (1917–2003), author of *Love and Death in
the American Novel* (1960); "The New Mutants" appeared in *Partisan Review*
in 1965.

457.33–34   Philip Rahv . . . Malcolm Muggeridge] Rahv (1908–1973),
cofounder with William Phillips of *Partisan Review*, author of *Image and Idea*
(1949); Howe (1920–1993), editor of *Dissent*, author of *Politics and the Novel*
(1957) and many other books; Muggeridge (1903–1990), English journalist,
later a convert to Catholicism.

457.37   SNCC] Student Nonviolent Coordinating Committee, civil rights
organization formed in 1960, which took a more radical turn under the leadership of Stokely Carmichael, 1966–67.

457.38   Conor Cruise O'Brien] Irish writer and politician (1917–2008), author
of *Writers and Politics* (1965), The Great M*elody: A Thematic Biography of
Edmund Burke* (1992), and many other books.

458.29   Mario Savio] Political activist (1942–1996), a major figure in the
Berkeley Free Speech Movement, 1964–65.

459.20   Edgar Z. Friedenberg] Sociologist (1921–2000), author of *The Vanishing Adolescent* (1959), *Coming of Age in America* (1965), and other works.

460.28   Leó Szilárd] Leó Szilárd, physicist (1898–1964) who developed the
idea of the nuclear chain reaction and played a major part in the research cul-
minating in the Manhattan Project; his eventual opposition to nuclear weapons
was expressed in the fiction collection *The Voice of the Dolphins* (1961).

460.28   Judith and Julian Beck] See note 166.12.

463.4   Andrew Kopkind] Journalist (1935–1994) who wrote at various times
for *The Nation, The New York Review of Books, The New Republic*, and *The New
Statesman*, and founded *Hard Times* in 1968.

465.8   Wilfred Burchett] Left-wing Australian journalist (1911–1983), active as a
war reporter from 1940 on, who was the center of controversy for his reporting
of the Korean and Vietnam wars.

465.9   Russell Foundation's International War Crimes Tribunal] Bertrand Russell (1872–1970) was the organizer of a tribunal established in 1966 to investi-
gate possible American war crimes in Vietnam. Two sessions were held in 1967.

471.33   *PM* and Corliss Lamont and the Webbs] *PM*, daily New York newspaper, 1940–48, founded by Ralph Ingersoll (1900–1985), whose regular
contributors included I. F. Stone, James Wechsler, and Theodor Geisel (Dr.
Seuss); Lamont (1902–1995), socialist and civil liberties activist; Beatrice Webb
(1858–1943) and her husband, Sidney Webb (1859–1947), central figures in the

Fabian Society and founders of the London School of Economics, authors of *Soviet Communism: A New Civilization?* (1935) and *The Truth About Soviet Russia* (1942).

471.35   Wallace campaign] Henry Wallace (1888–1965), after serving as vice president, 1941–45, and then as secretary of commerce, 1945–46, ran for president as the candidate of the Progressive Party in 1948, receiving 2.4 percent of the popular vote.

474.27   General Giap] Vo Nguyen Giap (b. 1911) commanded the Viet Minh army during the Vietnamese war of independence, 1946–54, and was the North Vietnamese minister of defense during the Vietnam War.

485.26   Howard Fast . . . Albert Maltz] Fast (1914–2003), author of novels, including *Conceived in Liberty* (1939), *Citizen Tom Paine* (1943), and *Freedom Road* (1944); Maltz (1908–1985), fiction writer, playwright, and screenwriter, blacklisted as one of the Hollywood Ten.

488.6   Norman Morrison] Morrison (1933–1965), a Quaker, immolated himself in front of the Pentagon on November 2, 1965, in protest against the Vietnam War.

494.4   *Kieu*] Written by Nguyen Du (1766–1820), the epic poem was translated into English as *The Tale of Kieu* in 1983.

503.37   Bao Dai] Last emperor of the Nguyen dynasty (1913–1997), who reigned as emperor of Annam, 1926–45, and subsequently as chief of state of South Vietnam until ousted in 1955.

513.18   Paulette Goddard] Movie star (1910–1990) who started her career as a dancer in the Ziegfeld Follies in the late 1920s, and later appeared in *Modern Times* (1936), *The Women* (1939), *The Great Dictator* (1940), and other films.

ON PHOTOGRAPHY

530.32   Chris Marker] See note 376.14–15.

531.31   Farm Security Administration photographic project] From 1935 to 1944, the Farm Security Administration's information division, under the direction of Roy Stryker, employed photographers to document the conditions of impoverished farmers.

539.38   Andersonville] City in Georgia, site of Confederate prison Camp Sumter.

540.18–19   one that made the front page . . . in 1972] The photo was taken by Associated Press photographer Nick Ut on June 8, 1972.

576.29   Reyner Banham] English architecture critic (1922–1988), author of *Los Angeles: The Architecture of Four Ecologies* (1971).

582.11   Viollet-le-Duc] Eugène Viollet-le-Duc (1814–1879), French architect associated with the Gothic Revival, extensively restored medievæl monuments, often adding original features.

584.8   Kitaj] R. B. Kitaj (1932–2007), American artist long resident in England.

595.20   "No truth but in things,"] Cf. William Carlos Williams, *Paterson*, Book One (1946): "Say it! No ideas but in things."

603.29   John Berger] English novelist and critic (b. 1926), author of *Toward Reality: Essays in Seeing* (1962) and *The Look of Things* (1972).

604.24   Gorin] Jean-Pierre Gorin (b. 1943), French filmmaker whose collaborations with Jean-Luc Godard, under the aegis of the Dziga Vertov Group, include *Wind from the East* (1970), *Tout va bien* (1972), and *Letter to Jane* (1972).

612.38–39   Viktor Shklovsky] Russian critic (1893–1984); his concept of defamiliarization (*ostranenie*) is explicated in *Theory of Prose* (1925).

618.31–32   John Szarkowski] Photographer and curator (1925–2007), director of photography at the Museum of Modern Art, 1962–91.

629.28–30   Photo-Secession . . . Magnum] Photo-Secession, group of American photographers formed in 1902 by Alfred Stieglitz; *f*64, San Francisco–based group of photographers organized around 1932, including Willard Van Dyke and Ansel Adams; New Objectivity (Neue Sachlichkeit), German photographic group including August Sander and Albert Renger-Patzsch; Magnum, cooperative photographic agency founded by Henri Cartier-Bresson, Robert Capa, and others in 1947.

631.6   Mario Praz] Italian critic (1896–1982), author of *The Romantic Agony* (1933).

ILLNESS AS METAPHOR

678.13–14   Karl Menninger] American psychiatrist (1893–1990), founder of the Menninger Foundation and the Menninger Clinic, author of *Man Against Himself* (1938), *Love Against Hate* (1942), *The Vital Balance* (1963), and other books.

682.31   Alice James] James (1848–1892), the sister of William James and Henry James and the subject of Sontag's play *Alice in Bed* (1991), kept a diary from 1889 until her death.

684.33–34   Katherine Mansfield . . . John Middleton Murry] Mansfield (1888–1923), the New Zealand–born author of *In a German Pension* (1911), *Bliss* (1920), and *The Garden Party and Other Stories* (1922) and wife of John Middleton Murry (1889–1957), was diagnosed with tuberculosis in 1917.

689.29   Murger] Henri Murger (1822–1861), whose story collection *Scènes de la vie de bohème* (1851) was the basis of Puccini's opera *La Bohème*.

692.10   Marie Bashkirtsev] Bashkirtsev (1858–1884), a Russian painter and sculptor, kept an extensive diary (sixteen volumes in the complete French edition of 2005) from 1873 on.

693.38–39   Praz . . . his famous book] See note 631.6.

700.18–19   Selma Lagerlöf's *The Phantom Chariot*] Lagerlöf's novel *Körkarlen* (*The Carriage*, 1912) was translated into English as *Thy Soul Shall Bear Witness!* and filmed in 1921 by Victor Sjöström as *The Phantom Carriage*.

701.11   *The Testament of Cresseid*] Narrative poem by the fifteenth-century Scots poet Robert Henryson.

701.12   *Les Liaisons dangereuses*] Epistolary novel (1782) by Choderlos de Laclos (1741–1803).

702.8   Émile] Boy whose upbringing is the subject of Jean-Jacques Rousseau's fictionalized treatise *Émile, or On Education* (1762).

702.21   Proverbs of Hell] Section of William Blake's *The Marriage of Heaven and Hell* (1790–93).

705.19   Jean Vigo] French filmmaker (1905–1934), director of *À propos de Nice* (1930), *Zero for Conduct* (1933), and *L'Atalante* (1934).

708.29   Milena] Milena Jesenská (1896–1944); Kafka's letters to her were collected in *Letters to Milena* (1952).

709.2   Keith Thomas] Welsh historian (b. 1933), author of *Religion and the Decline of Magic* (1971).

712.1–2   Charles-Louis Philippe's *Bubu de Montparnasse*] Philippe (1874–1909) published his novel in 1901.

725.1   *Quatre-vingt-treize*] French: *Ninety-three.*

726.29   Gang of Four] Radical political faction that rose to power during the Chinese Cultural Revolution before being arrested and publicly vilified in 1976 following the death of Mao Zedong; the most important member of the group was Jiang Qing (1914–1991), wife of Mao Zedong since 1938.

726.30   John Dean] Dean (b. 1938) was Richard Nixon's White House counsel, July 1970–April 1973.

727.10   Neal Ascherson . . . Slansky Affair] Ascherson (b. 1932), Scottish journalist; Rudolf Slánský (1901–1952), general secretary of the Polish Communist Party, 1945–51, and thirteen other prominent Czechoslovak Communists were convicted in 1952 after a public trial marked by open anti-Semitism for participating in a "Trotskyite-Titoist-Zionist" conspiracy against the regime. Slánský and ten other defendants were hanged.

727.38   *La Gangrène*] A collection of seven firsthand accounts by Algerians tortured in Paris by the French internal security service during the Algerian War; published in 1959, the book was confiscated by the French government and all unsold copies were destroyed.

UNCOLLECTED ESSAYS

733.25   Laura Riding] See note 314.11.

736.25–26   Maurice Blanchot] See note 102.27–28.

737.3–4   *Quer pasticciaccio brutto de via Merulana . . . Notre Dame des Fleurs*] *That Awful Mess on the Via Merulana; Our Lady of the Flowers.*

737.20   *Tirez sur le Pianiste*] *Shoot the Piano Player.*

740.22   Claude Ollier] French novelist and film critic (b. 1922), author of *La Mise en scène* (1958), *Le Maintien de l'ordre* (1961), and other works.

740.28   Brion Gysin] Gysin (1916–1986) was the author of *The Process* (1969) and other works; his collaborations with William S. Burroughs included *The Exterminator* (1960) and *The Third Mind* (1978).

740.33–34   *le cadavre exquis*] The exquisite corpse.

770.28–30   Trung sisters . . . Eberhardt] Trung sisters, Vietnamese national heroes who led resistance against China in the first century; Mademoiselle Maupin, born Julie d'Aubigny (1670–1707), French singer and fencer who sometimes wore male attire; Louise Michel (1830–1905), French anarchist leader active during the Paris Commune; Isabelle Eberhardt (1877–1904), Swiss-born writer and traveler who studied Arabic, converted to Islam, and settled in Algeria.

776.14   a poem by Brecht] See Bertolt Brecht, "An die Nachgeborenen (To Those Born After)," line 1: "Truly, I live in dark times!"

809.7   Lauren Hutton] American model (b. 1943) taken to exemplify a more natural look, notably for the uncorrected gap in her teeth.

Index

Kolbe, Maximilian, 126
Kommunismus, 84
Kopkind, Andrew, 463, 470, 477–78,
 482–83, 486, 490, 495, 515–16
Korean War, 540–41
Kornfield, Lawrence, 166
Kott, Jan, 132, 155
Kowal, Samuel J., 707
Kracauer, Siegfried, 376, 389
Krishnamurti, Jiddu, 310
Kroeber, Alfred, 78–79
Kubrick, Stanley: *Doctor Strangelove*,
 142–44
Ku Klux Klan, 146
Kun, Béla, 84
Kurosawa, Akira: *The Hidden Fortress*,
 230; *Ikiru*, 700; *The Lower Depths*,
 379; *The Seven Samurai*, 230; *The
 Throne of Blood*, 230, 379
Ky, Nguyen Cao, 471, 518

Laclos, Pierre Choderlos de, 65, 239;
 Les Liaisons Dangereuses, 38, 701,
 734–35
Lacouture, Jean, 464
Lacretelle, H. de, 661
Lagerlöf, Selma: *The Phantom Chariot*,
 700
La Lupe, 261, 266
Lamont, Corliss, 471
Land, Edwin H., 671
Landolfi, Tommaso, 442, 717; *Gogol's
 Wife and Other Stories*, 45
Lang, Fritz, 187, 414, 419, 425, 430
Langbehn, Julius, 726
Langdon, Harry, 151
Lange, Dorothea, 531, 540, 612–13,
 617, 661
Langlois, Henri, 440
Laos, 493, 495, 516–17
Lardner, Ring, 143
La Rochefoucauld, François de, 357
Lartigue, Jacques-Henri, 554, 567
Lassalle, Martin, 177, 184
La Tour, Georges de, 25, 263
Laughlin, Clarence John, 575, 584, 617,
 622, 658–59
Lautréamont (Isidore-Lucien Ducasse),
 231, 254, 297, 338; *Maldoror*, 256
Lawrence, D. H., 15–16, 256, 323, 507,
 596, 695, 727; *Apocalypse*, 237; *Lady

Chatterley's Lover*, 50, 241; *The Lost
 Girl*, 338
Lawrence, T. E., 72
Laydu, Claude, 177, 184
Leary, Timothy, 457
Lebanon, 727
Lee, Russell, 531
Leeds, Nina, 150
Leenhardt, Roger, 419
Léger, Fernand, 671
Lei Feng, 651
Leiris, Michel, 64–70, 333; *L'Afrique
 Fantôme*, 69; *Aurora*, 64; *Biffures*,
 68; *Fourbis*, 68; *Manhood*, 64–70;
 Simulacre, 64; *Vivantes Cendres,
 Innommées*, 68–69
Lely, Gilbert, 333
Lenica, Jan: *Labyrinth*, 216
Lenin, V. I., 84, 471, 497, 505, 772
Leningrad, Soviet Union, 389
Lenin Prize, 506
Leonardo da Vinci: "The Last Supper,"
 584
Leprosy, 710–11
Lermontov, Mikhail: *A Hero of Our
 Time*, 702
Lerski, Helmar: *Köpfe des Alltags*, 601
Le Secq, M., 661
LeShan, Lawrence: *You Can Fight for
 Your Life*, 706–7
Leskov, Nikolai, 91
Lesy, Michael: *Wisconsin Death Trip*,
 579–80
Leterrier, François, 184
Levine, Don Eric, 525
Levine, Les, 663–64
Lévi-Strauss, Claude, 71–82, 239,
 279, 358; *Le Cru et le Cuit*, 72; *Essai
 sur Quelques Formes Primitives de
 Classification*, 78; *La Pensée Sauvage*,
 72, 78–80; *Race et Histoire*, 72; *Struc-
 tural Anthropology*, 72, 75, 77–80; *Les
 Structures Élémentaires de la Parenté*,
 72, 78; *Le Totémisme Aujourd'hui*, 72;
 Tristes Tropiques, 71, 73–74, 78, 81
Lévy-Bruhl, Lucien, 76
Lewy, Guenter: *The Catholic Church
 and Nazi Germany*, 123
Leys, Simon: *Chinese Shadows*, 651, 727
Liberals, 456, 561, 770, 773, 787, 789,
 798

Libre, 769

Lichtenberg, Bernard, 126, 357

Life, 465

Lifeboat, 266

Life Is Beautiful, 256

Lillie, Bea, 152, 266

Lincoln Center Repertory Theater, 135, 138–39

Lindsay, John, 484

Little Gallery of the Photo-Secession, 548

Living Theatre, 166, 375, 385, 392

Loden, Barbara, 137

Lollobrigida, Gina, 263

London, England, 119, 125, 157, 160, 272, 388–90, 394, 538, 565–68, 629, 800–1

London, Jack, 485

Los Angeles, Calif., 576

Losey, Joseph: *The Damned*, 208

Louÿs, Pierre: *Trois Filles de leur Mère*, 320, 341

Lowell, Robert, 452

Lowie, Robert, 79; *Primitive Society*, 78

Lucretius, 237; *De Rerum Natura*, 74

Ludwig, Jack, 452

Lukács, Georg, 83–92, 128–29; *Aesthetics*, 85; *The Destruction of Reason*, 84–85; *Essays on Thomas Mann*, 85–86; *Goethe and His Time*, 85; *The Historical Novel*, 86; *History and Class Consciousness*, 84–85, 89; *History of the Evolution of Modern Drama*, 83; *The Metaphysics of Tragedy*, 83; *Realism in Our Time*, 85–89; *The Soul and Its Forms*, 83, 89; *Studies in European Realism*, 86, 88; *The Theory of the Novel*, 83, 89–91; *The Young Hegel*, 84–85

Lumière, Louis, 375

Luther, Martin, 245

Lutherans, 126

Luxemburg, Rosa, 770, 772, 776

Lyly, John: *Euphues and His England*, 263

Lynd, Staughton: *The Other Side*, 464

MacArthur, Douglas, 151

Machado de Assis, Joaquim, 101

Machiavelli, Niccolò, 131, 365, 722–24; *The Prince*, 129

Macmillan's Magazine, 670

Maddow, Ben: *Edward Weston*, 666

Mad Magazine, 143

Magee, Patrick, 157

Magnum Photos, 629

Magritte, René, 253, 418, 800

Maidman Theater, 252

Mailer, Norman, 67–68, 460, 485, 688; *An American Dream*, 28

Maistre, Joseph de, 365

Malina, Judith, 166, 385, 460

Malinowski, Bronislaw, 79

Mallarmé, Stéphane, 231, 309, 426, 545

Malle, Louis: *The Lovers*, 50

Malraux, André, 72, 91, 440

Maltese Falcon, The, 265

Maltz, Albert, 485

Mandelstam, Osip, 721

Mandiargues, André Pieyre de, 348

Manicheanism, 51

Manifesto of the 121, 76

Mann, Thomas, 14, 56, 86–88, 91; *The Black Swan*, 699; *Buddenbrooks*, 104; "Death in Venice," 697; *Doctor Faustus*, 698, 712; *The Magic Mountain*, 642, 682, 687, 695–97; "Tristan," 685

Mannerism, 24, 32, 263

Mannheim, Karl, 83, 89–90

Mansfield, Jayne, 263

Mansfield, Katherine: *Journal*, 684, 695, 703–4

Mantegna, Andrea, 603

Mao Zedong, 349, 419, 430, 432, 441, 448, 488, 496, 515, 786

Marais, Jean, 185

Marat, Jean-Paul, 158–59

Marcel, Gabriel, 236

March on the Pentagon, 470

Marcuse, Herbert, 89; *Eros and Civilization*, 239, 241–43

Marinetti, Emilio, 390–92, 721–22

Maritain, Jacques, 236

Marker, Chris, 376, 415; *La Jetée*, 578; *Si J'avais Quatre Dromadaires*, 530

Markopoulos, Gregory, 216

Marlowe, Christopher: *Doctor Faustus*, 128, 206

Marowitz, Charles, 155

Marsh, Mae, 229

Martin, Paul, 566

Martin du Gard, Roger, 86

THE LIBRARY OF AMERICA SERIES

The Library of America fosters appreciation and pride in America's literary heritage by publishing, and keeping permanently in print, authoritative editions of America's best and most significant writing. An independent nonprofit organization, it was founded in 1979 with seed funding from the National Endowment for the Humanities and the Ford Foundation.

To subscribe to the series or to order individual copies, please visit www.loa.org or call (800) 964.5778.

*This book is set in 10 point ITC Galliard Pro, a
face designed for digital composition by Matthew Carter
and based on the sixteenth-century face Granjon. The paper
is acid-free lightweight opaque and meets the requirements for
permanence of the American National Standards Institute.
The binding material is Brillianta, a woven rayon cloth
made by Van Heek–Scholco Textielfabrieken, Holland.
Composition by David Bullen Design. Printing and
binding by Edwards Brothers Malloy, Ann Arbor.
Designed by Bruce Campbell.*